MARKS & MONOGRAMS ON
POTTERY & PORCELAIN

CHELSEA GROUP
"Winter and Spring."

MARKS & MONOGRAMS
on *European and Oriental*
Pottery and Porcelain

By

WILLIAM CHAFFERS

The British Section edited by
GEOFFREY A. GODDEN, F.R.S.A.

The European and Oriental Sections
edited by
FREDERICK LITCHFIELD & R. L. HOBSON

15TH REVISED EDITION

VOLUME TWO

LONDON
WILLIAM REEVES

Published by William Reeves Bookseller Ltd.,
1a Norbury Crescent, London, S.W.16

© William Reeves Bookseller Ltd., 1965

Made in England
Second Printing

Printed in Great Britain by
Lowe & Brydone (Printers) Ltd., London

INTRODUCTION

In this revised edition of the British Isles section as much of the original material as possible has been preserved but errors have been corrected and many omissions repaired. As a result of the considerable amount of fresh information now available on Bow, Longton Hall and Lowestoft it has been found necessary to rewrite the sections dealing with these factories. The histories of other factories have been brought up to date and the relevant modern reference books cited in the text. The bibliography has been extended and rearranged for easy reference.

A complete list of potters working in the years 1900 and 1964 has been added, and the list of sale prices has been enlarged and now covers a period of fifty-five years. As so many pieces mentioned in the previous editions have now changed hands any information on their present where-abouts would be welcomed.

Wherever possible an approximate period or date has been given to each mark reproduced. The sections on Mintons and Worcester are particularly complete in this respect. Mintons private system of yearly dating is repro-duced, and methods by which Royal Worcester specimens may be dated are also fully explained. Messrs. Josiah Wedgwood's " three letter " dating system has been incorporated in the Wedgwood section.

It will be noted that many dates for Staffordshire potters and partner-ships differ from those given in earlier editions (and other reference books). The dates now recorded are based on transcriptions of Staffordshire yearly rate records in my possession. The originals of these invaluable documents were destroyed during the war.

Many nineteenth century objects are found bearing a diamond shaped stamp indicating that the design had been registered with the Patent Office. By using the table of Registration Marks given, the earliest possible date of manufacture can be ascertained.

The adoption of the following general rules would save many common errors in the dating of English trade marks.

1. The occurrence of " Limited," in full or in abbreviated form, in a ceramic mark indicates a date after 1855.
2. The words " Trade Mark " added to a mark indicate a date after 1862 and were not generally used before 1875.

3. The addition of " R^d no. ... " under a mark signifies a date after 1884, see table of registration marks.

4. It is often claimed that the word " England " was added to most marks from 1891 (to comply with the American McKinley Tariff Act). In fact, " England " may occur from about 1887 onwards but probably does not occur before this date. " Made in England " is a twentieth century form.

While every effort has been made to ensure that only correct information is contained in the present volume it may be that some errors have escaped the Editor's attention and he will be grateful to hear from anyone in a position to correct these or who can supply any information not available to him at the time of publication.

Valuable assistance has been forthcoming from the following persons who have specialised knowledge of their subjects: E. A. Lane, Keeper of the Department of Ceramics, Victoria and Albert Museum; G. Scholfield, Salisbury City Librarian; Cyril Shingler, Curator, Worcester Works Museum; Hugh Tait, F.S.A., Assistant Keeper of British and Mediaeval Antiquities, British Museum; F. G. Taylor, Curator, Minton Works Museum, Stoke; A. L. Thorpe, F.M.A., Curator of the Museum and Art Gallery, Derby; Donald Towner, Hon. Secretary, The English Ceramic Circle; Dr. Bernard Watney, F.S.A.; and my special thanks are due to Mr. John Cushion of the Department of Ceramics, Victoria and Albert Museum, who kindly checked my additions and corrections. The writer is also most grateful to Messrs. Scott, Greenwood & Son Ltd. for permission to use and reproduce from their *Pottery Gazette Reference Book* current ceramic marks and to extract lists of British potters working in 1900 and in 1964.

Many examples cited in the text, as well as a wide range of typical specimens, will be found illustrated in *British Pottery and Porcelain: an Illustrated Encyclopaedia of Marked Specimens*, in preparation.

14 Sompting Avenue, GEOFFREY A. GODDEN
Worthing, Sussex.

CONTENTS

STAFFORDSHIRE — THE EARLY POTTERS

When Dr. Plot published his *Natural History* of the county in 1686, it does not appear that there were many manufactories of pottery; he speaks of one at Amblecott, and another at Wednesbury, but he says, " The greatest pottery they have in this county is carried on at Burslem, near Newcastle-under-Lyme." His account of the various clays used is interesting, but he gives no information about the potters then engaged. The following is his account :—

" 25. Other potter's clays for the more common wares there are at many other places, particularly at Horsley Heath, in the parish of Tipton; in Monway Field above mentioned, where there are two sorts gotten, one of a yellowish colour, mixt with white, the other blewish : the former stiff and heavy, the other more friable and light, which, mixed together, work better than apart. Of these they make divers sorts of vessels at Wednesbury, which they paint with slip, made of a reddish sort of earth gotten at Tipton. But the greatest pottery they have in this county is carried on at Burslem, near Newcastle-under-Lyme, where for making their different sorts of pots they have as many different sorts of clay, which they dig round about the towne, all within half a mile's distance, the best being found nearest the coale, and are distinguish't by their colours and uses as followeth :—

1. *Bottle clay*, of a bright whitish streaked yellow colour.
2. *Hard-fire clay*, of a duller whitish colour, and fully intersperst with a dark yellow, which they use for their *black wares*.
3. *Red blending clay*, which is of a dirty red colour.
4. *White clay*, so called, it seems, though of a blewish colour, and used for making yellow-colour'd ware, because yellow is the lightest colour they make any ware of.

All which they call *throwing* clays, because they are of a closer texture, and will work on the wheel.

" 26. Which none of the three other clays they call *Slips* will any of them doe, being of looser and more friable natures ; these, mixt with water, they make into a consistence thinner than a syrup, so that being put into a bucket, it will run out through a quill. This they call *Slip*, and is the substance wherewith they *paint* their wares, whereof the

1. Sort is called the *Orange Slip*, which, before it is work't, is of a greyish colour, mixt with orange balls, and gives the ware (when annealed) an orange colour.

2. The *White Slip*: this, before it is work't, is of a dark blewish colour, yet makes the ware yellow, which being the *lightest* colour they make any of, they call it, as they did the clay above, the *white slip*.

3. The *Red Slip,* made of a dirty reddish clay, which gives ware a black colour.

Neither of which clays or slip must have any gravel or sand in them. Upon this account, before it be brought to the wheel, they prepare the clay by steeping it in water in a square pit till it be of a due consistence; they then bring it to their beating board, where, with a long *spatula,* they beat it till it be well mixt; then, being first made into great *squarish* rolls, it is brought to the *waging board,* where it is slit into thin flat pieces with a *wire,* and the least stones or gravel pick't out of it. This being done, they *wage* it, *i.e.* knead or mould it like *bread,* and make it into round *balls* proportionable to their work; and then 'tis brought to the wheel, and formed as the workman sees good.

" 27. When the potter has wrought the clay either into hollow or flat ware, they set it abroad to dry in fair weather, but by the fire in foule, turning them as they see occasion, which they call *whaving.* When they are dry they *stouk* them, *i.e.* put ears and handles to such vessels as require them. These also being dry, they *slip* or *paint* them, with their several sorts of slip, according as they designe their work; when the first slip is dry, laying on the others at their leisure, the *orange slip* making the ground, and the *white* and *red* the paint; which two colours they break with a *wire brush,* much after the manner they doe when they *marble* paper, and then *cloud* them with a *pencil* when they are pretty dry. After the vessels are painted they *lead* them with that sort of *Lead Ore* they call *Smithum,* which is the smallest *ore* of all, beaten into dust, finely sifted, and strewed upon them; which gives them the *gloss,* but not the colour; all the colours being chiefly given by the variety of slips, except the *motley colour,* which is procured by blending the *Lead* with *Manganese,* by the workmen called *Magnus.* But when they have a mind to show the utmost of their skill in giving their wares a fairer gloss than ordinary, they lead them then with lead calcined into powder, which they also sift fine and strew upon them as before, which not only gives them a higher gloss, but goes much farther too in their work than the lead ore would have done.

" 28. After this is done they are carried to the oven, which is ordinarily above 8 foot high and about 6 foot wide, of a round copped forme, where they are placed one upon another from the bottom to the top; if they be ordinary wares, such as *cylindricall butter pots,* &c., that are not leaded, they are exposed to the *naked* fire, and so is all their *flat ware,* though it be leaded, having only *parting shards, i.e.* thin bits of old pots, put between them to keep them from sticking together; but if they be *leaded hollow wares,* they doe not expose them to the *naked* fire, but put them in *shragers,* that is, in coarse metall'd pots made of *marle* (not *clay*) of divers formes, according as their wares require, in which they put commonly three pieces of clay, called *Bobbs,* for the ware to stand on, to keep it from sticking to the *shragers;* as they put them in the *shragers,* to keep them from sticking to one another (which they would certainly otherwise doe by reason of the leading), and to preserve them from the vehemence of the fire, which else would melt them downe, or at least warp them. In twenty-four hours an oven of pots will be burnt; then they let the fire go out by degrees, which in ten hours more will be perfectly done and then they draw them for sale, which is chiefly to the poor *Crate-men,* who carry them at their backs all over the countrey, to whome they reckon them by the piece, *i.e. Quart,* in *hollow ware,* so that six pottle, or three gallon *bottles,* make a *dozen,* and so more or less to a *dozen,* as they are of greater or lesser content. The *flat wares* are also reckoned by pieces and dozens, but not (as the *hollow*) according to their *content* but their different *bredths.*"

In a document drawn up by Josiah Wedgwood himself in 1776, we have the following list of the potters in his grandfather Thomas Wedgwood's time, with the weekly expenses and profits of each pot-work. (Meteyard's *Life of Wedgwood*, vol. i. p. 191.)

POT-WORKS IN BURSLEM ABOUT THE YEARS 1710 TO 1715

Potters' Names.	Kinds of Ware.	Supposed Amount.			Residence.
		£	s.	d.	
Thomas Wedgwood..............	Black and mottled.......	4	0	0	Churchyard.
John Cartlich.............	Moulded	3	0	0	Flash.
Robert Daniel (Small).............	Black and mottled.......	2	0	0	Hole House.
Thomas Malkin (Small)...........	Ditto ditto........	3	0	0	Hamel.
Richard Malkin........................	Ditto ditto........	2	10	0	Knole.
Dr. Thomas Wedgwood............	Brown stone..............	6	0	0	Ruffleys.
William Simpson....................	... ...	3	0	0	Stocks.
Isa Wood..............................	... ...	4	0	0	Back of George.
Thomas Taylor....................	Moulded	3	0	0	Now Mrs. Wedgwood's.
William Harrison....................	Mottled....................	3	0	0	Brown's Bank.
Isaac Wood..........................	Cloudy....................	3	0	0	Top of Robin's Croft.
John Adams..........................	Black and mottled.......	2	10	0	Brick House.
Marshes	Not worked...............	...	...		Top of Daniel's Croft.
Moses Marsh.......................	Stoneware	6	0	0	Middle of the town.
Robert Adams.......................	Mottled and black.......	2	10	0	Next on the East side.
Aaron Shaw.........................	Stone and dipt wt........	6	0	0	Ditto.
Samuel Cartlich (Conick)...........	Mottled....................	3	0	0	Next to the South.
Aaron Wedgwood....................	Mottled and black.......	4	0	0	Next to the Red Lion.
Thomas Taylor.......................	Stoneware and freckled	...	...		Next to the North.
Moses Shaw..........................	Ditto ditto........	6	0	0	Middle of the Town.
Thomas Wedgwood..................	Moulded	2	10	0	Ditto, now Graham's.
Isaac Ball...........................	... ...	4	0	0	South-West end of Town.
Samuel Edge.........................	Stoneware..................	6	0	0	Next to the West.
Thomas Locket.......................	Mottled....................	3	0	0	Late Cartlich's.
Turnstalls.............................	Not worked............ ..	3	0	0	Opposite.
John Simpson (Double Rabbit)...	... ...	3	0	0	West end of Town.
Richard Simpson....................	Red dishes &c..............	3	0	0	The Pump, West end.
Thomas Cartwright.................	Butter pots.................	2	0	0	West end of Town.
Thomas Mitchell.....................	Not worked...............	...	...		Rotten Row.
Moses Steel..........................	Cloudy....................	3	0	0	Ditto.
John Simpson, Chell...............	Mottled and black.......	4	0	0	Ditto.
John Simpson, Castle................	Red dishes and pans....	3	10	0	Ditto.
Isaac Malkin.........................	Mottled and black.......	3	0	0	Green Head.
Richard Wedgwood..................	Stoneware	6	0	0	Middle of Town.
John Wedgwood.....................	Not worked...............	(supposed)			Upper House.
John Warburton......................	... ...	6	0	0	Hot Lane or Cobridge.
Hugh Mare...........................	Mottled....................	3	0	0	Ditto.
Robert Bucknal.......................	Ditto......................	4	0	0	Ditto.
R. Daniel..............................	... ...	3	0	0	Ditto.
Bagnal	Butter pots.................	2	0	0	Grange.
John Stevenson........................	Clouded	3	0	0	Sneyd Green.
	Ditto......................	3	0	0	Ditto.
H. Beech..............................	Butter pots	2	0	0	Holdin.
		139	10	0*	

* £139, 10s., at forty-six weeks to the year, is £6417, being the annual produce of the pottery in the beginning of the eighteenth century in Burslem parish. Burslem was at this time so much the principal part of the pottery that there were very few pot-works elsewhere.

MEN NECESSARY TO MAKE AN OVEN OF BLACK AND MOTTLED, PER WEEK, AND OTHER EXPENSES

	£	s.	d.
Six men—three at 4s. per week, and three at 6s.	1	10	0
Four boys at 1s. 3d.	0	5	0
1 cwt. 2 qrs. of lead ore at 8s.	0	12	0
Manganese.	0	3	0
Clay, 2 cart-loads, at 2s.	0	4	0
Coals, 48 horse-loads, at 2d.	0	8	0
Carriage of ditto, 1½d.	0	6	0
Rent of works, at £5 per annum.	0	2	0
Wear and tear of ovens, utensils, &c., at £10 per annum.	0	4	0
Straw for packing—3 thraves of 24 sheaves to the thrave, at 4d.	0	1	0
The master's profit, besides 6s. for his labour	0	10	0
	£4	5	0

N.B.—The wear and tear, master's profits, and some other things, are rated too high. £4 per ovenful is thought to be sufficient, or more than sufficient, for the black and mottled works of the largest kind, upon an average, as the above work was a large one for those times.

POTTERS AT HANLEY IN THE BEGINNING OF THE EIGHTEENTH CENTURY

Joseph Glass, cloudy, and a sort of dishes, painted with different coloured slips, and sold at 3s. and 3s. 6d. per dozen.

William Simpson, cloudy and mottled.

Hugh Mare, black and mottled.

John Mare, black and mottled.

Richard Marsh, mottled and black, lamprey pots and venison pots.

John Ellis, butter-pots, &c.

Moses Sandford, milk-pans and small ware.

Only one horse and one mule kept at Hanley. No carts scarcely in the country. Coals carried upon men's backs. Hanley Green like Wolstanton Marsh. Only two houses at Stoke (meaning potteries), Ward's and Poulson's.

The reader should refer to "Slip Decorated Ware" for notices on the work of some of the above-named potters.

1750

POTTERS IN THE TOWN OF BURSLEM IN OR ABOUT 1750.

From the information of persons long since dead, given in Ward's " History of the Burgh of Stoke."

Ralph Allen.	Samuel Cartlich.	Josiah Simpson.
Moses Marsh.	Maria Lockers.	Richard Parrott
Aaron Shaw.	Taylors.	John Heath.
John Daniel.	Clark Malkin.	William Burn.
John Adams.	Joseph Simpson.	Thomas Cartlich.
Robert Daniel.	Thomas Mitchell.	Richard Onions.
Thomas Steel.	John Mitchell.	Thomas Taylor.

1770

A List of Potters in Staffordshire who bound themselves on the 4th February 1770 in the sum of £50 not to sell their wares under the specified prices, viz., dishes 10 to 21 inches, from 3d. to 3s.; worser dishes, half-price of best; snyeapp and baking dishes, 7 to 12 inches, 1s. 6d. to 6s. 6d.; tureens, 2s. to 3s. 6d.; sauce-boats, 1s. 3d. to 2s. 6d.; twyflers, 7d. to 1s. 4d.; plates, 1s. to 2s.; cups and saucers, 7d. to 1s. 10d.; butter tubs and stands, 5d. to 9d., &c.; to allow no more than 5 per cent. for breakage and 5 per cent. for ready money; to sell to the manufacturers of earthenware at the above prices, and to allow no more than 7½ per cent., besides discount for breakage and prompt payment; John Platt, John Lowe, John Taylor, John Cobb, Robert Bucknall,

John Daniel, Thomas Daniel, jun., Richard Adam, Samuel Chatterley, Thos. Lowe, John Allen, William Parrott, Jacob Warburton, Warburton & Stone, Jos. Smith, Joshua Heath, John Bourn, Jos. Stephens, William Smith, Jos. Simpson, John Weatherby, J. and Rd. Mare, Nicholas Pool, John Yates, Thomas Warburton, Thos. Hassels, Pr. Pro. of Ann Warburton & Son, and Wm. Meir.

I·H I·H HEATH
1 ⊙ 2 3

The Joshua Heath mentioned in the above list signed the oft-quoted "agreement as to prices," February 4, 1770, and worked from 1740-80. There were in the Sheldon Collection, a cream ware plate and a blue painted earthenware plate, bearing marks nos. 1 and 2. These marks are attributed to John Heath by Mr. Burton, but they are more probably those of Joshua. See also mark no. 3.

1786
MANUFACTURERS OF POTTERY WARE, NEAR NEWCASTLE, IN STAFFORDSHIRE

(from *A Topographical Survey of the County of Stafford*, by William Tunnicliff, c. 1786)

Total number of potters, 80, which had increased in 1802 to 149.

In this Survey, under the heading Burslem, are included Tunstall, Longport, and all manufactories north of the town; Fenton includes Etruria and Lane Delph; Lane End, Longton and Foley.

BURSLEM

Adams, William, & Co., manufacturers of cream-coloured ware and china-glazed ware painted.
Bagley, William, potter.
Bourne, John, manufacturer of china-glaze, blue-painted, enamelled, and cream-colour earthenware.
Bourne & Malkin, manufacturers of china-glazed, blue and cream-colour ware.
Cartlidge, S. and J., potters.
Daniel, Thomas, potter.
Daniel, John, manufacturer of cream-colour and red earthenware.
Daniel, Timothy, do. do.
Daniel, Walter, do. do.
Graham, John, jun., manufacturer of white stone earthenware, enamelled white and cream-colour.
Green, John, potter.
Holland, Thomas, manufacturer of black and red china ware and gilder.
Keeling, Anthony, manufacturer of Queen's ware in general, blue painted and enamelled, Egyptian black (Tunstall, near Burslem).
Lockett, Timothy and John, white stone potters.
Malkin, Burnham, potter.

Robinson, John, enameller and printer of cream-colour and china-glazed ware.
Rogers, John and George, manufacturers of china-glazed blue painted wares and cream-coloured.
Smith, Ambrose, & Co., manufacturers of cream-coloured ware and china-glazed ware, painted blue.
Smith, John and Joseph, potters.
Stevenson, Charles, and Son, manufacturers of cream-coloured ware, blue painted, &c.
Wedgwood, Thomas, manufacturer of cream-coloured ware and china-glazed ware, painted with blue, &c. "Big House."
Wedgwood, Thomas, manufacturer of cream-coloured ware and china-glazed ware, painted with blue, &c. "Over House."
Wilson, James, enameller.
Wood, John, potter.
Wood, Enoch and Ralph, manufacturers of all kinds of useful and ornamental earthenware, Egyptian black, cane, and various other colours, also black figures, seals, and ciphers.
Wood, Josiah, manufacturer of fine black-glazed, variegated, and cream-coloured ware, and blue.

COBRIDGE

Blackwell, Joseph, manufacturer of blue and white stoneware, cream and painted wares.

Blackwell, John, do. do.

Bucknall, Robert, manufacturer of Queen's ware, blue painted, enamelled, printed, &c.

Godwin, Thomas and Benjamin, manufacturers of Queen's ware and china-glazed blue.

Hales & Adams, potters.

Robinson & Smith, ditto.

Warburton, Jacob, potter.

HANLEY

Bagnall, Sampson, potter.

Boon, Joseph, ditto.

Chatterley, C. and E., potters.

Glass, John, potter.

Heath, Warburton, & Co., china manufacturers.

Keeling, Edward, potter.

Mare, John and Richard, potters.

Mayer, Elijah, enameller.

Miller, William, potter.

Neal & Wilson, potters.

Perry, Samuel, potter.

Taylor, George, ditto.

Wright, Thomas, ditto.

Yates, John, ditto.

SHELTON

Baddeley, J. and E., potters.

Hassels, John, potter.

Heath & Bagnell, potters.

Hollins, Samuel, potter.

Kneeling, Anthony, ditto.

Taylor & Pope, potters.

Twenlow, G., potter.

Whitehead, Christopher Charles, potter.

Yates, John, potter.

STOKE

Bell, Sarah, potter.

Booth, Hugh, manufacturer of china, china-glaze, and Queen's ware in all its branches.

Brindley, James, potter.

Spode, Josiah, ditto.

Straphan, Joseph, merchant and factor in all kinds of earthenware.

Wolfe, Thomas, manufacturer of Queen's ware in general, blue, printed, and Egyptian black, cane, &c.

FENTON

Bacchus, William, manufacturer of Queen's ware in all its various branches.

Boon, Edward, manufacturer of Queen's ware and blue painted.

Brindley, Taylor, potter.

Clowes & Williamson, potters.

Turner, John, potter.

Wedgwood, Josiah and Thomas, potters.[1]

LANE END

Barker, John, manufacturer of cream-coloured china-glaze, and blue wares.

Barker, William, potter.

Barker, Richard, ditto

Cyples, Joseph, manufacturer of Egyptian black and pottery in general.

Edwards, William, potter.

Forrester and Meredith, manufacturers of Queen's ware, Egyptian black, red china, and various other wares.

Garner, Joseph, potter.

Garner, Robert, manufacturer of Queen's ware and various other wares.

Shelley, Michael, potter.

Shelley, Thomas, ditto.

Turner and Abbott, potters to the Prince of Wales.

Walklete, Mark, potter.

A COMPLETE LIST OF POTTERS' NAMES AND MANUFACTORIES,

1802, IN THE DISTRICT KNOWN AS THE STAFFORDSHIRE POTTERIES

Total number of manufactories in existence at that date, 149 : thus—unoccupied   4

6 firms or persons had 2 manufactories each 12

133 ditto   ditto   had 1   ditto   each 133

---

139 names as given in list.   Total . . 149

---

[1] They never had premises at Fenton. Etruria must have been omitted.

1802
LIST OF NAMES AND RESIDENCES OF THE EARTHEN-WARE MANUFACTURERS

No.	Name	Residence
1	John Lindop	Green Lane
2	John and Thomas Capper	Golden Hill
3	Thomas Tunstall	ditto
4	John Collison	ditto
5	Abraham Baggaley	ditto
6	Moss & Henshall	Red Street
7	Riles & Bathwell	ditto
8	Samuel and Thomas Cartlich	Tunstall
9	Thomas Baggaley	ditto
10	Caleb Cole & Co.	New-field
11	William Adams	Tunstall
12	John Breeze	Smith-field
13	Unoccupied	Pitts Hill
14	Jonathan Machin	Chell
15	John Horn	Brimleyford
16	Smith & Steel	Tunstall
17	A. and E. Keeling (2 factories)	ditto
18	John Wood	Brown Hills
19	John Davenport	Longport
20	Henshall, Williamson & Co.	ditto
21	Williamson & Henshall[1]	ditto
22	Shirley, Lindop, & Co.	ditto
23	John and George Rogers (2 factories)	ditto
24	Walter Daniel (Burslem)	Newport
25	Holland & Co.	Burslem
26	John and Ralph Wood	ditto
27	Ralph Wood	ditto
28	Wood & Caldwell	ditto
29	Isaac Leigh	ditto
30	Nathan and John Heath	ditto
30	John Taylor & Co.	ditto
31	William Dawson	ditto
32	Jacob Marsh	ditto
33	Robinson & Sons	ditto
34	Read & Goodfellow	ditto
35	Edward Bourne	ditto
36	Tellwright & Co.	ditto
37	Thomas Holland	ditto
38	Charles Davenport	ditto
39	Lewis Heath	ditto
40	Thomas Guest	ditto
41	John Gilbert	ditto
42	Thomas Wedgwood (Overhouse)	ditto
43	Daniel Steel	ditto
44	Unoccupied	ditto
45	William and John Stanley	ditto
46	Bagshaw & Maier	ditto
47	J. and R. Riley	ditto
48	Mort, Barker, & Chester	ditto
49	Joseph Machin	ditto
50	Arkinstall & George	ditto
51	Richard Ball	ditto
52	William Wood & Co.	ditto
53	Thomas Green	ditto
54	John Warburton (2 factories)	Cobridge
55	Thomas Godwin	ditto
56	Benjamin Godwin	ditto
57	Smith & Billington	ditto
58	Stevenson & Dale	Cobridge
59	J. and A. Blackwell	ditto
60	William Adams	ditto
61	John Mozeley	ditto
62	Hewit & Buckley (Booden Brook)	Shelton
63	Hollins, Warburton, & Co. (New Hall)	ditto
64	Booth & Marsh	ditto
65	Bourne & Co.	ditto
66	Edmund J. Birch	Hanley
67	Heath & Shorthose	ditto
68	John Mare	ditto
69	Yates & Shelly	ditto
70	Joseph Lees	ditto
71	David Wilson	ditto
72	Elijah Mayer	ditto
73	George Taylor	ditto
74	T. and J. Hollins	ditto
75	Valentine Close	ditto
76	Joseph Keeling	ditto
77	Boon & Ridgway	ditto
78	John Glass	ditto
79	James Keeling	ditto
80	Meigh & Walthal	ditto
81	Billings & Hammersley	ditto
82	James and Charles Whitehead	ditto
83	Mrs. Mellor	ditto
84	John Stanley	ditto
85	William Baddeley	ditto
86	Job and George Ridgway	Shelton
87	John Hammersley	ditto
88	J. and E. Baddeley	ditto
89	Unoccupied	ditto
90	Simpson & Wright	ditto
91	John and William Yates	ditto
92	Thomas Pope	ditto
93	James Greatbatch	ditto
94	Dorothy Whitehead	ditto
95	Samuel Hollins (Vale Pleasant)	ditto
96	Wedgwood & Byerley	Etruria
97	Unoccupied	Stoke Lane
98	Mrs. Ratcliffe	ditto
99	John Harrison (Cliffgate Bank)	Stoke
100	Booth & Sons, ditto	ditto
101	Josiah Spode	ditto
102	Wolfe & Hamilton	ditto
103	Smith & Jarvis	ditto
104	Minton, Poulson, & Co.	ditto
105	Harrison & Hyatt	Lower Lane
105	Robert Clulow & Co.	ditto
106	Bourne & Baker	Fenton
107	Chelenor & Adams	ditto
108	Bagnall & Hull	Lane-delf
109	John Lucock	ditto
110	William Pratt	ditto
111	Mason & Co.	ditto
112	Thomas Forester	ditto

[1] The name HENSHALL & Co., is stamped on a plate in the Sheldon Collection. Henschell was the maiden name of the widow of James Brindley, who afterwards married the potter Robert Williamson.

113 Thomas Shelly . .	Lane-delf
114 } Samuel Baker (2 factories)	ditto
115 }	
116 Samuel Spode (now spelt	
Foley) . . .	Foley
117 Joseph Myatt . .	ditto
118 Robert Garner (now called	
Longton) . . .	Lane End
119 Charles Harvey (2 factories)	ditto
120 Hewitt & Comer . .	ditto
121 John Aynesley . .	ditto
122 John Hewit . .	ditto
123 W. and J. Phillips .	ditto
124 Samuel Hughes . .	ditto
125 Samuel Dawson . .	ditto
126 Richard Barker . .	ditto
127 Booth & Co. . . .	ditto

128 Thomas Stirrup . .	Lane End
129 Charles Harvey . .	ditto
130 Samuel Bridgewood .	ditto
131 Johnson & Brough .	ditto
132 Mary Syples . .	ditto
133 J. and G. Locketts .	ditto
134 Chetham & Woolley .	ditto
135 J. and W. Berks . .	ditto
136 } William and John Turner (2	
138 } factories) . . .	ditto
137 George Barnes . .	ditto
139 Thomas Jackson & Co. .	ditto
140 Thomas Shelley . .	ditto
141 William Ward . .	ditto
142 —— Shaw . . .	ditto
143 George Weston . .	ditto
144 Mark Walklete . .	ditto

The signature and date, RICHARD MARE, 1697, occurs on a two-handled cup, 4½ in. diameter, decorated in buff slip, and Mr. A. J. de Bushnell, the former owner, who found it in a cottage near Cheltenham, suggested that this Richard Mare was the grandfather of the potter of the same name of Hanley, who worked at the end of the eighteenth century.

The following list of Staffordshire potters who worked at the end of the eighteenth and early part of the nineteenth century, specimens of whose productions will be found in the Victoria and Albert Museum, may also be added on the authority of Professor Church:—

Bott & Co.	Harley.	Ridgway.
J. Clementson.	Lakin & Poole.	Riley.
Clews.	Mason.	Rogers.
Cookson & Harding.	Mayer & Newbold.	Salt.
Green.	Meir.	Stevenson.
Hackwood.	Mohr & Smith.	Walton.
Harding.	Moseley.	Wilson.

The list given above and the following, from a map in the *Staffordshire Pottery Directory*, Hanley, 1802, as well as many important notices of the Staffordshire potteries, were communicated by Mr. Edwin Hewitt of Hanley.

TRADES IN CONNECTION WITH POTTERS IN 1802

Booth, George, packer and dealer in earthenware, Tunstall.

Shaw, Chas., packer and dealer, Tunstall.

Adams, James, engraver, Fields, Burslem.

Bold, J. G., colour-maker, Furlong, Burslem.

Greatbach, John, dealer in earthenware, Chapel Street, Burslem.

Greatbach, Oliver, oven-builder, Commercial Street, Burslem.

Johnson, Ralph, modeller, Mount Pleasant, Burslem.

Knott, William, colour-maker, Hill Street, Burslem.

Machin, Joseph, enameller, Strand. Burslem.

Machin & Co., colour-makers, Hill Street, Burslem.

Martin, George, engraver, Commercial Street, Burslem.

Preston, John, packer and clay agent, Furlong, Burslem.

Stannaway, J., colour-maker, Ham Hill, Burslem.

Walley, Peter, dealer in earthenware, Hanover Square, Burslem.

Wilson, Ann, enameller, High Street, Burslem.

Boot, Jonathan, modeller, Cobridge.

Baddeley, Thomas, engraver and black printer, Chapel Field, Hanley.

Baggaley, Thomas, enameller, Old Hall Road, Hanley.

Beech, Bagnall, dealer in earthenware, Upper Hanley.

Booth, William, colour-maker, High Street, Hanley.

Daniel & Brown, enamellers, Market Place, Hanley.

Downing, William, engraver, Old Hall Lane, Hanley.

Ledge, Charles, engraver, Sleek Lane, Hanley.

Shorthose, John, merchant, High Street, Hanley.

Sparks, George, gilder of earthenware, Sleek Lane, Hanley.

Thursfield, Richard, dealer in earthenware, Chapel Field, Hanley.

Wilson, David, enameller, Abbey Field, Hanley.

Brammer, George, black printer, Shelton.

Fletcher, Thomas, black printer and enameller, Shelton.

Heath, Thomas, modeller, Shelton.

Johnson, John, black printer, do.

Keeling, John, gilder, Shelton.

Mollart, John, engraver, do.

Morris, Francis, black printer, Vale Pleasant, Shelton.

Palmer & Wright, colour-makers, Shelton.

Radford, Thomas, engraver, do.

Ridgway, John, dealer in earthenware, do.

Stephen, John, dealer in earthenware, do.

Vernon, Samuel, engraver, do.

Forrester, Anthony, dealer in porcelain, Lane Delph.

Lucock, John, engraver, Stoke.

Radford, Thomas, engraver, Stoke.

Shufflebottom, William, engraver, Little Fenton.

Sparks, Thomas, engraver, Stoke.

Staley, Stephen, dealer in earthenware, Lower Lane.

Steadman, George, flint-grinder, Stoke.

Whitehouse, Edward, engraver, Little Fenton.

Young, John, dealer in earthenware, Penkhull.

Bailey, William, gilder of earthenware, Lane End.

Carey, John, dealer in earthenware, Lane End.

Hampson, John, enameller, Lane End.

Jackson, Benjamin, dealer in earthenware, Lane End.

Jevans, William, enameller, Lane End.

Lockett, Joseph, dealer in earthenware, Lane End.

Lockett, Samuel, do. do.

Lowe, John, do. do.

Ryles, Moses, engraver, do. do.

Wood, George, do. do.

MANUFACTURE OF EARTHENWARE

The following enumeration of the order in which various materials and kinds of manufacture were introduced into Staffordshire is from Dr. S. Shaw's *Chemistry of Pottery*:—

" In this succession I find the common *brown ware* till 1680; then the *Shelton clay* (long previously used by the tobacco-pipe makers of Newcastle), mixed with grit from Baddeley Hedge, by Thomas Miles; *coarse white stoneware,* and the same grit and can marl, or *clunch,* of the coal seams, by his brother, into *brown stoneware.* The *Crouch ware* was first made of common potter's clay and grit from Moel Cop, and afterwards the grit and can marl, by A. Wedgwood of Burslem, in 1690; and the ochreous brown clay and manganese into a coarse *Egyptian black,* in 1700, by Wood of Hot Lane. The employment of the Devonshire pipe-clay, by Twyford and Astbury of Shelton, supplied the *white dipped* and the *white stoneware;* from which the transition was easy to the *flint ware,* by Daniel Bird of Stoke; the *chalk body ware,* by Chatterley & Palmer of Hanley; and the *Queen's ware* of the celebrated Josiah Wedgwood.

" Mr. Thomas Toft introduced *aluminous shale* or *firebrick clay;* Mr. William Sans, *manganese* and *galena* pulverised; Messrs. John Palmer and William Adams, *common salt* and *litharge;* Messrs. Elers Brothers, *red clay* or *marl* and *ochre;* Mr. Josiah Twyford, *pipe-clay;* Mr. Thomas Astbury, *flint;*[1] Mr. Ralph Shaw, *basalts;* Mr. Aaron Wedgwood, *red lead;* Mr. William Littler, *calcined bone earth;* Mr. Enoch Booth, *white lead;* Mrs. Warburton, *soda;* Mr. Ralph Daniel, *calcined gypsum;* Mr. Josiah Wedgwood, *barytes;* Mr. John Cookworthy, *decomposed white granite;* Mr. James Ryan, *British kaolin* and *petuntse;* Messrs. Sadler & Green, *glaze printing;* Mr. Warner Edwards, *biscuit painting;* Mr. Thomas Daniel, *glaze enamelling;* Mr. William Smith, *burnished gilding;* Mr. Peter Warburton, *painting in gold;* Messrs. John Hancock, John Gardner, and William Hennys, *lustres;* Mr. William Brookes, *engraved landscapes* and *printing in colours;* Mr. William Wainwright Potts, *printing by machine* and continuous sheet of paper; and the same with Mr. William Machin and Mr. William Bourne, for *printing flowers, figures, &c., in colour,* by machine and continuous sheet of paper.

" John Potts, Richard Oliver, and William Wainwright Potts of New Derby, engravers to calico-printers, patented in 1831 ' An improved method or process of obtaining

---

[1] This only refers to its introduction into Staffordshire. See " Fulham,"where it was used fifty years before Astbury's time.

impressions from engravings in various colours, and applying the same to earthenware, porcelain, china, glass,' &c. This consists in employing a cylinder printing machine, such as is generally used by calico-printers," &c., &c.

4

Mark no. 4. The Sheldon Collection contained a blue printed earthenware plate with this mark in blue. W. W. Potts supplied printed patterns, or engraved copper rollers to various potters. He was not himself a manufacturer. W. W. Potts took out a patent in his own name in December, 1835, for a printing process. This mark with the Derbyshire address is prior to 1841.

The necessity of determining the heat of the kiln during the process of baking the ware, and of regulating it when necessary by the admission or exclusion of the external air, as required to be of a lower or higher degree of temperature, was soon found to be a desideratum, and the Messrs. Thomas and John Wedgwood, about the year 1740, invented trial-pieces made of prepared clay, which being placed in the kiln, indicated (although very imperfectly) the temperature. These trial-pieces were from their form called "pyrometrical beads," and were similar to small poppy-heads out of which had been cut the calices or cups, and the colours these beads assumed when submitted to the different degrees of heat was the test in firing the ware; subsequently other *pyrometers* were invented, formed of metal rods, tobacco-pipes, and glass tubes, which contracted or expanded according to the various degrees of heat; and eventually Josiah Wedgwood introduced a more perfect *pyrometer*, or measurer of heat, himself.

The introduction into Staffordshire in 1720[1] of ground flint for making the white ware, and which paved the way for the manufacture of fine fayence, was of great importance; but the method of pounding the flints by manual labour, and afterwards passing the powder through fine lawn, was so tedious a process, and so injurious to the health of the workmen engaged, that a mill was invented by Thomas Benson, an engineer of Newcastle-under-Lyme. His first patent is dated November 5, 1725, which was followed by another in January 1732, with certain alterations; the title is as follows :—

A.D. 1732, January 14.—No. 536. BENSON, THOMAS, Engineer. "A new engine or

---

[1] It will be seen hereafter that calcined and ground flint was employed as early as 1689 by Dwight of Fulham.

method for grinding of flint stones, being the chief ingredient used in making of white wares, such as pots and other vessels, a manufacture carried on in our county of Stafford, and some other parts of this our kingdom; that the common method hitherto used in preparing the same hath been by breaking and pounding the stones dry, and afterwards sifting the powder through fine lawns, which hath proved very destructive to mankind, occasioned by the dust sucked into the body, which, being of a ponderous nature, fixes so closely upon the lungs that nothing can remove it, insomuch that it is very difficult to find persons to engage in the said manufacture, to the great detriment and decay of that branch of trade, which would otherwise, from the usefulness thereof, be of great benefit and advantage to our kingdom; that by the petitioner's invention the flint stones are sprinkled with water, so that no dust can rise, and then ground as fine as sand with two large stones made to turn round upon the edges by the power of a wheel, worked either by wind, water, or horses, which is afterwards conveyed into large stone pans, made circular, wherein are placed large stone balls, which, by the power of such wheels, are driven round with great velocity, that in a short space of time, the flint stones so broken are reduced to an oily substance, which, by turning of a cock, empties itself into casks provided for that purpose; that by this invention all the hazards and inconveniences in making the said manufacture in the common way will be effectually prevented, and in every particular tend to the manifest improvement and advantage thereof, and preserving the lives of our subjects employed therein."

In the foregoing title is contained all the description given of the invention.

The white stoneware, salt glaze, was made from 1690 to 1780, and is thus described by Professor Church in his Catalogue:—

" This ware was made during a period of about ninety years, chiefly in Staffordshire, more particularly at Burslem. Sometimes it is erroneously termed *Elizabethan* ware. One well-known piece has been absurdly enough termed ' Shakespeare's Jug.' It was made not less than sixty or seventy years after Shakespeare's death. In its earliest forms and in the hands of some potters it was coarse in texture and clumsy in design, but improvements rapidly took place, more care being taken in the selection and preparation of the clays and in the manufacture of the moulds. Devon, Dorset, and local clays, with finely ground sand or pounded flint, were the chief materials for the body of the white ware, while its glaze was usually formed wholly or almost wholly by the action of the vapour of common salt at a high temperature on the silica of the paste. A sodium silicate was thus formed of great tenacity and hardness, and the ware was thus most effectually protected from absorption of liquids or mechanical injuries by an impenetrable and unattackable coating. (A small proportion of red lead seems to have been occasionally used with the salt.) This glaze or coating is often harder than felspar, and is only just scratched by quartz (rock crystal), though the body itself is abraded by felspar. The specific gravity of this salt-glazed white ware or fine white stoneware is about 2.2 higher than that of most English pottery, except Elers' ware, which owes its density in part to the ferric oxide, which it contains in considerable proportion.

" This early fine white stoneware may almost take rank as a porcelain. The better and whiter specimens of it, had a little more alkali entered into their composition, would be in reality a kind of hard porcelain.

" The peculiar glaze of this ware is unmistakeable; when not too thick it is characterised by numerous minute depressions, which give it the appearance of a piece of fine leather or the skin of an orange. The high fusing-point of the glaze, and the fact of its having been *formed* on the ware itself, caused this peculiarity of texture.

" Some of the patterns on this ware are embossed, others are encrusted, and others again have been etched—traced with a point and afterwards commonly coloured blue. The ornamentation is often identical with that of Elers' red ware; sometimes it has been derived from the silver plate moulds of the time of Queen Anne. Metal moulds as well as plaster of Paris moulds were employed for this ware.

"Much of this fine white salt-glazed ware was made by Aaron Wood (1750-70); the earlier makes seemed to have been termed *Crouch* ware.

"Salt-glazed white ware is seldom marked. A globular bottle in my collection is, however, marked at the base with some cursive letters; an enamelled milk-jug in my collection has a cross in green enamel on the bottom.

"A superb butter-boat is in my collection. It is decorated with various embossed ornaments, and notably with figures of the Seven Champions of Christendom.

"The gilding on this ware is secured with gold size only. The enamel paintings are, for the most part, distinctively Chinese in style; the colours are bright."

A portion of one of the old salt-glaze pot-works could be seen at Sneyd Green, near Hanley, but the building has long been converted into two small cottages. There were more than a hundred of the curious old saggars with perforated sides still to be seen serving as a fence to the garden; the owner, an old man more than eighty years old, said that it had been in this state for more than a hundred years, and also when a railway was being cut close by, that many curious specimens of lead-glazed pottery were found in the soil, but were all dispersed among the workmen.

A bottle of cream-coloured salt-glaze stoneware, with garlands and festoons of flowers, and birds in extremely sharp relief, executed by metal mould, like Elers' or Aaron Wood's work, is in the Schreiber Collection in the Victoria and Albert Museum. It is stamped underneath apparently "D.H. 1759"; the ornaments are not moulded on the surface, but laid on after being stamped out.

A mug of the same salt-glazed stoneware, etched or incised and coloured blue, in the same Collection, bears this inscription:—

> "This is Thomas Cox'es cup;
> Come my friend and drink it up;
> Good news is come'n, the bells do ring;
> & here's a health to Prussia's King.
>   February 16, 1758."

A further reference to the cream-coloured salt-glaze ware, and also that with cream ground enamelled in colours will be found on another page.

Professor Church also thus describes another sort of pottery which was much in vogue in the first half of the eighteenth century:—

AGATE WARE AND TORTOISE-SHELL AND OTHER COLOURED GLAZE WARES

"The patterns in *agate ware* go through the substance of the paste more or less completely. The colouring matters were either ferruginous ochres and clays, or clays mixed with oxide of iron and manganese, and preparations of cobalt, worked up together, and then cut by a wire into strings, convoluted ribands, &c. Sometimes the clays thus worked and variegated were applied as slip in irregular smears to the surface decoration of cream ware. Thus were formed the early Staffordshire marble wares. A rarer variety of this ware may be called tesselated, minute pieces of variously coloured dried pastes being encrusted on to the body of the ware. These pieces were cemented in their places either by a thin slip or by a glaze subsequently applied (see specimens in the Victoria and Albert Museum).

" Although *tortoise-shell ware* was glazed and tinted with lead ore (galena) and manganese (wadd), other metals were often used, namely, iron, copper, and cobalt. Some of the earlier examples of tortoise-shell ware, with ' flooded ' and deep colours, resemble certain kinds of Chinese work in tone and richness, the minute fissures in the thick glaze adding to the effect.

" We have included under the group of tortoise-shell ware those which are coloured blue only, or green only, or brown only, or are variously mottled with two or more colours : they are distinguished by their peculiar ill-defined colour-markings from nearly all other kinds of British pottery. It appears to have been in 1724 when this ware was first made; it commanded a good sale for some years, and is even now manufactured, though usually of very inferior quality. It originated in a discovery made by a Stafforc̣a-shire firm of potters, Redrich & Jones, for which they took out a patent. Their process is described as one for so ' staining, veining, spotting, clouding, damasking earthenware as to give it the appearance of various kinds of marble, porphyry, and rich stones, as well as tortoise-shell.' Much of the old Staffordshire agate, tortoise-shell, green-glazed and cauliflower ware may be attributed to Whielden (1740-60), of Little Fenton. Aaron Wood and Josiah Spode were apprenticed to him. Josiah Wedgwood was in partner-ship with him for a short time. Variegated inlaid or tessellated wares were made by Ralph Wood of Burslem (1730 to 1740)."[1]

Professor Church thought that this variegated English pottery was made in the sixteenth, if not in the fifteenth century, although subsequently the methods of its production were perfected by such skilful potters as Whieldon and the Wedgwoods. Ralph Wood of Burslem and Daniel Bird of Cliff Bank were also contemporary makers of Whieldon type ware. There are several excellent specimens of this mottled and tortoise-shell ware in the Schreiber Collection, Victoria and Albert Museum.

EARTHENWARE

" With respect to the manufacture of common earthenware, which is so consider-able in England, not only for home consumption but for exportation, being sent to various parts of the world in great quantity, and which is at the same time so cheap, the following sketch of the processes usually employed may be useful to the visitor.

" *a.* The *common body* or paste is usually composed of Dorset or Poole clay, Cornish or Devonian kaolin, and flint.

" *b. Best body* is formed of Dorset or Poole clay, Cornish or Devonian kaolin, Corn-ish china-stone, and flint.

" The Dorset or Poole clay, which may be regarded as the base or chief ingredient in the manufacture of English earthenware, is mixed with water, and reduced to a state in which it can be passed through sieves of various sizes, in order to clear it of all lumps and to render it of a fine general consistency. The kaolin requires no cleaning prepara-

---

[1] The historical collection of English pottery formed for purposes of scientific research by Professor Church, and which he has fortunately catalogued, with remarks and analysis of the bodies and glazes of the ware, was totally destroyed, with many other valuable contributions of china, in the disastrous conflagration at the Alexandra Palace in 1873.

tion, and the flints are used as they come, finely comminuted, from their deposit in water after passing the grinding-mills. The china-stone requires to be treated as the flints, with the exception of being calcined or burnt in kilns, having to be crushed and reduced to a fine powder in mills.

" The materials being all thus ready for use, the proportions of each considered requisite for the kind of ware to be made are taken, mixed with water and with each other, to the *slip-kiln,* a long brick trough heated by means of flues from a furnace. Here the mixture is kept simmering until it becomes something of the consistency of dough. It is then ready for use, and is placed until required in cold dark cellars. If coloured bodies or pastes are required to give a general tint to the ware, certain metallic oxides or coloured clays or marls are added to the prepared mixed clay as may be thought desirable.

" The body or paste of mixed materials being now prepared, it is either *thrown,* as it is termed, by means of the potter's wheel, that is, raised into circular forms of different kinds by means of the rotary motion of the wheel and by the action of the fingers, or moulded into forms; in the latter case the paste or body being first rolled into flattened pieces, which can be easily squeezed into a mould, commonly of plaster of Paris. When thought desirable, the ' thrown ' forms are finished by placing them on a lathe, and turning into more accurately circular shapes.

" The various forms of the paste or body being completed, the pieces are taken to be carefully dried in rooms prepared for the purpose, in order to deprive them as much as possible of moisture without causing disintegration; water in the paste or bodies being regarded only as a tool in the manufacture, to be laid aside when no longer required.

" The future pieces of earthenware being thus sufficiently dried, are placed in large flat-bottomed pans, oval or round as may be considered desirable, with vertical sides of sufficient height, termed *seggars,* made of refractory materials, such as fire-clays, the broken pieces of earthenware after the first firing, and also of broken seggars themselves, pounded up, and often mixed with a small portion of damaged Dorset, Devon, or Cornish clays. In these seggars the pieces of dried future ware are so placed as to allow as many as possible to be packed without injury to each other. The seggars are then arranged in a kiln called the *biscuit-kiln* one above the other, so that an upper covers a lower seggar. The kiln is then ' fired,' that is, the heat deemed proper is communicated to it, and ' the fire ' is continued for about three days; that is, a kiln ' fired ' on Monday evening will be ready to be ' *drawn,*' or the seggars and their contents removed, on Friday morning. The ware is then in the condition termed *biscuit,* white and porous, readily absorbing water.

' The *biscuit* is now in a state to be painted with certain colours which can be used ' *under the glaze,*' that is, before it is covered with a preparation which in another ' firing ' turns into a coating of glass, and for receiving the impressions from etchings and engravings introduced so advantageously into ceramic manufactures for about a century, producing the ' *printed ware.*' The colours which can be advantageously used ' under the glaze ' are few as compared with those employed above it.[1] In the latter case the paints used are enamel colours, that is, glasses of different kinds mixed with metallic oxides, giving the colours sought. The printing is but the employment of the colours that can be advantageously used ' under the glaze,' mixed with oil, and worked as ordinary printing ink for engravings. Care is required as regards the paper for pressing the print on the ware, and for the dexterous removal of the paper after the pressure, so that the impression be not injured. To drive off the soil used as a vehicle for the colours, the ware, after ' printing,' is exposed at a low heat on a kiln termed a ' *hardening-kiln* '; after which it is ready to be glazed. The materials of the glaze, which may vary accord-

---

[1] Cobalt blue, chrome green., &c., which the heat of the "*gloss*" or glazing kiln will not change. Red, from peroxide of iron, cannot be thus applied, the heat of the kiln converting the red into brown and black.

ing to the practice of different potteries, are mixed with water so as to form a substance of about the consistency of cream. Into this the earthenware, either painted with colours which will not injure in the heat of the kiln into which it is next placed, or printed with colours of the like general kind, is dexterously dipped. Upon removal, all traces of the colouring are lost under a general slight coating of the finely comminuted materials of the glaze, the water being readily absorbed by the porous ' biscuit-ware.' It is now placed in seggars in a ' gloss-kiln,' as it is termed, for about one day, exposed to a less heat than in the ' biscuit-kiln,' but at the same time sufficient to reduce the coating upon the ware to a glass, disclosing the painting or printing under it, and preventing the access of liquids to the porous ware beneath. The earthenware is then ready for the market."

PORCELAIN

" The manufacture of porcelain bears a general resemblance to that of earthenware, the differences relating chiefly to the composition of the pastes or bodies and glazes, to the arrangement of kilns fitted for greater heats, properly to act upon more refractory materials, and to muffles or kilns for firing the various enamel colours employed upon the different forms given to the porcelain. The ingredients employed are commonly Cornish or Devon kaolin, Cornish china-stone and flint, with prepared bones. According to Aikin the following was the composition of the body or paste of Staffordshire porcelain about 1840 : Cornish kaolin, 31.0; Cornish china-stone, 26.0; flint, 2.5; prepared bones, 40.5.

" M. Arnoux considers the soft porcelain commonly manufactured in England as nothing but that which is termed hard, from its greater hardness, modified by the presence of the phosphate of lime contained in the bones employed.[1]

" The soft paste of Chelsea, Bow, and Derby must be carefully distinguished from that now made, as other ingredients were then employed, to the entire exclusion of bones, which were a subsequent invention."

It is a curious circumstance in connection with the marks on English ceramic wares, especially porcelain, that several manufactories should have adopted characters as marks which are used as chemical signs. This has probably arisen from the peculiar nature of the materials employed, or from some supposed affinity with the metals thereby applied. For example, the Plymouth mark of the sign of Jupiter (tin) was adopted, it is supposed, in consequence of the stanniferous nature of the clay employed; the triangle, denoting fire, was the mark used sometimes at Chelsea; the signs of the planets Venus and Mercury (copper and quicksilver) are found on Bow porcelain; the sign of Mars (iron) is found on the Staffordshire iron-stone china; the sign of Luna (silver) is a mark of Worcester, and many of the workmen's marks given hereafter as being found upon Worcester porcelain bear a strong resemblance to others. For the sake of comparison with similar marks so frequently found on china, we here annex a list of the chemical signs:—

---

[1] Lecture on Ceramic Manufactures. As to the action of the bones M. Arnoux remarks that when the other materials " begin to combine at a certain heat, the bones being phosphate of lime, which cannot be decomposed by the silica, melt, without combining, into a sort of semi-transparent enamel, and being intimately mixed in the mass, give transparency in proportion to the quantity used."

A	Aer . . . . . . Air		♄	Saturn . . . . . Lead.
▽	Terra . . . . . Earth.		♂	Mars . . . . . Iron or Steel.
△	Ignis . . . . . Fire.		♀	Venus . . . . . Copper.
▽	Aqua . . . . . . Water.		☿	Mercury . . . . Quicksilver.
♂	Dies . . . . . Day.		♁	Antimonium . . . Antimony.
ρ	Nox . . . . . . Night.		◇	Orichalcum . . . Brass.
♀ᴜ	Fumus . . . . . Smoke.		⚹	Fæces Vini . . . Lees of wine.
⊏C	Cineres . . . . Ashes.		⊙	Albumen . . . . White of egg
⊖	Sal . . . . . . Salt.		⋮	Arena . . . . . Sand.
⊙	Sol . . . . . . Gold.		⟋	Arsenicum . . . Arsenic.
☽	Luna . . . . . Silver.		⊏⊐	Atramentum . . . Ink.
♃	Jupiter . . . . Tin.		⌐	Creta . . . . . Chalk.
			⌂	Borax.

SLIP-DECORATED WARE

This quaint and effective, though coarse and grotesque ware, is said to have originated in Staffordshire, although Professor Church divides the honours between that famous centre of potting and Kent. We know of at least one important pottery in the latter county, at Wrotham between Maidstone and Sevenoaks, of which there are a great many examples in our museums and private collections. Professor Church, writing in 1884, considered the first piece with a date, which had been identified as Wrotham, was a jug in the Maidstone Museum, 1656, and perhaps a specimen in the Victoria and Albert Museum (1621); but Mr. Hodgkin had described and illustrated a *tyg* with four handles, which is in the Liverpool Museum, dated 1612. Subsequently to Wrotham this mode of decoration seems to have been adopted in Cheshire and Derbyshire, and there are several specimens with dates as early as 1708 and as late as 1794 in the British Museum and the Liverpool Museum, which were attributed to the pottery

of Cockpit Hill in Derbyshire.   Professor Church thus describes the process: " Sometimes white and red clays were marbled upon a red or brown
clay basis, but more frequently the white or light-coloured clay was
used in the form of a ' slip,' that is, a thin creamy mixture of clay and
water, dropped or trailed from a spouted vessel upon the surface of
the piece to be decorated.   Slip-ware is a convenient term for pieces
decorated in this way, which, indeed, much resembles the process by which
the complex sugar ornaments on bride-cakes are laboriously built up from
a syrup, the syrup, alas! being too often blown from a quill held in the
mouth of a dirty old man, well practised in the curious art.   The slips
were not always white, but buff, yellow, brown, and even nearly black,
while the ground or body was frequently of a light colour.   Candlesticks
small and large, drinking vessels in the form of *tygs*, cups and posset
pots, jugs and piggins, large plates or platters, and cradles for birthday
gifts occur amongst the most usual pieces in slip-ware."

The decoration of such pieces was grotesque and fanciful, there being
apparently nothing but the taste of the operator to guide him in producing
figures, animals, birds, foliage, or conventional ornaments.   The ware was
afterwards glazed with sulphuret of lead, often mixed with manganese,
which gave the object a rich yellow tint of a transparent character, and
it was then fired.

METROPOLITAN SLIP-WARE.   Besides the slip-ware made in the centres
of pottery mentioned, there was a good deal of this kind of work done near
London, but of a less ornamental character, and this was distinctively
classed as " Metropolitan Slip " by Sir A. W. Franks.   The body of these is
of a darker colour than the Wrotham or Staffordshire ware, and the ornament, apart from the inscription, is simpler; wavy lines, herring-bone, and
very crude floral designs being the rule.   Specimens found from excavations in and near London are sometimes dated and bear legends and
inscriptions.   These are generally of a pious character, which lead us to
suppose that they were made by or for Puritans.   There are several specimens in the British Museum, and the legends " Obeay God's Wourd,"
" When this you see remember me," occur on one of them.   Another is in
the Guildhall Museum, which was dug up in Bishopsgate, and bears the
date 1650, and the inscription " The gift is small, goodwill is all."   In
Examples of Early English Pottery Named and Dated, by J. E. Hodgkin,
F.S.A., and Edith Hodgkin (1891), the authors have taken infinite pains to
reproduce by careful drawing a large number of dated specimens of slip-
ware, giving in facsimile the curious mottoes and legends which occur,
together with the dates.

It was to this class of ornamental pottery that the Tofts and those
potters, a list of whom has been given, which form what has been called
the Toft School, devoted their taste and industry.   This description
of slip-ware, dealing as it does with other potteries besides those of
Staffordshire, has been placed under this heading as convenient to the
reader, and should be referred to in connection with the notices of the other
potteries of Wrotham, Cockpit Hill, and many others which occur in their

proper places in the body of this work. Collectors of this early and very interesting form of ornamental English pottery should consult Mr. William Burton's excellent *English Earthenware and Stoneware*, 1902, and also Mr. Solon's *Art of the Old English Potter*, 1885. The British Museum is rich in specimens.

THOMAS TOFT   RALPH TOFT 1677

5   6

WILLIAM · SANS

7

STAFFORDSHIRE. Thomas Toft (about 1660 to 1689). Thomas Toft was a Staffordshire potter; he is spoken of by Shaw (*Chemistry of Pottery*) as having invented a new description of ware by the introduction of *aluminous shale* or *fire-brick clay*. There is a large earthenware dish in the British Museum signed on the border as mark no. 5; it has in the centre a lion crowned, buff-coloured ground, the ornaments laid on in black and brown-coloured " slip." A dish in the Sheffield Museum has in the centre a half-length crowned portrait of Charles II with a sceptre in each hand, and the letters C.R. with red and black trellis pattern on the border, and the name at length, as usual. Another of the same description of ware, with a mermaid in the centre, is in the Victoria and Albert Museum; illustrated in Church's *English Earthenware*, fig. 13. Toft's pot-works were reputedly situated at Tinker's Clough, in a lane between Shelton and Newcastle-under-Lyme.

STAFFORDSHIRE. Ralph Toft (c. 1670 to 1680). His name at length, with the date 1677 (mark no. 6), is on a dish, buff-coloured ground with figures in relief of brown outlined with black; in the centre a soldier in buff jerkin and full-bottomed wig, a sword in each hand; on one side a crowned head and bust (Charles II), chequered ornaments, and name on the border. (Chaffers, *New Keramic Gallery*, 1926, fig. 444.) In the Salford Museum is another platter, with a lady and gentleman in the centre, having on the border the name at length, and date 1676. Mr. John J. Bagshawe, of Sheffield, had also a similar specimen, but without date, bearing a full-length figure of a queen holding a flower in each hand, and two medallions of busts of gentlemen with large wigs and crowns on their heads.

STAFFORDSHIRE. William Sans (about 1670). His name occurs on earthenware dishes of similar character and ornamentation to that of Thomas and Ralph Toft; he is mentioned by Shaw (*Chemistry of Pottery*) as having used in the manufacture of this pottery *manganese* and *galena pulverised*. Up to 1680 the glazing employed seems to have been plumbiferous; the silica derived from the body of the ware in the firing, and the lead from the galena (sulphuret of lead) of the Derbyshire mines, dusted in a pulverised state upon the unbaked ware through a coarse cloth. Mark no. 7.

STAFFORDSHIRE. William Talor (about 1670). A dish in the Sheffield Museum has two full-length figures in the costume of the Stuarts, the gentleman holding his hat and feather, and the lady a nosegay; between them are the initials W.T., and on the rim, in precisely the same manner as the Toft dishes, the name " William Talor." Mark no. 8.

The name RALPH TURNOR occurs round the upper part of a *tyg* or drinking bowl, with four handles, of brown mottled glaze on yellow ground; whether made in Staffordshire or at Wrotham in Kent, it is impossible to say. (*Ker. Gall.*, fig. 442.) Mark no. 9.

WILLIAM · TALOR   8   R·A·L·P·H· T·A·Y·L·O·R

RALPH · TURNOR   9   1
                                            11   6
          1681   9
                                                              7

ŁOŚEPŃ.GŁASS.SŸ.H.G.X   10

HANLEY (about 1670). A potter of the name of Joseph Glass resided here towards the end of the seventeenth century; his manufactory was in existence in 1710, and produced a cloudy kind of ware (mottled), and dishes painted with different coloured slip (*see* List of Potters in 1710). There was in the collection of the Rev. T. Staniforth a large buff coloured *tyg* ornamented with brown slip designs and white dots; it has four handles, with as many crinkled projections between, very similar to Toft's earthenware. The name is painted round the body. Mark no. 10.

Mark no. 11. RALPH TAYLOR. A red ware puzzle jug with dark brown and cream-coloured slip was in the Sheldon Collection, the name is in brown slip and the date in cream slip.

Professor Church in *English Earthenware* gives a list of potters' names occurring on dishes, and other important pieces of this character, which may be called of the Toft School: it includes, besides those mentioned above, T. JOHNSON, 1694, W. RICH, 1702, THOMAS and WILLIAM SANS, RALPH SIMPSON, WILLIAM and GEORGE TAYLOR, JOHN WRIGHT, 1707, and to these may be added that of RICHARD MARE, 1697. See Godden's *British Pottery and Porcelain, an Illustrated Encyclopaedia of Marked Specimens.*

A class of slip-ware produced by Samuel Malkin of Burslem and often bearing the initials S.M. is discussed by Hugh Tait in *The Apollo*, January and February, 1957. These S.M. dishes have previously been attributed to Samuel Mier of Derby.

Mr. William Burton, in his work on *English Earthenware*, has called particular attention to greater refinement apparent in the work of Joseph Glass in the decorative use of " Slip " as compared with the ruder kinds of Toft ware. His lettering is of a better character, and the effect has been improved by his method of first tracing the letters in dark brown slip, which was then brightened by decorating them with drops of white slip, the whole being in relief, and he mentions a cradle formerly in the collection of Mr. Griffiths which bears the inscription " Joseph Glass 1703." Several specimens will be found in the Victoria and Albert Museum, and the British Museum.

DERBYSHIRE. In the absence of distinguishing marks it is difficult to prevent erroneous attributions of slip-ware specimens, but we know that a great deal of this kind of ware was produced in Derbyshire, and certainly at three centres, namely, the Cockpit Hill Pottery, Bolsover, and Tickenhall. In the British Museum is a fine dish with a trellis border, rather stiff floral design, and initials S. M. on a label, could relate to those of Samuel Meir, who was believed to have worked at this pottery. See note above on Samuel Malkin. There was also a dish in the Liverpool Museum (Mayer Coll.), dated 1749, with initials W. W., and Mr. Burton mentions others known to him bearing dates from 1740 until 1780, at which latter date Cockpit Hill works were closed. Of the Bolsover works little is known, but Mr. Burton mentions that during some local excavations in 1894 fragments of ware were discovered, and that authenticated specimens are in the hands of local collectors.

Pottery which can safely be assigned to the Tickenhall craftsmen of the end of the seventeenth century is very rare, and the dish in the British Museum, dated 1643, which Mr. R. L. Hobson illustrates in his guide, is marked with a note of interrogation. For information about the slip decorated ware made at Wrotham in Kent, the reader should refer to the notice under that heading, and for excellent specimens he should visit the British Museum. The works on English earthenware by Mr. William Burton, Mr. Solon and Professor Church should also be consulted.

BRADWELL ELERS WARE. Established about 1690 by John Philip Elers, who accompanied his countryman, the Prince of Orange, to England, when he came to take possession of the English throne. Elers was descended from a noble family of Saxony. His grandfather, Admiral Elers, married a princess of the royal house of Baden; his father, Martin Elers, born in 1621, married the daughter of a rich Burgomaster of Amsterdam, and was ambassador to several Courts of Europe. Martin Elers had a daughter, who married Sir W. Phipps, ancestor of the Marquis of Normanby, and two sons—David, who settled in London as a merchant, and John Philip, who settled in Staffordshire in the secluded villages of Bradwell and Dimsdale. John Philip Elers was a man of great abilities, a good chemist and a clever mechanic; his knowledge of chemistry enabled him to discover the art of mixing the clay of the neighbourhood in greater perfection than had ever been attained in Staffordshire.

They introduced the delicate patterns in relief made by metal moulds, afterwards brought to great perfection by Aaron Wood and others. From clays found at Chesterton and Bradwell, near Burslem, carefully levigated and passed through fine hair-sieves, and then artificially evaporated, they manufactured to a considerable extent an improved kind of red unglazed porcelain in imitation of the red pottery of Japan, and they succeeded wonderfully in the attempt, insomuch that some of their elegant tea-pots are said to have been sold as high as a guinea a piece; the genuine specimens which still remain show their perfection, as well with respect to the texture and quality of the ware itself, as to the form and workmanship. They were ornamented in relief with sharp and well-designed flowers, etc., being formed in copper moulds, and sometimes of pierced work. By the addition of manganese to the clays they produced a fine black ware, a knowledge of which components was the origin of **Wedgwood's** black Egyptian or basalts.

The sharply-moulded ornaments on Elers's red Staffordshire ware were but a continuance of the moulded enscrollments of the stoneware of Germany. They took every precaution to prevent the secrets of their processes becoming known, but from the inquisitiveness of their neighbours, who clandestinely obtained a knowledge of their methods of mixing the clays (not having secured them by patent), they were driven from the locality. A story is told that the Elers, to keep the secret from the knowledge of other manufacturers, employed only ignorant people, or even idiots, to work for them; but one Astbury, counterfeiting idiotcy, was engaged, and after two years of dissimulation and deceit, possessed himself of the method and process, and left, to open an establishment at Shelton, where he turned the theft to his own advantage.

Astbury's son, Thomas, who was afterwards in business at Shelton, made several improvements in the manufacture of the earthenware, and is said to have produced a cream-coloured ware which afterwards in Wedgwood's hands became the celebrated Queen's ware.

Dr. Martin Lister, in his *Journey to Paris*, in the year 1698, says: "As for the red ware of China, that has been and is done in England, to a far greater perfection than in China. We have as good materials, viz., the soft hæmatites, and far better artists in pottery. But we are in this particular beholden to two Dutchmen, brothers, who wrought in Staffordshire (as I have been told), and were not long since at Hammersmith." From these quotations it would appear that his brother David was connected with him in the manufacture, and being a merchant in London, it is probable that he acted as agent.

There is a jasper cameo medallion of John Philip Elers, which was produced by Wedgwood; a specimen was in Sir J. D. Hooker's Collection. In a letter from Wedgwood to Bentley, July 19, 1777, he thus refers to the improvements made by John Philip Elers in the manufacture of pottery :—

"It is only now about eighty years ago since Mr. Elers was amongst us, when there were as many pot-works in Burslem as there are now, and had been from time immemorial; and the reason for Mr. Elers fixing upon Staffordshire to try his experiments seems to be that the pottery was carried on there in a much larger way and in a more improved state than in any other part of Great Britain. The improvements made by Mr. Elers in our manufactory were precisely these : Glazing our common clays with salt, which produced *pot de grey* or stoneware, and this after they (the two Elers) had left the country was improved into white flint stoneware. . . . I make no doubt but glazing with salt by casting it amongst the ware whilst it is red-hot came to us from Germany, but whether Mr. Elers was the person to whom we are indebted for this improvement I do not know. . . . The next improvement introduced by Mr. Elers was the refining our common red clay by sifting and making it into tea and coffee ware, in imitation of the Chinese red porcelain, by casting it in plaster moulds and turning it on the outside upon lathes, and ornamenting it with the tea branch in relief, in imitation of the Chinese manner of ornamenting this ware. For these improvements, and very great ones they were for the time, we are indebted to the Messrs. Elers; and I shall gladly contribute all in my power to honour their memories, and transmit to posterity the knowledge of the obligations we owe them, &c." (alluding to the publication of his bust in the jasper ware).

From the particulars given by Richard Lovell Edgeworth (father of the authoress Maria Edgeworth), who married the daughter of Paul Elers and granddaughter of John Philip (Miss Meteyard's *Life of Wedgwood*, vol. ii. p. 436), we learn that John Philip Elers had been in distressed circumstances, and was taken notice of by Lady Barrington, a whimsical, good sort of lady, and by her set up in a glass and china shop in Dublin. He was very successful in business, which enabled him to send his son Paul to the Temple in London, where he made great proficiency in his studies, and became a first-rate counsel. Previous to his residence in Dublin, John Philip Elers was for some time with Sprimont at Chelsea; so it is handed down.

Peter Elers, another branch of this family, came over to this country when George I. was called to the throne, and settled at Chelsea; he was a Justice of the Peace for the county of Middlesex, and in 1715 married a daughter of Thomas Carew, Esq.; he was buried in Westminster Abbey in March 1753.

Besides the red stoneware which is known so well as Elers's ware, there are in many public and private collections beautiful specimens of white and coloured salt glaze. The white is really of a slightly greyish hue, not unlike the colour of *putty;* the body is extremely hard, and the surface has been not inaptly compared to that of a lemon, the glaze being granular rather than smooth and even. The tea-pots, mugs, posset pots, and dishes which one finds of this class of old salt glaze are fine and thin and *very light,* altogether charming examples of the potter's art, and the decoration is either moulded, incised, scratched, embossed, or enamelled in colours.

In the coloured specimens enamel colours are used with excellent effect, and a result not unlike the fine old Chinese enamelled porcelain has been produced. There are many examples in the Victoria and Albert Museum and the British Museum, and Mr. J. E. Hodgkin has illustrated specimens from his own collection in his *Examples of Early English Pottery.* The earliest date he has found is that of 1701, and the quaintest example he has is dated 1749. Professor Church possesses also some charming specimens both of the white and coloured salt glaze.

The white and coloured salt glaze ware described above is never marked, but one finds occasionally on the red ware first made by John and

Philip Elers, the mark no. 12 which occurs on a red Elers ware coffee-pot with small figures stamped upon it by way of decoration.

An interesting paper on Elers type wares written by W. B. Honey is printed in the *Transactions of the English Ceramic Circle*, vol. i, part 2. See also vol. iv, part 5 and vol. v, part 3.

12

WEDGWOOD

John Wedgwood, eldest son of Thomas Wedgwood and Margaret Shaw, born in 1654, had a pottery at Burslem, called the *Upper House Works*, but it was "not worked" when Josiah Wedgwood's list was made in 1710, as he died a few years before, viz., in 1705. He was the father of Catherine Wedgwood, who was thrice married—1st, to her cousin, Richard Wedgwood; 2nd, to Thomas Bourne; 3rd, to Rowland Egerton. In the Victoria and Albert Museum there is an interesting relic of this John Wedgwood; it is a green glazed, brown earthenware puzzle jug, with pierced neck, the hollow channel running up the handle and round the mouth, on which there are three spouts, inscribed "*John Wedgwood*, 1691."

THE CHURCHYARD WORKS, BURSLEM. It appears from the document drawn up by Josiah Wedgwood, that in 1710 his grandfather, Thomas, then occupied these works; they descended to his eldest son, Thomas, father of Josiah, and eventually to Thomas, the elder brother of Josiah, in 1739, who also had the Overhouse Works. It was at the Churchyard Works that Josiah served his apprenticeship to his brother, which expired in 1749. Some years afterwards these works were taken by Josiah, who carried them on together with the Bell or Brickhouse Works and the Ivy House; on his removal to Etruria they were occupied by his second cousin, Joseph, who made jasper and other fine bodies for and under the direction of Josiah. About 1780 the latter purchased and conveyed them to his brother John, who in 1795 sold the property to Mr. Thomas Green.

Mark no 1, on a blue printed earthenware plate, formerly in the Sheldon Collection, has been attributed to Thomas Green, but is probably the mark of Thomas Godwin of Burslem, c. 1834.

In 1811 these works were purchased by a manufacturer named Joynson, or Johnson, who in turn sold them to Mr. Moseley. In the Victoria and Albert Museum there is a large tea-pot in black Egyptian ware, with fluted body and raised classic figures, impressed mark no. 2 "MOSELEY," which was probably made here, c. 1811-22. About the year 1857 the Churchyard Works were occupied by Messrs. Bridgwood & Clarke, who remodelled the buildings and erected others. Messrs. Bridgwood & Clarke also had extensive works at Tunstall and employed nearly 400 hands. Their services bear the impressed mark of "Bridgwood & Clarke," or a printed mark of the royal arms, and the words " Porcelain opaque, B. & C. Burslem." Bridgwood died in 1864 and the firm was carried on by Edward Clarke at various addresses until 1887; the wares were marked in full.

1

2

THE OVERHOUSE WORKS belonged for more than two centuries to the Wedgwood family. In 1756 they passed by inheritance to Thomas, the elder brother of Josiah; at his death, in 1772, to his son Thomas, who did not enjoy long the possession, for he died in 1786, leaving them to his son Thomas. In a Survey of the County in 1786 we find " Thomas Wedgwood, *Overhouse*, manufacturer of cream-coloured ware, and china-glazed ware, painted with blue." He occupied the property until his death in 1809, when it was sold successively to Christopher Robinson, John Wood, and in 1819 to Mr. Edward Challinor. The following inscription was placed over the entrance to these works: " Edward Challinor commenced business here A.D. 1819, and rebuilt the premises 1869." Messrs. Allman, Broughton & Co., who marked their ware A. B. & Co., with or without " Wedgwood Place, Burslem," carried on business after Mr. Challinor's retirement, until about 1874. They were succeeded by R. Hammersley & Son.

Dr. Thomas Wedgwood, of the Red Lion Works at Burslem, so called from being next to an inn of that name, was son of the first Aaron Wedgwood: he was born in 1655, and manufactured the ordinary lead-glazed ware of the day.

Dr. Thomas Wedgwood, jun., son of Dr. Thomas before named, carried on a pot-work at a place called Ruffley's in Burslem; his name will be found in Wedgwood's list of potters in 1710. He married Catherine, daughter of the first Thomas Wedgwood, of the Churchyard Works. In addition to stoneware he made marble, agate, cauliflower, and melon ware in great perfection; he also paid great attention to the construction of moulds and the art of modelling. His apprentice, Aaron Wood, acquired celebrity for his cutting of moulds for the stamped and other wares.

Richard Wedgwood, son of the first Aaron Wedgwood, born in 1668; he was a potter in the " middle of the town," making stoneware, which from the list already given was one of the most important in 1710-15.

Aaron Wedgwood (the second) of Brown Hills, established about 1688. He was son of Aaron, the sixth son of Gilbert Wedgwood and Mary Burslem; he was born in 1667, and married Mary Hollins: they both died in April, 1743, and were buried on the same day.

In Shaw's *Chemistry of Pottery* we find mentioned among the improvements in the manufacture of earthenware, that " the Crouch ware was first made of common potter's clay, and grit from Mow Cup, and afterwards the grit and can-marl by A. Wedgwood of Burslem 1690." His manufactory is included in the list of potters at Burslem in 1710. This Crouch ware, made by Aaron Wedgwood, was a coarse sort of ware of brick clay and fine sand, covered with a salt glaze, which gradually superseded the lead glaze. The account given of this discovery is, that at Mr. Joseph Yates', at Stanley, near Bagnall, the servant was preparing in an earthen vessel a salt ley for curing pork, and during her temporary absence the liquid boiled over and the sides of the earthen pipkin became red hot from intense heat, and when cold it had acquired an excellent glaze. This story Professor Church has proved to be fabulous, for the heat would not have been sufficient to effect the chemical change, and if the heat had sufficed and other conditions been favourable, a common brown pot is not likely to have stood the temperature. A more probable origin of the introduction of salt glaze into England is that told to Wedgwood by an old workman named Steel, and noted by him in 1775, that the brothers Elers had brought the process over with them in 1688, and that it soon became adopted at Burslem, which was only two miles from Elers's pottery. The ovens employed for the purpose were large and lofty, and constructed with a scaffold round them, on which the firemen stood to cast in the salt through holes made in the upper part of the cylinder, the saggars having holes in their sides to allow the vapours of the salt to circulate freely and act upon the surfaces of all the vessels in the oven. In 1700 twenty-two ovens were employed in Burslem; they were usually fired on Thursday night, finishing about midday on Saturday, and from eight o'clock until twelve on that morning, at which time the salt was cast upon the ware, the dense white cloud arising from the " firing up " so completely enveloped the town as to cause persons to run against each other in the streets.

William Littler, and Aaron Wedgwood, who succeeded his father about 1743 at Burslem, made many experiments in the manufacture of porcelain, which are said to have been very successful both as to the body and the glaze. In Shaw's enumeration of the order in which various materials were introduced into Staffordshire, we find, "Aaron Wedgwood, *red lead*, and William Littler, *calcined bone earth*. A pint of red lead in powder to each bushel of salt formed a fine fluid glaze, and the calcined bones gave transparency to the ware, but their experiments occasioned heavy losses, and the manufacture was discontinued." (See notice on Longton Hall, *post*.)

Thomas and John Wedgwood, of the Big House, Burslem, were sons of the second Aaron Wedgwood: Thomas born 1703; John born 1705. About the year 1740 it is said the two brothers left their father's employ and commenced the manufacture of white stoneware upon their own account; they subsequently built a new and commodious manufactory.

In 1750 they erected a large dwelling-house, adjoining their manufactory, which so far exceeded the other houses in point of size that it was called the *Big House*. In 1769 these gentlemen retired from business with ample fortunes, and Josiah took possession of the premises. Josiah took his cousin Thomas Wedgwood into partnership about 1769, and the business was carried on in Thomas's name (for the manufacture of cream-colour was the only one in which he was interested). In a Survey of the Potteries in 1786 we find "Thomas Wedgwood, *Big House*, manufacturer of cream-colour ware and china glazed ware, painted with blue."

HILL WORKS. Ralph Wedgwood (about 1790). He was the son of Thomas Wedgwood, partner of Josiah in the manufacture of Queen's ware, and was brought up with his father at Etruria; he was born in 1766. He was a man of great ability, and originator of many scientific inventions; he carried on business as a potter under the style of Wedgwood & Co., but was ruined through losses during the American War. In 1796 he took out three patents: the first was a " new discovered and invented method of making earthenware, whereby articles may be made at a less cost than hitherto, to the great advantage of the manufacturer thereof and of the public." This consists " in casing over inferior compositions with compositions commonly used for making cream-coloured ware, white ware, or china; " thick bats or laminæ of the inferior being covered on each side with thin bats of the superior clay, etc. The second was for making glass upon new principles, composed of alkaline salts or borax, in a state of solution, into which were cast pieces of china or earthenware pitchers, pieces of clay heated red hot; to these were added calcareous earth, slaked in a solution of borax, silicious earths, etc. The third was a newly-invented stove, " calculated principally for the use of manufacturers of earthenware and china," and " consisting in part of a potter's oven of any shape or size, with the fireplaces situated within, and adjoining to the interior diameter of the exterior walls, or under the bottom," instead of being placed, as was usual, outside. In 1796 he removed into Yorkshire, where, having entered into partnership with some other potters, he again commenced business at Ferry Bridge. In 1806 he established himself at Charing Cross, and patented his invention of the " Manifold Writer," and intently applied himself in perfecting his scheme of an electric telegraph, and tried to induce the Government to assist him, without success. In 1814 he applied to Lord Castlereagh, who told him that " the war being over, the old system was sufficient for the country." In more enlightened times Professor Wheatstone again brought forward the subject, and it became eminently successful. Ralph Wedgwood died at Chelsea in 1837.

JOSIAH WEDGWOOD

BURSLEM AND ETRURIA. JOSIAH WEDGWOOD was born in August 1730, at Burslem; he was the youngest of thirteen children. His father, Thomas Wedgwood, died in 1739, when Josiah was only nine years old. His eldest brother, Thomas, succeeded his father in business as a potter, and Josiah was bound apprentice to him in November 1744, being then fourteen years old. The indenture binding him to his brother for five years is preserved in the Museum of the Hanley Mechanics' Institution, and is signed by himself, his mother, and his brother Thomas, attested by Samuel Astbury and Abner Wedgwood. During his apprenticeship he was seized with a violent attack of smallpox, and was laid up for a considerable period; although he recovered, the disease left a humour which settled in his leg; this disorder continued with him until manhood, when, in consequence of a bruise on his leg, which aggravated his complaint and settled in his knee so as to endanger his life, he was advised to have his leg amputated, which he submitted to in the thirty-fourth year of his age. In 1748 he lost his mother. His apprenticeship expired in 1749, but he remained with his brother a few years longer, and then left home to manufacture knife handles, imitation agate, tortoiseshell small wares, &c., at Stoke, where, in 1752, he entered into partnership with John Harrison, of Stoke-upon-Trent, in a pot-work belonging to Thomas Alders, but in two years they separated. In 1754 Josiah Wedgwood went into partnership with Thomas Whieldon, of Fenton Low, one of the most eminent potters of his day, and they remained together at this place for five years; their principal manufactures were tortoiseshell plates and dishes, cauliflower jugs, teapots with crab-stock handles, imitation agate knife handles, snuff-boxes, &c. While here, Wedgwood succeeded in producing that fine green glaze which covered dessert plates and dishes in imitation of leaves and fruit. The partnership expired in 1759, and Josiah Wedgwood immediately returned to his native town of Burslem, and at twenty-nine years of age commenced business entirely on his own account at the Churchyard Works, where he was born and apprenticed; he also shortly after took other premises in the middle of the town called "The Ivy House Works." Here he set himself earnestly to work, improving the manufacture of pottery, and soon became so successful that he was compelled to enlarge his establishment: his principal products were ornamental flower vases, green glazed dessert services, &c.

In 1759 he entered into an arrangement with his second cousin, Thomas Wedgwood, to take him as journeyman on the following terms:—

"Memorandum of Agreement between Josiah Wedgwood, of the parish of Stoke, in the county of Stafford, potter, and Thomas Wedgwood, journeyman, now living at the city of Worcester, potter. The said Thomas Wedgwood engageth to serve the said Josiah Wedgwood as a journeyman from the 1st of May 1759 to the 11th November 1765, and is to receive of the said Josiah Wedgwood twenty-two pounds of lawful money for every year's service.

(Signed)   JOSIAH WEDGWOOD,
                THOMAS WEDGWOOD."

Thomas was an excellent potter, having gained his experience in porcelain works at Worcester at a time when great attention was paid to the execution and finish of the ware. He has the reputation of being the inventor of the electric telegraph.

In 1762 Josiah Wedgwood produced his fine cream-coloured ware, which gained him great reputation, and it remained a staple article to the time of his death; after it had been patronised by royalty the name was changed to *Queen's ware*. This ware is composed of the whitest clays from Devonshire and Dorsetshire mixed with a due proportion of ground flint; the pieces are fired twice, and the glaze applied after the first firing, in the same manner as on porcelain. The glaze is a vitreous composition of flint and other white earthy bodies, with an addition of white lead for the flux, analogous to common flint glass; so that when prepared in perfection the ware may be considered as coated over with real flint glass. This compound being mixed with water to the consistence of cream, the pieces, after the first firing in a biscuit state, are separately dipped into it; being somewhat bibulous, they absorb the water, and the glaze which was mixed with it remains adherent uniformly all over their surface, so as to become by the second firing a coat of perfect glass. The ware was at first made quite devoid of colour, and Wedgwood had at that time no enamelling or painting executed on the premises. Messrs. Sadler & Green, of Liverpool, having invented a method of transferring prints to the surface of the ware *upon the glaze*, Mr. Wedgwood employed a waggon once a fortnight to take down a load of cream-colour to be decorated in this improved manner by Messrs. Sadler & Green, and return with the load previously taken for that purpose. (*Ker Gall.*, fig. 451.)

The ware in imitation of granite, porphyry, and other marbles was made into most elegant forms, the handles, festoons, etc., being gilt to imitate metal mountings. The finest of these were produced by Wedgwood & Bentley. (*Ker Gall.*, fig. 453.)

About 1764 he rented the premises of John and Thomas Wedgwood, called the *Big House*. In 1764, being then in his thirty-fourth year, he married, at Astbury Church, his cousin, Sarah Wedgwood, by whom he had four sons and four daughters. In 1765 he made a tea service for Queen Charlotte; it was gold outside, with raised green flowers.

The manufacture of Queen's ware having increased enormously, he took into partnership his cousin, Thomas Wedgwood, who had, from 1759 to 1765, been articled to him, and subsequently had the superintendence of that particular branch; this was about 1766: he was a man of high scientific attainments, son of the third Aaron Wedgwood of Burslem, potter, and was born in 1734. The business of cream-colour ware was carried on in his name at the Big House. (See Survey of 1786, pp. 641-42.)

Wedgwood also produced about this date a sort of *red china engined*, formed of the same fine ochreous clay used by the Elers nearly a century before; it required no glaze, except what it received from friction on the wheel and lathe; its chief beauty was derived from the form and the manifold effects of the turner's lathe; it was made into tea and coffee pots and services. This manufacture was not confined to Wedgwood; Henry Palmer of Hanley and Baddeley of Shelton made a vast amount of it. In

1766 he produced his celebrated *basalts* or black Egyptian ware. (*Ker. Gall.*, fig. 447.)

His brother, John Wedgwood (nine years his senior), who resided at the sign of the Artichoke in Cateaton Street, greatly assisted him in his export and retail business until his death in 1767, which happened by his slipping into the river, where he was found the next morning, whether accidentally drowned or not was never known.

In 1768 Josiah took Thomas Bentley into partnership to assist him in the *ornamental* branches of his extensive manufactures; Thomas Wedgwood being a partner in the Queen's ware or useful branches. This gentleman had been the agent of Josiah Wedgwood for some years at Liverpool, of the firm of Bentley & Boardman; he was born at Scrapton, in Derbyshire, on January 1, 1730.

"Josiah Wedgwood, in the county of Stafford, potter to Her Majesty the Queen," took out a patent for encaustic painting, which is here given :—

"A.D. 1769, November 16.

"WEDGWOOD, JOSIAH.—' The purpose of ornamenting earthen and porcelain ware with an encaustic gold bronze, together with a peculiar species of encaustic painting in various colours, in imitation of the ancient Etruscan and Roman earthenware.' In carrying out this invention, the patentee first prepares ' ten ingredients,' among which is bronze powder; some of these are one chemical substance, whilst others are composed mostly of several chemical substances in certain proportions, and generally calcined together. The substances used are *ayoree*, a white earth in North America, gold, aqua-regia, copper, oxide of antimony, tin ashes (oxide of tin), white and red leads, smalts, borax, nitre, copperas, flint, manganese, and zaffer. By mixing these ' ingredients,' with the exception of the bronze powder, in different proportions, he obtains several colours, which he names as follows : Red, orange, dry black, white, green blue, yellow, and he produces another colour, which he names shining black, by mixing some of these ingredients and one of the colours, namely, the green," &c.

ETRURIA. In 1769 the new manufactory at Etruria was opened, and on the 13th of June Wedgwood's first productions were thrown; having, as we have seen, taken out his patent for the encaustic painting on Etruscan vases (the only invention he ever secured by patent). To commemorate the opening of the works, he inscribed on some of these elegant vases the following appropriate record :—

"June XIII, MDCCLXIX. One of the first day's productions at Etruria, in Staffordshire, by Wedgwood and Bentley.
"Artes Etruriæ renascentur."

They are of *basalts*, ornamented with encaustic paintings of classical subjects, 10½ in. high. An example in the Wedgwood Works Museum is illustrated in many books on Wedgwood. An interesting incident connected with these vases is recorded in the *History of the Borough of Stoke*, that Wedgwood himself threw the first specimens of the black Etruscan vases while Bentley turned the lathe. The colours employed in his encaustic paintings were principally derived from oxides of iron. Dr. Bancroft, in his *Philosophy of Permanent Colours*, says, " I remember having been told by Mr. Wedgwood that nearly all the fine diversified colours applied to his pottery were produced only by oxides of this single metal." Mr. Bentley resided in London, and a branch establishment was opened at Chelsea about 1770, for finishing and painting the best pieces; both these were under his immediate superintendence. There are two very elegant and probably unique Wedgwood ware tablets, each 11 in. by 7¼ in., finely painted in enamel colours, by one of his best artists, on slate-coloured ground, with oval medallions of Diana and Melpomene *en grisaille* on black and ornamental borders on red, formerly in Mr. John J. Bagshaw's Collection.

In 1773 another improvement was made, which was called "a fine white terra-cotta, of great beauty and delicacy, proper for cameos, portraits, and bas-reliefs"; this was the forerunner of the jasper ware, which became, by constant attention and improvement, the most beautiful of all Wedgwood's productions. About the year 1776 the solid jasper ware was invented, which, however, attained its greatest perfection ten years later, consequently it may be observed that the pieces signed "Wedgwood and Bentley" have not that delicate colour and semi-transparency which after Bentley's death they had acquired. In the manufacture of this beautiful jasper ware Wedgwood largely employed sulphate of barytes, and for a long time derived great profit, none of the workmen having any idea of the nature of the material upon which they were operating, until a letter containing a bill of parcels of a quantity of the article fell unfortunately into the hands of a dishonest servant, who told the secret and deprived the inventor for ever of that particular source of emolument; for when the same article was made by those who employed inferior workmen, to whom they did not pay one-fourth of the salary given by Wedgwood, the price of jasper ware became so reduced that he was unable to employ those exquisite modellers whom he had formerly engaged to superintend that branch of the manufacture (*Parkes*). The blue jasper was produced by adding to the mixture of clays *oxide of cobalt* in proportions varying from one-third of a part to one part in every hundred, according to the depth of tint required; the green jasper was obtained by the admixture of *protoxide of chrome*. The white figures and cameos of the early Wedgwood are made of a kind of soft porcelain, called *white body* of jasper, the composition of which is said to be as follows : 10 of native sulphate of barytes, 10 of blue clay; 5 of burnt bones, and 2 of flint.

The Empress Catherine II of Russia, a great patroness of the ceramic art, had a remarkable service of Wedgwood ware made for her Grenouillière Palace near St. Petersburg. This splendid service was commenced in April, 1773, and had upwards of 1,200 views of the seats of noblemen and gentlemen in England, and a green frog was painted on each piece. The form chosen was the royal pattern, and was made of the ordinary cream-colour ware with a delicate saffron tint; the views were in purple *camaieu*, bordered with a gadroon pattern, in Indian-ink, and round the edge a running wreath of mauve flowers and green leaves. The two services, for dinner and dessert, consisting of 952 pieces, and 1,244 enamel views, which cost on an average 21s. each, the borders and frogs to each about 15s. more: making the entire cost, with £51 8s. 4d. for the cream ware itself, a total of £2,359 2s. 1d., without calculating many extras; the price ultimately paid by the Empress was stated to be £3,000. In June, 1774, the service was sufficiently completed to exhibit it at the New Rooms in Portland House, No. 12 Greek Street, Soho, where it remained on show for nearly two months. The Empress showed it to Lord Malmesbury when he visited the Grenouillière Palace in 1779. It is still proudly displayed in Russia today.

A cup and saucer of the same pattern, *without the frog*, is figured in Meteyard's *Life and Works of Wedgwood*, vol. ii, p. 296.

Josiah Wedgwood, in a letter to Bentley dated 25th June, 1769, discusses the employment of Ralph Willcox and his wife as artists:—

" A Worcester china painter of the name of Willcox applied to me; he had served his time to Mr. Christian of Liverpool. He has a wife who paints and is very ingenious: she is at present finishing some work at Worcester. Willcox says she is an excellent copier of figures and other subjects, and a much better hand than himself. He showed me two heads of her doing in Indian-ink, which are very well done. She is a daughter to that Frye who was famous for doing heads in mezzotints, which you have seen. Willcox is at present employed by Twemlo's, but not engaged; he wants to be fixed, and would article for any time. I like his appearance much: he seems a sober, solid man, and has nothing flighty or coxcombical in his dress or behaviour, of which most of his class are apt to contract a small tincture. His wife and he have very good wages at Worcester, better he believes than ever he must expect again; they would now be content, both of them, at 25s. per week, which is low enough, if they will be tolerably diligent." Mrs. Catherine Willcox proved to be an admirable artist, and her services extended over a considerable period, probably until her death in 1776; she painted the best single figures, groups, and borderings on the Etruscan ware, between 1769 and 1776, and headed the group of female painters who were engaged on the great service for the Empress Catherine. The name is also spelt Wilcox.

We read in the *Gentleman's Magazine*, vol. xlvi, p. 350, that in the year 1776 " Mr. J. Bradley Blake, a resident of Canton, brought to England and presented to Mr. Samuel More, secretary to the Society of Arts, specimens of the earths, clay, stone, sand, and other materials, used by the Chinese in making the true Nankin porcelain, which he placed in the hands of Mr. Josiah Wedgwood, the most celebrated potter of this country. This ingenious artist from these materials produced some pieces of excellent porcelain, and declared them to be so complete a set of specimens, and yet so simple, as beyond a doubt to be the true porcelain materials, desiring nothing more than a large quantity to distribute among the different counties of England, in order that they might search for the like materials, and wishing further information of the nature of the land where they were found and what mines or minerals accompanied them, plans and sections of the kilns, etc. Mr. Blake's death, which happened shortly after his arrival, prevented any further investigations at that time."

In 1780, on the 26th November, Thomas Bentley, the friend and partner of Josiah Wedgwood, died at his residence at Turnham Green; and on the 3rd December 1781, the stock of Wedgwood & Bentley, their joint property (which did not include the Queen's ware), was sold by auction by Messrs. Christie & Ansell, the sale occupying two days. The several divisions are as follows: Bouquetières and myrtle pans; écritoires, ink-pots, &c.; tea-pots, &c.; ornamental vases in imitation of crystalline stones and in basalts; painted Etruscan vases; bas-reliefs in jasper for chimney-pieces; busts in basalts; statues, figures, candelabra, &c., for chimney ornaments; seals in basalts, lamps, &c.; medallions in basalts; encaustic paintings.

The encaustic paintings, in sets of five, brought from £2 to £15; bas-reliefs in sets, consisting of the tablet, frieze, and blocks, from £3 to £10; black seals averaged 8s. per dozen; busts 30s. to 70s.; vases in imitation of marbles, the set of five, 40s. to 60s.; one large vase with bas-reliefs, 5 feet high, bought by Nixon, £20 9s.; large cameo medallions, 15s. to 30s. each; tea-pots, 42s. per dozen.

The principal buyers were Flaxman, who was a large purchaser, as also was Nixon, Sir Harbord Harbord, the Duke of Devonshire; Sir Thomas Rumbold, Sir T. Gascoyne, Sir Joseph Banks, Sir H. Englefield, Councillor Dagge, Mr. Byng, Mr. Spode, Mrs. Moody, &c.

The modelling bills for the years 1770, 1771, and 1772 are missing, and even those of 1773, 1775, and 1779, which we here quote, are un-doubtedly but a small part of the whole, but they permit us to individualise many well-known and interesting objects (*Mayer MSS.*, Meteyard's *Life of Wedgwood*, vol. ii. pp. 324 to 326.)

1773. Hoskins and Grant for plaster casts prepared to mould from. Busts of Zeno, Pindar, Faustina, Germanicus, Antoninus Pius, Seneca, Augustus, Cato, Marcus Aure-lius, Homer, Antinous, Solon, Plato, at 21s. each. Inigo Jones, Palladio, Epicurus, Mar-cus Brutus, and Junius Brutus, 25s. each; Venus de Medicis, 15s.; Minerva, 12s.; Agrip-pina, 12s.; large Marcus Aurelius, £1 11s. 6d.; four ovals of the Elements, £1 16s.; Tablet of Cupid and Psyche, 7s.; Sphinx and Lyre, 6s.

1775. Hoskins and Grant. Two busts of the Madonna, in pairs; Swift and Milton; Virgil and Horace; Galen and Hippocrates; Sappho and Vestal; Spenser and Chaucer; Addison and Pope; Locke and Newton; Dryden and Dr. Johnson; Demosthenes and Democritus; Ben Jonson and Sir W. Raleigh; Prior and Congreve; Beaumont and Fletcher; Seneca and Cicero; Mark Antony and Cleopatra; Julia; all these at 10s. 6d. and 12s. 6d. each. Larger busts of Bacon and Boyle, 50s. the pair; Harvey and Newton, 50s.; Socrates, 15s.; Venus and Adonis, 15s. the pair.

1779. Large bust of Bacchus, 42s.; ditto Ariadne, 31s. 6d.; Vase, 31s. 6d.; large antique bust of Mercury, 21s.; ditto Alexander, 42s.; two busts of Shakespeare and Garrick, 36s.; six bas-relief figures, 63s.; two figures, Zingara and Chrispagnia, 42s.; cast of an oval Psyche and Cupid, 52s. 6d.; cast of the Aurora and a small tablet, 21s.;

sitting figure of Venus, 42s.; mould of Sterne, 42s.; sitting figure of Mercury, 42s.; bust of Julius Cæsar, 14s.[1]

Webber, a modeller of uncommon ability, was strongly recommended to Wedgwood by Sir W. Chambers and Sir J. Reynolds, and shortly after the death of Mr. Bentley he took the management of the ornamental department, about 1782. In June 1786, when Wedgwood acquired the loan of the Portland Vase, Webber was engaged in modelling a copy of it, which he seems to have completed in 1787, and in the autumn of the same year visited Italy with Wedgwood's eldest son. While there he engaged a first-rate artist named Angelo Dalmazzoni, and several other artists, to work under him in copying the fine works of art in that country. Webber himself assisted in making copies at the Museum Capitolinum, and took sketches of everything of interest that came in his way. The bas-reliefs which we can safely attribute to him, are a Triumph of Mars, a boy leaning on his quiver with doves, a Cupid drawing his dart, Hebe (the companion), Apollo and Daphne, Cupid, a sacrifice to Hymen, a sacrifice to Concordia, medallion of Hope addressing Peace, Labour, and Plenty; he also modelled vases, cups, chimney-pieces, &c.

Flaxman was engaged by Wedgwood & Bentley as early as 1775, and he continued furnishing them with drawings and models up to the time of his departure for Rome in 1787. After Bentley's death in 1780, his fame as a sculptor procured him other more important and lucrative work, but still, as time permitted, he worked for Wedgwood, as the cheques and receipts in the Mayer MSS. testify. Many of the bills are also preserved, and we quote them to show what subjects he executed, and the prices he received for some of them. (See Miss Meteyard's *Life of Wedgwood.*)

The first bill is dated 1775, at which time he worked for his father : A pair of vases, one with a Satyr, the other with a Triton handle, 3 guineas; Bas-reliefs of the Muses and Apollo; Hercules and the Lion; Hercules and the Boar; Hercules and Cerberus; Bacchus and Ariadne; Jupiter; Juno; Minerva; Justice and Hope : for each of these he received 10s. 6d. Tablet of the Four Seasons, £2 2s. Subsequently he produced a tablet of Silenus; two Fauns; the figure of Day; a set of models of the English Poets, for which he received 10s. 6d. each, were executed in 1777. A Sacrifice to Pan; the Dancing Hours; Greek Heads; the Marriage of Cupid and Psyche; the Apotheosis of Homer; the Apotheosis of Virgil; Boys and Goat; Triumph of Ariadne; Homer and Hesiod; an Offering to Flora, and a Bacchanalian Sacrifice.[2]

In 1781 we find a bill for a shell Venus, 25s.; a Bacchante, 25s.; moulding a " Turin " (old way of spelling tureen), 18s.; Cast of a fragment by Phidias, 10s. 6d.

In 1783, a figure of a Fool for Chess, 25s.; a Bas-relief of Boys in wax, £11 0s. 6d.; three Drawings for the Manufacturers' Arms, 20s.; three days employed in drawing

---

[1] "All these busts," Wedgwood says in a letter to Bentley, August 1774, "are much better finished than the plaster casts or busts we take them from. Hackwood bestows a week upon each head in restoring it to what we suppose it was when it came out of the hands of the statuary. Pray do not let our labour be unobserved when they are under your care. It is a fortnight's work to prepare and mould one of these heads."

[2] The latter, with others, seem to have been adapted to chimney-piece tablets, and one of the largest known is 23 inches by 9½ inches. Engraved in Miss Meteyard's *Life of Wedgwood*, vol. ii. p. 368, from the Collection of Mr. John J. Bagshawe of Sheffield.

Bas-reliefs, &c., £3 3s.; Bas-relief of Octavia and Volumnia entreating Coriolanus, £9 9s.; Drawing of Chessmen, £6 6s.; Drawing of a Chimney-piece, 10s. 6d.; Model of Peace preventing Mars from bursting the door of Janus's Temple, 15 guineas; a model of Mercury uniting the hands of England and France, 13 guineas; Bas-relief of Hercules in the Hesperian Garden, £23; small Bas-reliefs for Tea-pots, Mug, &c.; Children playing at Marbles; Blindman's Buff; Cupids at play; Triumph of Cupid; Cupid sacrificing to Hymen; Triumphal Procession of Cupid; Bust of Mercury; the Muses watering Pegasus on Mount Helicon.

The following portraits are by Flaxman : —

Mr. Banks, 42s.; Dr. Solander, Lord Chatham, Rousseau, and Sterne, 16s.; a bust of Dr. Fothergill, 24s.; a bust of Mrs. Siddons, 31s. 6d.; Portrait of Dr. Herschel, 42s.; Model in wax of Captain Cook, 42s.; Dr. Johnson, 42s.; C. Jenkinson, Esq., 42s.; Governor Hastings, 63s.; King of Sweden, 42s.; Mr. and Mrs. Meermans, 5 guineas; Sir Joshua Reynolds, Josiah Wedgwood, Mrs. Wedgwood, and Sir W. Hamilton.

When Flaxman went to Italy in 1787, he arranged to execute occasionally, when his other engagements permitted, some models for Wedgwood, but principally to suggest, overlook, and give finishing touches to the work of such artists as were employed expressly in copying from the antique, under the direction of Angelo Dalmazzoni. John de Vaere was a friend of Flaxman's, and was sent to Rome by Wedgwood at a salary; he returned to England prior to Wedgwood's death, and succeeded Webber at the ornamental works, Etruria. Some of his works were Proserpine; copy of the Borghese Vase; Discovery of Achilles; Judgment of Paris; the well-known "wine and water" ewers, &c., &c.

ITALIAN ARTISTS. (From letters and accounts of Dalmazzoni, *Mayer MSS.*) Pacetti's works were very numerous; Figures reclining over the Muses; Figures from Homer; Copies from Herculaneum; Copies from bas-reliefs in the Museo Capitolino; Priam kneeling before Achilles begging the body of his son Hector; the fable of Prometheus; Luna, Diana, and Hecate; Æsculapius and Hygeia; a Faun with three Spartan Bacchantes; Endymion sleeping on the Rock Latmos; Marcus Aurelius and Commodus; Apotheosis of Faustina; a series of the Life of Achilles, &c.; the Sacrifice of Iphigenia, &c.

Angelini's works were—Apollo with the Muse Erato; Pluto and Proserpine; the fable of Meleager; Apotheosis of a young Prince; two Fauns, two Bacchantes; Silenus; the Elysian Fields, &c.

Fratoddi and Mangiarotti were cameo engravers; they copied on shells some of the finest antique gems.

Manzolini and Cades were also artists employed by Dalmazzoni for Wedgwood at Rome.

The greater part of the models were procured from Italy, and the large majority of tablets and medallions assigned to Flaxman were in reality the work of other artists. The models which came from Rome were executed in red wax on fine slates, of which casts were also sent by a separate conveyance, in case of loss or damage during the transit. About twenty-five years ago, a number of these original tablets were offered for sale to the author by a member of the family; they were at that time packed in separate wooden cases with the name of the artist upon each case, being all Italian. Having first offered these most interesting objects to our National Museum, they were declined, and they passed into the possession of Sir D. C. Marjoribanks, afterwards Lord Tweedmouth. They are now in the Lady Lever Art Gallery, Port Sunlight, Cheshire.

Dr. Shaw says that Flaxman employed Mr. Jo. Lucock, and that he in November 1836 showed him and a friend, his account for work done for Flaxman for Wedgwood. In 1802 John Lucock, engraver, was living at Stoke.

In the year 1785 Wedgwood introduced a "jasper dip," in which the white clay vessels were dipped and received a coating of jasper, instead of being, as hitherto, of that body throughout. This description of jasper ware was almost universally adopted after 1785 down to 1858, when the solid jasper was revived; its adoption rendered an increase of price necessary, as we see by the following extract from his *Correspondence*: "The new jasper, white within, will be the only sort made in future; but as the workmanship is nearly double, the price must be raised; I think it must be about 20 per cent."—*Nov.* 21, 1785. Wedgwood also invented an iridescent glaze like mother-of-pearl, which he usually applied to dessert services, the pieces being in form of shells of great variety, the nautilus, &c.

In April 1787, the Portland Museum, the property of Margaret Cavendish, Duchess Dowager of Portland, was sold by auction by Messrs. Skinner & Co., at her house in Privy Gardens, Whitehall, by order of the acting executrix, and continued for thirty-eight days; the collection was extremely rich in natural history, conchology, mineralogy, &c.; this portion occupied thirty days, articles of vertu, eight; the sale concluded with the celebrated Barberini Vase, which was purchased from the Barberini family by Sir William Hamilton, who sold it to the Duchess of Portland. It is thus described in the catalogue, lot 4155: "The most celebrated antique vase, or sepulchral urn, from the Barberini Cabinet of Rome; it is the identical urn which contained the ashes of the Roman Emperor Alexander Severus, and his mother Mammæa, which was deposited in the earth about the year 235 after Christ, and was dug up by order of Pope Barberini, named Urban VIII., between the years 1623 and 1644. The materials of which it is composed emulate an onyx, the ground a rich transparent amethystine colour, and the snowy figures which adorn it are in bas-relief, of workmanship above all encomium, and such as cannot but excite in us the highest idea of the arts of the ancients. Its dimensions are $9\frac{3}{4}$ inches high and $21\frac{3}{4}$ inches in circumference," &c.

This gem of ancient art, which may still be seen in the British Museum, though broken to fragments many years ago by a mischievous visitor, and afterwards carefully pieced together, was composed of glass of two strata, dark blue and opaque white, the surface being cut from the solid in the same manner as an antique onyx cameo, and Wedgwood, in his enthusiasm for his art, desired to become the possessor, for the purpose of reproducing it in his jasper ware. He hastened to the sale, resolved upon its purchase, but was doomed to disappointment, for the Duchess of Portland as eagerly opposed him until the biddings reached to 1,000 guineas, when her Grace, upon being informed of the motive of Wedgwood's opposition, the loan of the vase was offered on condition of his withdrawing from the contest, to which arrangement he acceded.

Wedgwood immediately set to work to produce a copy of this gem and devoted all his energies to do justice to the task, at great labour and expense, employing only the most skilled workmen. The body used for his copy was jasper, apparently black, but with the slightest possible tinge of blue; it was, in Wedgwood's own words, " a mixture of blue and black, and then dipped in black "; the figures being modelled and cut to the utmost degree of sharpness and finished by the gem engraver. Eventually he produced fifty copies, which were sold to subscribers at fifty guineas each, but his expenditure considerably exceeded that amount. Mr. Parkes, in his *Chemical Essays*, says that he paid Mr. Webber alone 500 guineas for making the model, not being allowed to mould it lest it should sustain any injury. From a note in Wedgwood's catalogue of 1788, it appears that the subscription copies were not entirely completed then, and it was not till 1790 that they were actually issued. The original moulds are still in existence, and have frequently been used and amended by his successors, both in black and deep blue, but from their finish are easily distinguishable from the " fifty." It is asserted by some that Wedgwood did not complete more than half that number, and only those with pencilled numbers on, or inside, the vase are originals. (*Ker. Gall.*, fig. 450.)

Copies of this vase (first issue) are in the British Museum, Victoria and Albert Museum, the Wedgwood Works Museum, etc. Miss Meteyard says that a mould of the vase had been previously made by Pichler, the gem engraver, whilst it was in the possession of the Barberini family, and from this, on its first arrival in England, a certain number of copies were taken in plaster of Paris by Tassie, who afterwards destroyed the mould. These are now of extreme rarity.

The principal productions of Wedgwood, which were at this time in the greatest state of perfection, were:—

1. The cream-coloured table ware afterwards called Queen's ware.
2. Terra-cotta, made to represent porphyry, granite, &c.
3. Basalts, or black Egyptian ware, imitation bronzes, &c.
4. White porcelain biscuit.
5. Bamboo, a cream-coloured porcelain biscuit.
6. Jasper, a porcelain that would receive throughout its whole substance, from the mixture of metallic oxides, the same colours as they would communicate to glass or enamels in fusion, very applicable to the production of cameos, portraits, &c., that require to be shown in bas-relief, since the ground can be made of any colour, while the raised parts are pure white.
7. A porcelain biscuit, exceedingly hard, resisting the strongest acids or corrosive substances, very useful in laboratories and for mortars.

In Wedgwood's catalogue of antique ornaments, &c., published in

1788 in French and English, he gives the following notification of his productions, which gives an idea of the great variety of models of all kinds employed at his vast manufactory at Etruria, the importance of which has not been surpassed either at Sèvres or Dresden. Independent of numerous models of lamps, candelabra, cabarets, flower vases, Etruscan vases, plaques, &c., there were about 2300 models of statuettes, gems, &c. The impressions of antique gems were copied from the originals, lent to him for the purpose. He divides the different species of his fabrication into six, the varieties, before noted, and the forms into classes in the following order : —

CLASS I.—*Cameos and Intaglios.*—Egyptian Mythology, 13; Greek and Roman Mythology, 220; Sacrifices, 11; Portraits of Philosophers, Poets, and Orators, 46; Macedon, 25; Fabulous Subjects of Greece, 22; Trojan War, 25; Roman History, 180; Masks and Chimeræ, 13; Portraits of Illustrious Men, 81; Intaglios, 392.

CLASS II.—*Bas-reliefs, Cameo Medallions, and Tablets,* chiefly of Classical Subjects, 275, varying from 3 in. diameter to 18.

CLASS III.—*Kings and Illustrious Persons of Asia, Egypt, and Greece,* 108.

CLASS IV.—*Roman History Medals,* after Dassier, 60.

CLASS V.—*Busts of Illustrious Romans,* sizes 2 in. by 1¾, 3 by 2½, and 4 by 3 in.

CLASS VI.—*The Twelve Cæsars and their Empresses,* four sizes, 24.

CLASS VII.—*Emperors from Nerva to Constantine the Great,* 64 portraits.

CLASS VIII.—*Busts of the Popes,* from Dassier's medals, 253 pieces.

CLASS IX.—*The Kings of England,* 36, *and Kings of France,* 67; of various sizes.

CLASS X.—*Heads of Illustrious Englishmen*—Poets, Painters, Philosophers, Artists, Divines, Princes, and Statesmen, 228.

CLASS XI.—*Busts, Statuettes, and Animals,* in black basalt, in imitation of bronze, 130.

CLASS XII.—*Lamps and Candelabra,* after antique models of various kinds and patterns.

CLASS XIII.—*Cabarets, or Tea and Coffee Services,* in bamboo, basalt, and jasper of two colours, enriched with ornaments.

CLASS XIV.—*Flower-Pots.*

CLASS XV.—*Ornamental Vases* of antique form of every variety, polished, not glazed, imitating porphyry, agate, jasper, and other variegated stones of the vitrescent or crystalline kind, with handles, bas-reliefs, &c.

CLASS XVI.—*Antique Vases of black basalt,* highly finished, with bas-relief ornaments.

CLASS XVII.—*Painted Etruscan Vases, Pateræ, &c.,* exactly copied from the antique, chiefly from the Collection of Sir William Hamilton, painted in encaustic colours, without glaze, invented by Wedgwood, and for which he took out a patent.

CLASS XVIII.—*Vases, Tripods, and other ornaments in jasper,* with coloured grounds and ornaments in relief in white, called by Wedgwood his *later productions.*

CLASS XIX.—*Vessels for Chemical Purposes, Mortars, Inkstands, &c.*

CLASS XX.—*Thermometers,* for ascertaining degrees of heat, &c.

The celebrated painter, George Stubbs, is also mentioned in this catalogue as a painter on enamel, whose plaques of the size of 36 in. were exhibited in the Royal Academy; he was a painter of animals, born at Liverpool in 1724, and died in 1806. The catalogue finished by observing that all these as well as the Queen's ware for table and tea services, were to be obtained at his magazine in Greek Street, Soho, which was called Portland House, or at the manufactory, Etruria, Staffordshire.

The treaty of commerce between England and France was concluded about this time (1790), by which English ware might be imported into France, and the French china into England, on certain conditions. This was of immense benefit to English potters, and to none more than Josiah Wedgwood, whose beautiful products were in such great request on the Continent. France became, therefore, inundated with every description of English pottery, which could be produced here at a cheaper rate, having all the materials at hand, and the price of lead and tin, which came principally from England, was greatly increased abroad. The manufacturers in France were up in arms when they found the result so prejudicial to them, and petitions were presented against the treaty to the National Assembly, stating their grievances. In consequence of this, a great many of the French potters were ruined and their works entirely ceased.

In 1792 a similar treaty was made with Saxony, viz., to admit English pottery into that country, provided England would allow the importation of their porcelain at a duty of about 12 per cent. This was of course of far greater advantage to the makers of earthenware than to the makers of porcelain, as the latter could not compete with the Royal manufactory of Dresden and other German states, and was therefore strenuously opposed by them. The treaty was supposed to have been promoted by Wedgwood himself, who would necessarily be the greatest gainer.

An intelligent foreigner, M. Faujas de Saint-Frond, speaking of this ware (*Travels in England and Scotland*), says, " Its excellent workmanship, its solidity, the advantage which it possesses of sustaining the action of fire, its fine glaze, impenetrable by acids, the beauty and convenience of its form, and the cheapness of its price, have given rise to a commerce so active and so universal that in travelling from Paris to Petersburg, from Amsterdam to the farthest part of Sweden, and from Dunkirk to the extremity of the South of France, one is served at every inn with English ware. Spain, Portugal, and Italy are supplied, and vessels are loaded with it for the East and West Indies and the Continent of America."

Thomas Wedgwood, the relative and partner of Josiah, died in October 1788. In the obituary of the *Gentleman's Magazine* for that year we find, " At Etruria, Thomas Wedgwood, Esq., partner with Josiah in the manufactory of Queen's ware there." His eldest son, Ralph, was born in 1766.

On the 18th January 1790, Josiah Wedgwood took his three sons, John, Josiah, and Thomas, and his nephew, Thomas Byerley, into partnership by the name of " Josiah Wedgwood, Sons, and Byerley."

Thomas Wedgwood, the youngest son of Josiah, was, as well as a skilful artist, a very scientific man; he invented the silver ornaments on the black ware about 1791; he made numerous experiments on the action of light on paper prepared with nitrate of silver, and he made certain discoveries which led practically to the first principles of photography; he advanced so far as to throw objects with the camera obscura on paper and temporarily fix them there; but although he experimented with Sir Humphry Davy in order to give them permanency, he could not succeed. The process was called heliotype. Although almost obliterated, yet two specimens are still preserved in the family.

The manufacture of porcelain, which was never attempted by Josiah Wedgwood, was commenced at Etruria by Thomas Byerley about 1812, and was carried on for nine or ten years, when it was discontinued. Specimens are therefore scarce. The Right Hon. W. E. Gladstone had a coffee mug, the ground of a small blue pattern, with Chinese figures in tablets, in red and other colours. Mrs. W. Chaffers had a dessert service painted in colours, with birds after Bewick; others are in the Victoria and Albert Museum. All these are simply stencilled WEDGWOOD in small capitals on the bottom in red or blue. Porcelain was reintroduced about 1878.

In 1793 John Wedgwood retired from the concern, and the firm consisted of Josiah Wedgwood, Josiah Wedgwood, Jun., and Thomas Byerley. On the 3rd of January 1795, Josiah Wedgwood died, and was buried in the Church of St. Peter, Stoke-upon-Trent, in the 65th year of his age. In 1800 the partners were (Thomas having retired) Josiah Wedgwood and Thomas Byerley; in the map of 1802 the firm is styled Wedgwood & Byerley, Etruria. In 1810 Byerley died, and the business was carried on by Josiah alone until 1823, when he took his eldest son, Josiah, into partnership under the name of "Josiah Wedgwood & Son."

The business established by Josiah Wedgwood at Etruria is still carried on by his descendants under the style of "Josiah Wedgwood & Sons, Limited," the firm having been made into a private limited company for family reasons.

With regard to the scratched letters and numerals which one finds on old Wedgwood in addition to the impressed fabrique mark, Miss Meteyard has pointed out that the letters $\frac{o}{3}$ and 3 are only found upon good pieces, and are the mark of expert workmen. A rather rudely scratched K found on some fine busts is attributed to Keeling, the modeller.

Collectors should note that the three capital letters which occur as supplementary marks are evidence of the piece being nineteenth century or later, their use having only commenced in 1860 with the letter O, P denoting 1861, and so on, like the year marks on silver. See the table given later.

By the courtesy of Mr. Frederick Rathbone, who made Wedgwood his special study, and whose large folio work with superb coloured plates was published in 1898, this list of marks is quoted, together with Mr. Rathbone's notes thereon.

WEDGWOOD & BENTLEY PERIOD, c. 1769–1780. Mark no. 3 with the word "Etruria" impressed on a bat, and fixed in the corner inside the plinth of old basalt ware vases and on other large pieces, occasionally on the pedestal of a bust, the letters being in relief; used between 1769 and 1780.

Mark no. 4 is the most usual stamp on the basalt vases, with inner and outer lines always placed round the screw at the bottom, the letters in relief as before; used during the same period. It may be remarked that the " and " is always contracted thus, " &."

Mark no. 5 upon the Wedgwood and Bentley intaglios, with the catalogue number, varying in size. Very small intaglios are sometimes marked W. & B. with the catalogue number, or simply with number only.

Mark no. 6. This rare mark is found upon chocolate and white seal intaglios, usually portraits, made of two layers of clay; the edges polished for mounting.

Only the blue and white jasper plaques, medallions, and portraits have the Wedgwood and Bentley mark. Jasper vases of blue or any other colour, made in the old period, carry only the word " Wedgwood."

Marks no. 7, varying in size, attributed to the period after Bentley's death, and probably used for a time after Wedgwood died. These marks and others were used by chance—a small piece often bearing a large stamp, and a large one a minute stamp, not easily read.

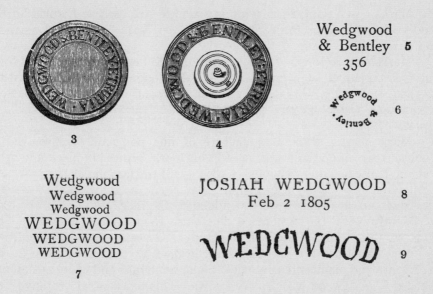

3

4

Wedgwood
& Bentley **5**
356

6

Wedgwood
Wedgwood
Wedgwood
WEDGWOOD
WEDGWOOD
WEDGWOOD

7

JOSIAH WEDGWOOD **8**
Feb 2 1805

WEDCWOOD **9**

Mark no. 8. Sometimes " 2nd Feby.," the mark of Josiah Wedgwood the younger. Supposed to be the date of some new partnership or change in the firm. Being found only upon some basalt tripod incense burners; it may be the date when the design was introduced.

Mark no. 9 is very rare in this form; it occurs on a large cream ware dish, black transfer decoration, made at the Bell Works, and is referred to by Mayer and Jewitt.

Marks nos. 10 to 12, rarely found upon pieces of a very high character
—usually upon dark blue stoneware vases and glazed ware—were adopted
about 1840, but soon disused. A plate from the series made by Wedgwood
for George III has a W only stamped upon it.

Mark no. 13 on the porcelain made from about 1812 to 1822, always
printed, either in red or blue, sometimes in gold.

WEDGWOOD	WEDGWOOD	Wedgwood	WEDGWOOD
ETRURIA	ETRURIA	Etruria	(*in red or blue*)
10	11	12	13

| WEDGWOOD | WEDGWOOD | *Emile Lessore* |
| 14 | 15 | 16 |

| *E Lessore* | *B* | 19 | ENGLAND |
| 17 | 18 | WEDGWOOD | 20 |

Marks nos. 14 and 15 varying in size, are still used at Etruria for the
modern jasper and useful ware of all varieties, with " Made in England "
and date marks.

Marks nos. 16 to 18. The celebrated Émile Lessore, who painted some
fine vases, plaques, etc., for Messrs. Josiah Wedgwood & Sons, from 1859
to 1875, signed his works in this form. Typical examples may be seen
in Godden's *British Pottery and Porcelain, an Illustrated Encyclopaedia of
Marked Specimens*.

Mark no. 19. The manufacture of fine porcelain was revived at
Etruria, 1878, and is still continued. This mark, printed in black and other
colours, is used. Later versions, c. 1891+, have stars under the vase, also
" England " or " Made in England."

Mark no. 20. This word was added to the mark WEDGWOOD in 1891,
to comply with the American Customs Regulations, known as the
McKinley Tariff Act. " Made in England " is a twentieth century addition.

The Wedgwood mark has been forged or imitated both in the
eighteenth and nineteenth centuries. Some small blue and white medallions,
marked " Wedgwood & Co.," are known. This mark is said to have been
used by some potters at Stockton-on-Tees, who were compelled to disuse
it by legal injunction. About the year 1840, a man named Smith set up a
factory in Holland, and stamped his ware " Wedgwood." The Staffordshire firm added Etruria to their mark, but it was soon abandoned, and the
simple word Wedgwood used again; foreign merchants and buyers not
understanding the addition. There is a tradition that a foreign dealer,
anxious to purchase Wedgwood, travelled to Italy to look for the Staffordshire Etruria! The forged marks are so rarely seen, they are almost worth

collecting as curiosities: the pieces bearing the mark, however, are of such poor quality as works of art, that no one would care to put them in the same cabinet with the genuine examples.

Any unmarked piece must not be condemned upon that account alone. Undoubted pieces of genuine old Wedgwood—many of fine quality —are at times met with without any mark. The omission may occur from various causes—carelessness, putting the piece to the lathe after marking, thinning down medallions, or the lapidaries' work grinding it down to fit to a metal mount. If made at Etruria, either in Josiah's time or later, it will carry its own marks of identification. It should be noted that the early Portland vases are not marked.

In the earlier specimens, the O in Wedgwood is generally found to be rounder than in later stampings. Sometimes, as shown in the examples given, the initial letter only is a capital, but generally the name is stamped in capital varying in height from $\frac{1}{32}$ to $\frac{1}{4}$ in. each (Miss Meteyard gives about 100 varieties on several portrait medallions). Other minor marks appear, such as H_3^o, and also initials of modellers, but Wedgwood discountenanced any such individual signatures.

The prices of fine specimens of Wedgwood's jasper ware have fluctuated considerably. Copies of the Portland Vase were sold in 1849 for £20, and early in the present century for about £160, whilst in 1956, £480 was paid for an example. Some years ago, owing to the deaths of several admirers of old Wedgwood jasper ware, their collections were thrown upon the market one after the other, with the natural result that with a greater supply than could be readily absorbed, prices dropped for a time. Now that there is but little really fine Wedgwood in the market, the values of good specimens are steadily rising.

It needs the accustomed eye and hand of the connoisseur to appreciate the merits of a genuine fine old piece, and no description can take the place of experience.

The jasper ware was made in seven colours. Blue of varying tints and depths, lilac pink, sage green, olive green, black and yellow, the latter colour being exceedingly rare. Amongst the best collections of old Wedgwood in England, the following may be referred to:—

The Wedgwood Works Museum
The Isaac Falcke Collection in the British Museum
Victoria and Albert Museum
The Lady Lever Art Gallery, Port Sunlight
Leith Hill Place, Surrey
The Nottingham Museum.

WEDGWOOD DATE LETTERS

Date letters, impressed in sets of three, were used from 1860. The first letter usually denotes the month, the second letter is the potter's mark and the third letter denotes the year.

1			2			3			4		
First Letter	Third Letter	Year	First Letter	Third Letter	Year	First Letter	Third Letter	Year	First Letter	Third Letter	Year
			(b)	A	1872	(b)	A	1898	4	A	1924
			(b)	B	1873	(b)	B	1899	4	B	1925
			(b)	C	1874	(b)	C	1900	4	C	1926
			(b)	D	1875	(b)	D	1901	4	D	1927
			(b)	E	1876	(b)	E	1902	4	E	1928
			(b)	F	1877	(b)	F	1903	4	F	1929
			(b)	G	1878	(b)	G	1904	4	G	1930
			(b)	H	1879	(b)	H	1905	(c)	31	1931
			(b)	I	1880	(b)	I	1906	(c)	32	1932
			(b)	J	1881	(b)	J	1907	(c)	33	1933
			(b)	K	1882	3	K	1908	and so on		
			(b)	L	1883	3	L	1909			
			(b)	M	1884	3	M	1910			
			(b)	N	1885	3	N	1911			
(a)	O	1860	(b)	O	1886	3	O	1912			
(a)	P	1861	(b)	P	1887	3	P	1913			
(a)	Q	1862	(b)	Q	1888	3	Q	1914			
(a)	R	1863	(b)	R	1889	3	R	1915			
(a)	S	1864	(b)	S	1890	3	S	1916			
(b)	T	1865	(b)	T	1891	3	T	1917			
(b)	U	1866	(b)	U	1892	3	U	1918			
(b)	V	1867	(b)	V	1893	3	V	1919			
(b)	W	1868	(b)	W	1894	3	W	1920			
(b)	X	1869	(b)	X	1895	3	X	1921			
(b)	Y	1870	(b)	Y	1896	3	Y	1922			
(b)	Z	1871	(b)	Z	1897	3	Z	1923			

The second letter is always the potters mark.

(a) =letter indicating the month as shown in the table below for the period 1860-64.

(b) =letter indicating the month as shown in the table below for the period 1865–1907.

(c) =figure indicating the month as shown in the table below for the period after 1930.

(a)   Months, period 1860-64:—

J = January	Y = May	S = September
F = February	T = June	O = October
M = March	V = July	N = November
A = April	W = August	D = December

(b)   Months, period 1865–1907:—

J = January	M = May	S = September
F = February	T = June	O = October
R = March	L = July	N = November
A = April	W = August	D = December

(c)   Months, period after 1930:—

1 = January, 2 = February, and so on in sequence to 12 = December.

The months were not recorded from 1907 to 1930, the figure 3 or 4 being substituted.

Examples: VAO = July, 1860 (A being the potter's mark).

LAS = July, 1890

3AS = 1916

4AB = 1925

1A32 = January, 1932

" England " often appears from 1890 onward. These tables should be used carefully, because O to Z in cycle 1 can be confused with cycle 2 but some of the month letters differ. So also can A to I in cycle 2 be confused with cycle 3.

BURSLEM, TUNSTALL, LONGPORT, HANLEY, SHELTON, etc.

BURSLEM. Ralph Shawe. On the 24th April, 1733 he took out a patent as follows: " Whereas Ralphe Shawe, of Burslem, on our county of Stafford, earth potter, hath by his petition humbly represented unto us that he hath for many years been a maker and dealer in earthenware, and during the long course of his trading hath, with great pains and expenses in making tryalls, found out various sorts of minerals, earth, clay, and other earthy substances, which being mixed and incorporated together, make up a fine body, of which a curious ware may be made, whose outside will be of a true chocolate colour, striped with white, and the inside white, much resembling the brown China ware, and glazed with salt." Being of a litigious disposition, he was continually objecting to the improvements made by other manufacturers, and in 1736 commenced a suit against John Mitchell of Burslem for an infringement of his patent at Stafford. The defendant was supported by all the potters of the district, and Astbury's invention and prior usage of that or similar materials being proved, a verdict was given against Ralph Shawe, and the judge thus addressed the manufacturers present: " Go home, potters, and make whatever kind of pots you please." He afterwards went to France, where he continued his manufactory. This salt glazed ware of Ralph Shawe's is never marked, but a few specimens attributed to him are in various collections.

Shaw (*Chemistry of Pottery*) says that Ralph Shawe introduced *basaltes* into the body of his ware.

BURSLEM. Ralph Wood. Mark no. 21 is stamped on a square pyramid, painted in imitation of granite, on a blue pedestal, with a white medallion in relief on each side, gilt leaf borders; and on a statuette of Chaucer; formerly in possession of the Rev. T. Staniforth. (*Ker. Gall.*, fig. 459.) The earthenware is of the same character as Whieldon's and Wedgwood's agate knife handles, etc. (c. 1730 to 1750). The same stamp is on a bust of Neptune

This potter received scant notice in earlier editions. He was responsible for some of the finest English earthenware figure models, decorated with translucent coloured glazes. Three potters of this name and family worked at Burslem, i.e. Ralph Wood I (1715-72) Ralph Wood II (1748-95) and the grandson Ralph Wood III (1781-1801). Various marks and model numbers occur impressed in the base of figures, etc. See *The Wood Family of Burslem*, by F. Falkner, 1912.

Aaron Wood commenced here about 1750. He served his apprenticeship to Dr. T. Wedgwood, jun., of "Ruffleys," one of the principal potters of this town in the early part of the eighteenth century. The indentures given by Simeon Shaw *(History of Staffordshire Potteries)* are dated the 23rd of August 1731, "Between Ralph Wood of Burslem, miller, and Aaron, his son, of the one part, and Dr. Thomas Wedgwood, jun., of Burslem, potter, on the other part, for the term of seven years. That he, the said Ralph Wood, shall provide for his son all sorts of apparel, meat, drink, washing and lodging, and in consideration thereof he is to be taught turning the lathe, handling, throwing, &c., and he engages to pay the said apprentice for every week's work in the first three years one shilling weekly, and for every week's work in the next three years one shilling and sixpence, and in the seventh and last year the sum of four shillings per week, and the said Dr. Wedgwood is to give yearly in addition one pair of new shoes."

83	E. WOOD.
Ra. Wood 21	22
Burslem	

On the conclusion of his apprenticeship, he served the same master for five years at five shillings per week. Aaron Wood was a very clever cutter of moulds for white salt-glazed stoneware plates with raised pattern borders which have been erroneously termed "Elizabethan," and found constant employment from different masters, among whom was Thomas Whieldon, the partner of Josiah Wedgwood. He was afterwards engaged by Mr. John Mitchell of Burslem, an extensive potter, in 1743, to work for him only for seven years, in a penal bond of £10 (who engaged him to be the better able to compete with Dr. T. Wedgwood), at the rate of seven shillings weekly, and ten and sixpence every 11th of November with the proviso that he should have no person to work with him. About the year 1750 Aaron Wood commenced business on his own account, and made embossed earthenware of old English white stoneware, *salt glaze*. There is a dish in the Victoria and Albert Museum thus inscribed: "*This dish was modelled by Aaron Wood about the year 1759 or 1760, and was deposited in this building by his youngest son, Enoch Wood, 1836, who at this date was Chief Constable of Burslem and Treasurer to the market.*" In the same museum are numerous specimens of Wood's ware, and types or moulds for tureens, sauce-boats, cream-jugs, tea-cups, etc. Cream ware is said to have been invented by Aaron Wood, and much improved by Wedgwood. He died in

1772. (*Ker. Gall.*, fig. 458.)

Enoch Wood commenced business in 1784, and eventually was called the Father of the Pottery; he greatly enlarged the business, the manufactory occupying the site of five old factories. He was a good modeller; his name occurs on a bust of John Wesley, mark no. 22, which was much admired at the time; on the back is an inscription stating that Wesley, " sat to Enoch Wood, sculptor, of Burslem, in 1781," he being at that time a working modeller. The word " sculpsit " sometimes accompanies the name " Enoch Wood " on medallions produced by him. He died in 1840. Shaw says, " About 1780 John Proudlove, the best mould-maker in that part, was hired by Mr. Wood for three years at 12s. per week." In a Survey of the county in 1786 the firm is thus described: " Wood (Enoch & Ralph), manufacturers of all kinds of useful and ornamental earthenware, Egyptian black, cane, and various other colours, also black figures, seals, and ciphers."

It is not generally realised that Enoch Wood made fine quality creamware dessert and dinner services, this is because the mark was rarely used. A unique dated (1792) creamware service of over a hundred and twenty pieces has only one piece marked in full, although other items have a small impressed " W." This service includes openwork baskets, moulded leaf dishes, sauce tureens, condiments, etc. See *English Pottery and Porcelain*, 1780-1850, in preparation.

Mr. Percy Fitzgerald, the well-known author, whose collection of some 300 or 400 specimens of Staffordshire pottery was sold at Christie's in January 1908, contained many portrait busts of notable celebrities of the last century, among them two of Wesley and Whitfield by Enoch Wood. They are powerfully modelled, and at the back of each is a roundel with the following inscriptions stamped in the paste. At the sale these busts realised £14 14s. :—

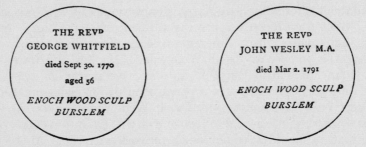

In 1790 Enoch Wood took into partnership James Caldwell of Linley Wood, and the business was carried on in their joint names until 1818. Messrs. Wood & Caldwell continued the manufacture of earthenware busts of celebrated characters, and produced some well-modelled portraits of Wellington, Napoleon as First Consul, the Emperor of Russia, etc.; on that of the Emperor Alexander is written, " Alexander I., Autocrat of all the Russias, born December 23rd, 1777. Moscow burnt September 14th, 1812. Paris entered March 31st, 1814. Europe preserved." In 1818 Enoch Wood purchased Mr. Caldwell's interest in the concern, and a few years after took his three sons into partnership. Their names are on a large bowl, blue inside, and on the exterior raised foxgloves and primroses, in white on a light blue ground, formerly in the possession of Mr. Egerton Leigh, and also on a figure of a girl reading, from the Sheldon Collection, which contained a great many specimens of figure work by the Woods variously marked as nos. 23 to 26; one of these is curiously marked with W***, supposed to be the work of Enoch Wood. In 1816 Mr. Wood formed a collection of pottery, select portions of which are now in the Victoria and Albert Museum. Enoch Wood died in 1840, ætat. 83; the works were continued by his sons until 1846, when they were finally closed.

BURSLEM. Daniel Steel had a manufactory here in the eighteenth century; his name is mentioned in a map of 1802 as then occupying the Scotia Works, erected in 1766 opposite the Overhouse; he afterwards removed to Nile Street, and is described in a Directory of the year 1821 as a jasper and ornamental earthenware maker. The works ceased in 1824. His name occurs, mark no 27, on a match-pot with dark blue figures, cupids, etc., on pink ground, in the style of Wedgwood's jasper, formerly in Dr. Diamond's Collection; and in the Victoria and Albert Museum is a small vase with white relief on blue. (*Ker. Gall.*, fig. 460). Two rare oval medallions of Earls St. Vincent and Howe in white cameo on blue ground, the name STEEL impressed, with three others by Wedgwood, were sold in March 1873 for twenty-five guineas.

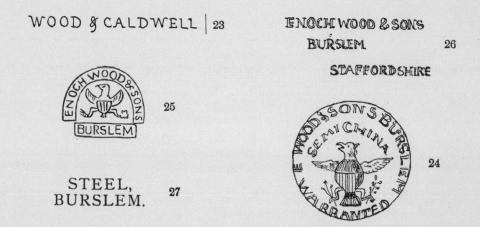

WOOD & CALDWELL | 23

ENOCH WOOD & SONS
BURSLEM 26
STAFFORDSHIRE

25

24

STEEL,
BURSLEM. 27

In Wedgwood's list of potters in Burslem in 1715 we find Moses Steel as a maker of cloudy ware of the period, and in Ward's List of 1750, Thomas Steel, a manufacturer of moulded ware.

BURSLEM. John Mitchell had his manufactory on the highest land in Burslem; it was established in the beginning of the eighteenth century. The ware principally made by him was the white stoneware, salt glaze. As his trade rapidly increased, he was obliged to enlarge his premises; and as only one hovel was thought requisite for all who made salt-glaze ware, the potters vied with each other who should excel in the size and

height of the hovel. Mr. Mitchell (says Shaw) erected the most enormously
wide and high one ever attempted to be built.   He was the greatest
manufacturer of that day: he had four travellers, and the practice
customary then was, not to take out invoices or to render an account of
the sales, but merely to empty out their pockets, after which they received
their wages (five or six shillings a week) for the time of their journey, their
expenses having been paid out of the cash received : he, notwithstanding
an apparently prosperous business, died in reduced circumstances.

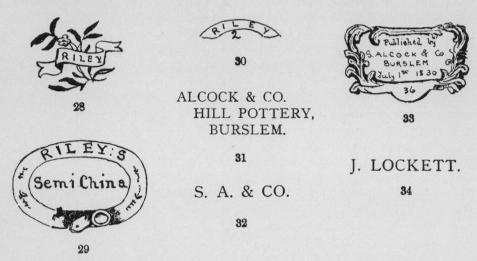

28

29

30

ALCOCK & CO.
HILL POTTERY,
BURSLEM.

31

S. A. & CO.

32

33

J. LOCKETT.

34

BURSLEM.—The Waterloo Potteries, established 1842, by Messrs.
Thomas and Richard Boote, of Nantwich, Cheshire.   They were the inventors and patentees, in 1843, of a new process of inlaying and ornamenting flooring tiles in different colours; thus, the proposed design is cut out
in paper or parchment, and laid in the mould, which is then closed, and
the ground colour poured in, after which the paper is removed and another
colour poured in to fill its place; or compositions of the required varieties of
colour are fixed in the mould, and the slip suitable for the groundwork
poured in; mosaics and low reliefs were also produced.   This patent with
improvements was renewed in 1857; prize medals were obtained in the
International Exhibitions of 1851 and 1862.   Earthenwares and stonewares
were produced in variety.   The Waterloo Works were closed in 1906.   The
firm has subsequently specialised in the manufacture of tiles.

BURSLEM. John Riley and Richard Riley were extensive manufacturers
in the last century; their names are found in the map of 1802.   Shaw says,
" By perseverance they amassed a very considerable property, but both
died in the vigour of manhood," about the year 1826 or 1827.   Their
premises were taken by Messrs. S. Alcock & Co.   Marks nos. 28 to 30,
c. 1802-26, occurred on specimens in the Sheldon Collection.

BURSLEM. Messrs. Samuel Alcock & Co., of the Hill Pottery, commenced business about 1830 in premises formerly occupied by J. & R.

Riley and John Robinson & Sons; they were exhibitors at the Great Exhibition of 1851. Messrs. Samuel Alcock & Co. made porcelain of a fine quality; M. Protat modelled for them; they also produced some fine biscuit figures modelled from historical subjects, and Parian vases and figures. Mark no. 31. The initials only, as mark no. 32, were sometimes used. An early impressed mark of this firm was a beehive with the name above. Mark no. 33 occurs on Parian jugs with figures in relief. See Godden's *British Pottery and Porcelain, an Illustrated Encyclopaedia of Marked Specimens.* At the sale which followed their failure in 1859, their models and moulds were dispersed. Subsequently the works were taken over by Sir James Duke & Nephews, and then by Bodley.

BURSLEM. Joseph Machin had a manufactory here in 1802. Joseph Machin & Co. are mentioned by Shaw as possessing extensive premises in 1828.

BURSLEM. In the Survey of the Potteries in 1786 we find Timothy and John Lockett described as *white stone potters* at Burslem. Mark no. 34, c. 1821-51 occurs impressed on a plaque of chocolate-coloured ware with a spirited relief of a drunken Silenus on a donkey, and other figures. A finely-executed and very large cider-barrel of *white stoneware, salt glaze,* with vine leaves and grapes in relief and medallions on the ends, of Toby Fillpot and a Bacchanalian group, the cask surmounted by a statuette of Bacchus, measuring 18 in. long by 15 in. diameter, was in Mr. Chaffers' possession; it bears J. Lockett's name impressed. In 1802 they appeared to have moved to Lane End, for the firm is described in the Directory of that year as Messrs. J. & G. Lockett, and in 1829 it was J. Lockett & Sons. From about 1836 to 1889, the title was J. & T. Lockett and from 1889 to the present day, John Lockett & Co.

BURSLEM. The Burslem patent encaustic tile-works were commenced by Messrs. Malkin, Edge & Co. about 1867. The speciality of these works was the rapid manufacture of tiles by the pressure of prepared clay dust, instead of the much slower process of slipping. Upon a level block of iron surrounded by a movable iron box of the size of the tile required, was placed a sheet of brass with the design cut out, the spaces were filled in with pulverised dust of different colours, and, with a counterpart of the design placed on the top, subjected to a slight pressure of the hand; the brass plate was then removed and the movable box raised; the space thus created above the level of the block was filled up with dust to form a base or background, and pressed under a screw by a wheel lever; it then became quite hard and firm, requiring only to be passed through the kiln. The present company, The Malkin Tiles (Burslem) Ltd., was formed in 1928. A separate nineteenth century company, Edge, Malkin & Co., worked The Newport & Middleport Potteries from about 1865.

BURSLEM. John Walton commenced business here about 1790 as a maker of common ware, such as marbles, whistling birds, and similar toys; shortly afterwards he produced coloured figures, which must have had a considerable sale; many of them were sent to London, and Mr. Jesse Philips and a Mr. Brunell bought largely; some of the figures were called

Shepherd and Shepherdess, Falstaff, Piper and Wife, Gardener, Fishwoman, Lions and Animals, the Evangelists, the Seasons, Man on Horseback, etc.; the name impressed or moulded within a scroll is frequently found upon them; he also made Egyptian black, etc. His name occurs in a Directory of 1822, and the manufacture was probably discontinued about 1835.

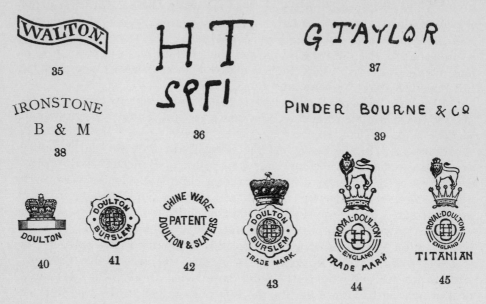

Mark no. 35 is the normal mark as found on a set of four coloured earthenware figures of the Evangelists holding books, with emblems at their feet, of coarse work. Toby jugs are known with this mark. The shape of the scroll varies, c. 1790-1830.

OBEDIAH SHERRATT commenced as a maker of figures about 1822; his early productions were of rather coarse work, but certainly not without merit in the modelling, etc.; he produced some good busts of Wesley and others. One of his most important groups was a representation of a bull-bait, produced at a time when that sport was still indulged in by the lower orders of Burslem. Another fine and colourful group depicts a menagerie. Obediah Sherratt died about 1846. No marked specimens are recorded, but typical specimens can be seen in the Willett collection in the Brighton Museum.

THOMAS HOLLAND. Mr. Fenton, of Cranbourne Street, mentions mark no. 36, slightly raised, evidently from a roughly made stamp, on the base of a Toby jug, which being read backwards, as seems to be intended from the way the date is indicated, is probably the mark of Thomas Holland, 1792, included in the list of potters of that date. He worked c. 1784-1812.

G. TAYLOR. There is in the Hanley Museum a pottery teapot with mark no. 37 impressed, probably the mark of the G. Taylor included in same list of potters. He worked from about 1784 and died in 1811.

BAGSHAW & MAIER is the name of another pottery firm working in Burslem about 1802. Their initials and the word " ironstone " on a stamp with scrolls occurs on some plates with blue decoration. Mark no. 38, but this attribution is now subject to doubt. The partnership ceased about 1808.

The following manufacturers of artistic products not previously mentioned possessed extensive works at Burslem:—

Bates, Elliot & Co., decorated earthenware, c. 1870-5.

Hope & Carter, decorated earthenware, c. 1862-80.

Pinder, Bourne & Co., decorated earthenware, c. 1862-c. 1882 (since transferred to Doulton's, and under their management nearly trebled in size, and the manufacture of china added).

PINDER, BOURNE & CO. A blue printed sauce-dish on feet in the Sheldon Collection had mark no. 39 in brown colours PINDER, BOURNE & CO. Various printed marks occur, c. 1862-c. 1882.

DOULTONS. From 1882 Messrs. Doultons took over Messrs. Pinder, Bourne & Co.'s factory in Nile Street (they had had an interest in this firm from 1877). The factory was enlarged and remodelled, excellent artists were employed and the quality of the earthware body was remarkable. In 1884 the production of porcelain was commenced and in the following years made a name for itself in the excellence of texture and in the style and quality of the decoration. Doultons exhibits at various international exhibitions were warmly praised. Of the many artists employed mention should be made of the following, all of whom normally signed their work: Harry Allen, Harry Betteley, Harry Birbeck, Edward Birks, Wilmot Brown, Percy Curnock, David Dewsberry, Arthur Eaton, Frederick Hancock, Henry Mitchell, J. H. Plant, Edward Raby, John & Walter Slater, George White and Samuel Wilson. The firm prospers to this day under the title Doulton Fine China Ltd. In the latter part of 1958 they introduced a revolutionary new translucent body called (and marked) " English Translucent China," having the qualities of porcelain without the high cost normally associated with the production of bone china. So successful was this new body that the production of earthenware was terminated in 1961.

The marks employed are generally similar to the Doulton marks on Lambeth wares (Stonewares, etc., porcelain was not made at Lambeth). The earliest Burslem mark was DOULTON impressed; other marks were no. 40, c. 1882+; no. 41, c. 1885+; no. 42, c. 1895+; no. 43, c. 1885+; no. 44, c. 1902 to the present day, the crown being omitted from c. 1922-27; and no. 45. Various other marks occur with the names of special effects, i.e. FLAMBE, etc.

TUNSTALL. Enoch Booth had a pottery here, established about 1750. He made great improvements in the manufacture of pottery, by carefully levigating and uniting the clays of the neighbourhood with those of Devon and Dorset, and introducing certain proportions of flint and white-lead; mark no. 46 is on a large dish, dated 1757, in the Victoria and Albert Museum. Enoch Booth first introduced that most important improvement, the *fluid glaze*.

Anthony Keeling, son-in-law of Enoch Booth, succeeded him in the business, which he carried on successfully for many years; he employed enamellers of porcelain, then commenced making under Champion's patent,

Enoch Booth.   ♣ A & E Keeling ♥
46   47

to which industry he joined about 1777 in copartnership with Samuel Hollins, Jacob Warburton, and William Clowes, whose name, W. CLOWES, is stamped on a black basalt candlestick formerly in the Sheldon Collection. The china manufactory was worked at his premises until his retirement from the concern, when it was transferred to New Hall, Shelton, under the firm of Hollins, Warburton & Co. In the Topographical Survey of the Potteries in 1786 we find " Anthony Keeling, manufacturer of Queen's ware in general, blue painted and enamelled, Egyptian black, etc., Tunstall near Burslem." In 1802 Anthony and E. Keeling had two manufactories here: they were succeeded by Mr. T. Goodfellow, who was in possession in 1828. Mr. Fenton, of Cranbourne Street, had two plates with printed decoration, stamped with the name BATHWELL above the name GOOD-FELLOW, probably the same potter in partnership. The period is c. 1818–22.

Mark no. 47 in red is on a tea-set richly gilt and painted in bright colours with Oriental figures and landscape, red and gold border; formerly in possession of Mr. Wake, Cockermouth, c. 1795–1811.

LOWNDS & BEECH.—A manufactory was carried on early in the nineteenth century by James Beech and Abraham Lownds. In the Directory of 1821 the firm was " Lownds & Beech, earthenware manu-factories at Sandyford, Tunstall." In 1823 they were doing a large trade: in 1834 it was James Beech alone, who retired about 1845.

SAMUEL MARSH & CO. At Brown Hills, in the vicinity, in 1829 there was a manufactory belonging to Samuel Marsh & Co., which in 1837 was Marsh & Heywood.

ADAMS. Potteries owned and worked by different members of the family of Adams existed from about the middle of the seventeenth century, and there has been some confusion by different writers in noticing their respective work and also that of William Adams of Burslem. The following information was supplied by Mr. Percy W. L. Adams, the great-grandson of the first William Adams of Stoke. It will be seen that at the end of the eighteenth century there were *three* William Adams, each of them manu-facturing pottery on a considerable scale, viz., William Adams of Stoke, William Adams of Cobridge Hall Potteries, formerly of Burslem, and William Adams of Greengates, Tunstall, the one best known to collectors as the maker of jasper ware. These were all members of the same family, and the present firm, Wm. Adams & Sons Ltd., now represents all three potteries.

" The Brick-House Works were established in the year 1657 by John Adams, of Burslem, a member of one of the oldest families in North Staffordshire. Ward in the

History of the Borough of Stoke-upon-Trent gives John Adams as the occupier of the Brick-House Potteries, Burslem, in 1657 and Ralph Adams in 1742; indeed it was worked by several generations until 1757, when the heir, William Adams (born 1750, son of John Adams by his wife Dorothy, d. of Wm. Murrell of Bagnall Hall, J.P.), being only seven years old, it was proposed to let the property for a term of years, and Miss Meteyard in her *Life of Josiah Wedgwood*, vol. i, page 239, tells us that John Adams *leaving his heir a minor, the premises were to let, and that Josiah Wedgwood took them on lease, in great probability some time prior to his marriage* (1760), *until* 1773 (a little over ten years' time), although, again quoting Miss Meteyard, vol. ii, page 126, in the reproduction of a letter dated November 11, 1769, from Josiah Wedgwood to his partner, Thos. Bentley, he says, ' . . . *I have notice to leave the Brick-House Works the next year, my Landlord has got married and will come to them himself* . . .' But from the above date (1773) it appears Mr. Wedgwood stayed on a little longer. William Adams did not stay long at the Brick-House Works, but built himself larger Potteries at Cobridge, and the Brick-House Works were again let and eventually sold. The Brick-House Works have long since been taken down, and the Wedgwood Memorial Institute stands upon the site.

" Potteries were also established by the Adams family (William Adams of Fenton Hall, born 1772, died 1829, being son of Richard Adams, a manufacturer of white stoneware, salt glaze, born 1739, and who was son of William Adams of Bagnall, gentleman, and cousin of Wm. Adams of the Brick-House and Cobridge Hall) at Stoke-upon-Trent towards the close of the last century, and also at Greenfield Tunstall. There were four separate Potteries at Stoke worked under the name of William Adams & Sons for the manufacture of earthenware and porcelain, *vide* Shaw's Hist. Staff. Potteries, page 67, and Ward, page 505. Parian statuary was also made, indeed a very extensive trade was done in all kinds of pottery and porcelain then in vogue, and at that time the firm was one of the largest producers of pottery and porcelain. One of their most important productions was the blue printed ware, decorated with views of well-known country places and English landscapes, which is now so largely collected in America, William Adams of Cobridge being the first to introduce printing from copper plates in Staffordshire in 1775. In 1819, four of the sons of William Adams (born 1772) were taken into partnership. The third son, Lewis Adams, was Chief Bailiff (equivalent to Mayor) of Stoke in 1840-42. Soon after his death in 1863 the Stoke Potteries were given up, and only the Tunstall Works were kept on, as they still are.

" William Adams of Greengates, Tunstall (born 1745, died 1805), who established the Greengates Potteries, Tunstall, in 1789, manufacturer of jasper ware, blue printed, &c , specimens of which are in many of our Museums, was a distant cousin of William Adams of Stoke and Greenfield, Tunstall, and tho' the Greengates family gave up being Manufacturers and sold the Pottery in 1820, it has been within the last five years amalgamated with the Greenfield Pottery, and is therefore again worked by the Adams family, who own both the Greenfield and the Greengates Potteries, which cover some 8 or 10 acres.

" The Greenfield Works and Estate (founded by Theophilus Smith and in his day called Smithfield) belonged at one time to the Breezes (as also did the Knowle Works, Burslem),[1] but became the property of the Adams' by marriage in 1827."

In 1786 the firm was " William Adams & Co., manufacturers of cream-coloured ware and china-glaze ware painted." " This jasper," says Shaw, " would have been more highly esteemed had it been *alone* before the public, but in this, as well as most other instances, the imitation very rarely equals the original." There are, however, some exceptions to this rule; we have seen examples quite equal, if not superior, to anything produced at Etruria, notably a blue and white jasper plaque with Diana

---

[1] The Knowle Works were for many years leased to Enoch Wood and Sons.

reclining after the chase, holding up her bow, a greyhound in front; signed W. Adams & Co.; was sold at the sale of Mr. John J. Bagshawe's Collection, and realised £171. (*Ker. Gall.*, fig. 474.)

The blue and white jasper ware of Adams, in the form of drums for the bases of candelabra (generally mounted with cut-glass lustre drops) and of vases, is the nearest approach to Wedgwood's productions both in colour and execution; and being unmarked, it would pass for Wedgwood but for the fact being known to experts that real Wedgwood is almost always marked.

The various marks used by the Adams firm, Tunstall, Stoke-upon-Trent, since 1770 are as follows:—

Mark no. 48, for cream ware, plain and enamelled, c. 1770–1800.

Mark no. 49, earlier mark used for the solid jaspers, c. 1780 to probably as late as 1790.

Mark no. 50, for printed ware, fine stoneware, and jaspers, both surface colour, and solid jasper, 1787 to about 1805.

Mark no. 51, for jaspers, very occasionally.

Adams & Co.	ADAMS & Co.	ADAMS	W. ADAMS & Co.	ADAMS ESTBD 1657 TUNSTALL ENGLAND
48	49	50	51	52

ADAMS, TUNSTALL.

53

ADAMS WARRANTED·STAFFORDSHIRE

54

W. ADAMS & SONS STOKE.UPON.TRENT

55

ADAMS

56

TRADE MARK
ADAMS. ENGLAND.

57

ESTBD 1657 IMPERIAL STONE WARE ADAMS TUNSTALL

58

CROWN SEMI·PORCELAIN W. ADAMS & CO. ENGLAND.

59

W. ADAMS & CO. 1657

60

Mark no 52, for jaspers, Egyptian black (basaltes) and Grecian red. A late mark, c. 1896.

Mark no. 53, still used for a variety of productions, impressed.

Mark no. 54, used for the deep blue printed ware, 1810-64.

Mark no. 55, printed in brown or black, used from 1809-64 for porcelain, semi-porcelain, ironstone ware, etc.

Mark no. 56, impressed, on parian wares, etc., c. 1845-64.

Mark no. 57, printed, from 1879, used for plain and painted earthenware, " England " from 1891.

Mark no. 58, printed, used for " imperial stoneware." and for " royal ivory," etc., c. 1899 onwards.

Mark no. 59, on semi-porcelain tablewares, etc. Late 19th century.

Mark no. 60, on royal iron-stone china, white granite, etc., from about 1881.

Marks nos. 61 to 63 are twentieth century marks of the present William Adams & Sons (Potters) Ltd.

W. Adams & Sons
England

61

W^M ADAMS & SONS,
ENGLAND

62

ESTP 1657
ENGLAND

63

RUBELLA

64

G. F. BOWERS

TUNSTALL

POTTERIES.

65

CHILD.

66

67

TUNSTALL. G. F. Bowers. Mark no. 64 occurs on an English porcelain cup and saucer, painted with blue grapes, scrolls, etc. The mark consists of the Staffordshire knot; in the three spaces are the letters G F B and below the word RUBELLA. The last word applies to the pattern; on another part of a tea service the word CLERMONT is under the knot, and the manufacturer's name is stamped in full. Mark no. 65. G. F. Bowers worked c. 1842–60, and was succeeded by his son Frederick, who failed about 1871.

SMITH CHILD. A manufactory was built at New Field about 1763 by Smith Child, Esq. Mark no 66 impressed is on a Queen's ware soup plate, octagonal, with embossed band round the rim; formerly in Mr. T. Fisher's possession. It was carried on from about 1790 by Mr. J. H. Clive, one of the earliest and most successful introducers of ornamental engraving into the blue printing department of pottery. The manufactory was occupied in 1829 by Joseph Heath & Co., and specimens sometimes bear the name *Heath* impressed. Some of this cream-coloured ware of Heath's was decorated in Holland with biblical subjects quaintly rendered.

WEDGWOOD & Co. Mark no. 67 was attributed, in earlier editions to Enoch Wedgwood (" It is probably an old imitation of Wedgwood's work.") The printed Unicorn mark is the registered trade mark of Wedgwood & Co. (Ltd. from 1900) of Tunstall, and has been used in various forms by this firm up to the present day. This firm was established by Enoch Wedgwood about 1835, the mark here reproduced dates from c. 1870.

" England " occurs on similar marks after 1891. It cannot be said that this firm copied the better known wares of Josiah Wedgwood & Sons Ltd. In the example reproduced " Indiana " refers to the name of the pattern.

J. MEIR & SONS. Various printed marks incorporating the initials J. M. & S. have previously been attributed to J. Meigh & Sons of Hanley. Tnese initials were also used by J. Meir & Sons of Greengates Pottery, Tunstall, from c. 1844 until 1897 and great care must be exercised in attributing examples bearing J. M. & S. marks. Mark no. 68. J. Meigh & Sons ceased c. 1834.

J M & S   ROGERS   ROGERS 20   ♂ ROGERS.   J·R L·

68   69   70   71   72

LONGPORT. Messrs. John & George Rogers had a large manufactory here in the eighteenth century; in the Survey of 1786 they are described as " manufacturers of china, glazed blue painted wares and cream-coloured," and in the map of 1802 they had two manufactories. Mr. John Rogers resided at the Watlands, which was afterwards occupied by his successor, Mr. Spencer Rogers, who had retired in 1829 after the fatigues of commercial activity.

Mark no. 69 is stamped on inferior imitations of Wedgwood. An earthenware plate painted with roses, bearing his name, was in Mr. Baldwin's Collection; a pair of sugar vases and covers, with transfer engraving of fruit and flowers, marked *Rogers*. Mark no. 70, late eighteenth to early nineteenth century.

Mark no. 71 (which is the character for iron) is found in blue on ironstone china, or opaque hardware so called; it is on some blue printed stoneware, the name stamped in the clay, early nineteenth century. It is found also on that of other manufacturers. See also *Donovan*.

Mark no. 72. The attribution of this mark is of some doubt, but is probably that of J. Rogers, c. 1814-36. It is found on an earthenware butter dish (Begonia ware), impressed.

E. & G. PHILLIPS. About 1760 a son of Mr. Phillips of Lane Delph commenced the manufacture of white stoneware, salt glaze, at Green Dock, Longton, and he afterwards made cream-colour at the same place.

Mark no. 73. There was in the Sheldon Collection a small blue printed ware dish with the words *E. & G. Phillips, Longport*, within a floral frame, c. 1822-34.

There is in the Victoria and Albert Museum a dish of common white ware, willow pattern, printed in blue, impressed mark, " *Phillips, Longport*." Edward and George Phillips were manufacturers at Longport from 1822 to about 1834. George Phillips continued until 1848.

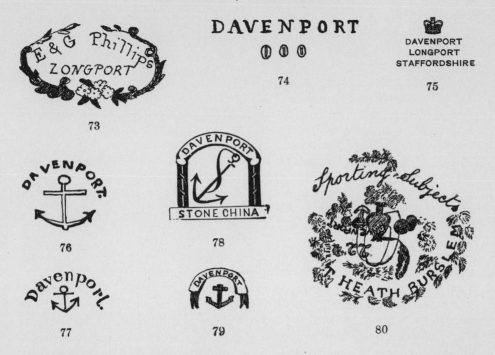

DAVENPORT

E & G Phillips
LONGPORT

73

Ⓞ Ⓞ Ⓞ

74

DAVENPORT
LONGPORT
STAFFORDSHIRE

75

DAVENPORT

76

DAVENPORT
STONE CHINA

78

Sporting Subjects
HEATH BURSLEM

80

Davenport

77

DAVENPORT

79

DAVENPORT.—These works were erected for the manufacture of pottery about the year 1773, and came into Mr. John Davenport's hands in 1793; they were considerably increased by purchase, and covered a large space of ground at Longport. The style of the firm since 1835 was William Davenport & Co.; subsequently Davenports Ltd., c. 1881–87. The manufactory ceased about 1887.

The specialties of their manufacture was excellence of material, combined with elegance and appropriateness of form in useful services. (*Ker. Gall.*, figs. 477–8.) Mark no. 74. The works were visited by the Prince of Wales and the Duke of Clarence in 1806, who were pleased with their progress in making porcelain; a magnificent service was ordered for use at the coronation banquet of William IV.

H.M. Queen Victoria used a " Davenport " service at the Civic Banquet in 1837. The late Mr. C. Wentworth Wass possessed a specimen plate decorated with the monogram V.R., the crown, and the city arms.

The words DAVENPORT, LONGPORT, STAFFORDSHIRE, surmounted by a crown, as mark no. 75, was the mark used from c. 1860. An earlier version does not include the crown, or the word Staffordshire.

The name DAVENPORT is both impressed in the clay and also painted and printed. Early porcelains before about 1820 may bear an impressed anchor only.

Mark no. 76, an early mark (c. 1805–c. 1825), impressed and also stamped in colour. The word LONGPORT was a so occasionally used above the anchor. The name is frequently printed in small Roman letters as mark no. 77. This mark has been erroneously attributed to Liverpool, from the word being misread in consequence of the erasure of the first two and last two letters. Various slight variations occur.

Mark no. 78 was used after 1805 for ironstone china, which was then very much improved.

Mark no. 79, printed, occurs on a pair of jugs in the Godden Collection and these are dated 1856. Most mid-nineteenth century Davenport porcelains bear this mark. See Godden's *British Pottery and Porcelain, an Illustrated Encyclopaedia of Marked Specimens.*

Mark no. 80. The Sheldon Collection contained an earthenware blue printed dish with the Davenport mark showing underneath the device of Heath, who evidently decorated the specimen. Various Thomas Heaths were potting early in the nineteenth century. This mark probably refers to Thomas Heath of Hadderridge, Burslem, c. 1812–35.

COBRIDGE. R. Daniel was established before 1710 at Hot Lane or Cobridge. Ralph Daniel, his son, about 1743, during a visit to France, ascertained that the moulds used in the porcelain works was formed by mixing calcined gypsum reduced to powder (plaster of Paris) with water, poured in a liquid state on the types of models, and allowed to dry. There is a story told how the Burslem potters, hearing that the French manufacturers employed moulds of plaster of Paris, determined to follow their example, with a view of improving the art, so as not to be behindhand with their French rivals; solid blocks of gypsum or sulphate of lime were obtained, which they ingeniously carved out into the required patterns; great was their surprise to find the moulds did not come up to their expectation. Mr. Daniel (Ralph) of Cobridge happened to visit a porcelain manufactory in France, when, among other information relative to their processes, he ascertained that the moulds were formed by mixing the gypsum in a pulverulent state with water. On his return home he exhibited plaster of Paris moulds from finished pieces of ware, and explained the discovery and its advantages, and the manufacturers being convinced of their error, were eager to possess moulds, because of the great facility with which any productions could be formed in them.

MESSRS. T. HALES AND W. ADAMS were potters here in the last century; they are mentioned as being present at the Hanley feast in 1783, and in the Topographical Survey of 1786. In the map of 1802 it was W. Adams alone at Cobridge, but he must not be confounded with the W. Adams who was then living at Tunstall.

HOT LANE or COBRIDGE. In 1710 John Warburton had one of the most extensive manufactories in " the Potteries "; after his death it was carried on by his widow, under whose supervision great improvements were made in cream-coloured ware; she having been present at the trial of the patent right of Ralph Shaw of Burslem in 1736, when all restrictions were taken from other potters, and the memorable fiat of the judge was pronounced, " Go home, potters, and make whatever kind of pots you please." In 1751 Mrs. Warburton made the last improvements of cream-coloured ware (previous to those of Josiah Wedgwood), by the use of Enoch Booth's fluid glaze. For some years this branch of enamelling or painting in colours on the ware was conducted by persons wholly unconnected with the manufacture, in some instances solely for the manufacturers, in others on the private account of the enamellers; a few of the more opulent connected this branch with the others when there became a great demand for it. Her son, Jacob Warburton, succeeded; he was born in 1740, and in 1777 joined the partners of the china works, on their purchase of Champion's patent. " Jacob Warburton, potter, Cobridge," is found in the list of 1786; he died in 1826, ætat. 86. In the map of 1802 we find that John Warburton had two manufactories at Hot Lane. Shaw tells us that the firm in 1828 was Warburton & Co. This firm ceased about 1829.

WARBURTON.

81

82

83

84

85

It has previously been stated that Mrs. Warburton decorated Wedgwood's creamwares, but Donald Towner has shown in the *Transactions of the English Ceramic Circle*, vol. 4, part 4, that David Rhodes decorated large quantities at Leeds before he moved to London, where he continued to decorate for Wedgwood.

Marks nos. 81 and 82. This name occurs impressed on a pair of two-handled oviform vases, of elegant form, white with bands of black, pencilled with gold. This mark may be found in various forms.

STEVENSON. There were in the Sheldon Collection two plates and a dish of blue printed earthenware, marked STEVENSON, also " Stevenson & Williams, Cobridge, Staffordshire," the words being enclosed in a fancy scroll, mark no. 83, c. 1818. Another specimen in the same collection has the words, STEVENSON, STAFFORDSHIRE, and a crown, mark no. 84, and can be dated c. 1810–c. 1830.

In a directory of 1802 we find the names of Stevenson & Dale as earthenware manufacturers at Cobridge, and in 1815 it was Ralph Stevenson alone: so also is it described in Shaw in 1828.

Mark no. 85 is stamped in the clay, and probably refers to Andrew Stevenson (c. 1816–36). A plate, raised scroll border, painted in the centre with a man riding on a velocipede, inscribed " Velocipede or Accelerator," and beneath, " Going to Brighton at the rate of ten miles an hour," was in Mr. Baldwin's Collection.

A similar plate in the Victoria and Albert Museum has a steamboat printed in brown and coarsely coloured, inscribed " On her passage from Belfast to Liverpool at the rate of ten miles an hour," and another, in a private collection, with a transfer view of the grand front of Claremont House, raised vine-leaf border.

Mark no. 86 is stamped on a blue printed dish formerly in the Sheldon Collection.

Mark no. 87 is stamped on a cream-coloured earthenware supper set of shaped pieces. This mark and the preceding are on portions of the same service, painted with Chinese figures, in the Victoria and Albert Museum, c. 1810–30.

STEVENSON

86

87

CLEWS
Warranted Staffordshire

88

89

Shaw says that in 1828 Messrs. Alcock & Stevenson published at Cobridge a series of busts of the most eminent characters of the time, executed in the best manner of the art in regard to accuracy of delineation and taste and elegance of workmanship; many of them being finished in dead gold, they are a very chaste, elegant, and beautiful ornament, equally for the drawing-room or the library. We have no other notice of Mr. Alcock having been in partnership with Stevenson, but they may have published these in conjunction. In 1834 the firm was Ralph Stevenson & Sons, and they gave up business about 1840.

Mr. Fenton, of Cranbourne Street, had a small bust of George IV. on a pedestal marked Saml. Alcock & Co., Cobridge, Staffordshire. Similar busts will be illustrated in Godden's *English Pottery and Porcelain*, 1780–1850.

J. & R. Clews, manufacturers of pale cream-coloured ware, established about 1814. Mark no. 88 is stamped on a piece formerly in the possession of Mr. C. B. Carruthers. About 1821 they made china, but only for three or four years; they returned to their cream-colour, for which they were noted, and retired about 1835.

Mark No. 89 is impressed on a blue printed earthenware tureen stand. The " coronation " is doubtless that of William IV. Other specimens have the words Clews warranted in a circle with a crown. N.B.—G. Clews of Tunstall is a later firm.

Mons. Voyez was a Frenchman some time in the employ of Josiah Wedgwood in the manufacture of his jasper ware for cameo busts, etc., and was a valuable servant, but he was discharged.

Wedgwood, writing to Bentley (March 31, 1768), says, "I have hired a modeller for three years; the best, I am told, in London. He served his time with a silversmith; has worked several years at a china work; has been two or three years carving in wood and marble for Mr. Adam, the famous architect; is a perfect master of the antique style in ornaments, vases, &c., &c., and works with equal facility in clay, wax, wood, or stone." According to Wedgwood's correspondence, which must be accepted *cum grano salis*, he for some malpractices was imprisoned for three months in the spring of 1769. Wedgwood was even after this unwilling to lose the services of Voyez; in fact, he feared he might, by leaving, do him a serious injury by imparting his secrets to others; for W. says, "to rival us the most effectually, our competitors stand most in need of some person to instruct them to compose good forms and to ornament them with tolerable propriety. Voyez can do this more effectually than all the potters in the country put together, and without much personal labour, as the ornaments may be bought or modelled by others." However, the engagement to work for Wedgwood solely for three years seems to have been broken, for we find him in 1769 working both for Wedgwood and for Palmer of Hanley. He afterwards worked for others, and finally set up in business for himself. A catalogue of his productions was issued by Voyez, which will give an insight as to his multifarious compositions, and the great sale he must have had for them; it was issued in 1773; the title is as follows:—

" A CATALOGUE of INTAGLIOS and CAMEOS, after the most esteemed of the Antiques, made by J. VOYEZ, Sculptor, Member of the Royal Society of Artists of Great Britain, and to be sold at his house, at COWBRIDGE near Newcastle, Staffordshire, and at M. Swinney's in Birmingham. BIRMINGHAM : Printed by M. Swinney, No. 76 High Street. MDCCLXXIII.

" INTRODUCTION.—The composition of these *Intaglios* and *Cameos* are a fine black porcelain, about the hardness of Cornelian, and having nearly the same properties as the Basaltes, resisting the attacks of all acids, the strongest Aquafortis having no more effect upon this composition than water; it is a touchstone to gold and all metals, and on the whole is esteemed the purest and most durable composition ever invented, being nearly (as we said above) as hard as the gems themselves from which they are taken.

" Any of the following subjects may be had either in Cameo or Intaglio.

" 1. Equestrian statue of Marcus Aurelius in Cornelian.

" 3. A man making a vase, Emerald, &c.

(Here follows a list of 560 subjects, chiefly from antique gems.)

" An appendix of about 500 more will be subjoined as soon as the list can be made out.

" Intaglios for seals.—They are sold unset at one shilling each, or neatly set in gilt metal from two shillings and sixpence to three shillings and sixpence.

" Antique ornamental vases, tablets for chimney-pieces, pictures and picture frames gilt, and equal to the best wood-carving, round statues, or in bas-relievo, from one inch to as big as life," &c., &c.

His name occurs on a jug with rustic characters in relief, coloured, in the Victoria and Albert Museum. A rare teapot, cover and stand of similar type was sold for £155 in 1959.

His name, mark no. 90, is stamped on an earthenware vase of good form, ornamented with leaves in relief, masks and festoons round the drum, of cream-colour, mottled brown and yellow at the top and bottom. Formerly in the Collection of the Rev. T. Staniforth. (*Ker. Gall.*, fig. 470.)

Mark no. 91 is on an earthenware flask moulded and painted with

J.VOYEZ   ɪ.ᴠoʏᴇᴢ,   E.MAYER.   E.Mayer.
                                    1784
    90   91   92   93

scenes from Shakespeare, from the Sheldon Collection.

John (Jean) Voyez produced some excellent vases. There was in the possession of Sir T. W. Holbourne a lofty black basalt vase, with a finely-sculptured medallion on each side of Prometheus attacked by a vulture: at the bottom is the signature " J. Voyez, sculp. 1769." The handles are of female terminal figures; on the square plinth is " H. Palmer, Hanley, Staffordshire." (*Ker. Gall.*, fig. 471, now in the Holburne of Menstrie Museum, Bath.) A vase of good form, in variegated marble ware, bearing his name, was in the Collection of Mr. E. Hailstone. Some " Fair Hebe " jugs also bear the mark of Voyez, see an authoritative paper by R. J. Charleston, published in the *Transactions of the English Ceramic Circle*, vol. 5, part 1, 1960. The name of Hawley is also found impressed on " Bacchus " jugs of the Voyez type.

HANLEY. Elijah Mayer commenced business about 1770; he was a contemporary of Wedgwood and noted for his cream-coloured ware, black basalt and *brown line* ware, but he produced many other varieties. In the Victoria and Albert Museum is a vase of unglazed drab terra-cotta, with festoons, etc., in relief, coloured. The basalts or black Egyptian ware tea services, with animals, etc., in relief, are well known. Another popular service was one made to commemorate Nelson's victories of the Nile and Trafalgar, with crocodiles, pyramids, Britannia, Fame, and monument inscribed " Pro Patrie," and tablet with Nelson, etc. These are usually impressed with E. Mayer's name, both in capital letters and lower-case, marks nos. 92 and 93. In the Survey of 1786, Elijah Mayer is styled enameller. He died in January 1813, and was succeeded by his son Joseph; but the names of E. Mayer & Son were retained some years longer. They ceased about 1830.

Elijah Mayer, of the High Carr, the father of the one here mentioned (of the firm of E. Mayer & Son), was unfortunately overtaken by the tide in crossing the sands near Ulverston, and perished along with some others. Simeon Shaw says that this Elijah Mayer and a potter named Moss, during the early part of the eighteenth century, fabricated greater quantities of pottery at Red Street than any others of the whole district.

Some brown ware plaques with cupids in relief, one dated 1784, marked E. MAYER, was sold at Sotheby's in 1905. Specimens of pottery stamped MAYER, STOKE, have also been seen and may be dated c. 1826–35.

The name of "*Joseph Mayer & Co., Hanley,*" occurred on some pieces in the Liverpool Museum. Mayer Collection, mark no. 94.

Mark no. 95, impressed without colour, is frequently found underneath earthenware services, especially upon wares made by E. Mayer; but it scarcely may be designated as a trade-mark, and was used by other makers.

Joseph Mayer made a transparent stoneware, a true Parian, in fact, forty years before the rediscovery of this body, a specimen of which is in the Victoria and Albert Museum, viz., a tea-pot, the body ornamented in relief with figures of Cupid and a female and a girl reading, the cover surmounted by a woman and infant. In 1860, on the death of Joseph Mayer (the son), a large quantity of the productions of this firm were sold by auction that had remained locked up for thirty years; a great deal was purchased by foreign artists and workmen residing in the Potteries and sent to their friends in France and Germany. These works were taken in 1830 by W. Taylor, Son, & Co., and subsequently by Messrs. W. Ridgway & Son, of the Bell Bank.

Joseph Mayer & Co., *Hanley.*	❋	MEIGH
94	95	96

MEIGH. The "Old Hall" works, where formerly the old Crouch and white stoneware, salt glaze, were made, and then conducted by Christopher C. Whitehead, were taken by Mr. Job Meigh about 1780; he afterwards took into partnership his sons, Job and Charles. Mark no. 96. In the map of 1802 we find the names of Meigh and Walthall, potters at Hanley. Job Meigh died 6th February, 1817, aged 67 years.

It is well known that the coarse red and mottled pottery, of which many utensils were made for cooking food by the lower grades of the community, is covered with a very pernicious glaze, of which litharge or lead ore is one of the principal components; when vessels of this kind are used for baking or boiling, the heat renders the glaze soluble, and it mixes with the animal fat, or the acid juices of fruits, or vinegar when cold, and is partiallys o even when they remain in the vessels cold; its effects are consequently very deleterious. Mr. Job Meigh, jun., received the gold medal of the Society of Arts in 1822 for giving to the public a glaze, for common pottery entirely free from the deleterious qualities of the usual red glaze. According to the Belle Vue Papers, the firm in 1823 was Job Meigh & Sons; in 1829 the firm was J. Meigh & Sons; in 1843 it belonged to Charles Meigh. The works were carried on by the "Old Hall Earthenware Company, Limited," from 1861 to 1866 and subsequently by the "Old Hall Porcelain Works Ltd." to 1902. A misleading late mark includes the date 1790 and the title OLD HALL inside a rope, surmounted by a turreted castle. This mark was not used before 1885.

A white stoneware mug with Bacchanalian subject in relief, and at the bottom, burnt in, a printed facsimile of the Society of Arts' medal of 1851, and the inscription, "Presented to Charles Meigh for the best model of a mug ornamented in relief," was formerly in the Editor's possession.

Mark no. 97, impressed (previously attributed to Minton) is found on Meigh earthenwares, c. 1820–50. Slight variations occur. For further information on Charles Meigh's wares see Godden's *English Pottery and Porcelain*, 1780–1850 (in preparation).

Mark no. 98 (previously given as undoubtedly Meigh) was used by J. Meir & Son, Greengates Pottery, Tunstall. The editor has seen this mark on a service bearing the impressed mark " Meir & Son." The initials J. M. & S. were used by both firms. 1841–97.

LAKIN & POOLE; established about 1790. The name of Lakin occurs in Hanley also in 1783, but is not found in the Survey of 1786, nor in the map of 1802. The Lakin & Poole partnership ceased about 1794.

Mark no. 99 impressed on a black vase, like Wedgwood's Basaltes, of sharp and good work with raised groups and basket-work, and on Queen's ware, etc. They made groups, one of which is the " Assassination of Marat by Charlotte Cordé " (*sic*). One of these groups, representing Marat in his bath, and Charlotte Corday in the act of stabbing him was in the Collection of Staffordshire pottery formerly belonging to Mr. Percy Fitzgerald. Mr. Edwin Hewitt of Hanley had a very carefully-painted figure in the costume of that period, with shoe-buckles, etc., marked with their names. Cream-ware and other varieties then in vogue were also manufactured to a considerable extent. In Mr. Jewitt's sale there was a tea-pot and stand, eight-sided and covered, divided into compartments; on one side and in the centre of the stand a finely-painted bird and landscape, on the other a flower; it had a sliding metal lid fitting into a groove in the body; marked " Lakin & Poole." In the Victoria and Albert Museum is a dish, shell pattern, of common ware, printed in blue with classic ruins and English landscape; impressed mark " Lakin."

STEVENSON. Mark no. 100 is on a square china pedestal, blue glazed ground, white figures in relief of Ganymede, a butterfly, milkmaid and dog; in the Victoria and Albert Musuem.

LAKIN & POOLE.

99

97

98

W. STEVENSON
HANLEY.
MAY. 2.
1802.

100

BIRCH. Established in the eighteenth century. The name of Edmund John Birch is found in a map of potters at Hanley in 1802, and the initials E.I.B. are frequently found stamped on his ware. Mark no. 1, c. 1796–1813.

Mark no. 2 stamped on a black Egyptian ware milk-pot, with figures in relief from Wedgwood's designs; formerly in Rev. T. Staniforth's Collection. The Sheldon Collection included a black basalt sucrier and cover with this mark. This pot-work was afterwards taken by Christopher Whitehead, and subsequently by Messrs. Thomas Dimmock & Co. (c. 1865).

E. I. B.   Birch   SHORTHOSE   Shorthose.

1   2   3   4

SHORTHOSE & HEATH   Shorthose & Co

5   6

GLASS. The name of Glass as a manufacturer of earthenware is perhaps of longer continuance than any in the Potteries with the exception of Wedgwood, having existed for a period of nearly 150 years. The first notice we have is in Thomas Wedgwood's list of 1710, as Joseph Glass, a maker of cloudy ware, etc. In 1786 John Glass was a potter at Hanley, also in 1802; in 1818 and 1821 it was John Glass & Sons, and down to 1838 a John Glass still continued the manufacture; in that year the name disappeared, but the premises were taken by Samuel Keeling & Co., who occupied it in 1842. The factory was pulled down in 1872, but the name of Glass has been given to a street upon its site.

J. SHORTHOSE. Established in the second half of the eighteenth century, and doing business in 1783. The name of Shorthose is found stamped on cream-coloured ware, pierced wicker-pattern baskets, etc. Mark no. 3, used to about 1802.

Mark no. 4, impressed on a small black Egyptian sugar-vase, beehive shaped, with lion's head handles; formerly in Mr. T. Fisher's possession.

The names of Heath and Shorthose are found in the map of potters in 1802 at Hanley. A cream-coloured ware dish of embossed wicker pattern, pierced border, in the Victoria and Albert Museum has the mark no. 5 impressed " Shorthose & Heath "; and on open-work cream ware baskets and stands. In the Belle Vue Papers the firm is spoken of as " T. Shorthose or Assignees " in 1823. Mark used c. 1795–c. 1815. The firm was succeeded by Shorthose & Co.

Mark no. 6 is on an earthenware vase, urn shaped, printed with a female figure in a medallion holding an urn and flowers, formerly in the possession of Mr. John J. Bagshawe. Shorthose & Co. ceased about 1823. In 1821 the Directory names John Shorthose & Co. in Tontine Street at Hanley.

RALPH SALT had a small manufactory on Miles's Bank in 1820, for the manufacture of various kinds of figures; he was also an enameller and lusterer. In 1834 he had removed to Marsh Street, where he added porcelain tablets to his other business; he died 21st November, 1846, ætat. 64, and was succeeded by his son Charles Salt, who had previously worked with his father, and was a skilful modeller. Parian was made to some extent;

a bust of Wesley of that material was in the possession of his nephew. Charles Salt died in April 1864, ætat. 54, when the manufacture entirely ceased.

SALT   M 15

7   8

An earthenware figure of a shepherdess, painted in colours, in the Victoria and Albert Museum, has mark no. 7 impressed, height 5 in. Other marked examples are known and are similar to those made by Walton.

MR. CHARLES CHATTERLEY and DR. SAMUEL CHATTERLEY were both potters at Hanley, the latter making excellent black Egyptian for tea and coffee sets. Mr. Charles Chatterley made some very beautiful articles. Simeon Shaw notes especially that in 1829, the date of his book, he had " two candlesticks near sixty years made, one of bisquet finely ornamented; the other glazed, the column very neatly fluted, the circle beneath the bowl well turned and ornamented with rosettes. A fine vase of extremely white bisquet, *pearl*, I believe, has some blue fern leaf ornaments on the lower parts and the cover; and the handles have scrolled work on them, the blue is very fine, and particularly strong in quality." He was the first to fix an agent in Holland. Elijah Mayer was some years his representative there; he subsequently admitted his brother Ephraim into partnership, who survived him, and continued until about 1797, when he transferred the business to his nephews, James and Charles Whitehead, sons of Mr. Christopher C. Whitehead of the " Old Hall," one of the early and most eminent salt-glaze potters. Charles and Ephraim Chatterley were both present at the Hanley Feast in 1780, the former being chosen mayor. Charles Chatterley died at Bath in 1786, ætat. 42; Ephraim died in 1811, ætat. 66. Their names are in the map of potters in 1802; they were succeded by J. & W. Handley, and in 1848 Messrs. Thomas Dimmock & Co. took the premises, who had two other manufactories close by.

MILES. Shaw mentions a Mr. Miles, of Miles's Bank, Hanley, who produced the brown stoneware about 1700; probably the same as the Thomas Miles of Shelton, the works having been on the boundary-line between the two townships. They have long since disappeared, but the names Miles's *Bank*, which is a local term for *manufactory*, still remains.

There is in the Victoria and Albert Museum an earthenware barrel supported by four cupids of brown glaze, with gilt hoops, resting on a stage of four supports, of good work, apparently the second half of the eighteenth century, impressed with the letters M. 15 and M. 22, mark no 8. (See *Ker. Gall.*, fig. 466.) There does not appear sufficient authority for attributing this barrel to Miles of Hanley; they are probably marks of the workmen only, for it is the custom in potteries not to pay the workman for his work until it comes out of the biscuit oven; hence it frequently happens that two workmen may be engaged in making the same sort of ware, and each affixes his mark, that he may know his own: it belongs to a much later period—first, it has a coating of fluid glaze, which was not introduced until 1745 or 1750; second, it is gilt, and gilding with burnished gold was not practised until about 1760 on Staffordshire pottery.

PALMER. Church Works was established by Humphrey Palmer about 1760 for the manufacture of ware in the style of Wedgwood; he made cream-coloured ware, red engined tea sets, black Egyptian, etc. His father, John Palmer, is spoken of by Shaw as having introduced *salt and litharge* in the glaze. Mark no. 9 is on a black Egyptian vase, 12½ in. high, with elegant festoons and medallions.

9

Neale & Palmer.

10

Simeon Shaw mentions the names of Chatterley & Palmer of Hanley as the inventors of the *chalk body ware*, and Henry Palmer and Chatterley were in some way related. Chatterly married a sister of Mr. Samuel Hollins. Henry Palmer copied many of Wedgwood's patterns, and Mrs. Palmer (who was a Miss Heath, the daughter of Mr. Heath, the potter of Lane Delph) seems to have been the active manager of her husband's business. She engaged persons to obtain the new pieces of Wedgwood & Bentley's as soon as they arrived at the London warehouse, for the purpose of copying them. The first attempts were to imitate the black Etruscan-shaped vases with medallions; but as the material of the black basalts was not an invention of Wedgwood, and had been known for many years, no steps could be taken to prevent his imitating them. Wedgwood says in a letter to Bentley, October 1769: " The body is very good, the shape and composition very well." But he adds, " We must proceed, or they will tread upon our heels." Palmer and his London partner, Neale (mark no. 10, c. 1769–76), whose shop was in Shoe Lane, next copied his Etruscan painted vases, the body being made in Staffordshire and painted in London by a man in Vine Street. An injunction was served upon them for an infringement of Wedgwood's patent, which ended in a compromise; Palmer purchasing a share in the patent. They subsequently discovered the secret of the jasper body. From the specimens we have seen, they were formidable rivals of Wedgwood, and considerable allowance must be made for the harsh words used by him in his published letters, which were never intended for any other eye except that of his partner Bentley, or his expressions would have been more guarded; but they were evidently engendered by trade jealousy, for, as he says, they were " treading upon his heels."

Palmer got into difficulties in 1776, and Neale (who had married his wife's sister, and was a large creditor) went from London to Hanley to settle his affairs, and the business was carried on by James Neale alone from 1776 to 1778.

The Sheldon Collection contained a black basalt cream ewer with figures in relief. Impressed under the handle is the letter N (mark no. 11), which is attributed to Neale; it is a rare mark.

Mark no. 12 is stamped on a blue mottled vase, with white and gold festoons, eagle-neck handles, in imitation of Wedgwood.

In 1778 Robert Wilson was associated with Neale at Hanley, and the style of the firm from 1778 to c. 1788 was Neale & Co., other partners having joined the concern. In a Directory of 1788 we find the firm spoken of as Neale & Wilson.

Mark no. 13 is on a jelly mould and core in cream-coloured earthenware, enamelled in colours, formerly in the possession of Mr. A. H. Church, c. 1788-90.

There were other partners in the London warehouse, who were probably not connected with the Hanley manufactory, unless they were included in the firm Neale & Co. Between 1780 and 1790 the London firm was styled " Neale, Maidment & Bailey," and subsequently " Neale & Bailey "; the warehouse for the sale of Staffordshire ware was in St. Paul's Churchyard.

Mark no. 14 of Neale & Co., with date 1789, was on a cream ware plate in the Sheldon Collection; as the firm of Neale & Co. ceased in 1788, the decoration must have been done the year following. Also on some blue & white vases, like Wedgwood's jasper, and on green glazed ware in the Victoria and Albert Museum. One of these is a very important vase, 18 in. high, light green, with richly-gilt female heads and festoons in full relief, of elegant form. Another very fine example of their manufacture is a large punch barrel painted with fruits, flowers, and a trophy of musical instruments, by one of the Chelsea artists, surmounted by a figure of Bacchus, and on the pedestal satyrs and children in relief, inscribed " Neale & Co." (*Ker. Gall.*, fig. 468.) Some of the Toby Fillpot ale-jugs were made by them. A pyramidal-shaped jelly mould in two pieces, the inner one painted with flowers, so as to show through the clear jelly, marked " Neale & Co.," was in the Baldwin Collection. Mark no. 15, c. 1778-88.

They also produced figures; a set of the Seasons, coloured and gilt, is in the Victoria and Albert Museum (Schreiber Collection), stamped NEALE & CO. The name sometimes occurs in italics.

Their names are impressed on a service of cream-coloured ware, like Wedgwood's Queen's ware; also on black Egyptian vases, with ornaments in high relief and highly-finished black ware medallions of Inigo Jones, etc. Two ovals, 12 in. by 9, of Dr. Franklin and Washington, stamped Neale & Co., were in Mr. John J. Bagshawe's Collection. They also imitated Wedgwood's blue jasper ware, even copying the designs, as on a jardinière in the Victoria and Albert Museum, and a set of five vases, formerly in the late Mr. D. W. Macdonald's Collection.

After the retirement or death of Neale, Robert Wilson continued the manufactory alone; he brought to perfection that kind of pottery known as *chalk body*, of excellent quality for fineness of grain and smooth beautiful glaze, of a fine cream colour; he married a daughter of Elijah Mayer.

WILSON

16

WILSON

17

Mark no. 16 is on an earthenware plate, white ground, raised ornaments, dolphins, etc., on the border, in the centre a Gothic castle, in the Victoria and Albert Museum; and on a large copy of the Portland Vase 12 in. high, white figures on grey ground, beautifully executed, the name impressed; the name is also found on copper lustre ware.

Mark no. 17 is on a pair of elegant earthenware jardinières, square, with wide mouths, leaf borders, in festoons in relief, in blue, green serpent handles. The meaning of the letter C under the crown is conjectural; it may perhaps refer to the chalk body, for which he was celebrated. The crown and C are sometimes found impressed without the name. A piece in the Victoria and Albert Museum has the figure 4 impressed beneath C and a crown. Mark prior to 1820.

Robert was succeeded by his brother, David Wilson, who also inherited his fortune; his name alone occurs in the map of 1802; he eventually took his sons into partnership. In a Directory of 1810 we find " D. Wilson & Sons (Assignees of)." In 1820 the manufactory was taken by Jacob Philips and John Denton Bagster, under the firm of Philips & Bagster, earthenware manufacturers; they left the works in 1828, which remained unoccupied for two years. In 1830 they were taken by W. Ridgway, the firm being W. Ridgway Son & Company, this being one of the six Ridgway works at Hanley and Shelton. In or about 1848 William Ridgway retired from the concern, leaving his son, E. J. Ridgway, in partnership with Mr. Abington; the firm was styled Ridgway & Abington; the last-named gentleman retired in 1860, leaving E. J. Ridgway alone. Mr. E. J. Ridgway reintroduced the jasper body, for which this firm was celebrated in the time of Neale, and vases and other elegant objects were manufactured in great variety. This firm had long been noted for stoneware jugs of elegant designs, some of which are engraved in the *Art Journal* for 1851; in 1866 he removed to the large manufactory which had been completed in Bedford Place, Hanley.

A correspondent mentions a buff-coloured jug with the mark no 18. Similar impressed marks occur, c. 1830 +.

MARE. In Thomas Wedgwood's list of potters about 1710, Hugh Mare and John Mare were makers of black and mottled wares at Hanley, and at Hot Lane or Cobridge. Messrs. J. & R. Mare were potters here about the middle of the eighteenth century; in 1770 they signed an agreement with other potters to sell their wares at stated prices; they were both present at the Hanley feast in 1763. In the map of 1802 we find John Mare alone; he was doing a good business in 1823. The name MARE occurs impressed on the tureen of a service, other pieces of the same set being marked SPODE.

WILLIAM BADDELEY is in the map of 1802, having a manufactory at Hanley; he was a brother of Messrs. J. & E. Baddeley of Shelton. His works were situated at Eastwood, now called Eastwood Mill; he was a maker of black ware, cream, ware, etc. The word EASTWOOD is frequently found on this description of ware, but no potter is known of that name. In the Directories for the years 1818 and 1822 William Baddeley is described as a " Manufacturer of fancy and ornamental earthenware at *Eastwood* "; and probably he adopted this mark to distinguish it from his brothers, J. & E. Baddeley of Shelton. On vases, the word is usually impressed on the plinth. Mark no 19, c. 1802–22.

Mark no. 20 is impressed on a match-pot of yellow clay, ornamented with blue raised leaves and figures.

PUBLISHED BY
W. RIDGWAY & Co.,
HANLEY,
October 1, 1835.

18

Eastwood.

19

EASTWOOD.

20

Simeon Shaw tells an anecdote of one of this family which occurred about 1750; he says:—

" About this time the lathes for turning were made at Congleton, because the secret of properly tempering the spindle and collar was possessed only by a smith resident there. In Hanley there resided a very ingenious smith (proved since to be Mr. John Baddeley of Eastwood), to whom the business was suggested; on a certain day he dressed himself as a potter, with white apron, and also white gloves on the hands, to prevent them being noticed by the smith at Congleton, and having a spindle, &c., with him, he accompanied Mr. W. Brooks and Mr. Thomas Greatbatch of Hanley, each having his spindle, &c., to the shop of the mechanic and smith, where he witnessed the several operations, and afterwards practised them at Hanley; and so careful was he to preserve the secret, that, according to the statement of his daughter (the late Mrs. Poulson of Stoke), he frequently performed the most particular operations about midnight, having only the company and help of his daughter. Thomas Greatbatch suggested the movement of an engine lathe to Mr. Baddeley, which was successfully constructed and was publicly sold in 1828."

RICHARD HOLLINS of the Upper Green established a manufactory about 1750; he died in 1780 aged seventy-eight years, and was buried in Hanley Churchyard. He was succeeded by his sons, T. & J. Hollins, whose names are shown in the map of 1802; they subsequently admitted their brother, Richard Hollins, into partnership, the firm being T. J. & R. Hollins, and continued so to the close of 1820. The finer productions of this manufactory date from 1790 to 1800; latterly they produced goods of a common description. John Hollins died in December 1855, at the advanced age of ninety-six years. We find Samuel Hollins, another brother, occupying the manufactory at the Vale in Shelton in the Directories of 1786 and 1802, and in the Sheldon Collection there was an earthenware cup and saucer with metallic decoration on a buff ground stamped S. HOLLINS, see notes in Shelton section later.

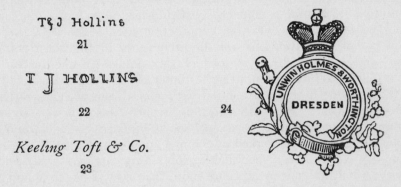

T & J Hollins
21

T J HOLLINS
22

24

Keeling Toft & Co.
23

Mark no. 21 is on a basin in jasper ware, white ground with cameo figures in blue, representing a female weeping at a tomb, children, etc.; mark impressed. Mark no. 22 is on a bowl in the Victoria and Albert Museum, white body and blue raised figures, highly finished in imitation of Wedgwood, c. 1795–1820.

KEELING, TOFT & CO. were potters from 1806 to 1824; they made Egyptian black and other wares of the period; their names are stamped on a black ware tea set, mark no. 23. In 1823 they are named by Mr. Bell of the Bell Vue Works as being then in business. See Godden's *British Pottery and Porcelain, an Illustrated Encyclopædia of Marked Specimens.* Toft & May were successors from 1824 to 1830.

VALENTINE CLOSE was a potter here in the last century; he was present at the election feast in 1783, and in 1796 took out a patent in conjunction with James Keeling of Hanley for improvements in kilns; his name is also in the Directory of 1802.

UNWIN, HOLMES & WORTHINGTON, makers of an ordinary description of earthenware for domestic use, but not of an artistic character; the imposing mark no. 24 is on an earthenware cup and saucer, red leaf border; the word *Dresden* refers to the pattern merely, not to its origin, c. 1865–68. Subsequently Unwin & Holmes, c. 1868–78 and then Holmes, Stonier & Hollinshead, etc., The Upper Hanley Pottery Co., c. 1895+.

T. Sneyd. Hanley (Miles Bank). The name impressed, as mark no. 25, of Sneyd occurs on jugs of red and other colours, in bad imitation of the Portland Vase, of nineteenth century manufacture, c. 1846. There was an earthenware dish with coloured transfer with this mark in the Sheldon Collection.

25

Edward Keeling's name is in the Directory of 1786 as a potter at Hanley; he was succeeded by James Keeling, who in 1802 was then in the business, and in the Belle Vue Papers, 1823, he is named as being proprietor. In 1796 he patented a substitute for the lead glaze on Queen's ware, and in the same year, in conjunction with Valentine Close, took out a patent for inventions and improvements in the construction of ovens and kilns, and the saving of fuel. Mr. James Keeling, in the latter part of 1828, produced, by printing, a dinner service which was at the time much esteemed; it was ornamented with views from the illustrations of Buckingham's *Travels in Mesopotamia*; which was followed by other manufactures, completing services of views in Turkey, Persia, and Hindustan. In 1843 it was worked by Samuel and John Burton.

Mann & Co. had a manufactory of a very common description of pottery, which was not in existence more than two years, 1858 and 1859.

The following manufacturers, not previously mentioned, were located at Hanley:—

Messrs. J. Adams & Co., jasper and majolica, c. 1864–73.
    ,,   T. & C. Ford, decorated china, c. 1854–74.
    ,,   J. & T. Bevington, Parian, c. 1865–76.
    ,,   Powell & Bishop, decorated china and earthenware, c. 1866–78. Subsequently Powell, Bishop & Stonier, c. 1878–90.
    ,,   R. Scrivener & Co., decorated china, c. 1870–83.

Shelton. Josiah Twyford is mentioned in Simeon Shaw's list of improvers of pottery as having introduced the use of pipe-clay from Devonshire in the making of white stoneware; he is also mentioned as having gained access to the works of Messrs. Elers to obtain their secrets, as well as his neighbour Astbury. There is in the Victoria and Albert Museum an octagonal plate of delft ware painted in blue with river scene, marked in blue under the glaze " I. T. March 1, 17$\frac{39}{40}$ "—which is attributed to him.

In a monograph by Mr. William Watkiss Lloyd, entitled *Elijah Fenton, his Poetry and Friends*, there is described and illustrated an old porringer of red clay body, with black glaze ornamented with yellow devices; it bears this superscription—" Mr. Thomas Ffenton," and was presented to Mr. Fenton (an ancestor of the poet Elijah's) by Mr. Twyford about the year 1700.

John? Astbury had a pottery here in the beginning of the eighteenth century. Mr. Burton says that the Christian name of the elder Astbury is given variously as John, Thomas or Samuel by different writers. He made red, crouch, and white stoneware; he died in 1743, aged 65. It is said that by pretending to be an idiot, he obtained employment at the Elers's manufactory at Bradwell, and thus became possessed of the secret of making their red and salt-glazed stoneware, which was very much in request for its fine quality and elegant forms. His son, Thomas Astbury, in 1725, commenced business at Lane Delph, and made a cream-coloured stoneware. A mug, dated 1730, has on it a tulip rose, and auricula, fairly designed and executed; some specimens have a red body with white ornaments. It is the pieces made by the son, Thomas, which are marked, and each letter was stamped separately, as mark no. 26, which occurs on a cream ware plate, blue painted (formerly in the Sheldon Collection). Two specimens in the same collection had a seal mark no. 27 copied from the Chinese, and another square mark no. 28.

ASTBURY

26

27

28

Wedgwood, in a letter to Bentley, July 19, 1787, attributes the discovery of the improvement in the white stoneware by the addition of calcined flint to Mr. Heath, although Simeon Shaw and Parkes speak of the younger Astbury as the inventor.[1] He says:—

"The *white stoneware* was produced by using the white pipe-clay instead of the common clay of this neighbourhood, and mixing it with flint stones calcined and reduced by pounding into a fine powder. The use of flint in our pottery is said to have proceeded from an accident happening to one of our potters, a Mr. Heath of Shelton, on his way to London. His horse's eye becoming bad, he applied to an hostler on the road, who told him he would cure the horse and show him what means he used. Accordingly he took a piece of black flint stone and put it into the fire, which, to our potter's great astonishment, came out of the fire a most beautiful white, and at the same time struck him with an idea that this fine material might improve the stoneware lately introduced among them. He brought some of the stones home with him, mixed them with pipe-clay, and made the first *white flint stoneware.*"

SAMUEL HOLLINS, a son of Mr. Richard Hollins of the *Upper* Green, Hanley, established about 1774 a manufactory of fine red ware teapots with figures in relief, black basalts, etc.; he procured the clay from Bradwell, being the same formerly used by the Elers. He joined the New Hall Company in 1777, but continued his private works as before. We find his name mentioned at Vale Pleasant in Shelton in a map of the year 1802;

---

[1] 'It will be seen hereafter, in speaking of Dwight of Fulham, that he used "calcined beaten and sifted flints" in the composition of his wares nearly fifty years before either Astbury or Heath are here stated to have made the discovery.

he retired from business c. 1813, and died in 1820, at an advanced age, and is buried with his two wives in Hanley churchyard.

Mark no. 29, c. 1784–1813, is on a jug of maroon ware with embossed hunting scene, name impressed; and on a basin of sage green ware, fluted and embossed with flowers, decorated with dark blue bands; in the Victoria and Albert Museum.

S. HOLLINS.

29

EDWARDS. The Bell Bank in Albion Street was in the first half of the eighteenth century carried on by Mr. Werner Edwards, for the manufacture of the various kinds of pottery then in demand with lead ore glaze; he was a good practical chemist, and produced fine enamel colours, and presented Mr. H. Daniel of Stoke with his drawing-book, containing also his receipts for enamels; he died in 1753.

RIDGWAY. About 1790 the Bell Works were taken by Job and George Ridgway. Job was an apprentice at Wedgwood's and George was his elder brother. They continued in partnership until 1813, when Job left to build the Cauldon Works, leaving George to conduct the Bell Works alone. On the death or retirement of George Ridgway his nephews, John and William Ridgway, the sons of Job, sometime previous to 1824 succeeded to the Bell Bank. In 1830 they separated, John leaving to conduct the Cauldon Works, while William remained to manage the Bell. William Ridgway extended the business considerably, and occupied five other works, combining three or four firms, of which he was the head:—

1. China works (formerly Geo. and Thos. Taylor), W. Ridgway & Son.
2. Pot work (formerly Elijah Mayer), W. Ridgway & Son.
3. Pot work (formerly Palmer and R. Wilson), W. Ridgway & Son.
4. Pot work (formerly Toft & May), W. Ridgway.
5. China and earthenware works (formerly Baddeley, and afterwards Hicks, Meigh and Johnson), taken in 1836 under the firm of W. Ridgway, Morley, Wear & Co.

Some of the marks of this firm are very elaborate: a dessert service, painted with flowers, has the mark of an elegant vase, against which rests an anchor and W. R. & Co., c. 1830+.

The firm was dissolved in 1854, and the Bell Works, after being closed for a short time, were purchased by Joseph Clementson in 1855, who at the time was a manufacturer of white granite ware, etc., for the American market, at a manufactory nearly opposite, called the Phœnix Works; he was thus enabled to extend his business largely; he died 22nd August, 1871. The Bell Works were carried on by his sons, under the style of Clementson Bros., until 1916.

There was an earthenware printed cup and saucer in the Sheldon Collection, with the printed mark no. 30, c. 1841–64.

CAULDON PLACE WORKS. These works were built in 1813 by Job Ridgway from the Bell Bank, who took into partnership his sons, John and William Ridgway; Job died 30th May, 1814, aged fifty-four years. Mark no. 31, c. 1808–33.

The name of this firm, Job Ridgway & Sons, is on a pair of porcelain urns and covers, very much like that of Swansea, painted with bouquets of flowers and gilt borders, made about 1813, formerly in Dr. Diamond's Collection.

Mark no. 32 was found on an earthenware plate, blue printed, c. 1814–30.

From 1814 to 1830 the sons, John and William Ridgway, continued in partnership, but in the year 1830 they separated, William being considered too wild and speculative by the steady-going John, who remained at Cauldon Place; Williams taking the Bell Works under his control. The words " India Temple " on mark no. 33 refer only to the pattern.

Mark no. 34 is impressed on an earthenware inkstand, buff coloured and gilt, with the name, W. Ridgway & Co., on the riband.

Mark no. 35 was on an earthenware plate in the Sheldon Collection, blue printed, the J.W.R. being John and William Ridgway, c. 1814–30.

John Ridgway remained alone from 1830 until he retired in 1858. Mark no. 36 is one of his early marks; it occurs on an earthenware plate of the blue printed willow pattern; stamped in the paste. John Ridgway was a party to several patents, one in 1825 for an improved china tap; another in 1840 for improvements in the moulds used for earthenware and porcelain; two others, in conjunction with George Wall, for improvements in apparatus and machinery in the manufacture of china, etc., and improving and preparing bats of porcelain and earthenware, and shaping them into articles, etc. In 1847 John Ridgway obtained a patent for improvements in the manufacture of paste boxes and similar articles in china or other plastic material with moulds and pressing apparatus, etc. In 1852 another patent for " improvements in the method of ornamenting china, earthenware, and glass, by applying the art of electrotype or electro-metallurgy, etc." A dessert service decorated with the royal arms with the mark " *John Ridgway* " was made for the Queen in 1855. A specimen plate was in the Sheldon Collection.

37

38

39

41

40

Mark no. 37 was used when royal patronage was accorded about 1850. Mark no. 38 is one of many used from 1830 to 1860; these various marks include the initials J. R.

John Ridgway died without issue in 1860; he retired from the Cauldon Place Works in 1858, and they were taken by Messrs. T. C. Brown-West-head, Moore & Co., who in 1872 took also the Victoria Works at Shelton, formerly occupied by Mr. Thomas Cooper. Mark no. 39 is one of their marks. From 1904 the firm was Cauldon Ltd.

Mark no. 41 occurs on wares of the 1817–38 period made by Reuben or Phoebe Johnson of Hanley; examples are in the Godden and other collections.

R. & J. BADDELEY. Established about 1750 or earlier. Shaw speaks of the surprise occasioned by their extravagance in having their manu-factory covered with tiles instead of thatch, as formerly used, and for being the first who erected four hovels in a row behind, instead of two. R. Baddeley retired about 1780; he died in 1810 or 1812. Printing with oil is said to have been first practised here about 1780. The first copper plates were engraved by a person named Oliver Dixon. Mr. William Smith, an engraver of considerable merit in Liverpool, was engaged to execute plates in a superior style for Mr. R. Baddeley, and the excellence of the pottery and the decoration were unrivalled for a considerable time. The firm from 1780 to 1806 was John & Edward Baddeley. Mr. John Baddeley for some time employed Thomas Radford to print tea services by an improved method of transferring the impression to the biscuit, which was attempted to be kept secret, but was soon developed.

In 1806 the Baddeleys retired, and they were succeeded by Hicks & Meigh, who carried on the business until 1822, when they took into partnership Mr. Johnson, who was traveller for them. The firm from 1822 to 1836 was Hicks, Meigh & Johnson, who produced excellent pottery, porcelain and stone china. They employed pre-Victorian royal arm marks such as no. 40. In the Sheldon Collection was a plate (blue printed) with the letters H.M.J. in a floral frame.

R. M. W. & Co.   Morley & Ashworth, Hanley.

42

43

They retired in 1836 and were succeeded by W. Ridgway, Morley, Wear & Co., who carried it on from 1836 to 1845 (mark no. 42) when W. Ridgway left the concern and the firm was F. Morley & Co. In 1850 Mr. F. Morley took Mr. G. L. Ashworth into partnership. Mark no. 43.

In 1862 G. L. & T. Ashworth (Ashworth Bros.) took the business. A transfer printed and coloured plate with Chinese subject has the mark of a crown and " Mason's Patent Ironstone China, Ashworth's." Sometimes only the name ASHWORTH appears. (See notice on Masons'.)

NEW HALL. The New Hall works were built by Mr. Whitehead, a celebrated maker of the white stoneware salt glaze, and carried on successfully by him for many years. The premises were taken about 1781 by a company of potters who had purchased Champion's (Cookworthy's) patent for the manufacture of porcelain, which had been renewed in 1775 in spite of the opposition of Wedgwood and others, and sold to them in 1777. The company consisted of Messrs. Samuel Hollins, of Shelton; Anthony Keeling, of Tunstall; John Turner, of Lane End; Jacob Warburton, of Hotlane; William Clowes, of Port Hill; Charles Bagnall and Mr. Heath, of Shelton. It was first carried on at the establishment of Anthony Keeling at Tunstall, and it is stated Champion himself undertook the superintendence, and continued to do so from the date of the purchase in 1777 until 1781.

Mr. Owen (*Two Centuries of Potting at Bristol*) has, in defiance of all the authorities, boldly asserted that Champion did not dispose of his patent to the Staffordshire Company until 1782, but that he continued working it at Bristol up to that date. We do not consider that he has proved this satisfactorily, and we therefore place greater reliance upon Shaw's account that Champion sold it to them in 1777, for this reason—Shaw's information was derived from persons who were living at the period of the establishment of the china manufactory in Staffordshire, and from one in particular whose valuable remarks he acknowledges, viz., Mr. Jacob Warburton, an original proprietor and who lived to see its extinction in 1825; he was born in 1740, and died in 1826, aged 86 years.

After Champion's retirement some misunderstanding arose among the proprietors, which caused Anthony Keeling and John Turner to retire from the concern: the others took the New Hall at Shelton about 1781, and it was then called the New Hall China Manufactory. In a Survey of the Potteries in 1786 the firm is described as Heath, Warburton & Co., china manufacturers; subsequently it was Hollins, Warburton, Clowes & Daniel. The *Staffordshire Pottery Directory of* 1802 says:—

" The porcelain or china manufactory is at Shelton, carried on under the respectable firm of Hollins, Warburton & Co. The china made here is very little if at all inferior (especially in the colours) to that of the East Indies. The kingdom produces all the various stone and clay which are used in this manufactory, and from the number of years it has already been established (written in 1802), added to a regular increase of encouragement and demand for their porcelain, there is no doubt but the worthy proprietors will reap the fruits of their spirited adventure in fame and emolument. The ingenious Mr. Champion of Bristol, who discovered the art of making this porcelain, expended an ample fortune in the various trials. He had the good fortune, however, of bringing it to perfection, and obtained a patent for the exclusive privilege of making it, which he sold to the above gentlemen for such a sum of money as enabled him to retire to America."

The most extensive as well as the most profitable branch of the Company's business was the manufacture of a glaze called " composition "; this composition doubtless included the materials of the ware itself, which was supplied to potters all over England in very large quantities, and as they do not appear to have monopolised the patent, they no doubt granted licences for the employment of hard paste materials. After the expiration of Champion's patent in 1796 the New Hall Company still continued to supply *composition* to other manufacturers.

In 1810 the firm was Samuel Hollins, Peter Warburton (son of Jacob), John Daniel, and William Clowes, about which time bone paste was introduced into their manufacture. In 1810 Peter Warburton, of Cobridge, in the county of Stafford, china manufacturer, took out a patent on behalf of the company for his " new invented method of decorating china, porcelain, earthenware and glass, with native, pure or adulterated gold, silver, platina or other metals, fluxed or lowered with lead or any other substance; which invention or new method leaves the metals after being burned in their metallic state." Granted for fourteen years. Mr. John Daniel was the managing partner for many years prior to his death in 1821.

A service made for John Daniel, manager of the works, painted with figures by Joshua Cristall, consisting of forty-two pieces, was sold at Sotheby's in 1909 for £27.

Mark no. 44 was used about 1820. Earlier wares have only the pattern number, prefixed by " N " or " No." In 1835 the entire stock was sold and the manufacture of china ceased. For typical examples see Godden's *British Pottery and Porcelain, an Illustrated Encyclopædia of Marked*

Specimens. The works having been closed for a time, were opened about 1837 by W. Ratcliffe, and about 1846 passed into the hands of Messrs. Hackwood and Sons, the name impressed; and seven years after Mr. Hackwood, senior, dying, the firm was Thomas Hackwood.

Mark no. 45. A pair of small oval dishes in cream-coloured ware, artistically painted with knights and armed figures by George Eyre, whose monogram is added, have the name *Hackwood* impressed.

HACKWOOD & CO.
(sometimes without
the " Co.")

45

HACKWOOD.
C. & H.
late
Hackwood.

46

44

HARDING.

47

In 1856 the firm was Cockson & Harding, mark no. 46. In 1862, Mr. Cockson having retired, it was continued by W. & J. Harding until c. 1872, mark no. 47. A sugar-basin in pale blue glazed earthenware, with white ornaments in relief, has the name impressed, and a cream-jug of brown glazed ware in the Victoria and Albert Museum. Subsequent manufacturers have been T. Booth & Son; A. Bevington; Plant & Gilmore, and The New Hall Pottery Co. (1899–1957).

CHARLES BAGNALL was a potter at Shelton about 1760, and is probably the same spoken of by Wedgwood in a letter to Bentley in 1768 as Bagnall & Baker, who were copying his patterns, especially what he calls the " blue-necked vases." As early as 1715 there was a potter named Bagnall at the Grange, Burslem, a maker of butter-pots, no doubt a progenitor. Charles Bagnall, of Shelton, joined the New Hall works in 1777. In the survey of 1786 the firm was described as Heath and Bagnall; this was perhaps the " Joshua Heath " who signed the bond regulating the trade prices in 1770, and who with his partner joined the New Hall works in 1777. The late Mr. Bernal had a yellow drab bowl-shaped mug, inscribed round the top, " JOSHUA HEATH, 177–," the last figure being obliterated; this may have been the person referred to.

THOMAS FLETCHER & Co. resided at Booden Brook, Shelton. They were established about 1786, but did not manufacture pottery; they were " black printers," and purchased the ware they decorated from other manufacturers, and printed it at their own house. There was living in Hanley a person who was with them in 1806; he said they were in business until about 1810. " Thomas Fletcher, black printer and enameller," of Shelton, will be found in the Directory of 1802. The name of this firm is on a mug, underneath an engraving in black of Louis XVI taking leave of his family on the morning of his execution: the mug is of Queen's ware, apparently of the latter part of the eighteenth century, in the Victoria and Albert Museum. Mark no. 48.

PHILLIPS. Mark no. 49, c. 1855–62, is on a group of flowers in biscuit, finely modelled, and a basket of biscuit flowers; formerly in J. Mills's Collection, Norwich.

Fletcher & Co.   Edward Phillips,
Shelton.   Shelton, Staffordshire.

48   49

T. TWEMLOW had a manufactory here, which was being carried on in Josiah Wedgwood's time, about 1770, and is referred to in his letters, but particulars are wanting; he was present at the Hanley Feast in 1780. In the Survey of 1786 given earlier we find G. Twemlow, potter, at Shelton, but his name is absent from the list of 1802. A John Twemlow is listed in the mid 1790's.

YATES. An old-established china and earthenware manufactory is alluded to by Ward as being then worked by Messrs. Yates & May (1828–43), heretofore by John and William Yates, and previously by their father; John Yates's name is mentioned in the lists of potters in 1770 and 1786; in the map of 1802 we find John and William Yates at Shelton.

In the Sheldon Collection there was a blue printed earthenware plate with the letters J. Y. in a band, and the words " Warranted Stone China, Fenton," which is attributed to John Yates.

MINTONS

The Minton firm was established in 1793 by Thomas Minton (1765–1836). He was an apprentice of Thomas Turner of Caughley, having been articled as an engraver; he was a native of Shropshire, and on the expiration of his term of service went to London as a free lance master engraver and worked for Spode and other manufacturers. In 1788 Thomas Minton came to Stoke and bought land belonging to a Mr. Hassall, and built a house and works on the site which has since become so celebrated. He entered into partnership in 1793 with Joseph Poulson, who had been manager at Spode's works and with Mr. Pownall, who retired c. 1800. Poulson died in 1809, leaving Thomas Minton alone to conduct the business. His second son, Herbert, was born on 4th February, 1793. Up to the year 1798 earthenware alone had been made at the Stoke Works, and the staple product of the business consisted of white earthenware ornamented with blue, in imitation of Nankin wares. In that branch of production the abilities and experience of Thomas Minton as an engraver had acquired for the firm a good commercial reputation. Herbert Minton was educated at Audlem School in Cheshire. The manufacture of porcelain was reputedly commenced in the year 1798, but owing to its proving unprofitable, that department of production was abandoned in the year 1811, to be resumed about 1821. In 1817 Herbert Minton and his elder brother, who subsequently entered the Church, were admitted into partnership with their father. About 1825 a marked improvement was effected in printed earthenware, both in the body, which was made whiter and purer, and in the glaze, in which borax to a great extent took the place of lead. On his father's death, in 1836, Herbert Minton succeeded to the business.

Shortly after his father's death in 1836 Herbert Minton admitted as a partner John Boyle, who remained for about five years, and then joined the firm of Wedgwoods. Boyle's place at Stoke was taken by Michael Daintry Hollins. The next phase of the firm, for about ten years previous to Herbert Minton's death in 1858, consisted of Herbert Minton and his nephews, M. D. Hollins and Colin Minton Campbell, the latter for many years represented North Staffordshire in Parliament, and was the head of Mintons until his death in 1885. The above changes in partners were reflected in the marks given later in this section.

After the year 1825, when the Derby manufactory began to decline rapidly, many skilful workmen joined Mintons and the class of goods involving artistic decoration rapidly improved. Among the best painters employed by Minton at that time were Steele, Bancroft and Hancock; these artists specialised in fruit and flowers (*Keramic Gallery*, fig. 613). John Simpson held the position of principal enamel painter of figures, and he achieved the highest standard of decorations from about 1837 to 1847, when he went to London to take charge of the department of enamel painting on porcelain at the Government School. Samuel Bourne remained as chief designer to the firm until 1848; the lead was then taken by M. Jeannest until c. 1854. M. Carrier de Belleuse (died 1887), a very clever sculptor, was subsequently employed to design many graceful objects, and M. Protat became principal modeller. No less than fourteen of Minton's employees received medals and other rewards at the 1867 Paris Exhibition. After the troubles of 1848 in France, Minton was so fortunate as to secure the services as Art Director of Leon Arnoux, a gentleman who had long enjoyed the reputation of being perhaps more versed in the mysteries of ceramic manufacture than any one else in France. Leon Arnoux (1816–1902) was a born experimenter, and there was scarcely any known type of ceramic decoration that Mintons did not attempt to emulate through their resourceful art director. Arnoux introduced Mintons' world famous " Majolica " earthenware body in time for its inclusion in the 1851 Exhibition. This " Majolica " body and the parian body were to form an important part of Minton's products for the rest of the nineteenth century. For an account of the parian body see Copeland section. Arnoux retired in 1895 but continued his association with Mintons up to the time of his death in 1902.

The fact that Leon Arnoux was successfully established at Mintons induced several Continental ceramic artists of the highest repute to follow his example. Several of these artists, notably Antonin Boullemier (and Emile Lessore), were trained at the Sèvres factory and were indispensable in the successful reproductions of the finest Sèvres style vases and services for which Mintons were so famous. A check list of the many famous artists whose work may be found on Mintons vases is here attached; fuller details concerning these artists may be found in Godden's *Victorian Porcelain* (Herbert Jenkins, 1961). Typical examples are illustrated in Godden's *British Pottery and Porcelain, an Illustrated Encyclopædia of Marked Specimens.*

LIST OF MINTON ARTISTS WHOSE SIGNED OR INITIALLED WORK MAY BE FOUND

" S " indicates that the artist normally signed his work in full.
" I " indicates that the artist normally signed his work with his initials only.

Thomas Allen, c. 1845–75. S—rarely. Figures.

Leon Arnoux, c. 1848–92. S or I—rarely. Experimental designs.

E. S. Bayley, c. 1890–1905. S. Flowers.

Lucien Besche, c. 1871. S. Figures.

Alboine Birks, c. 1876–1937. S and I. Pâte-sur-pâte.

Lawrence Birks, c. 1876–95. I. Pâte-sur-pâte.

Antonin Boullemier, c. 1871–1900. S and I. Figures.

Lucien Boullemier, early 20th century. S and I. Figures.

Richard Bradbury, c. 1927–39. I. Pâte-sur-pâte.

Helen C. Coleman, c. 1872. S and I. Floral patterns.

Rebecca Coleman, c. 1870–80. S. Figures.

William S. Coleman, c. 1870–73. S and I. Figures.

J. Edward Dean, c. 1882–1927. S and I. Animals, fish, etc.

Myer Dudley, early 20th century. S. Flowers.

John B. Evans, c. 1865–85. S. Landscapes.

John Eyre, c. 1872. S and I. Figures.

Herbert W. Foster, c. 1872–93. S and I. Figures, animals, etc.

W. J. Goode, c. 1865–90. S and I. Figures, animals, etc. (not a factory
    artist).

A. Gregory, c. 1890. S. Flowers.

Arthur Holland, c. 1951+. S. Landscapes, fish, etc.

H. Hollins, c. 1873–85. I. Pâte-sur-pâte.

Thomas Kirkby, c. 1845–87. S and I. Figures, cupids, etc.

Desire Leroy, c. 1874–90. S—occasionally. Floral and bird motifs in
    white enamel.

Emile Lessore, c. 1876. S and I. Figures, etc. Subsequently at Wedg-
    woods.

Arnold Machin, R.A., c. 1925–31. S. Figures, etc.

Henry S. Marks, c. 1870–80. S and I. Figure designs.

Thomas Mellor, c. 1873–80. I. Pâte-sur-pâte.

Henry Mitchell, c. 1860–72. S and I. Animals, birds, etc.

A. Morgan, c. 1873–80. I. Pâte-sur-pâte.

William Mussill, c. 1871–1906. S and I. Floral and bird compositions.

Richard Pilsbury, c. 1866–92. S and I. Flowers.

Edward G. Reuter, c. 1875–95. S and I. Floral and figure designs.

Frederick Rhead, c. 1873–78. I. Pâte-sur-pâte.

T. H. Rice, c. 1873–80. I. Pâte-sur-pâte.

Edouard Rischgitz, c. 1864–70. S. Figure and landscape subjects.

L. Rivers, c. 1890–1910. S and I. Flowers.

H. Sanders, c. 1870–76. I. Pâte-sur-pâte.

John Simpson, c. 1837–47. S. Figure subjects, etc.

T. H. Simpson, c. 1850–60. S. Flowers and fruit.

M. L. Solon, c. 1870–1904. S and I. Pâte-sur-pâte artist.

Leon Solon, c. 1897–1909. S and I. Figure subjects and Art Nouveau
    designs.

Charles Toft, c. 1872–77. S and I. Pâte-sur-pâte and copies of Henri
    Deux wares.

R. Walklett, c. 1894–1910. S. Flowers.

Albert H. Wright, c. 1871–1915. S and I. Birds, fish, etc.

Modellers, such as Paul Comalera, John Henk and John Bell, should also be mentioned.

Numerous other artists were employed by Mintons but did not normally sign their work. From about 1870 onwards many amateur artists painted on marked Minton blanks.

The most important of the foreign artists employed at Mintons was undoubtedly Marc Louis Solon, formerly a sculptor and decorator at Sèvres; he commenced at Mintons in 1870 and continued at the same kind of work until his retirement in 1904. The decoration for which he is so justly famous was achieved by applying white slip or engobe (china clay diluted to the consistency of cream) with a brush on to grounds of celadon toned grey, green and chocolate, and is called pâte-sur-pâte (paste on paste).

The invention (if it may be so called, having been adopted by the Chinese centuries before) dates from about 1860. It was employed by M. M. Regnier, Choiselat and Gely with varied success; but M. Solon almost made it his own by the skill and taste which he displayed. Numerous oxides may be employed, and the half-tones are very effective. The most exquisite shade, however, has been compared to a " cloud of cream " in a cup of tea. The white paste of slip is applied with a brush, in successive layers on the coloured paste, thus making a rough shape which is afterwards rounded and trimmed with sharp cutting implements or a small scraper until it has attained a given thickness and sharpness. When this bas-relief is completed, it is subjected to the first firing, which enables it to be dipped at once into the glaze. Lastly comes the final firing, and provided the piece has successfully withstood the firing nothing can exceed the charm of the result; the thicker portions in fusing retain a relief which forms the actual outline, and these form the flesh, a cloud of floating draperies reminding us of Wedgwood's white reliefs on blue jasper, although totally differing in construction, the latter being moulded and applied to the surface. M. Solon usually signed his name " Solon " (or " L. Solon "), or used mark no. 21.

With regard to the signature of this celebrated ceramic artist, the work he did for the Sèvres factory was usually marked with the monogram, mark no. 21, or with his initials, M. L. S. (Marc Louis Solon). The work he executed for the trade in Paris was signed " Miles." After he joined the staff of Mintons he generally signed L. Solon, but one piece, formerly in the collection of Mr. Herbert Eccles, of Neath, has mark no. 22, which is believed to be the only specimen so signed. Some of his plaques are dated, and a pair of very handsome vases with pâte-sur-pâte subjects, representing " Bondage " and " Freedom " from Mr. Eccles' Collection, are dated 1904, the year of his retirement. After his retirement he produced only plaques. M. L. Solon died in 1913. (*Ker. Gall.*, fig. 614.)

Owing to the success of this style of pâte-sur-pâte decoration and the slow painstaking process involved Solon trained various apprentices to assist him. These included Alboine Birks (c. 1876–1937), Lawrence Birks (c. 1876–95), H. Hollins (c. 1873–85), T. Mellor (c. 1873–80), A. Morgan

(c. 1873–80), Frederick Rhead (c. 1873–78), T. H. Rice (c. 1873–80), H. Sanders (c. 1873–76) and C. Toft (c. 1873). Richard Bradbury worked in the twentieth century. The apprentices sometimes signed their work with initials.

The varied products of the Minton factory are amongst the finest examples of nineteenth century ceramic art. Their wares occasioned the highest praise in all Exhibition reports and the list of medals won is almost endless. A student writing without prejudice in 1876 recorded:—

" . . . In high class pottery Mintons are to the china trade what the light of the sun is to the earth. Withdraw the house of Mintons from the firmament and the other firms now existing would only supply the place of the moon and the stars. Potteries seem to have their rise, their day of glory, and their decline, and just now the star of Minton is in the ascendant. One reason why certain manufacturers excel others in artistic pottery is that they engage the best artists to decorate for them. Some small firms make very good china, but they hesitate about paying so very highly for the best talent, fearing they may not recoup themselves for their outlay. Messrs. Mintons have not hesitated to employ the best talent that came to their hand, as they have by this means succeeded in gaining for their house a prestige above that of any other English firm."

The Minton Works Museum at Stoke-on-Trent houses a fine collection covering all periods; representative specimens may also be seen at the Victoria and Albert Museum, Room 140. L. Jewitt's *Ceramic Art of Great Britain* contains a good account of the factory and its productions up to the date of its publication in 1878. The subsequent history may be found in G. Godden's *Victorian Porcelain* 1961.

The products of the Minton factory may be readily dated by reference to the following changes in the marks employed.

MINTON MARKS

The early earthenwares were not marked. The Sèvres type marks nos. 1 and 2 occur on early 19th century porcelains (prior to 1830) and were hand painted. The pattern number under mark no. 2 naturally varies and was sometimes omitted.

1

2

From about 1826 a number of printed marks occur, incorporating the name or number of the relevant pattern. These various marks also incorporate the initials of the firm and these give a reliable guide to the date of the example.

Marks 3 and 4. " M " occurs from c. 1822–36. " M & B " (Minton & Boyle) from c. 1836–41. " M & Co " (Minton & Co) from c. 1841–c. 1873. " M & H " (Minton & Hollins) from c. 1845–68. It will be noticed that M & Co was used concurrently with M & H. The M & H mark usually occurs on earthenware. These two latter marks should also have year cyphers as given in the table reproduced.

From 1842 Mintons employed a private system of dating by impressing into the unfired wares cyphers and letters showing the month and year of potting and the potter. On porcelains from 1842 to 1862 these date cyphers may be the only means of identification. The key chart is reproduced as no. 5 in the table of marks.

They occur impressed into the clay with two other marks which denote the potter and the month. The figures 43, etc., have been used from 1943 onwards and are preceded by a workman's number, i.e. 1–45.

MONTH LETTERS OCCURRING WITH YEAR CYPHERS AS GIVEN IN THE YEARLY MARKS TABLE

J = January	E = May	S = September
F = February	I = June	O = October
M = March	U = July	N = November
A = April	Y = August	D = December

Earthenwares sometimes bear impressed month and year numbers, e.g. 7.27 for July 1927.

A table of Mintons year cyphers from 1842 to 1942, each year shown in a box with its symbol.

5

From 1845 to 1861 some Mintons earthenwares were impressed with " B.B. New Stone." The month and year cyphers also occur with this mark. B.B. denotes best body. Mark no. 6.

Mark no. 7 incised or impressed occurs on early (c. 1845-55) parian figures and groups which are, apart from the month and year cyphers, unmarked.

Mark no. 8 in relief is found on parian figures produced by Minton for " Summerly's Art Manufactures," c. 1847-8.

Mark no. 9, ermine mark, painted in colours or gold, or printed, on porcelains bearing a special soft glaze, from c. 1850 onwards. Some of the finest examples of Mintons hand painted porcelains were glazed with

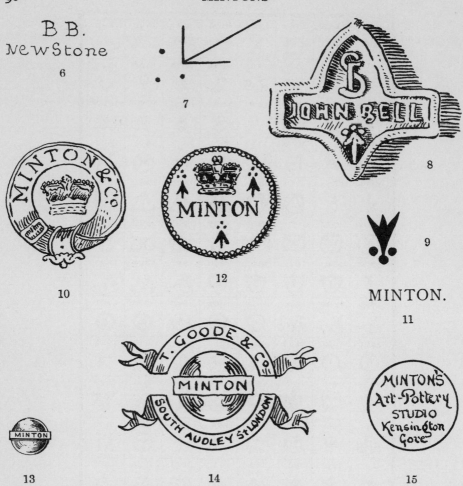

6

7

8

10

12

9

MINTON.

11

13   14   15

this special glaze and bear this device, often in addition to other marks.

Mark no. 10, printed, found on two plates in the Godden Collection. These plates are painted with interior views of the 1851 Exhibition and bear year cyphers of 1851.

Mark no. 11, impressed, in general use from c. 1862 to 1872 when " s " was added. Impressed year cyphers normally occur with this mark.

Mark no. 12, printed, used in the 1860's on fine quality specimens. This mark occurs on a pair of Sèvres style vases in the Godden Collection which were originally included in the 1862 Exhibition. Other special marks were used on wares made for later exhibitions; these are self explanatory and include the date.

Printed Globe mark no. 13 used from c. 1863 to 1872. Mark no. 14 incorporates the name of the London retailer, Thomas Goode & Co. Other marks occur incorporating the names of other firms. This mark was occasionally used after 1872 when it appears on an example decorated with a *printed* pattern.

Mark no. 15, printed, used at Mintons Art-Pottery Studio at Kensington Gore, London, c. 1871–75. This interesting venture is discussed at length in *Victorian Porcelain* (Jenkins, 1961).

Mark no. 16, impressed, found on Sèvres type wares c. 1868–80. The date is normally given with this mark, as drawn.

Mark no. 17 is a new form of the printed globe mark. There is now a crown and an " s " added to Minton. This mark was the firm's registered trade mark from 1873. However, occasionally the crown does not appear on this later version of the globe mark, but the title has the " s " added. " England " appears under this mark from 1891. " Made in England " appears from about 1902.

Mark no. 18, impressed, from 1873 (replacing the earlier form MINTON), found in conjunction with year cyphers.

Mark no. 19, printed, revised form of globe trade mark used from c. 1913 to 1951.

Mark no. 20 in use from early 1951.

Marks nos. 21 and 22 are the marks of the artist Solon and are referred to in more detail earlier in this section.

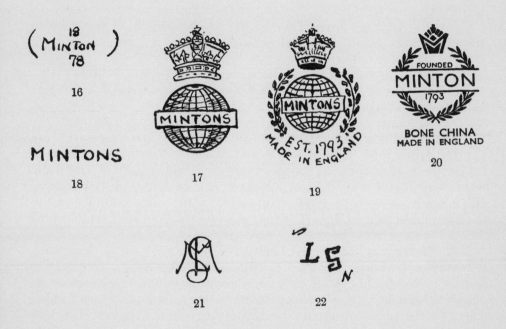

STOKE-ON-TRENT
INCLUDING SPODE, COPELAND, LONGTON HALL AND OTHER STAFFORDSHIRE POTTERIES

SPODE. The first Josiah Spode entered this manufactory about 1770; he was an apprentice of Mr. Whieldon, of Fenton, in 1749. In his account-book, quoted by Mr. Jewitt (*Art Journal*, May 1864), are the following entries referring to him:—

" 1749, April 9. Hired Siah Spode, to give him from this time to Martelmas next 2s. 3d., or 2s. 6d. if he deserves it; 2nd year 2s. 9d.; 3rd year 3s. 3d.; paid full earnest 1s."

The hiring was per week. Another entry, 1752, 22nd February:—

" Hired Josiah Spode for next Martelmas, per week, 7s.; I am to give him earnest 5s.; paid in part 5s.

" 1754, Feb. 25. Hired Siah Spode, per week, 7s. 6d.; earnest, £1. 11s. 9d.; paid in part 16s."

Mr. Spode took the works of Messrs. Banks & Turner. He is said to have introduced about 1784 the blue printed old willow pattern, and made cream-ware, black printed, black Egyptian, etc.; he also made jasper-ware. His name is stamped on a jasper incense or scent vase, with *amorini* on the sides and bands of flowers round, in white relief on blue, white lizard handles; in a private collection.

The mark also occurs of " Felspar Porcelain " in a garland, sur-mounted by the name " Spode." Spode died in August 1797, ætat 64, and was succeeded by his son Josiah, who commenced the manufacture of porcelain, and introduced bones into the paste as well as felspar, which increased the transparency and beauty of his ware. This porcelain had a very extensive sale, and to meet the taste of the day, much of it was profusely gilt and painted with flowers.

At this period the London dealers were principally supplied with porcelain from Worcester, Derby, and Caughley; he therefore exerted all his efforts to produce varied shapes, engaging the best modellers and artists to compete with them. His enameller, Henry Daniel, here first introduced in 1802 the present method of ornamenting porcelain in raised unburnished gold, similar to embossed dead gold or frosted work on silver.

In the year 1805 he also made a sort of fine ware, called opaque porcelain (or " stone china "), which was sold to a great extent throughout England and on the Continent. Spode and other manufacturers inundated France with this description of ware, which almost entirely superseded their fayence, being so much more durable, and inflicted great injury upon the trade of the French potters, many of whom were compelled to abandon the manufacture. The Prince of Wales visited the works in 1806, and Mr. Spode was appointed potter to his Royal Highness. The second Josiah Spode died in 1827, and his cousin, Josiah Spode the third, died a few years after.

The second Josiah Spode was the most successful china manufacturer of his time, and acquired a large fortune in business. He erected a noble mansion at Penkhull, called the Mount, about 1803; he also contributed largely towards the building of the new parish church of Stoke: the four corner stones of the church and the chancel, each about 16 in. by 12 in. superficial measure, were made by him and laid by the Dean of Lichfield, Mr. Spode, Mr. Kirkham, and Mr. Tomlinson. One slab was of the best porcelain, with bas-relief inscription and a landscape with a view of the old church and town of Stoke, embossed and gilt border; the second was of rich brown porcelain; the third of jasper; the fourth of patent stone porcelain; the fifth of blue painted pottery.

He established a regular London business, which was very successful, the clear profits of this alone in the year preceding his father's death exceeding £13,000. A confidential manager was mainly instrumental in effecting it, and Mr. Spode's satisfaction was evinced by a most substantial mark—a present of £1000, and a further reward for his assiduity and integrity by a share of the London business. Mr. Spode went to reside at Stoke, leaving his partner, Mr. William Copeland, to manage the town trade.

Mr. William Copeland, who had been in partnership with Spode, died in 1826, and was succeeded by his son, William Taylor Copeland, who became Lord Mayor of London in 1835. He purchased the entire concern from the executors of the third Josiah Spode, and took into partnership his principal traveller, Thomas Garratt, and from 1833 until 1847, when a dissolution of partnership took place, the style of the firm was " Copeland and Garrett," which is the mark distinguishing the productions of this period. Under the title of W. T. Copeland, late Spode, the firm continued to trade until 1867, when Alderman Copeland took his four sons into partnership, under the present style and title of W. T. Copeland & Sons. The Alderman was M.P. for many years, representing Stoke-on-Trent from 1837–52, and again from 1857–65. He died in 1868. The products of this old-established firm command a high reputation in the markets of the world. The manufactures may be divided into six classes: porcelain, ceramic statuary, ivory, majolica, ironstone, earthenware. The fruit and flower painting of C. F. Hurten during the 1859–97 period is worthy of note. The best specimens of this celebrated artist's work are signed.

We cannot close the account of this important manufactory without describing the beautiful parian biscuit, which, if not invented by Copeland & Garrett, was carried to the greatest perfection by them from about 1842. M. Léon Arnoux thus describes the manufacture:—

" Returning to the present manufacture, the first that we shall mention amongst the class of vitrified bodies is the biscuit, which is now so extensively used to make ornaments, figures, and decorative pieces for our dessert services. This biscuit is called *Parian Carrara* or *Statuary Biscuit;* these names indicating the similarity existing between it and the best marbles that it is intended to represent. This process is chiefly the result of the employment of a soft felspar instead of Cornish stone. Although this biscuit is fired to a heat which is not very high, if we consider its compound, we shall see that there is very little difference from the true porcelain—a very fusible one if you like, but it will have nearly all its characters. The fabrication of parian figures requires a much greater capacity and dexterity than any other branch of manufacture; for the figures are cast in a great number of separate pieces, and their joining and repairing requires a certain knowledge of the human figure. As these figures, instead of being pressed in moulds in the regular way, are cast with the compound prepared in a liquid state, the consequence is a considerable diminution of their bulk in the firing process, no less than a quarter of the model. These figures contracting so much in the fire, and being made of a fusible material, would lose their shape, and fall in many cases, if not supported all round with props of the same material. The firing itself requires great attention, for on the way it is managed depends the colour of the biscuit. This colour is not given by any material mixed in the compound, but by the small quantity of oxide of iron which is contained in the clays and felspar, pure as they may be. During the firing, as the atmosphere of the inside is oxidising, this small quantity of iron forms with the silica a silicate of peroxide of iron, which, like all peroxidised salts of this metal, has a yellowish-red colour. It is the small quantity of that salt spread in the mass which gives that yellowish-white colour which is so agreeable. If, on the contrary, by neglect or any other reason, there should be a great amount of smoke or flame, the nature of the atmosphere changing, the peroxide of iron would be partly reduced, and the result would be a salt of protoxide of iron, manifest by its bluish-green colour. In this last case, the parian loses the greatest part of its beauty.

" If we compare our parian with the biscuit made on the Continent—in Copenhagen, for instance—we shall perceive the enormous difference in their relative appearance; whilst the Continental biscuit acquires in firing a greater sharpness, it is the reverse in the parian; whilst the former, with its hard, cold appearance, will reject the light, this light, penetrating into the latter to a certain depth, gives it a softness which has never been realised before. By these precious qualities this article is in very great favour at the present time, and is manufactured with a good deal of taste by Messrs. Copeland, Minton, Rose, Wedgwood, and others."

For a full account of the introduction of the parian body see Godden's *Victorian Porcelain,* 1961.

MARKS ON SPODE AND COPELAND'S CHINA AND EARTHENWARE

For the information of collectors and connoisseurs of pottery, we give below the various marks which have been used on the ware produced by the firm from Spode's days to the present time.

Mark no. 1. This was sometimes stamped in the clay, and at others printed at back in the colour of the pattern. On china it was usually done

SPODE
1

2

Spode
Felspar
Porcelain
3

SPODE
Felspar Porcelain
4

SPODE
Stone-China
5

SPODE
Stone-China
6

SPODE
7

Spode's
NEW FAYENCE
8

Spode's
Imperial
9

SPODE, SON
& COPELAND.
10

SPODE & COPELAND
11

COPELAND AND GARRETT
12

COPELAND
& GARRETT

C & G

with the name
of the pattern.

13

COPELAND & GARRETT
LATE
SPODE
14

COPELAND & GARRETT
NEW FAYENCE
16

Copeland
Late Spode.
17

Copeland Late Spode
18

COPELAND & GARRETT
+ NEW +
JAPAN STONE
15

COPELAND
21

Copeland
Stone China
22

COPELAND late SPODE
19

COPELAND
LATE SPODE
20

CO
COPELAND
Mark used 1847-56.
23

COPELAND
24

COPELAND.
B
25

SPODE
COPELAND
26

W.T. COPELAND & SONS
27

COPELAND LATE SPODE
TRADE MARK.
28

SPODE
COPELANDS CHINA
ENGLAND
29

COPELAND
late
SPODE
ENGLAND
30

with the pencil by the decorator. The painted SPODE mark normally occurs in red with the pattern number, and is one of the earliest form of Spode mark on porcelains.

Mark no. 2, impressed. One of the early Spode marks, c. 1795–c. 1815.

Marks nos. 3 and 4. These were printed on the china when felspar was introduced, c. 1810.

Marks nos. 5 and 6. These were the stamps on the celebrated Stone-China, c. 1805+.

Marks nos. 7, 8 and 9. These were all printed on the ware, c. 1810–20.

Marks nos. 10 and 11, both impressed and printed. Probably used prior to 1816.

Marks nos. 12 to 16. Used during the Copeland & Garrett partnership from 1833 to 1847.

Marks nos. 17 to 30. Used from 1847. Mark no. 23, 1847–50. Ornate version, mark no. 24, c. 1850–85. Mark no. 26, c. 1850–90. Mark no. 27, c. 1867–c. 1900. Mark no. 28, c. 1894–c. 1910. Marks nos. 29 and 30, from c. 1891.

Twentieth century marks usually include the name Spode with the name of the type of body or decoration.

Typical examples of Spode and Copeland & Garrett wares are illustrated in Godden's *British Pottery and Porcelain, an Illustrated Encyclopædia of Marked Specimens*.

This is still one of the most important china manufactories in the kingdom; the best artists and modellers have always been employed; their jewelled ware is exceedingly ornate.

In the Schreiber Collection (Victoria and Albert Museum), and also in several private collections, there are early specimens marked with the word " Spode " written in red in ordinary manuscript, and having a number as well as the name. These are prior to 1820.

CLIFF BANK. At Cliff Bank was the manufactory of Thomas Mayer, formerly occupied by Daniel Bird, who first ascertained the exact quantity of flint required by the several kinds of clay to prevent the pottery cracking in the oven, for which he was first called the *flint potter*; he made agate buttons, knife hafts, and flint ware, salt glaze, by which he speedily realised a handsome fortune. Shaw writes, " We shall just notice here that Mr. T. Mayer (1829) has succeeded in a *chef-d'œuvre* of the art of pottery, by many considered as the best specimen of solid earthenware hitherto produced. It is a table of truly elegant workmanship, 32 in. in diameter, on a pedestal, painted with subjects from natural history."

31 T. Mayer.

Mark no. 31 and MAYER, STOKE in a circle, impressed, also occurs, c. 1826–35.

HENRY DANIEL, the enameller from Spode's, commenced the manufacture of fine porcelain at Stoke about 1823, and in 1826 the stone china at Shelton, the shapes and patterns being of the improved kind so much approved by the public. But, says Shaw, in addition to the various methods of enamelling then practised, he introduced the practice of *laying grounds* of different colours, and ornamenting them with gilding, both burnished and embossed, or *frosted* work as applied to plate. The porcelain fabricated at the manufactory of Messrs. H. & R. Daniel will bear a comparison for excellence with that of any other manufacturer. In 1827 they completed for the Earl of Shrewsbury different services of porcelain of the most costly kind ever made in the district, and probably the largest order ever received at that time. Mark no. 32. An ornate printed mark occurs on some fine quality pieces prior to 1830. Examples are in the Godden Collection, see Godden's *British Pottery and Porcelain, an Illustrated Encyclopædia of Marked Specimens*. Shaw says that the firm was in 1829 " Henry Daniel & Sons "; they retired from the concern about 1845. Richard Daniel worked to about 1854.

BOOTH. Hugh Booth was an eminent potter at Cliff Bank. In the Topographical Survey of 1786 he is described as " Maker of china, china glaze, and Queen's ware in all its branches." He died a bachelor in 1789, and was succeeded by his brother, Ephraim Booth, who associated with him in the business his sons, Hugh and Joseph; they carried it on successfully for many years. In the map of 1802 the firm was Booth & Sons. The manufactory was subsequently taken by W. Adams & Co. A firm entitled Booth & Son was working at Lane End, about 1830-35. Mark no. 33, printed in blue on an earthenware plate, blue printed decoration, formerly in Dr. Sidebotham's Collection, attributed to Ephraim Booth. This mark would seem to date from the early 19th century. The initials also fit the firm of Edge Barker & Co., c. 1835-7.

H. & R. Daniel.

32

33

WOLFE. Thomas Wolfe was an extensive manufacturer at Stoke, established about 1776. In the Topographical Survey of 1786 he is thus described: " Thomas Wolfe, Stoke, manufacturer of Queen's ware in general, blue printed and Egyptian black, cane coloured, etc." The orange-coloured enamel ware made by him mostly found its way to the Persian market; he entered largely into the Irish and American trade. He is stated to have been the first potter who employed steam-power for grinding calcined flints, about 1790. The first silver lustre was produced here by Mr. John Gardner while in Mr. Wolfe's employment. About 1790 he was in partnership with a Mr. Hamilton, and the firm is so styled in the Directory of 1802. Mark no. 34, in red is on an earthenware punch-bowl painted with Chinese figures and landscape, brick-red and yellow being the prevailing colours. The partnership ceased about 1811.

The Sheldon Collection contained specimens impressed with a W for Wolfe, the name in full, WOLFE AND HAMILTON, STOKE.

Mr. Wolfe claimed relationship with the celebrated General Wolfe who was killed at Quebec in 1759. There is a large jug with a fine engraving after West's picture of the death of General Wolfe, made by him, which remained in the family until 1860; there is also a smaller one in the Victoria and Albert Museum. He acquired an ample fortune, and died in 1818.

Wolfe & Hamilton,
Stoke.

34

CLOSE & CO.
LATE
35 W. Adams & Sons,
Stoke-upon-Trent.

W. ADAMS carried on a large business at Stoke; he died in 1829, and was succeeded by his sons, who retained the father's name in the concern as W. Adams & Sons. In 1843 their works comprised four separate buildings, three of which formerly belonged to Thomas Wolfe, and another at Cliff Bank, formerly Hugh Booth's. They were succeeded by Messrs. Close & Co. Mark no. 35, impressed on a fish plate in white ware, with a fish painted in brown (Victoria and Albert Museum), mid-nineteenth century.

ZACHARIAH BOYLE, near the churchyard, had a manufactory for porcelain and pottery of very excellent quality. In 1829 the firm was Z. Boyle & Son. Z. Boyle died in 1841. The firm probably continued to 1850. Examples in the Godden Collection bear initial marks Z.B. and Z.B. & S.

BERNARD MOORE WARE. Among early twentieth century producers of artistic pottery the name of Bernard Moore is of the first rank, and with Howson Taylor, and the Pilkington Pottery Company, whose productions are akin, carried off the highest awards at early twentieth century exhibitions. The specialité of Bernard Moore was in the successful reproduction of the glorious *flambé* glazes of the old Chinese Khang-hsi period, and although many more or less successful attempts had been made within the past hundred years to produce these wonderful colours, it was not until Bernard Moore astonished us with his rich red *Sang de bœuf* that the reproduction of the old glazes was achieved. William Burton in describing some of the effects realised by this potter by the scientific treatment of copper and other metals says: " The way in which the colour deepens and lightens over the piece, passing from the faintest grey to the richest brown or ruby red by imperceptible gradations, recalls the colouring of some piece of precious sardonyx or jasper, and is the final reward of days and nights of labour spent at the potter's kiln." Bernard Moore was a juror of award in the Turin International Exhibition of 1911, when his fine exhibit was *Hors Concours*. Production of these Moore glaze effects was from about 1900 to 1915.

Bernard Moore's pottery is marked with his monogram, mark no. 36, or with his name in full. Many talented artists and designers worked for Moore and signed their work with monograms.

The following manufacturers of artistic wares at Stoke have not been previously mentioned: George Jones produced a wide range of wares from the 1860's onwards. Mark no. 37. " England " occurs after 1891. Robinson and Leadbeater, parian wares which were sometimes marked with the initials R & L, c. 1865 into twentieth century.

THE COALPORT CHINA COMPANY. In 1926 the Coalport Company (purchased by Cauldon Potteries Ltd.) was moved to Stoke and did an extensive business in the manufacture of table services and ornamental wares of good quality. Its mark was then an Imperial Crown with the words MADE IN ENGLAND and COALPORT above and below the crown. The earlier 1891–c. 1920 version had only the word ENGLAND. This firm changed hands in 1958 but continues.

BRADLEY & Co. A pair of cream-coloured pottery candlesticks of " Adam " design, with mark no. 38 impressed, was in the possession of Mr. Fenton of Cranbourne Street. This potter does not appear to be mentioned in any work on English earthenware, although a decorating firm of this name is recorded.

FENTON. Ralph Bourne and William Baker were established here towards the end of the 18th century. In the Directory of 1802 the firm was Bourne & Baker, afterwards Bourne, Baker & Bourne, whose productions, says Shaw, were in estimation in both the home and foreign markets. They had in his time (1829) two extensive manufactories, and a mill and two spacious mansions as residences. In 1843 it was carried on by William Baker alone, the only surviving partner; subsequently by Challinor & Co. from about 1862 to about 1896.

36

37   ENGLAND.

BRADLEY & CO.
COALPORT.

38

FENTON. William Greatbatch, an apprentice to Mr. Whieldon, was a man of great ability and an excellent modeller; he commenced business at Fenton, on what was afterwards a portion of the extensive establishment of Bourne, Baker & Bourne, where he produced numerous articles of improved kinds and patterns; and, according to Shaw, he for some time

had a most rapid sale of teapots, on which was printed in black, by Thomas
Radford, the history of the Prodigal Son. A teapot with coloured mas-
querade figures of columbine, clown, etc., was in the possession of Jno. J.
Bagshawe. A pint mug of fine quality of Greatbatch's make has an engraving in transfer-printing of the " World in planisphere," engraved by
Thomas Radford; on one side of the mug are the initials E.T. on a roll, the
other has the two hemispheres. In 1802 Thomas Radford, engraver, was
living at Shelton, and had another house at Stoke. Mr. Wedgwood, aware
of the talents of his former servant, Greatbatch (while in partnership with
Whieldon), who was ruined by heavy losses in trade, engaged him for life
at the very high wages of five shillings per diem, whether at work or play,
and a house rent free, which sum was regularly paid him to the time of his
death. Specimens are sometimes signed Greatbatch cursive. See mark
no. 39, late eighteenth century. For further information on William
Greatbatch see D. Towner's *English Cream-coloured Earthenware.*

Greatbatch   Pratt

39   40

FENTON. William Bacchus had a pottery here in the second half of
the 18th century. In the Survey of the Potteries in 1786 it is thus described:
" William Bacchus, manufacturer of Queen's ware in all its various
branches." Shaw says that a portion of the extensive premises of Bourne
& Baker were built on the site of T. Bacchus's manufactory.

Felix Pratt's manufactory was built on the site of Thomas Heath's
pottery: he married a daughter of Heath.

The work of Felix Pratt deserves more attention than it has hitherto
received from writers on the subject, and probably the absence with some
exceptions, of any distinguishing mark accounts for this, and specimens
which should be attributed to him have been credited to Newcastle, Sunderland, or generally, and somewhat vaguely, to Staffordshire. An article
in *The Connoisseur* in June 1910, contributed by G. Wooliscroft Rhead,
contained many interesting items gleaned from an interview with the
representatives of the Pratt family.

The period of his work was from 1775 to about 1810, and the specimens
in the Victoria and Albert Museum, and in various private collections which
we now recognise as of Pratt's productions, are chiefly cream-tinted earthenware with a bluish glaze, decorated with ornamentation modelled in relief—
a jug formerly in Mr. Clarke's Collection modelled with " the farewell " and
" the return " of a sailor sweetheart is impressed on the bottom, with
the name Pratt (mark no. 40) and this acts as a means of identification
with similar jugs.

The busts of Nelson, Admiral Duncan, Lord Jarvis, and Wellington
appear on jugs, and quaint caricatures of figures wearing the extravagant
head-dress of the period are moulded in relief on teapots. A circular flask
in the Victoria and Albert Museum is decorated with an equestrian portrait
of the Duke of York.

Pratt also used the method of transfer printing, and some specimens have painted landscapes. Some of the Toby jugs may also be attributed to him, and Mr. Rhead tells us that one of his characteristic details of decoration was the zigzag or pointed borders top and bottom of his jugs, the plain zigzags being alternated or entirely replaced by acanthus leaf decorations.

Felix Pratt's successors, F. & R. Pratt & Co., continued the business of potting, and in the 1851 Exhibition the firm was awarded a medal for their system of transfer printing in several colours (under glaze) of pot-lid type. See Clarke's *The Pictorial Pot Lid Book*, 1955 and 1960. Nineteenth and twentieth century marks have the title in full.

LITTLE FENTON (WHIELDON WARE). Thomas Whieldon had a pottery here in 1740; he made agate knife-handles, toys, ornaments, black glazed tea and coffee pots, tortoise-shell and melon plates, etc. Wedgwood was in partnership with him until 1759. Aaron Wood was his apprentice, and made moulds for his wares, such as pickle leaves, crabstock handles, cabbage-leaf spouts for teapots, etc. Josiah Spode, Robert Garner, J. Barker, William Greatbatch, and Uriah Sutton were also his apprentices. Whieldon acquired a large fortune; he died in 1798 at a very great age. He never marked his ware.

FENTON. About 1750 John Barker, with his brother and Robert Garner, commenced the manufacture of shining black and white stoneware salt glaze at the Row House, near the Foley, Fenton, and where they afterwards made tolerable cream-ware. They realised a good property here, and R. Garner erected a manufactory and the best house of the time in Lane End. Both John Barker and Robert Garner were apprenticed to Thomas Whieldon of Little Fenton.

A blue printed earthenware plate stamped BARKER was in the Sheldon Collection.

T. Green
Fenton Pottery

41

1870

42

1890

43

1906

Staffs

44

45

1900

CROWN

ENGLAND.

46

FINE BONE CHINA CROWN

ESTᴰ 1801

ENGLAND

47

T. GREEN. This name occurs on a piece of china, with buds and Chinese flowers in a garter surmounted by a crown and " fine China "; mark no 41 stamped in black underneath. Other marks include the initials T.G. and date from c. 1847 to 1859. The firm was continued by the widow under the title M. GREEN & Co. from c. 1859 to c. 1877 and subsequently by T. A. & S. GREEN, c. 1877 to c. 1890. Their marks include the initials T.A. & S.G. Mark no. 42.

The firm was re-titled THE CROWN STAFFORDSHIRE PORCELAIN CO. about 1890. They carried on an extensive business in the manufacture of domestic ware, but they also made a speciality of the reproduction of old English pottery, and of the old Chinese forms and colours. The firm was originally established in 1801. The marks in use for the past seventy years are nos. 42 to 46. No. 44 was for reproductions of old English pottery. From 1948 the firm has been THE CROWN STAFFORDSHIRE CHINA CO. LTD. Mark no. 47 is the latest mark from about 1945.

LANE DELPH. Thomas Heath in 1710 made a good kind of pottery by mixing with his other clays a special kind obtained from the coal-mines; his pottery is of a durable kind, not easily affected by change or excess of temperature. Shaw says his three daughters were married to persons who afterwards became celebrated potters, Mr. Neale of London, Mr. Palmer of Hanley, and Felix Pratt of Fenton, one of whose descendants occupied the premises since erected on the site of Heath's manufactory. Shaw describes a plate, one of the earliest attempts at *white ware* and *blue painting* upon the face; the effect is pleasing, although the outline is very rude. In the landscape mere lines or strokes form the edifice; the clouds seemed formed by the finger's end and a soft rag or sponge, with a very tall thin woman and a low stout man in the costume of the time. Specimens are rarely stamped HEATH.

WILLIAM EDWARDS made very good coloured earthenware at Lane Delph in 1750 (says Shaw). Two plates of his manufacture were in the possession of George Forrester of Lane End; they are about 12 in. in diameter, with basket-work border, painted with a melon, harp, apple, pear, and two cherries, of lead glaze, quite green; the centre has manganese to give it a brownish cast; the green has been partially washed off, so as to appear white and green alternately, and there is no glaze on the under surface.

Mr. Phillips was also a very eminent manufacturer at Lane Delph; a fine cream-coloured inkstand, made by him in 1760, was in Mr. Forrester's possession; its ornamental work is very elegant, and it evinces much excellence of material.

W. Matthews of Lane Delph made excellent mottled and clouded pottery; his drinking-mugs are well handled and finely rolled, but without *spout* or *snip*, as in similarly-shaped vessels of later date.

LANE DELPH. John Adams and John Price were manufacturers here about 1750–60 of red porcelain and white stoneware, salt glaze, and realised large fortunes.

LANE DELPH. The Foley. The manufactory erected by the elder Josiah Spode for his second son, Samuel, whose name is in the map of 1802, was in 1829 occupied by Charles Bourne, but in 1843 it was empty. Some plates with green borders, and centres of flowers and fruits marked C. B. No. 20 underneath, are attributed to this manufacturer. The number varies and relates to the pattern.

LANE DELPH. Elkin, Knight & Bridgwood of the Foley Fenton (c. 1827–40). Their names are printed on some pottery which was in the

Staniforth Collection. Mark no. 48. The name of BRIDGWOOD & SON is stamped on a porcelain cup and saucer formerly in the Sheldon Collection and dates from 1853.

48 ELKIN
KNIGHT & Co.   49 |MYATT|

LANE DELPH. The Foley. Shaw, writing in 1826, says: " At the southern extremity is the house and factory of the late Mr. Joseph Myatt; he was one of the few persons who received the Wesleyan Methodist preachers, and in whose parlour the late Rev. J. Wesley stood while from the window he preached to a vast congregation only a few months prior to his decease." The name of Myatt is on a red earthenware teapot of engine-turned ornament, like those of Wedgwood, mark no. 49. This mark was also used by the Myatt Pottery Company, Bilston, c. 1845-94. In the map of 1802 Joseph Myatt had a manufactory at Foley, close to Lane Delph. According to Ward's *History of Stoke*, the manufactory was in 1842 occupied by R. Gallimore.

LANE DELPH (now Middle Fenton). A manufactory was established in the eighteenth century by Miles Mason; several early pieces have his name alone on the ware; in 1802 the firm was Mason & Co. The ironstone china was brought to perfection by Charles James Mason, who took out a patent in 1813 for " A process for the improvement of the manufacture of English porcelain. This consists in using the scoria or slag or ironstone, pounded and ground in water, in certain proportions with flint, Cornwall stone, and clay, and blue oxide of cobalt." At this time he probably went into partnership, the firm being G. M. & C. J. MASON until about 1829, when the title became C. J. MASON & Co.

In connection with Mason's early china it may be interesting to quote the following advertisement from the *Morning Herald* of Monday, 15th October, 1804:—

" MASON'S CHINA.—It has hitherto been the opinion, not only of the public, but also of the manufacturers of this country, that the earths of these kingdoms are unequal to those of foreign nations for the fabrication of china. Miles Mason, late of Fenchurch Street, London, having been a principal purchaser of Indian porcelain, till the prohibition of that article by heavy duties, has established a manufactory at Lane Delph, near Newcastle-under-Lime, upon the principle of the Indian and Séve (*sic*) china. The former is now sold only at the principal shops in the City of London and in the country as British Nankin. His article is warranted from the manufactory to possess superior qualities to Indian Nankin china, being more beautiful as well as more durable, and not so liable to snip at the edges, more difficult to break, and refusible or unitable by heat, if broken. Being aware that, to combat strong prejudices with success, something superior must be produced; he, therefore, through the medium of his wholesale friends, proposes to renew or match the impaired or broken services of the nobility and gentry, when, by a fair trial or conjunction with foreign china, he doubts not that these fears will be removed, and in a short period the manufactories of porcelain, by the patronage of the nobility of this country, will rival, if not excel, those of foreign nations. *N.B.*—The articles are stamped on the bottom of the large pieces to prevent imposition.''

MILES MASON.
Stamped, Earliest Mark.

50

FENTON
STONE WORKS
1805.

51

52

C.J. MASON & C?
LANE DELPH

53

After the death of Miles Mason the business was carried on by his sons, Charles James, and George Miles, at new and larger works at Fenton, but in 1805 these were given up, and the business transferred to new works. Charles James Mason was the brother who took the more leading part in the works, and he it was who made those enormous vases of an oriental pattern standing about 3 feet high, which we see sometimes, and also the chimney-pieces of ironstone china, some of which are still in existence.

A pamphlet entitled *The Mason Family and Pottery* was published by Geo. L. Ashworth and Brothers, of Broad Street Works, Hanley, where the pottery works are still carried on, which will give the collector many interesting facts about this family of potters which we have no room to chronicle here. The marks are given on this authority. Mark no. 50, impressed, the earliest mark, c. 1800+. Mark no. 51, 1805. Mark no. 52, printed, 1820+. Mark no. 53, 1829–45. Other Mason marks are nos. 54–57. See also *The Masons of Lane Delph*, by R. G. Haggar, 1952.

Miles Mason produced some very good ironstone semi-porcelain, usually printed in red and blue, with Chinese designs of landscapes and figures with gilt line borders. He opened a shop in 1780 in Fenchurch Street for the sale of Chinese porcelain. The business, however, came to grief owing to the heavy duties brought about by our increased national expenditure caused by Napoleon's ambitious schemes. He then removed to Lane Delph or Middle Fenton, where he bought a plot of land and erected the Minerva works. There is an invoice of his extant, dated 1797, enumerating blue dessert sets of 1 centre, 4 shells, 2 hearts, 2 cucumber tureens, and other useful pieces for domestic use.

C. J. Mason became bankrupt in 1848. Francis Morley of Shelton purchased many of the Mason moulds and copper plates and examples may be found bearing the F. M. & Co. marks of Francis Morley & Co. (c. 1846–59). The greater part of the Mason designs and working material was, however, subsequently passed to G. L. Ashworth & Bros. by the partnership between Morley & Ashworth (c. 1859–62). Messrs. Ashworth, moving on modern lines, have maintained the traditions of the past and for the past 100 years manufactured " Mason's Ironstone " earthenware, often with the old traditional patterns.

Mark no. 54 in blue is on a teaset formerly in the possession of John Bagshawe. The willow pattern and many other varieties of china were also produced here. Mark no. 55 is on part of a china service with a version of the willow pattern. This is evidently an imperfect impression of the mark copied from Chinese porcelain. It occurs on various varieties of Mason's Ironstone china. The colourings of some of these services are particularly bright and the ware is well potted and finished (c. 1805–15).

Mark no. 56, " Mason's Cambrian Argil," is a clay probably brought from Wales. This mark occurs on vessels and dinner services with designs like the willow pattern, c. 1820.

Typical examples of Mason's wares are included in Godden's *British Pottery and Porcelain, an Illustrated Encyclopædia of Marked Specimens*.

Many " Ironstone " marks occur. The plain impressed mark no. 57 is the earliest, c. 1814–25. Other impressed marks are of the same early period. The printed marks were generally used from c. 1820 onwards.

The whole story of the Masons is complicated; several members of the family worked five different factories. C. J. Mason re-established himself after the bankruptcy and sale, and showed wares at the 1851 Exhibition.

FENTON. The firm of C. Heathcote & Co. was established in Lane End. Mark no. 58. The feathers and Cambria may refer to the pattern or to the clay, as the words " Cambrian Angil " were used by Mason of Lane Delph, q.v. A specimen with the name only was in the Liverpool Museum. The period is c. 1818–24.

M. Mason.

54

MILES

MASON

55

MASONS'
CAMBRIAN-ARGIL.

56

Mason's
Iron Stone China.

57

58

LONGTON HALL. With recent years our knowledge of the Longton Hall products and the proprietors has been greatly enlarged. Some interesting excavations have been carried out on the factory site (the first in March, 1955) and the discovery of factory wasters on the site has confirmed, and in some cases increased, our knowledge of the porcelains made by this factory from c. 1749 to c. 1760. Other important discoveries have been made by Dr. Bernard Watney and are contained in his *Longton Hall Porcelain* (Faber & Faber, 1957). This work should be consulted for a full history of Longton Hall porcelain and for numerous illustrations of the wares.

Former notices have given great prominence to the association of William Littler to the Longton Hall factory. While it is true that Littler was the guiding hand and the practical potter in the concern, Dr. Watney's researches have established that the original partners were William Jenkinson, William Nicklin and William Littler. It was William Jenkinson who " had obtained the Art Secret or Mystery " of making porcelain and who rented the Longton Hall premises at a date prior to 1751. Jenkinson sold his shares in the company in 1753 and he was then replaced by a new partner, Nathaniel Firmin. In 1755 a further partner, Robert Charlesworth, was admitted and supplied much needed financial backing to the company.

It was Mr. Charlesworth who dissolved the partnership in May 1760 although William Littler continued the works for a few months. It has recently been established that Littler later worked in Scotland (see Scottish chapter). The final sale of the Longton Hall stock was transacted at Salisbury in September 1760.

Several contemporary advertisements have been discovered and are interesting in that they include descriptions of the Longton Hall products. Aris's *Birmingham Gazette* on 20th June, 1757, had the following announcement:—

" At the China manufactory, by William Littler, at Longton Hall, near Newcastle, Staffordshire, there is now upon sale all sorts of china, both useful and ornamental, as well plain blue and white tea china of all sorts, coffee cans, chocolate cups and saucers, punch bowls and mugs, as finely enamelled and curiously modelled fruit dishes, leaf plates, saucer boats, and variety of curious useful ornaments for dessert, with figures and flowers of all sorts made exactly to nature, allowed by the best judges to be the finest in England, where all gentlemen and ladies who please to honour him with their commands may depend upon having the favour greatly acknowledged, and all tradesmen who favour him with orders may depend upon having them faithfully executed by their most obedient humble servant,   WILLIAM LITTLER."

In the year following another advertisement appears in Aris's *Birmingham Gazette* of 12th June, 1758:—

" This is to acquaint the public that there is now to be sold by William Littler & Co., at Longton Hall, near Newcastle, in Staffordshire, a great variety of all sorts of useful and ornamental porcelain or china ware, both blue and white, also enamelled in the best and most lively colours.

" *N.B.*—The Longton porcelain is vastly improved and is now allowed by all judges to be the best made in England. The prices are lowered, and are now very reasonable."

The final sale notice appears in the *Salisbury Journal* of 8th September, 1760:—

" To the Nobility, Gentry, Shopkeepers and others. Mr. Samuel Clarke sworn Exchange-broker of Cheapside, London, will sell by Publick auction, on Tuesday the 16th inst. and the four following Days at the Great Sale Room at the Sun at Fisherton adjoining the city. The Genuine large and valuable stock of the Longton Porcelaine China Factory, which, as the partnership is dissolved, will be sold without reserve or the least addition; containing upwards of ninety thousand pieces of the greatest variety of Dresden Patterns in rich enamel'd, pencil'd, Blues and Gold; as Figure and Flowers, mounted in Chandeliers, Essence Jars, Beakers, Vases, and Perfume Pots, magnificent Dessert Services, sets of Bowls, Mugs, Dishes and Plates, ornamented with Columbines and Central Groups, Tea Coffee and Toilet Equipages, of elegant patterns superbly finished, equal to a national Factory, so elegantly distinguish'd with a profusion of useful and ornamental articles. Particulars will be mentioned in the Catalogue which may be had at the place of Sale. The whole may be viewed the Friday, Saturday and Monday preceding the Sale, which begins each day at ten in the morning and at five in the Evening."

Typical specimens of Longton Hall porcelain are heavily potted although, of course, there are exceptions to this general rule; a streaky underglaze blue is the characteristic colour and this had a tendency to run. The wares of the factory are now avidly collected and on account of their rarity, high prices are given for good examples.

The majority of Longton Hall porcelain is unmarked. Apart from numbers and letters (probably workmen's marks) which sometimes occur on blue and white examples and several versions of a cross mark, the factory mark may be said to be the crossed " L " mark (capable of being read as J.L. for Jenkinson-Longton), which occurs painted in underglaze blue on some specimens, marks nos. 59 to 62.

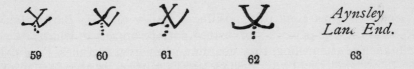

| 59 | 60 | 61 | 62 | 63 |

LANE END (now LONGTON). John Aynsley, established towards the end of the eighteenth century; his name is found in the map of 1802; it also occurs on a melon-shaped teapot, with portraits of a young gentleman and lady of about 1790, inscribed with mottoes, as " Keep within compass," " Fear God," etc. Mark no. 63. A plate of coloured transfer has a young lady within a large pair of compasses; around is this distich:—

> " Keep within compass and you shall be sure
> To avoid many troubles which others endure."

> " Prudence brings esteem," etc.

These portions of a tea service with mottoes were made for schools, and were presented to scholars as tokens of approval on leaving, with hints for their future guidance, being suitable both for boys and girls. John Aynsley also employed silver lustre on his ware; he died about 1826. Another specimen, a barrel-shaped mug, is in the Victoria and Albert Museum, printed and rudely painted in colours with a drinking party, with the song " Here's to the maid of bashful fifteen," etc. The manufactory has been continued by the family for over a century; the style of the firm is now John Aynsley & Sons Ltd., of Longton.

A curious pint mug with a transfer-printed subject tinted in colours representing a prize-fight between Humphreys and Mendoz, 9th January, 1788, their named supporters standing around, is signed *John Aynsley, Lane End*.

Nineteenth century firms of this name include H. AYNSLEY & Co., Commerce Works, Longton. Established about 1869, this firm continues to the present day. Their nineteenth century mark was the initials H. A. & Co. within a Staffordshire knot with L under.

Mark no. 64 is printed in blue on an earthenware jug of coloured transfer. The letters are believed to refer to BAGGERLEY & BALL of Longton, c. 1822–36. A marked jug in the Godden Collection is dated 1823. See Godden's *British Pottery and Porcelain, an Illustrated Encyclopædia of Marked Specimens*.

64

Bailey & Batkin.

65

May' & Newb^a.

66

M & N.

67

LANE END (now LONGTON). William Bailey and W. Batkin (mark no. 65) were the sole patentees of lustred pottery objects in which, as well as the branch of enamelling, they acquired competent fortunes. The partnership dates from about 1814. Shaw speaks of them as carrying on business there in 1827, and having then been so for nearly a quarter of a century, and passes high encomiums on their public spirit and private social virtues. The name of BAILEY & HARVEY, impressed or moulded in relief, occurs on lustre ware and this partnership dates from c. 1843–c. 1845.

LANE END (now LONGTON), opposite the church. Thomas and Joseph Johnson in the 18th century made salt-glaze white stoneware as well as crouch ware; they were succeeded by Mayer & Newbold, who greatly enlarged the works in the commencement of the last century. The name of this firm is found in red on a pair of porcelain match-pots, painted with roses on blue ground, gilt leaves, green and gold borders, formerly in Rev. T. Staniforth's Collection, mark no. 66. Their jugs were in great repute; they were doing a good business in 1823. The porcelain was of a fine translucent quality; pieces marked with initials only are rarely met with, mark no. 67. From about 1833, Richard Newbold was sole proprietor. The name *Mayer & Newbold* in full is on some specimens, and there was a jug in the Sheldon Collection with the letters M. & N. and the words "new opaque."

LANE END (now LONGTON). HARLEY'S name occurs on a curious painted jug, with a caricature of Bonaparte and the Quaker; about 1809.

Also on an earthenware tea service with blué and gold border, the name
stamped in the ware, and also on an earthenware teapot with a swan knob
in the Victoria and Albert Museum. See Godden's *British Pottery and
Porcelain, an Illustrated Encyclopædia of Marked Specimens.* Marks nos.
68 and 69, c. 1805–8.

LANE END. In the Survey of 1786 we find Forrester & Meredith, manufacturers of Queen's ware, black Egyptian, red china, etc. George Forrester
had a manufactory here in the first part of the 19th century; he was doing
a good business in 1823 and in 1829. " The premises were not large," says
Shaw, " but very convenient, being arranged on a regular plan, with
separate places for the distinct processes," c. 1805–31.

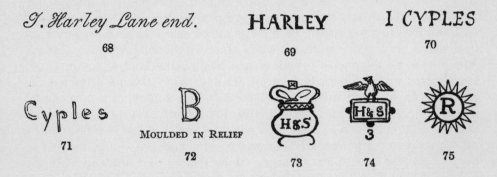

I. Harley Lane end.　　　　**HARLEY**　　　　**I CYPLES**

68　　　　　　　　　　　　　　69　　　　　　　　　　　　70

Cyples　　　　B　　　　　　　　　　　　　　　　　R

71　　　　MOULDED IN RELIEF

　　　　72　　　　　　　H&S　　　　H&S　　　　

　　　　　　　　　　　　73　　　　3　　　　75

　　　　　　　　　　　　　　　　74

LANE END. Joseph Cyples is described in the Topographical Survey of 1786 as a " Manufacturer of Egyptian and pottery in general."
Mark no. 70, impressed, is on a tea service on a chocolate basalt body in
imitation of Wedgwood, with raised figures of Grief; etc. The works were
continued after his death by Mary Cyples (c. 1795+) and then by Jesse
Cyples (c. 1805–c. 1811). William and Richard Cyples worked the factory
until about 1840. Mark no. 71. The Market Street Works at Longton were
sold to a Mr. Barker, and he afterwards sold them to a Thomas Barlow
(c. 1849–c. 1888), who was a maker of porcelain, and it is to this pottery
that Edward Sheldon attributes a mug with a face modelled the full size
of the mug. These were made in large quantities, but are seldom marked,
and are therefore attributed to better known makers. Mark no. 72 is on a
porcelain " face " mug, is *in relief*, which is very unusual. (Sheldon Collection.) The works were carried on by the firm of G. L. Bentley & Co.
from c. 1898 to c. 1912.

LANE END. Hilditch & Martin were china manufacturers here,
c. 1815–22, and were succeeded by Hilditch & Son, c. 1822–32. Mark no.
73 occurs on a white china teapot painted in white, blue and gold, and on
other porcelains. Mark no. 74, their initials surmounted by an eagle,
also occurs. Subsequently Hilditch & Hopwood, c. 1832–58.

Mark no. 75, in blue, has previously been attributed to Hilditch,
R the sign of Thomas Radford the printer. However, it is more probable
that this is the factory mark of William Ratcliffe of Hanley, c. 1831–40.

LANE END (now LONGTON). Benjamin Plant, potter. His name occurs on a jug in the form of a lioness, passant regardant, one foot raised, resting on a globe, 12 in. high; white glaze like the basketware, made about 1780; formerly in the possession of Jno. Plant, of Salford. Mr. Hailstone had a pair of lions inscribed " Benjamin Plant, Lane End." Mark no. 76.

B Plant
Lane End. 76

LANE END (now LONGTON). About 1756 R. Bankes & John Turner were manufacturers of white stoneware at Stoke, on the spot, part of the premises of Josiah Spode. They dissolved partnership and Turner removed to Lane End in 1762, where he manufactured every kind of pottery then in demand, and also introduced some other kinds not previously known. About 1780 he discovered a vein of fine clay on the land of Green Dock, the property of Ephraim Hobson of Hanley; from this he obtained the materials for his beautiful and excellent *stoneware pottery*, of a cane colour, which he formed into jugs, with ornamental designs, and the most tasteful articles of domestic use; some are wine-coolers, tureens, butter-coolers, others represent different kinds of pastry, etc., and are well calculated to deceive the eye at a short distance. Shaw relates that one cup made by Turner for the late Viscount Creamhorn (qu. Cremorne?) has never been equalled in the district, though formed of the common clay of Lane End; this was once produced by Jacob Warburton, at a meeting of potters, to show to what a degree of perfection even common pottery may be carried; it became so estimable in the opinion of its owner, that to prevent the possibility of injury, he had a proper-sized mahogany box made for its reception, and in the door is a pane of glass, through which alone he permits it to be inspected. Simeone Shaw also related the following anecdote: " Mr. Fletcher of Edinburgh, of sporting celebrity, having given an order to a tradesman at Edinburgh for a very large punch-bowl, the order had been forwarded to different celebrated potters and remained not executed; application was ultimately made to Mr. Turner, whose throwers attempted by different processes to accomplish the object, but it was only fully and satisfactorily got into form by the ingenuity of Mr. William Massey, the modeller; it holds twenty-two gallons imperial measure, and is now preserved in the Museum at Edinburgh; on its outside is a kind of tablet, on which are beautifully enamelled a Chinese town and the names of the persons and place as well as the date." The William Massey here mentioned was born in 1770, he was seventh son of the seventh son, in the twenty-seventh year of his mother's life; in 1834 he was the survivor of seventeen children, and the father of seven children, and altogether an eccentric. A unique self portrait plaque is in the Godden Collection.

Mr. Turner was deputed with Wedgwood to oppose the extension of Champion's patent in 1775; they visited Cornwall; the result was that

Wedgwood and Turner became joint-lessees of some clay mines at St. Austell and Redruth; and although unsuccessful in their opposition to the renewal of Champion's patent, they succeeded so far as to secure him a sole right to the use of Cornish clay only in *transparent ware*, leaving it open to the other manufacturers to employ it in opaque pottery and glazes of every kind. Mr. Turner died in 1786. Mark no. 77, impressed, c. 1770+. Among the numerous specimens of Turner's ware are some marked Turner & Co. In the Survey of 1786 a Mr. Abbott was in partnership; the firm is described as " Turner & Abbott, Potters to the Prince of Wales, Lane End." Turner's ware is the most successful imitation of Wedgwood's jasper, and, in fact, many of his examples are superior in point of finish; its chief excellence lies in the fine quality of the body used for the figures and ornaments in relief; it has the tone and apparent texture of fine ivory, and the reliefs are characterised by their sharpness and well-defined outline. The peculiar blue of the ground colour of some of his jasper ware is different from any other. The black Egyptian, as plinths for the jasper vases, etc., will bear the polish of the lapidary's wheel. (*Ker. Gall.*, enlarged edition, figs. 475 and 476.)

TURNER.

77

John Turner of Lane End, though he had not a workshop at Delft, had at least a depôt there, and he manufactured many goods at Longton for the Low Country market; specimens of cream-coloured ware, with his name, TURNER, impressed upon the paste, are not uncommon on the Continent, and may otherwise be readily recognised by the grotesque caricatures which they nearly always exhibit, with inscriptions in the Dutch language. Two polychrome plates with his name represent the Prodigal Son; on one is inscribed in Dutch *His departure*, on the other *His poverty;* another plate represents the celebration of a wedding; the bride and bridegroom are dressed in the fashion of the time. Many of the plates manufactured by Turner are painted with portraits of the reigning family of Orange; upon one we may see the bust of Prince William V., Stadtholder in 1766, then nineteen years of age; at his side is the bust of Sophia Wilhelmina, a Prussian princess, whom he married in 1767; the two busts face each other, and are separated by an orange; the whole is surrounded with a quantity of lines in Dutch, the last couplet of which is as follows : —

" As long as the sun and moon exist, so will the orange colour."

Another plate, also fabricated on the occasion of this marriage, which seems to have been a most popular one in Holland, shows the Stadtholder and the Princess separated by a candle, while lines in Dutch surround them. The same portraits on a similar plate have an inscription which translated is : —

> "That your sword may be like that of Gideon,
> That your wisdom may be that of Solomon."

The letters P. W. D. V., which we see on many of these services, are the initials of Prinz Willem Den V.

His sons, William and John Turner, succeeded him, and continued successfully all the various sorts of pottery for which their father was so celebrated; they also employed gilding; their jasper and black Egyptian were second to none. Mr. John Hancock was for some time prior to 1800 employed by them, and introduced the method of gilding with burnished gold. On 9th January, 1800, William Turner and John Turner, of Lane End, in the parish of Stoke-upon-Trent, in the country of Stafford, potters, patented "a new method or methods of manufacturing porcelain and earthenware, by the introduction of a material not heretofore used in the manufacture of those articles." The material is known in Staffordshire by the names "Tabberner's Mine Rock," "Little Mine Rock," and "New Rock." It is generally used as follows: Ground, washed, dried in a potter's kiln, commonly called a slip-kiln, afterwards mixed with a certain proportion of growan or Cornish stone, "previously calcined, levigated, and dried "; a small quantity of flint similarly prepared is also added, but in different proportions, according to the nature of the ware and the heat required in burning it; this was called "patent stone," but differing from the later "ironstone china." The rare mark no. 78 was adopted for their patent stoneware, usually in red, c. 1800–03. Their principal modeller was John Lucock. A fine vase, 18 in. high, has been seen by the editor. The patent was sold to Spode and from about 1805 appears as their "Stone China."

78   Turner's Patent.

In consequence of great losses occasioned by the French Revolution, they were compelled to give up their works in the year 1803. Their names, William and John Turner, are found in the map of 1802, at which time they had two manufactories. A mark in imitation of the Worcester well-known "square-mark," accompanied by the words TURNER'S PATENT, has been recorded.

ABBOTT & MIST. This firm produced some good earthenware; we have met with a tea set, white ground with a broad band of pink wavy line, like coral branches with wreath of gold leaves over it. The principal pieces have their names in pink. The name of Mist occurs on some pieces in the style of Wedgwood or Adams. A Mr. Abbott was in partnership with Turner of Lane End in 1786, in which year the latter died, and the business was carried on by his sons. It is probable that Abbott left the firm and went into partnership with the Mist above named, who was probably a London dealer or agent. All the goods partake of the character of Turner's wares. Examples by Mist are illustrated in Godden's *British Pottery and Porcelain, an Illustrated Encyclopædia of Marked Specimens.*

LANE END. *Pearl ware.* Chetham & Woolley, c. 1795–c. 1811. Simeon Shaw informs us that about 1795 a new kind of pottery, a *dry* body " without glaze or smear," was introduced into the market by Chetham & Woolley of Lane End. It is to the white pottery what jasper is to the coloured; not being affected by change of temperature, but very fine in grain, durable in quality, and of a most beautiful and delicate whiteness, it received the name it still bears of *pearl* from Mr. J. Spode, at that time resident in London. It is used, like jasper, for the finest description of ornaments, and is in general estimation among all ranks of society. Very few of the different attempts to produce pearl ware of equal excellence to that produced by this firm have been attended with success. Mark no. 79 dates from c. 1811.

79   CHETHAM

A beautifully-modelled bust and pedestal of this fine material was in the possession of the author; it is life-size, and is inscribed on the back of the pedestal, " Admiral Lord Viscount Duncan, who defeated the Dutch fleet, commanded by Admiral De Winter, off the coast of Holland, on Wednesday, the 11th of October, 1797." On the side is stamped, " *Chetham & Woolley, Lane End, 1798.*" The partnership dates from c. 1795 to c. 1811.

There were several other potters of more or less note established at this place in the first quarter of the nineteenth century, of whom we have no particulars. Among these may be named John Bill, earthenware manufacturer (c. 1832), who died in 1836. Johnson and Brough are in the map of 1802, succeeded by Benjamin Singleton Brough; Samuel Bridgwood; Goodwin & Orton; A. & J. Shaw; T. & J. Carey (c. 1823–42); Mr. H. Simpkin, who made a superior kind of china; and Ducroz and Millidge, makers of new stone china.

The following Longton manufacturers were listed in earlier editions, dates are now added:

Harvey, Adams & Co., decorated china, c. 1870–c. 1885.

Thomas Barlow, decorated china, from 1849, now T. W Barlow & Son Ltd.

Hammersley & Asbury, decorated china, c. 1872–c. 1874, then Hammersley & Co.

Moore Brothers, decorated china, c. 1873–1905.

This firm used impressed name marks, also a printed globe mark.

STAFFORDSHIRE. The name of R. B. Decarle occurs on some beautifully-modelled brown stoneware jugs, barrel-shaped, with vine leaves, grapes, cornucopiæ, etc.; under the spout a cherub's head. On the front of one formerly in Mr. Willett's possession is inscribed on an escutcheon, " John Samuel Clack, January 16th, 1781," on the handle is the artist's name; another formerly in the Owles Collection had in front " R.A.D. 1781," and the artist's name.

Mark no. 80 impressed on a white oviform vase of two handles, with figures in oval medallions and festoons in relief, like Wedgwood. These initials fit Peter & Francis Warburton of Cobridge, c. 1795–c. 1802.

Mark no. 81 occurs on fine cream-coloured ware, with raised oak-leaves. No details are known.

Mark no. 82 impressed on a blue painted dish, open-work border. George Harrison worked at Lane End and Lane Delft late in the eighteenth and early in the nineteenth centuries.

The following are marks of potters not hitherto mentioned who are believed to have worked in Staffordshire. These were included in former editions and some dates are now added:—

Mark no. 83, on a stone china plate, coloured transfer and yellow painted rim. Stephen Folch, Church St., Stoke, c. 1820–30.

Mark no. 84, on an earthenware basin, transfer-painted decoration.

Mark no. 85, on a blue printed earthenware dish. Mark printed in blue.

Mark no. 86, on a blue printed earthenware dish. Mark printed in blue. A John Tams was a nineteenth century potter at Longton.

Mark no. 87, impressed on earthenware pepper-caster and salt-cellar, marbled decoration, c. 1852–68. The firm was James Macintyre & Co. from 1868 to 1928. Various marks were used and incorporate the name or initials.

P & FW.	FREELING & Cọ	G. Harrison.
80	81	82

FOLCH'S GENUINE STONE CHINA.	Hillcock. and Walton.	ᶜ TAMS & Cº
83	85	86

]Hɪ̈ewson		MACINTYRE
84	STUBBS.	87
	88	

STUBBS. Mark no. 88, impressed on a blue printed earthenware dish. This potter is mentioned by Mr. Rhead as of Dale Hall, Burslem, retired before 1829, and died in 1836. Benjamin & Joseph Stubbs produced some fine printed earthenwares, many examples of which were decorated for the American market from 1818 onwards.

Mark no. 89. Martin Shaw & Cope. This firm of potters is mentioned by L. Jewitt as at the New Market Street Works, Longton. The mark occurs on a china jug, painted decoration in the Godden Collection, c. 1816–24.

Mark no. 90, scratched in the paste of a coloured earthenware plaque. This potter is mentioned by Jewitt, vol. 11, p. 297, as having signed the price agreement of 4th February, 1770. A potter of this name also worked c. 1811–2.

Mark no. 91, scratched in the paste of a painted earthenware plaque, the name of the potter (?) is mentioned in Freeth's *Old English Pottery*, p. 32. The name does not occur in available records of Staffordshire potters.

Mark no. 92. This mark is impressed on a printed plate of " Saxon stone " body. Made by T. & J. Carey, Anchor Works, Lane End, c. 1823–42. John Carey was potting from 1813. Mentioned by Jewitt, vol. ii, p. 409. The works were closed c. 1842.

Mark no. 93, impressed on an earthenware figure of a gardener, painted in colours. Early nineteenth century.

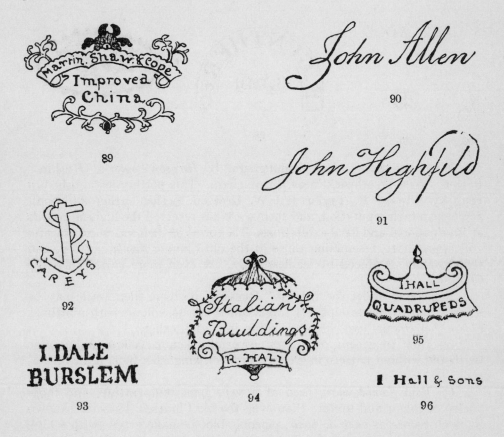

Marks nos. 94 to 96 are given by Jewitt, vol. ii, p. 281, as those of John Hall and John Hall & Sons of the Sytch Pottery, Burslem, working from about 1810. They are impressed on two earthenware plates and a jug, the plates blue printed and the jug buff colour with green lines and hunting scenes, having a greyhound handle. The " & Sons " mark was used from c. 1828 to the bankruptcy in 1832. Ralph Hall of Swan Bank, Tunstall, worked from about 1822 to about 1849 (" & Co." from 1846). Various marks were used incorporating the title.

Mark no. 97 is stamped on a black basalt vase and is attributed to S. Greenwood, who worked at Fenton about 1780–90. The specimen is in the British Museum and is said to be the only piece marked. Illustrated in Grant's *Makers of Black Basaltes*, and Godden's *British Pottery and Porcelain, an Illustrated Encyclopædia of Marked Specimens.*

Mark no. 98, on an earthenware jug, in the form of a man's head, with helmet, covered with drab glaze; the mark impressed; formerly in Lord Cadogan's Collection. The name Gunther does not occur in Staffordshire rate records.

Mark no. 99 is attributed to Lockett & Hulme of Lane End, c. 1822–26. Various marks of this form occur with other initials.

S. GREENWOOD.

97

100   101   98   99

WEST SMETHWICK, near Birmingham. *W. Howson Taylor's* " Ruskin " Pottery, West Smethwick, near Birmingham. This pottery, established in 1898 by Edward R. Taylor and W. Howson Taylor (father and son), achieved a high reputation, and their work has received the highest awards at international and local exhibitions. The forms of their vases are graceful and appropriate, resembling those of the old Chinese *flambé* pottery, and their colours, produced by leadless glaze, are even more varied than the Chinese.

Registered under the title of " Ruskin " pottery, their ware may be classed under three groups: (1) Single colour effects, colours with mottlings of another colour, two colours shading into each other.

(2) New treatment of lustres, especially lemon yellow and orange (with and without pattern in green or bronze), kingfisher blue, pearl blister, etc.

(3) Real *flambé* ware, fired at a very high temperature, and more varied in colour and texture than even the old Chinese. These are known by such names as *sang de bœuf*, pigeon's blood, snake green (with white, grey, puce, or *sang de bœuf* diaperings), dove grey, crushed strawberry, pearl blister, peach bloom, deep maroon, ivory, celadon, and others.

The paste or body of the ware is hard and thin, and has the appearance of being exceedingly well potted.

Some of the earlier pieces were marked with a monogram, but many were unmarked. Three main marks were used, namely, the Scissors (mark no. 100), " RUSKIN POTTERY " impressed in an oval, and the monogram mark no. 101. Various self-explanatory marks also occur. Production ceased in July 1935.

LOWESBY, Leicestershire; established by Sir Frederick Fowke, c. 1830–40. Mark no. 102, sometimes without the fleur-de-lis, is stamped on red terra-cotta with black enamelled ornaments in imitation of Wedgwood. There was a marked pair of vases in the Sheldon Collection (*Ker. Gal.*, figs. 513–4).

SWADLINCOTE, Burton-on-Trent, about thirty miles from Hanley. Thomas Sharpe. Mark no. 103 occurs on a bottle in the form of a man, bright yellow glaze, and well modelled; on the back is SOUTER JOHNNY, and on the front, " The Souter told his queerest stories." Sharpe (established 1821) was an exhibitor at the International Exhibition of 1851.

ASHBY-DE-LA-ZOUCH, Leicestershire. Wilson & Proudman worked the Coleorton Pottery in 1835 to about 1842. The firm was Wilson Bros. from c. 1880 to c. 1895. Stonewares were produced.

LOWESBY

102

SHARPE,
MANUFACTURER,
SWADLINCOTE.

103

LIVERPOOL, CAUGHLEY, COALPORT, ETC.

During recent years much new and interesting research has been carried out on the products of the various Liverpool factories. The Liverpool manufacturers seldom marked their wares and the following notices have not been amended.

The reader seeking further information on the various Liverpool wares is recommended to study the following papers read to the English Ceramic Circle and published in their transactions:—

Liverpool Porcelain, by Dr. T. Knowles Boney. Vol. 4, part 1, p. 7.

Liverpool Saltglazed Wares, by Dr. T. Knowles Boney. Vol. 4, part 2, p. 51.

Four Groups of Porcelain, possibly Liverpool, by Dr. Bernard Watney. Vol. 4, part 5, p. 13, and Vol. 5, part 1, p. 42.

Liverpool Delft Ware, by F. H. Garner. Vol. 5, part 2.

Also *Liverpool Porcelain*, by B. Rackham and W. B. Honey in *English Porcelain Circle Transactions*, no. 2, p. 27.

And Dr. T. Knowles Boney's reference book, *Liverpool Porcelain of the Eighteenth Century and its Makers*, 1957.

Recent research has identified a class of Liverpool saltglaze stoneware. A tea caddy with incised decoration (in the collection of Mr. E. Allman) is signed (?) " Henry Muskit 1760. L." A firm·trading under the title Okill & Co. are believed to have made similar wares at Liverpool. See an article by Dr. T. Knowles Boney in the *Apollo* magazine, December 1960.

Some early fayence punch-bowls of the first half of the seventeenth century are attributed to Liverpool; they are generally painted in blue *camaieu*, with ships and inscriptions. There is a very large bowl, capable of holding at least two gallons, in the Victoria and Albert Museum, and another bowl, coarsely painted in blue, with medallions of flowers, inscribed " Parliament bowl, free without excise, 1736," alluding to the taking off the duty by Walpole's Bill. Another bowl, of the same description of ware, in the Victoria and Albert Museum, praises the fine tin of Luxillion in Cornwall for making the opaque white tin glaze which *glidered* its surface, which the owner of the mine thus immortalises in verse : —

John Uddy of Luxillion,
　his tin was so fine,
It glidered this punch-bowl,
　and made it to shine.

Pray fill it with punch,
　let the tinners fill round,
They never will budge
　till the bottom they sound.　1731.

The beer mugs were frequently printed with rhymes suitable for landlords and quaint devices; here are some examples : —[1]

More	Beer	Score	Clerk
for	my	my	his
do	trust	pay	sent
I	I	must	has
shail	if	I	brewer
what	for	and	the

These lines are read from bottom to top, beginning at the right-hand lower corner. On another we have—

THE LANDLORD'S CAUTION

Customers came, and I did trust 'em,
So I lost my money and my custom;
And to lose both it grieves me sore,
So I'm resolved to trust no more.

Chalk's useful, but say what you will
Chalk never paid a malster's bill;
I'll strive to keep a decent tap
For ready money, but no strap.

These two specimens were formerly in the Baldwin Collection.

A Liverpool jug printed with a scene in a justice-room, has on the reverse " The Bachelor's Wishes in Rhyme ":—

　　" One female companion to soften my cares,
　　Two thousand a year to support my affairs,
　　Three dogs and a gun when to sport I incline,
　　Four horses and chaise to indulge me and mine,
　　Five jolly companions with whom to make merry,
　　Six dishes each day, with six glasses of sherry."

LIVERPOOL.　Mr. Richard Chaffers was the principal manufacturer; he was born in Mersey Street in 1731, one year after the birth of his contemporary, Josiah Wedgwood; his father was an eminent shipwright. Mr. Chaffers served his apprenticeship with Alderman Shaw. About 1752 he established a bank for the manufacture of pottery, and made blue and white earthenware, which was exported to our American colonies, now the United States. Shortly after, hearing the report of the great improvements made by Wedgwood in the body of the ware, and finding him a formidable

---

[1] These landlords' rhymes on the matter of " No trust " are very numerous, and many are highly suggestive. The barbers, too, were not behind in giving hints of the due time for payment, for we find on the barbers' basins which were placed under the customer's eyes this seasonable hint, " Sir, your quarter's up."

rival in the art of which he was then at the head, Mr. Chaffers was induced to aim at making a higher class of ware than had ever yet been produced. His endeavours were now turned to the production of china, the manufacture of which required an ingredient called soapstone, of which he could not procure a supply.

Mr. Podmore had been in the service of Mr. Wedgwood, but left it from a wish to establish himself as a manufacturer in America. On coming to Liverpool to embark for that country, he called upon Mr. Chaffers as the leading man in the trade. They entered into a long conversation, in the course of which Podmore exhibited so much intelligence and practical knowledge, that Mr. Chaffers, by a most liberal offer, induced him to forego his American project and enter into his service.

Mr. Chaffers's object now was to come into the field with Staffordshire; he therefore determined to set out for Cornwall, upon the forlorn hope of discovering a vein of soap-rock. The operations would be most expensive and laborious. He obtained letters of introduction from the Earl of Derby and other men of consequence in the county, and some of the leading landowners in Cornwall, then attending their duties in Parliament.

In those days there were no coaches and railways to aid the weary traveller; a stout horse was the only means of conveyance for a man of the higher class. Imagine Mr. Chaffers, having taken leave of his wife and numerous family and friends, mounted with a pair of saddlebags under him, containing a supply of linen, etc., a thousand guineas, the first instalment, to pay the wages of the miners, a brace of pistols in his holsters, pursuing his journey to London. He had made considerable progress in practical geology, though the science was then but little cultivated. Having, during his stay in London, obtained permission to bore for soap-rock from more than one of the principal proprietors of the mountain land he judged most likely to yield it, he proceeded to Cornwall and commenced operations. His first efforts were not successful. He moved to another quarter, with no better result: in a word, he expended large sums of money without finding the wished-for vein. Somewhat disheartened, but not subdued, he determined to return home, where his presence was much wanted. He did not, however, intend to abandon, but only suspend, his operations. He accordingly assembled all the miners in his employ, and announced to them, to their great regret, his determination. Previously to his departure he scrupulously paid every man his wages; one of them was missing: he was told the man in question was gone up the mountain to try another place. He then left that man's wages in the hands of the " captain " of the gang, and mounting his horse with a heavy heart, took leave of the men, to whom his animated and conciliatory manners had greatly endeared him.

The road to the nearest town was precipitous and rugged : a traveller on horseback made so little progress that a mountaineer on foot, by taking a short cut over the rocky crags, could easily come within ear-shot of him. After journeying for some time he thought he heard a faint cry in the distance; he dismounted, and ascending a hill, plainly saw the signal of discovery flying from a lofty peak. It appeared that the man who had separated from his fellow-miners and pursued his researches alone had discovered a vein; and on coming back to headquarters and finding that Mr. Chaffers had left them, he hoisted the preconcerted signal, and pursued him across the mountain with the pleasing intelligence, shouting, at times, to attract the somewhat dispirited traveller's attention.

Mr. Chaffers immediately returned, took the whole gang into permanent employment, and obtained an ample supply of the long-sought-for clay, which was conveyed to the nearest port, and thence shipped to Liverpool; on his arrival, the vessel entered with its precious freight into the Old Dock, dressed in colours, amidst the cheers of the spectators.

During his absence, Mr. Chaffers had regularly corresponded with his wife; but on his arrival in London, on his return homewards, the continued fatigue he had endured, together with anxiety of mind, brought on a dangerous fever, under which he laboured for several weeks. He was unknown at the inn where he stayed; but the landlord seeing that his guest —a very handsome man—had the dress and demeanour of a gentleman, called in an eminent physician, who sedulously and skilfully attended his patient. The doctor examined his saddle-bags, and, having ascertained his name and address from the letters and papers therein, communicated to his anxious wife all the particulars of his illness, and concluded with the consoling intelligence, that "he could that day pronounce him out of danger." As soon as he could travel he delighted his family and friends with his presence in Liverpool. No sooner had he arrived at home than he set to work with his new materials, and soon produced articles that gained him much reputation, as was frankly acknowledged by the great Wedgwood, to whom he presented a tea-set of his china ware, and who, on looking at one of the cups, admiring the body, and examining the colours used in decoration, exclaimed: "This puts an end to the battle. Mr. Chaffers beats us all in his colours, and with his knowledge he can make colours for two guineas which I cannot produce so good for five!"

But of how short duration was this distinguished progress! The sad tale of the sudden death of this eminent citizen remains to be told. Podmore, his favourite foreman, was seized, some years after the events narrated, with a malignant fever, without hope of recovery. The unfortunate sufferer sent a message declaring "his wish to see his dear master once more before their final separation." Mr. Chaffers, a man of full and sanguine habit, most imprudently complied, and shortly after took the fever to which he fell a victim; he was interred in the old churchyard of St. Nicholas, near the grave of his faithful servant. This expedition, so graphically narrated by Mr. Joseph Mayer, as will be seen by extracts from the letters of his agent at Mullion (quoted in the following pages), took place in 1755, and Chaffers lived ten years longer, sufficient to enable him successfully to mature his important discovery. He died in December 1765.

It is said that when Wedgwood heard of his sudden death, like a generous competitor he exhibited sincere regret, and acknowledged that he must ultimately have yielded the palm to his rival in certain branches, from his superiority as a chemist, his profound knowledge of the art of compounding colours, and their more economical preparation. This unfortunate event, by taking away both master and principal assistant, put an end to the prosecution of the trade, and was the commencement of the breaking up of that branch of the art which Chaffers had mainly brought to such a high state of perfection. A great number of the potters ultimately emigrated to America, whilst many of the best hands transferred themselves to the service of Wedgwood, or were hired by other Staffordshire manufacturers.

Another piece is a tea-cup, painted with a figure and landscape, after the style of Indian china, which, for cleverness of manipulation in the throwing, the almost egg-shell thinness of its sides, the compact solid body, with the smoothness of the glaze, and the deep richness of the brilliant colours, may be compared, without any fear of disparagement, with the large punch-bowl of Oriental make that he kept as a pattern for his workmen to copy from. It was preserved in his family until presented to Mr. Mayer, along with the pounce-box and tea-cup, by his grandson, John Rosson, Esq., of Moor Hall, near Ormskirk, whose mother was the daughter of Mr. Chaffers, and who related many of the particulars of his career. Other pieces in the same collection are—a teapot, a tea-caddy, and a cream-jug, painted with figures and landscapes after the Chinese style; also a large punch-bowl, painted with flowers and festoons, presented by Miss Mather of Mount Pleasant; also a quart jug, having a portrait of Frederick the Great, King of Prussia, on each side of which are trophies of war; in the inside are painted a war trophy and sprigs of flowers, and at the bottom is a Prussian eagle. This was given by Charles Chandos Pole, Esq., a descendant of one of the early Liverpool families, whose grandfather was the Member of Parliament to whom the letter was addressed in favour of Messrs. Sadler & Green, the inventors of printing on pottery.[1]

The foregoing interesting notice is taken from the *History of the Art of Pottery in Liverpool*, by Joseph Mayer, F.S.A., Liverpool, 1855. In Mr. Mayer's account of Mr. Chaffers we have unfortunately no dates, and the only evidence is the pounce-box, bearing date 1769, which was made

---

[1] In the *Liverpool Advertiser* for 18th December 1756 we find, "Chaffers & Co., China Manufactory.—The porcelain or china ware made by Messrs. Richard Chaffers & Co., is sold now here in the town; but at the manufactory on Shaw's Brow considerable abatement is made for exportation, and to all wholesale dealers. *N.B.*—All the ware is proved with boiling water before it is exposed for sale."

In the same paper we read that on the evening of March 7, 1782, at ten o'clock, a fire was discovered at the china works on Shaw's Brow, but was happily prevented from spreading farther than a part of the building.

by his son and successor four years after his father's death.

Through the kindness of R. Assheton Cross, Esq., M.P., we are enabled to give the date of his operations in Cornwall; he has favoured us with the perusal of a bundle of letters from one Gauregan Teppit, a miner, addressed to Mr. Chaffers in Liverpool, by whom he was engaged to draw soap-rock at Mullion, in Cornwall, on some land which he had leased for the purpose. These letters range over a period of eleven years, from July 1756 to December 1767; it was therefore about 1755 that the expedition to Cornwall just described was undertaken.

These letters show that in 1756 he was procuring soap-rock from Mullion in large quantities, for making his porcelain at Liverpool, which was some time before Cookworthy had commenced his experiments in the composition of *hard paste* porcelain. Borlase informs us that in 1758 Mr. Cookworthy of Plymouth had made experiments on the Breage china stone, and that it had been found useful in the making of porcelain; and we have no other correct data until his patent in 1768, ten years afterwards. Lord Camelford says, "The porcelain manufactory at Plymouth was attempted to be established and was undertaken by Mr. Cookworthy, upon a friend of his having discovered on an estate of mine in the parish of St. Stephen's, a certain white saponaceous clay, and *close by it* a species of granite or moor-stone, white with greenish spots, which he immediately perceived to be the two materials described by Père d'Entrecolles as the constituent parts of Chinese porcelain, the one giving whiteness and body to the paste, the other vitrification and transparency." These materials are described in his patent of 1768 as the kaolin or china clay or soap-rock, which was infusible, and the growan or moor-stone or decomposed granite, which was fusible; and the patent was for the combination of these two ingredients, the latter constituting what is called *hard paste*, previous to which fine white sand or calcined flints had been used as a substitute for the *petuntse* or growan. The china clay or soap-rock had been used, as we find, thirteen years previously by Mr. Chaffers, and from the juxtaposition of the growan or china stone much of it was mixed with the clay, hence the cause of the hard paste of which much of his porcelain was composed.

Extracts from the letters of Gauregan Tippit, of Mullion, Cornwall, to Mr. Richard Chaffers at Liverpool:—

1756. 9th July. He speaks of Mr. Chaffers having recently left, and he hopes the drawing would answer the charges; he had set some men to work, and paid their wages, and was in good order for raising the clay, and had obtained two tuns or thereabouts.

1756. 2nd Oct. He will send about ten tuns of clay, but was afraid of a disturbance between the lords of the land when he weighed it off; his "charges out at this present was not much up nor down of thirteen pound." He sends his compliments to Mr. Podmoor.

1756. 22nd Nov. Teppit says he had "sent to Hail eight tuns and fourteen hundred of sopey rock"; he had put it into casks with directions upon each sort. During

1757 and 1758 they were still raising soap-rock in the summer months, and shipping it to Liverpool.

1759. Aug. 26th. " We are going on well with the sopey rock, and have placed tackle over the plate, and have a very good prospick of cleay now in sight, and hope we shall gaine sume of youre large charges that is past."

1759. Nov. 9th. " We have the finest parcel of clay that was ever found in *Penradock.*"

1759. Dec. 8th. Teppit had weighed of the clay 9 tons and 17 hundred of as nice a clay as ever was seen, and said that there was a man down in October who said he would give any money for such a parcel.

1760. Feb. 8th. " I hope we shall raise this summer so much as we did laste. We began in April and left over in November."

1760. Aug. 9th. " We are going on very well upon the sopey rock; hope to hear the last parcel of clay arrived safe and well; will send ten tun in the next."

1761. March. " 1 have sent the clay to Hail firmly caskt up; we are obliged to shoute night and day and pouder is dear. The cost of every thing from 1st March 1760 to March 1761 is £94."

1761. May 23rd. " We have found a verey good bunch of clay; if it holds we can rise two or three hundred a day, and when the level is in, I hope it will serve for many years."

1762. Sept. 9th. " We raise half a tun of a day."

1763. June 25th. " The quarterly charges are about £20. The place is worth a hundred pounds in sight now more than it was laste year, for wee have a deep adit in and we are rising of clay faste."

1763. July 14th. Teppit sends twelve tons of clay.

1763. Aug. 20th. He sends 10 ton of " sopey rock."

1763. Oct. 5th. Sends off 10 tons more in 35 casks. In 1764 the soap-rock yields well, and is duly shipped *via* Hail to Liverpool.

The last letter sent to Mr. Richard Chaffers is dated the 26th of November 1765, and contains an account of all the monies received and paid by Teppit up to that date. The balance was transmitted in January 1766 by Mr. Huniball Chaffers. It would therefore appear that in or about December 1765, Mr. Richard Chaffers died, and that Mr. Christian, the potter, of Liverpool, his intimate friend, in conjunction with Huniball Chaffers and Edward Chaffers, his sons, were the executors to his will. In January 29th, 1766, Teppit writes to Mr. Huniball Chaffers at Liverpool, that he has 20 tons to weigh off, and a very good vein in sight. Mr. Christian's name is mentioned as having some interest in the clay (perhaps only as executor), but not in some copper-works which they had just come across, which Teppit describes as being very rich, and had brought £96 a ton. He concludes, " As for your lease, no man shall see it without your orders."

1766. Feb. 27. Teppit, writing to Mr. Edward Chaffers, says, " The lease is entirely drawn upon Mr. Richard Chaffers and his Executors, Administrators, and Assigns, and to pay one pound of lawful money per ton to the Lords when the clay is weighed off. Mr. Christian has desired me to send him the account of what cash I received of Mr. R. Chaffers, which I have done to the best of my knowledge as follows : Received from May 1756 to February 1766, £730, 6s. 3d."

The last letter of the series addressed to Mr. Edward Chaffers is dated December 10th, 1767, and the works were still in operation at Mullion.

The lease of this mine of soap-rock was, in May 1775, sold by Mr. Christian to the Worcester Porcelain Company for £500.

SHAW. Alderman Thomas Shaw had a bank for making pottery, situated at Shaw's Brow, in the beginning of the eighteenth century. A large plaque, 2 ft. 7 in. long by 20 in., formerly in the possession of Mr. Mayer, with a view of Great Crosby, is dated 1716; other specimens are dated 1722 and 1756. It was probably continued by his son after the Alderman's death, for we find recorded in the papers of the time the following notice: " October 20, 1775. Died, Mr. Samuel Shaw, potter, Dale Street, Liverpool."

Shaw's pottery was unmarked.

JOHN SADLER. A pottery was established in Harrington Street by John Sadler, the son of Adam Sadler, a printer in the New Market, Liverpool. John Sadler having served his apprenticeship to his father, and learned the art of engraving, commenced business on his own account in Harrington Street. A book printed by him is entitled " Cato Major," a poem by Samuel Catherall, M.A. Printed and sold by J. Sadler in Harrington Street, Liverpool, 1755. Guy Green was also a printer and partner, and succeeded John Sadler.

John Sadler was the inventor of printing upon pottery from copper plates, in conjunction with Guy Green, and it is said to have originated by Sadler noticing some children stick some waste prints which he had given them on some broken pieces of earthenware from the potteries. The patent, dated 1756, which it was proposed to take out, was never enrolled, as Sadler & Green preferred keeping the invention secret to the doubtful security of patent rights.

This invention was the application to glazed earthenware of prints from engraved metal plates, the colour remaining on the surface after the paper was removed, when it was passed through the muffle or enamelling kiln to fix the colours.

AFFIDAVIT AND CERTIFICATE

I, John Sadler, of Liverpoole, in the county of Lancaster, printer, and Guy Green, of Liverpoole aforesaid, printer, severally maketh oath, that on Tuesday the 27th day of July instant, they, these deponents, without the aid or assistance of any other person or persons, did within the space of six hours, to wit betwixt the hours of nine in the morning and three in the afternoon of the same day, print upwards of twelve hundred earthenware tiles of different patterns, at Liverpoole aforesaid, and which, as these deponents have heard and believe, were more in number, and better, and neater than one hundred skilful pot-painters could have painted in the like space of time in the common and usual way of painting with a pencil; and these deponents say that they have been upwards of seven years in finding out the method of printing tiles, and in making tryals and experiments for that purpose, which they have now, through great pains and expense, brought to perfection.   JOHN SADLER.
GUY GREEN.

Taken and sworn at Liverpoole, in the county of Lancaster, the second day of August, one thousand seven hundred and fifty-six, before William Statham, a Master Extraordinary in Chancery.

We, Alderman Thomas Shaw and Samuel Gilbody, both of Liverpool, in the county of Lancaster, clay potters, whose names are hereunto subscribed, do hereby humbly certifye that we are well assured that John Sadler and Guy Green did, at Liverpoole aforesaid, on Tuesday, the 27th day of July last past, within the space of six hours, print upwards of 1200 earthenware tiles of different colours and patterns, which is, upon a moderate computation, more than 100 good workmen could have done of the same patterns in the same space of time by the usual way of painting with the pencil. That we have since burnt the above tiles, and that they are considerably neater than any we have seen pencilled, and may be sold at little more than half the price. We are also assured that the said John Sadler and Guy Green have been several years in bringing the art of printing on earthenware to perfection, and we never heard it was done by any other person or persons but themselves. We are also assured that as the Dutch (who import large quantities of tile into England, Ireland, &c.) may by this improvement be considerably undersold, it cannot fail to be of great advantage to the nation, and to the towne of Liverpoole in particular, where the earthenware manufacture is more extensively carried on than in any other town in the kingdom, and for which reasons we hope, and do not doubt, the above persons will be indulged in their request for a patent to secure to them the profits that may arise from the above useful and advantageous improvements.

The *Liverpool Guide*, by Mr. W. Moss, 1799, says: "Copper-plate printing upon china and earthenware originated here in 1752, and remained sometime a secret with the inventors, Messrs. Sadler & Green, the latter of whom still continues the business in Harrington Street. It appeared unaccountable how uneven surfaces could receive impressions from copper-plates. It could not, however, long remain undiscovered, that the impression from the plate is first taken upon paper, and from thence communicated to the ware, after it is glazed. The manner in which this continues to be done here remains still unrivalled in perfection." Wedgwood sent his Queen's ware to them weekly to be printed in this improved manner, and continued to do so until his death.

Mr. Mayer quotes several invoices and letters from Mr. Guy Green (Sadler's partner) to Josiah Wedgwood, as a proof that the ware of the latter was sent to Liverpool to be printed:—

1783.—I have put the tile plate to be engraved as soon as I received your order for doing it, but by the neglect of the engraver it is not yet finished, but expect it will be completed to-morrow.

1783.—Our enamel kiln being down, prevented us sending the goods forward as usual.

1783.—The plate with cypher was done here. I think it would be best to print the cypher in black, as I am much afraid the brown purple that the pattern was done in would not stamp an up and down heat, as it would change in being long in heating.

1783.—For printing a table and tea service of 250 pieces [D. G.] for David Garrick, £8, 6s. 1½d.

1783.—Twenty-five dozen half tiles printing and colouring, £1, 5s.

SADLER & GREEN. There are in the Schreiber Collection (Victoria and Albert Museum) several specimens of this joint-work.

Mr. Mayer adduces as further evidence of Sadler being the inventor of this art, showing that he could not only transfer prints to earthenware, but to enamelled plates on the same system as the manufactory at Battersea, an impression from a copper-plate, engraved after a portrait of Frederick II, King of Prussia, done from an original, painted at Berlin, in 1756, inscribed " J. Sadler, Liverp^l, enamel^r," on enamelled copper; another, in the same style, being a portrait of George II; also a specimen with the arms of the Bucks' Society. Mark no. 1 is on the mug, with a portrait of George II; sometimes the names of both are affixed to their ware.

Dr. Diamond had a barrel-shaped mug of Liverpool china, beautifully printed with masonic emblems and figures on scrolls; in the centre are the Freemasons' arms, inscribed " Saddler, En¹. Liv¹." (*Ker Gall.*, fig. 480.) In the sale in 1910 of the Thoms Collection several of these mugs fetched good prices. One with portraits of George III and Queen Caroline, signed " Sadler," 40 guineas; another 15 guineas; one with the Freemason's arms, 17 guineas; one signed " Gilbody, maker," being bought for the Liverpool Museum, 22 guineas.

There was in the Mayer Collection, Liverpool Museum, a toilet-box, enamelled on copper inside and out, with transfer printing in black, *The Ladies' Pocket Kalendar*, which covers the top and base, of the year 1760; it is signed " J. Sadler, enam¹." The signature, " Green, Liverpool," is also occasionally seen, but it is rare.

In the Schreiber Collection, Victoria and Albert Museum, a case containing several specimens of Liverpool pottery, there are mugs commemorating several illustrious persons and historical events, among others of W. Pitt, Lord Nelson, General Wolfe, signed " J. Sadler, Liverpool " (*Ker. Gall.*, figs. 481–2), " John Wilkes, Esq., the patriot," and John Wesley. The first attack of the Bastile (dated 14th July, 1789), also a curious mug with Liverpool lighthouse and the signals on Bidstone Hill, the colouring of the flags varying according to the names of the merchants represented, also several with the arms of private individuals and trade societies. This print also occurs on glass wares. Mark no. 2 is from a tin glazed tile. Printed in black, formerly in the Sheldon Collection; several other signed examples occur.

Green, Liverpool   *J Sadler Liverpool*

1   2

There is in the Victoria and Albert Museum a handsome bowl of this Liverpool delft, painted in blue, with a three-masted man-of-war, engraved in Church's book. There are evidences that the same methods of colour-printing or transfer were adopted by Sadler & Green at Liverpool to those in use under Alderman Jansen's proprietorship at the Battersea enamel-works about the same time.

The tiles, with transfer prints, are neatly executed, and very varied. Among these we find a number of celebrated actors and actresses in character by Sadler, Liverpool : —

Miss YOUNGE, in the character of Zara.

Mrs. HARTLEY, in the characters of Imoinda and Lady Jane Grey.

Mrs. WARD, in the character of Rodogune.

Mrs. BEASLEY, in the character of Mahomet.

Mrs. LESSINGHAM, in the character of Ophelia.

Mr. GARRICK, in the character of Sir John Brute.

Mr. LEWIS, in the character of Douglas.

Mr. WOODWARD, in the character of Razor.

Mr. LEE LEWIS, in the character of Harlequin.

Mr. MOODY, as Simon in " Harlequin's Invasion."

Mrs. BARRY, in the character of Athenais.

Mrs. CIBBER, in the character of Monimia.

Mrs. BULKELEY, in the character of Angelina.

Mrs. BARRY, in the character of Sir Harry Wildair.

Mr. WOODWARD, in the character of Petruchio.

Mr. LEWIS, in the character of Hippolitus.

Mr. FOOTE, in the character of Fondlewife.

Mr. KING, in the character of Lissardo.

Mr. GARRICK, in the character of Abel Drugger (engraved in Church's *English Earthenware*).

Mr. MOODY, in the character of Teague.

Mr. WROUGHTON, in the character of Barnwell.

Mr. SMITH. in the character of Lord Townley.

There are several of these tiles in the Schreiber Collection, Victoria and Albert Museum. They are about 5 in. square, very well potted, and were exceedingly popular for use in lining stoves and walls. One finds, as in other specimens of transfer, the details often filled in by the brush after the process of transfer. (*Ker. Gall.*, fig. 483.)

PENNINGTON. Seth Pennington was celebrated for his punch-bowls, which were well potted, of large size, and painted generally in blue, with shipping subjects, much in the style of Lambeth or Bristol delft, but having a slightly blue tint in the glaze. With the huge shipping trade at Liverpool these punch-bowls appear to have been made in honour of the occasion of launching a new vessel or in commemorating a voyage—" Success to the Monmouth, 1750," and other names of ships being inscribed on specimens in the Liverpool Museum. Pennington flourished about 1760. The industry was shattered by the increasing competition of the Staffordshire potteries, which, as will be observed in the notices of other English manufacturers, became all-powerful towards the end of the century, and brought about the extinction of their smaller rivals. The letter P (mark no. 3), varying in formation, in gold and in different colours, also impressed, occurs in the bases of sundry earthenware specimens—on a jug, on the figure of a greyhound, and others—but whether we can ascribe them to Pennington is uncertain.

3   P

Among the indentures of apprenticeship to Josiah Wedgwood, the name of John Pennington occurs, son of James Pennington, manufacturer of china at Liverpool, and brother to Seth; it is dated 1784, " to be taught the art of engraving in acquatint." Mr. Binns says, James Pennington (perhaps the same here spoken of) came to Worcester from Wedgwood's on completing his apprenticeship, and in 1792 was selected to paint an entire service for the Duke of Clarence, having in the centre a figure of Hope, a ship in the distance; he was afterwards chief artist, herald painter, and foreman in Messrs. Flight & Barr's works.

PHILIP CHRISTIAN, of Shaw's Brow, carried on an extensive business in manufacturing porcelain, and after Chaffers's death became the leading potter in Liverpool. He was Chaffers's executor, and disposed of his lease of the vein of " soap-rock," which that potter had discovered in Cornwall, to the Worcester Porcelain Company, for £500, in May 1775; it was situated in the parish of Mullion.

In Sadler's receipt-book of January 1769 we find: " Christian's china body—To 100 parts rock flint, 24 parts; best flint glass, 6 parts; crown glass, 6 parts. To every 20th of the above, put 1 lb. of salts. Glaze— 4 china body (foreign), 16 flint glass, 3 white lead, and 12 oz. of pearl ashes."

Among other ware made by him was the tortoise-shell, of round and octagonal forms; also some fine pattern services and chimney ornaments.

ZACHARIAH BARNES was a native of Warrington; he was born in 1743, and died September 1820. He commenced business as a potter in the Old Haymarket; at first he made china, but afterwards gave up that and confined himself to delft. He made Welsh ware dishes in large quantities; but his principal business was the manufacture of square tiles of excellent quality and durability: they were printed by Sadler & Green. So large was the sale of this article alone, that he made a profit of £300 per annum by tiles only; also large quantities of potting pots for char. Pharmacy jars, and labels for liqueurs were also made by him. This was the last pottery of the old-established locality carried on at Liverpool.

WILLIAM BALL AND THOMAS WOLFE, see the English Ceramic Circle's *Transactions*, vol. 5, page 42.

SAMUEL GILBODY AND EVANS, see the English Ceramic Circle's *Transactions*, vol. 4, part 5, page 20.

W. REID & Co., Liverpool, china manufactory, Castle Street. In the advertisements from 1756 to 1760 we find several from this firm, requiring "apprentices for the china work"—"A sober, careful man, who understands sorting and packing, and merchants' accounts"—"Apprentices for painters," etc. Their principal manufactures were " all kinds of blue and white china ware, not inferior to any make in England." See the English Ceramic Circle's *Transactions*, vol. 4, part 5, page 13.

ABBEY. A pottery was established on the south shore of the Mersey, near Liverpool, about 1790, by Richard Abbey, in conjunction with a Scotchman named Graham, where they carried on business with good success for some time.

Richard Abbey was born at Aintree, and served his time as an engraver to Sadler, in Harrington Street, where he engraved, besides many other works, a large quart jug, having upon it the Farmers' arms, and was considered very skilful in his art. A mug, formerly in E. Norman's Collection, had a transfer engraving commemorating the treaty of commerce between England and France; a figure of Hibernia, seated, with ships in the background, inscribed, " Ye sons of Hibernia, rejoice in the freedom of commerce." *R. Abbey, sculp*. He retired from the concern in 1796, when the works were taken by Worthington & Co., who called the site the *Herculaneum Pottery*; he died at Aintree in 1801, at the age of 81. J. Mayer says he was engaged for some time at a pottery in Glasgow to teach engraving, and also visited France for the same purpose; this must have been previous to 1790.

BOARDMAN. In the Sheldon Collection there was an earthenware plate, printed in black, with the rare mark no. 4. It is attributed to the firm of Bensley & Boardman of Liverpool. The specimen was exhibited at the Centenary Exhibition, 1907, in Liverpool.

BOARDMAN

4

HERCULANEUM

5

HERCULANEUM

7

6

8   HERCULANEUM
POTTERY.

HERCULANEUM POTTERY. This pottery was originally established by Richard Abbey about 1790; on his retirement in 1796, it was taken by Worthington, Humble & Holland, and they engaged as foreman Archibald Mansfield, a thrower of Burslem, and about forty operatives, men, women, and children, to be employed in various branches of the art, and the works were remodelled and enlarged. As Wedgwood had christened his settlemen "Etruria," Worthington & Co. christened theirs "Herculaneum"; it was carried on by them until 1806, when, requiring larger capital, an increase of proprietors took place, and it continued as a company until 1833, when the concern was dissolved and the property sold to Ambrose Lace, Esq., and others, for £25,000, who let the premises to Thomas Case, gentleman, and John Mort, potter, and they carried on the business until 1836; the firm was afterwards Mort & Simpson, who manufactured here until 1841; the site is now occupied by the Herculaneum Dock. The first wares made here in 1796 were Queen's ware and blue printed. About 1800 they commenced making china; at this period Ralph Cordon was manager; he came from Lane End, now Longton. Of the marks used here the earliest was "Herculaneum," printed in blue. By a resolution of the Committee of Management, dated 6th August, 1822, it was ordered that "to give publicity and identity to the china and earthenware manufactured, the words 'Herculaneum Pottery' be stamped or marked on some conspicuous part of all china and earthenware hereafter made at this manufactory." Marks nos. 5 and 6.

They made earthenware dinner and dessert services, painted and decorated in good taste; a service formerly in the possession of the Rev. T. Staniforth has a maroon border, painted with roses and buds; the mark no. 7 stamped on the back. This is the standard mark for the period c. 1796–1822.

Mark no. 8 was used from 1822 to 1833, according to the order quoted above. A favourite pattern was printed views of the principal towns in England, with the name in a medallion at the bottom of the piece.

The crest of the borough of Liverpool, of a bird called the liver, with wings expanded, holding a plant called the liverwort, was adopted by Case, Mort & Co. (1833–36), mark no. 9.

There was a cream ware dish in the Sheldon Collection with a mark of this factory, which is said to be unique. It is a monogram, which reads Mort Herculaneum Pottery Co., mark no. 10.

In the same collection was a plate, one of a set made from 1806–33, with mark no. 11.

The Rev. Septimus Firman of Liverpool possessed an oval sauce-boat dish, decorated in two shades of blue, and a medallion having the arms of the Corporation of Liverpool painted in their proper heraldic colours. Impressed mark " HERCULANEUM."

The bust of Admiral Lord Duncombe in the Schreiber Collection, Victoria and Albert Museum, is an excellent specimen of the higher class of production of this factory.

Mark no 12 is impressed, and has the appearance of being stamped with a button, the bird's head being to the right instead of the left, as it would be heraldically. Mr. Staniforth had a small set of brown printed tea things so stamped. Specimens of Herculaneum wares are illustrated in Godden's *British Pottery and Porcelain, an Illustrated Encyclopædia of Marked Specimens.*

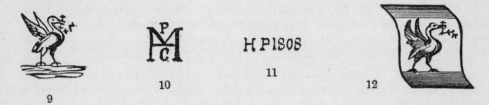

9   10   11   12

LANCASTRIAN LUSTRED POTTERY. CLIFTON JUNCTION, near Manchester. *Pilkington's Tile and Pottery Company, Limited*, was founded in 1892, and under the able directorship of William Burton, their technical and artistic director, the firm have produced some excellent results. Their chief speciality was a ware called " Lancastrian Lustred Pottery," which was remarkable for the fine polychromatic glazes reproducing the iridescence of the early sixteenth century Deruta and Gubbio majolica; next an infinite variety of shaded colours, good greens, reds, blues, yellows, and a new combination called orange-vermilion, varied by handsome mottled and opalescent effects. The forms of the vases, tazzi, and plates or bowls, are Oriental in inspiration, and while some of the painted lustres remind us of the old Italian maiolica, of old Persian or Hispano-Moresque effects, others are originally quaint and well adapted to the forms and colours of the specimens they decorate. Among the artists specially engaged were the following, each specimen bearing in addition to the impressed mark of the firm the mark or cipher of the individual craftsman. Pilkingtons received the highest awards at exhibitions, and at the Brussels Universal Exhibition in 1910 and Turin 1911 their exhibits were greatly admired.

List of Special Artists at the Pilkington Tile and Pottery Co.

W. S. Maycock.	R. Joyce.	T. Evans.
Miss A. Burton.	Miss J. Jones.	Lewis F. Day (designer).
E. Kent.	C. E. Cundall.	Miss D. Dacre.
Miss C. M. Rodgers.	G. M. Forsyth.	A. Hull.
A. Barlow.	J. Chambers.	Walter Crane, R.I. (designer).

13

14

Mark no. 13 from about 1904 to 1913, and roman numerals occur under the mark indicating the date, e.g. VII=1907. Mark no. 14 from about 1913. Production ceased in 1938.

CHESHIRE. ST. HELENS and SEACOMBE. There was a revival of the manufacture of pottery in this neighbourhood, and works were built at Seacombe, in Cheshire, on the opposite side of the Mersey from Liverpool, in 1851, under the proprietorship of Mr. Goodwin, who was formerly a manufacturer at Lane End, the workmen coming chiefly from Staffordshire; the first oven was fired on 19th June, 1852. There were advantages in this locality for such work, as coal could be had nearly as cheap as in Staffordshire; the quality, I believe, was not quite so good, being more gassy, and consequently not burning so clear as that used in the great pottery district. There was also a great saving in carriage, as the raw materials, such as clay, Cornwall stone, and flint, could be laid down on the quay close to the works; and again, when packed and ready for the market, vessels could load in the great float at Birkenhead, and at once proceed to sea without reshipment, as was the case with the Staffordshire ware on its arrival at Runcorn.

The ware manufactured here consisted principally of earthenware and stoneware, chiefly of blue and colour printed ware, and Parian of a good quality. Here was introduced one of the throwing tables for making hollow ware, cups, bowls, etc., by machinery, with the aid of which four boys, who were quite unacquainted with the art, could, in a day or two's practice, produce as much work as by the old process of hand-throwing could formerly be made by five men in the same space of time. A very large and increasing trade was carried on with the east and west coast of South

America, Turkey, California, and India. So admirably arranged were the buildings, that all the different parts worked together; the ware, after being fired, was carried direct from the ovens into the biscuit warehouses which adjoined them, and on the other side the coal was conveyed along a railway and deposited close to the mouths of the kilns. The whole was looked upon as a model for all future buildings and arrangements for pot-works; indeed, so perfect was it considered, that it was visited by several manufacturers from France and Germany, who by permission of Mr. Goodwin took plans of it as a guide for new works to be erected in those countries (J. Mayer's *History of Liverpool Potteries*, 1885.) The works closed prior to 1878.

WARRINGTON. The works were commenced here about 1797 by James & Fletcher Bolton, who obtained the services, as managing partner, of Joseph Ellis of Hanley, Staffordshire, a pupil of Josiah Wedgwood. It arose out of the idea that as the Cornish clay passed through Warrington *en route* to Staffordshire, potteries might be advantageously made to compete with that county, and export it to America. As England was at that time at war with America, it was sent over unmarked, and cannot therefore be now identified. The ware is described as a hybrid between pottery proper and china inferior, blue and white printed, an inferior black ware, etc. In 1812 the firm became bankrupt. Dr. Kendrick of Warrington made a collection of the productions, which he presented to the local museum.

JACKFIELD, Shropshire, was one of the oldest potteries in the county, and it is said that as early as 1560 entries occur in the parish registers of Stoke-upon-Trent of potters " from Jackfield." A few years ago a coal-pit at Jackfield, which was known to have been closed for two centuries, was opened, and in it was found a brown earthenware mug bearing the date 1634; an early jug was in the possession of W. F. Rose of Coalport. J. E. Hodgkin has illustrated in his book a double-handled posset-pot in his collection, dated 1760, and he mentions other pieces in the Liverpool Museum and some private collections bearing the following dates: 1766, 1767, 1769, and 1781. In 1713 the pottery was taken by Richard Thursfield, from Stoke-upon-Trent, and after his death in 1751, it was carried on by his son John until 1772. The early ware made about this time was a red earth covered with a very black glaze, sometimes with scrolls and flowers in relief, known in the locality as " black decanters." About 1780 the works were purchased by John Rose (who had served his apprenticeship with Turner of Caughley), in conjunction with a Mr. Blakeway, who greatly improved the character of the ware, and consequently the business was much extended; after a few years the manufactory was removed to Coalport, on the opposite bank of the Severn, where more convenient premises had been erected.

BENTHALL, Shropshire. John Thursfield established a manufactory here in the year 1772, on his retirement from the Jackfield works. Benthall is half a mile from Broseley, and the reason of his choosing this spot was the discovery of a fine bed of clay in the immediate vicinity suitable for making pottery. The clay drawn from this spot was used for the extensive manufactory of Maw & Co., from about 1852.

The productions of the Benthall manufactory were of the same character as those of Jackfield, and the secret of the black glaze was only known to the proprietor, and died with him; the establishment was known as *The Mug House*. At his death it was continued by his son, John Thursfield, in partnership with his brother-in-law, Mr. Pierce, under the firm of W. Pierce & Co., and it lasted until about 1818, when a person of the name of Bathurst succeeded. Mark no. 15.

15   *W. Pierce and Co.*

CAUGHLEY, near Broseley, Shropshire. Established about 1751 for the making of earthenware, but it does not appear to have been on a large scale; it was carried on by Mr. Browne of Caughley Hall, a man of good property, and after his death by Mr. Gallimore. It was not till 1772 that it rose to any importance, when Mr. Thomas Turner, Mr. Gallimore's successor, commenced operations; he came from the Worcester porcelain manufactory, which he left on the sale of the works in that year; he was an excellent draughtsman and engraver, and probably learned his art under Robert Hancock.

Thomas Turner, of Caughley Place, was the son of the Rev. Richard Turner, LL.D., Rector of Comberton, 1752, Vicar of Elmley, 1754; died 1791, and was buried at Norton, all in the county of Worcester; he was also chaplain to the Countess of Wigtown. Thomas Turner was born in 1749, and in 1783 was married to Miss Dorothy Gallimore, a niece of Mr. Browne of Caughley Hall, where she was residing at the time; he had two children, who both died young, and Mrs. Dorothy Turner also died in 1793.

Mr. Turner, in 1796, married Mary Milner, the widow of Henry Alsop, Esq., formerly of London, by whom he had two children: Catherine Georgina Cecilia, who married Mr. John Jacob Smith of St. James's, Bridgnorth (who was town-clerk of Bridgnorth for upwards of fifty years), she died in 1836; and George Thomas Turner, a solicitor, who died at Scarborough without issue in 1869, with whom also died out the family name of Turner. Thomas Turner resided at an elegant château, erected by a French architect, which was pulled down after his death; he died in 1809, aged sixty. Having married a lady of some property, he went to Caughley, and began to build suitable premises for the manufacture of porcelain, but it was some years in progress, and was not completed until 1775. We read in a paragraph in a newspaper of Nov. 1, 1775: "The porcelain manufactory erected near Bridgnorth, in this county, is now quite completed, and the proprietors have received and supplied orders to a very large amount. Lately we saw some of their productions, which in colour and fineness are truly elegant and beautiful, and have the bright and lively white of the so much extolled Oriental." These works, which were extensive, were pulled down some years after Mr. Turner's death; a few mounds only remain to mark the site, and the ground at the edge of a wooded dingle still bears the name of the Factory Field.

The excellence of Turner's porcelain, and the invention of the beautiful dark blue of the Caughley china, attributed to him, gained him great patronage. (*Ker. Gall.*, figs. 605–607.) In 1780 he produced the celebrated " willow pattern," which even at the present day is in great demand, and the " blue dragon," another favourite pattern, and completed the first *blue printed table service* made in England for Thomas Whitmore, Esq., of Apley Park, near Bridgnorth; the pattern was called *Nankin*. Thomas Minton of Stoke assisted in the completion of this service, being articled as an engraver there. These patterns remained universal favourites for many years; the *willow pattern* for dinner services, and the *Broseley* for tea and breakfast sets. Robert Hancock, the artist-engraver of better known Worcester fame, is also said to have worked with Turner some time after 1774, and is probably responsible for the good transfer decoration in blue under glaze which we find occasionally on some good Caughley specimens.

Chamberlain of Worcester, until the end of 1790, had their porcelain in the white from Thomas Turner of Caughley. He at first mixed all the bodies himself, but afterwards instructed his sister how to do it; subsequently a man named Jones mixed for him.

About the year 1780 Turner went over to France, and returned with several skilled artists and workmen. Of those engaged at the Caughley works the principal were Dontil, a painter, also John Parker, Thomas Fennel and Henry Boden for flowers, Thomas Martin Randall for birds, Muss and Silk for landscapes, Adams, a blue painter, De Vivy, and occasionally Stephan (a German), modellers. Peter Stephan, his son, later modelled at Coalport. John Rose, the son of a farmer in the neighbourhood, also learned his art under Turner; he left about 1780, and commenced a small business at Jackfield and subsequently moved to Coalport.

Perry, one of the workmen who was apprenticed to Turner, stated that in 1797 they had four printing-presses at Caughley, introduced by Davis: the patterns at that time and for years previously were birds and blue panels; that Turner had been an engraver at Worcester; and he recollected a slab on the front of one of the arches of the building at Caughley, stating the date of its foundation, 1772, which would be the time he succeeded Gallimore, but it was not finished for some time after.

Hubert Smith, formerly of St. Leonards, Bridgnorth, the grandson of Thomas Turner, and his only direct representative, kindly supplied the author with many of these particulars. The family was in possession of portraits of Thomas Turner and his wife, Gallimore, Dr. Turner, and others.

In 1799 Turner retired, and John Rose & Co. became proprietors of the Caughley works by purchase. They continued to make china there, but chiefly in the biscuit state, which was taken to Coalport to be decorated. They altogether removed them to Coalport about 1814 or 1815, and the materials were used for enlarging their premises there; at the present time no vestige of the house or works remains at Caughley.

CAUGHLEY. The word " SALOPIAN " impressed on blue Chinese

figures and landscapes, and on white china, with rich gilding, marks nos. 16 and 17, c. 1772–c. 1800.

The impressed marks TURNER or very rarely TURNER & GALLIMORE also occur in the 1770's, marks nos. 18 and 19.

The letter S, in blue, is sometimes placed alone, and was used at a very early period of the works; it is found on a white mug with blue and gold flowers, bearing the words Francis Benbow, 1776, surmounted by an anchor, formerly in the possession of Malcolm Benbow, his grandson, at Coalport. Marks nos. 20–24, 1772–1785.

The crescent and the word SALOPIAN are sometimes found together, the former in blue, the latter impressed; this occurs on a fruit dish, painted in blue and gold, mark no. 25, c. 1772+.

Mark no. 26 is on a cup and saucer of English china, in imitation of Oriental, with blue stripes and red flowers, c. 1780.

The series of Arabic numerals from 1 to 8, with flourishes, give them something of an Oriental character. All these marks are printed in blue on early blue printed ware, with Oriental designs in the blue, which was brought to such perfection by Turner. Marks nos. 27–36, c. 1772–c. 1785.

The crescent marks nos. 37–40 with faces, letters, and numerals are sometimes attributed to Worcester, but the former Editor and other authorities catalogued them as Caughley, c. 1772–c. 1785.

The crescents nos. 41–46 with numerals also occur on specimens, c. 1772+.

It may be observed with regard to Caughley ware, that there is considerable difficulty with regard to some of the sparsely decorated blue and white specimens, as to whether they are Worcester or Caughley (Shropshire) china. The crescent mark accompanied by a capital letter, which the reader will find included among the Worcester marks, is by several authorities believed to belong to Caughley. The letter C, mark no. 47, may certainly be ascribed to this factory. It is generally found on such specimens as trellis pattern baskets or tea services of Worcester-like china, decorated with blue in the Worcester manner. Caughley wares are illustrated in Godden's *British Pottery and Porcelain, an Illustrated Encyclopædia of Marked Specimens.*

41   42   43   44   45   46   47

COALPORT, in Colebrook Dale, Shropshire. These works were established by John Rose between 1780 and 1790, when he removed his manufactory from Jackfield, where he had commenced business in or about the year 1780, but remained there only a few years; he carried on these and the Caughley works (purchased in 1799) simultaneously, until the latter were finally removed to Coalport in 1814. Having purchased both the Swansea and Nantgarw manufactories, they were incorporated with Coalport, and Billingsley and Walker, proprietors of Nantgarw, were both engaged, and remained until Billingsley's death, which happened in 1828, see notice of Billingsley's career in the notice of Nantgarw porcelain.

In 1820 Rose received the gold medal of the Society of Arts for his felspar porcelain and an improved glaze, which is found recorded on some pieces, by a mark 2 in. in diameter, as follows: " Coalport Felspar Porcelain; J. ROSE & Co. (The word is sometimes spelt ' Feltspar.') The gold medal awarded 30th May, 1820. Patronised by the Society of Arts." Several variations of these 1820 marks occur. Services are met with, the principal pieces being so inscribed. The Society of Arts had offered a premium " to the person who shall discover the cheapest, safest, most durable, and most easily fusible composition fit for the purposes of glazing earthenware, without any preparation of lead, arsenic, or other pernicious ingredients, and superior to any hitherto in use." The gold Isis medal was awarded to John Rose. The composition being—felspar from Welshpool, 27 parts; borax, 18 parts; sand from Lynn, Norfolk, 4 parts; Cornish china clay, 3 parts; nitre, 3 parts; soda, 3 parts: this mixture was fritted, and 3 parts of calcined borax then added.

About 1821, Walker of Nantgawr reputedly introduced at Coalport a maroon-coloured ground, which became a speciality; they not only copied the patterns of Dresden and Chelsea china, but counterfeited the crossed swords and the gold anchor, a practice which ought to have been avoided. The proprietors copied the Sèvres china both in form and decoration, and produced some exquisitely-painted pieces by first-rate artists; great attention has also been paid to the grounds, and the beautiful *rose Pompadour* has been imitated here more successfully than by any other manufactory.

Billingsley's original recipes for making his china ware were in the possession of the late Mr. Rose, and it can be made at Coalport of as fine a quality as ever, but it is too expensive a process to be followed to any great extent; it is easily identified, whether made at Pinxton, Nantgarw, Swansea, or Coalport.

Coalport marks were as follows:—

Mark no. 48, in red, is on a porcelain tea set, painted with ribbons and roses, thought from the quality of the china to be the mark of Rose, the proprietor of the Coalport works, early 19th century.

A porcelain basin, printed decoration, formerly in the Sheldon Collection, has the mark no. 49, evidently the copy of a Chinese mark, and another piece has the Dresden crossed swords. Early 19th century.

COLEBROOK DALE is synonymous with Coalport, but the different titles have caused confusion. Mark no. 50 is a usual one, c. 1820.

Mark no. 51, on a scent-bottle, flowers printed on maroon, ground, and gilded, c. 1820.

Mark no. 52 is on a china basket of flowers, finely modelled and painted, c. 1820.

Mark no. 53, in blue is on a pair of china vases, with leaves and flowers in relief. Several examples of floral encrusted wares are marked with a crossed swords mark in blue.

The elaborate mark no. 54 appears on many fine specimens, c. 1820–30. Slight variations occur. The peculiar spelling of feltspar has already been noticed.

Mark no. 55 occurs on a pair of porcelain tulip-shaped cups and other specimens, c. 1820.

Various printed marks occur in the 1830–1850 period. These are self explanatory and include the title " John Rose & Co." Some specimen plates presented to the Victoria and Albert Museum in 1850 are marked ' John Rose & Co., Colebrook Dale, 1850."

Another mark of CBD (Colebrook Dale), in monogram was used, c. 1851 to c. 1861, see mark no. 56. It occurs on fine quality specimens in the Godden and other collections. This mark is often in gold. Many Coalport wares are illustrated in Godden's *British Pottery and Porcelain, an Illustrated Encyclopaedia of Marked Specimens.*

Several copies of Chelsea, Sèvres and Dresden factory marks were used by the Coalport firm in the middle of the nineteenth century.

Lord Tweedmouth had a very large Sèvres set, the English supplements to which bear in some cases the double L of Sèvres. To the expert, however, the signs of English paste, glaze, and painting are at once apparent.

A monogram mark no. 57 was used from 1861 to about 1875. This mark, often in gold, may be termed the ampersand mark. The initials C.S.N. stand for Coalport, Swansea and Nantgarw.

From c. 1875 to c. 1881, the mark was "Coalport, A.D. 1750." The crown was added to the above mark about 1881. " England " was added in 1891, mark no. 58. " Made in England " occurs from c. 1920 onwards. Various versions of these marks occur. Mark no. 59 is used after World War II.

The style of the firm was Messrs. John Rose & Co. John Rose died in 1841; he was succeeded by his nephew, W. F. Rose, who was succeeded by William Pugh. In 1889 Charles Bruff was managing director of the new Coalport China Company. In 1925 the firm was purchased by Cauldon Potteries Ltd. and re-established at Stoke-on-Trent in 1926. Various changes have since taken place and the firm was taken over by E. Brain & Co. Ltd. in 1958.

BENTHALL, near Broseley. Maw & Co. were makers of the encaustic tile pavements in the mediaeval style, for public or private buildings; their productions had a very extensive sale. George Maw presented to the Geological Museum a very important collection of raw materials of pottery and porcelain, as well as specimens of the clays and plastic strata of Great Britain, which has been rendered all the more valuable by the catalogue and description, written by himself, a practical potter, printed in an appendix of the second edition of the Museum Catalogue, revised and aug-

56

57

ENGLAND

COALPORT.
A.D. 1750.

58

59

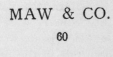

MAW & CO.

60

mented by Trenham Reeks and F. W. Rudler, London, 1871. Maw & Co. also contributed numerous examples of modern enamelled majolica, manufactured at the Benthall works, consisting of vases, pateræ, medallions, friezes, tiles, etc.

Mark no. 60, c. 1852+. The firm of Maw & Co. Ltd. still continues.

MADELEY (Salop). Thomas Martin Randall, like Billingsley, was a most energetic potter, though equally restless. He and his brother, Edward

Randall, practised their art first in the Caughley manufactory; thence Thomas Martin Randall went to Derby, and then to Pinxton. He afterwards went to London with Mr. Robins, and carried on a business at Islington, using Nantgarw white china, and decorating it especially after the manner of Sèvres.

It was to this firm that the Mortlock of those days sent white Nantgarw china to be decorated, and it is also to Randall's skill that we owe a good deal of so-called " Sèvres " porcelain which was decorated by him for some of the London dealers. Genuine old soft paste Sèvres, with a slight amount of decoration, was bought, and any enamel colour removed by the application of powerful acids, and Randall then added some of the beautiful ground colours for which the Sèvres factory was famous, and the cupids, birds, and flowers on the white reserves. That he declined from conscientious scruples to forge the Sèvres mark is quite probable; but when the former Editor's father, Samuel Litchfield, was a young man, the expression applied to a certain class of redecorated Sèvres was that of " quaker," alluding to Randall's work. In 1813 there was a sale at Sèvres of a quantity of undecorated china, and doubtless some of this was afterwards embellished by Randall. He also decorated some of Minton's productions in the Sèvres manner, and there are many doubtful specimens in our public and private collections which may be imputed to him.

Robins and Thomas Martin Randall dissolved partnership about the year 1826, and the latter set up in Madeley, Shropshire, a china manufactory complete in all its branches. Thomas Wheeler, William Roberts, and F. Brewer were potters there. Philip Ballard, Robert Grey, and John Randall (later a painter at Coalport, and author of several works on local matters) were the principal painters.

A beautiful body was the characteristic of this manufactory; it was in appearance a body partaking of the character of Nantgarw and Sèvres, and has often been mistaken for the latter, especially as Sèvres decorations were very successfully imitated there.

They turned out a variety of fine wares, dogs and other animals, after the manner of the Derby, very carefully modelled. Only one marked example is recorded: a lion—" T M R Madeley S."

Statuettes of the human figure were also made in this factory, besides the ordinary wares for table use and ornament. The manufacture of this Madeley paste was, like that of Nantgarw, very costly, and heavy losses occurred in the firing processes, so much so that occasionally the whole contents of a kiln melted together, and the débris was wheeled into the canal hard by. Mr. Randall subsequently went to Shelton.

In the *Gentleman's Magazine* for October 1859 we find the following : " At Shallowford, in the Quakers' burying ground, a quiet sunny spot, within hearing distance of the murmurings of the Trent, were laid the last remains of a good and clever man,—Thomas Martin Randall. Born at Broseley, he served his time, like the late Herbert Minton's father, at Caughley, the earliest of our Shropshire porcelain works, and the nursery of a class of very clever men. From thence he removed to Coalport, thence to London, afterwards to Madeley, and thence to the Potteries, where he succeeded, after great perseverance and expense, in producing specimens of porcelain equal to those he made his model,—the highest productions of the Royal Sèvres Works in the palmy days of Louis XIV. [XV.]. 'Ay, sir,' said a well-known dealer in the Strand in our hearing, 'the old Quaker stands first, at the top of the tree, but he will not put the French mark on his ware (the double L), or I could sell any quantity at the tip-top price old Sèvres china sells for. He has a conscientious objection, and would not be a party to deception.' For a quarter of a century he was the advocate and supporter of the Temperance cause. When the movement first came up, he emptied his barrels, cut them in two for tubs, and had the mashing-stick made into a good stout walking-staff, which until his death he carried as a trophy of the victory he had achieved over popular prejudice and long-continued habit." His nephew, John Randall, is at present engaged at the Coalport works as an artist, and is the author of an interesting illustrated work entitled *The Severn Valley*, published in 1862.

WORCESTER

Collectors of some years standing may have noticed with regret that the time honoured term " Dr. Wall period " (1751–1783) has been generally replaced by the more accurate but less interesting descriptive designation " First period." This covers the period until Dr. Wall's death in 1776.

The first indication of this change became apparent on the publication in 1954 of H. Rissik Marshall's *Coloured Worcester Porcelain of the First Period*. Mr. T. Leonard Crow, in an article in *The Antique Collector*, February 1960 (reprinted in *BADA* the journal of the British Antique Dealers' Association), gave added publicity to the inaccuracy of the old term and the reader will now find the use of " First period " rapidly spreading.

The extensive mansion, afterwards called " The Royal Worcester Porcelain Works," was a fine specimen of ancient domestic architecture; it was situated near the Bishop's Palace, and faced the river Severn. The view from the back commanded the whole range of the Malvern Hills. The house was formerly the residence of the " Warmstreys," but its history can be traced back to the reign of Henry VII, when it was occupied by Sir William Windsor (second Lord Windsor), ancestor of the late Earl of Plymouth. In 1751 this mansion was taken for the establishment of a manufactory of porcelain by Dr. John Wall, a physician and good practical chemist, who, in conjunction with others, formed the Worcester Porcelain Company. The original factory was demolished early in 1960 and a new technical college built on the site. There was an important early link with Benjamin Lund's factory at Bristol where the soap rock body was first introduced. Worcester porcelain is of a compact, soft paste body which included soap rock.

Dr. Wall was born at Powick, a village near Worcester, in 1708. His father was a tradesman in Worcester, and served the office of Mayor in 1703. Dr. Wall's father dying while he was young, he was educated at the King's School, and in 1726 went to Worcester College, Oxford. In 1735 he became a Fellow of Merton College, and in 1739 he took his degree and commenced practice at Worcester. He married (in 1740) Catherine Sandys, cousin of the first Lord Sandys. Independent of his being an excellent chemist, he was an artist of great ability. He painted several historical pictures, among which may be mentioned that of the Founder of Merton in his robes, which he presented to that college in 1765; the Head of Pompey brought to Caesar, now at Hagley; the Judgment of Brutus; the Return of Regulus to Carthage; Queen Eleanor sucking the Poison from the Arm of Edward I, and many others; he etched several plates, and made some designs for stained glass windows. Dr. Wall died at Bath on 27th June, 1776.

Dr. W. Bayliss .	.	£675 0 0
Edward Cave .	.	. 562 10 0
Richard Holdship .	.	562 10 0
Richard Brodribb .	.	225 0 0
John Brodribb ⎱	.	. 225 0 0
John Berwick ⎰		
Josiah Holdship .	.	450 0 0
John Thorneloe .	.	337 10 0

Dr. John Wall .	.	. £225 0 0
William Davis	.	. 225 0 0
Edward Jackson	.	. 225 0 0
Samuel Bradley	.	. 225 0 0
John Doharty, junior	.	225 0 0
Samuel Pritchett	.	. 225 0 0
William Oliver	.	. 112 10 0

The above is a list taken from the partnership deeds or " articles for carrying on the Worcester Tonquin Manufacture," which bears the date 4th June, 1751, and is taken from a copy of the original, kindly supplied by R. W. Binns. In the copy of " the partnership deeds," the signatures of the partners are all in facsimile.

The entire property of the Worcester Porcelain Company was sold by auction in January 1772 for the sum of £5250; it was purchased nominally by the Rev. T. Vernon, who gave up possession in favour of Dr. Wall, but he was only taking charge of the works until the new company could be formed. In January 1773 the following gentlemen were selected : —

John Wall the elder, M.D.	Rev. Thomas Vernon.
William Davis the elder, apothecary.	Robt. Hancock, engraver.
William Davis the younger, gent.	Richard Cook, of London.

A cylindrical mug, painted with blue flowers, of the well-known Worcester type, formerly in the possession of Mr. J. L. Baldwin, has deeply scratched in the paste the date "July 13, 1773," which probably refers to the first issue of the ware made by the new firm, on which occasion a number of these common mugs may have been distributed to the people connected with the works as mementoes of the event. In 1774 Hancock sold his share in the manufactory for £900. On the 10th of April 1783 the entire property was sold to Messrs. Flight for £3000.

BLUE AND WHITE. There is great variety in the blue decorated Worcester, or " blue and white " as it is generally called, not only in design and merit of execution, but in kind and quality of paste. The most complete collection of the various kinds is that in the Dyson Perrins Museum at the Royal Worcester Porcelain Works, which contain between 300 and 400 specimens, from fine eggshell porcelain equal to Oriental and most carefully printed with blue transfer, to pieces of more ordinary domestic ware. The " Workmen's Marks " (marks 51 to 123) are generally found on these early pieces of blue and white. The painted examples are distinguished from the printed by having, as a rule, the open or outlined crescent on the former and the filled-in crescent on the latter. Under glaze blue decoration was cheap to produce as it only required two firings.

One can only ascribe a date to those specimens by considering the kind of decoration and the shape of the piece on which it occurs. Generally speaking, the blue decoration is supposed to be that adopted in the earlier period of the works, but some finely-painted blue and white specimens which, judging from the moulds of the articles decorated, would point to the blue decoration being used for a long period. The Dyson Perrins Museum contains a mug painted in blue with St. George and the Dragon dated 1776 and other late examples of good blue and white Worcester porcelain.

A noteworthy class of early Worcester porcelain is decorated with over-glaze transfer printed motifs. R. W. Binns, speaking of the transfer-printed Worcester china, says: " It may be well to note that all the black printing was done on the glazed surface of the ware, and passed through the enamel kiln fire only." There are a few specimens which show that Dr. Wall was desirous of introducing an underglazed colour in addition to blue for these engraved patterns.

The Worcester transfer-printed " King of Prussia " mugs may be thus described: They are printed in black, and commencing from the handle to the left we find a three-quarter portrait of Frederick the Great; he is in armour, with a cloak lined with ermine thrown over his shoulder, pointing with his finger, and a full-bottomed wig on his head, without any hat; the inscription is " King of Prussia," and at the bottom is R.H. in mono-gram and an anchor, the rebus of Richard Holdship, and the date 1757; above, to the left, is a small cupid. The next subject is a large trophy of arms, among which are three flags, enumerating his nine great battles; and thirdly, a large figure of Fame; they are printed over the glaze. (*Ker. Gall.*, fig. 573.) Slight variations occur, some examples are not dated.

Formerly undue importance has been ascribed to Richard Holdship (and his anchor rebus) in connection with Worcester printed wares. Hold-ship went to Derby in 1764. The true spirit behind the Worcester printed decorations was Robert Hancock, who had earlier worked at the Battersea enamel factory, and at the Bow works up to about 1756.

Robert Hancock was the most skilful engraver employed at Worcester in engraving copper plates for the purpose of transfer. The excellence for which Worcester printed porcelain has always been distinguished is due to his super-vision; he sometimes included his name in full in the design. It is not known at what time he first worked there, but it was previous to 1757. Hancock was celebrated as a line engraver, and in 1765 instructed pupils in his art; he became a proprietor and director of the works in 1772, but his partnership was not of long duration, as he left in consequence of some disputes with the other partners in 1774.

A complete list of known Hancock prints (with much relevant informa-tion) is contained in Cyril Cook's *The Life and Work of Robert Hancock* (1948) and in the 1955 supplement to this work.

These transfer prints were sometimes overpainted with semi-trans-lucent colours, but the pieces on which colouring appears are now extremely rare. Frederick Litchfield had a complete porcelain tea-service of printed transfer, beautifully painted in colours heightened with gold, of landscapes, ruins and figures, evidently in imitation of Dresden; and to carry out the similarity every piece has underneath the imitation Dresden mark of the crossed swords as copied at Worcester, with the figure 9 beneath. In the Museum at Worcester are good specimens of this coloured-over transfer printing. (*Ker. Gall.*, fig. 579.)

The Dyson Perrins Collection includes an important hexagonal vase of yellow ground (very rare), with the views and ruins in coloured transfer, and also a pair of vases of similar shape and views, but with the ground of blue salmon-scale. There is a companion to the Dyson Perrins' yellow vase in the Victoria and Albert Museum (Schreiber Collection). It is very seldom that we find this transfer decoration with coloured grounds.

BAT-PRINTING succeeded the printing from engraved or etched copper plates about 1795. This new style, instead of being first printed upon paper and then transferred, was accomplished thus: The plate was stippled with a fine point by London artists, after designs by Cipriani, Angelica Kauffmann, and Cosway, and the engravings of Bartolozzi, so fashionable about the beginning of the last century—landscapes, shells, fruit, flowers, etc. The copper-plate being carefully cleaned, a thin coating of linseed oil was laid upon it, and removed by the palm of the hand from the surface, leaving the oil in the engraved crevices; instead of paper, bats of glue were used, cut into squares the size of the engraving; one of these bats was pressed on to the plate, so as to receive the oil out of the engraved parts, and laid on the china so as to deliver the oil marks on to its surface; it was then dusted with the colour required, the superfluous colour being removed carefully with cotton-wool, and then placed in the kiln. Some specimens of bat-printed Worcester are also in the museum of the Royal Porcelain Works. Bat-printing went out of favour about 1830.

Besides the decoration of Worcester porcelain by transfer-printing, the earlier specimens were also decorated in imitation of Chinese and Japanese specimens, and not only the patterns copied, but the marks also. The conventionalised chrysanthemum (so common on Japanese porcelain) we find introduced into the designs of tea and coffee services.

From about 1768 the Chelsea influence made itself felt and some very fine and valuable specimens were produced. Vases and services with rich scale grounds of blue, and (very rarely) pink, apple green, canary yellow, crimson lake (rare), turquoise blue, and a pale orange generally in bands, also rich dark mazarine blue (without scale), having panels of exotic birds and flowers with enrichments of gold most carefully and elaborately executed—this class of Worcester (*Ker. Gall.*, plate 7), so well known and highly prized by collectors, was made at this time. The directors of the Worcester factory during this, the period of their greatest excellence, drew their inspiration from many sources. The Chinese figures with pagodas, etc., and quaint birds are quite in the rococo style affected by Thomas Chippendale, which was the decorative fashion of the time; sometimes the oriental designs are more strictly copies of Chinese patterns. The designs of Sèvres were copied, and can trace the influence of the Meissen School, also that of Venice, in many of the Worcester styles of decoration.

Figure subjects are very rare. Apart from the work of John Donaldson, which has been more fully noticed in a subsequent paragraph, and the work of O'Neale, which was generally represented by animal painting, there are, only two main kinds of figure painting on the typical blue-scale ground Worcester. Chinese figures, rendered somewhat in the European manner, appear on pairs of vases and on some large-sized breakfast cups and saucers, and figures in conversational subjects after the manner of Watteau on only two services of tea and coffee sets with the blue-scale ground. There are some illustrations in R. L. Hobson's book, and when any specimens of these figure-painted services appear a very high price is given. This figure painting was executed by artists engaged from the Chelsea Works, and the date of their first migration to Worcester is said to be about 1763, but it may have spread over a considerable period. In the reply to the advertisement by Giles, which is alluded to below, the Worcester proprietor especially mentions the engagement of painters from Chelsea.

The Worcester Works Museum includes a magnificent vase of rich dark blue ground, 14½ in. high; this was originally one of a set of three, painted with lion, bear and boar hunting scenes, and signed " O'Neale pinxt "; also another pair with Aeneas bearing Anchises, and the rape of Helen, signed by the same artist and dated 1769; and these are evidence that O'Neale did more important work for Worcester than he has hitherto had credit for. This set of vases is illustrated in Litchfield's *Pottery and Porcelain*, revised edition, 1953.

There are some Worcester vases with finely-painted classical subjects and figures by John Donaldson, who obtained medals from the Society of Arts for the best enamel paintings in the years 1765 and 1768, formerly in the possession of the Right Hon. W. E. Gladstone. It would appear from the evidence of an unfinished vase that Donaldson painted, or at least had his work fired at the factory. But if Donaldson was not engaged at Worcester, it is probable that these vases were purchased there in the white and decorated in London—a common occurrence. Binns was of this opinion; he says: " The peculiar character of Worcester china was generally acknowledged about the year 1760, for both prior and subsequent to that date an artificer named James Giles of Kentish Town advertised to " procure and paint for any person, Worcester porcelain to any or in any pattern! " This is the " Gyles " alluded to by Thomas Craft in his account of the Bow bowl in the British Museum, and here, no doubt, were fired the fine vases by Donaldson, and many other specimens which occasionally puzzle us as to their parentage. Donaldson was born in 1737, and died in destitute circumstances in 1801, brought about by his developing a religious mania, which ruined his work. Duvivier also painted figure subjects on Worcester porcelain in the 1770's. Examples are very rare.

In R. L. Hobson's important work on Worcester porcelain, published in 1910, he mentions that this advertisement of Giles produced an immediate challenge from the Worcester Factory in the announcement that the proprietors " had engaged the best painters from Chelsea, etc., and that any orders will be executed in the highest taste, and much cheaper than can be afforded by any *Painters in London*."

In 1770 the stock-in-trade of this Giles was advertised for sale " at the large warehouse in Cockspur Street, near Mr. Pinchbeck's, the whole consisting of elegant dessert services, fine tea sets, caudles curiously enamelled in figures, birds, flowers, etc., and ornamented with mazarine, and sky blue and gold. Every article in this sale is the sole property, and has been enamelled in London by, and under the proprietor of the said warehouse, who having at present a large quantity of white china, continues to execute all orders to any pattern, at the shortest notice, and may be spoke with daily at the above warehouse."

The varied work of the decorator, James Giles, is discussed at length in a paper by the late W. B. Honey printed in the *Transactions of the English Ceramic Circle*, vol. 1, part 5. See also a paper by W. H. Tapp printed in the same *Transactions*, vol. 3, part 5.

The Sheldon Collection contained a cup and saucer which bears two marks of considerable interest in connection with Giles' mark. The seal mark is in red, and the crescent is in blue; on the one piece the two marks are distinct (marks 33 and 34), while in the other the blue crescent shows distinctly through the red seal mark (mark 35). A red anchor and a gold crescent also occur on some outside decorated Worcester porcelain.

FIGURE WORK AT WORCESTER. In previous editions of Chaffers attention was drawn to the strong evidence of figures and groups having been made at the Worcester factory. The examples ascribed to Worcester in these earlier editions are Bow. Worcester figures are generally simple; the models include a pair of Turks, a gardener and companion. These and other rare models are illustrated in H. R. Marshall's *Coloured Worcester Porcelain of the First Period* (1954). Attention was first drawn to the true Worcester figures by the late Wallace Elliot in a paper published in the *Transactions of the English Ceramic Circle*, vol. 1, part 2.

PASSAGES FROM THE DIARY OF MRS. PHILIP LYBBE POWYS

(in which " china ornamental figures " are mentioned)

A.D. 1771, p. 125 (Longmans & Co.)

" *Aug. 28th.*—Our next stage to Pershore, through the Vale of Evesham, so famed of old for fine grain of all kinds. Our last stage that night was by moonlight. Got to Worcester about nine, ourselves nor little companion not the least fatigued, though a long journey for a boy of 6 years old, but novelties took up his attention, and the day passed agreeably even without sleep.

" Worcester city in some parts well built, fine Assembly room, excellent town hall. Cathedral indifferent and a large infirmary now building. As to its China Manufacture 'tis more worth seeing than anything I hardly ever did see. They employ 160 persons, a vast number of them very little boys. There are eleven different rooms in which the employment is as follows : First room; a mill for grinding the composition to make the clay. 2nd : the flat cakes of clay drying in ovens. 3rd : the cakes worked up like a paste and formed by *the eye only* into cups, mugs, basins, teapots; their ingenuity and quickness at this appear like magic. 4th : making the things exactly by moulds all to one size, but they are seldom different, so nice is their eye in forming. 5th : paring and chipping coffee cups and saucers in moulds, a boy turning the wheel for each workman. 6th : making the little vases, handles, twists and flowers one sees on the China fruit baskets, all these stuck on with a kind of paste. 7th : scalloping saucers, &c., with a penknife while the composition is pliable, and in this room they make the *China ornamental figures;* these are done in moulds; separate moulds for the limbs and stuck on as above. 8th : the heat of this eighth room was hardly bearable, filled with immense ovens for baking the China, which is put in a sort of high sieve about 6 ft. long. 9th : glazing the china by dipping it into tubs of liquor and shaking it as dry as they can. 10th : some sorting the China for painting, others smoothing the bottom by grinding. 11th : painting the China different patterns. I rather wondered they did not in one room exhibit their most beautiful china finished. They did, it seems, till finding people examined it too long and so took up too much of the men's time, so now they send it to the shops in Worcester for sale. You pay for seeing the Manufacture by putting what you please in a box at the gate."

FLIGHT and later periods. In 1783 Flight, the company's London agent, purchased the entire property, and placed his two sons, Joseph and John, in the business, which continued increasing in prosperity, a new life being instilled into the works, and the ware as well as the decoration improved greatly.

George III visited the works in August 1788, and gave his patronage to Flight, after which they were called the Royal Worcester Porcelain Works, and the crown was added to the mark. In 1793 Martin Barr was taken into partnership. Some very expensive services were made for the royal family and the nobility, the Emperor of Russia, etc.

In the museum at the Worcester factory there are specimen plates of some of the special services made for royalty. George III, George IV (as Regent), with royal arms richly emblazoned, and also a very beautiful service made in 1792 for H.R.H. the Duke of Clarence, with rich blue and gold border, and a figure of Hope in different positions, painted in sepia by John Pennington, who was engaged in 1789. Presentation services were also made about this time for Lord Nelson, of which there are specimens in the Worcester Works Museum, besides those in several private collections.

One of the most noteworthy of these Nelson services is that inscribed " Nelson, 2nd April, Baltic," within oak and laurel wreaths, and having also a large anchor. This service was in Lord Bridport's possession until July 1895, when it was sold at Christie's, and the thirty cups and saucers with ten other pieces realised a total of £700.

Another of the " Nelson " services is that which was presented by the Corporation of the City of London after the battle of Copenhagen. The service is decorated with oak leaf and acorn border, laurel wreath and anchor in the centre of each plate, with dates commemorating the battles of the Nile, Baltic, and St. Vincent. Continental (hard paste) copies of these " Nelson " services exist.

From about 1792 to about 1807 the Worcester factory was carried on under the title Flight & Barr. In 1807 to 1813 the firm was (Martin) Barr, (Joseph) Flight and (Martin) Barr (junior). In 1813 to 1840 it was (Joseph) Flight, (Martin) Barr, and (George) Barr.

Solomon Cole, who was a pupil of Thomas Baxter, the accomplished artist of the Worcester porcelain manufactory, and who was himself for many years a painter there, gave us many particulars of the works while under the management of Flight, Barr and Barr. He being as it were the last link of the old works, his personal reminiscences will be read with interest. He says:—-

" The painting-room was a hundred feet long. There were several peculiarities. connected with the manufactory of Messrs. Flight, Barr & Barr, one of which was that of paying the painters by *time* and not by *the piece*. This plan was wholly confined to them, and they adopted it to secure the greatest possible degree of excellence in all that they produced. Their business too was strictly of a private character; their orders came from the nobility and most of the distinguished families of the United Kingdom; they kept no traveller, nor did they transact business with retail houses.

" The slightest patterns produced by them were always painted, not printed, as is often the case, consequently their ordinary services were expensive. The quality of their gold has never been surpassed. Mr. Barr always prepared the gold himself, and obtained the best possible quality, which was used as well for the slightest patterns as for the most elaborate.

" The colours, too, were always ground as fine as possible, and fully prepared for the painter's use. The *bleu du roi* was painted upon the biscuit, and consequently under the glaze : hence arose the extreme purity and brilliancy of the gold laid upon it.

" Before grounds were dusted upon the border of the plate or upon vases, they were laid of one uniform even tint with a large flat brush. This was very skilfully done by James Tomlins, who excelled all others in this peculiar branch. It was the custom of Messrs. Flight, Barr & Barr to select those best qualified to paint the different parts in any rich piece, and who excelled in some particular branch. One was chosen to paint the embossed parts to receive the gold, another would be engaged in laying on the gold in armorial bearings, a third would shade the gold, another would be selected to paint the supporters, varying according to the design. If the subject was the royal arms, one would paint the lion in flat gold, another would shade the gold and give expression to the lion after the piece had been burnt. Another would paint the unicorn. The best flower-painter would be selected to paint the rose, thistle, and shamrock, and another would write the motto. By these means the greatest perfection was obtained.

" Frequently, on Messrs. Martin and George Barr going round the painting-room, which was their custom twice a day, they would say to the painters engaged upon the richest services, ' We want you to consider this as jewellery—we wish you to take all possible pains.' This was particularly the case when the dessert service was being executed for his Majesty William IV., a plate of which service, that was retained by the manufacturers as an example of their productions, has since realised by auction no less a sum than £34. Another mark of distinction was that of never employing females to paint. None were ever employed except as burnishers; and this branch of the manu- facture is particularly suitable to them. The burnishing room was over the painting room, and occupied one half the length, 50 feet; the other half was devoted to the finished productions and private use of the firm.

" The burnishers were presided over for many years by Mrs. Hunt, who devoted most of her time in skilfully papering up the finished pieces ready for the packer. The only other female employed was Mrs. Lowe, who had a room to herself, and was engaged principally in printing the names of the firm in a circular form on the back of each rich and important piece, and in occasionally printing shells and figures, as already described, in one colour, sometimes in a grey tint, and at others in a warm self-colour. On each plate of the very rich services, the names of the firm, &c., were written with a pen in gold by Joseph Cotterell. He also wrote with a pen in colour the subjects of the figure pieces and the names of the views. John Bly, who came from Lowestoft, excelled in shading the gold in arms, and was unequalled in giving a natural expression to the lion in the royal arms or wherever it occurred, and took that part in the grand service made for his Majesty William IV. above alluded to. His son John continued with the firm until the breaking up of that establishment. He painted landscapes, and was occasionally otherwise engaged. Ishmael Sherwin was chiefly engaged in designing patterns and in decorating the rich pieces with gems, &c., and attended principally to the embossed gold. He was a fine ornamental gilder. Thomas Baxter, who was first employed in Worcester in 1815, may be said to stand unrivalled in this country as a classical figure-painter on porcelain. He had one advantage over others, that of being a student of the Royal Academy for some years, and was esteemed one of the best draughtsmen of his time.

" Mr. Baxter's father had workshops at No. 1 Goldsmith Street, Gough Square, London, for painting and gilding china, obtained principally from France and Staffordshire. Mr. Baxter, jun., his son, established a school of art during his stay at Worcester, from 1814 to 1816; among other of his pupils were Doe, Astles, Webster, Pitman, Lowe, and Cole. His fine productions on porcelain elevated the taste, and his tuition cultivated the talent of several others of that period; two of whom succeeded him as figure-painters after his death, which occurred in 1821—viz., Thomas Lowe and Solomon Cole.

" It may be said of this manufactory that it was a school of art; not only were those engaged in the higher branches emulated byBaxter's works, but those who ornamented his productions by gilding and adding gems round the subjects were stimulated to the greatest possible pains—taking care to render their part of the performance worthy of him who, by his excellent productions, was setting them so good an example; even the potters could not fail to receive benefit from those for whom they were producing such excellent forms, the like of which up to that period had never been produced in this country. Examples of them are rarely to be found except in the collections of the nobility.

" It is not always the most elegant forms that are best adapted for porcelain. Messrs. Flight, Barr & Barr, knowing that the Etruscan shapes presented a greater amount of plain surface than any other, had the good taste to adopt them, being desirous of introducing as much art as possible into their manufacture. These classical forms admitted of figures being painted upon them without the disadvantage of the limbs being distorted by the curvature of the lines, or the building in landscapes losing their perpendicular. The most elegant form in porcelain that can possibly be produced is of little value compared with what it becomes when colour and artistic decoration are added to it; and upon the quality of these is the value of the vase estimated.

" While these Etruscan shapes are classical and severe in form, they may be also said to be complex, always having handles, and great skill being required in their production; while ornaments without handles, however elegant in form, cannot please in the same degree, because they can be produced by far more simple means, viz., by the thrower on the wheel in clay or the turner in wood.

" At the same time that Thomas Baxter was engaged in painting classical figure subjects on vases, some of which were 22 inches in height, John Pennington was devoting his talent to rustic figures, while Samuel Astles and Henry Stinton were painting groups of flowers on similarly shaped vases. There were also flower-painters subordinate to them. Then there were also Messrs. Thomas Rogers, John Barker, and John Smith at the same time painting landscapes. Barker excelled in painting shells, and was engaged in that part of the celebrated service made for Watson Taylor, Esq.; William Doe painted natural birds, feathers, insects, &c.; Charles Stinton painted fancy birds, &c.; Thomas C. Crowther painted flowers, and was particularly gifted in painting the cowslips with great delicacy. At the same period the celebrated bird-painter, George Davis, usually called Dr. Davis, added his brilliant colouring in the rich plumage of his birds to the decoration of these Etruscan forms, a beautiful example of which, painted on one side with exotic birds by Davis, and on the other a group of flowers by Stinton, with a garnet ground, is in the possession of Mr. R. C. Tennant of Kensington

" In the collection of Sir Arthur Guinness (Lord Ardilaun) are three of these Etruscan-shaped vases of the larger size painted by Baxter, and by the same hand, upon smaller vases, are seven other figure subjects set round with pearls and gems.

" A fourth vase of an extremely elegant shape, also in the same collection, is painted with flowers by Astles. These choice specimens, with many others, were produced between the years 1815 and 1821, in which latter year Baxter died.

" Soon after Baxter arrived at Worcester, and was engaged by Messrs. Flight, Barr and Co., he painted a cabinet plate, the subject of which was Mrs. Siddons in the character of the ' Tragic Muse,' which the then Marquis of Stafford purchased for fifty guineas. A second plate was afterwards painted by Baxter, precisely the same in all respects, which was in the collection of Mr. H. Rokeby Price. Mr. H. T. Hope, the great virtuoso, invited Baxter to view his collection of pictures, china, &c., and during the inspection he handed a plate to Baxter, remarking how much it was to be regretted that we had no artist who could paint on china in so good a style, at the same time saying, ' I bought this in Paris,' and that ' the like had never been seen in this country '; when Baxter said, ' I have seen this plate before.' ' No,' said Mr. Hope, ' that is impossible.' Mr. Baxter replied, ' I have not only seen this plate before, but I painted it.' This was no doubt a French plate painted by Baxter for his father before he left home for Worcester. The painters never marked the pieces at Barrs', not even the superior and highly-decorative specimens. The name of the artist was always sent to London with the vase that was painted by him."

Painters employed at Messrs Flight, Barr & Barr's in 1819, and who continued until the breaking up of their establishment, except Billingsley, who established works at Nantgarw, and Cole and Lowe, who left to pursue a higher line of art:—

JOHN PENNINGTON (painted the beautiful service of H.R.H. the Duke of Clarence).
SOLOMON COLE (pupil of Baxter).
CHARLES STINTON (flowers).
WILLIAM RICHARDS (flowers).
WILLIAM TAYLOR (blue paintings).
JOHN BARKER (shells).
WILLIAM WOODS figures).
GEORGE DAVIS (exotic birds after the Chelsea style until 1816; he afterwards worked for Chamberlain).
WILLIAM DOE (figures and landscapes).
SAMUEL ASTLES (flowers).
THOMAS RICHARDS (flowers).
BILLINGSLEY (celebrated flower-painter, also of Derby and Nantgarw).
BREWER (from Derby, painted landscapes in a style peculiar to himself.

JOSEPH COTTRELL.	JAMES TOMKINS.	JOHN SMITH.
THOMAS ROGERS.	THOMAS HOLLOWAY.	ISHMAEL SHERWIN.
THOMAS LOWE.	WILLIAM HOLLOWAY.	THOMAS PEUGH.
JAMES LOWE.	JOHN LEAD.	JAMES BRADLEY.
DARBY ROGERS.	THOMAS DOBBS.	THOMAS BAXTER.
JOHN JONES.	THOMAS DUTTON.	CHARLES RICHARDS.
J. C. CROWTHER.	THOMAS DUTTON, Jun.	JOHN BLY.
WILLIAM MANASON.	THOMAS SMITH.	JOHN BLY, Jun.
HENRY MANASON.	SAMUEL SMITH.	JOS. TAYLOR.
NICHOLAS PENINGS.	HENRY STINTON.	JOS. NIBLETT.
THOMAS CARADINE.	JOSEPH JONES.	JOS. DOVEY.

Mr. Flight, though in London, never took an active part in the business; Mr. George Barr resided in London for some years, managing the sale of the finished productions, while Martin Barr and a younger brother superintended the manufactory at Worcester. After Mr. Flight's death George Barr went to Worcester, and took his part in the management, leaving a confidential person to preside over the London house, which was situated at No. 1 Coventry Street.

The two principal manufactories of Messrs. Flight & Barr and Messrs. Chamberlain continued working separately until 1840, when the two firms were amalgamated, the plant and stock removed to the premises of the latter, and it was styled Chamberlain & Co. The tile business of Mr. Chamberlain was removed to the old manufactory and worked by the firm; subsequently this section was given up to Messrs. Maw, who about 1853 removed the manufacture to the Benthal Works, near Iron Bridge, in Shropshire. The period 1840–52 is dealt with in the history of Chamberlains later in this chapter.

KERR & BINNS period, 1852–62. It was about that time that Kerr & Binns, the then proprietors, brought into notice the beautiful decoration on porcelain called the "Worcester Limoges," or white enamel painting on dark blue ground. These were principally executed by Thomas Bott, a student of the School of Art, whose works are now eagerly sought after, but whose merit was not perhaps sufficiently estimated as it deserved until his death. These are usually enamelled in light-blue or white camaieu, on dark-blue ground.

George Wallis, in his account of Worcester Porcelain at the International Exhibition of 1862, says: " The examples exhibited amply prove what can be done by an intelligent and earnest continuity of action; and whilst the specimens themselves are of a very varied character, some of them are the most perfect things of the kind ever produced. The dark-blue ground contrasts admirably with the gold enrichments, dead and burnished, whilst the white enamel in its various delicate gradations, from the extremely relieved high light downward, gives a delicacy and purity to the general effect of each piece which renders them covetable objects to all persons of taste." A collection of Bott's enamels can be seen in the works museum; other examples are in the Godden Collection of Victorian ceramics at present displayed at Ragley Hall, Alcester, Warwickshire.

The various styles of porcelain—Ivory body, parian wares, Raphaelesque body, and the normal decorated porcelains produced by Kerr & Binns from 1852 to 1862 are amongst the finest examples of 19th century ceramic art. The shapes and decoration was pleasingly restrained and elegant, the painting and gilding of the highest quality. Marks nos. 135-7.

ROYAL WORCESTER. In 1862 W. H. Kerr, of Kerr & Binns, retired, and on 24th June, 1862, R. W. Binns formed a new joint stock company under the title, the Worcester Royal Porcelain Company—its subsequent products are known, far and wide as "Royal Worcester." Thomas Bott continued to paint his Limoges enamels until his death in 1870 at the age of 41. His work for the " Royal Worcester " company was acclaimed in all the international exhibitions of the period.

Apart from the normal day to day productions, always of the highest quality in finish and design, the Worcester company specialised in exquisite gilt and jewelled work often with reserve panels of classical heads, etc.

About 1870 R. W. Binns, who was continually seeking new ideas, experimented with Japanese motifs. The fashion quickly caught the public's fancy and the Worcester models in this style received world-wide publicity at the International Exhibitions of 1872 and 1873. One critic of the exhibition of 1873 wrote: " We must all feel glad that a works so renowned as the Worcester factory has again taken its legitimate place amongst the chief potters of the world; but what is most interesting in view of our present consideration is the fact that all the finest of the Worcester works have been suggested by oriental examples, and chiefly by works in Japanese lacquer; but the application is both new and clever." It should be stressed that these Japanese wares are not slavish copies of the originals. " . . . he (Binns) has seen and appreciated the value of Japanese Art, and here it is fair to say he has improved where he has borrowed, taking suggestion rather than models." These remarks are equally applicable to the other styles which influenced later Worcester—Persian, Italian, Indian, etc. These Japanese models, figures, vases, centrepieces, gilt services, etc., brought deserved fame to the Worcester modeller, James Hadley, who for a number of years until 1896 modelled a fine range of objects for the company. Many of these pieces incorporate Hadley's signature, see mark no. 162. In 1896 James Hadley and his three sons established their own works at Worcester, see end of this section. The quality of the gilding on the Japanese designs is remarkable.

Towards the end of the 19th century the Royal Worcester excelled in a class of reticulated porcelain. The delicately pierced designs were hand cut by George Owen (given in previous editions as " Allen ") and are marvels of craftsmanship. Inferior wares in this style were produced at the Grainger and Locke factories, also at Worcester. The popular cream ground Worcester with floral sprays was introduced in the late 1880's and continued in production well into the 20th century. This cream ground ware and the cattle and fruit painted pieces are probably the best known examples of Royal Worcester porcelain.

R. W. Binns retired in 1897 and he was succeeded by E. P. Evans, who retired in 1914. Subsequent directors were G. Solon (1914–1927), J. B. Moore (1927-1930) who was succeeded by J. F. Gimson. A list of the more noteworthy Worcester artists of the Kerr & Binns and " Royal Worcester " periods includes:—

BAKER	Floral artist, Kerr & Binns period, 1852–62.
BALDWYN, C. H. C.	Bird subjects, swans, etc., c. 1879 to c. 1904.
BATES, David	Floral artist, c. 1868–80.
BEJOT, E.	Gilder, designs in chased gold, etc., c. 1869–80.

BINNS, Albert	Son of R. W. Binns, rare experimental work, c. 1800, d. 1882.
BOTT, Thomas	B. 1829. Famous for his enamel painting, c. 1852–70, d. 1870.
BOTT, Thomas John	B. 1854, employed c. 1870–85, later Brown-Westhead, Moore and Coalport, d. 1932.
BRADLEY, James	Animal, portrait and floral artist, c. 1852–60.
BRECKNELL, Joseph	Designer and decorator, Chamberlains and Kerr & Binns.
BROCK, Thomas R. A.	B. 1847. Modeller at Worcester, c. 1860, d. 1922.
CALLOWHILL, James	Figure subjects, heads, chased gilding, etc., c. 1855–85.
CALLOWHILL, T. S.	Figure subjects, leads, enamels, gilding, etc., c. 1855–85.
CHIVERS, F. H.	Fruit painter, late 19th century. Later worked for Coalport.
COPSON, Octar H.	Fruit painter, c. 1880.
CROOK, James	Gilt decorative motifs, c. 1885.
DAVIS, Harry	Landscape and general artist of repute, c. 1898–present day.
DAVIS, Josiah	Fine gilder and designer, b. 1839, d. 1913. Employed c. 1855 onwards.
DOE, E., senior	Scenic and figure painter, Chamberlains and earlier.
DOE, E., junior	Scenic and figure painter. Chamberlains and Kerr & Binns period.
EVANS, George	Modeller, c. 1870–1910.
EVANS, David	Floral artist, early Grainger (also Copelands).
FREEMAN, John	Floral and fruit artist, c. 1925–present day.
HAWKINS, William	Figure and fruit painter, c. 1874–1928.
HADLEY, James	B. c. 1837. Modeller. After 1875 worked on his own account. D. 1903.
HOPEWELL, John	Bird subjects, c. 1855–1890.
JOHNSON, George	Exotic and game bird painter, c. 1900–1938.
KIRK, W. B.	B. 1824. Sculptor, modeller. Kerr & Binns period, 1852–62. D. 1900.
LAWTON, Stephen	Enamel and gilt decorations, c. 1857–1870.
LOCKE, Edward	B. 1829. Floral compositions, later on his own account. D. 1909.
LOCKYER, Thomas.	Fruit painter, c. 1900–1935.
OWEN, George	Celebrated designer of openwork cut patterns. Late 19th century, early 20th century. D. 1917.
PALMERE, C.	Figure subjects, etc., c. 1870–80.
PERLING, Robert F.	Landscape and animal subjects, c. 1855–85.
PHILLIPS, Ernest	Floral artist, c. 1890–1935.
POWELL, Walter	Hadley artist, c. 1900.
POWELL, William	British birds, c. 1890–1950.

PRICE, Horace	Floral and print artist, c. 1912–present day.
RABY, Edward	Floral artist, c. 1870–92. Later at Doultons.
RANFORD, Samuel	Gilder and designer, c. 1855–1890.
ROBERTS, Frank	Floral and fruit painter, c. 1900–1920.
RUSHTON, Josiah	Figure painter, c. 1854–71.
SALTER, Edward	Landscape and English cattle, c. 1893–1902.
SEABRIGHT, Richard	Fruit artist, c. 1900–1940.
SHERRIFF, James	Senior: Floral artist, c. 1852–c. 1862.
(senior and junior)	Junior: Butterflies, etc., c. 1880.
STINTON, James	Game bird painter, c. 1900–1951.
STINTON, John	B. 1854. Landscapes, cattle, etc. Originally with Graingers. Late 19th to c. 1938. D. 1956.
STINTON, H.	Landscape and cattle painter, c. 1900–present day.
TAYLOR, William (?)	Floral painter, c. 1845–55.
WEAVER, James	Bird painter, c. 1853–70. Subsequently at Copelands.
WELLS, Luke	Animal subjects, etc., c. 1852–65.
WILLIAMS, Joseph	Animal subjects, scenic, etc., c. 1860–75.

The Harry Davis mentioned in the above list was training in 1961 two promising young artists to follow his style. They were Frank Higgins and Milwyn Holloway.

A fine collection of Worcester porcelain of all periods may be seen in the Dyson Perrins Museum at the factory in Worcester, and at the Victoria and Albert Museum, London. For further information on the 18th century wares, the reader is referred to Marshall's *Coloured Worcester Porcelain of the First Period*, 1954, and to Barrett's *Worcester Porcelain*, 1953, and for the later wares to Binns' *Worcester China—a Record of Forty-five Years*, 1852–1897, and to Godden's *Victorian Porcelain*, 1961. Important specimens of Worcester porcelain of all periods are included in Godden's *British Pottery and Porcelain, an Illustrated Encyclopaedia of Marked Specimens*.

MARKS—FIRST PERIOD. The manufacturers of Worcester seem to have copied the marks of most of the celebrated fabriques in their turn. We find the Oriental and the Dresden, both the caduceus and crossed swords, and sometimes the Chelsea anchor.

Mark no. 1 is one of the earliest marks: a crescent outlined in blue, frequently used, together with other marks, down to 1793, but not after; it is most likely taken from the Warmstrey arms, that being the house where the manufactory was first established. This same mark occurs in gold on dishes and plates painted in fruits, and on a dessert dish of a set made originally for Bishop Sumner, in the Japanese taste, now in the Dyson Perrins Collection. The noted service made for the Duke of Gloucester also bore the gold crescent.

Marks nos 1, 2 and 3 (the open crescent) are the most usual marks on painted wares. The hatched or filled-in crescent (mark no. 4) occurs on blue printed examples. The crescent, incised, is very rare, and occurred on specimen in the Drane Collection.

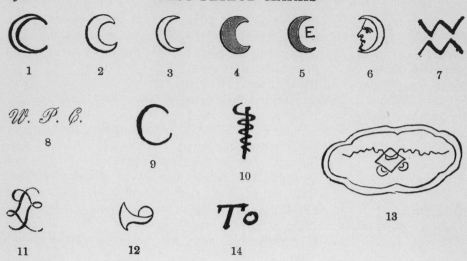

Mark no. 7 is given by R. W. Binns (*A Century of Potting in the City of Worcester*, page 346) as occurring on jugs belonging to the Corporation of Worcester. These are emblazoned with the city's arms and dated 1757. The bowls belonging also to the Corporation are of much later date (1792).

Mark no. 8 (Worcester Porcelain Company). These initials occur on the bottom of a round inkstand painted in blue with flowers (Dyson Perrins Collection). The same letters are placed on the Worcester money tokens mentioned by R. W. Binns.

Mark no 9 in gold, rare.

Mark no. 10, the Dresden mark of the caduceus or wand of Aesculapius is sometimes found, as well as the crossed swords. This, in blue, is on an early basin, moulded pattern and painted in blue flowers.

Mark no. 11. Imitation of the Sèvres mark on a small Worcester tea-cup.

Mark no. 12. Imitation of the Chantilly mark. Two small plates with scalloped edges decorated in flowers, painted in blue, gold, and Indian red. (Dyson Perrins Collection.)

Mark no. 13 and also another very similar occurs on a sauce tureen of an old silver shape, and on the plate decorated in blue and white, in the manner of the old Chinese. The marks are evidently careless copies of those found upon the Chinese specimens from which they are taken. A similar mark occurs on Derby porcelains.

Mark no. 14, c. 1770, is on a quatrefoil-shaped basket pattern tureen of undoubtedly Worcester porcelain. This mark impressed in the paste occurs in the rim of the base, and affords proof that " Tebo," the modeller, whose mark we know on Bristol and Bow specimens, must have also worked at Worcester. Such specimens of Worcester bearing this mark are very rare. R. L. Hobson illustrates an important vase of Worcester, which he attributes to Tebo.

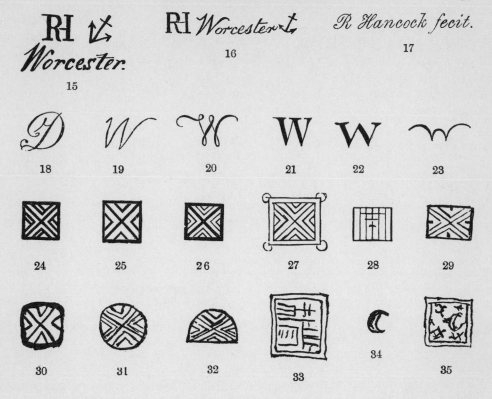

Mark no. 15 occurs on a jug, with portrait of the King of Prussia, dated 1757, in the Victoria and Albert Museum; and on similar mugs both bell-shaped and cylindrical included in many collections.

Mark no. 16 is the anchor rebus mark of Richard Holdship, on a jug with vignettes in black of a child with the cap of liberty and martial trophies, and a portrait of George II and two men-of-war; executed previous to 1760, as the King died in that year.

Mark no. 17 of R. Hancock, found on printed subjects only; his subjects are generally garden scenes and figures. Several pieces of transfer thus signed are in the Worcester Museum, c. 1757+.

Mark no. 18, c. 1770. The initials of John Donaldson, the painter on Worcester porcelain, is occasionally found, as on a set of three vases, gros bleu ground with medallions of mythological subjects.

It may be added here that one of the most decorative and valued patterns of Old Worcester, that of dark Oriental " powder " blue, with fan-shaped panels of birds and flowers, is seldom marked. The apple-green ground Worcester is also usually unmarked.

Marks nos. 21 and 22, the printed W, are very rare. Marks nos. 27, 30, 31 and 32 are all very scarce renderings of the square seal mark. The other square marks nos. 24–26 and the mock Chinese marks nos. 36–41 are more usual. Excellent Worcester is frequently unmarked.

It is not an unusual occurrence to find a pair or set of vases, or parts

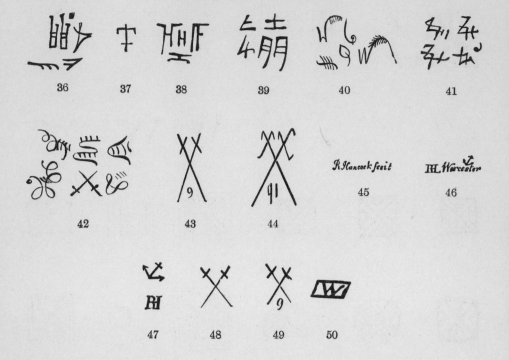

36   37   38   39   40   41

42   43   44   45   46

47   48   49   50

of the same service, with different marks—the W, the crescent, and the square seal. There is a teapot in the Worcester Museum which bears both the square seal and the crescent. Alfred Trapnell had a dish of oriental decoration with the square seal mark in blue and the crescent in *red*. In the same collection were other specimens of blue and white oriental character with both marks (seal and crescent) in blue, and on some of these the seal mark varies considerably. Double marked specimens are also found in the Dyson Perrins Museum. Marks nos. 33, 34, 35 are found on double marked specimens in the Sheldon Collection, and are described earlier in this section in connection with Giles.

Marks nos. 43, 44, 48 and 49. These crossed swords marks vary as regards the numerals between the points of the swords, and sometimes there is a dot between the hilts.

Marks are sometimes inconsistent with the decoration; thus the crossed swords will be found on a black transfer cup and saucer, and the square Chinese seal on a piece decorated in a pattern anything but oriental. This is on account of the blue fabrique mark having been put on before the piece was glazed or decorated.

Marks nos. 51 to 123 are workmen's marks found on specimens of printed and painted blue decoration, c. 1750–65 in the Museum of the Worcester Porcelain Works and in well-known private collections. The Dyson Perrins Collection includes several specimens (blue and white) with marks not quite the same as these but similar.

Mark no. 75 was also used at the Bow factory.

51	52	53	54	55	56	57
58	59	60	61	62	63	64
65	66	67	68	69	70	71
72	73	74	75	76	77	78
79	80	81	82	83	84	85
86	87	88	89	90	91	92
93	94	95	96	97	98	99
100	101	102	103	104	105	106	107
108	109	110	111	112	113	114	115
116	117	118	119	120	121	122	123

FLIGHT, BARR, and FLIGHT & BARR PERIODS. These works were purchased for Joseph and John Flight in 1783, when marks nos. 124 and 125 were used until 1788. The crescent sometimes appears alone. Mark no. 125 is also found in impressed capitals. John Flight died in 1791.

Mark no. 126 was used after the King's visit in 1788 until 1792. Note the addition of the crown. Occasionally we find the older marks occurring in conjunction with the mark of Flight; this is owing to some of the older stock of white china being decorated after the concern was purchased by Flight.

Marks nos. 127 and 128. This letter B is found indented on pieces of this ware between 1793 and 1807, Mr. Barr, senior, having the entire management of the works for a short period, during which this letter was scratched on the clay. The letter B was the initial of Martin Barr, who joined the firm in 1792.

Mark no. 129. At the same period, c. 1792–1807, marks incorporating the names Flight & Barr or the initials F & B may occur.

BARR, FLIGHT & BARR PERIOD. From 1807 to 1813 the firm was Barr, Flight & Barr. The standard mark was the letters B.F.B., with a crown above, impressed or incised in the ware without colour.

Several printed marks occur at this period, all include the name Barr, Flight & Barr or the intials B.F.B. and can consequently be dated 1807–1813. Marks nos. 130, 131, 132.

FLIGHT, BARR & BARR PERIOD. From 1813 to 1840 the firm was entitled Flight, Barr & Barr. Various printed marks may be found incorporating these names. Marks nos. 133 and 134. The impressed initials F.B.B. (with or without crown over) is the mark most frequently met with at this period. When this occurs on B.F.B. shapes, the pieces may be dated c. 1813–25. Later wares may be heavier in feeling. For marks of the 1840–1852 period see the Chamberlain section which follows later.

KERR & BINNS PERIOD. Mark no. 135 was used (both impressed and printed) by Kerr & Binns for porcelain from 1852 to 1862. It has the letter W for Worcester, and in the centre the crescent and 51, representing 1751, the first year that porcelain was manufactured at Worcester.

Mark no. 136 is a printed mark used by Kerr & Binns, the proprietors of this time, for fancy goods, from about 1854 to 1862. This mark was used on the finest specimens, the artist's signature or initials were sometimes placed in the bottom left-hand segment. The last two numerals of the year occur in centre of this mark. These are often indistinct. A special large elaborate mark was used for specimens made for Queen Victoria.

During the Kerr & Binns period (1852–62) several printed marks were employed where the title appears as " W. H. KERR & CO." as mark no. 137. It should be noted that a proportion of Kerr & Binns products were unmarked, but these can be identified by their forms, quality and style of the decoration and gilding.

135   136

137   138

ROYAL WORCESTER PERIOD. In 1862 another joint-stock company was formed, called the Worcester Royal Porcelain Company, R. W. Binns having the direction of the artistic department, for which he was so well qualified. W. H. Kerr withdrew from the old concern on the formation of the new company in 1862.

Under R. W. Binns' direction great improvements were affected, good modellers' and painters' services were secured, and fine work was produced.

The Kerr & Binns circular mark was retained by the new company but a crown was added at the top (mark no. 138). This crowned mark has been used from 1862 to the present day—with various amendments which are here recorded.

A private system of dating was emploqed from 1867 (previous to this, from 1862, the last two numerals of the year may occur under the mark). This dating system was alphabetical, the key is as follows:—

A — 1867	H — 1873	P — 1879	W — 1885
B — 1868	I — 1874	R — 1880	X — 1886
C — 1869	K — 1875	S — 1881	Y — 1887
D — 1870	L — 1876	T — 1882	Z — 1888
E — 1871	M — 1877	U — 1883	o — 1889
G — 1872	N — 1878	V — 1884	a — 1890

a(1890) is in old English script.

Mark no. 139 illustrates the mark for 1890.

In 1890 " ROYAL WORCESTER ENGLAND " was added to the above mark and from 1891 a new system of year dating was introduced:—

In 1892 one dot was added above " Royal."

In 1893 one dot was added above " England," making two in all. One dot was added for each successive year (either at each side or below) until by 1915 there were 24 dots. Mark no. 140 with eleven dots illustrates the mark for 1902.

In 1916 a star was placed below the mark and until 1927 one extra dot was added each year to this star.

In 1928 these were replaced by a square.

In 1929 the square was replaced by a diamond.

In 1930 this was changed to a circle.

In 1931 this was replaced by two interlaced circles.

In 1932 a third circle was added, making three in all.

In 1933 one dot was added to the three interlaced circles. A further dot was added for each year up to 1941 when there were nine dots with the circles.

From 1941 to 1948 annual modification of the trade mark was suspended.

139   140

Subsequent year marks were:—

    1949 — V
    1950 — W
    1951 — W and 1 dot
    1952 — W and 2 dots
    1953 — W and 3 dots
    1954 — W and 4 dots
    1955 — W and 5 dots
    1956 — R in a circle and 6 dots
    1957 — R in a circle and 7 dots
    1958 — R in a circle and 8 dots
    1959 — R in a circle and 9 dots
    1960 — R in a circle and 10 dots
    1961 — R in a circle and 11 dots
    1962 — R in a circle and 12 dots

Other marks were occasionally used from 1862; these all incorporate the words " WORCESTER ROYAL PORCELAIN WORKS." See mark no. 141.

Mark no. 142 is a later " Royal Worcester " mark. The words " Bone China " were added in 1938.

142

141

CHAMBERLAINS. Robert Chamberlain, who was the first apprentice at the Old Worcester Porcelain Company, commenced business with his brother Humphrey, in new premises in High Street about 1789. At first they decorated porcelain, which they bought from Turner of Caughley, who not only supplied the ware from his works to Chamberlain's orders, but sent large quantities to be decorated and returned for his own trade. They took larger premises and their business increased greatly, being honoured with orders from various members of the royal family. A complete service for the East India Company at Madras was supplied at £4,190; another for the Prince Regent cost £4,000. The well-known breakfast service made at Chamberlain's, which is generally supposed to have been presented by the ladies of England to Lord Nelson, was ordered by Nelson himself in 1802, with a dinner service, a pair of vases, with miniatures of Nelson and Lady Hamilton, etc.; but the breakfast set alone was completed, his death occurring in the meantime. This service, in some way, passed from the family, and pieces may be found in the cabinets of most collectors of Worcester china. To give some idea of the prevailing taste for showy china from 1804 to 1811, Chamberlain paid on an average for wages £4,500 per annum, and the amount for gold alone to decorate the porcelain was £900 per annum.

The principal painters were in the first place Humphrey Chamberlain, son of the senior proprietor, whose paintings were of exceedingly high finish; he died in 1824 at the age of 33. The others were Wood and Doe, for landscapes and figures; Davies and Rogers, birds, etc., Steel, fruit; Plant, heraldy. Examples mentioned in previous editions as being signed by E. Doe and " Doe and Rogers " were examples painted independently by these artists; they are interesting but not true Chamberlain pieces.

In the 1820's and 1830's the products of the Chamberlain factory closely followed those of Flight, Barr & Barr. Some magnificent pieces were produced, but the ordinary pieces were generally inferior to those of Flight, Barr & Barr.

In 1840 a joint-stock company was formed with a capital of £40,000, for the purpose of uniting the Flight, Barr & Barr company with that of the Chamberlain company. From this period the marks read " Chamberlain & Co." with the exception of an impressed " CHAMBERLAINS " mark used from 1847 to 1850 (marks nos. 147–150).

Among the new innovations mention should be made of the manufacture of door furniture, porcelain buttons, and openwork designs. Examples exhibited in the 1851 Exhibition included: a tea service of egg-shell china, china plaques finely painted, china bracelets and brooches, inkstands, baskets and large vases variously decorated.

The general reaction to the Chamberlain porcelains of the 1840's and early 50's was not, however, encouraging and one by one the original partners retired, leaving only W. H. Kerr. In 1852 Kerr invited R. W. Binns to join him, and form a completely new company, Kerr & Binns. This new venture was entirely successful and from it rose in 1862, the Worcester Royal Porcelain Company, still in operation.

CHAMBERLAIN MARKS. The early marks from about 1789 to about 1808 are the name Chamberlains Worcester written by hand in enamel colour or in gold. The pattern number was often added to this mark. In common with other porcelains of the period the mark was not always placed on the wares, in some cases only the pattern number was painted near the footrim. Mark no. 143.

From about 1807 various printed marks occur; all marks incorporating the Royal Crown are subsequent to 1811. Particular attention should be paid to the addresses that occur in these marks for by these the period of the piece can be ascertained. Marks nos 144 to 147.

" 63 Piccadilly " was used from 1814 to 1816.
" 155 New Bond Street " occurs from 1816 to 1845.
" No. 1 Coventry Street " occurs from c. 1840 to 1845.

Chamberlains
Worcester
No 70.

143

Chamberlain's
Worcester
& 63, Piccadilly,
London.

144

CHAMBERLAIN & CO.,
WORCESTER
155, NEW BOND STREET
& NO. 1,
COVENTRY ST.
LONDON.

147

145

Chamberlain's
Regent China
Worcester
& 155
New Bond Street,
London.

146

From c. 1811 to c. 1820 a special body term " Regent China " was introduced, mainly for tea, dessert and dinner services. The appearance of this body is hard and glossy. Special marks were used on this ware, and include the name Regent China.

After 1840 and the amalgamation of the Flight, Barr & Barr firm Chamberlain marks read " Chamberlain & Co." (the exception is the impressed " CHAMBERLAINS " mark of 1847–1850). Marks nos 148, 149, 150.

On the cessation of the Chamberlain company in 1852, the works were continued by Kerr & Binns.

THE GRAINGER FACTORY. In 1801 a third Worcester china manufactory was established in St. Martin's Street by Thomas Grainger, nephew of Humphrey Chamberlain. The firm was successively Grainger & Wood, and Grainger, Lee & Co., Mr. Lee having joined about 1812. The early wares were rarely marked. The names as on marks 151 to 153 give the various periods and assist the dating of marked specimens.

George Grainger succeeded his father in 1839. Mark no. 153 is on a mug with a well-finished painting of the city of Worcester, inscribed

Chamberlain & Co; Worcester.
148

CHAMBERLAINS
149

150

Grainger Wood & Co
Worcester Warranted
151

Grainger Lee & Co
Worcester.
152

G GRAINGER
19 FOREGATE
WORCESTER.
154

George Grainger.
Royal China Works,
Worcester.
153

GRAINGER
WORCESTER .
155

G & Co. W.
157

G GRAINGER & CO
MANUFACTURERS
WORCESTER.
156

" Worcester Regatta, 1846," in the Victoria and Albert Museum.

Amongst a collection of several specimens of biscuit china of different factories, including Sèvres, Dresden, and Derby, which is at Knole House, Sevenoaks, there is a set of three ewers and vases with grapes in high relief, marked in cursive letters, " Grainger, Worcester." Similar objects occur in the Grainger pattern books. From 1839 to the period of the 1851 Exhibition the Grainger products closely followed in style those of the Chamberlain factory. The mark prior to 1851 is generally written overglaze as mark no. 153.

Various printed marks occur on mid-nineteenth century wares and incorporate any of the forms of title given by marks nos. 154 to 157.

In 1848, a new body, named " semi-porcelain," was introduced; this had remarkable utilitarian value for it proved extremely durable. Special printed and impressed marks were used for this ware, and date from 1848

G G & Co
SP

158

CHEMICAL PORCELAIN
GRAINGER & Co
MANUFACTURER
WORCESTER.

159

160

162

161

The (experimental) pieces made in 1896 bear a mark either painted or stamped with rubber.

163

From Feb., 1897 to June, 1900, a printed mark

164

From June, 1900 to August, 1902.

165

And from August, 1902 to June 30th, 1905.

166

167      168

onwards. The term " chemical porcelain " also occurs in printed marks from this period. Marks nos. 158 and 159.

The Grainger company produced a wide range of open-work porcelain. Such pieces won high praise at the 1862 Exhibition and were a feature of the factory's productions until the closure. Good parian ware was also made during the second half of the nineteenth century. Pâte-sur-pâte was also produced, and is mainly floral in design. Two versions of a printed shield shaped mark occur on examples from about 1870. Mark no. 160, c. 1870–90, and mark no. 161, c. 1890–1902.

In 1889 the Grainger Company was incorporated in the larger Worcester Royal Porcelain Company, but the works continued in production until 1902.

HADLEY WARE. The celebrated Royal Worcester modeller, James Hadley, established himself in 1875 as an independent designer and modeller but until 1894 his entire output was absorbed by the Royal Worcester Company, mark no. 162. In 1896, with the assistance of his three sons, he began manufacturing on his own account. His products were termed " Hadley Ware " and mainly comprised decorative vases with coloured clay enrichments painted with floral compositions. Many of these are of high quality and are often painted in monochrome. James Hadley died in December 1903 and the business was taken over by the Worcester Royal Porcelain Company in 1905. Mark no. 163 painted or rubber stamped on experimental pieces made in 1896. Mark no. 164 printed, February 1897 to June 1900. Mark no. 165, June 1900 to August 1902. Mark no. 166, August 1902 to 30th June, 1905.

Wares in the Hadley tradition were produced by the " Royal Worcester " company after 1905 and bear the normal Worcester mark, sometimes with the addition of the words " Hadley Ware." Several " Hadley " shapes are used to this day.

A contemporary account of the small factory reads " In his pleasant studio in the High Street of Worcester, and at his new works just built at Diglis you may see his beautiful process carried through from the modelling of the forms to the final burnishing of the completed work of art. . . . To-day (October 1898) may be seen a complete little manufactory with two large kilns, painting room, electric polishing lathe, and grinding machinery complete . . . the ware of Mr. Hadley and his three sons, each of whom has a complete knowledge and direction of his special branch, shows nothing of the amateurism often characteristic of new ventures. It has found its way to appreciation without advertisement of any kind." A fuller account of this quotation is incorporated in G. Godden's *Victorian Porcelain* (1961) and gives an interesting account of the methods of manufacture of " Hadley ware," with its mixture of coloured clays.

LOCKE & COMPANY. In 1895 Edward Locke (b. 1829, d. 1909) established the Shrub Hill Works, assisted by his large family of eleven, many of whom, like Edward, had been trained at the Royal Worcester factory or at Graingers. His products were mainly floral in character and follow closely the Royal Worcester style.

A contemporary (1899) review reads: " In addition to the most costly art pieces which they pride themselves most upon, Messrs. Locke & Co. are producing a very large assortment of fancy goods at very moderate prices." This small factory was closed soon after 1904, mainly due to the fact that Locke lost a law action with the Royal Worcester Company over the use of the word " Worcester " to describe his products. The marks are nos. 167 (c. 1895–1903) and 168 (c. 1903–06).

LEEDS, ROCKINGHAM, SUNDERLAND, HULL, CASTLEFORD, etc.

BISHOPS WALTHAM (Hampshire). This pottery was established in September 1862, when the " Bishops Waltham Clay Company, Limited," was formed, having been promoted by Mr. Helps (author of *Friends in Council*), who at that time owned the Vernon Hill estate, on which the clay works are situated. The manufacture at first consisted of ordinary red ware, red and black bricks, tiles, etc.; and the black bricks used in the construction of Blackfriars Bridge were the production of these works.

In February 1866 the manufacture of *red ware* or *fine art pottery* was commenced. A few hands only were employed upon this branch as an experiment, which, though fairly successful, had only a short existence.

No porcelain was ever made, the terra-cotta jugs, water-coolers, tea-cups and saucers, etc., are of elegant and classical design. A handsome dessert service, intended as a present to the Queen, was contemplated, and it was proposed to have a different design on each plate; only one pattern, however, was struck off, and of this several plates were originally sold at 10s. 6d. each.

The *Art Pottery* manufacture was discontinued in December 1867, the company having gone into liquidation in April of that year, the business being then continued by the liquidators. Examples in the Godden collection bear a printed mark, " Bishops Waltham " within a double lined oval. See Godden's *British Pottery and Porcelain, an Illustrated Encyclopædia of Marked Specimens*.

POTTERS PURY (Northamptonshire). A pottery existed here, as its name indicates, at an early period, but there have been no potters for many years. An old earthen jug was found in the vicinity and was in the possession of Mr. Wake, of Cockermouth; it is of a dark-brown coarse ware, glazed, 8 in. high; the name " Robin Woodward, Yardley Gobion, 1761," is inscribed on the upper part. Yardley Gobion is near Potters Pury.

LITTLE BROUGHTON (Cumberland). About five miles from Cockermouth there was a pottery, established in the beginning of the eighteenth century. The early ware was coarse, with yellow glaze and chocolate ornamentation in dishes, puzzle jugs, &c. The Wedgwoods were concerned in the works, and they also dealt in Burslem wares. *The Cockermouth Guide*, page 127, thus refers to it: "We now proceed direct through the village of Little Broughton towards Dearham. From the first cross-road, distant nearly two miles from the village, we see, four fields beyond, a low, dark-looking building. This is called 'Whistling Syke,' a house built by the grandfather of Josiah Wedgwood, the great potter, in the year 1708. The Wedgwoods were a race of potters, and carried on a small manufactory of earthenware. The father also resided here at the birth of his son Josiah in 1730."

PLACE WARE. YORK. There was a manufactory established at the Manor House, York, about 1665, of which little is known except the mention of its existence by Ralph Thoresby and Horace Walpole. In Walpole's *Catalogue of Engravers* we learn that "Mr. Place was a gentleman of Yorkshire, and had a turn for most of the beautiful arts. He painted designs and etched. . . He was a younger son of Mr. Rowland Place, of Dimsdale, in the county of Durham, and was placed as clerk to an attorney in London until 1665."

Ralph Thoresby, in his *Ducatus Leodiensis*, often mentions Mr. Place with great encomiums, and specifies various presents that he made to his museum. He tells us too that Mr. Place discovered an earth for and a method of making porcelain, which he put in practice at the Manor House of York, of which manufacture he gave Thoresby a fine mug. "His pottery cost him much money; he attempted it solely from a turn for experiment, but one Clifton of Pontefract took the hint from him and made a fortune by it." Mr. Place died in 1728, and his widow (by whom he had a daughter, married to Wadham Wyndham, Esq.), quitting York, disposed of his paintings.

Thoresby says: "WORTLEY PARISH.—Here is a good vein of fine clay, that will retain its whiteness after it is burnt (when others turn red), and therefore used for the making of tobacco-pipes, a manufacture but lately begun at Leeds. . . . As to this manner of making of pipes, I can add nothing to what Mr. Houghton has writ in his very useful collections for the *Improvement of Husbandry and Trade* (vol. 4, No. 154), where he tells us also that the pint mugs, and even china ware, were made of this sort of earth, of which, saith he, we may make as good in England as any in the world. And this I am fully convinced of, having a specimen in this museum, made of English materials, in the Manor House at York, by the very ingenious Mr. Francis Place, who presented it to me, with one of the outer covers (seggars) purposely made to preserve it from the violence of the fire in baking." In the catalogue of his museum (p. 477) is described "one of Mr. Place's delicate fine mugs, made in the Manor House at York; it equals the true china ware;" he adds, "Mr. Houghton, in his Collection, tells us that there were very good made at Fulham," &c.

Lord Orford says, " I have a coffee-cup of his ware; it is of grey earth, with streaks of black, and not superior to common earthenware." This specimen was sold at Strawberry Hill, and is now in the Victoria and Albert Museum, presented by Sir A. W. Franks; it is of very fine stoneware, of light fabric, but perfectly opaque, ornamented with black streaks, and similar in composition to the small specimens of Dwight's early Fulham ware. A. J. Toppin (*York Herald*) read an interesting paper on Francis Place to the English Ceramic Circle in 1948, *Transactions*, Vol. 3, part 1.

LEEDS. Pottery of a refined nature was first made at Leeds in 1760, by two brothers named Green, at Hunslett. The pottery was conducted at an early date by Humble, Green & Co. Thomas Wilson, of Leeds, has the draft of an agreement, dated 11th November, 1775, by which the firm of Joshua Green, of Middleton, gent., and John Green, potter, of Hunslett, agree with Messrs. Hutchison and Evers to erect and maintain at their mill a water-wheel, with the necessary machinery for grinding flints. The firm was subsequently Hartley, Greens & Co., who published in 1783 a book of patterns of ware made by them, entitled: *Designs of sundry articles of Queen's ware, or Cream-coloured Earthenware, manufactured by Hartley, Greens & Co., at the Leeds Pottery: with a great variety of other articles; the same enamelled, printed or ornamented with gold to any pattern; also with Coats of Arms, Cyphers, Landscapes, etc.* This ware has much perforated or basket work. The name of the firm is also occasionally seen impressed on the ware; they had an extensive trade with Russia.

The partners in 1783–84 comprising the firm were William Hartley, Joshua Green, John Green, Henry Ackroyd, John Barwick, Samuel Wainwright, Thomas Wainwright, George Hanson and Savile Green. In 1800 two fresh partners joined the concern, Ebenezer Green and E. Parsons; a great extent of business was carried on, but in consequence of disagreements among the numerous persons interested, the concern was thrown into Chancery, and in 1825 it was purchased by Samuel Wainwright, and for a short time was styled S. Wainwright & Co. At his death in 1832 the trustees carried on the business under the style of the " Leeds Pottery Company," managed by Stephen Chappell, and shortly after the whole concern was transferred to Stephen and James Chappell, and continued by them until 1841, when they became bankrupt.

The assignees carried it on for a few years, managed by Richard Britton, and in 1850 Samuel Warburton bought the works in partnership with Britton, under the style of Warburton, Britton & Co.

Marks 1 (many reproductions bear this impressed mark), 2, 3 and 4, c. 1780+. From about 1861 the title was Richard Britton, and from 1872 " & Sons " was added. Various marks were used until 1878 and these include the initials " R B & S."

Mark no. 5 occurs on some wicker pattern plates and baskets, with perforated borders, with a sort of diamond ornament in the centre, impressed, the *twigs* are formed in strips by the hand, not made in a mould and require considerable skill in manipulation, being sometimes plaited or twisted in open work round the sides. This being a favourite pattern, it was made by most of the makers of Queen's ware. They are found so much alike as to pattern and quality as to render it almost impossible to distinguish one maker from another.

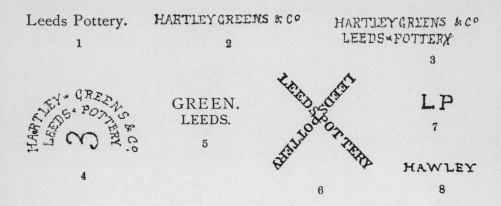

Leeds Pottery.　　HARTLEY GREENS & Cᵒ　　HARTLEY GREENS & Cᵒ
1　　　　　　　　　2　　　　　　　　　　LEEDS · POTTERY

3

GREEN.　　　　　　　　LP
LEEDS.　　　　　　　　7
5

HARTLEY · GREENS & Cᵒ LEEDS · POTTERY
4

LEEDS POTTERY
6

HAWLEY
8

Mark no. 6 is on a pair of green and white shell-shaped dishes of Leeds pottery and other examples. The Sheldon Collection contained specimens of Leeds pottery marked with the names of Hartley, Greens & Co. in various ways, and also a cream ware plate painted with a coat of arms stamped as mark no. 7 (Leeds Pottery), which is rare. Other specimens have some curious workmen's marks.

In the Schreiber Collection, Victoria and Albert Museum, there is a case containing several specimens of Leeds pottery.

The Hon. Roger G. Molyneux had a white earthenware tobacco pot, with a landscape and figures in blue transfer printing upon it, with the following names on the bottom scratched under the glaze: " Richard Craven, Hunslett, 18th October, 1815. W. Houlden." Hunslett is a suburb of Leeds, and this may have been a gift from one of the workmen of the Leeds Pottery to a friend. This specimen is now in the collection of Mr. Donald Towner.

The well-known " frog " mugs, in which the model of a frog is attached to the interior of a pint mug, were made at Leeds as well as at Newcastle and other places.

The reader is referred to Donald Towner's *Handbook of Leeds Pottery*, 1951, and to his *English Cream-coloured Earthenware*, 1957, for all aspects of Leeds pottery. Examples are illustrated in Godden's *British Pottery and Porcelain, an Illustrated Encyclopædia of Marked Specimens.*

HAWLEY. Kilnhurst Old Pottery, Kilnhurst, Yorkshire. A potter named Hawley worked here from 1750–90, and made good cream ware moulded and painted. He is mentioned by Jewitt, vol. 1, page 527, and a cream ware teapot, impressed mark, no. 8, was in the Sheldon Collection. Owing to many pieces being unmarked, they are attributed to Palmer, Neale, and others. Other potters of this name are recorded. For the history of this and other Yorkshire Potteries, the reader is referred to O. Grabham's *Yorkshire Potteries, Pots and Potters*, 1916.

RAINFORTH & Co. (Petty's Pottery, Holbeck Moor). This name is impressed (mark no. 9) on a cream ware painted mug formerly in the Sheldon collection. The pottery was close to the old Leeds works, and is mentioned in Kidson's *Old Leeds Pottery*. It was working from about 1780 to about 1800. The title Petty & Rainforth occurs in 1792, Rainforth & Co. mark after 1792.

RAINFORTH & Co   DON POTTERY.   GREEN.

9   10   DON POTTERY.

                      11

12   13

DON POTTERY, near Doncaster. There was a pottery on the river Don, established by John Green, of Newhill, who came from the Leeds Pottery about 1790. In 1807 some other members of the family joined, and the firm was for a short time " Greens, Clarks & Co."

John J. Bagshawe, of Sheffield, had a pattern book containing designs of nearly 300 specimens; the title is as follows: " Designs of sundry articles of Queen's or cream-coloured earthenware, manufactured by Greens Clarks & Co., at DON POTTERY, near Doncaster, with a great variety of other articles. The same enamel'd, printed or ornamented with gold or silver to any pattern, also with coats of arms, cyphers, landscapes, etc." The Don Pottery was very similar to that of Leeds—pierced work, baskets, vases, dinner, dessert, and tea services, etc. In 1834 the works passed by purchase to Samuel Barker, of the Mexborough Old Pottery, in whose family it remained until about 1896. The products of the early period were cream-coloured and fine earthenware and the usual mark was " Don Pottery." The marks included one of the crest of the fore part of a lion rampant holding a flag, inscribed DON POTTERY, mark no. 12, sometimes with his name above, or the intials S. B. & S. from 1851 to 1896, and an eagle displayed rising out of a ducal coronet; this last was only used for a short period, the demi-lion within a garter being resumed.

It has been stated that some experiments were made in the manufacture of china, but it must have been to a very small extent. Two examples were catalogued in Llewellynn Jewitts' sale July 1871, but they were extremely doubtful, having no mark by which they could be identified; one was a jug painted with flowers, on which it was remarked: " The china body for this jug was mixed by Godfrey Speight and Ward Booth, and it was painted by Taylor Booth." The curious part of the story connected with this jug is, that in the body of which it is composed are two of the fingers of a noted malefactor, Spence Broughton, who was gibbeted on Attercliffe Common at the close of the eighteenth century. Jewitt relates that a party of drunken potters passing by the spot, threw stones at the skeleton and knocked off two fingers, which were taken home as trophies, and afterwards calcined and mixed with the paste of which the jug was made.

Mark no. 10 is stamped on an earthenware plate, with a coloured print of a landscape, of cheap character, formerly in Bohn's Collection. Mark no. 11 is stamped on a canister of octagonal form, of yellow clay, ornamented with a chocolate-brown appliqué, musical trophies, and medallions of female figures in relief, fine work, in emulation of Wedgwood. (*Ker. Gall.*, fig. 503.)

An earthenware plate formerly in the Sheldon Collection bears mark no. 12, impressed 1820–34.

Mark no. 13 on an earthenware goblet on foot, pale pinkish glaze, white band, with branched stem in red and green, round top, green bands, white inside. Dr. Brameld's Collection.

14

HULL (Belle Vue Pottery). An extensive manufactory was carried on here by William Bell; it was situated on the Humber Bank. He had a depôt at Hamburg under the management of Edward J. Bell. John J. Bagshawe, of Sheffield, had the receipts for the various bodies and glazes of the ware made here from 1826 to 1841; the principal varieties were cream-colour, common painted, blue or brown printed, with landscapes, etc. Mark no. 14, used c. 1826–41 with or without title Belle Vue Pottery.

Bell had as many as thirty apprentices. In his prospectus he undertakes to supply earthenware 30 per cent cheaper than Staffordshire, and as there are always Danish and German ships, which usually return empty, the freight is very low. He exported largely to Germany, and dealt also in potter's materials and colours, and had flint mills at the Humber Bank. W. Bell also did business in supplying potter's materials and colours, with the following well-known potters in Staffordshire:—

Forrester, Lane End; James Keeling, Hanley; J. & W. Ridgway, Cauldon Place; T. Shorthose (or assignees); Mayer & Newbold; T. Dimmock; Handley, Burslem; Bourne, Baker & Bourne; Locketts; Keeling, Toft & Co.; Wood & Brittell; Henshell & Williamson; Bailey & Batkin; Ratcliffe & Blood; John Mare; Enoch Wood; Bagster; T. Weston; Hollins,

Warburton & Daniel; Lownds & Beech; F. & R. Pratt; Job Meigh & Sons;
Elijah Mayer & Son; Hackwood; Pratt, Hassall & Gerrard.

NOTE.—To give an idea of the working of such an establishment, we
here quote the expenses for the year 1837, extracted from the books of the
Belle Vue Pottery formerly in the possession of John J. Bagshawe:—

Slip kiln	.	.	.	.	£96 19 0
Flat men	.	.	.	.	144 4 9
Pressers .	.	.	.	.	47 1 10
Throwers and turners	.	.	.	376 5 6
Seggar-making	.	.	.	.	33 15 11
Cock spurs	.	.	.	.	26 18 10
Modelling	.	.	.	.	21 0 0
Printing	.	.	.	.	164 0 11
Biscuit firemen	.	.	.	.	59 16 11
Biscuit painting	.	.	.	.	89 18 8
Gloss firemen .	.	.	.	.	113 9 4
Packing, etc. .	.	.	.	.	104 19 8
Engineer	.	.	.	.	79 10 5
Enamel painting	.	.	.	.	76 17 9

£1434 19 6

This amount does not include rent, steam mills, sheds, kiln, wear and
tear, or materials, etc. The "cock spurs" are the small triangular or
pyramidal pieces of clay, three of which are placed under each piece in the
saggars to prevent adhesian in the kiln.

The works closed in 1841. The "Belle Vue" mark probably dates
from 1826.

CASTLEFORD, twelve miles from Leeds, established about 1790 by
David Dunderdale, for the manufacture of the finer kinds of pottery,
especially Queen's ware and black Egyptian. Dunderdale took into partnership a Mr. Plowes, and in 1803 the firm was D. Dunderdale & Co. The
works were closed in 1820, and a part of them was taken by some of the
workmen, whose names were George Asquith, William and Daniel Byford,
Richard Gill, James Sharp, and David Hingham. They were succeeded by
Taylor Harrison & Co.; and in 1854 by Thomas Nicholson & Co.; their
mark was T. N. & Co. in a garter surmounted by a crown, until 1871.

CASTLEFORD   D. D. & Co.
POTTERY.   16

15

The name, impressed as mark no. 15 (c. 1803–20), occurs on a black
Egyptian earthenware service, with raised flowers, like Wedgwood; the
coffee-pot has on the cover a female figure seated. The late Rev. R.

Pulleine had a mug with raised figures, white, with brown rim similar to Wedgwood, and part of a dessert service, painted with landscapes and views in bistre, on white ground; these all have the initials of the name impressed as mark no. 16. Stoneware teapots, with subjects in relief and blue line borders, have a hinge of earthenware attached to the lid, through which a metal pin is passed and fastened to the rim; sometimes the lid slides in a groove towards the handle. (*Ker. Gall.*, fig. 504.) Such pieces often have numbers, such as 22, impressed into the base. On several examples the name Castleford is added below the initial mark, no 16.

MIDDLESBRO
POTTERY CO.

17

18

WEDGWOOD & CO   FERRYBRIDGE.

19   20

MIDDLESBROUGH POTTERY CO. Mark no. 17 impressed on a white cup and saucer, embossed with flowers on the borders, formerly in the possession of the Rev. T. Staniforth. The initials M. P. Co. also occur. An earthenware dish with blue printed English landscape has the impressed anchor mark with " Middlesbro Pottery " (Victoria and Albert Museum), c. 1834–44, mark no. 18. Subsequent firms working the Middlesbro Pottery have been the Middlesbrough Earthenware Co. (1844–52) and Isaac Wilson & Co. (c. 1852–c. 1887). These firms used the initials M. E. & Co. and I. W. & Co.

A mark of an anchor below the word " London " was formerly attributed to this pottery but, on the evidence of a plate in the Godden Collection, this impressed mark was used by Malkin, Walker & Hulse of Longton, c. 1858–64.

FERRYBRIDGE, by Knottingley, near Pontefract; established in 1792 by Wm. Tomlinson, with whom were associated Mr. Seaton, a banker, Mr. Foster, a shipowner, Timothy Smith, a coal proprietor, and a retired gentleman named Thompson, under the firm of Tomlinson & Co. In 1796 they took into partnership Ralph Wedgwood, son of Thomas Wedgwood, partner of Josiah, the firm being Tomlinson, Foster, Wedgwood & Co. During this time they imitated Josiah's ornamental jasper and other wares, to which they were very inferior, and placed upon these articles the name of Wedgwood & Co. alone, omitting the names of the other partners. Until 1804 the works were known as the KNOTTINGLEY POTTERY, but they were then altered to FERRYBRIDGE POTTERY. In 1826 the style of the firm was for a short time Wigglesworth & Ingham, and afterwards Reid, Taylor and Kelsall until 1851, when the words were purchased by Lewis Woolf, who carried on the works under the title Lewis Woolf & Sons until 1883. Subsequent owners were Sefton & Brown and Joseph Horn. There is a large figure group, 16½ in. high, in coloured glazed earthenware, representing two cupids struggling for a heart; it has the impressed mark no. 19

of " Wedgwood & Co." This was probably made at Ferrybridge. The name of the place is occasionally found impressed as mark no. 20; a specimen is in the Victoria and Albert Museum. C. 1804+.

YEARSLEY. Wedgwood; *circa* 1700. There was a manufactory of pottery here in the beginning of the eighteenth century on the estate of Sir George Wombwell, adjoining New Burgh Park. Where his tilery stood " Old Wedgwood made *pancheons* "; a pancheon was a sort of deep pan. Several earthenware pitchers and fragments have been dug up on this spot of a coarse brown ware with lead glaze. There is a traditionary distich in the district as follows:—

> " At Yearsley there was pancheons made,
> By Willie Wedgwood, that young blade."

A brown earthenware oven, green glaze, semi-circular, opens at the top, with a hollowed edge round the inner side about half-way, and a flat bottom, having two handles at the sides, and between them a crinkled ornament, was dug up at Yearsley, near Easingwold, Yorkshire, together with a plain earthen crock or *pancheon* of red earth, green glaze, having a handle on each side. Mark no. 21 incised before glazing is on the upper part inside the oven. They were bought at the sale of Mr. Scott, steward to Sir George Wombwell, on whose estate the pottery of Wedgwood was.

21   ꝅꝏ 1712 ATIC   REED.   22

MEXBOROUGH, near Swinton. A manufactory of pottery, established towards the end of the eighteenth century, for a common description of pottery, by a person named Beevers, trading as Beevers & Ford; being built close to a rock, it was called the " Rock Pottery." Subsequently it was Ford, Simpson & Beevers, who made cane-coloured jugs, dishes, etc., for household use. In the Sheldon Collection there was a blue painted earthenware plate impressed SOWTERS & CO., MEXBRO. The works passed into the hands of Reed & Taylor, who also owned some works at Ferrybridge; they introduced a finer ware. In 1839 it belonged entirely to John Reed, and was successfully carried on by his son until 1873. Mark no. 22. Sidney Wolfe & Co. continued from 1873 to 1883.

At the sale of the Rockingham Works, about the year 1842, Reed purchased many of the moulds, among which were Conisburgh Castle, and some large vases in close imitation of the Oriental, called the " lotus vases." Reed kindly presented the author with a pair made from these moulds, but without the coloured decorations they were wont to be adorned with at the Rockingham Works.

SWINTON. This manufactory appears, from the specimen we now describe, to have been originally established by a Mr. Twigg. An earthenware dish marked " TWIGGS " has a large view, 10 in. by 8 in., of the Swinton Works, beneath which on a scroll is written, " North-west view of the Earthenware Manufactory at Swinton, near Rotherham in Yorkshire;

established in the year 1745." However, the "Twigg" marks are not necessarily early Rockingham as is generally understood by this name because Joseph Twigg established the separate Newhill pottery in 1822 and worked until 1866. The Sheldon Collection contained two specimens impressed TWIGG and TWIGG, NEWHILL (marks 23, 24, c. 1822+) made by this Joseph Twigg of the Newhill Pottery.

23   (TWIGG)   TWIGG   24
                             NEWHILL

In the year 1757 the Rockingham pottery was conducted by Edward Butler. In 1765 it was carried on by William Malpass (who had another manufactory at Kilnhurst in the neighbourhood). In 1778 the works were taken by Thomas Bingley & Co., who enlarged them, and made earthenware of a superior quality, and stoneware, blue and white dinner and tea services; they also made the brown tea and coffee services, pitchers, etc., which obtained the name of " Rockingham ware."

From about 1790 to 1800 the firm was Greens, Bingley & Co., one of the Greens of Leeds having joined it. The works afterwards passed entirely into the hands of John and William Brameld, and subsequently Thomas George Frederick, and John Wager Brameld became the tenants. L. Jewitt mentions a posset pot with two handles and incised floral decorations dated 1759, and a drinking-cup of fine white earthenware ornamented with blue transfer inscribed William Brameld, 1788, from which it would appear that Brameld was connected with the works rather earlier than has generally been supposed.

The Rockingham teapots were in great repute for extracting the full flavour of the tea; they were taller than usual, and in form more like a coffee-pot, which was considered a great improvement. Mortlock, the china seller, is said to have ordered of this article alone £900 worth for one season's demand. These tea or coffee pots were of a chocolate-coloured glaze, lined with white; occasionally we find the name of MORTLOCK stamped upon them, sometimes they are stamped " Brameld."

Sometimes the teapots were of a peculiar shape, in form of a fruit with leaves and flowers in relief, in imitation of Japanese; they were filled from beneath the vessel; they were called " CADOGANS " and were frequently stamped with the word. " MORTLOCK'S CADOGAN " is stamped on one in the Victoria and Albert Museum; occasionally the coffee-pots had " NORFOLK " stamped underneath, in reference to the pattern. (*Ker. Gall.*, fig. 506.)

About the year 1823 Thomas Brameld directed his attention to the manufacture of porcelain of the finest description, employing the best artists, and sparing no expense to bring it to perfection. John Wager Brameld was himself a painter on porcelain; there are some authenticated pieces presented by him to Robert Allen, of Lowestoft, formerly a painter in that manufactory, viz., a snuff-box and a set of vases. In 1826 they became embarrassed, but the works were continued by the assistance of Earl Fitzwilliam till 1842.

There is a very lofty Rockingham vase in the Victoria and Albert Museum; it is nearly 4 ft. high. It is most elaborately painted with flowers and small medallions of landscapes; the three handles are formed of gilt oak branches, and it rests on three lions' paws on maroon ground; the cover is surmounted by a rhinoceros. The companion vase was at Wentworth Hous ᵉ. Walter Joy, of Leeds, had a compotier of blue and gold trellis ground, bordered with flowers in relief, with views of Lowther Castle, etc. This is part of a service made for King William IV in 1832, and which, from its expensive character, is said to have caused the ruin of the firm: it was painted with views of the seats of the nobility and gentry. (*Ker. Gall.*, figs. 580, 581.)

Before the order for the King's service was actually given, some trial plates were made, elaborately painted with the royal arms and richly gilt. Two of these, and also a portion of one of the plates actually chosen, were in the Museum of the Royal Worcester Porcelain Works. The broken plate was sent there from Buckingham Palace for the Worcester factory to match, but the cost was so great that the order was not given.

In Emerson Norman's Collection were some fine sets of Rockingham china tazzas, designed for dessert services, the stems having plants and fruit in relief coloured after nature, especially the mulberry, painted with views of gentlemen's seats; also a lofty centrepiece, light blue ground, and acorns in relief, painted with " The Tight Shoe " and " The Young Soldier."

Rockingham Works.
Brameld.

25

Mark no. 25 of a griffin, the Rockingham crest, was usually placed on china; it was adopted about 1825, the commencement of the manufacture of porcelain under the patronage of Earl Fitzwilliam, whose second title is Marquis of Rockingham; this early mark is in red. The name is also found on tea services of yellow clay, glazed inside, with figures outside in blue of children playing, in the style of Wedgwood. In some specimens of Rockingham china in the Schrieber Collection, the mark varies somewhat in details, "Royal Rock m Works, Brameld," and "Manufacturers to the King" being below the crest of the griffin. This was added to the former " Griffin " mark about 1830. The later version was printed in purple, not red.

A great many figures being unmarked have been ascribed to other factories which are probably Rockingham. Dudley W. Macdonald had a figure of a woman drawing water at a well, 7 in. high, with an incised mark (which is very rare), " No. 22 " Rockingham Works, Brameld, and the griffin. The same collector had also several other figures, one of which in biscuit, of a girl with a basket of flowers, has an incised number 31— others are unmarked, and amongst them a rare figure of Dr. Penglass, formerly in Dr. Diamond's Collection. A portion of the works was subsequently occupied by Isaac Baguley, formerly in the employ of Messrs. Brameld, who purchased earthenware and china in the biscuit state and decorated it. Baguley was a painter of birds; Speight painted interiors and figures, copies of Wilkie, etc.; Cordon painted landscapes and views of gentlemen's seats, in which he was succeeded by Lucas. Thomas Steel painted flowers and fruit for a brief period before 1830. Typical examples of Rockingham porcelains are illustrated in Godden's *British Pottery and Porcelain, an Illustrated Encyclopædia of Marked Specimens*.

Mark no. 26. The impressed word " Rockingham " also occurs on a marked " Wedgwood " green glazed teapot in the Godden collection.

Marks nos. 27 to 31, c. 1815–30. The Sheldon Collection contained specimens marked BRAMELD, with the word in a cartouche and also plainly stamped. The " Brameld " mark predates the Griffin mark. Many Rockingham specimens are unmarked.

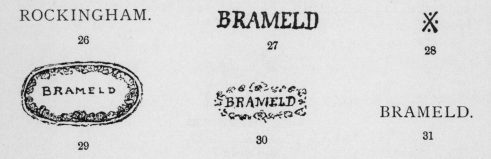

ROCKINGHAM.

26

BRAMELD

27

28

29

30

BRAMELD.

31

HOLMES POTTERY, near Rotherham. A manufactory of earthenware was carried on at this place, by various owners from about 1850, including J. Jackson & Co. (c. 1865–87).

WAKEFIELD. Thoresby, in his Diary, writes: " March 16, 1702.— From Wakefield, then by Allerthorp and Silkhouse to the *Pot-ovens* (Little London, in the dialect of the poor people), where I stayed a little to observe, not only the manner of forming their earthenware, which brought to mind the words of the prophet, ' As clay in the hands of the potter, so are we in the Lord's,' but to observe the manner of building the furnaces, their size and materials, which are small, and upon the surface of the ground, confirming me in my former apprehensions that those remains at Hawcaster-rigg (*Philosoph. Trans.* No. 222) are really the ruins of a Roman pottery."

Dixon & Co.
Sunderland Pottery.

32

Scott Brothers & Co.

33

SCOTT

34

Scott
xi

35

Phillips&Co Sunderland.1813.

36

Dixon co

37

Dixon, Phillips & Co

38

Phillips & Co.
Sunderland, 1813.

39

PHILLIPS & Co.
Sunderland Pottery.

40

J. PHILLIPS,
Hylton Pottery.

42

MALING

43

41

DAWSON.

44

45

DAWSON & CO
5

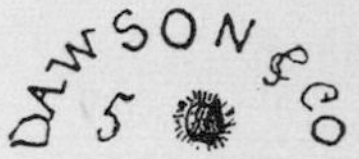

46

SUNDERLAND. The *Sunderland Pottery* was established by Dixon, Austin & Co. in the early part of 19th century, doing a considerable trade in 1824 and in 1837, some earthenware figures of the Seasons are in the Victoria and Albert Museum. The ware made here was also frequently decorated with the pink metallic lustre so usual on the Sunderland jugs, etc.; one favourite pattern was a ship of war, accompanied by verses suitable for sailors. A butter dish, showing the character of the ware, may here be given; it has " The Northumberland, 74 guns," printed in colours:—

> " The troubled main, the wind and rain,
>   My ardent passion prove;
>   Lash'd to the helm, should seas o'erwhelm,
>   I'll think on thee, my love."

Underneath is the manufacturer's name as mark no. 32. For full information on all Sunderland potteries, the reader is referred to *The Potteries of Sunderland and District*, published by the Sunderland Library.

Some marked examples are reproduced in Godden's *British Pottery and Porcelain, an Illustrated Encyclopædia of Marked Specimens.*

SUNDERLAND. The *Newbottle Pottery* was established about 1755 by Mr. Byers, and carried on by Anthony Scott; it was removed in 1788 to the *Southwick Pottery*, the works being then newly built, and was continued by his descendants under the name of Scott Brothers (& Co.), and in 1837 Anthony Scott & Sons. Marks include nos. 33–35.

SUNDERLAND. The *Garrison Pottery* was established about 1807 by a Mr. Phillips, who produced Queen's ware, etc.; the marks in transfer were as nos. 36, 38 and 41. Mark no. 41 is on a pair of earthenware slabs painted in black, with ships and verses in metallic lustre frames, c. 1840–65. Various firms operated this pottery until 1865.

Carr's Hill Pottery, near Gateshead, on the Durham side of the Tyne. A manufacture of white earthenware was established as early as 1730 or 1740 by Mr. Warburton, which, after having been successfully conducted for seventy years, gradually declined, and was closed in 1817.

There was in the Sheldon Collection a rare and interesting yellow ware jug decorated with a transfer signed J. Warburton, N. on Tyne, with an inscription—

" Have communion with few,
 Be familiar with none,
 Deal justly with all,
 Speak evil of none."

In 1762 Christopher Thompson and John Maling erected potteries at North Hylton, near Sunderland; there was also the *Hylton Pottery*, established about 1762, and carried on for some time by J. Phillips and Mr. Maling (mark no. 42). There was in the Sheldon Collection a ware plate painted with a Dutch scene impressed with his name, MALING (mark no. 43). In 1815 Robert Maling removed the business from Hylton to the Tyne. A fish-pot, in Llewellynn Jewitt's sale, with two handles, ornamented in pink lustre, has on one side a ship in full sail, on the other a view, above bridge, of the *Hylton Pot Works*, with long inscription.

SUNDERLAND, LOW FORD. A manufactory of pottery and earthenware services was flourishing here in the beginning of the nineteenth century, and it is spoken of in the papers of the Belle Vue Company. A specimen of the ware, a cup and saucer formerly in Dr. Diamond's Collection, has a coloured transfer of figures bordered with the pink metallic lustre; the name stamped in the clay (mark no. 44). The firm was Thomas Dawson & Co., from c. 1830 to 1864.

There was in the Sheldon Collection a large cream ware mug with coloured transfer, bearing mark no. 45, said to be the work of John Dawson & Co. about 1800; made at the Low Ford Pottery, Sunderland. Also, in the same collection, a pink lustred cup and saucer impressed DAWSON & Co. (mark no. 46).

NEWCASTLE-UPON-TYNE. Thomas Fell & Co., proprietors; it was called " St. Peter's Pottery "; they exhibited earthenware at the International Exhibition in 1862. This pottery was established about 1817. (*Ker. Gall.*, figs. 507, 508.) Marks nos. 47 and 48.

FELL & Co., with anchor and cable, stamped on a willow pattern plate; sometimes the arms of the town of Newcastle in blue, and Fell on the label below the shield; on others, F. & Co. Marks of the 1869–1890 period have the initials T. F. & Co.

NEWCASTLE-UPON-TYNE. About 1838 J. Wallace & Co. had a pottery at Forth Bank. The impressed mark WALLACE & CO. is recorded.

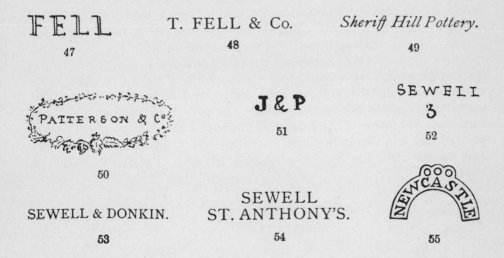

FELL
47

T. FELL & Co.
48

Sheriff Hill Pottery.
49

PATTERSON & C°
50

J & P
51

SEWELL
3
52

SEWELL & DONKIN.
53

SEWELL
ST. ANTHONY'S.
54

NEWCASTLE
55

Directories list J. Wallace & Co. from 1838 to 1857, subsequently Wallace & Co., at various addresses until 1902.

NEWCASTLE-UPON-TYNE. Sheriff Hill Pottery. This pottery was carried on by Edward Lewins in partnership with George Patterson. Mark no. 49.

A Mr. Jackson also appears to have been in partnership with Patterson in 1833, and there were in the Sheldon Collection two earthenware cups and saucers, the one printed in blue, PATTERSON & Co., and the other impressed with J. & P. for Jackson & Patterson, c. 1830–45. Marks nos. 50 and 51. Members of the Patterson family worked the Sheriff Hill Pottery until about 1903, when the Sheriff Hill Pottery Co. succeeded.

NEWCASTLE-UPON-TYNE. Established about 1780 at St. Anthony's, about 2½ miles from Newcastle; makers, Sewell & Donkin; Queen's ware and pink metallic lustre, also printed subjects; sometimes SEWELL alone, the name stamped. A jug of his make has Cupids in relief, coloured with pink metallic lustred clouds and bronzed borders. (*Ker. Gall.*, fig. 509.) He also produced ware like that of Leeds, pierced wicker baskets, etc. Marks nos. 52 to 54. In 1891–2, Patterson & Parkinson worked this pottery and from 1893 to about 1908, T. Patterson & Co.

NEWCASTLE. Mark no. 55 occurs on an earthenware fruit dish on a stand embossed with wicker-pattern sides and pierced border, a group of fruit in the centre (date about 1800). The ware is like Leeds pottery, but of a whiter and better colour; there are numbers underneath the mark, all impressed.

SOUTHWICK, near Sunderland. The *Wear Pottery*, established in 1789 by Brunton & Co., succeeded by Moore & Co. in 1803. Their names occur on jugs, with prints of a view of the bridge over the Wear at Sunderland, commemorating the erection and opening of the potteries at Southwick, which are alluded to in the *Penny Cyclopædia* among other manufactories. These transfers of Nelson's victories and other popular subjects were surrounded by a pink metallic lustre. On a mug, with a toad inside the cup, which is discovered when the drinker has half emptied it, is inscribed:—

"Though malt and venom seem united,
Don't break my pot or be affrighted."

Two of these jugs were in the possession of Mr. Hawkins of Grantham; they are of a creamy-white colour, similar to the Leeds pottery. The manufactory is mentioned in the Belle Vue papers as doing an extensive business. The name of the makers is impressed as mark no. 56 on a blue printed cup and saucer formerly in the Sheldon Collection. Mark no. 57 and various other similar marks occur, c. 1803–81. The factory closed in 1881.

ᴴᴼᴼᵀᴱ ᵋ ᶜ 4 ᶜ	MOORE & CO. SOUTHWICK.	STOCKTON POTTERY.
56	57	58

WEDGEWOOD.	W. S. & Co.
59	60 QUEENS WARE. STOCKTON.

STOCKTON-ON-TEES. This South Stockton pottery was established in the early part of the nineteenth century by William Smith of Stockton, in conjunction with John Whalley, a Staffordshire potter. They entered into partnership with William and George Skinner. In 1833 the firm was " Messrs. J. Smith & Co., Stockton Pottery." Mark no. 58.

About the year 1848, Wedgwood of Etruria applied for an injunction against W. Smith and others, of Stockton, for using their name stamped or printed on pottery made to imitate their productions; the stamp used by them was WEDGEWOOD instead of WEDGWOOD. Mark no. 59.

Mark no. 60 is impressed on a plate, with embossed Mayflower border painted in purple *camaieu*, with Virginia and her goats; formerly in the Rev. T. Staniforth's Collection. They also made great quantities of cobble boats, which were purchased by sailors and others to give as presents on long voyages; one of these, painted with green stripes, was in E. Hailstone's Collection. C. 1826–50. There was a separate factory at North Shore, Stockton.

NOTTINGHAM. In Deering's *Historical Account of Nottingham*, 1751, he speaks of potter's ware being made here. Under the year 1757, in Bailey's *Annals of Nottinghamshire*, we read that " Mr. Morley was a manufacturer of brown earthenware, carrying on his works in the lower part of Beck Street, and by this business he amassed a very considerable fortune. This ware was at one time of great celebrity throughout the whole of the Midland counties, especially its famous brown mugs for the use of public houses," and the brown ware is still called " Nottingham ware," although the manufacture has been discontinued for nearly a century. Morley's pottery was situated in Mug-house Yard, Mug-house Lane, Beck Street. No manufactory exists at the present day. There is a specimen in the Victoria and Albert Museum—a large brown earthenware bowl, with " *November* 20, 1726," incised on the outer rim.

61 *John. Smith Jun.ᵉ of Basford near Nottingham. 1712.*

NOTTINGHAM. The inscription, mark no. 61 incised, is round an earthenware jug of light brown glaze and has a light metallic lustre. These names refer to the persons for whom the vessels were made, not those of the maker, and are usually scratched into the ware before glazing.

A brown stoneware mug with subjects in relief; in front, a bust of Queen Anne between two *Beef-eaters*; dogs and hare round the bottom; on the rim is this portion of an old song:—

" On Banse downs a hair wee found,
　Thatt led uss all a Smoaking Round."
" Wm. Marsh 1729."　　　　　　　　　　　　Height 9 in.

Another of the same character, with hare hunt, etc., is inscribed:—

" Southwell for ever.　W. C. M."　1739.　　　Height 10 in.

A brown stoneware mug in the Victoria and Albert Museum has a number of stamps in relief of figures, houses, hounds, stag, etc., and the names scratched on the outside:—

" Edw. Slark, 1727."　　　　　　　　　　　　Height 9 in.

A brown ware mug, with subjects in relief, has in the centre Hogarth's " Midnight Conversation," a stag hunt, and a medallion, with *two* busts of men; underneath is written:—

" We Three Loggerheads.　G. Ieffrey, 1761."　Height 8½ in.

These mugs are in the Schreiber Collection, Victoria and Albert Museum.

The ware made here in the first half of the eighteenth century is very hard and durable, and has usually a light-brown lustrous glaze, and a peculiar smoothness of surface. It is frequently ornamented with dotted designs, or incised outlines of stalks and flowers, especially the carnation. The earliest dated specimen we have met with is a posset-pot, described by Jewitt, inscribed and dated 1700:—

> Samuel Watkinson, mayor of Nottingham.
> Sarah, his wife, mayoress.

John Hawkins of Grantham had a tobacco jar in form of a bear, of brown lustrous glaze, his head being the cover, a collar round his neck, and a chain to which is attached a large hollow ball, containing stones and holes, used as a rattle; on the ball is impressed the name " Elizabeth Clark, Decr ye 25th 1769 "; also a neatly-made puzzle jug, of the same lustrous glaze, ornamented with a vase of pinks and scrolls round the lower part, the flowers being a dark red colour: on the front is the date 1755, underneath the bottom the initials G.B. Nottingham stonewares do not bear a maker's mark.

LANGLEY MILL, near Nottingham. A firm of potters named Lovatt & Lovatt carried on from about 1895 the manufacture of useful and decorative pottery at this address. From 1931 the title has been " Lovatts Potteries Ltd."

At the Brussels Exhibition, 1910, they exhibited " Langley " stoneware glazed without the use of lead, vases of antique shapes in different glazes, plant holders, bulb holders, tea and coffee pots, etc. Marks nos. 62 to 69. No. 62, c. 1895+. No. 63, c. 1900+. No. 69, from 1931.

CHESTERFIELD. In this neighbourhood many pot-works were established in the eighteenth century, the principal productions being a brown ware of particularly hard and durable quality, as well as stoneware. The clay was obtained from the East Moor, Derbyshire, and from Brampton, a few miles away; the former standing a higher degree of heat, they were usually mixed and covered with a salt glaze. A number of quaint vessels and " bears," like those of Nottingham, were made here.

WHITTINGTON, near Chesterfield. The manufacture of pottery was carried on in the early part of the 19th century by William Johnson and Aaron Madin.

BRAMPTON, near Chesterfield. Potteries were established here in the early part of the eighteenth century, the principal ware produced being the ordinary brown, of hard and close texture and reddish glaze. About 1800 these works were carried on by William Bromley, who, in addition to the brown ware, made a cream-coloured earthenware with transfer prints; they were subsequently worked by Robert Bambrigge & Co.

There were six earthenware manufactories at this place, conducted by Mrs. Blake, William Bridden, Luke Knowles, Thomas Oldfield, John Wright, and Wright & Co., producing brown-ware filters, jugs, tobacco jars, puzzle jugs, etc. In John J. Bagshawe's Collection there was a brown-ware posset-pot made at Brampton, decorated with raised ornaments, dated 1774; and Mr. Hodgkin mentions a two-handled posset-pot incised, " Robert Bruston, March the 2nd, 1749, Derby." The firm of Oldfield & Co. is mentioned by Brongniart as located in 1843 at Chesterfield.

The ware made here is similar in many respects to the old Nottingham stoneware, but is less hard, thicker and not so well potted; the glaze is very slightly iridescent, and the decoration not so well executed; the bands of lineal design and dotted work is clumsier and less attractive. Oldfield & Co. worked from c. 1838 to c. 1888 and mark no. 70 and various other marks were employed; all include the name. The works were established in 1810 by Oldfield, Madin, Wright, Hewitt & Co.

A mug, formerly in Mr. Lucas's Collection, of ware like that of Chesterfield, ornamented with hunting scenes, has mark no. 71, which dates from about 1818. Later the title was Thompson Brothers, subsequently Messrs. Holland & Thompson worked this pottery until the closure in 1882.

TICKENHALL POTTERY, supposed to have been established as early as the sixteenth century, produced articles of a coarse, hard body, of a dull brown colour, sometimes decorated with yellow slip.

OLDFIELD&CO
MAKERS
70

71

DERBY

COCK PIT HILL. The earliest manufactory at Derby was called the " Derby Pot Works," situated on Cock Pit Hill. The first notice we have of it, although it must have been established long before, is in 1750, when is was held by John & Christopher Heath, who were persons of considerable importance as bankers, moneylenders, and scriveners, residing in Full Street, Derby, and also owners of considerable house property in the vicinity. John Heath twice served the office of Mayor of the borough, namely, in 1763 and 1772, and his brother Christopher received a similar distinction in 1774. It is in connection with William Duesbury that we first hear of what the *Derby Mercury* of 1780 describes as " the great and extensive factory, commonly known by the name of the Derby Pot Works." The name of its founder and the date of its establishment have not yet been discovered.

Alfred Wallis and W. Bemrose, jun., in their *History of the Pottery and Porcelain of Derby*, to whom we are indebted for these notes, continue: " It may have been that Duesbury, who was at the outset of his career simply a ' toy figure ' maker, was also a salesman of ware made at the Pot Works, Keys stating that when the Heaths failed, Duesbury had a stock of goods by him, and was entrusted with more ware from the Pot Works for sale in Ireland; the voyage was successful, and the debt was discharged ' with satisfaction to the bankruptcy.' This occurrence (the bankruptcy) took place about 1780, as we learn from the advertisements in the *Derby Mercury*: ' To be sold without reserve at the Derby Pot Works a large quantity of earthenware, being the whole stock in trade of that great and extensive factory, consisting of an assortment of enamelled and blue and white useful china, a large quantity of enamelled cream ware and plain cream tea-table ware; a great quantity of white, stone, and brown ware, etc., the property of Messrs. John and Christopher Heath, of Derby, bankrupts.' " Christopher Heath died at the vicarage, Duffield, in 1815, at the age of 97 years.

Rare examples of transfer printed creamware are marked with Radford's signature and " Derby Pot Works " (in various forms). An example is in the British Museum. See *Transactions of the English Ceramic Circle*, Vol. 3, part 4. See also the following pages on Derby porcelain. Marks 1, 2 and 3, c. 1760–71. Thomas Radford was only the engraver of the printed pattern.

DERBY   POT WORKS IN DERBY.   RADFORD Sc
                        2   DERBY POT WORKS.

1   3

THE DERBY PORCELAIN WORKS

Among the collection of papers relating to pottery and porcelain which belonged to Jacob Burn there are two letters containing reminiscences of the old Derby manufactory in the Nottingham Road; one by Mr. Locker, who was apprenticed there in 1809, and subsequently carried on a smaller business in King Street, Derby, about 1849; the other notice is by Samuel Keys, apprenticed to the first William Duesbury in 1785. From these documents, written about 1855, we quote the following interesting extracts:—

Locker, who was clerk to the factory in 1809, tells us that " the earliest manufactory of earthenware at Derby was carried on by a Mr. Heath at Cock Pit Hill. This gentleman was also a banker in Full Street; it was on a very extensive scale, but we have no record of the date of its establishment. Mr. Duesbury was a clever man, and took a fancy to the pot and china business, and he became acquainted with Mr. Heath with a view to carrying out his own idea of china-making, which he did successfully, by first making animals in a small way, and by degrees building a very extensive manufactory himself.

" About 1745 a man, said to be a foreigner in very poor circumstances, living in Lodge Lane, made small articles in china, such as birds, cats, dogs, sheep, and other small ornamental toys, which he fired at a kiln in the neighbourhood belonging to a pipe-maker named Woodward. Mr. Duesbury frequently visited this image-maker and took great interest in his small manufactory, and becoming desirous of improving the art, he engaged his services on his own account, and, with the assistance of Mr. Heath, at that time considered a man of large property, he soon added considerably to his stock of useful and ornamental articles. The Cock Pit Hill manufactory, however, began to decline, and from a variety of causes Mr. Heath, to the surprise of everybody, became bankrupt. At the sale which ensued, M. Duesbury was a large purchaser, and he took the earthenware over to Ireland, which proved for him a very fortunate speculation. Mr. Duesbury commenced building a manufactory over St. Mary's Bridge, which was finished in 1751, and he made porcelain there in the same year." However, according to William Bemrose's more recent information, Duesbury was at this time (1751–3) employed in London as an " enameller to the trade," and therefore this date is incorrect. Jewitt thinks the foreigner mentioned in the above paragraph was a French refugee named Andrew Planché, having in his possession the draft of a deed (which was never executed) of partnership for ten years between Heath, Duesbury, and Planché.   Probably Heath's bankruptcy about 1780 altered all these arrangements, for Planché's name never appears again in connection with the works.   The early Derby porcelains and the connection with Planché is discussed in a paper by Mrs. MacAlister in the *Transactions of the English Porcelain Circle*, no. 2, 1929.

Mr. Locker says, " It was a remarkable thing that the old hands could never furnish any precise data about the Derby factory prior to 1751; not even Keys, who was an apprentice to the first Mr. Duesbury as far back as 1785.   I have had many conversations with Miss Duesbury, who is the daughter of the second Mr. Duesbury, and used to sell china at the warehouse over St. Mary's Bridge about the time Isaac Farnsworth was the leading man for her father in the figure trade, but I could glean nothing, for she and other branches of the family, when they were at fault for data, always applied to me, as I was the person employed to look over all the old documents when the Derby factory unfortunately got into Chancery, and everything relating to the figure trade was required by the Chancellor in order to ascertain the value of the models, for that was the bone of contention between the second Mr. Duesbury and Mr. Kean, so that the historical part was destroyed; but I have no doubt in my own mind that, china was made at Derby some five or six years before Worcester.   I however, did not take any particular notice of dates, for I did not like the job of looking over books and papers above one hundred years old— they were very dirty, and injured my clothes very much.   With regard to printing, I know comparatively little as to its rise; I, however, *do* know that there were things *printed* amongst the stock removed from Cock Pit Hill to the factory, and wooden sort of things they were.   I have seen cups and saucers and plates *all printed*—they were chiefly water-fowl, such as ducks, etc.; they remained in the back office, and must have been done at least a century ago."

Samuel Keys tells us that " about the same time there was an excellent china manufactory at Chelsea, where a variety of splendid figures, vases, and other beautiful ornaments were produced, and also a great assortment of useful china.   They employed first-rate artists in the painting, gilding, and general decoration, then superior to anything of the kind in England; but from some mysterious cause, at the time unknown, the Chelsea manufactory suddenly ceased working, although producing excellent ware, and being greatly encouraged and highly patronised. . . . Mr. Duesbury became the purchaser of the whole stock of models, moulds, and unfinished ware, etc., belonging to the concern."   Mr. Locker adds, " Mr. Duesbury bought all the stock in trade, finished and unfinished, had it sent to Derby, and engaged the hands employed at Chelsea, and the first painter of that day was brought down to Derby to finish all their first-rate things: his name was Bowman," [sic] Boreman.

Keys continues, " A small manufactory at Bow closed about the same time, and Mr. Duesbury had several beautiful figures and ornaments from there. The Derby manufactory very soon after began to make a conspicuous figure in the town of Derby and in the china trade of England. Mr. Duesbury lived to an advanced age, when, by paralysis, he was deprived of speech and the use of one side, and in a few months died, sincerely regretted (Mr. William Duesbury, senior, died 30th November, 1786). He left two sons, William and James, and two daughters: William, the elder, succeeded his father, and in a short time married Miss Edwards, an amiable and beautiful young lady; they had several sons and daughters. Mr. W. Duesbury, junior, was a persevering man of very superior talent. Patronised by the King, the royal family, and the principal nobility and gentry, he advanced the porcelain manufactory of Derby in every branch to very great perfection. The Duchess of Devonshire honoured him with very extensive orders. Chaste and classical figures in great variety were modelled by first-rate artists, and produced a white biscuit, as well as being richly painted; and in the figure trade Derby was at that time without a rival; dinner, dessert, breakfast, and tea services, with ornaments of the most splendid description, graced the showroom, which at that time was superior to any in the kingdom.

" I was the last apprentice bound to the first Mr. Duesbury in 1785 or 6, and it was soon perceptible that the constitution of his successor being naturally very delicate, the anxieties of business, and too close application and study, were becoming too powerful; he was therefore advised to take a partner, and selected Mr. Michael Kean, a gentleman in every respect, and a first-class artist [who married Miss Duesbury, October 29, 1798]; he was an excellent designer, and introduced a great variety of new and splendid specimens of ornamental and useful articles. Mr. Duesbury got gradually worse, and died in the prime of life, leaving very few his equals.

" The management of the concern for the widow, her family, and himself devolved upon Mr. Kean, and in a short time Mr. Duesbury's son William assisted in the business. It was so conducted for several years, until some family disagreements took place, which caused Mr. Kean to withdraw rather hastily from the connection, and it was disposed of to Mr. Robert Bloor about the year 1815 [The chronology quoted from Mr. Bemrose's book corrects this date to 1811.—ED.] who had been clerk and salesman to the firm for several years. He greatly increased the business, employing fifty painters and gilders, besides a great number of apprentices, and several females, burnishers, potters, etc., to correspond. In 1820 he manufactured to a great extent, and selling largely by auction, dispersed his wares over all parts of England.

" That system proved destructive to the reputation of the manufactory, which began to decline, and his health failing, he was compelled to relinquish taking an active part in the business, and there being no one capable of conducting it with any spirit, it of course fell off, and Mr. Bloor after a distressing and protracted illness died. [From 1828 till the time of his death in 1849, Mr. Bloor was mentally incapable of taking any part in the business, and during that time Mr. Thomason had the entire management of the concern, until a few years before Mr. Bloor's death when a statute of lunacy was taken out.—ED.]

" The business was continued for a short time for the widow and two children, until they also died, leaving a granddaughter of Mr. Bloor's, who married Thomas Clarke, a maltster and corn-factor at Derby; but not understanding the business, and having no inclination to persevere, he sold the entire plant, models, moulds, ware, tables, stools, in short, every movable article, *even to the old clock*, to Mr. Samuel Boyle, a china manufacturer of Fenton, Staffordshire potteries; and the Derby, china manufactory is no more." To continue Key's narration, Boyle subsequently failed, and the models, etc., were laid by as useless; they then became the property of the Copelands, by whom various articles were very creditably revived.

In 1769 Mr. Duesbury, of Derby, purchased the Chelsea China Works, and carried on both manufactories simultaneously until 1784; the date of the agreement to purchase was 17th August, 1769, and on 5th February, 1770, the Chelsea Porcelain Manufactory and its appurtenances were assigned to Mr. William Duesbury. This purchase entailed upon him some heavy law proceedings against M. Sprimont, for the recovery of a quantity of goods made by him, which Mr. Duesbury considered as part of the purchase. M. Sprimont died in 1771, and we find in the *Westminster Magazine* that in April 1773 John Chetwood, Esq., counsellor-at-law, married Mrs. Sprimont, widow of Nicholas Sprimont, Esq., proprietor of the Chelsea porcelain manufactory. In 1784 the works were discontinued, the kilns and every part of them pulled down, and what could be made available sent to Derby.

The following is a list of the principal artists engaged in the Derby Works:—

PAINTERS.—Zachariah Boreman, landscapes, flowers, and birds, from Chelsea; Hill, landscapes; Brewer, landscapes and figures; Thomas Steel, fruit; Bancroft, flowers, insects, etc.; George and John Hancock, flowers; Moses Webster, flowers; Edward Withers, flowers; Robinson, landscapes; Cuthbert Lawton, hunting subjects; E. Prince, landscapes; William Corden, flowers; Stanesby, flowers; George Mellor, insects and flowers; William Pegg, still life; Thomas Pegg, gilder; Samuel Keys, ornamentalist; John Keys, flowers; Holland, flowers; William Billingsley, flowers; Thomas Soar, gilder; Joseph Stables, gilder; William Taylor, Oriental subjects and patterns; John Haslem, flowers, afterwards figure painter; Cotton & Askew, figure painters. Others of less note were William Cooper, William Yates, John Yates, Joseph Dutton, John Blood, William Smith, William Longden, etc.

MODELLERS OF FIGURES, ETC.—Spangler, Stephen, W. J. Coffee, Hartenberg, Complin, Duvivier, Webber, Dear, and others, including

Bacon the sculptor, who is supposed to have sent models occasionally, and John Duesbury, overlooker.

William Billingsley, son of Mary Billingsley of Derby, was apprenticed to Duesbury of Derby, china or porcelain maker, 26th September, 1774, for five years, " to be taught the art of painting upon china or porcelain ware," and to receive 5s. per week during the whole of the five years. Billingsley was sixteen years of age when apprenticed, having been born in the parish of St. Alkmund, Derby, in 1758. He left Derby in 1796 to join Mr. Coke in starting the Pinxton factory, a connection which only lasted four years, and about 1800 he appears to have established a small works in Belvedere Street, Mansfield, an old-fashioned town some seven miles from Pinxton, where, with some of the workmen whom he had induced to accompany him, he decorated china in the Pinxton manner. John Ward, F.S.A., to whom the previous Editor was indebted for many interesting details of Billingsley's chequered career, mentions two excellent specimens in the Cardiff Museum signed " Billingsley, Mansfield," the one a covered cup richly diapered with gold, and the other a large jug with monochrome views of Nottingham Castle and Sherwood Forest. These are illustrated in Godden's *British Pottery and Porcelain, an Illustrated Encyclopædia of Marked Specimens*.

The venture was not a success, and after three years Billingsley left it, and is next heard of at Torksey, a village near Gainsborough. Samuel Walker (who, by the way, has hitherto been erroneously called George by Marryat, Professor Church, Jewitt, and others) worked at Torksey with Billingsley, and married his daughter some years later, and is the same man, says Ward, of whom we afterwards hear so much in connection with the Nantgarw and Swansea china. The Torksey scheme was a failure, and Billingsley and his family became involved in great financial difficulties, and travelled about under an assumed name, enduring great hardships until Billingsley and Walker obtained situations at Worcester. Here they worked for some time, and Binns mentions them in his *Century of Potting*. They introduced a system of firing called the " reverberating kilns," which had been in use at London and Derby, but were new to Worcester. They built them both for Flight, Barr & Barr, and also for the Chamberlains.

Billingsley appears to have been a man whose undoubted great abilities were spoiled by a hot temper and a restless ambition, and in 1813 we find him disregarding his engagement, and leaving Worcester to start manufacturing porcelain in Wales. He and his son-in-law, Walker, selected Nantgarw, on the banks of the Glamorgan Canal, in the Taff Valley, for their operations; but their small capital was soon exhausted, and they sought the aid of William Weston Young, a native of Gloucestershire, who had long resided in Glamorgan. He advanced some money, but the concern was a losing one, and an agreement was then made with the proprietors of the Swansea Pottery, where the works were transferred.

It was while experiments were being made at Swansea that Dillwyn, the proprietor, received a letter from Flight, Barr & Barr stating that " the parties calling themselves Beeley and Walker had clandestinely left their engagement at Worcester," and forbidding him to employ them; and as it was not worth while to prosecute them, Dillwyn adds in a letter to Dr. Lardner, that the runaways went back to Nantgarw. The revival of the Nantgarw works is told under the notice of that factory, but it was short-lived, and Rose of Coalport purchased the stock and plant of the works either in 1820 or 1822, and Billingsley entered his service until he died in 1828, and thus, to quote Jewitt, " one of the most remarkable men in the whole line of English potters passed away in complete obscurity, and in much greater poverty than his talents deserved." For further particulars of Billingsley's career, see also Swansea and Nantgarw section.

Coffee was formerly a painter in oil; he also was a modeller, especially of animals. W. Bemrose, jun., of Derby, had several examples of dogs and a bull in terra-cotta, on which was written in the clay, " W. T. Coffee, fecit, 1811, published." He left the works about 1790, and subsequently worked on his own account. We have seen a wolf, wild boar, and other animals bearing his name, W. T. Coffee, Derby.

A writer in the *Derby Mercury* of 10th May, 1865 (F. J. Jessop) says that Duesbury was proprietor of some china works at Longton as well as Derby. He also alludes to a china jug made in commemoration of Admiral Rodney's victory over the French fleet under De Grasse, which was presented to a club of Derby china workmen, called the " Sick Club "; the spout is a head of Rodney, under which is the date 12th April, 1782, and it is ornamented with groups of flowers painted by Withers. A similar jug is in the Schreiber Collection at the Victoria and Albert Museum. He also speaks of a " prentice plate " painted by Billingsley, which was kept as a pattern in the old Derby manufactory until its close in 1848. (*Ker. Gall.*, figs. 561, 571.)

There was another painter, named William Pegg, a Quaker, who was clever in painting single flowers and plants, but from a singular notion that it was sinful " to make the likeness of anything," retired from the profession, and kept a shop, which, however, barely kept him; his conscientious scruples did not prevent him from occasionally indulging in the *sin*, for he painted a water-colour group of red-herrings, which was placed in his window to intimate that he dealt in that savoury edible. Mr. Haslem of Derby had a thistle plate or square china tray painted by Pegg, with one gathered from " Nun's Green." (*Ker. Gall.*, fig. 563.)

Shortly after the purchase of the Chelsea Works, new premises were taken in London for the sale of porcelain from the manufactories of Chelsea and Derby. This was in June 1773, on which occasion a large engraved card was issued by Mr. Duesbury; one of these has a deep border, grounded in green, with designs of amphoræ, flower vases, tripod candelabrum, obelisk, ewer and basin, cabaret, tureen, dishes, &c.; at the top are two amorini holding festoons, to which are attached medallion busts; on an oval in the centre is written : —

" Duesbury & Co., Manufacturers of Derby and Chelsea Porcelain, most respectfully beg leave to inform the Nobility, Gentry, and the Public in General, that they have fitted up the large and elegant *Suit* of rooms at No. 1 Bedford Street, Covent Garden; which are now opened with a great variety of capital as well as useful and Ornamental Articles. A fine assortment of Biscuit *groops* and single figures; Also a curious Collection of Derbyshire Fluors Mabasters *(sic)*, Marbles, &c. *N.B.*—The rooms are well air'd."[1]

At the same time a catalogue in small 4to of 20 pages, comprising nearly 200 objects, was published; the title states:—

" Messrs. Duesbury & Co., proprietors of the Derby and Chelsea Manufactories, most respectfully beg leave to acquaint the Nobility, Gentry, and the public in General, that they have now opened a commodious warehouse in Bedford Street, Covent Garden, with large assortments of the following articles specified in this Catalogue : The ornamental part consists of Jars, Vases, Urns, Tripods, Altars, &c. Designed in the Antique and Modern taste, &c. The useful part furnishing an extensive variety of rich and select Table and Desert Services, &c. Great choice of Biscuit Groups and figures in a Grotesque style, from accurate designs, elaborately finished even to the minutest imitation of lace. Also a collection of Derbyshire Fluors worked into slabs, obelisks, vases, &c. &c."

Our limits will not allow of a lengthened extract from this list, the more especially as the objects are so minutely described, but we will copy a few important specimens:—

" 1. Their present majesties the King and Queen and royal family, in 3 grouped pieces in biscuit—the centre piece represents the King in a Vandyke dress, on a blue and gold basement, supported by 4 lions, leaning on an altar richly ornamented in blue and gold, with hanging trophies of the polite arts and sciences. The crown, munde, and scepter reposing on a cushion of crimson, embroidered, fringed, and tasselled in gold. Height 14 inches.

" 13. A set of three crimson-coloured crown topped *urns,* with white and gold buttoned square anses, and circular cartouches, representing on the centre urn Venus and Adonis, painted after a drawing of Boucher, and a bouquet; the two side urns of the same form represent Dido receiving Æneas, Vertumnus and Pomona, and two landscapes, white and gold festoons pass through the anses; height 13¾ and 9¾. *N.B.*—Two other vases, No. 28, being added form a set of five.

" 96. A pair of mazarine blue and gold Chelsea jars, with white and gold foliage anses and bottoms; the two cartouches represent a shepherd filling the lap of a sleeping shepherdess with flowers, and a nymph uncovered in her sleep by a curious satyr;— both are matched with flower pieces on the opposite cartouches.

" 101. A pair of crimson-coloured cabinet cups and saucers, spangled with gold; the cups with two white gold-tipped foliage handles; cups and saucers embellished with white compartments to detach two antique heads framed in gold, and suspended on a green and red laurel festoon tied with blue knots."

There are no groups or figures enumerated in this list, but in a catalogue of a sale by auction by Mr. Christie in Pall Mall, on the 9th and 10th February 1773, being of the last year's produce of the Derby and Chelsea porcelain manufactories, we find, among various ornamental and useful objects, the following biscuit and coloured groups, which the catalogue states "are modelled with the greatest nicety, and particularly suited for the embellishment of desserts."

1. A pair of sitting figures, finely enamelled, and richly finished with gold.

---

[1] The manufacturing of vessels and ornaments from solid fluor spar (called Blue John) was begun in Derbyshire in 1765.—Watson's *Chemical Essays,* ii. 227.

2. Apollo and four Muses : Calliope, Terpsichore, Urania, Melpomene, finely modelled in biscuit.

3. A pair of sitting figures, with a dog and cattle, enamelled, and richly finished with lace.

4. A group of two figures (Spring), finely modelled in biscuit.

5. Four groups of the elements (Earth and Air, Fire and Water), finely modelled in biscuit.

6. Five Muses : Euterpe, Polyhymnia, Thalia, Erato, and Clio, finely modelled in biscuit.

7. A pair of sitting figures : gentleman singing, and lady playing on the guitar, finished with lace in biscuit.

8. Two groups, Poetry and Grammar, finely modelled in biscuit.

9. A pair of elegant sitting figures, finely enamelled, gentleman reading and lady knotting, richly finished with gold.

10. An altar dedicated to Bacchus, enamelled in figures, a fine crimson ground, superbly decorated with gold.

11. A pair of French horn and guitar figures, finely modelled in biscuit.

12. A pair of sitting figures, with a dog and cat, finely modelled, and finished with lace, in biscuit.

13. A fine figure of Garrick in the character of Richard III., in biscuit.

14. Two groups, Music and Painting and Sculpture, finely modelled in biscuit.

15. A set of antique Seasons on pedestals, finely modelled in biscuit.

16. A pair of small sitting figures, finely modelled and finished with lace, in biscuit.

17. A pair of elegant dancing groups, enamelled and finished with gold.

18. A pair of figures, Prudence and Discretion, finely modelled in biscuit.

19. A pastoral group, finely modelled, with an antique vase, enamelled.

20. Four groups of the Arts and Sciences, viz., Painting and Sculpture, Poetry and Music, and Astronomy, in biscuit.

21. A bust of Voltaire, finely modelled in biscuit.

22. A pair of sitting figures, gentleman playing on the flute and a lady singing, enamelled and decorated with gold.

23. A large group, Jason and Medea vowing before the altar of Diana, enamelled and richly finished with gold.

The Derby figures are seldom marked with the crown, cross, and D, as the services were, but underneath the base we find three large round blotches or pad marks on which the figure rested in the kiln, and the number of the pattern scratched in the clay, and sometimes the size, as mark no. 17. Mr. Bernard Rackham first drew attention to the " patch " marks on early figures and the subsequent identification of Derby figures and groups of the 1750–70 period. See Godden's *British Pottery and Porcelain, an Illustrated Encyclopædia of Marked Specimens.*

Collectors of old Derby figures should consult Haslem's *The Old Crown Derby Factory,* 1876, for the interesting information he gives us with reference to these incised marks.

From the old books of the factory he has extracted the original description, numbers, and prices of the various models, and the following quotation will show how one may refer from a specimen purchased at the present-day prices, and see exactly what it was originally published at. Thus:

No.	Names of Groups and Figures.	Size.	Height, Inches.	Enamelled and Gilt.			Biscuit.		
				£	s.	d.	£	s.	d.
1	Group of the Virtues	1st	11½	2	2	0	...		
	Do. do.	2nd	...	...			...		
3	The Elements (Stephan)	1st	...	3	3	0	3	13	6
	Do. do.	2nd	...	2	12	6	3	3	0
	Do. do.	3rd	7⅛	1	16	0	2	2	0
4	Pastoral Group	...	...	2	12	6	3	3	0
5	Four Antique Seasons in a set	1st	8	1	4	0	1	8	0
	Do. do.	2nd	6½	0	16	0	...		
	Do. do.	3rd	4⅞	0	12	0	...		
6	Four Seasons in a set	...	4	0	10	6	...		
7	Gardening	1st	6¾	0	15	0	0	16	0
	Do.	2nd	5	0	8	0	0	9	0
8	Fruit and Flowers	...	5¾	0	10	6	0	12	0
9	Music	1st	6¼	0	14	0	0	16	0
	Do.	2nd	6	0	10	6	0	12	0
	Do.	3rd	4⅝	0	6	0	0	7	0

It will be observed from these prices that the cost of the figures and groups in *biscuit* were higher than those "enamelled and gilt," or, as we should say, the coloured specimens. This was, it has been said, on account of the great difficulty in producing perfect specimens of *biscuit*, and the many trifling flaws from firing, which could not be remedied in the white, could be filled in and concealed by the colouring.

These groups and figures of Derby biscuit are among the most beautiful objects of a collector's possessions. The paste is soft and pleasing, the modelling careful and finished in the minutest details; they are preferred by many to the coloured porcelain. In addition to an incised number denoting the pattern, we find another number indicating the size, as figures were made in several sizes, and sometimes also the fabric mark of the crown and crossed sticks. Thomas Boynton mentions a figure of Shakespeare in his collection, with Nos. 305, No. 6, and in black the mark no. 16.

These incised numbers, the particulars of which are given by Haslem, run as high as No. 390, besides a lengthy list of articles not numbered, and he also quotes from some old Derby factory books (which were shown to the former Editor by R. W. Binns) the numbers of different patterns of tea, coffee, dinner, and dessert services. One of these books contains the numbers of tea services up to 770, and another with dinner and dessert services up to 400. The works were, therefore, very productive, although, of course, only some of these services were of such decoration as would render them valuable in a collector's eyes, a large number being of a purely domestic character.

Among the splendid services executed at Derby, the following may be particularly noticed:—

An elegant dessert service of 120 pieces, for the Prince of Wales, in 1788.

A service for the Earl of Shrewsbury, upon a rich ground of chrome green, embellished with fruit subjects.

Another for the Duke of Devonshire, enriched with original views of Chatsworth, Hardwick, etc.

Elegant services for Lord Muncaster and for Lord Ongley, richly and tastefully embellished with historical designs.

A service consisting of numerous bowls and dishes for the Persian Ambassador was, in 1819, executed in a style of superior splendour; the ground was gold, chased, and inscribed with Persian characters.

Among statuettes we may allude to two quaint figures of dwarfs, represented in the Derby porcelain, the history of the production of these oddities being that two similar figures stood formerly outside the Mansion House, and to which public advertisements were frequently attached. Illustrated in Litchfield's *Pottery and Porcelain*. These models have been re-introduced by the present company.

Towards the end of the eighteenth century it was very much the fashion for ladies to paint china, not only cabinet specimens, but sometimes whole services, elaborately covered with flowers and fruit; these were painted in mineral colours, and afterwards burnt in or set in a muffle kiln. The white Derby china was a favourite medium of handing down to posterity these proofs, if not of the taste, at least of the industry and perseverance of their grandmothers and maiden aunts, who employed their leisure hours in this way. Many of these anomalous and frequently gorgeous relics present themselves to the perplexed collector

The following advertisement occurs in the *Derby Mercury*, April 5th, 1810:—

"ENAMELLED CHINA.—Thomas Soar, with the greatest respect, begs leave to inform the Nobility, Gentry, and Public at large, that he enamels Dessert, Breakfast, and Tea Services, with arms, crests, cyphers, &c., in the most elegant manner and on the most reasonable terms. His long experience at the Derby Porcelain Manufactory encourages him to look with confidence for support. *N.B.*—Ladies instructed to paint china at their own apartments on reasonable terms. Navigation Row, near St. Mary's Bridge, Derby."

We have before us an advertisement of a sale by auction, by Mr. H. Phillips, on the 4th July 1798, at his great room, New Bond Street:—

"Part of the stock of a White Derby China Manufactory, comprising tea and coffee services, many hundred cabinet cups and saucers and ornamental articles, the property of the manufacturers. The above affords to the gentry a favourable opportunity of providing themselves with white porcelain, either for immediate use or to paint upon as specimens of ornament."

W. Bemrose, jun., kindly inquired of an old man who was engaged at the Old Works about this "White Derby China Manufactory," of which he gives the following explanation:—

"At the Old Works in the Nottingham Road there was a workman employed in the ornamental room named Wm. Duesbury; he was a relation of the Wm. Duesbury in partnership at that time with Mr. Kean, carrying on the works. When Coffee, the modeller, left the Derby China Factory, Wm. Duesbury, who was a potter, left also, and Coffee and Duesbury became partners and manufacturers in a small way in the neighbourhood of Friar Gate; their partnership was of short duration, for Messrs. Duesbury and Kean, thinking these men were likely to become their rivals in the china trade, induced their relative to return to their employment and cease to be a partner with

Coffee. This broke up the Friar Gate Factory, where, I believe, Coffee afterwards manufactured terra-cotta ornaments and figures. The above facts I have frequently heard related by the old potters at the china works in the Nottingham Road. I have no doubt this is the ' white Derby china ' named in the advertisement; the articles named are exactly what I should expect a small establishment to produce, and the date corresponds so far as I can ascertain, with the time Coffee ceased to be employed at the Old Derby China Works."

The old Derby manufactory in the Nottingham Road was advertised for sale or to be let in December 1846, as there stated, " in consequence of the death of the late owner and occupier, Robert Bloor, Esq.; formerly the property of Messrs. Duesbury and Kean. To treat for the purchase or to rent, apply to Mr. James Thomason, executor of the late Robert Bloor, Esq., or to Mr. Thomas Clarke, corn factory, Derby." It was subsequently pulled down, and a covent was erected on its site. This building was also demolished in 1863. (Specimens of Derby china, see the *Ker. Gall.*, figs. 560–571.)

In a more recent contribution to our information about Derby porcelain, William Bemrose, in *Bow Chelsea and Derby Porcelain*, London, 1898, quotes from Duesbury's work-books and from other documents which had recently come into his possession, to prove that the date of 1751, which has been generally accepted as that of the foundation of the Derby factory by William Duesbury, is not correct. It should be noted that the incised date 1750 occurs. From the years 1751–53 Duesbury was at work in London as an enameller to the trade, and the quotations from his work-books include several such items as the following:—

" 6 doz flowrs," 6s.; " a pair of imbost jars," 3s.; a pair of leaf jars, 4s. And there is also a receipt for a sum of £6, 19s. for " collors " paid by Duesbury to " Frederick Vorgewits."

Bemrose thinks that Duesbury worked for the different factories which are mentioned by him in his work-book, namely, " Bow or Bogh," " Chellsea," " Darbey," " Darbishire and Staffordshire," and then with the money he had saved and some assistance from Heath he purchased some seven houses at Derby, and transformed them into workshops, and started a manufactory in the year 1756. Whether about the same time Duesbury had any connection with the Longton Hall works is open to question. In 1756, he was living at Longton Hall and is described as " enameller." If he did, he was concerned in four of our English factories, and the following chronology, as given by Bemrose, may be of interest:—

1725. William Duesbury born.
1751–53. William Duesbury working in London as an enameller to the trade.
1754–55. Starting the Longton Hall works. (?)
1756. Starting the Derby works.
1770. Purchases the Chelsea works.
1776. Purchases the Bow works.

1784. Closes the Chelsea works.
1786. Dies, and is succeeded by his son, William Duesbury II.
1795. William Duesbury II enters into partnership with Michael Kean.
1796. William Duesbury II dies, succeeded by William Duesbury III.
1811. Partnership dissolved between Duesbury and Kean.
1811. Robert Bloor purchases the Derby works.
1846. Robert Bloor dies.
1846. Thomas Clarke carries on the works.
1849. Boyle buys models, moulds, etc. Derby factory closed.

MARKS ON DERBY AND CHELSEA-DERBY PORCELAIN

Marks 1 and 2. An early mark (c. 1750+) was either a simple *D* or the word *Derby*; the latter occurs on a very old Derby white china cream-jug, decorated with fruit and leaves. The incised mark " New D " occurs on an early pair of figures in the Derby Museum.

This early mark no. 1 of a *D* is generally somewhat roughly scratched in the paste and is found on some early experimental pieces. Bemrose describes a white cream jug with strawberries in relief, something like the Chelsea Bee and Goat jugs. A similar white jug in the Victoria and Albert Museum has the " D " mark and date 1750.

Mark no. 3, in pink on a semicircular porcelain jardinière, painted with detached flowers in natural colours and small gold sprigs between, gilt borders, and a gilt ram's head at each end; formerly in the possession of Mr. Jeans. C. 1760–70. This mark may occur on other wares.

Mark no. 4. This cursive *N*, incised in the paste, is on a pair of cups and saucers painted in colours with festoons of flowers suspended from the beaded gilt edge. The same mark occurred also upon a very beautiful set of two ewers and a vase in Borradaile's Collection, and also on many other specimens. This *N* must not be confounded with the *No.* signifying the number so frequently found on Derby figures. C. 1770–c. 1790.

Mark no. 5. The Chelsea Works was united to Derby in 1769, and the moulds and models from Chelsea were subsequently transferred to Derby, which then became an important manufactory; this union is denoted by the anchor of Chelsea crossing an italic capital *D*, c. 1770–84.

This mark, in gold, is also on every piece of a dessert service of forty-four pieces purchased of W. Duesbury & Co., Derby, for £33 8s. in June 1773; in the centre is painted a large bunch of grapes, and round the border medallions of cameo busts of Roman Emperors, in white on chocolate ground, connected by festoons; formerly in the possession of Sir Philip de Malpas Grey Egerton, and now in a Sussex collection. The invoice is still preserved, and as it alludes to other pieces, some of which are well known, it is here given entire:—

PHILIP EGERTON, Esq.   *Bot of* WILLIAM DUESBURY & CO., Derby.

		£	s.	d.
1771.				
Nov. 7.	Pair of knotting figures, finely enamel'd & gilt	2	2	0
1773.				
Jan. 28.	Large Tea Pot, enamel'd blue and gold, chased and burnished .	1	11	6
April 7.	A Tythe pig groupe	0	16	0
	A pair—the Welch taylor and family	1	1	0
April 2.	A pair of small Prudence and Discretion	0	12	0
June 22.	24 Disert plates in medallions and grapes @ 13/	15	12	0
	2 Large Oval Comports at 25/	2	10	0
	2 Large heart-shaped Comports at 25/	2	10	0
	16 Smaller, different shapes, @ 16/	12	16	0
Dec. 1.	4 Baskets and stands @ 31/6	6	6	0
	3 Large punch bowls, painted; yᵉ allusion of stag hunting, hare hunting, and fishing, @ 42/	6	6	0
	2 Quart Jugs with the word *Fiat* and rose and thistle . .	2	2	0
	2 Half pint mugs do. do. do. . .	0	10	6
	A nest of mugs, 5 pieces, finely painted with heads and trophies .	3	3	0
	3 Jugs, various sizes, painted in flowers and gold . . .	3	0	0
	Boxes . .	0	4	6

A trident for Neptune gratis.
                                                           £61 2 6

Received SARAH DUESBURY, 9 July 1774.

The Quart Jugs referred to in the above invoice were made for a Jacobite Club of the border counties and North Wales, called the *Cycle*, of which many relics were preserved at Oulton Park, especially a portrait of Prince Charles Edward, enclosed in a walnut wood cabinet, which, according to tradition, was placed upon the table and unlocked when the health of Prince Charlie was given; and some drinking-glasses with the same motto. The Miss Sarah Duesbury who signed the invoice, was the daughter of the second William Duesbury, who managed the sale business over St. Mary's Bridge, Derby, for many years.

6

Mark no. 6 is an anchor painted in gold. It occurs on fine quality Derby porcelains decorated at the Chelsea works from about 1770 and during the Chelsea-Derby period. A garniture of three vases and two ewers, decorated with pale blue and gold stripes, with medallions of figure subjects and landscapes, have the anchor in gold on the stands of the vases, and in the paste the No. 98 incised, also the kiln mark of three blisters in the paste. These are of the transition period, and may be classed as Chelsea-Derby. Several other examples can be cited of the gold anchor mark occurring on Derby or Chelsea-Derby wares, c. 1770–84.

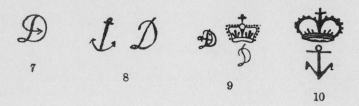

Mark no. 7, on part of a service, marked with the double anchor, painted with flowers, and the gold unusually thick; formerly in Dr. Diamond's Collection. This may be regarded as a variation of no. 5. C. 1770–c. 1784.

Mark no. 8. The mark of Chelsea-Derby, when represented by the anchor and " D," is almost invariably a combination of the two, as in the above marks, but a fine sucrier and cover with turquoise colourings and the " hop trellis " pattern with gold ornaments was purchased by Albert Amor of St. James Street, bearing the anchor and letter D in gold separated.

Mark no. 9. These two marks are on a fine quality cup and saucer in the British Museum, decorated with blue and gold spiral flutings, and it is evidently part of a service which was produced at the time when Duesbury had just purchased the Chelsea works and amalgamated them with those at Derby.

Mark no. 10, in gold occurs on a set of four oviform vases, made in August 1777, for Philip Egerton, Esq., of Oulton Park, with portraits of himself, his wife, and two children; the invoice of William Duesbury of Derby is also still preserved, and they are thus described: *four cups and covers enamel'd with portraits in compartments and striped with gold*, £6 6s. od. The following items occur in the same bill:—

2 Trouts' heads for Drinking cups	.	.	.	.	.	£0	11	0
Pair of Duck Sauce Boats	.	.	.	.	.	0	5	0
Dejeuner enamel'd Chantilly pattern	.	.	.	.	1	11	6
Punch Cask, enamel'd with oak leaves and acorns, mounted with a silver cock, gilt	.	.	.	.	4	14	6
2 Druid Cups in compartments, green ground	.	.	.	1	11	6

The receipt is signed by W. Duesbury, jun.

The same mark occurs on a Derby-Chelsea plate, painted with vases of flowers in the centre and festoons with gilt ornaments, formerly in the

Sheldon Collection. The Countess of Essex had a dessert service, bearing this mark, which is rare, and may be dated c. 1770–84. The pieces bearing the anchor and crown (without the *D*) were probably made at Chelsea by Duesbury, after his purchase of the works in 1769, as they were continued by him at Chelsea for more than ten years, and not finally abandoned until 1784.

No. 60
3d size.

Mark no. 11, c. 1770–80. This mark was used on porcelain, painted in the Chinese style in fine enamel colours, scarcely distinguishable from the Oriental, except in the softness of the paste. This mark and no. 3 are copied from the Chinese, representing, apparently, an incense burner. There are five plates in the Victoria and Albert Museum so marked, finely enamelled in colours, with Chinese flowers, amorini in the centre. Slight variations of this mark occur.

Mark no. 12. Crown-Derby. This mark was on a handsome gilt Derby tea service, in the possession of the Earl of Chesterfield. This should not be regarded as a factory mark as it seems unique to this special service.

Mark no. 13. The crown and letter painted red, the square impressed, on a porcelain plate, of oriental pattern, in the Victoria and Albert Museum. A very rare mark.

A similar seal mark in blue, also accompanied by the usual Derby mark in red, is on a plate of oriental design formerly in the collection of Captain Sharp of Bellshill, Northumberland.

Mark no. 14. Standard Crown Derby mark painted in blue, c. 1770– c. 1782.

Mark no. 15. This Crown-Derby mark, in purple, with DK, is on a large china mug painted with a landscape and rainbow, gilt edges, formerly in the collection of the Rev. T. Staniforth. The mark of Duesbury & Kean, used occasionally after 1795. Very rarely used as a factory mark.

Mark no. 16 is a variation of the standard mark no. 18.

Mark no. 17, with variations, is incised on the base of figures and relates to the model number and size.

Mark no. 18. The standard mark from c. 1782, in blue or puce, the latter colour being the oldest and most prized by collectors. A crown above a cross, and three dots in each side angle, below which is a capital *D*, used from about 1782 by the Duesburys, and continued in red by Robert Bloor as late as about 1825; sometimes the cross is omitted, and only the crown and letter pencilled upon the ware. Lord Tweedmouth had a very beautiful dessert service with a violet mark, with richly-jewelled border and medallions of landscape views. Mark no. 16 is a variation of this standard mark.

Mark no. 19, reputedly used in 1803. Part of a set made for the second W. Duesbury; on a green leaf dessert dish, veined and coloured after nature. This mark also occurs on some pieces of a beautiful service, evidently made at Derby to match the Tournay service at Windsor Castle; the names of the birds represented are also written at the back of each piece.

Mark no. 20. This rare mark in blue is on a tea service, blue and gold border but should not be regarded as a standard mark.

An unglazed vase, with flowers, taken from a sulphur mould, formerly in the collection of W. Bemrose, jun., is marked in the clay with a triangle, and underneath " No. 115," as well as the usual Crown-Derby mark (no. 18). This triangle mark was the sign of Joseph Hill. There is frequently found on Crown-Derby china in the centre, at the bottom of the piece, a star of six points stamped in the ware; usually without the painted mark in red, but occasionally with it. This was the mark of Isaac Farnsworth, one of the repairers or assembler of figures.

19   20   21   22

Mark no. 21. The words " Duesbury, Derby," in addition to the usual Derby mark, occur on a can and saucer of pale salmon colour and gold decoration, formerly in the collection of Dudley W. Macdonald. In previous editions Chaffers considered that this mark was only a design of Duesbury's which had not been used, but the specimen here mentioned goes to prove the contrary.

Mark no. 22. Jewitt gives this mark, which he thinks may have been used at Caughley to pass as Chelsea-Derby; it occurs on a copper-plate for a mug, with landscape and figures, but it is doubtless the mark of Richard Holdship, who worked both for Derby and Worcester, placing the name of each town under or by the side of his rebus, the anchor (Holdship), according to his engagement. It will be observed that this anchor (in both instances) differs from that of Chelsea, by the omission of the ring at the top, and in the angle of inclination. Jewitt had in his possession an agreement between Duesbury of Derby and " Richard Holdship of the city of Worcester, china maker," to print such china as may be required, and this was one of his copper plates; the date of this deed is 1764, after he retired from the Worcester works.

Mark no. 23. This interesting inscription is on a small porcelain cup 2¾ in. high, diameter at base 1⅞ in. and at the mouth 2½ in., straight sides, without a handle. It bears, printed in lilac under the glaze, the bust of the King of Prussia, somewhat similar to the type used at Worcester, but evidently not from the same plate. Under the bust is a ribbon inscribed " The King of Prussia," and underneath at the right-hand corner is written " Derby, 1757 "; on the other side of the cup is the figure of Fame with two trumpets, differing materially from the Worcester copperplate. The Derby cup above referred to was doubtless an experiment of Holdship's to produce a colour under the glaze, which, however, was not perfectly successful, the figure of Fame having changed in the kiln from lilac to brown.

Mark no. 24. This counterfeit mark of the Meissen factory is some-times found upon Derby as well as Worcester; it occurs on several pieces of a service, the greater portion being marked with the Crown-Derby mark in red; also on some copies of Chelsea plates, crimson and gold borders, painted with exotic birds. The Sèvres mark has also been found in some specimens of Derby. C. 1800+.

About 1825 we meet with the " thumb-printed " marks nos. 25–27 of the late Bloor period, to secure a uniform trademark; these were affixed to the porcelain by taking off the impression with the thumb from a copper-plate charged with vermilion.

Mark no. 25. Derby. Robert Bloor succeeded Duesbury & Kean about 1815, but continued using the marks adopted by them of the crown, crossed batons, and dots, with the D (no. 18), until about 1825, when he discontinued it, and substituted his own name as mark no. 25.

Mark no. 26. Bloor's mark, used about 1825+.

Mark no. 27. On a statuette formerly in the possession of Mr. Kidd of Nottingham. It may be as well to note that all the Derby marks previous to 1825 were *painted* by a brush, the later ones were *printed* in colour.

Mark no. 28. This mark, painted in green except the " IN," which is in red, is on a dish, painted and gilded, formerly in the Sheldon Collection. The *IN* and *gb* are supposed to represent the letters of Sèvres artists. A special mark probably to match a Sèvres original.

Mark no. 29 which is also a colourable imitation of a Sèvres mark, also the word BLOOR, occurs on a late Derby figure of a girl in the attitude of listening. C. 1830+.

Mark no. 30. A mark used by Bloor from about 1835; sometimes this scroll is found under the crown.

Mark no. 31 was used by Bloor about 1839. The works in the Nottingham Road were closed in 1848; Bloor died in 1845.

Mark no. 32. Locker & Co. succeeded Bloor when his works were discontinued, and opened a manufactory in King Street, Derby, in 1849, and worked until 1859.

Mark no. 33. Courtney was Bloor's London agent, and after the works closed, carried on the business in his own name at 34 Old Bond Street, London, c. 1846–49. Specimens are rare.

Mark no. 34. The mark of Stevenson, Sharp & Co., successors to Locker in King Street, who died in 1859. The subsequent proprietors were Stevenson & Hancock. For some years the old mark of a crown and *D*, with the cross and dots, had been used on ornamental porcelain; but it having been suggested to Stevenson & Hancock that such a practice was calculated to mislead collectors, they adopted mark no. 35 in 1861, which identifies them with the old-established works, while the addition of the initials of their names, sufficiently marks the difference of the epoch. Stevenson died in 1866; the works were until 1898 carried on by Sampson Hancock, who used the same mark, being the initials of his own name. This was continued until 1935 when the King Street works were taken over by the Royal Crown Derby Porcelain Company.

In 1878 a new factory had been started in premises erected upon the site of the old Workhouse, by a Limited Liability Company, entitled the " Crown Derby Porcelain Company," with E. Phillips, formerly of the

Worcester Porcelain Works, as managing director and W. R. Ingram as modeller; the capital being £67,850, subscribed by local gentlemen interested in reviving upon a large scale the important industry which had formerly flourished at Derby.

36   37

Mark no. 36. The mark of the Derby Crown Porcelain Co. from 1878–90.

Mark no. 37. The new company prospered and in 1890 adopted, by permission of her Majesty, the prefix " Royal," with an alteration of the trade mark as shown.

In previous editions of Chaffers this Limited Company was erroneously stated to have purchased the business of Sampson Hancock who has been referred to above, but the previous Editor received a communication from Mr. Hancock pointing out that he had no connection whatever with the Royal Crown Derby Porcelain Company, but that his business in King Street, Derby, was quite distinct; and further, that his great-great-grand-father was the first apprentice of the original William Duesbury of the first Derby china factory. His productions were on the old lines, and his work, although not on a large scale, was of considerable merit and similar to the old Crown-Derby of the time preceding the " Bloor " period. The two firms were, in fact, amalgamated in 1935. Good examples of all Derby porcelains are illustrated in Godden's *British Pottery and Porcelain, an Illustrated Encyclopædia of Marked Specimens.*

PINXTON. Established about 1796 for the manufacture of porcelain by John Coke and William Billingsley. The latter was a practical potter, having been engaged at the Derby China Works as a flower-painter; he brought with him a staff of workmen and their families to assist in the manufactory. It went on successfully, and as many as fifty to sixty men, women, and children were employed, and twelve or fourteen painters. In the British Museum are three tokens of Pinxton porcelain, circular, about 1⅜ in. diameter respectively, for 5s., 7s., and 10s., marked in figures in the centre, with this inscription, " Let the bearer have in goods 7," and on the other side, " Which place to the account of John Coke, Pinxton, Dec. 4, 1801." In April 1799 Billingsley left the concern, and it was carried on by Coke alone for seven or eight years. Cutts, a painter, who had been his foreman, then took the works; they were altogether discontinued about the year 1818, and Cutts went into Staffordshire. The life and work of William Billingsley was described by Major W. H. Tapp in a paper read to the English Porcelain Circle in 1929, *Transactions*, no. 2.

The china made here was similar to that made at Derby, but lacking the high finish of the best old Crown-Derby work. A favourite pattern was called the " French sprig," being an imitation of the Angoulême china, painted with a forget-me-not or small blue corn-flower, and a gold sprig laid on the white, edged with gold; groups of flowers, and occasionally landscapes, but never with raised flowers, like the Derby, and the ware when not edged with gold was usually blue, but sometimes a maroon colour. After Billingsley's retirement, another description of china was made, of a more opaque character, as he kept the recipe for mixing his ingredients entirely in his own possession, and never divulged the secret; at his death it came into the hands of his employer, Rose of Coalport. An aged widow named Vallance, who worked there many years as gold burnisher (of whom there were about a dozen), possessed several pieces, presented to her when she left. She said she well remembered Billingsley, Slater, Marriott, and Musgrove as painters, and several hands from Derby; George Mellor was one of them. She also remembered Sir Joseph and Lady Banks visiting the works in 1810, when they purchased three hampers of china; they were received during their stay at the house of Mr. and Mrs. Simpson, who lived close by, and Mr. Cutts, the proprietor presented the latter with a quart jug with the letters JMS entwined in gold (Joseph and Mary Simpson), which was in the possession of E. M. Kidd of Nottingham, their grandson, who has several other specimens of Pinxton china, especially a piece marked with an italic *P* purchased at the works by his grandfather. Mrs. Vallance thought they never made china at Mansfield, though they might paint and enamel it there.

The site of the manufactory is well known, being close to the canal, and the tenements built upon it were called the Factory Square and China House Square; they were inhabited by the colliers of the neighbouring coal-mines. Mr. Hawkins, of Grantham, to whom we are indebted for the above information, possessed some specimens purchased on the spot, and E. Norman, of Norwich, had a large coffee-pot, of fine glaze, painted with the " French sprig " pattern, and a tea service, well painted with landscapes and gold borders, marked *P*. and *N*. 300, and sometimes the word " Pinxton." Dudley Macdonald had also a bowl, two plates and a cup and saucer belonging to this service similarly marked. W. Bemrose, of Derby, whose collection was sold at Christie's in 1909, had a set of three flower vases of the sprig pattern with ring handles. There is a covered bowl and a cup and saucer in the British Museum.

The Rev. Septimus Firman of Liverpool had a cup and saucer with finely-painted scenes, marked with a P 108, in red.

38   39

Mark no. 38 in puce, is on a boat-shaped tray, with a landscape well painted in an oval medallion, quite in the character of old Derby, and in

Bemrose's catalogue of the Kidd Collection he finds this mark on some specimens of a service, other pieces of which bear the ordinary Pinxton mark. This device is taken from the Coke Arms.

A cream jug, yellow ground painted in landscape on one side and view of Pinxton Church on the other in dark violet colour bears mark no. 39, the letter P being formed to look like a B. Underneath is written *inxton Church, D   hire*, the missing letters having slipped in firing. This specimen was described in Bemrose's book. Various small impressed letters occur under the bases of specimens. The mark " Pinxton " painted in gold is recorded but is very rare. Interesting articles on Pinxton are contained in *The Connoisseur*, January and February 1963. Many documentary specimens of Pinxton porcelain will be found illustrated in Exley's *Pinxton China Factory*, 1963.

BURTON-ON-TRENT. This factory was established for the manufacture of a yellow earthenware in garden vases, flower-pots, and similar objects. W. Bemrose, jun., informs us that a manufactory of porcelain was situated on the Hay, Burton-on-Trent, established about the year 1839 by a Mr. William Edwards, a lawyer of Derby, assisted by the capital of Mr. Tunnicliffe, and carried on about seven years. Bemrose continues, " The packer informed us that Mr. Edwards would have the wares dipped in skimmed milk, which he thought improved the appearance of the goods, but the packer said ' it only turned 'em mouldy.' " Washing in hot skimmed milk was, however, adopted by Wedgwood to improve the appearance of his black Egyptian ware.

Edwards obtained his potters from Staffordshire: the principal modeller was Wornall Hayes; a person named Malkin mixed the body; the painters were George and John Hancock and Joseph Bentley, from the Derby Works, and William Watson from the Coalport; Isaac Bentley was the manager.

WIRKSWORTH. About the year 1770 there was a manufactory of china here, said to have been established by a person of the name of Gill; pottery was first made, and a punch-bowl of copper-coloured lustre, in the possession of Mr. Lucas, of Bentley Hall, Ashbourne, is believed to be a specimen of the manufacture; they afterwards made porcelain (soft paste), the usual decoration being flowers, roughly painted, and shells, tea services, white and gold borders. No mark is known. The following sale advertisement appeared in the *Derby Mercury* of 16th May, 1777, and may refer to the Wirksworth works. " A great number of elegant Plaister moulds, for toureens, plates, dishes, sauceboats, teaservices and equipages with all other sorts required for a manufactory of china or potwork. A few very large Figures, Vases, Urns, Lamps. . . . Throwing wheels, laths and other implements necessary. A quantity of Zaffer, Borax, Red Lead, Lynn sand . . . with some fine Fritt, ready made. Enquire of Mrs. Dickens, the three crowns, Wirksworth."

CHURCH GRESLEY, Derbyshire. There was reputedly a manufactory of china established at Gresley Hall, the seat of the Gresley family, in

1795. Sir Nigel Gresley, Bart., was lord of the manor of Burslem; his seats were at Knipersley, Drakelow, and Gresley Hall. Wedgwood, writing to his brother in 1765, says: " Sally and I are taking a ride to look at poor Sir Nigel's goods, etc., which are to be sold in a fortnight. He had left Knipersley with his family, and it is much feared his affairs will never suffer his return." The factory was in existence for about twenty years, and the property was sold in 1825 on account of the business not being remunerative. My informant, Mr. W. Brown, says, " Part of the buildings were standing as stables in the farmyard, and were repaired in 1848. My mother told me about the Miss Gresleys painting china for themselves when she went over the works. Gresley Hall was bought by my father from the Gresleys, and was occupied by my grandfather, and we retained it until 1851; we had many dozens of *wastrels*, plates of very fine transparent china, white with a deep blue tree with birds; they were all said to be imperfect, or they would have received a second colour in gold." No mark is recorded.

DENBY (Denby Pottery, near Derby). A manufactory of stone bottles, etc. A better description of ware was attempted here, in imitation of Wedgwood's black Egyptian, by Mr. Bourne. In the 1851 Exhibition J. Bourne, of the Denby Pottery, near Derby, exhibited fine stoneware, garden labels, etc. A stoneware flask moulded as Lord Brougham, with mark no. 40, may be dated c. 1812–34. It is illustrated in Downman's *Pottery* and in Jewitt's *Ceramic Art*. Joseph Bourne & Son Ltd. continue to produce Denby pottery in a variety of useful stoneware articles.

BURTON-ON-TRENT, Woodville. The Ashby Potters' Guild. This industry was founded in 1909 by Pascoe H. Tunnicliffe, who acquired some premises in the village of Woodville, near Swadlincote, in the heart of the Derbyshire potteries. His " Vascoe " ware was produced in a series of crystalline, opalescent, and *flambé* glazes. They were all hand-made, i.e. thrown on the wheel. Specimens are impressed in the clay with the words Ashby Guild, and important pieces bear also the initials of the artists, marks 41 and 42. In 1922 the firm amalgamated with the Ault Pottery and traded as Ault & Tunnicliffe Ltd. until 1937. The marks include the trade name " Aultcliffe."

BELPER & DENBY
BOURNES
POTTERIES
DERBYSHIRE

40

PhT
ω12c

41

ASHBY
GUILD

43

JwD ABR.

42

LOWESTOFT

Previous editions have closely followed William Chaffers' original writings, in which he attributed a class of hard paste Chinese porcelain (decorated for the European market, with armorial bearings, etc.) to the Lowestoft factory. Former editors have added notes in an endeavour to correct Chaffers' serious error but confusion still arises. The time has now arrived to rewrite the Lowestoft section and in so doing all mention of the confusing hard paste myth has been deleted.

Many superstitions have grown up over the establishment and subsequent history of the small " soft paste " porcelain factory at Lowestoft in Suffolk. The basic facts concerning this unpretentious but very interesting manufactory, which over a period of nearly fifty years produced a large range of porcelains, is set out in Gillingwater's *History of Lowestoft* published in 1790:—

" The only manufactory carried on at Lowestoft is that of making *porcelain* or *china ware*, where the proprietors have brought this ingenious art to a great degree of perfection, and from the prospect it affords, promises to be attended with much success. The origin of this manufactory is as follows : In the year 1756, Hewlin Luson, Esq., of Gunton Hall, near Lowestoft, having discovered some fine clay or earth on his estate in that parish, sent a small quantity of it to one of the china manufactories near London, with the view of discovering what kind of ware it was capable of producing, which, upon trial, proved to be finer than that called the Delft ware. Mr. Luson was so far encouraged by this success as to resolve upon making another experiment of the goodness of its quality upon his own premises; accordingly, he immediately procured some workmen from London, and erected upon his estate at Gunton a temporary kiln and furnace, and all the other apparatus necessary for the undertaking; but the manufacturers in London being apprised of his intentions, and of the excellent quality of the earth, and apprehending also that if Mr. Luson succeeded he might rival them in their manufacture, it induced them to exercise every art in their power to render his scheme abortive; and they so far tampered with the workmen he had procured that they spoiled the ware, and thereby frustrated Mr. Luson's design. But, notwithstanding this unhandsome treatment, the resolution of establishing a *China Manufactory at Lowestoft* was not relinquished, but was revived again in the succeeding year (1757) by Messrs. Walker, Brown, Aldred, and Richman, who, having purchased some houses on the south side of Bell Lane, converted the same to the uses of the manufactory, by erecting a kiln and other conveniences necessary for the purpose; but in carrying their design into execution they also were liable to the same inconveniences as the proprietor of the original undertaking at Gunton was; for being under the necessity of applying to the manufactories in London for workmen to conduct the business, this second attempt experienced the same misfortune as the former one, and very nearly totally ruined their designs; but the proprietors happening to discover these practices of the workmen before it was too late, they took such precautions as to render every future attempt of this nature wholly ineffectual, and have now established the factory upon such a permanent foundation as promises great success. They have now enlarged their original plan, and by purchasing several adjoining houses and erecting additional buildings have made every necessary alteration requisite for the various purposes of the manufactory. They employ a considerable number of workmen, and supply with ware many of the principal towns in the adjacent counties, and keep a warehouse in London to execute the orders they receive both from the City and the adjoining towns, and have brought the manufactory to such a degree of perfection as promises to be a credit to the town, useful to the inhabitants, and beneficial to themselves."

The early products of the Lowestoft factory were without exception decorated in underglaze blue, generally with patterns that were Chinese in feeling. It is recorded that women were employed in painting much of the blue and white ware, which continued to be the staple mode of decoration throughout the factory's life, and which proved so suitable for the decoration of utilitarian porcelains for the local middle class clientele. Tea services formed a large part of the factory's output, plates and dishes are rarely found.

A charming series of pieces decorated with moulded relief motifs and ornate scroll cartouches framing Chinese style underglaze blue scenic and figure-subject panels, are noteworthy; the early pre-1775 examples in this style are amongst the most attractive of English blue and white porcelains. See Godden's *British Pottery and Porcelain, an Illustrated Encyclopædia of Marked Specimens*.

Before about 1773 the above-mentioned blue and white, and moulded specimens were often marked with small, workmen's numbers painted in underglaze blue on the inside edge of the footrim. (*N.B.* Similar Bow workmen's numbers generally occur painted on the base of the article, not on the rim.) Examples of these numbers are marks 1 to 7.

| 1 | 2 | 3 | 4 | 5 | 6 | 7 | 8 | 9 | 10 |

It should be noted that the numbers " 3 " and " 5 " are frequently found, and occur on the majority of inscribed and dated pieces. The number " 5 " was often painted half on and half off the footrim, giving a distorted appearance. Initials may also appear on the footrim.

In 1771, Robert Browne, the manager and technical expert, died, and was succeeded by his son Robert. Shortly after Robert Browne junior succeeded his father, the system of workmen's numbers on the footrim was discontinued; no dated examples after 1773 bear such a mark. At the same period underglaze blue printing was introduced and copies of Worcester and other factories' patterns and shapes were reproduced; such examples often bear the crescent mark of Worcester or the crossed swords of Dresden. Such pirated marks belong to the period c. 1770–1790 and only appear on blue decorated examples. Marks no. 8, 9 and 10.

William Chaffers recorded that in the 1780 period between sixty and seventy persons were engaged at the factory and that two travellers were constantly employed. In 1770 the factory had a warehouse in London, a contemporary advertisement reads:—

" Clark Durnford, Lowestoft China Warehouse, No. 4. Great St. Thomas the Apostle, Queen Street, Cheapside, London. Where Merchants and Shopkeepers may be supplied with any quantity of the said ware at the usual prices. N.B.—Allowance of Twenty per cent for ready money."

The first dated examples of Lowestoft porcelain bearing over-glaze enamel colours occur in 1774; these are quite accomplished and it would appear that over-glaze enamel decoration was commenced in about 1770. The London warehouse would require such decorative pieces in order to compete with other establishments. The enamelled patterns were in the main simple floral or Chinese figure subject compositions. More pretentious motifs occasionally occur—ruins, English views, European figure subjects and bold floral sprays, including prominent tulips, are all note-worthy. As with the blue and white pieces, many special commemorative orders were undertaken and these depict such subjects as local churches, farms, ships, etc. Several patterns were decorated in black enamel, slightly heightened with gold.

Apart from some early enamelled pieces with underglaze blue borders, the enamelled Lowestoft porcelain was not marked. The only exceptions to this rule would appear to be some formal Chinese styled patterns associated with the Redgrave family of painters employed at the factory; these patterns occasionally bear a small cross in red enamel on the inside edge of the footrim. A floral bowl in the collection of Noel H. P. Turner, Esq., of Ipswich, bears the number 2 on the footrim; this is the only known example of a number mark occurring on a purely over-glaze enamelled example. Mugs, inkwells, etc., were sometimes inscribed " A Trifle from Lowestoft " (pieces were also made for other East Anglian towns—Bungay, Hingham, Holt, Lynn, Wangford, etc.); these are all rare. See Godden's *British Pottery and Porcelain, an Illustrated Encyclopædia of Marked Specimens*.

Some coloured figures, putti, swans, cats and sheep have been identified but in the main the factory concentrated on the useful wares. For the recently attributed figures the reader is referred to *The Connoisseur Year Book*, 1957.

The Lowestoft factory produced an interesting range of miniature, children's, tea ware and small circular inscribed birth tablets (unique to the Lowestoft factory). The most important feature of Lowestoft porce-

lain lies in the number of special documentary inscribed and dated specimens, made from 1761 onwards; these enable the gradual changes in
style and taste to be seen. A list of the documentary specimens was compiled by A. J. B. Kiddell, Esq., and is included in The English Porcelain
Circle's *Transactions*, no. III, 1931.

The Lowestoft factory was closed about 1802, probably due to the
growing competition from the Staffordshire manufacturers, who with their
earthenware were able to undersell the Lowestoft porcelain.

In 1902 and 1903 a quantity of moulds, broken fragments and factory
wasters were found on the site. These moulds and fragments enabled the
positive identification of Lowestoft wares to be made. The " soft paste "
porcelain body was found to contain a relatively high percentage of bone
ash (about 19 per cent) and as such is chemically (and visibly) similar to
that employed at the Bow factory.

A fine and large collection of Lowestoft porcelain (and moulds) is
permanently displayed at the Castle Museum, Norwich; other collections
may be seen at the Victoria and Albert Museum, London; the Fitzwilliam
Museum, Cambridge; Christchurch Mansions, Ipswich; and at the
Lowestoft Borough Library. Many illustrations of original moulds and
fragments are included in W. W. R. Spelman's otherwise unreliable *Lowestoft
China*, 1905. A selection of blue and white specimens are illustrated in
Godden's *Illustrated Encyclopædia of Marked Specimens*.

The following notes on the proprietors of the Lowestoft factory, and
on the artists are largely taken from earlier editions of this work.

PROPRIETORS OF THE LOWESTOFT WORKS

PHILIP WALKER. Walker was of a good family at Lowestoft. In
1768 we find his name mentioned as one of the feoffees of the church
property. He was still living in 1790, as we find his name " Philip Walker,
gentleman," among the subscribers to Gillingwater's *History of Lowestoft*.
He, like many others of the gentry, had a boat, which was occasionally
engaged in the mackerel and herring fisheries, from 1770 down to the year
1790.

ROBERT BROWNE, one of the original proprietors, was a good chemist,
and had the management of the works, superintending the mixing of the
clays and the colours. He died in 1771, and was succeeded by his son,
Robert Browne, junior, who was also a clever practical chemist, and was
constantly making experiments to improve the body of the ware; he died
in 1806.

OBED ALDRED, partner in the Lowestoft china manufactory. " Obed
Aldred, bricklayer," was appointed one of the feoffees of the church
property in 1768; he died 22nd July, 1788.

Stannard and Aldred had boats engaged in the herring-trade from
1769 to 1778, when they seem to have dissolved partnership. In 1779 we
find Obed Aldred as a shipowner, and he continued so until 1786; at his

death in 1788 his share and interest in the china manufactory, as well as his share of the water-mill at Gunton, stock, outstanding debts, and effects thereto belonging, were left to his widow, Triphena Aldred, which at her death, in January 1791, were assigned to her son, Samuel Higham Aldred, who remained in it until its close in or about 1803.

JOHN RICHMAN was an extensive merchant, and employed several boats in the herring-fishery; in 1748 he had four, and more or less up to 1756, when he seems to have discontinued the trade, and probably devoted himself to the interests of the porcelain manufactory. He was perhaps succeeded by his son James, but we have no precise information on this point.

Robert Browne of Lowestoft has kindly furnished us with the following particulars: The first Robert Browne, who died in 1771, left by his will to his son his fourth part share or interest of and in the water-mill at Gunton, together with the gears, tackle, and furniture, also his interest in the lease of the ground on which the same stands. And being entitled to one-fourth part or share of and in the stock in trade of the china manufactory carried on at Lowestoft, he directs his executors to adjust and settle with his partners concerned therein all accounts; this he also leaves to his son. The executors were Philip Walker of Lowestoft, gentleman, and Obed Aldred, of the same place, bricklayer, two of the partners in the factory.

ARTISTS

RICHARD POWLES. Gillingwater says, " A beautiful view of the light-house hill, with part of the German Ocean, also of the town, the church, etc., has lately been taken by the very ingenious Mr. Richard Powles, a native of Lowestoft, but now resident in Elsingeur, in Denmark, an artist well known to the curious from his elegant drawings." Mr. Davey, super-intendent of the lighthouses of the district, had a china mug which was made at the manufactory in the 18th century for his grandfather, who had the same appointment; it has a large medallion painted with a view of Lowestoft, showing the high and low lighthouses and cottages below the cliff, shipping in the roadstead, etc., above the arms of the Trinity Company; it was probably painted by Powles from that referred to above. One of these mugs can be seen in the Victoria and Albert Museum, and another specimen in the Castle Museum, Norwich.

The Fitzwilliam Museum at Cambridge possesses a porcelain teapot, exquisitely painted on both sides with marine views, shipping, and figures, apparently of Yarmouth roadstead; under the spout are the initials W. J. S. (William and Jane Simpson), for whom it was expressly painted. This piece may also be attributed to Richard Powles (c. 1764, d. 1808) as can other fine figure and shipping subjects occasionally found on Lowestoft porcelain. An interesting paper on the life and work of Richard Powles is included in the English Ceramic Circle's *Transactions*, Vol. 2, No. 7, and was written by the authority on Lowestoft porcelain, A. J. B. Kiddell, Esq.

THOMAS ROSE. Another artist who reputedly painted the beautiful floral patterns which decorate the greater portion of this ware, was named Thomas Rose, a clever painter on porcelain, who, it is said, fled from France previous to the great Revolution. A porcelain smelling-bottle painted with Chinese figures, inscribed W. J. S. (made for the same parties as the teapot just described), is dated 1784; and a scent-bottle painted by Rose, with three fleurs-de-lis and a crown, bearing the initials S. C. (Samuel Chambers), is also dated 1784. It is difficult to identify the work of the painter with certainty.

THOMAS CURTIS. Thomas Curtis (born 1759) was one of the painters at Lowestoft. It is stated by Jewitt (*Art Journal*, July, 1863) that Thomas Curtis was a " silent partner " in the Lowestoft works; but this statement is erroneous, for in an extract from the accounts of Robert Browne, acting as executor of the will of Obed Aldred, who died 1788, reference is made to a mortgage from Thomas Curtis to the said Obed Aldred for £45, which was then, in 1795, unsatisfied, and was not paid until 1796. In the will of Thomas Curtis he is styled " porcelain painter" only. A mug, painted by him for his father and mother, is inscribed, " James and Mary Curtis, Lowestoft, 1771."

Thomas Curtis is associated with a class of formal floral patterns in enamel colours usually in conjunction with wide ornate borders. Many examples in this style were included in the sale of the effects of his son in 1887. A teapot in the Godden collection comes from this source; the original catalogue description reads " A Tea Pot painted by Thomas Curtis, with wide border and festoons and cornucopia of flowers. . . ."

ROBERT ALLEN. Robert Allen worked in the manufactory from its commencement to its close; he entered it as early as 1757, then only twelve years old, as an under-glaze blue painter. There was in his grandson's possession a small china cup on which he proved the colours; on each side is written " Robert Allen, 1760," and in the divisions are a bird flying, a cutter, and flowers. This cup is interesting, as it gives evidence of the china made at Lowestoft at that date, a fine transparent quality of soft paste; the colours then employed and the style of the painter, which may be recognised on other finished pieces. In a service painted for his aunt, Elizabeth Buckle, in 1768, he being then twenty-three years old, we find a great improvement; and on another formerly in Mr. Seago's Collection we find pastoral figures in the Watteau style as well as flowers; a basin with blue and white decoration in the style of the early Worcester has underneath the name E. Buckle. Allen afterwards became foreman of the manufactory; he was thoroughly acquainted with all the various processes; superintended, under Mr. Browne, the mixing of the earths, and assisted him in carrying out his experiments; mixed the colours employed in the decoration, and eventually was manager of the works. We do not know when he became manager, but it was probably about 1780. His grandson, Robert Allen Johnson, had in his possession a small oval palette of enamelled copper, on which are burnt in the various shades of colour employed in the manufactory, each having a number affixed; on the back was written " Griffiths, 1792."

The same gentleman had a sketch-book of Robert Allen's with fruit, flowers, insects, landscapes and figures, ships and animals, all painted in colours; one of these sketches is copied on a plate made for his aunt Buckle in 1768, formerly in Mr. Seago's Collection. There are also coloured portraits of Philip Walker and Robert Browne, two of the original proprietors of the factory, by Robert Allen.

After the close of the works Allen opened a shop in Lowestoft as stationer and china dealer, and having erected a small kiln in his garden, he decorated Wedgwood, Turner, and other Staffordshire wares. His daughter, Mrs. Johnson, who lived at Lowestoft, had a set of twelve Queen's ware plates, painted with English flowers in blue camaieu, which she remembered seeing him paint and bake many years after the works had ceased; these have on the back his initials, " R. A. 1832."

His intimate knowledge, acquired in the preparation of colours as used on porcelain, was turned to account in the art of painting on glass, to which he paid especial attention for amusement rather more than profit.

Allen painted the east window of his parish church in 1819. A Chinese porcelain teapot, in the Victoria and Albert Museum, should be mentioned as it bears Allen's name, and was probably the initial cause of the myth that hard paste porcelain was made, or decorated at the Lowestoft factory. Robert Allen died in 1835, at the age of ninety-one.

Other artists reputedly employed at Lowestoft include: John Sparham, a flower painter. (A John Sparham was born in 1758 and died c. 1786, a son of the same name was born in 1784); Abel Bly (d. 1793); John Bly (b. 1792), who went to the Worcester factory on the closure of Lowestoft, and was known for his shading of gilding and armorial work; Richard Phillip, an early blue and white painter; the Redgrave's—James (b. 1778); John, Margaret (or Mary); James Balls (d. 1774?). Thomas Mortershed, William Hughes (b. 1768) and John Stevenson were modellers, who with other workers later went to Worcester. The female blue painters include Mrs. Cooper, Mrs. Simpson, Mrs. Stevenson and daughter.

YARMOUTH. There was a gloss-kiln here for burning in the decorative colours of earthenware about the end of the eighteenth century. The arrow seems to have been the mark used by some other manufactory at present unknown; it occurs on a dessert service, with flowers and plants painted in front and their names written on the back in red. Mark no. 1, c.1785+.

A decorator named Absolon worked at a place called " The Ovens." Mark no. 2 is found on cream-coloured ware like Wedgwood's Queen's ware, and also on some plates formerly in the possession of J. Mills of Norwich, painted with fruits and flowers, the arrow impressed. Mrs. Wade of Brantingham Thorpe, East Yorkshire, possesses a dish marked " W. Absolon, Yarm." Mark no. 3 is on a specimen in the Sheldon Collection. " No. 25 " occurs on marks after 1790 and before about 1815.

Mr. E. Norman had in his possession some specimens of this so-called Yarmouth ware, which have TURNER stamped on them, and the name of " Absolon " painted; this proves that they were made at Lane End, Staffordshire, and decorated at Yarmouth.   In fact, it was distinctly averred by the Absolons that no ware was ever made there, but that it was

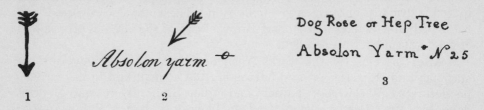

Dog Rose or Hep Tree
Absolon Yarm⁺ N° 25

1   2   3

procured " from the North," and painted and burnt in at the Ovens.   The Absolons seem to have carried on a considerable trade in the sale and decoration of china and glass.   Among a curious collection of tradesmen's notes, issued when the copper currency was at a very low ebb, and quite insufficient for the required change of small sums, we find the following printed note, which has on the left margin a hand holding a cup and " Success to Trade," also the arms of Yarmouth:—

CANNON COURT BANK, YARMOUTH.
I promise to pay *Mr. Brittle* or Bearer, on demand, the sum of Fourpence, at No. 25 Market Row, or at the Norfolk and Suffolk Cut Glass Manufactory.

Value Received.
For China, Delf, Crockery and Self.
M. N. Absolon.

There is also a copper token; on the obverse is a ship in full sail with the words " Yarmouth Halfpenny," 1792; on the reverse are the arms of the town and " Let Yarmouth flourish "; on the edge, " Payable at the Glass Warehouse of W. Absolon."   See *Transactions of the English Ceramic Circle*, Vol. 5, part 1.

CADBOROUGH, near Rye, in Sussex.   " The Cadborough Pottery " was established about 1807 for common descriptions of earthenware; but little is known of its early history until W. Mitchell took possession, about 1840. The clay was evidently suitable for ornamental objects, and great care and attention was bestowed by him in producing them; the artistic productions were very limited—it is a red ware like that used for flower-pots. The vases are of elegant forms, with highly-glazed green or brown mottled surfaces; there are some specimens in the Victoria and Albert Museum, and Dr. H. W. Diamond had a brown jug equal in appearance to the " Rockingham ware."   The name was formerly scratched in the clay, but the retailers objecting, it was omitted.   William Mitchell and his son continued at the Cadborough Pottery until William's death in 1871.   The wares were similar to the Rye pottery examples.

RYE. Frederick Mitchell established the now better known Rye, or Bellevue Pottery, in 1869, and this became famous for " Sussex Rustic Ware," mark no. 4, produced up to about 1920. After various changes in ownership, the factory was closed from 1940 to 1947, when it was re-opened by W. V. & J. R. Cole, who are today producing well-designed decorative earthenware. Their marks are self-explanatory.

4

A very curious vessel called a " Sussex pig " emanates from this factory, and was used at weddings in that county: the body forms the jug and stands on end; the head takes off, and a *hog's head* of beer is drunk off to the bride's health by every person present. One of these pigs is in the Victoria and Albert Museum. These pigs were produced into the twentieth century.

KENT, DEVONSHIRE, CORNWALL
AND PLYMOUTH

In connection with the history of mediæval pottery in Kent (which is very meagre), it may be observed that records are extant proving that in 1582 a Dutch potter was established at Maidstone.

WROTHAM had a manufactory for earthenware jugs, tygs, posset-pots dishes, candlesticks, and other domestic vessels, about the middle of the seventeenth century, which, from the dated pieces here alluded to, continued in operation for more than fifty years, the earliest being, according to the piece so described by Mr. Hodgkin in the Liverpool Museum, 1612, the latest 1739. This name is pronounced *Rootham* in the county. The ware made here is of a coarse brownish-red clay, ornamented with designs, letters, and dates in yellow slip, sometimes with incised or scratched patterns and raised tablets, the whole being covered with a lead glaze. The Rev. Canon Lane, Rector of Wrotham, informed us that the site of the pottery was known, and that fragments were constantly turning up on the spot. The name of an earlier manufacturer was Jull. The vessels are very similar to those made about the same date in Staffordshire bearing the names of Thomas and Ralph Toft, etc., but of greater interest, having frequently the name of the locality. Wrotham is between Sevenoaks and Maidstone. See description of slip decorated ware under notice of Staffordshire pottery—

1656. A jug, ornamented with yellow slip on reddish-brown ground, with an oval tablet enclosing a heart, the initials H · I and date 1656. Maidstone Museum.

1657. A jug, similar, differing only in date. Maidstone Museum.
      A candlestick, undated, but of the same period, with the initials H · I on the upper part, and on the body towards the bottom M. N. I. Maidstone Museum.

1659. A tyg, of brown earthenware and yellow slip, with four double handles, similar to those usually called Staffordshire; round the top is written WROTHAM, and between the handles a fleur-de-lis, the letters C.R., and the owner's name, W.R.S. and the date 1659.

1668. A large round plateau of brown earth and yellow glaze, with incised
       pattern of rosettes and geometrical designs, dated 1668, and the
       letters H.I. in the centre, and I.A., with the sacred monogram
       and date on the border. It was formerly in the possession of a
       family at Tunbridge Wells, where it had remained for more than
       a century, and was traditionally believed to have been made at
       Rootam.

1681 or 1686. A double-handled posset-pot, dark brown body, ornamented
       in yellow slip with fleur-de-lis, the initials I · E and E · C. with
       the date 1681. Two heraldic devices have been laid on the clay,
       but are mostly chipped off, a crown and unicorn alone remaining.
       Victoria and Albert Museum.

1699. A large reddish-brown dish, mottled with yellow slip and orna-
       mented with similar devices, inscribed with the initials E.W.E.
       and WROTHAM, 1699. British Museum.

1703. A double-handled posset-pot in coarse red earthenware, with raised
       ornaments, and inscription laid on in yellow slip before glazing,
       inscribed in rude characters WROTHAM, with I.E. 1703. Victoria
       and Albert Museum.

1707. A tyg, with ornaments of a similar character in yellow slip on
       brown ground, inscribed as mark no. 1. Maidstone Museum.
       A tyg, similar but undated, inscribed I.E. WROTHAM. Maidstone
       Museum.

1710. A large drinking mug, with two knobs serving as handles, height
       7 in., ornamented with yellow slip on brown ground with fleur-
       de-lis, has the same initials I.E. and date 1710, is doubtless from
       the Wrotham pottery.
       Another tyg of this manufactory is preserved at Penshurst, which
       has been in the mansion ever since it came from Wrotham, a
       short distance from thence, and is now one of the heirlooms.

₮E 1707

1

WROTHAM

In the collection of the late Rev. H. Lindsay, Rector of Sundridge,
was a curious specimen of the Wrotham ware, consisting of four mugs,
each with two handles entwined within those of the others, forming a
square; the pattern has been copied in porcelain by modern manufacturers
(engraved in Marryat, 3rd edit. p. 187).

Lord Wimborne possessed three brown ware tygs or bowls, two with
six handles and one with four, two of them being provided with whistles;
that with four handles is 8 in. in diameter, and is inscribed with the fol-

lowing couplet:

> COM . GOOD . WEMAN . DRINK . OF . THE . BEST
> ION . MY . LADY . AND . ALL . THE . REST.

and there are some specimens in the Pitt-Rivers Museum at Rusholt near Salisbury. A very full account of the Wrotham wares is given by A. J. B. Kiddell in a paper in the *Transactions of the English Ceramic Circle*, Vol. 3, part 2. A list of 104 documentary pieces is given. Examples are illustrated in Godden's *British Pottery and Porcelain, an Illustrated Encyclopædia of Marked Specimens.*

DEVONSHIRE AND CORNWALL

Although Cornwall was the county where the principal ingredients for the manufacture of pottery and porcelain were obtained, viz., the lead and tin necessary for the glaze and the best description of clay for the purpose, especially the Cornish *kaolin* or soap-rock, and the moorstone or *petuntse*, a decomposed felspar for making porcelain, yet there do not appear to have been any early manufactories of importance established here. No doubt the reason of this may be traced to the reluctance of the tinners and workmen employed in the mines to adopt earthenware vessels of any kind, being naturally inclined to use those only made of pewter, considering pottery an innovation calculated materially to injure their trade. This dislike is exemplified in the following paragraph from an Exeter paper of 4th April, 1776:—

" Last week the tinners in Cornwall rose, in consequence of the introduction into that county of such large quantities of Staffordshire and other earthenware. About a hundred in a body went to Redruth on the market-day and broke all the wares they could meet with, the sale of which had been intended in that town. From thence they went to Falmouth for the same purpose, and because they could not force their way into the town-hall, where a large parcel of Staffordshire and other wares were lodged, they were about to set fire to it, had not Mr. Allison, the printer and alderman of that town, with another gentleman, pacified them, by promising to discourage the sale and use of these wares by every means in their power, and by going to a pewterer's and bespeaking a quantity of pewter dishes and plates, to evince their readiness to serve them, on which they happily dispersed."

St. Ives. Bernard Leach (b. 1887) established his now famous Studio Pottery at St. Ives, Cornwall, in 1920. He had studied at the Slade School, London; he also studied pottery in Japan and has since re-visited that country on several occasions. Bernard Leach's pots and useful wares display a simple natural feeling for the true potter's craft and his work is widely appreciated and may be seen in museums in many countries.

Several famous English studio potters have been trained at the Leach Pottery—these include Norah Braden, Michael Cardew, Katherine Pley-dell-Bouverie, Harry and May Davis, Dorothy Kemp and many others. David Leach, the eldest son of Bernard Leach, worked with his father for many years, but in 1956 he established his own " Lowerdown Pottery " at Bovey Tracey. David's personal marks are nos. 7, 8 and 9. For further information on Bernard Leach and his pottery the reader is referred to *The Work of the Modern Potter in England* by George Wingfield Digby (1952) and *Artist Potters in England* by Muriel Rose (1955). All the marks are incised or impressed into the clay. Leach Pottery marks are nos. 2 and 3. Bernard Leach's personal marks are nos. 4, 5 and 6.

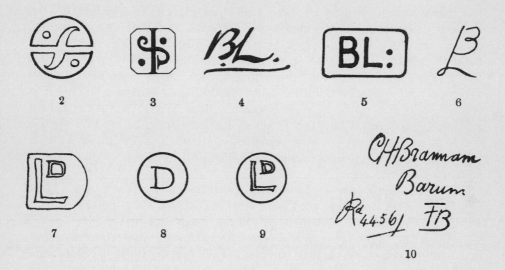

BOVEY-TRACEY, Devonshire. A manufactory of pottery was carried on by John and Thomas Honeychurch; as will be seen by the following extract from an advertisement, it was on a large scale:—

" To be sold by public auction, as directed by the assignees of John and Thomas Honeychurch, bankrupts, at the Union Inn, Bovey-Tracey, on the 2nd May 1836, *The Folly Pottery*, situate in the parish of Bovey-Tracey, in the county of Devon. This may be designated one of the largest and most complete potteries in the West of England, fourteen miles from Exeter and twenty-eight from Plymouth; its situation being in the *land of clay*, from which nearly all the potteries in Staffordshire draw their supply, with coal-mine, and railroad, &c." After describing the premises and its conveniences, it refers to a gloss-kiln and a biscuit-kiln capable of containing 1600 seggars of ware, flint-kilns, a quantity of Cornish flint and clays, copper-plates, moulds, and every implement necessary for carrying on an extensive business.

BOVEY TRACEY. A manufactory of pottery was carried on here by Mr. Divett and Capt. Buller under the title " Bovey Tracey Pottery Co." from about 1842 to 1894. The Bovey Pottery Co. Ltd. continued from 1894 to 1956.

DEVONSHIRE. There were several potteries in Devonshire which turned out a considerable quantity of artistic and useful wares of quaint forms and good glazes of various colours in the nineteenth century. The chief of these was C. H. Brannam's " Royal Barum Ware," made at Barnstaple. His wares were marked *C. H. Brannam, Barum, N. Devon*, scratched on the bottom of each piece, often with the year. Mark no. 10 is on Brannam's Royal Barum Ware. The initials of the decorators differ on each piece. Brannam also made the Devonshire pottery ovens of local fame for bread-baking. The firm continues to produce useful and decorative wares.

In the same town W. L. Baron also made glazed art ware for the shops of the Devonshire watering places. His mark was *Baron, Barnstaple*, with the addition of a number, scratched in the clay. The Rolle Quay Pottery was established about 1899 and continued until 1939.

FREMINGTON, NORTH DEVON. This is the place from which comes the red clay used in the above-mentioned potteries, and it is also of interest on account of the work of a local potter named E. B. Fishley, who worked single-handed and produced some good copies of the old " motto " and fancy jugs of an earlier time; also sgraffitto and " slip "-decorated ware in the manner of the seventeenth century Staffordshire potters. His name is scratched in the paste of each specimen, from 1861 to 1911. Edwin Fishley's grandson, W. Fishley Holland, has continued to produce similar wares at various west country potteries. His book, *Fifty Years a Potter* (1958) is a most interesting account of a life spent in producing hand-made country pottery.

Further south were the Devonshire potteries of THE WATCOMBE TERRA COTTA CO., THE ROYAL LONG PARK, and THE ALLER VALE potteries, with works at Torquay. All of these produced cheap and artistic wares of a decorative character, tea-sets and pieces for table use, with mottoes incised and having glazes of various colours. Their productions are generally stamped or incised with the name of the manufacturing company. In addition to its cheaper wares of this kind, the Watcombe Terra Cotta Co. is well-known for much more important work of both an architectural and a domestic description. This firm ceased in 1903, when it was combined with the Royal Aller Vale Pottery, and as such continues to this day.

At SALISBURY, or somewhere in the vicinity, there was, no doubt, at a very early period, a manufactory of pottery, although no record exists of its locality; fragments of vessels, puzzle jugs, etc., are frequently found in the immediate neighbourhood.

Mr. Nightingale of Wilton kindly forwarded a photograph of a vessel of greenish ware, in the form of a mounted knight, with pear-shaped shield, cylindrical helmet, and prick spur, evidently of the twelfth century; also some puzzle jugs of a fine compact ware and excellent glaze of a brownish red; one of these has scratched under the glaze " W. Z. When this you see, Remember me, 1603 "; another is inscribed " W. Z. maker, 1604," and others with initials only. Another example is dated 1799. These are in the Salisbury Museum. It would seem that Zillwood worked in the late 18th and early 19th century and that the earlier dates are spurious.

Mr. Payne of Salisbury was not a manufacturer, but his name was stamped or printed upon the china made for him, especially on services with printed views of Stonehenge and Salisbury Cathedral; he kept a warehouse for the sale of china and glass in a fine old hall with a timber roof, called the " Halle of John Halle." Mark no. 11.

11   **PAYNE,**
SARUM.

WINCANTON, Somersetshire.   From information supplied to the previous Editor by local antiquaries, it would appear that a potter named Ireson, who had formerly worked at Nuneaton in Warwickshire, carried on at the Somersetshire town of Wincanton a factory of " Delft ware " which achieved a high local reputation.   Specimens, generally bowls, jugs, or plates, described as of a body similar to pie crust, but with a good glaze, and decorated by stencilled process in oriental subjects, and also painted in rustic scenes, fruits and flowers, are in the cabinets of Devonshire collectors.   Such pieces as are marked have the potter's name " Ireson," or the name " Wincanton," or sometimes its Latin equivalent " Wincanto." One piece has the name and date, " G. S. Clewill, 1737 " (Clewill worked for Ireson).   Ireson worked in Wincanton from about 1737 to about 1748.

The previous editor was indebted to W. P. Ivatts for several press cuttings from local papers and some useful letters, with reference to the above hitherto unrecorded pottery.   A documentary example and many fragments found on the factory site are illustrated in Godden's *British Pottery and Porcelain, an Illustrated Encyclopædia of Marked Specimens.*

PLYMOUTH

William Cookworthy was born at Kingsbridge, in Devonshire, in 1705.   His discovery of *kaolin* and *petuntse*, the ingredients of Oriental china, or rather of "moorstone or growan and growan clay," materials which produced porcelain similar to the Chinese, being of hard paste, took place about 1765.   In a letter from Cookworthy dated 1760, he says he has just returned from Cornwall, where he has been for the benefit of his health, and gives an account of a method of distilling sea-water, but not a word about china-clay or china-stone.   An earlier date of his discovery has been assigned, but we have no distinct information on this point.

In 1768 he, in conjunction with Lord Camelford, took out a patent for the use of kaolin and porcelain granite, called china-clay; it is dated the 17th of March 1768.   "William Cookworthy of Plymouth, in the county of Devon, chemist," took out his patent for "a kind of porcelain newly invented, composed of moorstone, or growan and growan clay." The *moorstone* stone, or growan, is said to be known as such in the counties of Devon and Cornwall, and is generally composed of grains of stone or gravel of a white or whitish colour, with a mixture of talcky shining particles; these stones are fusible. "The earth or (growan) clay for the most part lyes in the valleys where the stone forms the hills." "The stone is prepared by levigation in a potter's mill, in water, to a very fine powder." The clay is prepared by diluting it with water, allowing the gravel and mica to subside, pouring the water, white with clay, into vessels, and allowing the clay to settle. It is said that the earth "gives the ware its whiteness and infusibility," and the stone "its transparence and mellowness," and they are mixed in the methods used by potters, in different proportions, as the ware is intended to be more or less transparent. The articles formed, "when biscuited," are dipped in a glaze made of levigated stone, with the addition of lime and fern ashes or *magnesia alba*, and then baked.

The following advertisement appeared in Berrow's *Worcester Journal*, February 22, 1770: "China painters wanted. For the Plymouth new invented patent porcelain manufactory. A number of sober, ingenious artists, capable of painting in enamel or blue, may hear of constant employ by sending their proposals to Thomas Frank in Castle Street, Bristol."

Cookworthy engaged the assistance of a French artist, whose ornamental delineations on the articles produced here, were extremely beautiful. Some elegant salt-cellars, in form of open conch-shells resting on a bed of coral shells, etc., all well modelled in white hard porcelain, were made here, and became great favourites of the table: a pair of these salts was in the collection of the Right Hon. W. E. Gladstone; another china sauce-boat of elegant design, resting on a stem and foot, formed of groups of shells, is in the collection of Mr. James Carter of Cambridge. In the Schreiber Collection there is a Plymouth mug inscribed " Josiah and Mary Greethead, March 13, 1769." The centre-pieces, salt-cellars, etc., of rock-work and shells just noticed, were also made at Bow fifteen or twenty years before the opening of the Plymouth factory.

The ware made at Plymouth was allowed to be a complete porcelain, inasmuch as it would bear a heat which melted other china ware placed inside it, and was of uniform texture and quality from the inner to the outer surface. They continued to work this manufactory until 1770, but it not answering their expectations, and having expended nearly £3,000 in perfecting the discovery, they disposed of their interest in the patent to Richard Champion, of Bristol, and these works ceased. It was then transferred to Bristol, under the firm of Champion & Co., and on the retirement of Cookworthy from the partnership, the patent was assigned by him in 1773 or 1774 to Champion alone. (*Ker. Gall*, figs. 592–598.)

It is doubtless due to this sale of the Plymouth factory to Champion that we find some of the models of figures made in both Plymouth and Bristol china. There is a general overlap of styles between the hard paste Plymouth and Bristol wares which makes it difficult to ascribe unmarked pieces with certainty.

Marks 12 and 13 occur on a porcelain cup, decorated in blue; in the

centre is a shield of four castles with "PLYMOUTH" above, and underneath
some letters which are illegible, but the word is probably "*Manufac^y*."
The initials and date are on the bottom of the cup. The patent was taken
out on 17th March, 1768, and this was probably a trial-piece made three days
previously. It is now in the British Museum.

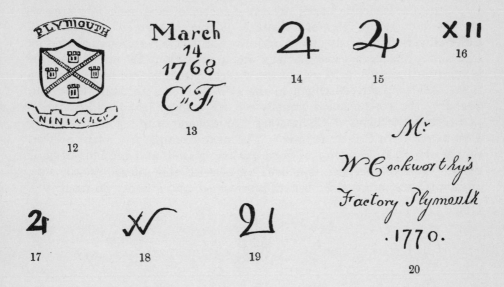

Mark no. 14 may be regarded as the stable Plymouth factory mark,
and has been copied on reproductions. It is the chemical sign for tin,
perhaps in consequence of the stanniferous character of that part of the
country where the materials were obtained. Usually marked in red or
blue on the bottom of the pieces.

Many variations of this tin mark (nos. 14 and 15) occur as they were
hand painted, see also nos. 18 and 19. Mark no. 16, on a cup of English
porcelain with blue Chinese figures. Mark no. 17, on a saucer of the same
pattern, formerly in the Reynolds Collection. Mark no. 18 is a variation
in form, from the carelessness of the painter. Mark no. 19, in brown on a
hard porcelain shell dish, supported on three feet of coral and mussel
shells, painted inside with lake and blue flowers and green leaves, formerly
in the Staniforth Collection. Mark no. 20, in red underneath a china butter-
boat, painted with detached flowers.

There are a great many interesting specimens of Plymouth porcelain
in the Schreiber Collection (Victoria and Albert Museum); some of which
are illustrated in Church's *English Porcelain*, and also in the British
Museum. The Trapnell Collection included many specimens, the models
of which were made first at Plymouth and afterwards reproduced at
Bristol. For a very full account of the Plymouth factory, the reader is
referred to *Cookworthy's Plymouth and Bristol Porcelain*, 1946, by F.
Severne Mackenna. Plymouth, Bristol and the New Hall factory in Staf-

fordshire are the only English factories to have produced true or hard paste porcelain.

BRISTOL POTTERY OR DELFT.

BRISTOL, Redcliffe Backs. The first record of Bristol pottery appears to have been in the reign of Edward I. Mediæval earthenware vessels of different periods, probably made in the locality, have been found at Bristol, and under Elizabeth a manufactory was in operation. At the close of the seventeenth century delft was made; the earliest notice we have met with is the following advertisement in the *Post-Boy* for 25th April, 1699, but probably the word china is actually put for delft or fayence in imitation of oriental porcelain: " China ware, far beyond white Japan, sold by Pattenden, Corn Street, Bristol." The next example is a plate marked on the rim S. M. B., 1703, of good quality, glazed, and the blue of good colour; another specimen is a delft high-heeled shoe, dated on the sole, 1722, with the initial M.S., beautifully formed, and a buckle in front.

E.

1   M. B.

1760.

In the Victoria and Albert Museum there is a delft plate painted in blue with Chinese subjects, and initialled in blue. This was painted by Michael Edkins of Bristol, and the initials are those of Michael and Betty Edkins his wife (mark no. 1). A delft election plate, painted in blue and purple, has in the centre the words, " Nugent only, 1754," and on the rim, " T. B. 1754," attributed to Bristol. These specimens are illustrated in Litchfield's *Pottery and Porcelain*. For the identification of Bristol and other English delft wares, the reader is referred to *English Delftware*, 1948, by Professor F. H. Garner.

The delft works were carried on at Redcliffe Backs in the eighteenth century by a Mr. Frank, and produced plates, dishes, Dutch tiles, etc. There is in the Victoria and Albert Museum a slab composed of twenty-four tiles, with a view of Redcliffe Church, Bristol; they were made by Richard Frank during the Bishopric of Butler (1738–50), whose arms are upon one of the tiles. It is stated that these delft potters were preceded by a maker of salt-glazed pottery named Wrede or Read. (*Ker. Gall.*, fig. 515.)

" Richard Frank, the Bristol delft potter, was a man of great energy. He resided at Brislington, and summer or winter, fair or foul weather, he always walked to Bristol to begin his day's work at six o'clock in the morning. It is not known when he took his son, Thomas Frank, into partnership, but in the year 1777 the firm removed to other premises, No. 9 Water Lane, occupied in 1775 by James Alsop, a brown stoneware potter, who removed to Temple Street." (*Owen*.)

BRISTOL, Temple Backs, Water Lane. Richard Frank & Son removed their business here in January 1777, as shown in the following advertisement in Felix Farley's Journey of January 2, 1777:—"Richard Frank and Son, earthen and stone pot-works, are removed from Redcliffe Backs to Water Lane, where they continue the same business in all its branches." On the 20th September 1784, Mr. Joseph Ring, vinegar-maker, who had married a daughter of Richard Frank, purchased the business of Frank and Co. at a valuation of £669, 1s. 3½d.; it was called the "Bristol Pottery." The following advertisement appeared in the *Bristol Gazette* for January 1787: "Bristol Pottery, Temple Backs. Joseph Ring informs merchants and others that he has established a manufactory of the Queen's and other earthenware, which he will sell on as low terms, wholesale and retail, as any of the best manufacturers in Staffordshire can render the same to Bristol."

2

3

Marks 2 and 3, which occurred on specimens of early Bristol delft in the Sheldon Collection, are attributed to Richard Frank, but cannot really be regarded as factory marks.

On the 9th January 1788, Mr. Ring took Messrs. Taylor & Carter into partnership under the firm of Ring & Taylor, Water Lane. Mr. Ring was connected by marriage with Cookworthy, his nephew, Frederick Cookworthy, being married to Mr. Ring's daughter Sarah, on the 11th August 1789. Mr. Ring was killed by the fall of a roof while superintending some alterations in the pottery on the 5th of April 1788. Mr. Owen (*op. cit.*) says: "Mrs. Ring, being left a widow with nine children, resolved to carry on the business; the daughter of Richard Frank, inheriting the energy of mind and strength of purpose of her father, she lost no time in taking up her lot in life. The works were continued by the widow for many years after his death: we have an invoice before us for china and glass to the amount of £12, 17s. 6d. The heading is: "Bought of Elizabeth Ring & Co., Earthenware, China & Glass Rooms, 8 High Street, Bristol," dated 4th January 1817; and in the account of Bristol by Corry and Evans, edition 1816, speaking of the potteries of Bristol, it adds, "Nor must the pottery of Mrs. Ring be omitted, for of the articles made here, it is little praise to say that they combine elegance with taste, and consequently a visit to the pottery is now generally among the objects which are pointed out to the notice of the stranger."

There was in the Rev. Septimus Firman's Collection a half-pint jug, decorated with a monument on which is inscribed " Peace signed at Amiens between England, France, Spain and Holland, March 27, 1802," with G. R. at the top, and on the other side are two figures of Peace and Liberty backed by the flags of the four nations. There is also a view of Ring's Pottery and the Temple Church. This specimen is marked " Bristol Pottery."

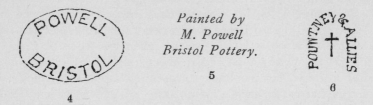

Painted by
M. Powell
Bristol Pottery.

5

4

6

POUNTNEY & ALLIES. From Chilcot's *Guide to Bristol,* and Matthew's *Guide,* we learn that the Bristol pottery at Temple Backs was then, in 1825–26, occupied by Pountney & Allies (c. 1816–35), employing about 200 men, women, and children, and had been established several years. The articles they produced were similar to those of the superior potteries in Staffordshire, and, in addition to the home trade, a considerable export business was carried on. In 1837 the firm was Pountney & Gouldney, who continued to about 1849. They were succeeded by the present firm, Pountney & Co. Ltd. The marks are self explanatory.

A plate painted in coloured flowers in E. Broderip's Collection had mark no. 6 impressed. A similar plate has the date 1831 without the maker's name, while a third only bears the initial letter *P* impressed. This maker's mark also occurs on some jugs made at the time of Dickens' first popularity, with subjects from *Nicholas Nickleby.*

Among other workmen engaged here were Thomas Patience and a family of the name of Hope.

Mark no. 4 (c. 1830) was impressed on a Bristol stoneware jar in the Sheldon Collection. Powell is said to have founded the Temple Gate pottery, and to have been the inventor of a peculiar glaze. He is mentioned by Jewitt, Vol. 1, 1878, pp. 402, 403, 407.

A painted plate (flowers), garish colourings, inscribed on the back as mark no. 5, was formerly in the Broderip Collection.

In the sale of Llewellyn Jewitt's Collection in 1871 there was a plate of Pountney's earthenware, painted with groups of flowers in brilliant colours, by William Fifield—mark P impressed and date 1829 in red. Also one of Pountney's jugs " painted in groups of roses and other flowers by William Fifield, in the 75th year of his age and without glasses." In front are the initials W. F. and date 1853. Fifield painted a great many pieces of pottery for a curiosity dealer named H. James of Bristol, whose name is occasionally found written in red upon them. H. L. Phillips had a lofty vase and cover painted by Fifield, with large flowers, dated 1825. The Editor has seen pieces fully signed.

William Fifield was a painter at the Water Lane pottery; he worked as an enameller for fifty years, and died in 1857, ætat. 80. He is said to have worked for Champion at Castle Green, but this is impossible, as he was not born till 1777, and Champion's labours concluded a few years after that date.

During Mr. Pountney's time some fine parian figures were produced, especially by a workman named Raby, who removed into Staffordshire; some excellent imitations of the Etruscan and other antique styles were also made. The work was carried on by his widow, who employed a large number of hands in the ordinary classes of earthenware, principally for exportation.

Bristol Glass. Michael Edkins was a painter of delft; he remained at Bristol until the pottery declined, and in 1761 he became a coach painter and decorator, and being employed about most public works in the city, he soon rose to eminence; he painted the bas-reliefs to the altarpiece in St. Mary Redcliffe Church; he also enamelled glass for Messrs. Little and Longmans, and their successors, Vigors & Stevens, whose glass-house adjoined the pottery at Redcliffe Backs.

" The glass made at Bristol at this time was particularly good and has become very scarce. The highest class of goods produced by Mr. Edkins was beautifully and perfectly enamelled: the colours were remarkably good and thoroughly incorporated in the glass." This glass is of an opaque white body, beautifully painted in enamel colour in flowers, and much resembles porcelain. His books, containing the prices charged for painting and enamelling glass from 1762 to 1787, are preserved. Of course, common descriptions were also made, but the colours not being properly fixed by heat, are soon rubbed off. Many of the specimens formerly in the Edkins Collection passed to the collection of Alfred Trapnell. Only a small proportion of Bristol type glass attributed to the hand of Edkins can have been decorated by him, and may well have been produced at glass houses other than at Bristol.

BRISTOL PORCELAIN

The earliest information we have of the manufacture of porcelain at Bristol is that derived from Dr. Richard Pococke's *Travels through England during 1750 and 1751*, issued by the Camden Society in 1888.

Under date 13th October, 1750, Dr. Pococke mentions that soapy-rock at the Lizard was used " for the manufacture of porcelane now carrying on at Bristol." He says: " I went to see a manufacture lately established here by one of the principals of the manufacture at Limehouse, which failed. It is a glass house, and is called Lowris (?) China House. They have two sorts of ware, one called stone-china, which has a yellow cast both in the ware and the glazing, that I suppose is made of pipeclay and calcined flint. The other they called old china. This is whiter, and I suppose this is made of calcined flint and the soapy-rock at Lizard Point, which 'tis known they use. This is painted blue and some in white like the old china of a yellowish cast. Another kind is white with a bluish cast, and both are called fine ornamental white china." The factory's correct name was Lowdin's China House, owned by William Lowdin until about 1745, and subsequently by Benjamin Lund and William Miller. Their stock was sold in 1752, and a close association or agreement entered into with the proprietors of the Worcester factory.

In R. L. Hobson's book, a sauce-boat in the British Museum is stated by him to be the product of this small factory. Hobson quotes from Dr. Pococke's diary: " They make very beautiful white sauce-boats adorned with reliefs of festoons, which sell for sixteen shillings a pair."

Mark no. 7 occurs " on a moulded cream-boat, one of the early trial pieces, of dry opaque body, made wholly of kaolin without the addition of petuntse, and answers exactly to the description given by Champion of this trial of the Carolina clay. The mark having been incised in the mould, is reproduced in relief." The words in inverted commas are those of Hugh Owen, who made a special note of this early specimen, which was at the time of his writing in Mr. Edkin's possession. His description of the body is open to doubt. A cream-ewer of this very early Bristol china was in the Sheldon Collection, with the word *Bristol* spelt with one *l*, which differs from the ones usually known (mark no. 8).

Bristoll.   Bristol

7   8

Various rare pairs of white figures of chinamen with an inscription, " Bristoll 1750," are recorded. These are very interesting specimens, because they are of soft paste and excellent glaze. They represent the fine porcelain which was made at Bristol before Champion's time, and probably were from the small factory already referred to. There was an important connection between this early Bristol factory and the Worcester works. The Bristol stock was sold in 1752.

CHAMPION'S, BRISTOL, Castle Green. Hard Paste. These works were founded by a company before 1765 for the manufacture of porcelain, but they failed to surmount the difficulties and expenses attending the manufacture, and according to Hugh Owen (*Two Centuries of Ceramic Art in Bristol*), the factory was taken by Champion in conjunction with others in 1768. Richard Champion was a merchant of Bristol; he is described as a man of great activity of mind and a constant projector. In 1743 he had a zinc manufactory on the banks of the Avon, about two miles from Bristol; and in 1767 we read in Corry and Evans's account of Bristol, that he published a plan, which had nearly been adopted, for improving the port of Bristol. In Barrett's *History of Bristol* (ed. 1789, p. 701) we find that in 1764 the great new dock was begun by Richard Champion. In 1769 he separated from certain partners; in March 1770 we find him advertising for china painters, and in October of the same year he built a new enamelling kiln; in 1771 his works are named in the rate books.

Champion had been a partner with Cookworthy in his porcelain manufactory at Plymouth, and it was removed to Bristol c. 1770 under the firm of Champion & Co., the patent being assigned to Champion when Cookworthy gave up his interest in the concern in May 1774. The works were transferred to Bristol about 1770, and carried on there four years before the patent was assigned to Champion solely.

In January 1772 Champion began to take apprentices, the first of whom was Henry Bone, the enameller, and in 1773 three china painters were added, and in the following year several more. In 1774 Burke presented the well-known Bristol china service to Mr. and Mrs. Smith; in 1774 also, the beautiful service was completed which Mr. and Mrs. Champion presented to Mrs. Burke (hereafter described), being the year in which Edmund Burke was elected member for Bristol; both these important services were commenced doubtless before the transfer of the patent from Plymouth in May 1774.

Henry Bone, the celebrated enameller, was born at Truro, in Cornwall, on February 6, 1755; in 1767 his parents moved to Plymouth, where, in consequence of his showing an early inclination for painting, and having copied a set of playing cards, he was engaged by Cookworthy in the china manufactory at Plymouth in January 1771. It has been stated that he was apprenticed in that year to Cookworthy, and about the end of the same year, on the establishment being transferred to Bristol under the direction of Messrs. Champion & Co., Henry Bone at their request accompanied it, and was there apprenticed in January 1772 for the completion of his term, viz., six years. His apprenticeship therefore expired in 1778, as stated in the *Annual Biography* for 1836, and the Bristol factory having failed, he came to London in 1779, and for many years was engaged in painting devices in enamel for jewellery; he subsequently attained considerable eminence as a miniature portrait painter on ivory as well as on enamel. Increasing the size of his enamel plates beyond anything before attempted, he copied pictures of the best masters. The first which obtained particular attention was the Sleeping Girl of Sir Joshua Reynolds in August 1794; another which he painted, Titian's Bacchus and Ariadne, on a plate 18 by 16 inches, he sold for 220 guineas. He was elected Associate of the Royal Academy in 1801 and R.A. in 1811; he died in December 1834.

Cookworthy's patent was assigned to Champion in May 1774. The latter says, in his petition in answer to the memorial of Wedgwood and the Staffordshire potters against the extension of the patent in 1775, when seven years out of the fourteen originally granted would expire, that—

" He had been many years concerned in the undertaking, nearly from the time the patent was granted to Mr. Cookworthy, in whose name it continued until assigned over to Champion. One part of the benefit of every work from whence profit may be derived is the power of assignment, and if, in fact, the manufacture could not be completed, nor the inventor, of course, derive any profit from it, without the expense, care, and perseverance of the assignee and once partner, the merit of that assignee who both completes the manufacture and rewards the discoverer is equal in equity to that of the discoverer himself—equal in every respect, except the honour that attends original genius and power of invention. Mr. Champion can assert with truth that his hazards and expense was many times greater than those of the original inventor. . . . He claims the merit of supporting the work, and when the inventor declined the undertaking himself, with his time, his labour, and his fortune, improved it from a very imperfect to an almost perfect manufacture. Mr. Champion at this moment allows him and is bound to his heirs, &c., in a profit equal to the first cost of the raw material, and as Mr. Champion's manufactory is encouraged, must increase to a very great degree."

Wedgwood, in his memorial, taunts the discoverer and the purchaser that, for want of skill and experience, they had not been able during the space of seven years already elapsed to bring it to any useful degree of perfection, and that if Mr. Champion has at length perfected it, the unexpired term of seven years ought to be enough to enable him to reimburse himself. To this Champion replies that—

" He submits to a discerning and encouraging Legislature whether a seven years' sale is likely to repay a seven years' unproductive, experimental, and chargeable labour, as well as the future improvement to grow from new endeavours. Until he was able to make this porcelain in quantities to supply a market, it was rather an object of curiosity than a manufacture for national benefit."

The opposition offered by Wedgwood to the passing of the bill, although of no avail, resulted in the introduction of two important clauses; the *first* made it imperative on Champion to enroll anew his specification of both body and glaze within the usual period of four months; the *second* throwing open to potters generally the use of the raw materials for any purpose except the manufacture of transparent porcelain. The Act was passed, specimens of porcelain submitted and approved, and the specifications duly enrolled on the 15th September 1775, thereby extending the patent for twenty-one years from that date.

The following extracts from the specification are interesting :—

" NOW KNOW YE THEREFORE, that I, the said Richard Champion, do hereby testify and declare that the specification hereinafter contained is the true and just specification of the mixture and proportions of the raw materials of which my porcelain is composed, and likewise of the mixture and proportions of the raw material which composed the glaze of the same, and which, at the time of passing the before-mentioned Act, was in the hands of the Lord High-Chancellor of Great Britain (that is to say) :—

" The raw materials of the above porcelain are plastic clay, generally found mixed with mica and a coarse gravelly matter. It is known in the counties of Devon and Cornwall by the name of growan clay. The other raw material is a mixed micarious earth or stone called in the aforesaid counties moorstone and growan. The gravel found in the growan clay is of the same nature, and is used for the same purpose in making the body of my porcelain as the moorstone and growan. The mixture of these materials to make the body of the porcelain is according to the common potter's method, and has no peculiar art in it. The proportions are as follows : The largest proportion of the stone or gravel aforesaid to the clay aforesaid is four parts of stone to one of clay. The largest proportion of clay to stone is sixteen parts of clay to one part of stone mixed together. I use these and every proportion intermediate between the foregoing proportions of the stone to the clay and the clay to the stone, and all this variation I make without taking away from the ware the distinguishing appearance and properties of Dresden and Oriental porcelains, which is the appearance and are the properties of mine. The raw materials of which the glaze is composed are the stone or gravel aforesaid and the clay aforesaid, magnesia, nitre, lime, gypsum, fusible spar, arsenic, lead, and tin ashes.

"The proportions of our common glaze are as follows, together with every intermediate proportion, videlicet :—

Growan gravel	128 parts	
Growan or moorstone . . .	112 ,,	The materials
and I vary it from 96 to	144 ,,	ground and mixed
Magnesia	16 ,,	together with
and I vary it from 14 to	18 ,,	water.
Gypsum	3 ,,	
Lime	8 ,,	

"But I also use the following materials for glaze :—

Growan clay	128 parts	
Growan or moorstone . . .	112 ,,	
and I vary it from 84 to	140 ,,	
Magnesia	20 ,,	
and I vary it from 16 to	24 ,,	The materials
Lime	8 ,,	ground and mixed
and I vary it from 6 to	10 ,,	together with
Nitre	1 ,,	water.
and I vary it to	2 ,,	
Fusible spar	20 ,,	
Arsenic	20 ,,	
Lead and tin ashes	20 ,,	
and I vary it from 16 to	24 ,,	

"I have described truly and justly the raw materials, the mixture and proportions of them which are used in making my porcelain, which has the appearance and properties of Dresden or Oriental porcelain, and which porcelain may be distinguished from the frit or false porcelain, and from the pottery or earthen or stonewares, as follows :—

"The frit or false porcelain will all melt into a vitreous substance, and lose their form and original appearance in a degree of heat which my porcelain, agreeing in all properties with Asiatic and Dresden, will not only bear, but which is necessary for its perfection. My porcelain may be distinguished from all other wares which are vulgarly called earthen or stone wares, which can sustain an equal degree of heat, by the grain, the colour of the grain, and by its semi-transparency; whereas the earthenwares, such as Staffordshire white and yellow earthenwares and all other earthenwares which sustain a strong heat without being fused, are found, when subjected to the most intense heat, to appear cellular or otherwise, easily by the eye to be distinguished from the true porcelain."

In a letter from Wedgwood to Bentley, dated August 24, 1778, he says : "Poor Champion, you may have heard, is quite demolished; it was never likely to be otherwise, as he had neither professional knowledge, sufficient capital, nor scarcely any real acquaintance with the materials he was working upon. I suppose we might buy some *growan stone* and *growan clay* now upon easy terms, for they have prepared a large quantity this last year."

It does not, however, appear that he was " quite demolished," for his friends rallied round him, and he continued business for a few years after that time, having got over his pressing difficulties. In 1776 he had opened a warehouse in London for the sale of his true china. In 1779 he made a statuette commemorative of his daughter, which is preserved in the family. In 1781 he was in a way of disposing of his business profitably. Britain, the foreman, who resided on the premises, voted on that qualification, and the works were still rated to the poor in September 1781. His London warehouse remained open in 1782. These facts are quoted by Owen, *Two Centuries of Potting at Bristol*, with a view of showing that Champion continued to manufacture his china at Bristol down to 1781 or 1782, and he then sold his patent to the Staffordshire China Company now known to collectors as the New Hall Company.

By the following list it will be seen that no apprentices were bound to Champion at Bristol after 26th July, 1777; but he retained his premises for the purpose probably of disposing of his stock in trade; and there is no record of his manufacturing any china after that date, except the above statuette commemorating his daughter's death.

Champion received the appointment of Deputy Paymaster of the Forces through Mr. Burke's influence in 1782, but the Ministry being dissolved shortly after, he was thrown out of office, and he emigrated to America on 7th October, 1784. His death is thus recorded in the *Gentleman's Magazine* of December 1791: " October 7th, 1791, near Camden, South Carolina, Richard Champion, Esq., late Deputy Paymaster General of His Majesty's forces, and proprietor of the china manufactory formerly carried on at Bristol."

Owen (*op. cit.*) gives the following list of workmen and apprentices, 1768 to 1777:—

> Anthony Amatt, thrower and painter.
> Moses Hill, china maker. John Britain, foreman.
> Thomas Briand of Derby, a flower modeller, 1777.
> B. Proeffel, a German.
> Lequoi (?) and Philip James, china painters.

APPRENTICES *bound to Richard Champion and Judith, his wife, for seven years, with dates of indentures.*

1772.	Jan. 20.	Henry Bone, son of Henry Bone of Plymouth, cabinetmaker.
,,	,,	William Stephens and John Hayden.
,,	Jan. 23.	Samuel Daw.
,,	Dec. 31.	Samuel Andrews Lloyd, paid as merchant, £472, 10s.
1773	June 18.	Jacob Allsop, as a china painter.
,,	,,	Samuel Banford, as china painter.
,,	,,	John Garland, as china painter.

1775. April 8.   William Wright, as china painter.
  ,,   Nov. 22.   John Parrot, as burner of china.
  ,,   Dec.   5.   Benjamin Lewis, as china painter.
1776. Jan. 29.   Samuel Beynon, as china painter.
  ,,   Sept. 19.   Thomas Williams, as china repairer.
  ,,   ,,   John Jones, as thrower.
  ,,   Oct. 24.   Samuel Ffiander Paglar, as china painter. ·
1777. July 26.   John Webb, as china painter.
  ,,   ,,   William Webb, as china painter.
  ,,   ,,   James Saunders, as china painter.

At this date there is a sudden stop, as if some great event had happened, either the close of the Bristol manufacture or the transfer of the
patent rights, or probably both; and to our mind this fact is conclusive,
and tends to show that the patent was about that time sold to the Staffordshire China Company.

Horace Walpole mentions in his Catalogue " a cup and saucer, white
with green festoons of flowers, of Bristol porcelain." We have seen many
similar specimens, bearing the mark of a cross, well painted and richly gilt.
There are also reproductions of this type of Bristol porcelain.

The sale by auction of Champion's stock-in-trade took place on 28th
February, 1780, and two following days at Christie and Ansell's rooms in
Pall Mall, and comprised some 300 lots, which sold for prices which would
now be considered absurdly small. In the *catalogue raisonnée* of the Trapnell Collection there is a reprint of this interesting catalogue, with sale
prices and purchasers' names attached. Mr. Amor, who purchased this
collection, republished Trapnell's catalogue together with this reprint of
the sale catalogue of Champion's stock. It is a valuable reference for
collectors of Bristol china. Rare examples of transfer printed Bristol
porcelain occur but are unmarked.

A very interesting tea service of Bristol china was sold at Messrs.
Sotheby's in April 1871, for the, at that time, unprecedented price of £565
the six pieces, viz., teapot, milk-pot, sugar-basin, three cups and saucers.
The teapot, which fetched £190, is thus described in the catalogue : it had
a yellow diapered border and gold scrolls, painted on both sides with an
altar, on which was Cupid holding a torch, supported by figures of
Minerva holding the cap of liberty and Plenty with a cornucopia; on the
front of the altar was a shield, bearing the arms of Burke impaled with
Nugent, and on the plinth the following inscription : —

I. BURKE. OPT. B. M.
R. ET. I. CHAMPION. D. DD.
PIGNUS. AMICITIÆ.
III. NON. NOV. MDCCLXXIV.

which is thus rendered into English : "Richard and Judith Champion gave
this as a token of friendship to Jane Burke, the best of British wives, on
the 3rd day of November 1774." It was also enriched with emblems, and

the cover surmounted by a wreath of flowers in biscuit; the decorations are attributed to Henry Bone, then an apprentice at the Bristol works.

A cup and saucer of this service realised £70 at the sale of Dr. Callender's Collection at Christie's in 1880, and was purchased at the sale of the Fry Collection at Sotheby's in 1889 for £42. A cup and saucer of this service was sold at Christie's in July 1899 for 48 guineas (see illustration), and in the sale of J. E. Nightingale's Collection, 7th December, 1911, a cup and saucer of this service realised £178. The teapot was sold at Christie's in the early part of the year 1907 for £440. Recent prices are given in the list of auction prices at the end of this book. The fairly complete service, including the teapot, cream-ewer, and other specimens, was in the Trapnell collection, see illustration.

This was by far the largest collection in the world of old Bristol china and glass, and comprised over one thousand specimens, including judicious selections from the sales which have taken place during the previous thirty years, in which time the Seymour-Hayden, Fry, Dr. Callender, and Edkins Collections were dispersed.

Besides the beautiful service here described, there are at least four other special tea and coffee services which deserve notice. They are all similar in design and vary in particular details.

The Burke-Smith service was presented by Edmund Burke to Mrs. Smith, the wife of Joseph Smith, a Bristol merchant, and friend of Champion's, who entertained Burke the parliamentary candidate, during his election in 1774. The shape of the cups and saucers is from a Dresden model, and the painting is of that school. Wreaths and festoons of laurel in green and S. S. (Mrs. Smith's initials) painted in bright blossoms with precision and delicacy. The gilding is excellent, the effect being obtained by being wrought in a burnished pattern on a matted ground. Two of these cups and saucers were in the Fry sale in 1889, and were purchased for £17, and £18, 15s.—a very great decline in price from that realised by one of them a few years previously at the first Edkins sale, when it brought £55. Borradaile has one of them in his collection, and two were in that of Alfred Trapnell. Another service is similar, but each piece has a crest, the Cornish chough holding an olive branch in a wreath.

Some other services believed to have been made for Bristol families may be shortly mentioned. The " Plumer " service, decorated with the initial P.; that made for Sir Robert Smith having the monogram R.S. entwined, and one which is said to have been ordered by William Clowes, of 33 Castle Green, Bristol, having the monogram W.C. in gold. Some of these specimens are decorated in Owen's book and others in Litchfield's *Pottery and Porcelain*.

Another notable service of Bristol porcelain is that known as the Gainsborough service, which is said to have belonged to that celebrated artist. The decoration is green bay leaves entwined round a gold band, with flowers in the centre. The mark is that of the Dresden crossed swords. Specimens of all these famous Bristol services were included in the Trapnell Collection which, as before mentioned above, was the most comprehensive

BRISTOL PORCELAIN
Portions of the " Burke " Service, all of which were in the Collection of
Mr. Alfred Trapnell.

and complete of its kind. Several other important services are listed and illustrated in F. Severne Mackenna's *Champion's Bristol Porcelain*, 1947, to which the reader is referred.

Mention should also be made of the delicately modelled plaques of biscuit china made by Champion. These are described by Owen and some illustrations given. They are found with coats of arms and medallion portraits, and have flowers in high relief most elaborately finished. Some of these were in the Fry and Edkins Collections, sold at Sotheby's in 1889 and 1891, and brought good prices; others were in Nightingale's Collection, which was sold in December 1911. One of these portrait medallions of Benjamin Franklin, which was formerly in the Edkins Collection, was marked with an *incised* cross, and is believed to be the only piece of Bristol porcelain so marked. A similar specimen, but unmarked, is now in the British Museum, having been presented by J. E. Nightingale. On one of these carefully modelled flower plaques from the Trapnell Collection, was written on the back the following inscription:—

From
E. H. Champion (daughter of Richard Champion)
to her much valued Friend
Mr. Wm. P. Lunnell (of Bristol)
June 7th, 1822.

" Daughter of Richard Champion " and " of Bristol " was written by Charles Edward Rawlins, grandson of R. C. The other writing is the autograph of Esther H. Champion to Wm. Peter Lunnell, father of John Evans Lunnell. For these plaques see *Transactions of the English Ceramic Circle*, Vol. I, part I.

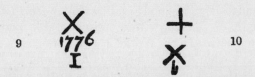

9   10

MARKS.—The mark adopted at the Bristol manufactory was a cross, usually painted in a sort of grey-blue colour, but occasionally it was blue, as on a Bristol tea service belonging to the late Lady Byron, afterwards in the possession of John J. Bagshawe of Sheffield, painted with flowers, the name of each flower being placed under it in blue colour. Dr. Diamond had a specimen with the cross stamped in the paste. Mr. Edkins of Bristol had a cup with initials J. H. and date 1774 inside it, made in the first year of Champion's purchase of the patent, for Joseph Harford, who was part proprietor, residing at Blaize Castle, near Bristol. There is in the Schreiber Collection (Victoria and Albert Museum) a similar cup, and also one bearing the date 1776, marked with a blue cross. Marks 9 and 10. Reproductions were made early in the twentieth century.

Mark no. 11 occurs on a cup and saucer of hard porcelain, painted with detached flowers, of undoubted Bristol manufacture.

The number I in gold is considered by many collectors to be the mark of Henry Bone, who was the first apprentice, and the number 2 that of William Stephens, the second apprentice (see list of apprentices given earlier in this chapter). For a very interesting paper on Stephens, by F. Severne Mackenna see *Transactions of the English Ceramic Circle*, Vol. 4, part 1.

Marks 12 and 13 occur on specimens in the British Museum, and are taken from R. L. Hobson's guide to that collection.

Some of the Bristol china was marked with the crossed swords of Dresden, a dot in centre; sometimes the pieces have numerals in gold, 1, 2, 3, and so on, with a dot below or at the side. Mark no. 14 and several variations.

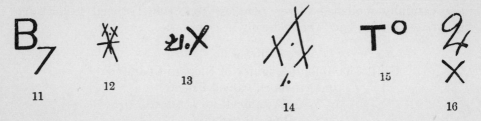

Mark no. 15 is sometimes found impressed on porcelain figures attributed to Bristol. It is generally thought to be the sign of the " repairer " (the assembler of the figure, etc., into its finished, complete form) Tebo. It is underneath a set of four figures of the Elements, 10 in. high; *Fire* is represented by Vulcan at his forge; *Earth* by a husbandman with spade, fruit, etc.; *Air* by a winged female figure holding Pandora's box, and Æolus below; *Water* by a Naiad holding a net with fish and a water urn, etc. These statuettes are of good quality and were in the possession of Mrs. Boddam Castle of Clifton, with an indisputable pedigree; they were purchased at the Castle Green Works by her mother's great-aunt, Mrs. Killigrew, and have been handed down as heirlooms.

Mr. Edkins of Bristol had some figures with the same mark impressed in the clay; a boy skating (Winter), 11 in. high, in white; finely glazed, and a boy playing on the hurdy-gurdy, 8 in. high; some of these were purchased at the sale of Edkins's Collection by Francis Fry, and again at the latter gentleman's death and consequent sale were added by Alfred Trapnell to his important collection, which includes a set of the " Classic Seasons," as illustrated, Plate X of Owen's book. Among others, a set of the " Quarters of the World," of one of which, "Asia," there is an illustration on Plate XII of Owen, two of the Element Series, *Air* and *Fire*, boy and girl with bird and bird-cage, Shakespeare and Milton, etc. In the Schreiber Collection there is also a set of the Elements. The mark no. 15 also occurs on Bow and Worcester porcelains.

Mark no. 16, forming a curious combination of that of Plymouth and Bristol, was probably used during the transition between the re-establishment of the works at Bristol and the assignment of the patent to Champion; it is in blue under the glaze, on a basin painted with Chinese flowers in the Schreiber Collection, c. 1770-2.

In the carefully compiled catalogue of the Trapnell Collection, edited by the Rev. A. W. Oxford, M.A., several additional variations of the crossed swords mark are given, which occur on specimens in that collection. We reproduce some of these which we believe have not been hitherto published. Mr. Oxford, in a preface which gives us much useful information about Bristol porcelain, states that as the result of his notes on some 1,500 specimens, he has observed that—

(1) The mark of a cross occurred on 867.

(2) This cross was accompanied by a number on 459, while there was no other mark on 288.

(3) The other specimens were variously marked with crossed swords, or the letter B, or else unmarked. Of the series of 459 marked with numbers the highest was no. 24.

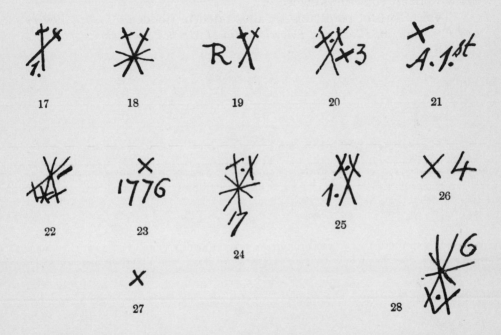

Mark no. 17, on portions of the Gainsborough service. Mark no. 18, on a chocolate cup and saucer, with gold border, entwined with gold and lake. Mark no. 19 was previously attributed to Bristol but this is subject to some doubt. Mark no. 20 occurs on a pair of exceedingly rare chocolate cups and saucers, with the letter B painted in forget-me-nots; the figure 3 is in gold. Mark no. 21, on several pieces of the celebrated Burke-Smith service. Mark no. 22, on a chocolate cup of a service painted with natural flowers, and border of heavy gold ornamentation.

Mark no. 23, on a chocolate cup of great rarity, with W.C. monogram, gold border, and flower painting, figures in gold. Mark no. 24, on a pair of sauce-boats of rather inferior quality, with flower ornamentation, surrounded by a raised margin. The × and figures 17 are in red. Mark no. 25, on a *cabaret* complete, finest quality, ornamented alternately with gold bands, laurel leaves, and sprays of flowers. The figure 1 is in gold. (Henry Bone's mark?) Mark no. 26, on a coffee can and saucer, band of pink salmon scale, with green laurel leaves. The can is marked with cross only, no. 27. Mark no. 28, on a quart jug, with mask under lip, ornamented with sprays of flowers, 7½ in. high.

Thomas Pardoe, a Derby man, removed to Bristol in 1809, where he had an enamelling shop in Bath Street in 1812–16 and in Long Row in 1820–21. He afterwards went to Nantgarw and became manager to Mr. Young, and is said to have assisted Billingsley in painting the famous service made for the Prince Regent. As we have seen in the biographical notice of Billingsley and in the notices of the Nantgarw and Swansea works, their prosperity was very short-lived, and Pardoe died in 1823. Examples of his work are sometimes signed.

Typical Bristol porcelains are illustrated in Godden's *British Pottery and Porcelain, an Illustrated Encyclopædia of Marked Specimens.*

FULHAM, LAMBETH, VAUXHALL, MORTLAKE, etc.

John Dwight, M.A., of Christ Church College, Oxford, has been called *the inventor of porcelain in England*; he was secretary to Brian Walton, who died in 1660, and to Henry Ferne and George Hall, successive Bishops of Chester. He established a manufactory for the production of earthenware and porcelain at Fulham in 1671, and although his claim to have made true porcelain cannot be allowed, still he succeeded in producing a stoneware very superior to any which had been made before in England. His patent, granted 13th April, 1671, was for " the mistery of transparent earthenware, commonly knowne by the names of porcelaine or china, and of stoneware vulgarly called Cologne ware."

There are (or were) in existence two old books of receipts and accounts (which were purchased by Lady Schreiber from Mr. Bailey, the late proprietor of the Fulham Pottery), with memoranda bearing dates 1689 to 1695, and from these it has been assumed that Dwight actually produced true porcelain at this early period.

It is, however, now pretty well established that although his efforts were sufficiently successful in producing what Professor Church has aptly termed " a porcellaneous stoneware " sufficiently fine to be termed porcelain in those days, it was not the product which we should now classify by that name.

Besides the manufacture of this excellent earthenware, of which the specimens in our museums (mentioned a little later) are such good testimony, there were other discoveries made by John Dwight. His second invention was of even greater importance to the community at large, and the commercial interests of this country, viz., his successful imitation of the *grès de Cologne*. Several attempts had been made in previous years to compete with the potters of Cologne, but these endeavours had hitherto been unavailing, the durability, compactness of material, imperviousness of glaze, and consequent cleanliness of the vessels, could not be imitated: all England, therefore, continued to be supplied with German pots. Finding they could not manufacture them, the English potters tried to destroy the monopoly of the Cologne merchants who imported them, but the duty received by the English Government on the ware, formed too important an item to be abandoned, without sufficient cause. (See the petition of W. Simpson to Queen Elizabeth in Part III of the Introduction to this book.)

Dr. Plot states that Dwight's great difficulty was in the glazing of his "porcelain," which was the only obstacle that had prevented him *setting up a manufactory before*, but he had eventually overcome it. That his inventions were well known to and appreciated by the scientific men of the time, is evidenced from the following interesting notice by Dr. Plot in his *History of Oxfordshire*, published in 1677, which, from its important bearing upon these valuable discoveries, we quote at length:—

"§ 84. Amongst arts that concern *formation of earths*, I shall not mention the making of pots at Marsh Balden and Nuneham Courtney, nor of tobacco-pipes of the *white earth* of Shotover, since those places are now deserted. Nor indeed was there, as I ever heard of, anything extraordinary performed during the working these *earths*, nor is there now of a very good tobacco-pipe clay found in the parish of Horspath, since the first printing of the third chapter of this history. . . . Let it suffice for things of this nature that the ingenious John Dwight, formerly M.A. of Christ Church College, Oxon., hath discovered the *mystery of the stone or Cologne wares* (such as d'Alva bottles, jugs, noggins), heretofore made only in Germany, and by the Dutch brought over into England in great quantities; and hath set up a manufacture of the same, which (by methods and contrivances of his own, altogether unlike those used by the Germans) in three or four years' time he hath brought it to greater perfection than it has attained where it has been used for many ages, insomuch that the Company of Glass-sellers of London, who are the dealers for that commodity, have contracted with the inventor to buy only of his English manufacture, and refuse the foreign.

"§ 85. He hath discovered also the *mystery of the Hessian wares,* and vessels for reteining the penetrating salts and spirits of the chymists, more serviceable than were ever made in England, or imported from Germany itself.

"§ 86. And hath found ways to make an earth *white and transparent as porcellane,* and not distinguishable from it by the eye, or by experiments that have been purposely made to try wherein they disagree. To this earth he hath added the colours that are usual in the coloured china ware, and divers others not seen before. The skill that hath been wanting to set up a manufacture of this *transparent earthenware* in England, like that of China, is the glazing of the white earth, which hath much puzzled the projector, but now that difficulty also is in great measure overcome.

"§ 87. He hath also caused to be modelled *statues or figures of the said transparent earth* (a thing not done elsewhere, for China affords us only imperfect mouldings), which he hath diversified with great variety of colours, making them of the colour of iron, copper, brass, and party colour'd as some Achat-stones. The considerations that induced him to this attempt were the duration of this hard-burnt earth, much above brass or marble, against all air and weather, and the softness of the matter to be modelled, which makes it capable of more curious work than stones that are wrought with chisels or metals that are cast. In short, he has so advanced the *Art Plastick* that 'tis dubious whether any man since Prometheus have excelled him, not excepting the famous Damophilus and Gorgasus of Pliny (*Nat. Hist.*, lib. 35, c. 12).

"§ 88. And these arts he employs about materials of English growth, and not much applied to other uses; for instance, he makes the stone bottles of a clay in appearance like to tobacco-pipe clay, which will not make tobacco-pipes, although the tobacco-pipe clay will make bottles; so that that which hath lain buried and useless to the owners may become beneficial to them by reason of this manufacture; and many working hands get good livelihoods, not to speak of the very considerable sums of English coyn annually kept at home by it."—Dr. PLOT's *Natural History of Oxfordshire*, Oxford, 1677.

In Aubrey's *Natural History of Wiltshire*, written about 1670-80, whose MSS. were edited by John Britton in 1847, we read :—

"In Vernknoll, adjoining the lands of Easton Pierse, neer the brooke and in it, I bored clay as blue as ultra marine, and incomparably fine, without anything of sand, &c., which perhaps might be proper *for Mr. Dwight for his making of porcilaine.* It is also in other places hereabout, but 'tis rare."

The Editor in a note upon this passage remarks :—

"It is not very clear that 'blew clay,' however fine, could be proper for the 'making of porcilaine,' the chief characteristic of which is its transparent whiteness; apart from this, however, Aubrey's remark is curious, as it intimates that the manufacture of porcelain was attempted in this country at an earlier period than is generally believed. The famous porcelain works at Chelsea were not established till long afterwards, and, according to Dr. Plot, whose *Natural History of Staffordshire* was published in 1686, the only kinds of pottery then made in that country were the coarse yellow, red, black, and mottled wares, and of these the chief sale was to 'poor crate men, who carried them on their backs all over the country.'"

Mr. Britton adds :—

"I have not found any account of the Mr. Dwight mentioned by Aubrey, or of his attempts to improve the art of pottery."

It is remarkable that Britton, who has here quoted Dr. Plot's own words in his *History of Staffordshire*, should never have looked into the same author's *History of Oxfordshire*, published nearly ten years earlier; had he done so, he would have found Dwight's name honourably mentioned. Mr. Britton's doubt about the "blew clay" being fit for porcelain is easily explained; the blue clay is considered the best for making porcelain, and fetches the highest price; it not only burns *very white*, but forms a ware of great solidity, and will bear a larger proportion of flint than any other.

From the foregoing accounts it is perfectly clear that an attempt was successfully made to produce porcelain by John Dwight of Oxford as early as the year 1671. Dr. Plot says it was of "*transparent earth ooloured with metallic colours, like that of China.*" We may therefore assume that, having perfected his discoveries, and finding the sale of his newly-invented wares was likely to be of considerable magnitude, he removed his manufactory near the metropolis, and proceeded to secure his inventions by patent. His first patent is dated 23rd April, 1671, and runs thus:—

"John Dwight, gentleman, hath represented unto us, that by his own industry and at his own proper costs and charges, he hath invented and sett up at Fulham, in our county of Middlesex, several new manufactories," &c. "The mistery of transparent earthenware, commonly known by the name of porcelaine or china, and Persian ware, as alsoe the misterie of the stone ware, vulgarly called Cologne ware; and that he designed to introduce a manufacture of the said wares into our kingdom of England, where they have not hitherto bene wrought or made." "Granted for the tearme of fourteene years, paying yearly and every yeare during the said terme twentie shillinges of lawfull money of England."

That he continued these new manufactures successfully is proved by his obtaining at the expiration of this term of fourteen years a renewal of his patent: it is dated June 12, 1684 :—

" Severall new manufactures or earthenwares, called by the names of white gorges (pitchers), marbled *porcellane vessels, statues, and figures*, and fine stone gorges and vessells, never before made in England or elsewhere; and alsoe discovered the mystery of *transparent porcellane*, and opacous redd and darke coloured porcellane or china, and Persian wares, and the mystery of the Cologne or stone wares." Granted " for the term of fourteene years."

John Houghton, F.R.S., in his *Collection of Papers on Husbandry and Trade*, a close observer, and one who scrupulously mentions facts relating to these matters, thus speaks of the property of clays, with special reference to that found at or near Poole, in Dorsetshire, 12th January, 1693: " And there dug in square pieces of the bigness of about half a hundredweight each; thence 'tis brought to London, and sold in peaceable times at about eighteen shillings a ton; but now in this time of war is worth about three and twenty shillings." He continues: " This sort of clay is used to clay sugar, and the best sort of mugs are made with it, and the ingenious Mr. Dwight of Fulham tells me that 'tis the same earth china ware is made of, and 'tis made, not by lying long in the earth, but in the fire; and if it were worth while we may make as good china here as any in the world "; and it is fair to presume that the only porcelain made in England was that produced by Dwight, who, he says, " has made it and can make it again."

In spite of the mention of porcelain in the above contemporary report, there was, unfortunately, not a fragment of porcelain in the *Fulham trouvaille*, which we shall presently have occasion to notice; but we must not too hastily conclude that, because no specimen is yet known, there is none in existence. A few years since, if any collector had inquired where any pieces of Moustiers fayence could be procured, he would have been told that even the name had never been heard of as a pottery; yet now we know that this place was celebrated over Europe in the beginning of the eighteenth century as one of the largest emporiums of the fictile art, and numerous products can now be produced which had before been attributed to Rouen, St. Cloud, and other places. The same dark cloud hung over the productions of porcelain at Florence, made as early as 1575; the Henri Deux ware of Oirons, near Thouars, of the beginning of the sixteenth century; and other places which modern research has brought to light. Such was also the obscurity of the imitation of Cologne ware, so much lauded by Dr. Plot; but now we know that it was extensively made at Fulham; and although it has hitherto been confounded with the German *grès* itself, yet we can now easily distinguish and refer it to its original source. The Company of Glass-sellers of London, who were the dealers in that commodity, having " contracted to buy only his stoneware, to the entire exclusion of the foreign," its sale must have been very extensive.

The Fulham stoneware, in imitation of that of Cologne, is seen at the present day in some collections; it is of exceedingly hard and close texture, very compact and sonorous, and usually of a grey colour, ornamented with a brilliant blue enamel, in bands, leaves, and flowers. The stalks have frequently four or more lines running parallel, as though drawn with a flat notched stick on the moist clay; the flowers, as well as the outlines, are raised, and painted a purple or maroon colour, sometimes with small ornaments of flowers and cherubs' heads, and medallions of Kings and Queens of England in front, with Latin names and titles, and initials of Charles II, William III, William and Mary, Anne, and George I. The forms are mugs, jugs, butter-pots, cylindrical or barrel shaped, etc.; the jugs are spherical, with straight narrow necks, frequently mounted in pewter, and raised medallions in front, with the letters CR. WR. AR. GR., etc., in the German style of ornamentation; these were in very common use, and superseded the Bellarmines and longbeards of Cologne manufacture.

We must now direct especial attention to a most interesting collection of the early productions of the Fulham manufactory, formerly in the collection of Mr. Baylis of Priors Bank (which was sold by Messrs. Christie), who obtained it from the Fulham manufactory about 1862, in which year he communicated the discovery to the *Art Journal* for October. It afterwards passed into the collection of Mr. Reynolds, and dispersed at the sale which took place at his death. It consisted of about twenty-five specimens, which had been preserved and remained as heirlooms since the period of their manufacture.

The statuettes and busts are of *grès* or stoneware, beautifully modelled: a large bust of Prince Rupert, life-size, wearing the order of the George and collar; smaller bust of Charles II and Catherine of Braganza; James II and Mary d'Este, the large wigs, lace ties, etc., being minutely modelled; full-length figures of Flora, Minerva, and Meleager; a sportsman in the costume of Charles II's reign, a girl holding flowers, two lambs by her side; a girl with her hands clasped, drapery over her head and round her body, at her feet a skull and plucked flowers—the last two are probably members of Dwight's family; five stoneware statuettes in imitation of bronze, of Jupiter, Mars, Neptune, Meleager, and Saturn; these figures, from 7 to 13 in. high, are now in the British Museum, where is also the magnificent bust of Prince Rupert and several other most interesting specimens illustrated in Mr. Hobson's Guide to the British Museum Collection. There is in the *Portfolio* for 1894 an illustrated account of this factory, with representations of these statuettes and the bust. Some of them are also illustrated in Professor Church's *English Earthenware.*

The most interesting relic of the manufactory executed in the hard stoneware is a beautiful half-length figure of a lifeless female child, lying upon a pillow, with eyes closed, her hands on her breast, clasping a bouquet of flowers, and a broad lace band over her forehead, evidently modelled from the child after death. (*Ker. Gall.*, fig. 491.) This most touching memento of one of the earliest of England's potters, recalls the words of Dr. Plot, that " he had so far advanced the art plastic, that 'tis dubious whether any man since Prometheus ever excelled him," for the child seems almost to breathe again. Fortunately we are not left to conjecture its history: it tells its own tale, for on the back is inscribed in the clay, while yet moist before baking, " *Lydia Dwight, died March* 3, 1673."

It was therefore executed two years after he had taken out his first patent; it is preserved in the Victoria and Albert Museum.

There was also in the Reynolds Collection a large fayence plateau, 32 in. in diameter, in exact imitation of the early Nevers ware covered with the rich *bleu de Perse* enamel, for which that manufacture was celebrated, decorated with white flowers and scrolls, the centre being filled with the royal arms and monogram of Charles II, boldy sketched, said, with more than mere probability, to have been one piece of a dinner service made expressly for this king.

Among the minor productions are a slate-coloured bottle, with marble bands, and white figures in relief, of a church, birds, Merry-andrew, and in the centre the busts of William and Mary; another with white figures as the last, and the letter C; two marbled bottles; a cylindrical mug, with stamped ornaments, and in front Hogarth's "Midnight Conversation"; a butter-boat, the outside formed of leaves and stalk handle, like the early Chelsea pieces; and two open dishes in the form of leaves. Some of these pieces are obviously of a much later date than the time of the founder of the Fulham factory.

In looking over this collection we are astonished at the variety of Dwight's productions, and the great perfection to which he had brought the potter's art. The figures, busts, and groups are exquisitely modelled, and will bear comparison with any contemporary manufactures in Europe; and a careful inspection will convince any unprejudiced mind of the erroneous impression which exists, that, until the time of Wedgwood, the potter's art in England was at a very low ebb, and none but the rudest description of pottery was made, without any attempt to display artistic excellence. Here, however, we have examples of English pottery, a century before Josiah Wedgwood's time, which would have been a credit to the *atelier* of that distinguished potter himself.

A later proprietor of the Fulham Pottery, Mr. C. J. C. Bailey, possessed two of the old books of receipts and memoranda, bearing dates ranging from 1689 to 1695, among which the following headings may be especially noticed, claiming that Dwight actually made *transparent porcelain* at that early period, and corroborating the facts we before adduced— viz., his two patents of 1671 and 1684; the privilege extending for twenty-eight years, from 1671 to the year 1699.

These manuscripts having been discovered among some old account books, Mr. Bailey did not wish the receipts made public until he had himself made some experiments upon the materials thus unexpectedly brought to light. Mr. Bailey kindly placed these two most important books in our hands, to inspect and make some extracts for publication, under certain restrictions. But we are permitted to state that, from a careful perusal of the receipts relating to the making of porcelain, we have no hesitation in affirming that a translucent porcelain can be made from them—the materials stated being identical with those which constituted the paste of subsequent English manufacturers, with this exception, that the latter used white clay, fine white sand, and ground glass, while Dwight used the glass-making materials uncombined to mix with the calcareous white clay. These books would now seem to have been lost. Transcriptions made by Lady Schreiber in 1890 are, however, in the British Museum.

Small Book, bound in vellum.—All that is in this book was entred since 9ber 15th, 1695.

The fine stone cley. The fine white cley for gorges and cans. The fine white cley for dishes or tea pots to endure boiling water. To make *transparent porcelane* or china cley. To make another *transparent porcelane* or china cley. To make red porcelane cley. To make a bright red cley wʰ Staffordshire red cley. Light grey cley to endure boiling water. Mouse coloured cley to endure boiling water.

1698, April 6, p. 19.—To make Number Sixteen.

1698, April 6, p. 21.—The best white cley to make gorges, cans, or dishes to endure boiling water. To make yᵉ white earth. To make the dark earth. To make *fine white*.

NOTE.—This is the material or frit which, mixed with the clay, gives it translucency. We are not at liberty to give the receipt, but we may state that fine white sand is one of the ingredients; and a note is appended showing that calcined flints were sometimes used instead. " Calcined, beaten, and sifted flints will doe instead of the white sand and rather whiter, but the charge and trouble is more."

To make fine dark. To make calcined sand. To make white *pr* cyprus (per cyprus sieve).

Things necessary always to be in readyness.—White sand in some good quantity, in several boxes. Best white cley, dry'd and sifted. Iron scales, clean, dry, and sifted through a midling hair sieve. Coarse white. Fine white. White *pr* cyprus. Coarse dark. Fine dark. Saltpeter, dry'd, beaten, and sifted.

Small parchment covered Book, with silver clasp.—The first six pages are unfortunately torn out, but some, no doubt, referred to making china, from the following remark : " Note yᵗ in burning china you must set pots near the widenes of yᵉ arches and set them 6 inches distant from one another and from the wall. The little furnace where the last red tea pots were burnt, I take to be a convenient one for this use."

9ber, 1695.—An essay towards a china glasse (glaze).

1691, March 14.—To make a grey porcellane by salt.

NOTE.—This is a strong hardy cley, fit for garden pots, tea pots, dishes, &c.

1691, March 14.—To make a blew porcellane cley to be turned into vessels, or to spot and inlay pots on any other porcellane.

1692, July 16.—to make yᵉ black earth.

1692, July 5.—To make a fine bright and strong brown.

1692, July 16.—To make the brightest brown colour.

9ber, 29/95.—A fine grey cley for marbling stone pots.

1692, July 16.—To make a fine white porcellane cley to be burnt wʰ salt, fit only for things of ornament. A grey cley for yᵉ like use.

1692, Feb. 8.—A mouse colour'd porcellane wʰ white specks.

1692, July 27.—A bright mouse colour'd cley to endure boiling water.

1692, Aug. 15.—A fine porcellane cley fit for deep dishes, wʰout handles to be burnt wʰout *glaze* in the strongest fire that may serve to perfect yᵉ china ware.

Reversing the book, we have—

1692, 7ber 12.—The best dark earth. The best brown glasse (glaze) for stone pots. Note that stone pots having much cley in themselves doe retain the brown colour though it have less in it, and the less cley there is in the colour the more lustre it hath; the reasons I shall give elsewhere.

1692, 7ber 12.—The best brown glasse (glaze) for white brown pots.

1693, 9ber 14.—To make the dark earth.

1693, 9ber 14.—To make *transparent porcellane* or china cley :—Take *fine white earth* thirty pounds; cley, sifted, twenty pounds—mingle and tread. To make another *transparent porcellane* or china cley.

1693, 9ber 14.—A dark colour'd cley for marbled dishes and tea pots to endure boiling water.

1693, 9ber 14.—To make a deep red porcellane or china clay.

1693, 9ber 14.—To make a grey porcellane cley, hardy and fit for garden potts, and tea pots, &c.

1693, 9ber 14.—To make a deep red cley of the Staffordshire red cley.

1693, 9ber 14.—To make a cley to burn brown, strong and hardy, fit for tea pots, to be sprig'd white.

1695, July 2.—To make yᵉ best fine stone clay.

In one of the leaves of this book is written in a child's hand—

Lydia Dwight,   8

her book,   12

Fulham.   4

and on another page her name, unfinished, and her young friends'—

Miss Betty Osgood and Miss Molly Osgood.

Among the memoranda of this book are some very curious entries of hiding-places for money about the year 1693; as the moneys were withdrawn the entry was erased. We make a selection from these as follows : —

In the garret, in a hole under yᵉ fireplace, 240 G, in a wooden box.

In yᵉ old labouratory at the old house, in two holes under the fireplace, on both sides yᵉ furnace, in two half-pint gorges, cover'd, 460.

In the second presse in yᵉ's labora : under some papers at yᵉ bottom, in a bag, some mill'd money.

Behind yᵉ doore of the little parlor, old house, in a canne, some mill'd money.

In two holes of that great furnace running in almost to the oven, 2 boxes full of mill'd money, may be drawn out wʰ a long crooked iron standing behind yᵉ kitchen door.

Between a little furnace and great one that joynes to the oven, behind shovels and forks, a pott of Gui :

1698. In several holes of yᵉ ffurnace in yᵉ middle of the kitchen opening at the top where the sande lyes is a purse of 100 Guis. and severall cans cover'd. At yᵉ further end of yᵉ bottom hole of   ffurnace in yᵉ little parlour, a box of 200 G.

There is a tradition in the family that the production of the classic figures already referred to, together with the dinner ware, were made expressly for King Charles's own table, and the finely-modelled figures of grey clay, in substance something like the fine Cologne ware of the same period, were confined, or mostly so, to the life of the elder Dwight; for it is a fact well recorded in the family, that he buried all his models, tools, and moulds connected with this branch of the manufactory in some secret place on the premises at Fulham, observing that the production of such matters was expensive and unremunerative, and in order that his successors should not be tempted to perpetuate this part of the business, he put it out of their power, by concealing the means. Search has often been made for these hidden treasures, but hitherto without success, though no doubt exists as to their being still in their hiding-place.

In pulling down a range of old and dilapidated buildings to make the required improvements, excavators came upon a vaulted chamber which had been walled up; it contained a number of stoneware Bellarmines of exactly the same form and material as those of Cologne, with masks under the spouts and medallions in relief, and a quantity of fragments of stoneware, some inlaid with blue and the maroon red colour. Many of these had been dispersed before the author had an opportunity of inspecting them, but there were still left some with the characteristics just spoken of, viz., the crest of a stag's head, the interlaced C's and C. R. crowned, a fleur-de-lis crowned, rosettes inlaid with maroon and blue colours, etc. These were the " fine stone *gorges* never before made in England " alluded to in the patent of 1684. The term *gorge* was still used in the factory in the nineteenth century to denote a pitcher. (*Ker. Gall.*, figs. 493–4.)

John Dwight, the founder of the Fulham pottery, died in the course of 1703, and the business was subsequently carried on by his son Samuel, and afterwards by Samuel's widow, Margaret, in partnership with Thomas Warland. They were not successful, for in 1746 the *Gazette* informs us that Margaret Dwight and Thomas Warland, potters of Fulham, were bankrupts. Margaret's daughter Lydia married Thomas Warland, and after his death married a William White, who re-established the pottery. Lysons, writing in 1795, says, " The works are still carried on at Fulham by Mr. White, a descendant in the female line of the first proprietor. Mr. White's father who married John Dwight's granddaughter, obtained a premium in 1761 from the Society for the Encouragement of Arts, etc., ' for the making of crucibles of British materials.' " For further information of John Dwight and his stonewares, the reader is referred to a paper by Miss Mavis Bimson in Vol. 5, part 2 of *The Transactions of the English Ceramic Circle.*

In 1762, 25th January, William White of Fulham, potter, took out a patent for his invention of " A new manufacture of crucibles for the melting metals and salts, &c., called by the name of white crucibles or melting pottes, made of British materials, and never before made in England or elsewhere, and which I have lately set up at Fulham. Take Stourbridge clay and Dorsetshire clay, calcined; mix them with Woolwich sand and water; to be trodden with the feet and then burned."

In Mr. Jewitt's sale there was a gallon flip-can of stoneware, with strongly-hinged cover of the same material, and a grated spout, ornamented with raised borders and figures of a woman milking, a church in the distance, hunting-scene, Hope, Peace, and other figures, with a well-modelled head on the spout, marked at the bottom, in letters scratched into the soft clay, " W. J. White, fecit Dec. 8, 1800"; and on the heart-shaped termination of the handle is "W. W. 1800"; and a stoneware mug with crown and date 1662 and " God save the King."

In 1813 the manufactory was in the hands of Mr. White, a son of the above, and the articles then made were chiefly stoneware jars, pots, jugs, etc. The Fulham works remained in the family until 1862, when the last Mr. White died, and he was succeeded by MacIntosh & Clements; but in consequence of the death of the leading partner, the works were disposed of to C. J. C. Bailey, in 1864. This gentleman made considerable alterations, and fitted up a quantity of machinery with a view of facilitating the manufacture and extending the business. The business changed hands about 1889 and became the property of the present limited company, The Fulham Pottery and Cheavin Filter Company Limited. The Bailey marks are self-explanatory except for one, the monogram of the initials, C.J.C.B.

" A relic of Alexander Selkirk, a flip-can of stoneware, may here be noticed, as having been made for him at the Fulham factory. Howell, who wrote the introduction to the *Life and Adventures of Alexander Selkirk*, printed at Edinburgh in 1829, discovered his grand-nephew in the person of John Selcrag, a teacher at Canonmills, near Edinburgh; he was in possession of two relics which had formerly belonged to Selkirk, a walking-stick and his flip-can, which was of brown stoneware, holding a pint; it was inscribed—

> ' Alexander Selkirke, that is my one (own)
> When you take me on bord of ship
> Pray fill me full with punch or flipp.'—FULHAM.

This stoneware jug was (reputedly) obtained from the Fulham pottery about the middle of 1703, while waiting for the equipment and sailing of the Cinque Ports galley, to which he had been appointed sailing-master, and doubtless accompanied him on his voyage to Juan Fernandez, and was highly venerated in the family; it was kept locked up for fifty years by one of his nieces." (From a correspondent to *Willis's Current Notes*.)

A circular pocket-flask, of brown glazed stoneware, with flattened sides, made about 1810 by Mr. White, has in front a representation of a chronometer dial; on the back is inscribed, " *J. Drinkwater, Coach & horses, Notting Hill*," and underneath is stamped, " *Fulham Pottery*."

The earliest known date on Fulham stoneware is 1721, on a mug decorated with a ship and figure of a shipwright caulking the seams of a hull.

1
> *Robert Asslet,*
> 17 *London Street* 21

Mark no. 1 is inscribed in script on a mug formerly in the collection of Mr. J. E. Hodgkin, F.S.A. Probably not a maker's mark. Perhaps the most quaint and interesting specimen known to the Editor is the large mug with pewter mount; decorated in the centre with a medallion representing Hogarth's "Midnight Modern Conversation," on the mug is also a medallion bearing the old Butchers' arms of Hereford, and the quaint legend—

> Waller Vaughan of Hereford,
> His Mugg must not be brock.   1740.

There are specimens in the British, Victoria and Albert Museums, and also in several private collections.

FULHAM. There was a factory of stoneware, galley-pots, mugs, pans, dishes, etc., carried on by James Ruel at Sandford House, Sands End, King's Road, Fulham. This factory and all the effects, together with the lease of twelve years unexpired, plant and fixtures, were advertised for sale by auction, by order of the Sheriff of Middlesex, in May 1798, but they were sold by private contract previously.

WILLIAM DE MORGAN & CO. Another art pottery which since 1888 had been transferred to Fulham, was that of William De Morgan, whose work is now well known. William De Morgan began painting tiles and pots about 1870 in Fitzroy Square; he moved afterwards to Chelsea, and continued to decorate in an effective manner pottery made by Stiff & Co. of Lambeth, and by Staffordshire firms. He then, while at Orange House, Chelsea, built an oven, and, except for the lustred work, carried out all the processes himself. In 1888 he was joined by Halsey Ricardo, and the firm became W. De Morgan & Co., a new factory being built at Fulham, and the pottery stamped W. DE MORGAN & CO., SANDS END POTTERY, FULHAM, S.W., and also with the device as mark no. 2. The work executed at Chelsea was marked " W. DE MORGAN," in an oblong or oval lozenge. There is also a mark of his name, with " Merton Abbey," on tiles decorated by him about 1879, when he worked there in association with William Morris.

Besides the lustred decoration which is in imitation of the Hispano-Moresque work of the fifteenth and sixteenth centuries, William De Morgan has decorated pottery in the Persian style, with excellent results, also landscapes and Dutch scenes. He relinquished his business as a potter about 1907, and became a successful novelist. Charles and Frederick Passenger, his partners, continued decorating on a small scale in Brompton Road until 1911. (Ker. Gall., figs. 495–6.)

LAMBETH

In the *History of Lambeth* it is related that about 1650 some Dutch potters established themselves here, and by degrees, the manufacture of earthenware became important, for the " village " possessed no less than twenty manufactories, in which were made the glazed pottery and tiles used in London and various parts of England. The ware made here was a tin glazed earthenware with landscapes and figures painted in blue. The Dutchmen referred to were probably John Ariens Van Hamme (and his potters), who obtained a patent in England on 27th October, 1676; the preamble to which grant states: " Whereas John Ariens Van Hamme hath humbly represented to us that he is, in pursuance of the encouragement he hath received from our Ambassador at the Hague, come over to settle in this our kingdom, with his own family, to exercise his *art of making tiles and porcelaine, and other earthenwares after the way practised in Holland*, which hath not been practised in this our kingdom."—Granted for and during the term of fourteen years. The trade continued flourishing for more than a century, until about the year 1780 or 1790, at which time the Staffordshire potters, by the great improvements they had made in the quality of their ware, and its cheapness, completely beat them out of the field. There is considerable uncertainty as to the exact date of the first manufacture of Lambeth delft. A mug in the British Museum inscribed " William and Elizabeth Burgas," bears date 24th August, 1631; the mug with inscription " William Lambeth " in Mr. Willett's Collection, 1650; and the candlestick in the Victoria and Albert Museum with the Fishmonger's arms, 1648. Various early Lambeth potters are mentioned in a paper by Dr. F. H. Garner in *Transactions of the English Ceramic Circle*, Vol. 1, part 4.

The white bottles or jugs for wine, upon which are written the names of drinks, were probably made at Lambeth, having much of the delft character; they bear dates from 1635 to 1672. Walpole had one at Strawberry Hill, which he bought of Mrs. Kennon, the virtuoso midwife, inscribed *Sack*, 1647. Another of these bottles inscribed " Sack, 1646," and also one " Claret, 1647," are in the Schreiber Collection, Victoria and Albert Museum. In the Norwich Museum there are four of them, inscribed *Claret*, 1648; *Sack*, 1650; *Whit*, 1648; and another, of larger size, with the Grocers' arms, W. at top, and E. M. E. on each side, dated 1649. These were found at Norwich; the last-described belonged to Edward and Mary Woodyard, whose names appear on a token in the same museum—*ob.* a sugar-loaf and two doves, " Edward Woodyard of "—*rev.* " Norwich Grocer 1656," and the initials E. M. W. These delft type bottles, with narrow necks and handles, with a very white glaze, were used to contain wines, which were then sold by apothecaries. The dates, usually in blue, upon those which we have noted, are as follows: 1646, sack or claret; 1647, sack or whit; 1648, claret, whit, or sack; 1649, whit; 1650, sack; 1656, sack; 1659, sack. (*Ker. Gall.*, fig. 497.) An interesting paper by G. E. Howard discusses these bottles and associated wares in *Transactions of the English Ceramic Circle*, Vol. 1, part 3.

Mr. Emerson Norman had a Lambeth delft plate with a portrait of Queen Catherine of Braganza, wife of Charles II, inscribed K 2 R 1682, painted in blue and yellow; and another with portraits of William and Mary. There was at Strawberry Hill " a very curious old English dish, with portraits of Charles II and his Queen," probably of Lambeth delft. A mug of this ware is in the Victoria and Albert Museum, " Anne Chapman, 1649 "; another in Sir A. W. Franks's Collection, with the arms of the Bakers' Company, dated 1657; and another, with the arms of the Leathersellers' Company, has the motto " Be merry and wise 1660," formerly in the Rev. T. Staniforth's possession. We also find octagonal plates with short sentences or ciphers enclosed by grotesques; the dates upon them are from 1660 to 1690. Six delft plates, each with inscription and date 1738, are in the British Museum:—

1. What is a merry man?
2. Let him do what he can
3. To entertain his guests
4. With wine and merry jests.
5. But if his wife do frown
6. All merriment goes down.

In the same museum are also several other excellent specimens of this Lambeth fayence, a cup inscribed, "BEE MERRY AND WISE," a jug with an inscription, "DRINKE TO THY FRIEND BUT REMEMBER THY ENDE," and others, in all of which the same rather ornamental form of letters is to be noticed, and the peculiarities of the blue colour, which is of a grey tone. Without doubt, until so much was latterly written about this Lambeth "Delft," much of what may be justly claimed for our premier national pottery, was attributed to Dutch factories.

Mr. R. L. Hobson has illustrated many of the British Museum specimens in his Guide.

There are in the Schreiber Collection a series of tiles, twelve in number, *circa* 1680, painted in blue, with scenes from Titus Oates's Plot, probably executed at Lambeth. Mr. Nightingale had a pack of playing cards of the same period, the backs of which are printed with repetitions of the same subject.

The English potters about the end of the seventeenth century appear also to have copied the forms of the Palissy ware. A favourite pattern, of which we have seen several reproductions, rudely moulded from the French, probably at Lambeth, is a large oval dish, having in the centre, in relief, a nude female reclining on a couch, holding an infant on her breast, and four other naked children gambolling in the background, emblematical of Fecundity or Charity; the border is ornamented with eight round and oval cavities, separated by masks and baskets of fruit alternately. (*Ker. Gall.*, fig. 498.) Another dish, in the Victoria and Albert Museum, has the initials H. T. T. 1697; there is also one in the British Museum, with the date 1659, and initials I. C. E. Other examples are known.

They also made at Lambeth apothecaries' slabs, which were used for mixing conserves, pills, etc., and hung up in the shops; they were in form of a heart or an escutcheon, generally painted with the arms of the Apothecaries' Company, and the motto " Opifer que per orbem dicor." Dr. Diamond had one painted in blue *camaieu*; he remembered hearing an assistant lament that he had been the cause of a great discomfiture to his master, for he had broken " his heart," in allusion to a similar tablet, which he had accidentally let fall. There are two other of these apothecaries' tablets, with the arms of the Company, in the Victoria and Albert Museum; one is shield-shaped, the other octagonal.

A person of the name of Snizer had a pottery at Lambeth; we have no particulars, except that he is stated to have been the latest maker of delft in England. John J. Bagshawe had a honey jar with a green glazed cover, signed as mark no. 1.

Also at Lambeth was a manufactory of china (?) ware carried on by Mr. Crispe, of which we know little, except from the circumstance of the celebrated sculptor, John Bacon, having modelled groups of figures for him. John Bacon, subsequently R.A., was born in Southwark, 20th November, 1740, and was apprenticed in 1755 to Mr. Crispe of Bow Church-yard, who had a manufactory of china at Lambeth. He was a self-taught artist, and, among other things, he was reputedly employed in painting on porcelain and in modelling shepherds, shepherdesses, and such small ornaments; and when two years had elapsed he made all the models required for Crispe's manufactory. It is very doubtful that Bacon painted or modelled china. It is said that he went also for a short time to Coade's manufactory at Lambeth, and designed some important models to be reproduced in artificial stone.

1

Snizer,
Lambeth.

Coade's artificial Stone Works were established about 1760 at King's Arms Stairs, Narrow Wall, Lambeth. The preparation was cast in moulds and burnt, and was intended to answer every purpose of carved stone; it extended to every species of architectural ornament, and the price was much below that of stone. John Bacon, the sculptor, designed models, monuments, and tablets as early as 1762. Nichols (*Parish of Lambeth*) says it was carried on in 1769 by Mrs. Coade. "Here are many statues which are allowed to be masterpieces of art, from the models of that celebrated artist, John Bacon." Nichols engraves one of the trade cards, on which are allegorical figures, and in the centre is written, "Coade's Lithodipyra or Artificial Stone Manufactory." In 1811 the manufactory of artificial stone belonged to Messrs. Coade and Sealey.

Richard Waters, of Fore Street, Lambeth, took out a patent in June 1811 for a new method of manufacturing pottery. *First*, in the fabrica-tion of various articles of considerable magnitude, instead of throwing or moulding them on a revolving table, the clay is made into sheets and then applied upon moulds, and finished by beating or pressure or by turning while in a revolving state; *second*, forming delft pots and other articles by compression of the clay between suitable moulds; *third*, marking or clouding the "Welsh ware," by using a number of pipes instead of one in distributing the colour; *fourth*, *fifth*, and *sixth*, provides for making large figures, statues, &c., by the same process.

The "*Imperial Pottery*," Prince's Street, carried on by Stephen Green & Co., was established about 1820, and did an extensive business in the manufacture of glazed stoneware pipes, utensils for chemical purposes, and vessels of large and small size, from ink-bottles to jars made to contain upwards of 400 gallons. The works were sold to John Cliff in 1858 and closed in 1869. See mark no. 2.

Stephen Green Imperial Potteries Lambeth.

2

Fulham
Pottery

4

DOULTON & WATTS
LAMBETH POTTERY
LONDON

3

The " *Lambeth Pottery*," in High Street, was a very old-established manufactory of stoneware, and one of the most extensive in England: the firm of Doulton & Watts was known all over the world. James Watts died in 1858, having for upwards of forty-one years been connected with the firm. The first Mr. Doulton served his time with White of Fulham. Mark no. 3, c. 1826–58.

The Sheldon Collection of English Pottery contained some marked specimens of the stoneware made by Doulton at different times of their history and connections: A brown stoneware jug impressed DOULTON & WATTS, LAMBETH POTTERY, LONDON, made during Watts' partnership (mark no. 3, c. 1826–58); a stoneware flask impressed *Fulham Pottery* (mark no. 4), made about 1800, when the first Doulton was apprenticed to White.

DOULTONS. Doultons paid great attention to the improvement of stoneware from an artistic point of view, both as regards domestic utensils and external decorations. The material is almost identical with the German steingut or so-called *grès de Flandres*, the manufacture of which in the sixteenth and seventeenth centuries flourished to such an extent as almost to supersede other descriptions of ware which had not the peculiar strength and durability of the salt-glazed stoneware.

It is necessary to point out that the *grès de Flandres* being fired with wood, the difficulty of contending with deleterious coal gases did not exist. Despite this the Doulton ware palette has accomplished a notable advance. Professor Church, in Mackenzie's *Encyclopædia of Art and Manufacture*, p. 709, says: " Rix, the manager of this department, has succeeded in obtaining a greater variety of tints than were ever secured by the German potters of the seventeenth century." Rix resigned his position in 1897.

Up to about 1867 nothing but useful household wares, chemical vessels, sanitary works, and last, but not least, the Toby-Phillpot jugs, were manufactured; but in these last vessels Doultons had an interest to the extent of many thousands of pounds a year in the continual production and sale of them throughout the country, and so great was the demand

for those articles, that their travellers frequently requested them to produce a new variety of the time-honoured " Toby-Phillpot."

About 1856 a school of art was instituted at Lambeth, which, under
the superintendence of Mr. Sparkes, kept on steadily increasing in usefulness, and many art students acquired such proficiency in modelling and
design as to attract the attention of Mr. (afterwards Sir Henry) Doulton,
that he conceived the idea of introducing art work as a branch of his
business, and engaged some of the best hands to carry out his plans. The
results were some vases and jugs of ornamental form and character which
were sent to the Paris Exhibitior in 1867. The first attempt at art ornament was incised or *sgraffito* work, the design being scratched in with
a point while the pot was still wet, and filled in with a colour that would
stand the heat of the kiln and complete the process at one baking, called
by the French *au grand feu*. Subsequently another method was adopted
viz., after the vase was turned and still moist, moulded pieces of clay,
usually of a different colour to the body, were made in forms of dots,
discs, flowers, scrolls, and borders, and pressed on to the surface; carving
out the surface in low relief in leaves, etc., and other decorations too
numerous to notice here.

Sir Henry Doulton's efforts to promote the potter's art, both in
modelling and artistic adornment, resulting from the encouragement given
by him to the most successful artists in his special department, have been
acknowledged far and wide; but the highest compliment that could be paid
him has been worthily accorded by the presentation of the Gold Albert
Medal of the Society of Arts by H.R.H. the Prince of Wales, on the very
spot where his success has been attained, viz., " The Lambeth Works,"
on 21st December, 1885, " for the impulse given to the production of art
pottery in England."

5   7   8   9

6

Doultons laid down rules which materially tended to the improvement
of the art. Among these, no copy of a previous pattern was made, and
no duplicates, hence mechanical reproduction was avoided, the object
being to obtain variety and originality in every piece. The early examples
of art-stoneware are impressed with the name " Doulton Lambeth "
within an oval and with the date of production, from about 1877. This also
occurs in circular form. In 1880 the trade mark (no. 5) was adopted, the
word " England " being added in 1891. Mark no. 6 was used from about
1901.

Miss Hannah B. Barlow, who worked 1872–1906, cleverly and quickly delineated animal life with a point on the moist surface, which in a few strokes is wonderfully true to nature. In this branch she was assisted by her sister Florence. Hannah's mark is no. 7. Her brother, Arthur B. Barlow, modelled wreaths and ornaments on the ware; he was also an art student at Lambeth. His mark is no. 8. This artist died in 1879.

A talented artist at the Lambeth pottery was George Tinworth, originally a wheelwright, but not liking the trade, he entered the art school and became a first-rate modeller. His medallions of sacred and classical subjects are exceedingly clever, as are also his architectural decorations in terra-cotta relief on jugs, etc. He was employed from about 1866 to his death in 1913. Mark no. 9.

During the year 1879 Tinworth completed two important works in terra-cotta, viz., the reredos for York Minster, and a series of semicircular panels for the Guards' Memorial Chapel in Birdcage Walk, the latter being entirely Scripture subjects from the Old and New Testaments. Tinworth also modelled some amusing small animal figures and groups.

Among George Tinworth's later works are the Brazen Serpent in Sandringham Church, and the reredos and font presented by the then Princess of Wales to the English Church at Copenhagen.

E.S.   EDL

10   11

12

At the 1878 Paris Exhibition was introduced a new variety of Doulton ware in the " pâte sur pâte " style, this being entirely produced in salt-glazed stoneware, no colour being added further than that contained in the clay itself, and no glazing except that of the salt fumes. The chief artists in this ware were Miss E. Simmance (mark no. 10, c. 1873+)and Miss E. D. Lupton (mark no. 11, c. 1880+), both of whom were trained at Lambeth School of Art.

Doulton wares by Miss H. Barlow, George Tinworth and other artists are illustrated in Godden's *British Pottery and Porcelain, an Illustrated Encyclopædia of Marked Specimens*.

In the year 1872 Doultons turned their attention to a finer quality of ware, which in its " biscuit " state was submitted to the artist. To this ware the name of " Lambeth faience " was applied, and the distinctive mark (no. 12) from the commencement used.

The essential difference between this Lambeth faience and the Doulton ware is that the former is produced by painting the design on the form after it has been first fired to the biscuit state, and then submitting it to the second firing after dipping in a transparent glaze.

Since then various other developments have been made, one of which has been the introduction of yet another entirely distinct ware, termed " Doulton impasto " ware. This was introduced in 1879, the first pieces being drawn from the kiln and shown on the visit of the Princess of Wales and Crown Princess of Prussia to the Lambeth Works. The distinctive trade-mark used from the commencement has been as shown by mark no. 13.

This ware was produced by painting in relief on the ware in various shades of stained clay previous to the final firing and glazing, and was capable of very rich and spirited effects of decoration. The chief artists in this ware were Miss Collins (mark no. 14) and Miss F. Linnell (15). In Lambeth faience the chief decorative artists were Miss M. Capes (16), Miss Crawley (17), Miss F. Lewis (18), John Eyre (19), Miss Kate Rogers (20), Miss Rosa Keen (21), and Miss Mary Butterton (22 or 23). In Doulton ware, there were in addition to those already named, Miss Edwards (worked from c. 1873, no. 24), Miss Florence Barlow (died 1909, no. 25), Frank A. Butler (worked c. 1873–1911, no. 26) and Mark Marshall (worked c. 1876–1912, no. 27).

The following additional trade-names have also been introduced to distinguish some fresh features of art branches of their manufactures:—

Silicon Ware. Coloured vitreous stoneware in grey, buff, brown and black, was introduced in 1881 and continued to about 1912. Mark no. 28.

Chiné Ware. By this term is indicated all wares having textured backgrounds produced by the impression of lace and other textile fabrics on the soft clay. Mark no. 29, c. 1886–1914.

Marqueterie Ware. Produced with sections of parti-coloured clays of semi-geometrical designs ingrained through the mass, in effect not unlike wood marqueterie. Introduced in 1887, and used to about 1900. Mark no. 30. Similar marks without " England " are pre–1891.

Carrara body was introduced c. 1888 and continued until 1898; examples bear mark no. 31. " ENGLAND " was added to all trade marks from 1891 (no. 32). Subsequent marks include no. 33, impressed on small pieces of stoneware.

Early in the present century (c. 1902), mark no. 34, was adopted and was used until 1936. The bottom part of this mark was used at the same period for small objects. Other marks used from this period to the closure of the Lambeth factory in 1956 have been no. 35 on Persian designs, c. 1920–28, and no. 36, c. 1922–56.

Similar Doulton marks but including the word BURSLEM were employed at the company's large factory in Staffordshire. See Staffordshire section.

The *London Pottery* belonged to James Stiff from about 1840. The manufacture of stone ware drain-pipes and Doulton type wares was carried on until about 1913 when Doultons acquired the works. It was originally a delft pottery, established about 1751 and stood on the site of Hertford House.

Another pottery was established in the nineteenth century by Mr. Northen, who was an apprentice at White's Fulham Pottery; it was devoted principally to drainpipes, etc.

The Southern Embankment from Westminster Bridge to Vauxhall drove away many potters, who, for the convenience of transit, had established manufactories by the river-side.

SOUTHWARK. Gravel Lane. Nathaniel Oade was a potter here in 1718; this is made known to us by a paragraph in the *Post Boy* of March 1, 1718, from which we learn that he had four sons; and because the father would not turn over his house and trade to them, and be contented with what property he had, they swore they would have it in spite of him.

They consequently arrested him in a sham action in the Marshalsea Court
for £500, when the four sons and the attorney turned the mother and
servants out of the house and barricaded the doors, having conveyed into
it arms and provisions. In their rage they shot a woman who was passing
by, also their own mother and a servant, who would not give up possession
of the books of accounts. The constables and the military arrived; they
at length capitulated. They were subsequently tried; the youngest son
and a carpenter were found guilty of murder and hanged, the others of
manslaughter only.

A communication was made to the Royal Society, June 21, 1750, by
William Jackson, a potter, that the roof of a pot-house at Lambeth,
belonging to Mr. Oade, in Gravel Lane, was thrown down by the earth-
quake, March 1749-50.

10, 1876	9, 1880	10, 1896
R. W. Martin	R. W. Martin	Martin Brothers
London	London & Southall	London & Southall
1	2	3

MARTIN WARE. It is singular that a meritorious, albeit small *fabrique*
of stoneware, a revival in England of the old sixteenth and seventeenth
century Grès-Ceramique, should have escaped the notice of so many
writers on the subject. The four brothers Martin carried on from about
1873 a small pottery at Fulham and at Southall from 1878, and had for the
sale of their productions a little shop in Brownlow Street, Holborn. The
initiator of the business was Robert Wallace Martin, a Royal Academy
student, and pupil of Alexander Munro, the sculptor, and after the lapse
of a somewhat unsatisfactory co-operation with Mr. Bailey, who was then
proprietor of the Fulham Pottery, he was joined by his three brothers—
Charles Douglas, Walter Fraser, and Edwin Bruce. Meanwhile they had
spent a considerable time making experiments with clays and colours,
and with the firing of them, and so they were enabled, after many failures
and difficulties, to produce the ware which bears their name. These men
struggled on bravely, and their method reminds one of the earlier potters'
struggles with want of capital and meagre encouragement. A great point
with the Martins is that the decoration of a specimen was never repeated,
so that each piece is in its way a unique example of the handiwork of the
potter. The mark is a signature incised in the paste, and varies: sometimes
R. W. Martin & Brothers (or Bros), sometimes Martin Bros or Brothers in
full, and the words London and Southall, with month and year of production, these words being in cursive manuscript, and written, with but few
exceptions, by the youngest brother—Edwin. Some earlier pieces are
signed " R. W. Martin, Fulham," later " London," or " Southall," occurs.
Most examples are dated. Mark no. 1, c. 1874–78; no. 2, c. 1878–82; no. 3
from c. 1882 onwards.

The forms are from classical to quaint and grotesque; the colouring, though sometimes similar to the old stoneware, is more frequently as original as the decoration, which is incised, modelled, or carved, and the ware is both artistic and effective. There are specimens in the Victoria and Albert Museum and in private collections. Walter Martin died in 1912 and Edwin in 1915. The last successful firing was in 1914 for, with the loss of the experience of his brothers, Robert could do little but model his famous pieces. He died in 1923. An unsuccessful effort was made to restart the pottery in the 1930's. Typical examples are illustrated in Godden's *British Pottery and Porcelain, an Illustrated Encyclopædia of Marked Specimens.*

VAUXHALL

In *Houghton's Collections*, March 13, 1695-96, we read: "Of teapots in 1694 there came but ten, and those from Holland. To our credit be it spoken, we have about Faux Hall, as I have been informed, made a great many, and I cannot gainsay but they are as good as any came from abroad."

Thoresby, in his *Diary* on May 24, 1714, with his friend Boulter, "went by water to Foxhall and the Spring-garden. After dinner there, we viewed the pottery and various apartments. Was most pleased with that where they were painting divers colours, which yet appear more beautiful and of different colours when baked."

The Vauxhall Pottery abutted on the Thames, close to Vauxhall Bridge, and in the High Street, Vauxhall, and the delft manufactory in Princes Street, Lambeth, was included in it. It is probably the one spoken of in the preceding paragraph, but we do not know the names of the previous proprietors. Mr. Wagstaffe had the Vauxhall Pottery towards the end of the last century; he died about 1803 or 1804. The business and premises were left by Mr. Wagstaffe to his nephew, Mr. Wisker, who carried it on until his death in 1835

In 1833 John Wisker patented "certain improvements in machinery or apparatus for grinding covers or stoppers for jars, bottles, and other vessels made of china, stone, or other earthenware."

Mr. Alfred Singer, who has kindly responded to our inquiries relating to the Vauxhall Pottery, says: "I have always understood that it was in existence in the time of Charles II., but when it was first established I have no idea." He continues: "The Vauxhall Pottery was purchased for me in 1835 of the executors of Mr. Wisker; the business was carried on by me for thirty years, from 1835 to 1865. The premises are now pulled down and built over."

In April 1839, Alfred Singer, in conjunction with Henry Pether, patented "certain improvements in the preparation and combination of earthenware or porcelain for the purpose of mosaic or tessellated work." These are, first, "the mode of producing the pieces for the formation of mosaic work by cutting clay or other plastic material into rectilinear figures by means of intersecting wires stretched in a frame." Second, "the forming of ornamental slabs of mosaic work by cementing together small pieces of porcelain or earthenware of various figures and colours on slabs of slate, stone, or other suitable material."

This important revival of geometrical mosaic by Mr. Singer, aided by his ingenious assistant, Mr. Pether (although tessellated pavements of similar character had been in general use from the time of the ancients), literally "paved the way" for a beautiful and durable material for the floors of public and private buildings, and Mr. Herbert Minton was not slow in availing himself of Mr. Singer's patent, from whom he took out a license for laying small tiles and tesserae of coloured clay, which he brought to great perfection.[1]

Mr. Singer says: "For many years the only ware made at the Vauxhall Pottery was delf. At what date the salt-glazed stoneware was introduced I do not know, and have often tried to ascertain; but I know the delf business was removed to Mortlake long before Mr. Wisker's time, and stoneware only has been produced at the Vauxhall Pottery for nearly a hundred years.

"In 1820 the delf business was removed from Mortlake to Princes Street, Lambeth, opposite the pottery, and carried on there by Mr. Wisker, and Mr. Singer after him, until 1846, when the premises were sold to the South-Western Railway Company, and the manufacture, which had latterly diminished, was finally abandoned; this was the last and only delf ware pottery in England. The goods latterly produced were confined to pomatum pots, Dutch tiles, wine and butter coolers, etc., but formerly a great variety of domestic ware was made there."

MORTLAKE

The first mention we have found of this pottery is that, "on Friday, June 8, 1764, Mr. Jackson, potter at Mortlake, was found hanging in a hayloft belonging to Mr. Langton. No reason can be assigned for his committing this rash action, as he was in good circumstances."

We do not know the date of the establishment of the delft pottery at

---

[1] This patent, it must be remembered, is quite distinct from another (also a revival) taken out in January 1830, by Mr. Samuel Wright of Shelton, for making encaustic tiles or ornamental tiles, bricks and quarries for floors, pavements, and other purposes, and decorating them in various colours and patterns by impressing the patterns on the clay and filling up the cavities with clay or slip coloured with metallic oxides. It was subsequently purchased by Mr. Minton.

A third patent was taken out in June 1840 by Mr. Richard Prosser, for solidifying china clay in a dry powder by subjecting it to a great pressure in iron moulds, thus avoiding the shrinkage in the kiln by evaporation of moisture, and producing a substance of extraordinary density and evenness of texture throughout its body.

These three important patents of Mr. Singer, Mr. Wright, and Mr. Prosser were the groundwork of Mr. Minton's future excellence and perfection in the manufacture of coloured tesserae and encaustic tiles, which were laid out in exquisite patterns from designs of Mr. Owen Jones, Mr. Digby Wyatt, and other celebrated artists.

Mortlake, but it was not in existence early in the eighteenth century. The works were taken by Mr. Wagstaffe towards the end of the last century, but who his predecessor was we have no information; at his death they were left by will to his nephew, Mr. Wisker, together with the Vauxhall Pottery. Both delft and stoneware (but principally the former) were made at Mortlake. The business and all the materials, as well as all the hands employed, were removed to London by Mr. Wisker about 1820 or 1821, and continued on his premises in Princes Street, Lambeth, until 1846.

Lysons (edit. 1811) says: "The manufactory of delf is now carried on by Wagstaffe & Co. There is a small manufactory of white stoneware belonging to Mr. Joseph Kishire." A very large delft punch-bowl, of Mortlake enamelled earthenware, made about the middle of the eighteenth century, white ground, painted in blue with scrolls, medallions, masks, flowers, and birds, 21 inches diameter, and a framed panel of twelve tiles of Mortlake delft, of the same date, artistically painted in dark blue, with a rocky landscape, ruins, and figures, on white ground, 20 inches by 15 inches, were removed from Mortlake in 1820, and subsequently presented to the Victoria and Albert Museum by Mr. Alfred Singer; these are both painted by hand in a masterly manner.

Kishere

I K

I 8 2

Kishere Mortlake

1

2

3

MORTLAKE POTTERY. The pottery carried on by Joseph Kishere was apparently a small concern, and such specimens as the Editor has seen do not possess great merit, but collectors of marks like to identify their specimens. The ware was a salt glazed or enamelled pottery, brown and yellow, sometimes ornamented with figures in low relief. Mark no. 1. Early nineteenth century.

Major-General Astley Terry had a specimen impressed *Kishere Mortlake*, as mark no. 3, and Mr. Davis of Hampstead had a pair of yellow salt glazed earthenware candlesticks with lady and cavalier standing by columns, forming candleholders, with mark no. 2 impressed; probably the initials of Kishere.

ISLEWORTH. Established c. 1760. Porcelain discontinued about 1800; "Welsh ware" in 1825; established by Joseph Shore, from Worcester. The factory was situated at Railshead Creek, close to the ferry at Isleworth; it was on a small scale, employing from fifteen to twenty hands, and two kilns, one used for "biscuit," the other for "glazing." The principal painter was Richard Goulding, who married Joseph Shore's daughter, assisted by his son William, one or both of whom had probably been decorators at Worcester, and the factory came, by will, to the Gouldings, who carried it on after Shore's death. The superintendent of the works was Benjamin Quarman, who died in 1787; the manufacture of porcelain was, however, continued. Lysons, in his *Environs of London* (vol. iii, p. 122), published in 1795, says: " There is a china manufactory at Isleworth belonging to Messrs. Shore & Co." The stock of china remained in the factory unsold for more than thirty years, and was dispersed by auction at Isleworth about the year 1830. Mark no. 4, but should not be regarded as a true factory mark.

W.GOULDING   26   F. G.

June 20.1770.   S & G.   S & Co   73

                      5   6

                                                7

4

The late Mr. Thomson, great-grandson of Joseph Shore, possessed several specimens, among which was a basin painted with blue flowers in the Oriental style, of exactly the same fabric and similar in decoration to the porcelain of Worcester, bearing the early mark of a crescent; others are painted in colours, white china figures, etc.; they also decorated Oriental porcelain. The manufacture of pottery was carried on simultaneously, and continued to be made until about 1825; it was called Welsh ware, a strong and close earthenware, streaked with yellow and brown glaze in a zigzag pattern: jugs, dishes, shallow pans, etc., were made. The manufactory was removed to Hounslow, but the distance from the metropolis, and other causes, rendered it unprofitable, and it was given up about two years later.

A porcelain cup and saucer, in Mr. Tulk's possession, was painted with blue flowers and embossed leaves. A butter-boat which belonged to Mr. Chaffers, is of good glaze, embossed with daisies and leaves, and painted in blue, like Worcester, presented to him by Mr. Tulk, to whom he was indebted for calling his attention to the Isleworth porcelain manufactory.

An octagonal teapot of red ware, similar to Elers' ware, was in Mrs. Arthur Macdonald's Collection, impressed SHORE & Co., and specimens were in the Sheldon Collection, stamped S. & G., S. & Co., also F. G., which are attributed to this factory (marks 5, 6, 7). N.B.—The German firm of Schiller & Gerbing used the initials S & G on similar wares. The initials given here fit several firms.

ESSEX (CASTLE HEDINGHAM). The former Editor was indebted for the following particulars of a pottery, hitherto unrecognised, to Miller Christy, the editor of the industrial section of the *Victoria County History of Essex*. Edward Bingham, born in 1829, the son of a Lambeth potter, assisted his father in his business, which was that of making ordinary pottery. In 1837 the family settled at Hedingham, and Edward, when only a lad of ten years of age, is said to have shown his artistic taste by modelling such natural objects as flowers, vases, and snakes. The business was apparently not successful, for in 1859 Edward Bingham set up a school where he had some twenty-nine pupils. He was, however, a potter by intuition, and after a few years of school-keeping, he returned to his favourite occupation, and in 1864 was employing five or six assistants, progressing steadily until we read of his requiring no fewer than thirteen kilns in 1885. The peculiar grey-blues, greens, and warm browns that characterised his Castle Hedingham ware became known, and he received considerable patronage, Soden Smith, Sir A. W. Franks, and other influential people being personally interested in his works.

The failure of native clay caused him to procure material from Devonshire, and this altered the character of his pottery. After making over the business to his son, the works were sold to a Devonshire firm, who carried them on for a few years under the title of the " Essex Art Pottery," but the concern came to an end in 1905.

In the Corporation Museum of Colchester there is the " Essex Jug," bearing mark no. 8. It is decorated with medallions in relief illustrating the history of the county, the Boadicean revolt, the Dunmow Flitch ceremony, and the arms of Essex families. There is an illustration of this specimen in Litchfield's *Pottery and Porcelain*. Various incised marks and signatures occur. The castle mark is on a raised pad and has sometimes been chipped away from the ware.

8

BOW

It is not known exactly when the Bow porcelain factory was started, but we do know who was its leading spirit and driving force. He was the Irish painter and engraver, Thomas Frye, who was born of obscure parents in or near Dublin in 1710. He was a painter and engraver of considerable merit, who, in 1738, came to London, where he continued his profession. Amongst others, he painted a portrait of Frederick Prince of Wales for Sadler's Hall, and also published a number of fine life-size mezzotints of the heads of George III, Queen Charlotte, Garrick, the Duchess of Northumberland and others. It is said that no one was more happy in delineating the human countenance and that he had the correctness of Van Dyck and the colouring of Rubens. In miniature painting he equalled, if not excelled, the famous Cooper.

In 1744 Thomas Frye was associated with Edward Heylyn, a glass merchant of Bow, in taking out this patent for a material for making porcelain:—

" Edward Heylin, in the parish of Bow, in the county of Middlesex, merchant, and Thomas Frye, of the parish of West Ham, in the county of Essex, painter, took out a patent on the 6th of December 1744 for a new method of manufacturing a certain mineral, whereby a ware might be made of the same nature or kind, and equal to, if not exceeding in goodness and beauty, china or porcelain ware imported from abroad. *The material is an earth, the produce of the Cherokee nation in America, called by the natives* UNAKER. A glass is formed in the usual way with one part of either ' pot-ash, fern-ash, pearl-ash, kelp, or any other vegetable lixiviall salt,' and ' one part of sand, flints, pebbles, or any other stones of the vitrifying kind,' and reduced to an impalpable powder, and mixed in different proportions, according to the nature of the ware to be made, with *unaker*, from which sand and mica have been removed by washing. They are then kneaded together, thrown or moulded, and put into a ' kiln burned with wood,' called ' biscuiting,' then painted and glazed with *unaker* and the glass above described; ' they are not to be taken out of the kiln till it is thorough cold.' "

The unaker mentioned in this patent was a clay discovered in America about 1738 by Andrew Duché of Savannah, Georgia. Some porcelain was made there by him and in 1743 he brought samples to England. The circumstances are described in an interesting letter written by William Cookworthy of Plymouth on 30th May, 1745:—

" I had lately with me the person who has discovered the *china earth*. He had with him several samples of the china ware, which I think were equal to the Asiatic. It was found on the back of Virginia, where he was in quest of mines; and having read Du Halde, he discovered both the *petunze* and *kaolin*. It is this latter earth which he says is essential to the success of the manufacture. He is gone for a cargo of it, having bought from the Indians the whole country where it rises. They can import it for £13 per ton, and by that means afford their china as cheap as common stoneware; *but they intend* only to go about 30 *per cent. under the Company.*"

The company which the American intended to undersell may have been the Bow Porcelain Company. On the other hand, it may be that the company referred to was the East India Company, which was importing Chinese porcelain in quantity and may well have been importing kaolin itself from China.

Another partner in the firm at this early period was George Arnold, Master of the Haberdasher's Company and President of St. Thomas's Hospital. On his death in 1751, he was described as one of the principal proprietors of the Porcelain Manufactory at Bow. He was a man of substance and probably provided some of the finance required for the new venture.

George Arnold and Edward Heylyn bought a piece of land on the Middlesex side of Bow bridge in 1744, and Frye's experiments between 1744 and 1748 were probably carried out there. It was not known whether any saleable porcelain was produced at this time.

Frye's partner, Edward Heylyn, had a glass-kiln which, no doubt, was used considerably in their experiments in the search for a satisfactory porcelain, using the unaker or china-clay that Duché had discovered in America. However, they were not able to make hard porcelain.

In 1749 we find Frye taking out a second patent:—

" On November 17, 1749, ' Thomas Frye, of the parish of West Ham, in the county of Essex, painter, for a new method of making a certain ware, which is not inferior in beauty and fineness, and is rather superior in strength than the earthenware that is brought from the East Indies, and is commonly known by the name of China, Japan, or porcelain ware.' Animals, vegetables, and fossils, by calcining, grinding, and washing, are said to produce an insoluble matter named *virgin earth,* but some in greater quantities than others, as all animal substances, all fossils of the calcareous kind, as chalk, limestone, &c.; take therefore any of these classes, calcine it, grind and wash it in many waters; these ashes are mixed in certain proportions with flint, ' white pebble or clear sand,' and with water, made into balls, highly burned and ground fine, and mixed with a proportion of pipeclay; it is then thrown on the wheel, and when finished, dried, burnt, and painted with ' smalt or saffer,' when it is ready to be glazed with a glaze, made first by making a glass with saltpetre, red lead, and ' sand flint, or other white stones,' grinding it up well, and mixing it with a certain proportion of white lead, adding a little smalt to clear the colour. After dripping and drying, the articles are put in cases and ' burned with wood till the surface is clear and shining.' "

It will be noticed that whereas the first patent was for a material from which porcelain might be made, this second patent is specifically for making porcelain and it indicates the use of bone-ash, which gives Bow porcelain its phosphatic characteristics.

The earliest recorded reference to the Bow Porcelain Factory is contained in the fourth edition of Defoe's *Tour of Great Britain*, 1748, where it says ". . . the first village we come to is Bow, where a large Manufactory of Porcelain is lately set up. They have already made large quantities of tea-cups, saucers, etc., which by some skilful persons are said to be little inferior to those which are brought from China. . . ."

By 25th March, 1749, Frye was established on the Essex side of Bow bridge in the ward of Stratford (or Stratford Langthorne) within the parish of West Ham, on the north side of Stratford High Street and not, as has so often been stated, at Stratford-le-Bow in the parish of Bow. The firm traded as Alderman Arnold & Co., and the factory was given the name of " New Canton."

From Michaelmas Day, 1750, to Lady Day, 1752, the firm is recorded as Fry & Company. It is, therefore, doubtful whether Weatherby & Crowther took over the firm in 1750 as was thought previously. This is more likely to have taken place at some time between 1752 and 1757.

One of the managers or travellers for the company was John Bowcock, who left several books formerly in use at the Bow works, including books of designs, memorandum books, diaries and some account books relative to the business. These books and documents came into the possession of Lady Charlotte Schreiber, the enthusiastic collector of ceramics, but have since disappeared. However, before this happened the following extracts had been made and give valuable information as to the early history of the factory.

The first contains the accounts from January, 1750-51. From these it appears that a branch establishment was opened in London in 1753, which, no doubt, was that of St. Catherine's near the Tower, although the place is not mentioned. An account is given in separate columns of the bisket (unglazed) and glazed ware taken into the warehouses at Bow, and sold out of the warehouses at London and Bow in each year. A statement for the year 1754 is here given to show the extent of the business transacted:—

A WEEKLY ACCOUNT OF TRADE, &C., AT LONDON AND BOW

1754	Goods Credited with Discount			Credit without Discount			Retail Cash, London			Cash, per Journal			Cash Received, Bow			Goods Returned		
	£	s.	d.	£	s.	d.	£	s.	d.	£	s.	d.	£	s.	d.	£	s.	d.
January 5	134	15	5	1	1	0	20	4	3	11	1	6	28	17	9½	9	15	0
12	174	6	1	25	5	6	29	4	8	138	9	3	16	14	8	4	13	0
19	192	13	6	24	16	10	50	16	0	153	18	9	28	15	10½	15	5	0
26	115	14	4	1	0	0	59	6	2	94	13	0	20	8	9	16	16	3
February 2	50	16	11	15	19	3	26	2	6	86	15	0	30	9	6½	1	6	0
9	69	8	7	9	14	7	42	3	9	40	5	4	21	6	1	62	1	5
16	51	16	8	3	7	6	32	17	5	71	18	5	24	14	7½	7	16	6
23	48	9	11	71	1	8	38	12	8	58	17	7	22	10	7½	2	19	3
March 2	67	1	3	13	9	6	56	4	3	83	2	5	26	3	10	17	14	6
9	89	12	7½	8	9	4	44	11	9	145	14	2	35	5	1½		...	
16	136	17	0½	5	9	6	27	11	5	70	12	6	33	16	4	2	0	6
23	41	7	5	13	6	0	36	8	10	55	9	6	14	7	0	1	9	0
30	104	11	0	14	10	6	41	18	3	90	16	2	21	9	9		...	
	1127	10	9	211	7	2	506	1	11	1101	13	7	325	0	0	141	16	11

ANNUAL ACCOUNT OF THE PORCELAIN COMPANY'S TRADE FOR THE
YEAR 1754

	Sold with Discount			Sold without Discount			Cash Received, London			Cash Received, Bow			Debts Come in		
	£	s.	d.	£	s.	d.	£	s.	d.	£	s.	d.	£	s.	d.
1st Quarter	1277	10	9	211	7	2	506	1	11	325	0	0	1101	13	7
2nd Quarter . . .	2222	11	8	200	0	3	569	3	11	299	10	4	1434	10	1
3rd Quarter . . .	2647	18	1	385	2	2	381	18	11	150	4	0	2184	6	11
4th Quarter . . .	1982	3	8	189	0	0	353	5	8	77	8	11	2429	10	9
Total	8130	4	2	985	9	7	1810	10	5	852	3	3	7150	1	4
Discount 10% . .	813	0	0												
	7317	4	2												

	£	s.	d.
Cash received, Bow . . .	852	3	3
,, ,, London . .	1810	10	5
Sold without discount . . .	985	9	7
Sold with discount . . .	7317	4	2
Total	18,115	8	9

The following extract will show the actual cash receipts at Bow and London, 1751, to 1755, exclusive of the book debts received during the year, which, as will be seen in the preceding account for 1754, amounted to upwards of £7000. This statement gives us an idea of the steady increase of the business, which had nearly doubled itself in five years:—

O.S.	1750-1	.	.	.	.	.	£6,573	0	8
N.S.	1752	.	.	.	.	.	7,747	4	8
,,	1753	.	.	.	.	.	10,114	11	6
,,	1754	.	.	.	.	.	10,965	6	3
,,	1755	.	.	.	.	.	11,229	15	2

The next entry gives us the weekly account of the biscuit china made at Bow in 1754 and is interesting as it informs us that the name of the Bow factory was " New Canton, the model of the building being taken from that at Canton in China," so distinctly stated by Thomas Craft in his contemporary account of the factory given later in this section. It also enables us to appropriate with certainty the china inkstand formerly in the Worcester Porcelain Company's museum, decorated with the favourite and well-known Bow pattern of the prunus. It is inscribed on the upper surface " Made at New Canton, 1750."

New Canton or Bow Inkstand

Others of the same kind and with identical inscriptions are in the British, and Victoria and Albert Museums. The date 1751 also occurs. There is also an illustration of another in the *Ker. Gall.*, fig. 532. Other Bow specimens are illustrated in the same work, figs. 524-5, 530-44.

A WEEKLY ACCOUNT OF BISKET WARE MADE AT NEW CANTON

1754.			£	s.	d.	1754.					£	s.	d.
Jan.	5.	No kilns	.	.	...	April 6.	2 kilns	.	.	.	109	4	3
	12.	Do.	.	.	...		13.	Do.	.	.	140	13	3
	19.	Do.	.	.	...		20	Do.	.		128	8	6
	29.	Do.	.	.	...		27.	Do.	.	.	115	3	6
Feb.	2.	Do.	.	.	...	May 4.	Do.		.	.	121	13	3
	9.	Do.	.	.	...		11.	Do.	.	.	.	115	16	6
	16.	Do.	.	.	...		18.	Do.	.	.	128	5	0
	23.	2 kilns	.	.	128 15 2		25.	3 kilns	.	.	.	184	13	8
Mar.	2.	Do.	.	.	126 8 11	June 1.	Do.	.	.	.	177	0	8
	9.	Do.	.	.	134 9 10		8.	Do.	.	.	.	177	17	6
	16.	Do.	.	.	147 18 6		15.	Do.	.	.	.	181	14	5
	23.	Do.	.	.	129 0 6		22.	Do.	.	.		177	3	0
	30.	Do.	.	.	132 14 10		29.	Do.	.	.	.	169	9	1

£799 7 9

£1927 2 7
799 7 9

£2726 10 4

Amount one week with another for 19 weeks is £143, 10s. 0d. each week.

There is a cash-account book for 1757 and 1758, of receipts and payments of a London branch of the Bow factory, either at St. Catherine's or in Cornhill; it is balanced weekly. The moneys received are principally from customers, whose names are given, and ready money taken daily, cash received from St. James Street, &c., averaging about £120 per week; the bulk of the money was paid to Mr. Crowther every week, occasionally to Mr. Weatherby.

Mr. Frye frequently received sums varying from £15 to £30, possibly for expenses at Bow. Mr. Heylin's name occurs once or twice, only for small sums. Other payments are for powder gold and for grain gold for Bow; freight of clay; weekly wages—to Mr. Brown, 18s.; Mr. Sandys, 12s.; Hugh Williams, 12s.; Stephenson, 12s.; Burnett, 10s.; which average about 60s. per week.

The book we now refer to contains memoranda made by John Bowcocke in 1756; he was one of the managers, or perhaps travellers, for the Bow Works. In it we find orders from customers, and many interesting notes relating to the business. We shall have occasion to quote largely from this manuscript, as the items throw considerable light upon the various descriptions of ware made there, among which many will be identified by the curious reader.

" 1756. Insure £450 on board the *Antilope*. John Cowling. Mr. Crowther paid Thos. Osborne for an anchor for the ship *Antilope* £12, 1s. 2 doz. crimson buttons for Mr. Frye.

" Jan. 29. Mr. Fogg,[1] a sprig'd sallad vessel, 12s.; 1 pair sprig'd boats, 6s.; 16 cooks, 2s. each, abated; a swan; two harlequins (returned), 7s.

" March. Mr. Fahy: 9 gentlemen and ladies at 9s., £4, 1. Mr. White: 1 small flutter, white; 3 pair of boys and girls; 1 pair small fidler and companion; 1 pair tambourines; 1 cook. Mr. Fogg: 2 doz. odd cups and 2 doz. imag'd small; 2 pair image ewers; 6 swans; 6 white boars; 6 sprig'd handled cups and 6 cans; 1 pair sauce-boats, Mr. Vere's pattern, 4s.; 1 pair large ribbed boats, 4s.; 1 large dragon milk-pot; 12 dragon breakfast cups and saucers with good deep colour; 1 sprig'd upright tea-pot, 3s.; 1 sprig'd cream ewer; 24 octagon nappy plates, partridge pattern; 1 vine-leaf milk-pot.

" March 27. Mrs. Ann Howard, the Lamb, in Broad Mead, Bristol: 10 round dishes; 2 of each size from the smallest to the largest, both included; 1 largest octagon dish; 1 next less size dish; 36 table plates; 12 soup plates; 2 pair rib'd boats; 3 pair flat salts, without feet; they must all be the bordered image, blue and pale, as you please. She has it greatly in her power to serve the factory. I hope they will be very neat and charged reasonable; I have not told her any price. Add 1 soup dish, 13 or not above 14 inches over; 12 table plates. Imaged pale blue.

" Quy. What's to be done with white bud sprigs; what quy. of Cupids and B. is wanted white; what floras, &c.

" March 30. Lent Mr. Frye, cash £8.

" April 22. Colol. Griffin, Brook Street; 4 small upright pint mugs to be painted to the very fine landskip pattern, as soon as possible.

" April 22. 4 doz. blue plates, Newark pattern; 8 doz. mosaic do.

" April 28. Lord Southwell. Mr. Heylin has promised him to make an oval tureen, the image pattern, and to be done in 6 weeks without fail. Think of the Chinese head for Mr. Weatherby.

" May 4. Mr. Vanderkist: an enamelled partridge coffee-pot, 9s. Mr. White: 1 imag'd cup and 7 sprig'd chocolates. What is meant by 36 white men with salt-boxes? Mr. Hunter desires to have some mustard ladles as the cream ladles, only small boles and long handles; 6 enamelled roses, 2 pr. green leaf candlesticks, 4 white leaf candlesticks. Mr. Kentish: mandril coffee-pot. Mr. Fogg: 2 swans, wings open. Mrs. Whitfield to have 1 pr. white branch candlesticks. Mr. Williams: 1 pr. sporters; 1 enamelled pero, 6s.; 1 shepherd, imperial, 7s.; 1 shepherdess, 9s.

" May 7. Quy, whether any Windsor bricks were received at the glass-house which is charged to the porcelain compy. Paid Mr. Heylin, Minshull's draft, £10, 10s. J. B. Paid Sir Joseph Hankey for Messrs. Weatherby & Crowther, £348, 18s. Mr. Fahy: 1 pr. of the new shepherd and compn.; 1 pr. Dutch dancers, 9s.; 1 gentleman and lady, 18s.; 1 cook, 7s.; 1 boy and girl, 12s.; 1 Paris cries, 6s.; 1 woman with chicken, 7s. Whether any *bucks* is wanted? There was 5 pair sent down, and only 1 pair came back. Send down what *does* there is in town, and send down the Bow books.

" May 28. Patterns received from Lady Cavendish: a Japan octagon cup and saucer lady pattern; a rib'd and scollop'd cup and saucer, image pattern; a basket bordered dysart plate; a Japan bread and buttered plate. Mr. Williams: 12 setts blue teas, at 2s. 10d.; a sett compleat of the second *printed* teas.

" May 15. Recd. a pair of birds on pedestals, to be painted for Mr. Legg, corner of Birchen Lane. Lady Stairs: a compleat sett Dresden sprig, the canister top; partridge octagon plates. Mrs. Whitfield to have 1 p. white biscuit candlesticks.

" May 20. Duchess of Leeds: 2 square enamd. and sprig'd desst. 15s.; 1 blue dol-

---

[1] Mr. Fogg was a dealer in china, living in Swallow Street, nearer to Oxford Street than Vigo Lane. His son, after Regent Street was built, had a shop in it. Robert Fogg in Bond Street china-man, died at Reading in February 1806, in his ninetieth year.

phin pickle stand, 5s.; one white basin and cover, 3s.; the Duke of Argyle's acct.; £207, 5s. The Duchess of Portland's acct. to be made out, and wait on the steward, Mr. Guidon, in Privy Gardens, Whitehall, and will be paid when her ladyship returns.

"June 18. Mr. Fogg: 1 pint *printed* mug, 5s.; 1 half-pint do., 3s. 6d.; 1 fine plate, 4s.; 1 partridge handd. cup and saucer, 3s. 6d. Allowed Mr. Fogg. In a Pero's broken hat, 1s. (Pierrot); in 2 Turks, 3s.; octagon dysart partridge plate, 3s. 6d. Mr. Fogg to know the price of the best cock plates; 4 pair rib'd boats at 4s. good; 2 pr. small imaged boats and plates; 6 squirrels; butter tubs; 2 small dragon milk-pots; 2 do., a little larger; 1 dragon sugar-dish. Mr. Morgan lent me a leaf for the roses; 4 vauses; 1 pair Minervas of each size. 2 dcuble dozn. of lace and 2 double dozn. dysart rose pattern knife handles; to be mounted and sent in Baxter's parcel.

"July 24. Mr. Fogg to have one pair of ccloured squirrels. The knife-handles : how many sold of Dresden flowers? and to have a double dozn. mounted. Has Mrs. Bernardeau had what she ordered of the wheatsheaf? To buy a partridge either alive or dead. To bring down the Chelsea cabbage leaves and bason. Recd. and gave Mr. Beswick receipt for £107, 12s. in full to Sept. 1755, for Weatherby & Crowther. J. B. Mr. Coleman : harliquin, columbine, and Pero (Pierrot). 1 small sprig'd round tea-pot. Goats, swans, and every other sort of toys to be sent in Baxter's order, flat drawers to be made on purpose, and each kept separate. A plate of the Princess Wales' pattern, good.

"Aug. 30. Paid Mr. Heylin's draft on Mr. Crowther for £13, and charged Mr. Crowther's cash acct. with it : quy., how is Mr. Heylin made Dr. and J. C. Creditor?

"Nov. 29. J. Bowcocke borrowed of Mr. Crowther for Bow £30. Mr. Fogg : caudle-cups, white sprig'd and saucers; 3 pr. image cream ewers full blue; 4 white leaf candlesticks, 2s. 3d.; 1 set large sprig'd teas handled; 2 pr. rib'd boats, at 4s. 6d.; 1 sprig'd teapot, 4s. good. Patterns received from Lady Cavendish; a Japan octagon cup and saucer, lady pattern; a rib'd and scollop'd cup and saucer; a basket bordered dysart plate; a Japan bread and butter plate. To be returned in a month, May 28th, 1756."

On analysing these memoranda, although they are but imperfect and necessarily curt, being written only for the writer's guidance, we are made acquainted with many facts not before disclosed; for example, it has not been suggested hitherto that *printed* china was produced at Bow, yet it is evident that china was decorated with transfer engravings as early as the year 1756, as appears from the following entries :—

"One pint *printed* mug."   "One half-pint ditto."
"A sett compleat of the second *printed* teas."

As will have been seen from Bowcock's papers, the business prospered quickly and in 1754 the firm's sales amounted to about £18,000. A warehouse was opened in Cornhill, London, in 1753. Bow china was evidently well-known abroad because a Boston newspaper announced in 1754, "Just imported by Philip Breaching, and to be sold at his House in Fifth Street, a Variety of Bow China, Cup and Saucers, Bowls, etc." The wording of this announcement suggests that Bow china was already familiar to the inhabitants of Boston.

The company's need for more workpeople in this period is shown by their advertisement in the *Birmingham Gazette* in 1753 for painters in the blue and white pottery way and enamellers on china ware. Trade was good enough for a West End warehouse to be opened on the Upper Terrace, St. James's Street, where everything was to be sold at the same prices as at the factory or at the Cornhill warehouse.

In 1759, Frye had to give up management of the factory on account of ill health. He went to Wales for a change of air but by April, 1760, had sufficiently recovered to return to London and take a house in Hatton Garden, where he resumed his profession as an artist. He died of consumption on 2nd April, 1762.

He had two daughters, who assisted him in painting the china at Bow. They both married indiscreetly and gave their father much uneasiness. One of them married a Mr. Wilcox and they both subsequently worked at Worcester and for Wedgwoods.

The death of Frye, under whose management and by whose talents as an artist and practical knowledge the china had been brought to that perfection for which the factory had become so celebrated, must have proved a great blow to the concern. It may have caused the dissolution, for in the next year, 1763, Crowther was gazetted as bankrupt. Weatherby had died in 1762.

We have three advertisements of the sale of the stock of " Bow china porcelain," by order of the assignees of John Crowther, bankrupt; on the 12th March, 1764, and following days, at the Bow warehouse in Cornhill; on May the 19th, 1764, and on the 30th of the same month. The last took place at the great exhibition-room in Spring Gardens, "consisting of a large quantity of the finest porcelain, chosen out of the stock in curious figures, girandoles, and branches for chimney-pieces, finely decorated with figures and flowers, &c., dishes, compotiers, &c., beautiful desserts of the fine old partridge and wheatsheaf patterns, a quantity of knife and fork handles, some neatly mounted, and a variety of other porcelain."

However, the crash does not seem to have been serious and it appears that only the Cornhill warehouse was concerned and Crowther retained the works at Bow. In the *Directory* 1770–75 it is stated that John Crowther of Bow China Works had a warehouse at 28 St. Paul's Churchyard.

The factory is thought to have closed about 1776 and the moulds and implements bought by William Duesbury, the proprietor of the Derby China Works and transferred by him to Derby.

An important contemporary account of the factory by Thomas Craft, one of the factory painters, is given in a document which accompanies a Bow china bowl in the British Museum:—

" This bowl was made at the Bow China Manufactory at Stratford-le-Bow, Essex, about the year 1760, and painted there by me, Thomas Craft—my cipher is in the bottom; it is painted in what we used to call the old Japan taste, a taste at that time much esteemed by the then Duke of Argyle; there is nearly two pennyweight of gold, about 15s. I had it in hand, at different times, about three months; about two weeks' time was bestowed upon it. It could not have been manufactured, &c., for less than £4. There is not its similitude. I took it in a box to Kentish Town, and had it burned there in Mr. Gyles's kiln, cost me 3s.; it was cracked the first time of using it. Miss Nancy Sha *(sic)*, a daughter of the late Sir Patrick Blake, was christened with it. I never used it but in particular respect to my company, and I desire my legatee (as mentioned in my will) may do the same. Perhaps it may be thought I have said too much about this trifling toy. A reflection steals in upon my mind that this said bowl may meet with the same fate that the manufactory where it was made has done, and like the famous cities of Troy, Carthage, &c., and similar to Shakespeare's cloud cap't towers, &c.

" The above manufactory was carried on many years under the firm of Messrs. Crowther & Weatherby, whose names were known almost over the world; they employed 300 persons; about 90 painters (of whom I was one), and about 200 turners, throwers, &c., were employed under one roof. The model of the building was taken from that at Canton in China; the whole was heated by two stoves on the outside of the building, and conveyed through flues or pipes and warmed the whole, sometimes to an intense heat, unbearable in winter. It now wears a miserable aspect, being a manufactory for turpentine, and small tenements, and like Shakespeare's baseless fabric, &c. Mr. Weatherby has been dead many years; Mr. Crowther is in Moreden College, Black-heath, and I am the only person of all those employed there who annually visit him.

"T. CRAFT, 1790."

The bowl measures 8¾ in. in diameter. See *Ker. Gall.*, figs. 536–7.

WASTERS. The Bow Works were situated on the Essex side of the River Lea at Stratford Langthorne. The buildings, after the disposal of the goodwill and the probable removal of the implements to Derby about 1776, were turned to an entirely different purpose. The site of the china factory was purchased by E. L. Macmurdo, then of Old Ford, calico printer, and converted by him into a chemical works, which afterwards became Marshall's Emery Mills.

In 1868, during building operations at Bell & Black's match factory on the south side of Stratford High Street, a large quantity of wasters (fragments, etc.) were found at what is now thought to have been the site of a waste heap some distance from the works. Nearly a century after the extinction of the china factory, and when even the nature of the ware made there was problematical and scarcely known or remembered, a mere accident brought to light some of its long-hidden relics. Useless as these would appear to some people, and the merest fragments, fit only for the dustheap or to be immediately immured again, yet Charles Schreiber, M.P., thought the discovery of sufficient importance to mention it in the House of Commons. In trenching a drain from the factory into the sewer, the workmen, at about 8 to 10 ft. from the surface, came upon the debris of the old Bow China Works.

Mr. Higgins, jun., who was attached to the match factory, received his first intimation of the lucky find from perceiving fragments of delicate biscuit china in the hands of some children, who had picked them up as playthings. This led him to keep strict watch over the excavation, and, by permission of the proprietors, the ground remained open for a few months, and, as leisure permitted, he examined the earth for some distance immediately round the spot. Limited as the space was, he found a great quantity of specimens, which he and his sister, Miss Higgins, took the pains to arrange carefully in trays. Although fragmentary, they are particularly interesting, as showing us the various descriptions of ware made at Bow, verifying its products, and enabling us to identify not only the paste and glaze, but also the methods of ornamentation.

In the find were a quantity of bricks cemented together, the inner surface having become vitrified by the heat of the kiln, and also a vast number of broken saggars, or cases of baked earthenware, used to contain the china, and protect it from the flame and ashes in the kiln. One of these saggars, of cylindrical form, measures 10 in. in diameter by $8\frac{1}{2}$ in. in height; it has three rows of holes pierced through the sides, at equal distances from top to bottom, into which clay pegs (like large clout-nails) were inserted, to support the plates, etc., within, at convenient distances. The cockspur, or point used to separate the china, is a simple cone of baked clay, not the usual form, which is like the caltrop, having always three points below and one only uppermost. Large pieces of china clay were found, some in a soft soapy state, others hardened; bones of animals, which entered into the composition of the paste, as well as calcined flints and pieces of quartz, used in making the frit or glaze: a number of circular medallions of baked clay from 2 to 6 in. diameter; one was marked on each side with H and M, cut into the clay. All the fragments of vessels discovered are of porcelain biscuit, not a piece of delft or common earthenware being found among them; some few are glazed, but these form exceptions.

The first we shall notice, and probably the earliest manufactured, are the pieces decorated with blue painting; the designs are painted, in mineral colour, on the biscuit, and have not been glazed or burnt in. These designs are principally of Chinese landscapes, flowers, figures, and birds: a few examples are here given to show their general character: figs. 1 to 5.

A very frequent pattern, of simple character, in the blue ware, is three hanging branches of willow leaves. Among the rest is a mottled ground plate with white angular medallions of light blue scenery. The only variations in colour are a cup with green leaves and lake flowers, and a fragment painted in lake *camaieu* with a castellated mansion, of high finish: these two are glazed. Not a single specimen of blue printed china was discovered: all are painted with a brush.

The next division consists of biscuit china, fragments of services ornamented in relief, the favourite pattern being the prunus; the hawthorn is also represented, with its thorny branches and blossoms. About a dozen of the moulds for stamping these flowers were also found, quite perfect; they are of biscuit, 3 in. by $2\frac{1}{2}$in. in diameter. Fig. 6 is interesting, being the original mould of a biscuit cup which has its exact counterpart glazed. These pieces form a history in themselves.

Another mould is of two roses and leaves on a stalk (fig. 7). The raised figures on the biscuit are remarkably sharp, but the application of the glaze fills up the spaces; the other decorations in relief are the basket pattern, overlapping leaves, vertical bands overlaid with scrolls, ribbed cups and basins, a biscuit candlestick in form of a vine leaf, another of different pattern painted blue. In this extensive collection we find milk-pots, cups, cans, and saucers, open-work baskets and octagonal plates, cup handles, lion's-paw feet, small pots for colour or rouge; but not a single piece has any mark which can be assigned to the *fabrique*. One of the cups

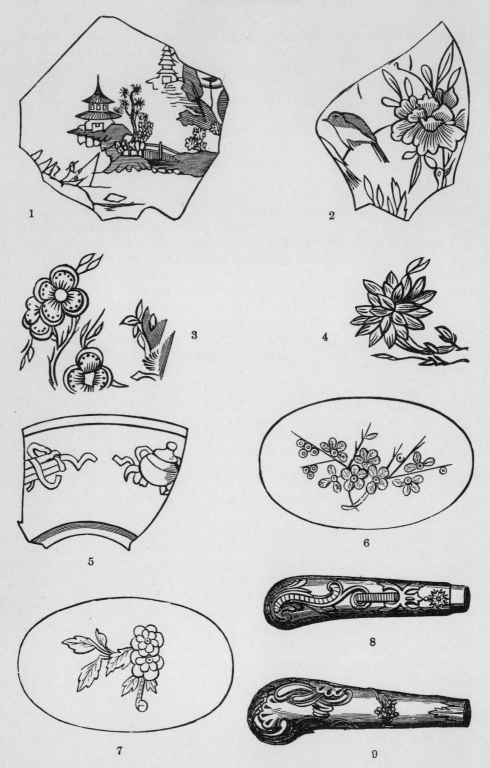

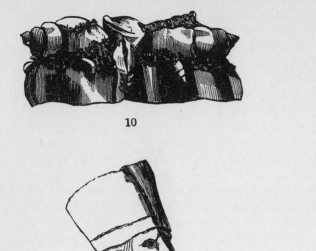

10

11

12

has the name of " Norman " written on it in pencil, perhaps the name of one of the painters. Among other relics are pieces which have been injured in the kiln by falling into ugly and distorted shapes, plates and saucers that have inadvertently come in contact with each other and could not be separated. There is a great variety of china biscuit knife-handles, some plain, others with rococo scrolls in relief heightened with blue; two specimens are here given (figs. 8 and 9).

Some few pieces of an ornamental character are among the débris. The foot of a salt-cellar, beautifully modelled in biscuit, formed of three shells, with smaller shells and seaweed between: the upper shell, to hold the salt, is wanting; a sketch of it is here given (fig. 10).

To these may be added the foot of a large centre ornament of the same character as the last, to hold sweetmeats, also modelled by hand, in shells of all sorts, rockwork, coral, seaweed, etc., with three escallop shells: this has had one or more tiers above, but is broken off at the stem; some natural shells were found which served as copies. There are two pug dogs nearly perfect, with collars, on which are roses; two handles in form of female heads in high relief, for tureens and other large bowls (fig. 11); and a man's head, with a high cap and feather, nicely modelled (fig. 12); also the body of a female figure in biscuit, with laced bodice. The head here sketched forms part of a salt-cellar: a man kneeling on one knee supports on the other a shell held with both hands, his body is bent forward, and he wears a high cap with a feather turned over the top; these are alluded to in Mr. Bowcock's memoranda quoted previously. A pair of these, of white porcelain, was in the possession of John J. Bagshawe of Sheffield, and a representation may be found in the *Keramic Gallery*, fig. 524.

THE SECOND EXCAVATION. In July 1921 demolition of buildings at Wilmer & Sons' Iron Foundry on the north side of Stratford High Street (the opposite side to Bell & Black's Match Factory) was taking place, and Mr. Aubrey J. Toppin discovered a considerable quantity of fragments. In the *Burlington Magazine*, 1922, p. 224, he gives a full description of the find which included pieces of blue and white, sprigged ware, moulded ware, coloured pieces and three fragments of transfer printing. The majority were unglazed. One or two moulds were also found, but were not identified. Workmen's marks noted on blue and white were 10, 12, 28, 30 and 31, all in underglaze blue. A portion of a rustic base in red clay biscuit, perhaps a model, marked with a crescent and a cross, each distinctly incised is important. Both these marks have occurred in blue on figures of un-doubted Bow origin. Also, fragments were found which corresponded with the well-known Negress with a Bowl, General Wolfe and the Marquis of Granby. It is considered that it is this site which corresponds with the position of the factory and not the site of the 1868 excavations.

EARLY WARES. Although the Bow factory produced many fine and interesting figures, it specialised in useful table wares. The porcelain made from bone-ash according to the patent of 1749 proved to be strong and durable and so ideal for the table ware which was the main output of the factory. In fact, the important English contribution to the development of porcelain making was this " bone china," of which Bow was the first source and Frye the discoverer.

Little is known of the wares produced before 1750, but a number of enamelled pieces attributed to this period were shown at the Bow Exhibi-tion arranged by Hugh Tait, F.S.A., at the British Museum in 1959. These early specimens all had a mushroom-grey or drab appearance, and also were phosphatic when analysed chemically. They comprised shell salts, partly enamelled in red and painted with flower sprays in green, yellow, blue and red, sauce boats and a tankard with spreading foot and silver-shape handle.

The earliest dated specimens belong to the year 1750 and include the fine undecorated figures of Kitty Clive and the actor, Henry Woodward, both of which are creamy-white in appearance. These two models were also made at the Derby factory. Also from the same year, 1750, is the Negress with Basket and Cover which is greyish-white. Three enamelled inkwells are known from this year. They bear the inscription " Made at New Canton 1750."

FIGURES. As the earliest figures were undecorated, it is assumed that the enamelling of figures was presenting difficulties at that time. There-fore the earliest enamelled figures probably belong to the period 1751–53. The enamelling was over the glaze. Some examples from the later period of the factory have part of the decoration in underglaze blue, the remainder being in overglaze colours.

A large range of figures were made in the early 1750's, and many of these were original and not derived from other factories such as Meissen. This can be attributed to Frye's artistic ability and familiarity with the engravings of Lancret, Boucher and Watteau as well as the contemporary English artists. From these engravings and paintings, he composed excellent figures and figure groups, such as Kitty Clive, Henry Woodward, La Bonne Aventure, Group Symbolical of Air, Lovers with Birdcage, etc.

Other figures were copied from Meissen models and they were frequently decorated by independent enamellers. It is known that William Duesbury (1725-86) painted Bow, Chelsea and Derby pieces between 1751 and 1753. James Giles (or Gyles) was another independent enameller working from about 1760 to about 1780. He had a kiln at Kentish Town for burning in the colours on porcelain. He obtained pieces from other factories and advertised both before and after 1760 to " procure and paint for any persons Worcester porcelain to any, or in any pattern." He decorated a considerable amount of Bow porcelain and it has been suggested that the anchor and dagger mark in red indicates his decoration.

TRANSFER PRINTING was an English contribution to the art of porcelain decoration and was either invented or perfected at the Battersea enamel factory about 1753. The process consisted in taking a print on thin paper from an engraved copper plate and transferring it on to the surface of the porcelain, where it would be melted into the glaze.

Robert Hancock (1730-1817) was an engraver for transfer printing on porcelain and it is thought that he worked for a time at Bow after the closing of the Battersea factory in 1756. A number of transfer printed Bow wares signed by Hancock are known about 1756, and other prints in Ravenet's style are probably his work.

The known prints of Hancock on Bow porcelain include The Tea Party, The Wheeling Chair, L'Amour, Garden Statuary, Aeneas and Anchises, and The Prussian Hero. The transfer method was also used to print the outlines of a design which could subsequently be painted over in colours, thereby enabling many more semi-skilled workpeople to be used.

The transfer-printed wares of Bow are rare and the colours are often russet or purplish black and are over the glaze. Examples printed in underglaze blue are very rare indeed. A specimen attributed to the Bow factory is illustrated by Figure 19 on Plate 5.

MARKS. Bow had no regular factory mark. The following marks have been recorded, many of which are workmen's marks rather than a factory device.

Marks nos. 1 and 2 are scratched in the paste under the glaze on a pair of large white porcelain figures of a lion and lioness couchant, 12 in. long by 5 in. high; formerly in the possession of John J. Bagshawe, and there is a similar pair in the British Museum. Early period, c. 1750.

The same mark occurs on a cup and saucer decorated with sprays of prunus blossom in low relief, formerly in the collection of the Rev. Septimus Firman of Liverpool, and on the white figure of an actress in Turkish costume in the British Museum.

Mark no. 3, incised on a hard white porcelain shell bowl, supported by smaller shells and rock-work. Early period.

The Countess of Hopetoun had part of a leaf-pattern dessert service; one of the butter-boats had mark no. 4 impressed in the clay; and Mr. E. Norman had a porcelain vase covered all over with leaves in relief, edged with green and purple stalks, white veins and white ground, with this mark impressed.

Mark no. 5 is on a butter-boat, embossed with leaves and painted in colours with a rose, butterflies, and insects, which we take to be Bow: it bears this mark in brown. Respecting it, Marryat writes: " I must contend that my vase and butter-boat are of Bow manufacture, whatever the mark may be." The same mark is stamped in the clay on a salt-cellar, formerly in James Sanders's Collection.

As regards the anchor mark, this was used at Bow as well as at Chelsea, but was of a different character. The anchor and dagger are now satisfactorily attributed to Bow, being on an altogether different ware to any ever produced at Chelsea.

Mark no. 6, impressed, is on a Bow china figure of an actor; also on part of a dessert service.

Mark no. 7, an anchor with a cable is on a porcelain caddy, painted with a landscape in orange *camaieu*, raised flowers on the lid; formerly in the possession of Miss Lovell.

Mark no. 8 (no doubt intended for *B*, for Bow) occurs on one of a pair of little vases of taper form, 6½ in. high, painted in flowers on white ground. The companion vase is marked with a *B*. Formerly in Louis Huth's Collection, and now either the same or one similar is in the British Museum.

Mark no. 9. The *B* is in blue under the glaze, the anchor and dagger are painted in red over it, and burnt-in in the muffle-kiln; it occurs on a china figure in the Victoria and Albert Museum. Several Bow figures with the anchor and dagger in both red and blue colours occur.

Mark no. 10 is on a set of four figures representing the Seasons on scroll stands; the colouring is exceedingly good; also on the figure of a Turk, and of a musician with lute and tambourine; all in the collection of Mrs. A. R. Macdonald, who also possessed a very fine double-spouted teapot, of deep powder-blue ground, with panels of exotic birds. This example is now in the British Museum. The anchor and dagger mark is the normal mark found on the later wares from about 1760.

Mark no. 11, the letter A, was until recently considered to be a Longton Hall mark. There are, however, in the British Museum two vases with dark blue ground, frill ornaments, and painted in bird subjects, quite in the Longton Hall style, which have this letter A in blue, and also (in red) the anchor and dagger of the Bow factory. Similar examples occur.

A pair of Bow figures in Eastern costume, 8½ in. high, formerly in the collection of Sir John Smiley, Bart, of Saxham Hall, Bury St. Edmunds, bears marks nos. 12 and 13 in blue, accompanied by the anchor and dagger in gold.

Mark no. 14. On a small Bow figure of a little girl (one of a pair) are two letters, A F, incised in the paste. Formerly in the collection of Sir John Smiley.

A cup and saucer, with impressed leaf surface and green border, is marked with an anchor and dagger, and a figure of a man playing on the bagpipes, emblematical of " Air," has in addition to the anchor and dagger, a cross in blue on one of the scroll feet.

In Dudley Ward Macdonald's Collection there was a pair of candlesticks with embowered birds of paradise, which have the anchor and dagger in red, and also mark no. 15 in blue.

In the Schreiber Collection there are three soft paste statuettes of Bow china, representing an actor in the character of Tamerlane, with turban and fur collar, all of the same model, some being coloured. One of these has mark no. 16 incised in the clay before glazing; it consists of a crescent at top, then a ring and stem in form of a cross, like a caduceus; the second figure, which is painted, has underneath an upright dagger and anchor pencilled in red, and a sword in blue placed horizontally (mark no. 18); the third figure is of white china, unmarked, but the man holds a scimitar in his right hand, the point resting on the ground; the companion figure to this is an actress with high head-dress; both of these are well known to collectors.

Mark no. 16 has never before been attributed to Bow; but we are, for many reasons, justified in doing so. In the Schreiber Collection there is a pair of white china pug-dogs with a similar mark, but the crescent at top is unconnected.

Mark no. 17 is also seen on Bow china; it is a variation of mark no. 16, having no crescent at top, but a dot on each side; it is given by Marryat as belonging to Bow.

The triple mark no. 18, sometimes with the dagger and sword only, is frequently seen on china figures. We may place it as a Bow mark, c. 1760.

Mark no. 19, with crossed arrows and an annulet, was on a Bow china saucer in the possession of Mr. Temple Frere.

The next mark no. 20 is a bow and arrow; it is pencilled in red on the back of an octagonal plate, painted with daisies and two quails, a favourite Bow pattern.

Mark no. 21. The letter G in blue occurs on an undoubted Bow group of a peacock with foliage and a scroll base. It is the stand for a candelabrum.

The crescent in blue, mark no. 22, is given by Professor Church as a Bow mark very rarely used. There is a figure of Ceres bearing this crescent mark in the British Museum.

The impressed mark " To " (no. 36), which we have noticed under the remarks on Bristol and Worcester, is also occasionally found on Bow figures, and leads one to the conclusion that the modeller, Tebo, of whose name the letters are supposed to be a contraction, worked for Bow as well as Bristol and Worcester. Mrs. Macdonald had a dancing figure with this mark, of a boy which is a well-known Bow model, and, moreover, had all the characteristics of that paste.

This mark has been included by R. L. Hobson in his book on Worcester porcelain as the mark of a modeller who worked at this factory, and he has

illustrated an important hexagonal vase with raised flowers, masks, butterflies, and insects.

A somewhat distinct type of Bow china is shown in a pair of octagonal
plates, painted in decorative borders and a monogram R. C., for Robert
Crowther. The body is opaque looking, and of quite different appearance
to the famous Craft Bowl, described previously, and to the glassy and
vitreous-looking paste of which the majority of Bow figures is composed.
One of these plates has painted on the back, " Mr. Robert Crowther,
Stockport, Cheshire, January, 1770." They were formerly in the collection
of Henry Willett, and were presented by him to the British Museum. Mrs.
A. R. Macdonald had one of these interesting plates bearing the same
decoration and inscription at the back.

The monogram T. F., mark no. 23, occurs on some Bow figures, and
such pieces must be attributed to an early period of the Bow Works
previous to 1760. Mrs. A. R. Macdonald had a small pair of dancing figures
of harlequins, with this monogram in red. A similar mark occurs on early
Worcester porcelain.

With regard to this monogram, it is of interest to collectors of English
porcelain to record the fact that the authorities at the British Museum
transferred a set of six pieces, including three dishes with elaborate borders,
a teapot, and two sauce-boats, all of which are moulded with raised designs
and painted in the Chinese taste in delicate underglaze blue, bearing a
similar mark to the above, from Bow to Worcester, and for the following
reason. A small fragment was taken from a tureen in the Dyson-Perrins
Collection, and on analysis was found to contain steatite in the body.
This ingredient, which was a feature of the composition of Worcester paste,
is said not to have been used at Bow, and as this tureen exactly corresponds
with the British Museum set, marked with what had hitherto been accepted
as the monogram of Thomas Frye, the founder of the Bow factory, it is
now considered to have been another signature of a Worcester painter or
decorator, and not that of Frye, or else was the mark of Jade copied from
other Chinese porcelain. While the Editor of " Chaffers " agrees with the
decision made for the reasons given, it must be distinctly understood that
on this account all figures and groups bearing a monogram of T. F. are not
to be classed as Worcester. In some cases the monogram is to be found in
conjunction with the anchor and dagger of Bow, and in others the paste
and colouring lead to the conclusion that they are of this make. The same
remark applies to some few pieces bearing the crescent mark, instances of
which have been given above. Paste, colouring, and some details, trifling
in themselves but important taken in conjunction with others, must be
carefully studied before we can attribute to either Bow or Worcester.

In the Schreiber Collection there are specimens bearing some of the
above marks, and also some others which are copied from the catalogue,
all of which are impressed in the paste.

Marks 24 to 36 are found on figures and groups in the Schreiber Collection. They are workmen's marks or modeller's initials. Similar marks
occur on other wares.

Various workmen's numbers occur on blue and white specimens. They are similar to those employed at the Lowestoft factory, but at Bow the numbers were placed on the flat part of the underside, not on the inside of the foot rim as at Lowestoft. Simulated Chinese characters also occur.

Mark no. 37, the letter R, roughly incised under the glaze, on a vase with cover painted in birds and flowers; in E. Broderip's Collection. Early period c. 1755.

The Bow porcelain body contains bone-ash and is therefore phosphatic on chemical analysis. It can appear exceedingly hard, and the fracture shows the texture to be very close and compact; consequently the pieces, as a rule, are very heavy for their size, but many of the cups and saucers are almost of eggshell thickness; the colour is a milky white.

ILLUSTRATIONS. A considerable number of rarer and more interesting early useful wares are illustrated by Plates 1 to 12. They originally formed part of the collection of Dr. John A. Ainslie and are described in the following notes condensed from Sotheby and Co.'s sale catalogue of this fine collection.

1. Cream Jug in underglaze-blue, black, red and gilding, c. 1750–3.
2. Cream Jug, transfer-printed in sepia with the Tea Party, The Wheeled Chair and a part of The Singing Lesson, all by Hancock, c. 1753–5.
3. Cream Jug, transfer-printed with three orientals in black outline and washed in colours, c. 1755–7.
4. Cream Jug, painted with flowers, c. 1758.
5. Cream Jug with straight sides, painted with two yellow and black aquatic birds in famille rose style, c. 1755.
6. Piggin, with upright fleur-de-lys handle, three applied prunus branches round the body, c. 1752–4.
7. Teabowl and Saucer decorated in shades of green, brown, iron-red and gilding outlined in black, c. 1754. Mark numeral 3 in brown.
8. Coffee Cup and Saucer, underglaze blue, black, red and gilding, c. 1752.
9. Cup and Saucer, pine cone moulded, green borders, c. 1765.
10. Teabowl and Saucer, famille rose style, c. 1752+.
11. Ecuelle, Cover, Stand and Ladle, painted with flowers in underglaze blue, c. 1757.
12. Sprigged Bowl, painted with peonies and prunus sprouting from the rockwork, c. 1754.
13. Cream Boat, peach-shaped, with applied flowering prunus branches, c. 1752.
14. Sauceboat, with moulded swags, painted with sprigs and garlands of famille-rose flowers, c. 1754.
15. Double-lipped Sauceboat, interior painted with green diaper border and a peony and magnolia, and black reeded leaves, c. 1752–4. Mark E in red.
16. Sprigged Sauceboat, creamy glaze, with applied flowering tree peony, interior with green diaper border.

BOW—Plate 3
11
12

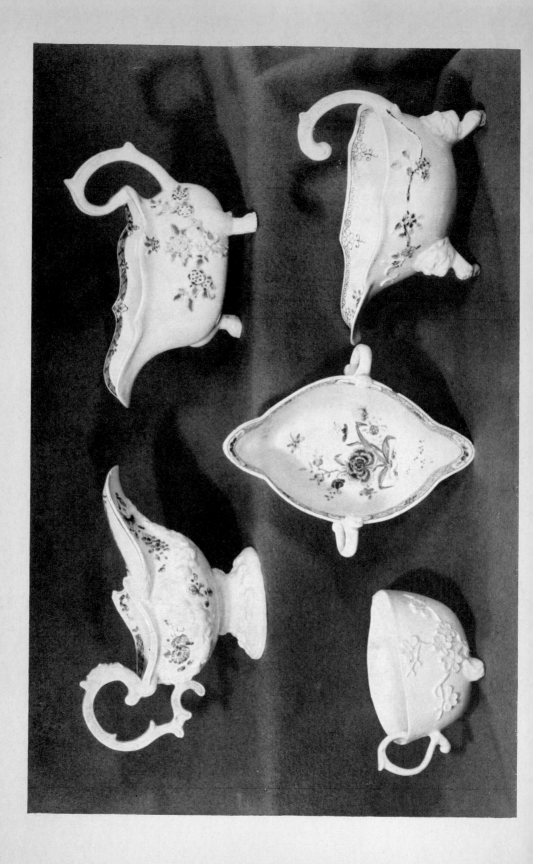

BOW—Plate 9

38

39

BOW—Plate 10
40
41

BOW—Plate 12

45
46

17.   Sauceboat, with applied branches of flowers, black pencilled scroll border with peonies, early period, c. 1750.

18.   Plate, transfer-printed in lilac with La Toilette du Matin originally engraved by J. P. le Bas after Chardin, c. 1753–5.

19.   Plate, transfer-printed in underglaze-blue with The Herdsman and the Spinning Maiden in oriental style, c.1760–5.

20.   Plate, transfer-printed in puce with the arms of the Anti-Gallican Society, c. 1753–5.

21.   Plate, transfer-printed in red, with L'Amour, border in red, yellow and blue, c. 1753–5.

22.   Plate, transfer-printed in lilac, with a Stag Hunt and three land-scapes on the rim, c. 1753–5.

23.   Plate, transfer-printed in black with masonic arms, c. 1760. No other of this pattern recorded.

24.   Cane Handle, enamelled with variously coloured prunus and peonies, double red line border, c. 1750.

25.   Cane Handle mounted as a seal, painted in bright colours, c. 1750.

26.   Inkstand, painted in Chinese style, c. 1754.

27.   Doll's Teapot, painted in famille-rose style, c. 1755. Part of a service.

28.   Stemmed Cup, painted with garden flowers, c. 1757.

29.   Small Teapot, 4½ in. high, painted in Worcester style, c. 1757.

30.   Teapot, painted in bright blue, with bamboo and a peony, large scratch cross mark, c. 1752–4.

31.   Teapot, decorated in striking shades of brown, green, yellow and iron-red and gilding with brown outlines, oriental landscapes and *shan shui*, c. 1752.

32.   Teapot, painted in the style of the New Canton inkwells and presumably of 1750 period.

33.   Mug, painted with flowering tree peony with red blooms, lime green border, c. 1750.

34.   Small Mug, painted in the style of the New Canton inkwells, painter's mark B, c. 1750.

35.   Tankard, drab appearance, painted in early enamel colours, early period, c. 1750.

36.   Mug, drab appearance, painted with pendant swags of flowers, interior black border, early period, c. 1748–50.

37.   Mug, painted in famille-rose enamels with large peony, c. 1755.

38.   Shell Sweetmeat, painted in famille-rose style with pink peony, etc., red and green floral border, c. 1754.

39.   Shell Encrusted Centre-piece, in blue and white, with incised nick mark, c. 1752.

40.   Shell Salt, enamelled in colours with oriental flowers, c. 1748–50.

41.   Shell Sweetmeat, painted in famille-rose style, c. 1754.

42, 43.   Cup, underglaze-blue, the base inscribed I: C 1763.

44.   Bowl, with *shan-shui* in blue, green, brown, etc., with inscription in underglaze-blue: Thos. Target 1754.

45, 46.　Bowl, underglaze-blue in Chinese style, with inscription:
William & Elisabeth Martin. November 20 1750.

EDWARD HEYLYN & Co.　Evidence has come to light of a rival
" Porcelain Company " (Edward Heylyn & Co.) operating in the early
1750's at Bow, Middlesex (within the parish of Bromley St. Leonards).　No
examples from this factory have so far been identified and the significance
of this firm has yet to be determined.　See *Apollo*, October, 1960.　The
reader is referred to a paper by Hugh Tait in the *Transactions of the
English Ceramic Circle*, vol. 5, part 4.

CHELSEA

It was probably in or about the year 1745 that the Chelsea Works were established, and workmen were obtained from the Staffordshire potteries. We have it upon record that "Carlos Simpson was born at Chelsea; to which place his father, Aaron Simpson, went in 1747, along with Thomas Lawton, slip-maker; Samuel Parr, turner; Richard Meir, fireman; and John Astbury, painter, all of Hot Lane; Carlos Wedgwood, of the Stocks, a good thrower; Thomas Ward, and several others of Burslem, to work at the Chelsea china manufactory." They soon ascertained that they were the principal workmen, on whose exertions all the excellence of the porcelain must depend: they then resolved to commence business on their own account at Chelsea, and were in some degree successful; but at length, owing to disagreement among themselves, they abandoned it and returned to Burslem. (See Shaw's *History of the Staffordshire Potteries*.)

In 1745 a company which at that time desired the exclusive privilege of establishing a porcelain manufactory at Vincennes (subsequently that of Sèvres), urged the benefit that France would gain by having works that would produce the fine porcelain, and thereby exclude that of Germany and England. We give the extract in the original words:—

"Il ose encore répresenter qu'il est d'autant plus advantageux pour l'état qu'il ait réussi, qu'un nouvel établissement qui vient de se former en Angleterre d'une manufacture de porcelaine qui paroit plus belle que celle de Saxe, par la nature de sa composition, occasionerait la sortie de fonds considerables de la France, s'il n'étoit parvenue à pouvoir procurer à ce royaume ce qu'on auroit été chercher à grands frais chez l'étranger."— *Arrêt du Conseil d' Etat du Roy*, qui accorde à Charles Adam le privilége pour l'établissement de la manufacture de porcelaine façon de Saxe, au Château de Vincennes du 24 Juillet 1745.

Faulkner (in 1829) says, "The Chelsea Porcelain Works were situate at the corner of Justice Walk, and occupied the houses to the upper end of the street; several of the large old houses were used as showrooms. Their ovens were in Lawrence Street. The whole of the premises have been pulled down and new houses erected on the site."

In Campbell's *London Tradesman*, 1747, we find the following: "Of late we have made some attempts to make porcelain or china ware after the manner it is done in China and Dresden. There is a house at Greenwich and another at Chelsea where the undertakers have been for some time trying to imitate that beautiful manufacture."

In the *London Magazine* of May 1753 we are told that at Chelsea and Stratford (Bow) undertakings were carried on in the greatest perfection, so as to emulate the elegancies of Dresden or Chinese porcelain.

Rouquet (*Present State of the Arts*, ed. 1755) says: "In the neighbourhood of London there are three or four manufactories of porcelain, among which that of Chelsea is the most considerable. It is carried on at the expense of a private person, and a French artist of great abilities furnishes or directs the models."

The following interesting account is from a statement made by Mr. Mason, who worked at the Chelsea manufactory, and whose son (also a china painter) worked many years at the Worcester manufactory, when conducted by Flight, Barr & Barr:—

"I think the Chelsea China Manufactory began about the year 1748 or 1749. I went to work about the year 1751. It was first carried on by the Duke of Cumberland[1] and Sir Everard Fawkener,[2] and the sole management was intrusted to a foreigner of the name of Sprimont, report says at a salary of a guinea per day, with certain allowances for apprentices and other emoluments. I think Sir Everard died about 1755, much reduced in circumstances, when Mr. Sprimont became sole proprietor; and having amassed a fortune, he travelled about England, and the manufactory was shut up about two years; for he neither would let it or carry it on himself. I then went to work at Bow for a short time, which was carried on by a firm, but I don't recollect their names. I went to work again at Chelsea for Mr. Sprimont, after being absent between two and three years, where I stopped till I engaged with Mr. Duesbury to go to Derby, which was about the year 1763. I think there was very little business done there after that time. What time Mr. Duesbury made a purchase of it I don't recollect, but some of the materials were taken to Derby."

A beautifully modelled bust of the Duke of Cumberland, patron and part proprietor of the Chelsea manufactory, was produced at the works; it is of plain white glazed porcelain; he is represented bareheaded with a cuirass on his breast. One of these is in the Victoria and Albert Museum.

It will be seen by the following advertisement that Mr. Sprimont was for a time seriously ill and unable to attend to business:—

1757. "The public is hereby acquainted that the Chelsea Porcelain Manufactory has been very much retarded by the sickness of Mr. Sprimont; nevertheless, several curious things have been finished, and are now exposed to sale at the warehouse in Piccadilly with the lowest price, for ready money, fix'd on each particular. All warranted true enamel."

The period of its greatest excellence was from c. 1750 to 1765. Three spots or blemishes, at equal distances, under plates and other pieces, where the glaze has been removed is one of the characteristics of Chelsea china, caused by contact of the three points on which it rested in the furnace,

---

[1] William, Duke of Cumberland, was born April 15, 1721, and died October 31, 1765.

[2] Sir Everard Fawkner, Knight, Postmaster-General, died at Bath, November 16, 1758.

showing the method adopted in its manufacture.

Mr. J. E. Nightingale in his *Contributions to a History of English Porcelain*, 1881, has quoted some advertisements showing that a "Cha˙ Gouyn" had preceded Sprimont as proprietor and director or manager of the Chelsea Works; but in a deed quoted by Mr. Bemrose from the original document in his possession, in which the Lawrence Street property is leased by Nicholas Sprimont to James Cox, 1769, it states "heretofore in the tenure or occupation of Mr. Lagrave and then of the said Nicholas Sprimont," and does not mention the name of Gouyn. Who this Lagrave was we do not know, nor have we any information as to the making of the china on these premises previous to Sprimont's occupation. Mr. Bemrose considers that from the wording of a deed quoted by him china must have been made by Sprimont some time previous to 1759, and he is also of opinion that Gouyn was manufacturing at another address (unknown) china which he was selling through a dealer named G. Stables. He quotes an advertisement headed "Chelsea Porcelaine" which appeared in the *Daily Advertiser*, 15th May, 1750, which states that the "Sale-warehouse of the manufactory there, will from henceforward be constantly open," but curiously and most unfortunately the advertisement gives no address as to the whereabouts of the sale warehouse or manufactory. Mr. Arthur Lane discusses this second Chelsea factory in his *English Porcelain Figures of the Eighteenth Century*, 1961.

Among the *Lansdowne MSS.* is a memorial from the "undertaker of the Chelsea manufacture of porcelain," who was "a silversmith by profession," and from a casual acquaintance with a chemist, who had some knowledge this way, was tempted to a trial, and upon the progress he made, he was encouraged to pursue it with great labour and expense. Neither the name of the undertaker nor the date of the memorial are given, but it is mentioned that the Duke of Orleans (who died in 1752) had tried the paste in his kilns. It states that "one hundred persons were employed, and a nursery of thirty lads from the parishes and charity schools, were bred to designing and painting." The memorialist complains of the smuggling sales of Dresden porcelain allowed to be imported for private use, but otherwise prohibited; "that a certain foreign Minister's house had been for a course of years, a warehouse for this commerce, and the large parcel advertised for public sale on the 7th of the next month was to come from thence." Dresden porcelain for private use only paid eighteenpence per pound, so that the competition was very injurious to the Chelsea china. He adds, he had sold during the previous winter of the value of more than £3500, which was a great deal, considering *the thing was new*, and was of so great extent that it was beyond the reach of his industry to produce such complete assortments as were required. Nicholas Sprimont was originally a silversmith by profession, residing in Compton Street, Soho. He entered his name at Goldsmiths' Hall on the 25th January, 1742, and deposited his mark or punch as by law required, which was *NS.* in italics, a star above. Several examples of his modelling in silver have come under our notice; they are chiefly remarkable for the representations in relief of shells, coral, rockwork, crawfish, and reptiles, &c. There are two oval silver dessert dishes with escalloped edges, ornamented in full relief and beautifully executed, of shells, corals, crawfish, &c., round the borders, diameter 11 by 9 inches, preserved in the Royal Collection at Windsor Castle. He was probably a pupil of Paul Crespin, a silversmith of Compton Street, who entered his name at the Hall in 1720, and who produced pieces of a similar character.

Sprimont undertook the management of the Chelsea porcelain manufactory, and on taking possession he issued the well-known " Case of the Undertaker of the Chelsea Porcelain," which, although undated, is evidently of that time. He states therein that " he was originally a silversmith by profession "; corroborative proof of Sprimont's identity with the writer of the " case " is found in the exact similitude of his works in silver to many that he produced in porcelain. The well-known centrepieces or sweetmeat stands of shells and rockwork and the beautiful crawfish salts described in a catalogue of 1756, and which we occasionally meet with, are evidently modelled by the same hand as those in silver. Again in the numerous announcements of the time, Sprimont styles himself " The undertaker of the Chelsea porcelain manufactory."

The undertaker had good cause of complaint; for Jonas Hanway, writing in 1750–51, in descanting on the manufacture of Dresden porcelain, observes: " It is with great satisfaction that I observe the manufactories of Bow, Chelsea, and Stepney have made such a considerable progress; on the other hand, it is equally a subject of horror to see so many shops in the streets of London supplied with the porcelain of Dresden, though it is importable only under oath of being for private use, and not for sale."

Marryat quotes part of a letter from Horace Walpole to Sir Horace Mann of 4th March, 1763, in which he mentions having seen a set of Chelsea porcelain about to be presented by the King and Queen to the Duke of Mecklenburg, which was to cost £1,200; this is perhaps the same service mentioned in the following advertisement of 21st March, 1764: " Exhibition Room, Spring Gardens, Charing Cross.—In this day's sale will be sold that magnificent and extensive table or desart service of the rare and curious Mazarine blue and gold, the same as the Royal pattern which was sold for £1,150. Also some desart plates of the inimitable crimson and gold." The major portion of this fine service is now in Buckingham Palace, and for a review of it, the reader is referred to Country Life Annual, 1960.

Mons. Groslet, who visited London in April 1765, speaks of the Chelsea manufactory as having just then fallen, and that the Comte de Lauraguais had endeavoured to treat with the proprietors. He had heard that the county of Cornwall furnished the proper clay for making the porcelain.

Mr. Sprimont made an attempt to dispose of the Chelsea manufactory in 1764, as appears from the following advertisement : —

" To be sold by Auction, by Mr. Burnsall, on the premises, some time in March next (1764), at the Chelsea porcelane manufactory. Everything in general belonging to it, and all the remaining unfinished pieces, glazed and unglazed; some imperfect enamelled ditto, of the useful and ornamental; all the materials; the valuable and extensive variety of fine models in wax, in brass, and in lead; all the plaster molds, and others; the mills, kilns, and iron presses; together with all the fixtures of the different warehouses; likewise all the outbuildings, &c., &c. And as Mr. Sprimont, the sole possessor of this rare porcelane secret, is advised to go to the German spaw, all his genuine household furniture, &c., will be sold at the same time.

" N.B.—Soon after, when everything is sold belonging to the manufactory, &c., and the large warehouse cleared, there will be some most beautiful pieces of the true inimitable Mazarine blue, crimson, and gold, that Mr. Sprimont has thought deserving finishing, that will be sold at Chelsea, as the whole remaining, and the last produce of that once most magnificent porcelane manufactory."

But he was evidently unsuccessful in finding a purchaser, for we find it advertised again in April 1769 in the leading newspapers, addressed, " To all Proprietors of Porcelain Manufactories and others : There is to be sold at Chelsea Manufactory, by order of the proprietor (having recently left off making the same), everything in general belonging to it; as all the plaster moulds, models in wax, lead, and brass; kilns, mills, iron presses, and a large quantity of biscuit-work, &c. Likewise all the buildings and many other articles. For further particulars, inquire of Mr. Thomas at the said manufactory."

On 17th May 1769, Mr. Burnsall again offers to sell by auction, " by order of Mr. Sprimont, he having entirely left off making the same, all the matchless pieces of that valuable manufactory, consisting of beautiful vases, urns, table, dessert, and tea services, &c., particularly two groups of the Roman Charity, all most highly finished in Mazarine blue, crimson, pea-green, and gold, &c.; likewise all fine models, kilns, mills, presses, buildings, &c."

In April 1769, Josiah Wedgwood, writing to Bentley, who was then at Liverpool, tells him, " The Chelsea moulds, models, &c., are to be sold, but I enclose you the advertisement. There's an immense amount of fine things." Of these it is evident he intended to become a purchaser of at least a portion, had the classes or articles been sold separately, for he writes to Cox, 24th July 1769, " Pray inquire of Mr. Thomas whether they are determined not to sell less than the whole of the models, &c., together. If so, I do not think it would suit me to purchase. I should be glad if you could send me any further particulars of the things at Chelsea." But they were sold in the lot, with the manufactory and all its appurtenances. (Meteyard's *Life of Wedgwood*, vol. ii, p. 120.)

Again, in March 1771, Mr. Christie of Pall Mall advertises the sale of the pictures of Mr. Nicholas Sprimont, *the late* proprietor of the Chelsea porcelain manufactory, who is retired into the country, brought from his late houses at Richmond and Chelsea. It may be noticed that he is here called the *late* proprietor, and it is probable that the buildings were privately sold to Mr. Duesbury in 1770, who took the unexpired term of the lease. The remainder of the stock of china from Chelsea was sold by Messrs. Christie & Ansell on 5th May, 1779, and following days, and was the property of Mr. Duesbury, for the advertisement states, " the lease of the premises being expired, they will be sold without reserve."

In *Bow, Chelsea, and Derby Porcelain*, Mr. William Bemrose has collected several additional facts about the history of the Chelsea Works, and as he quotes from actual documents in his possession, the dates given by him are reliable. From these the following quotations are of considerable interest.

Sprimont leased the Lawrence Street site of property for fourteen years, from 3rd March 1759, and re-leased it to James Cox, 29th September 1769, who again leased the property to William Duesbury and John Heath on 9th February 1770. This lease ran out in 1773, and then Duesbury carried on a lease for seven years more until 1780. After this there was a period of uncertainty as to carrying on the works or closing them, and this period lasted until 1784, when Duesbury ordered the sale of the moulds and the demolition of the kilns, in accordance with the terms of his lease.

Mr. Bemrose also gives us much detailed information respecting a lawsuit which was of a prolonged character between Duesbury and Heath as plaintiffs, and a Mr. Burnsall as defendant, respecting a quantity of "unfinished ware" which it was alleged should have been included in the sale of the factory plant, stock, &c., by Cox to Duesbury. This ware it was alleged had been alienated by one Francis Thomas, a servant of Sprimont's, and it was as Thomas's executor that Burnsall was sued. The litigation ultimately ended by Duesbury paying the costs. The matter is of especial interest to collectors, however, on account of the schedule of the articles claimed to have been "concealed," as we easily recognise many of the models now so much in request by those who collect old Chelsea, and the date of the litigation establishes the fact of these articles having been made previous to 1769.

A letter from Sprimont to Burnsall requests that this "very large quantity of my porcelain both finished and unfinished that are not yet delivered to Mr. Duesbury, this is to desire that you will deliver the whole to him immediately, being his property, and you will oblige," &c., &c.

After the purchase of the Chelsea factory by Duesbury, both that and the Derby Works were carried on conjointly, and many of the models transferred to Derby. This period, from 1770 to 1784, is the Chelsea-Derby period, and includes the time when some exceedingly fine work was produced. An advertisement undated, but which is supposed to have been circulated in the years 1774-75, informs the " Nobility, Gentry and Publick in general that Messrs. Duesbury & Co., proprietors of the Derby and Chelsea Porcelane Manufactories, have now opened a commodious warehouse in Bedford St., Covent Garden, with large assortments of the following articles specified in this catalogue."

The reader will find more detailed information on the Chelsea-Derby period of manufacture under the head of Derby.

The earlier productions of Chelsea are of great interest to the collector. For information on the early history of Chelsea porcelain the reader should refer to a paper by E. A. Lane and R. J. Charleston in *Transactions of the English Ceramic Circle*, vol. 5, part 3.

Chelsea porcelain, which, like that of Bow, was the result of private enterprise, ranks highest for beauty of decoration and careful finish, and is esteemed in proportion to its merit as a work of art. Some productions of the Chelsea Works bid fair to rival those of the far-famed Imperial manufactory of Sèvres, at any rate in the estimation of English connoisseurs, and the prices at which some have been recently sold have nearly equalled the sums paid for the finest specimens of Sèvres.

Two of the most important examples of Chelsea porcelain, both from their size and quality, are undoubtedly the "Chesterfield" vase and the "Foundling" vase. These veritable *chefs-d'œuvre* are two feet high, oviform, with bold rococo scroll handles, surmounted by dome-shaped covers : they are both exquisitely painted with classical or pastoral subjects on white medallions, probably by Donaldson (who also decorated some of the choicest Worcester vases), and they are equal, if not superior, to any other contemporaneous work at home or abroad; the reverse sides are painted with exotic birds of rich plumage, and the body or ground is of a rich *gros bleu* colour. The former of these was exhibited at the Loan Exhibition, South Kensington, in 1862, and again at Paris in 1867; it also formed a prominent object of attraction at the Leeds Exhibition of Works of Art in 1868.

The history of the companion vase now remains to be told. An extract from the minutes of the Hospital informs us that, "At a meeting of the Committee, Wednesday, 20th April 1763, the Treasurer acquainted them that he had received from Dr. George Garnier a fine vase of porcelain made at Chelsea. *Resolved*—That the Treasurer be desired to direct that a glass case be made for the safe keeping of the said vase, to be placed in the Committee-room of this Hospital." It does not even appear that a vote of thanks was accorded to the donor, so little was the gift appreciated at that time; it was allowed to remain as a chimney ornament, and, strange to say, for nearly a century did it survive the risks and chances of accident which china is heir to, with the exception of a fracture of the cover. Some twenty or thirty years ago, an amateur made what at that time was considered a liberal offer for the vase, but it was declined; this circumstance drew the attention of the committee to its value, and precautions were immediately taken, by placing it again under glass, to prevent further injury. A few months after, Mr. Chaffers, who, on behalf of Lord Dudley, had purchased the Chesterfield vase for £2000, applied to the trustees of the Foundling Hospital to purchase the companion, and made an offer of a very large sum; after mature consideration, they came to the conclusion that they were not justified in retaining a fragile object of such value, when they could with the proceeds increase the funds of the charity and enlarge the benefits for which this noble institution was founded. This vase was then placed by the side of its companion at Dudley House.

A considerable portion of the late Lord Dudley's old Chelsea was sold by Messrs. Christie in May 1886, and amongst the specimens offered were these two magnificent vases. The highest bid was 2100 guineas, and they were withdrawn. The same amount was offered for a similar pair which the Earl had purchased from the Hon. P. J. Locke-King, M.P. These vases became the property of Sir J. B. Robinson, of Dudley House, when he purchased that residence and its contents in 1895. Amongst some notable pieces of Chelsea china sold at the auction, was the beautiful vase on pedestal, about 15 inches high, which Mr. Samuel Willson gave 945 guineas for, and the companion to which is in the British Museum. The tea service, formerly the property of Lord Lonsdale, realised 1200 guineas, a pair of vases with open-work necks, and covers, painted in Watteau subjects, 16 inches high, 1071 guineas, and a set of three vases, with scroll handles in relief, 700 guineas. Generally speaking, these prices were considerably less than Lord Dudley had paid for them, but his Lordship always had the reputation of paying extravagant prices for specimens upon which he had set his mind.

Probably the most valuable set of vases in existence is the beautiful set of seven, of rare pink ground colour and exquisite painting in mythological subjects, which were formerly at Chesterfield House in Lord Burton's possession. They are illustrated in Litchfield's *Pottery and Porcelain* and are now on loan from Lord Bearsted, at the Victoria and Albert Museum.

A pair of famous vases, 20 in. high, was given to the British Museum on 15th April, 1763; the gift is thus recorded in the donation-book: " Two very fine porcelain jars of the Chelsea manufactory, made in the year 1762, under the direction of Mr. Sprimont, from a person unknown, through Mr. Empson." (*Ker. Gall.*, fig. 551.)

There is every reason to infer, from the date of presentation of these two vases to the British Museum, and the other to the Foundling, on the 15th April, 1763 (probably on the same day, for the committee did not meet till a few days after), that Dr. Garnier was the " person unknown," and that he purchased the set of three at the Chelsea Works, the Foundling vase forming the centre.

There is another style which, although it bears the anchor mark, differs entirely from the Chelsea manufacture previously spoken of; the vessels are of simple, elegant forms, with the frequent recurrence of gold stripes; these the connoisseur would at a first glance refer to Derby, but it is probable they were made at Chelsea, and are its latest productions, between 1770 and 1784, whilst under the direction of W. Duesbury, of Derby. Several examples of Chelsea-Derby porcelain bear the anchor mark in gold.

There is this peculiarity about the Chelsea porcelain, that it will not, like the *pâte tendre* of Sèvres, bear any fresh exposure to the heat of the furnace without splitting and cracking, so that it cannot be repainted and " doctored " like its French rival. (For examples of Chelsea china, see *Ker. Gall.*, figs. 547–9, 551–4.)

Jewitt, in his *Chelsea China* (*Art Journal*, April 1863), gives copies of two letters from Robert Boyer to Duesbury; he was one of the old Chelsea workmen, who remained there to superintend the removal of the kilns, moulds, etc., to Derby. In the first he says:—

"LAWRENCE STREET, CHELSEA, *February* 18, 1784.
"SIR,—I wright to inform you how we are pretty forward in the pulling down of the buildings at Chelsea. I think a little better than a fortnight they will be all down to the ground and cleared of the primeses, which I shall be glad to my hart, for I am tired of it.

"Mr. Lygo says you would wish to have the ion kiln come to Derby. Its hardly worth sending, for the corners are a good deail burnt at the bottom, and the sides are opend or drawd so much as 4 or 5 inches on each side. I wish yow will let me no if yow will have the mold of the large figur of Britania sent to the warehous or broake."

This was one of the largest figures produced at the Chelsea Works, and such pieces are now of great rarity. John J. Bagshawe, of Sheffield, had one of these figures; it represents Britannia seated on a lion, with trophies, etc.; she holds in her left hand a medallion of George II, and underneath the base is a *triangle* incised in the clay. The Mr. Lygo mentioned in the letter above was London agent and salesman to Duesbury.

A magnificent figure of a female with a lion, but not the usual Britannia model, of the very unusual height of 27 in., was in Frederick James Tompson's Hampstead Collection. It is very finely modelled. This important figure was purchased by William Chaffers at the sa e of the Tompson Collection and it is illustrated in Litchfield's *Pottery and Porcelain*.

Louis François Roubillac, French sculptor, the author of Handel's monument in Westminster Abbey and of the statue of Shakespeare in the British Museum, reputedly modelled for Sprimont, and some of the most important groups and figures produced at the Chelsea factory have been attributed to him. They are more graceful than the more commonplace Chelsea, and as a rule are richly gilt and decorated, and are almost invariably marked with the gold anchor. Sometimes they have an R impressed in the paste, as is the case with three beautiful figures of Apollo and two of the Muses, Erato and Clio, formerly in Claude Watney's Collection, and also with a small figure of a gleaner which was in Dudley W. Macdonald's Collection; but many which we cannot doubt are of Roubillac's modelling, have no such initial, and it is very doubtful if the " R " mark can be related to Roubillac. While he may well have modelled the originals of some Chelsea figures and groups, the " R " mark was added in the normal course of finishing each example. (This mark also occurs on models unrelated to Roubillac.)

There are some very fine specimens in the Schreiber Collection (Victoria and Albert Museum). The late Lord Romilly had a pair of groups of sportsman and lady, representing Summer and Winter. Mrs. Lionel Phillips had a remarkable pair of figures, shepherd and shepherdess.

Captain Thistlethwayte had a pair of shepherd figures formerly in the Mainwaring Collection, and there are others in good private collections. A pair of groups representing the Seasons, 12 in. high, marked R. were purchased by Mr. Amor, St. James Street, in 1911, for the very high price of 950 guineas, and this record was eclipsed a few months later by his purchase of Roubillac's group, *L'agréable Leçon*, for the enormous sum of 1,750 guineas. An example of the latter group may be seen in the Schreiber collection at the Victoria and Albert Museum. The three groups form a superb set of the best of Chelsea's productions. The reader will find in the Appendix a list of prices realised at auction by specimens of Chelsea.

EDITOR'S NOTE TO THE THIRTEENTH EDITION

The numerous historical facts concerning the history of the Chelsea factory, collected by Mr. Chaffers, and compiled in the foregoing pages, may perhaps be rendered of more value to the collector if a short note of the different products of this important English factory be added.

About 1745, which is the earliest authenticated date we have, there were produced those white undecorated specimens which are of a soft paste somewhat like the early St. Cloud porcelain, and somewhat resembling opaque glass. To this period belong the bee jugs, the busts of the Duke of Cumberland, the crawfish salt-cellars, and several specimens which should be carefully studied at the British Museum, and also in the Schreiber Collection in the Victoria and Albert Museum.

Then follows the period beginning about 1751, when the paste was thicker, heavier, denser, decorated generally in the Oriental taste (Kakiyemon style), or when European subjects such as birds and animals from Æsop's Fables were chosen, the drawing is archaic in character. This is the time of the oval medallion with anchor in relief, and may be said to have lasted until about 1758. It is the period of the " moons " or " discs," that is an effect of moons or discs inside the paste, visible when the specimen is held up to a strong light, and is caused by the incomplete mixing of the ingredients in the paste or body. The table services of this period have no gilding, but the edges of the cups and saucers and plates, have a thin reddish-brown colour. Towards the end of this second period the small red anchor was used, and the figures were delicately modelled in the style of the earlier Dresden or Meissen groups and figures by Kändler.

From 1759 to about 1770 we have the beautiful ground colours introduced, first the rich deep blue *(gros bleu)*, then a delicate pea green, and a year or so later the claret, which should be called a crimson lake, and is peculiar to Chelsea, also the turquoise colour. This is the period of the richest and most decorative of Chelsea porcelain, the time of Roubillac's modelling, the time of these numerous portrait statuettes, of the pieces made in the style of Sèvres, the quarters of the globe, the shepherds and shepherdesses, and the beautiful services, all of which now command such enormous prices. A specialité of the factory, too, was the making of those charming little flacons, and *étuis* sometimes mounted in gold, and decorated with French mottoes and legends which the collector prizes very highly, and which are equal in quality, and indeed very similar in effect to the finest specimens of Menécy and also of Meissen. In the latter part of this period gold was used more freely in the decoration of vases, figures, and services, and this last epoch of the Chelsea factory continued until the sale of the concern was advertised by Sprimont in 1769, and as will be seen in the foregoing notice of Chelsea-Derby, the works, models, plants, &c., passed into the possession of Mr. Duesbury in 1770.

EDITOR'S NOTE TO THE FIFTEENTH EDITION

It has only been necessary to make minor amendments to the preceding historical notes. For an appreciation of the interesting early products of the Chelsea factory, the reader is referred to *Chelsea Porcelain—the Triangle and Raised Anchor Wares*, 1948, and *Chelsea Porcelain—the Red Anchor Wares*, 1951. Both works by F. Severne Mackenna.

CHELSEA PORCELAIN MARKS

The early incised mark of a triangle (no. 1) is occasionally found, especially upon the little milk-jugs in form of a goat, with raised flowers and a bee perched upon one of them. A jug of moulded strawberry leaf design formerly in the Sheldon Collection bore this incised triangle. The incised triangle mark is found on wares of the 1745–49 period.

Sir A. W. Franks, in his *Notes on the Manufacture of Porcelain at Chelsea*, says: "As an additional confirmation that china of this kind (bearing the triangle) was made at Chelsea, I may mention that Walpole, in his *Description of Strawberry Hill*, speaks of 'two white salt-cellars with crawfish in relief, of Chelsea china,' a very uncommon design, which I have found only once, viz., at the Earl of Ilchester's at Melbury, where are four such salt-cellars, all marked with a triangle." A similar set, modelled by hand and not stamped in a mould, was in the collection of Dr. Diamond, marked with a blue triangle.

The interesting mark (no. 2) is on a milk-jug, of two goats, and in front a bee in relief, in the British Museum, formerly in the Franks Collection. A similar jug, with the same mark and date, was in the possession of Mr. T. Thornhill, jun., and other similar jugs, some white and some coloured, but with the incised triangle mark only, are in various collections. A similar jug is illustrated in *The Apollo*, July 1944, in this case the date could be interpreted as 1743. See also *Chelsea Porcelain—the Triangle and Raised Anchor Wares*, 1948, by F. Severne Mackenna. Mrs. A. R. Macdonald had a silver-gilt jug of this size and pattern which bore the London hall mark of 1724. Reproductions of the Goat and Bee jug were made in the nineteenth century at Coalport.

Mark no. 3, incised under the glaze, is on two small white Chelsea octagonal cups made in imitation of the white Oriental porcelain. The mark is evidently a copy of the Chinese seal. They are the only specimens so marked known to the Editor. Formerly in Frederick Tompson's Collection.

Mark no. 4, in underglaze blue, is found upon a very early white Chelsea group of two lovers, in the British Museum, and also upon a white tall-shaped cup with flowers in relief, formerly in the collection of Frank Hurlbutt, and there is also a similar cup, with the relief pattern tinted with colours, but unmarked, in the British Museum. Two similar cups are also mentioned by Solon in his *Old English Porcelain*. The Sheldon Collection contained a cream ewer of moulded strawberry leaf design, also bearing this extremely rare early Chelsea mark, c. 1745–9.

At the Marquis of Hastings' sale (15th January, 1869) there were two small white porcelain cups, each formed of four leaves, standing on eight feet, escalloped edges, marked with the triangle impressed; and over the triangle on one of them was the mark in blue as mark no. 4.

An early mark (no. 5) of the Chelsea factory is an embossed oval, on which is an anchor in relief, with or without colour. There is in the Schreiber Collection a piece of white glazed china, being an exact copy of the well-known French earthenware statuette, " La Nourrice," bearing the mark of the raised anchor. Dr. Diamond had two pheasants, coloured, with the raised anchor painted red, the rest of the medallion being left white. Mrs. A. R. Macdonald had two early specimens of birds on stumps with this mark, and there is a tea service bearing this mark, the cups of which are fluted, painted with animals, distributed in various collections; some cups and saucers are in the British Museum. This mark, is known as the raised anchor mark, the period is c. 1749 to c. 1753.

The anchor (marks nos. 6 to 11) may be regarded as the standard Chelsea mark. As it was painted by various hands several slight variations occur.

The anchor painted in red enamel (other colours were occasionally used) denotes examples made in the " Red Anchor " period, c. 1753 to c. 1757.

The " Gold Anchor " period (in which the anchor was painted in gold) embraces the period c. 1757 to c. 1769, but this also occurs on some pieces made in the " Chelsea-Derby " period c. 1770 to c. 1784. The anchor combined with the letter D or with a crown above also denotes the

" Chelsea-Derby " period, see Derby section.

The anchor mark was used by other factories and has been extensively used on reproductions of Chelsea porcelain. Examples should not be attributed to Chelsea on the evidence of the mark alone. There is no foundation for the statement made in previous editions that the colour of the anchor mark denotes the quality of the example.

Typical specimens of Chelsea porcelain are illustrated in Godden's *British Pottery and Porcelain, an Illustrated Encyclopædia of Marked Specimens*.

For the work of twentieth century Chelsea potters—Gwendolen Parnell, Harry Parr, Reginald Wells, Charles Vyse, etc., the reader is referred to *The Cheyne Book of Chelsea China and Pottery*, 1924.

WALES

SWANSEA

The manufacture of earthenware was carried on in the Strand, at Swansea, some few years after the date of a lease " granted for the erection of a pottery " in 1764, and on a small scale; between 1780 and 1790 the works were taken by George Haynes, who styled them the *Cambrian Pottery*. Donovan (*Excursions in South Wales and Monmouthshire*), who visited the works about the year 1800, describes at some length the Cambrian Pottery. It was conducted, he says, by Haynes & Co.; the plan upon which the works were carried on was similar to that of Wedgwood, comprising an extensive suite of rooms, furnaces, and baking-kilns, in which the various kinds of earthenware and porcelain were manufactured from the raw materials, the whole being moulded, formed, glazed, baked, printed, painted, and otherwise completely finished in the several apartments within the circuit of the works.

Donovan minutely describes the method of mixing and working the clays at Swansea, and forming the vessels of ordinary pottery. He says : —

" We now come to the last process, in which the *porcelain* of the most superior kinds are decorated with emblematical designs, landscapes, fruit, flowers, heraldic figures, or any other species of ornamental devices. The whole of this is executed by the pencil of the painter; the various objects are slightly sketched in black-lead upon the ware after it is glazed, and is only submitted to a certain degree of heat in the kiln when nearly finished, to fix the metallic colours in their proper tints."

The preparation of the colours is next spoken of, and the gilding; he tells us that gold also enters into the composition of their purples.

" A solution of tin is prepared with nitro-muriatic acid, and being saturated with a small proportion of gold held also in solution, deposits a crimson precipitate, which after a few days becomes a fine purple; copper calcined by acids and precipitated by an alkali forms a beautiful green; an oxide of iron produces brown or black; and various earths that are slightly ferruginous afford browns and yellows of various hues;" cobalt, the rich blue, manganese, &c. " Biscuit porcelain, or that without any glaze or painting, is also executed here in great perfection."

He then gives an interesting account of the process of printing the surface of the ware, and he concludes thus : —

"We are to consider the manufacture of the superior kinds of porcelain in our country as an improvement in our national art. The elegance of this ware is not to be denied; in one respect at least it has an advantage over the porcelain of India, its embellishments are certainly more chaste, more tasteful, and appropriate.

"Capricious fashion may for a time assign a preference to the manufacture of our Continental neighbours, but it will admit of doubt whether some of the better kinds of our home-made porcelain, under the management of such ingenious individuals as the conductors of those works, may not bid fair one day to vie with the boasted produce of the *Seive* (*sic* for Sèvres) pottery.

"We have no other rival on the Continent of Europe to dispute the palm with us."

The "porcelain" mentioned by Donovan was really a superior ironstone ware, and not the true Swansea porcelain now recognised by collectors, which was not made until 1814. In 1810 Haynes retired, leaving L. W. Dillwyn sole proprietor; there appears, however, to have been some difficulty connected with the dissolution of partnership, for in a letter from Dillwyn in our possesion he says, "*The Courier* contains a tolerably correct account of the late trial at Cardiff; the infamous conduct of my opponents during the trial is there mentioned, and I rather think it was inserted by the shorthand writer whom they employed; we had about 107 witnesses, and *I saddled Haines with above £1,200 costs*," etc. Dillwyn retired from the concern in 1813, leaving it to his son, L. L. Dillwyn.

As already noticed, it was in the year 1814 that the manufacture of what is now recognised as Swansea porcelain was introduced. At that time Billingsley or Beely (a contraction of his real name, and by which he was probably best known) had commenced making his beautiful porcelain, which was much admired, at Nantgarw. Dillwyn's attention was drawn to this, and conceiving that the kilns used by Billingsley & Walker might be considerably improved, he made arrangements with them to carry out their processes at Swansea. With this view two new kilns were erected at the Cambrian Pottery, and the manufacture was conducted by them for some considerable time. This was the origin of the Swansea porcelain; and under the personal direction of Beely, who possessed the secret of mixing the ingredients which compose this beautiful paste or body, several experiments were made, and the paste or body was rendered more compact and harder. Specimens produced about this time, say, after 1815, show a greenish tint (" duck's egg ") when held up to a strong light, and the mark after 1817 is the word SWANSEA, accompanied by one or two tridents (crossed) as mark no. 7; and this trident was to mark a supposed improvement in the manufacture. Baxter, a clever painter of figure subjects, left Worcester and entered Dillwyn's service in 1816, and continued there for about three years, returning to Worcester in 1819. Pollard and Morris were also noted flower painters who worked at this factory.

The histories of William Billingsley and of his son-in-law Samuel Walker, given at some length in the notice of the Nantgarw factory, should be referred to.

Marks nos. 1 and 2, the word SWANSEA, is frequently found impressed, written or stencilled in red on porcelain, c. 1814–22.

SWANSEA.

1

Swansea.

2

SWANSEA

3

DILLWYN & Cº

4

BEVINGTON & Co.,
SWANSEA.

5

6

7

8

9

10

11

12

13

14

15

16

17

18

NANTGARW.

19

NANT GARW
C.W.

20

Nantgarw

21

Cambrian
Pottery

23

CAMBRIAN

24

Dillwyn's
Etruscan Ware.

25

SWANSEA

26

22

Kalmbc
H
S

27

OPAQUE CHINA.

28

Dudley W. Macdonald had part of a breakfast service of fine quality, the remainder of which is in the Victoria and Albert Museum, and which is described and illustrated in Professor Church's *English Porcelain*. It is painted in wild roses. One of the plates is marked "Dillwyn & Co."; other pieces are stamped "Swansea."

Marks nos. 3 and 4 are separately impressed on two porcelain plates of the same service, painted with bouquets and groups of flowers in the centre by Pollard, a Swansea artist. (Franks Collection.) The same combination of marks occurs on a square plateau in Herbert Eccles' Collection. Mark no. 4, DILLWYN & Co., usually on earthenwares, c. 1811–17.

The name of Bevington is occasionally found on pieces of Swansea porcelain. The period of his work and influence was from 1818 to 1824, and is marked by the peculiar dead whiteness of the glaze. Mark no. 5 is impressed on a *biscuit* chimney ornament of a ram lying down; separated from the mark are the impressed letters I. W., which are those of the modeller, Isaac Wood. This specimen is in the Victoria and Albert Museum. With reference to Bevington & Co., the former Editor was indebted to the late Robert Drane of Cardiff, who paid very close attention to many details regarding the history of both the Swansea and Nantgarw factories and also to Herbert Eccles for the following information. There were two Bevingtons, Quakers; one was part proprietor of the works, and the other their commercial representative or "traveller." Both were essentially "business" men, and neither of them had anything to do, artistically, with the products of the factory. Earthenware from 1817 to 1824 may bear the "Bevington & Co." mark.

Marks nos. 6 and 7. The mark of a trident was adopted on the soap-rock body, c. 1817+. The word Swansea and a trident are impressed on several examples, c. 1817–22.

The word "Swansea" with a single trident occurs on two spill-vases painted with flowers and fruit by Morris, formerly in the collection of Dudley W. Macdonald.

N.B.—These marks appear on reproductions.

Marks nos. 8 to 18 are also found upon earthenware specimens in the collection formed with the advice and assistance of Mr. Drane for the Cardiff Museum, and in the private collection of Alexander Duncan, to whom the former editor was indebted for drawings and tracings of the marks.

The reader is also referred to E. Morton Nance's monumental work, *The Pottery and Porcelain of Swansea and Nantgarw*, 1942, for a full review of the various periods and owners of the Welsh factories and their productions.

The date of Evans & Glasson (mark no. 17) was quite late, c. 1850–62, and there was in the Sheldon Collection another variation of their mark, the names with the word SWANSEA being printed in a triangular frame. The marks of D. J. Evans are of the period c. 1862–70. Mark no. 18 of Baker, Bevans & Irwin may be dated c. 1813–38, other marks occur.

So far as the fine old Swansea porcelain made by Billingsley is concerned, the only mark known to the Editor is the impressed mark, SWANSEA. This was only made for a very short time, and, finding that on account of the peculiar composition of the body so many failures occurred in firing, the experiment was tried of using more china clay and flint, which had the effect of hardening the body. In some specimens of the trident marked "Swansea," one can see that the body almost resembles glass, and when others are held up to a strong light, there appears a dark, smoky effect.

Herbert Eccles of Neath, who had one of the largest collections of Swansea, numbering nearly a thousand specimens, has analysed powdered portions broken off different kinds of Swansea china specimens, and the Editor was indebted to him for the following chronological list of marks and the varying compositions of the paste—

	Date.	Composition.
No. 1. Porcelain made from the Nantgarw recipe; impressed mark SWANSEA.	1814–16.	Pure sand, bone ash, china clay, potash.
No. 2. (a) Porcelain with duck's egg, green tint; see previous note.	1815–17.	Ground flint, bone ash, china clay, potash.
(b) Porcelain made after sale of the factory to Bevingtons.	1817–24.	
No. 3. Porcelain after so-called improvement, that is, made harder, more durable, and less liable to failure in firing, marked with trident, generally impressed, and sometimes accompanied by SWANSEA, also impressed.	1816–17.	Pure sand, soap-rock, china clay, potash, *no* bone ash.

The SWANSEA mark, when not impressed, is written or printed in red chiefly, but also in gold, blue, black, green and yellow. A great deal of Swansea china is unmarked. Mark no. 4, " Dillwyn & Co., Swansea," is very rare on porcelain, but is common on pottery.

NANTGARW (Glamorganshire). This porcelain manufactory was established by Billingsley, a celebrated flower-painter of Derby, who served his time to Mr. Duesbury, and probably left his service about 1796. In some of the early Derby pattern books now at Worcester mentioned by Mr. Binns, is frequently written, " To be painted with Billingsley's flowers," so that he was an artist of high repute at that time. He was not only a first-class painter, but he thoroughly understood the manufacture of porcelain in all its branches. In 1796 he established a porcelain manufactory at Pinxton, in partnership with Mr. John Coke: here he remained about five years, dissolving partnership in 1801, but the works were continued until 1812. In 1800 we find him superintending a small decorating establishment at Mansfield, where he remained for four years. From 1803 to 1808 he was at Torksey, in Lincolnshire, engaged in a manufactory there, and upon the failure of the enterprise from lack of means, he was engaged by Messrs. Flight & Barr of Worcester. His son-in-law, Walker, was at Torksey, and also at the Worcester works, and made some improvements; he introduced that most important invention, the *reverberating enamel kiln*, already in use at London and Derby; the method of building this kiln was kept secret, Walker always working at night to complete it.

In 1813 Billingsley and his son-in-law, Walker, left the Worcester factory, breaking their engagement, and set up some kilns at Nantgarw for the manufacture of soft paste porcelain. Being in want of money to carry on their work, an application was made for Government assistance, and it was upon Dillwyn's investigation on behalf of the Board of Trade that they were induced to join the staff of his own factory at Swansea. Flight and Barr having acquainted Dillwyn with their breach of contract they were dismissed and returned to Nantgarw, but straitened means forced them to discontinue the struggle after two years, and thus they entered into an arrangement with Rose of Coalport to transfer their services to his factory. This happened about 1820.

The Nantgarw porcelain was of remarkably fine body and texture, but its composition, although highly artistic, was of an impracticable character, inasmuch as it would not always stand firm, being indeed more like glass than porcelain, it frequently cracked in the kiln. There was a great demand for it in London; it is said that Mr. Mortlock contracted to take the whole of it in its white state to decorate it in London. There are in the British Museum two elaborately painted plates of this description of Nantgarw china decorated in London.

Mr. Bemrose, jun., of Derby, wrote that Webster, a Derby painter, painted quantities of Nantgarw china in London for the dealer Mortlock of Oxford Street, who purchased all that Billingsley made at this time in the white glazed state: it was fired after being painted by Robins & Randall, enamellers, of Spa Fields. Both Robins and Randall worked at one time at Derby, and also at Pinxton. The former was a Pinxton man, the latter was from the Caughley Works. (See an account of Thomas Martin Randall under Madeley).

Billingsley died in 1828, when Walker went to America and established a pottery there. (*Ker. Gall.*, figs. 618–20.)

In Jewitt's sale there was a curious tea-cup of the usual Chantilly pattern, in blue, used by Billingsley as a trial-piece for colours and glazes; it had various washes of colours, with marks and contractions to show the mixture which had been burnt in; among these marks were NL FOB, NL FO, WITH CAL, etc.

Mark no. 19 is impressed; sometimes the letters C.W. are found stamped under the word " Nantgarw," which probably stand for "China Works," mark no. 20, c. 1813–c. 1822.

Sometimes we find the mark NANTGARW painted or stencilled in red, but the Editor is inclined to agree with Mr. Drane and other experts that these are probably not of Nantgarw make, but imitations. They must be viewed with suspicion.

Mark no. 21, written in red, is very rare, and occurs on a spill-holder formerly in the Sheldon Collection.

Collectors of Swansea and Nantgarw china will find additional information in *The Ceramics of Swansea and Nantgarw*, by W. Turner, and other books listed in the bibliography.

The best public collection of Nantgarw and Swansea is that in the Cardiff Museum, where specimens decorated by Billingsley, Baxter, Pardoe, Pollard, Morris, Latham, and Young may be seen and their different characteristics compared. There are also specimens in the British and Victoria and Albert Museums.

CAMBRIAN. At the commencement of the notice on Swansea there is mention of this CAMBRIAN POTTERY, which should be referred to. Some further particulars of the peculiarities and marks of its productions will be of interest to collectors. A thin earthenware of extreme lightness was manufactured at the Cambrian Pottery into tea services, jugs, etc., painted in vivid enamel colours, in landscapes, costume figures, flowers, and animals; the subjects are painted in a rough and careless manner, although very effective. The forms of the pieces are good, and carefully modelled; some few of these are marked " Cambrian Pottery," but the majority are unsigned, and like other doubtful pieces, are attributed to Staffordshire.

Mark no. 22, c. 1780. Factory unknown, but probably Swansea (Cambrian Pottery). It is on an earthenware jug or coffee-pot, painted with roses and pinks, formerly in the possession of E. Bourchier Savile.

Mark no. 23 appears on wares from c. 1783 to c. 1810, impressed or written.

Mark no. 24 is found on two large oviform vases of Cambrian pottery about 1790, finely glazed and well painted, with a large medallion of a passion-flower, roses, etc., and a butterfly, and is an excellent example of flower painting by Thomas Pardoe on Swansea earthenware. The body of the vases is *gros bleu*, but while in the case of one the gilding has not been properly fired, in the companion vase the " marbling " is in gold and the painting of the flower subject much better finished and shows substantial progress. There is an illustration of one of these vases in Litchfield's *Pottery and Porcelain*. The name " Young, pinxit," occurs on a pair of semi-circular jardinières of Cambrian pottery, beautifully painted with birds, butterflies, caterpillars, vine leaves, and grapes, on dark-brown ground; in the collection of Sir A. W. Franks (now in the British Museum). William Weston Young also decorated the " opaque china," and was occasionally engaged at Nantgarw; he left the Cambrian Works and joined Billingsley & Walker at Nantgarw, which manufacture he continued after their departure in 1820.

Mark no. 25 is found on pieces of Greek form and classic subjects; an elegant tazza shaped like the Greek calyx on a foot and two handles, with classical subject in the centre, and " key border painted in red on black ground; the mark underneath within a foliated border." Etruscan ware was not made at Swansea until about 1847. Other ornate marks occur on these Etruscan pieces, which were only manufactured for a few years and are of earthenware body.

From 1802 to 1810 the firm was HAYNES, DILLWYN & Co., CAMBRIAN POTTERY, SWANSEA, but we do not know when Louis Weston Dillwyn joined it. A trade card of the period has a view of the works engraved in the centre, as they appeared about 1802. The simple mark SWANSEA was normal at this period.

Mark no. 26 is standard impressed mark on earthenwares from c. 1783 to c. 1810 (later on porcelains).

Some cream ware dishes and plates with flowers painted, and the names of flowers inscribed on the backs have mark no. 27, and have been attributed to Haynes of Swansea.

Mark no. 28, Opaque China. This ware was introduced late in the eighteenth century, and was remarkable for the careful delineation of birds, butterflies, and shells, with which it was decorated.

THE YNYSMEUDW POTTERY, near Swansea, produced blue printed earthenware from c. 1850–c. 1859. Examples are recorded with the impressed initials Y M P or Y P.

LLANELLY, SOUTH WALES POTTERY. This pottery, formerly owned by Chambers & Co., produced a large quantity of earthenware. Herbert Eccles had several specimens of the older ware, which is of medium quality, the pattern best known to the Editor being one with encrusted flowers. These are marked with the impressed stamp, SOUTH WALES POTTERY, in a circle, and the name, W. CHAMBERS, in an inner circle. Other specimens have a word denoting the pattern, and the letters S. W. P. The CHAMBERS period was from about 1839·to 1854. Subsequent changes have been COOMBS & HOLLAND (c. 1854–c. 1858); HOLLAND alone from c. 1858 to c. 1869; HOLLAND & GUEST, c. 1869–c. 1877; GUEST & DUESBURY, c. 1877–c. 1927.

Earlier editions illustrated a mark incorporating a bee(?), the word " Cumae " and the initials M W & Co. These initials were attributed to a firm Woronzou & Co., but no pottery firm of this name can be traced in local records. It is probable that this was the mark used by Morgan, Wood & Co. of Burslem, c. 1860–70.

IRELAND

DUBLIN

We have no history of the manufactories of pottery in Ireland, although there must necessarily have been many in existence from the earliest times, but they have fallen into oblivion, and even during the eighteenth century we have been able to find scarcely any record of them. It is to be hoped some antiquary of Erin will turn his attention to the subject, and endeavour to identify the specimens, of which there must be many extant.

The following letters from Mr. Henry Delamain, of the India Warehouse, Abbey Street, Dublin, to Mr. William Stringfellow, at the Delft Manufactory in the Strand, Dublin, are of sufficient interest, we think, to give them entire. They are dated December 1753 and January 1754, and relate to the use of coals in heating potters' kilns instead of wood or turf, which Delamain states he had successfully adopted in his own manufactory. His aim appears to have been to obtain a reward from the English Parliament for his discovery, but it seems doubtful whether he was successful. Stringfellow, we may infer, was actually in his service, or at least under great obligations to him. Coal was used at Lille in 1784, and at Arras in 1785, but we do not think it was used, even in England, where coals are more plentiful, before the date of Delamain's letters. The first letter is from Delamain to Stringfellow, dated 19th December 1753 : —

" DEAR SIR,—I was obliged to go for England at an hour's warning, therefore had not time to bid you farewell, or settle any of my affairs. In my way to London I called at Liverpoole, where I was advised to petition the Parliament of England for a reward, for having burnt and glazed delft ware with *coals*, and at the same time to get the Magistrates and Corporation of Liverpoole to back my petition and to get the potters here to joyne them, all which I have effected; but some of the potters doubt the success of our large kiln, which I have assured them has answered as well as the small one did, and that it was twice burnt before I left Dublin. As they are in correspondence with you, they say you gave them no such information, therefore they will write to you by this post, to know whether it was twice burnt before I left Dublin, and how it succeeds; therefore I beg you will answer them by return of the post, that it was burnt before I left Dublin, with perfect ware, which turn'd out as well as ever it was done with *turf* and *wood,* and that you have burnt it since I left Ireland, and that it answers to all our wishes, and that not a bit of ware was smoaked, but all white, and better glazed than ever you saw it done with *wood* or *turf.*

"Suppose it has happened quite the reverse, do you write what I desire you for your own advantage as well as my credit, for I have set them all on fire to burn their ware with *coals,* and have come into this agreement with them, that you are to come over to build their kilns, for which they all promise to pay you handsomely; some offered me money, but I told them if they gave me £500, I would not touch a penny of it, but that it should be all for you; all that I desired of them was to back my petition to Parliament with the Mayor and Corporation, which they have promised to do, provided the great kiln turns out well, which they doubt; therefore by all means answer to them by return of the post all you can say in its favour, and more if necessary, for I know we shall make it do as well as the little one. It's the opinion of most people here the Parliament of England won't do anything for me, it being unusual, and this branch of trade thought nothing of by them; let that be as it will, I have pushed on your affaires here much better than ever you could do it yourself, and hope you will receive a large sum from them.

"I shall make what haste I can to Dublin, and be assured I will settle all your affairs to your satisfaction, and beg you will push on my business in the interim. They don't want you here these two months, before which time I hope to be in Dublin. Don't let any one know in Liverpoole I wrote to you on this subject. I beg to hear from you, directed to me, to George Fitzgerald, Esq., London. Let me know how everything goes on since I parted. My respects to Mr. Hornby, Mr. Shee, &c. Pray let me hear from you by return of the post, and let me know what's wanting for the manufactory, and whether the front of the house is finish'd.

"I am, &c.　　　　　　　　HENRY DELAMAIN.
"To Mr. Wm. Stringfellow, the Delft Manufactory,
　　in the Strand, Dublin."

The next letter to which I shall refer is written by Mr. Delamain to his wife, dated 18th December 1753, giving her directions to see String-fellow immediately, and "beg him to write to Liverpoole this night and say, right or wrong, that the large kiln was burnt twice before I left Ireland and once since, and that it succeeds so well that not a bit of ware was smoaked, and that it glazes the ware better than turf and wood, and makes it harder and less subject to peel, and that about 2 tons or 2½ tons of coal will burn it." He concludes, "I shall go to London this day, and shall call in my way at Wor'ster to see the fine new manufactory," &c. This letter is addressed to Mrs. Mary Delamain, at the India Warehouse, Abbey Street, Dublin.

The next letter is dated the 9th January 1754, O.S., which corresponds with 20th January 1754:—

"SIR,—I am glad you're safe arrived in England, and am surpriz'd you did not receive my 2nd letter before you parted. The gentlemen of Liverpoole will assure you, if they do me justice, that I beg'd nothing from them but to gratifye you for the trouble you may be at to build kilns and to sign a petition for me to Parliament, which can by no means prejudice you or them. I am informed this post they refuse to sign the petition, which I think ungrateful, for this secret would never have been found out only for me, who, contrary to your opinion and all others, I persued the scheme to burn with coal, which several of the workmen of my manufacturie made oath of before I left Ireland, and which is confirmed by the votes of the House of Commons of Ireland. As it has been always my intention to serve you and settle you master of the manufactorie, and that I have freed you from all your troubles, it will be the highest ingratitude of you to do anything to my disadvantage, therefore beg you will not enter into any agreement with the manufacturers at Liverpoole till my affair is decided in the House of Commons of England, which will be done in a few days, for if you do it without my approbation, the consequence may be your ruin, and perhaps won't hurt me, and there's no money they can give you can recompense the loss it may be to me, and I am both able and willing to pay you any sum they will give you, and even more. I now make it my request to you, that you will not inform them any part of the secret, and declare to them you never will, unless they sign my petition; and if the Parliament grants me a sum for this, whatever they have agreed to give you, I will immediately pay you down in cash that sum, which I promise by these presents, and also you will be recompensed by one man in London more to build him a kiln than all the people of Liverpoole together will give you. I have great friends here, and a strong interest is making for me, therefore entreat you will not do anything to hurt me. As soon as my affair is decided in Liverpoole you must come to London, where we will settle all our affairs, and as soon as the kilns are built and properly burnt, we must go to France together, on some extraordinary affairs to both our advantage; in the interim I will continue y'r guinea a week to y'r wife till our return to Dublin. Inclosed I send you a draught for five pounds, and beg you will get my petition signed, with an absolute promise that as soon as my affair is settled in Parliament, that you will build their kilns, and do them all the service in your power, but till then you can't do anything. As soon the Pet'n is signed, which must be done immediately, come up to me to London the next day, as fast as you can; you will perhaps get a horse at Liverpoole for London, if not, hire one to Warrington, and come up in the Stage Coach to London; you must leave Liverpoole on Sunday next to get to Warrington in the Monday's Stage, or you will be too late : if you can hire a good horse, you will be in London sooner than in the stage; if you can't, don't miss the Monday's Warrington Stage Coach, for I want you much here on several accounts, and as soon as my affair in Parliament is over, we can set people to work both here and at Liverpoole not to lose time, for we must go to Paris as soon as possible. Write to me Saturday's post what is done, and don't let any one in Liverpoole know y'r coming to London. As soon as you arrive, get a Porter or a Coach to show you the way to Mr. Chilton's, a periwig maker in Porter Street, near Newport Ally, just by St. Martin's Lane or Newport Market; if I am not at home, there's a Tavern next door to me where you may sup, and I have had a bed for you this fortnight past at my own lodgings. Don't let your wife know anything of your going to Paris for fear she should inform mine, which I don't chuse should know it; be assured while we are absent she shan't want for anything. By all means get the petition signed, and send it to me by Saturday's post. Apply to Mr. John Hardman, who is my friend, about it.

" I do assure you the manufacturers of Liverpoole, as I am well informed, have no other intention to serve you, but to get the secret out of you, and then to take you as a journeyman painter; therefore take care what you do, or this affair may be your perdition, but agreeing to what I would have you do, you can't fail of making your advantage of it, let things turn as they will. Since I wrote the above, I have consulted with one of the Members of Parliament of Liverpoole, who thinks it better you should not leave Liverpoole in so great a hurry after the petition is signed, for they are jealous people, and may raise numbers of false conjectures to my prejudice; therefore, don't come up to London till you hear further from me, unless you think your leaving the town will not hurt me, for I want you much, and wish you was here this moment, but would not chuse either of us should do anything to disoblige the manufacturers of Liverpoole, therefore, let us act with prudence, which will turn to both our advantage. I have wrote this post that your wife may receive a guinea every Saturday night till we return, and that all care may be taken of her and the children if wanted. As soon as you receive this, go with the inclosed bill to Mr. Sandford, Mr. Gibson will show you where he lives, and he will pay you five pounds English on sight. I will in a few days send you down a letter of credit in case you want more money, that you may take it up without writing to me or drawing for it.

" Pray observe what I have wrote, and don't do anything with the people of Liverpoole without my consent; I shall write to you constantly how my affairs go on in Parliament; push the manufacturers to sign my petition without delay, write to me every post what occurs. I believe I shall receive my money in Holland, as soon as we get over.

"I am, dear Sir, your assured friend, &c.,   HENRY DELAMAIN.

"To Mr. Stringfellow."

It seems from the following letter that his kindness to Stringfellow in settling his affairs was ill repaid, for he handed the preceding letters, written by Delamain, to the Committee appointed by Parliament to investigate his claim for the reward, which circumstance doubtless proved fatal to his cause so far, at least, as the Parliamentary grant was concerned.

LIVERPOOL, *February 12, 1754.*

"MY LORD,—I have only to enclose your Lordship the two letters of Delamain's own writing, and I have had Mr. Stringfellow with me, and said a good deal to him about keeping them from the Committee; he says the reason was that Delamain made him promise not to produce them, if possible to avoid it, or he would not sign his release, and when Delamain sent that order down here he knew Stringfellow had them. I shall also enclose you another of his letters to him.

"I hope this may prevent Stringfellow's coming up again, and that the original letters may do; no doubt Delamain will own them his own. Stringfellow says he would not have come, but he waited on your Lordship first, and you advised him not to come without release, which he obtained from Delamain, and he gave him Two Guineas to bear his charges, and he had no money to support himself longer than that. I fancy you had as good close the Committee, and excuse his appearing; however, I show'd him Sir Ch. Mordaunt's order for his appearance there.

"I am, my Lord,

"Your Lordship's m't obd't Serv't,

"JOHN HARDMAN.

"To Lord Strange, M.P., London."

In Sleater's *Public Gazetteer*, 11th March, 1760, the following notice may be found: "Tuesday last died Mrs. Mary Delamain, widow of the late Captain Henry Delamain, who was the first that brought the earthenware manufacture to perfection in this kingdom; and since his decease, his said widow (endowed with all the virtues of a good Christian, tender parent, and sincere friend) continued it with such advantage to the purchasers as to prevent the further importation of foreign wares," &c.

A fine documentary bowl was acquired by the British Museum in 1960. It is 16 in. in diameter and is inscribed on the base " Clay got over Primate's Coals, Dublin, 1753." This piece is an undoubted example of Henry Delamain's coal fired delft type ware. See Godden's *British Pottery and Porcelain, an Illustrated Encyclopædia of Marked Specimens.*

DUBLIN. In the course of the eighteenth century there must have been several manufactories of earthenware in Ireland. The Dublin Society having received in grants from the Irish House of Commons, from 1761 to 1767, the sum of £42,000, exclusive of an annual grant of £500 for the encouragement of various branches of trade in Ireland, gave away in 1766 £700 to encourage the earthenware manufacture in Ireland. There are several pieces of this Irish earthenware still extant; they are of a similar

Donovan,
Dublin.

2

DONOVAN

3

$\mathcal{D}ublin$

1

4

WADE(ULSTER)LTD.
PORCELAIN

5

Irish Porcelain

E

MADE IN IRELAND

6

Irish Porcelain

WADE. CO. ARMAGH.

7

Irish Porcelain

MADE IN IRELAND
R

8

kind of material to that now known as Leeds pottery, and are marked with a harp and a crown, with the word *Dublin* in italics. Mark no. 1 is on an earthenware bowl, like Leeds pottery, painted in blue, with a landscape on the inside and deep border of pierced intersecting annulets, formerly in the possession of Mr. Stopford of Drayton House, Northamptonshire, who had also a plate with the same mark.

Mr. Donovan of Poolbeg Street, on the Quay, does not appear to have been a manufacturer, but agent for several Staffordshire houses; among others he was agent for Mason of Stoke, whose ironstone china he stamped with his own name. About 1790 he had a glass manufactory at Rings End near Dublin, and he employed a painter to decorate pottery, and placed all sorts of fancy and imitation marks on china and earthenware.

Mark no. 2 is on a porcelain plate, with deep rose-coloured border, edged with gold, painted in the centre with a landscape. His name occurs on china bearing the mark of two italic *S's* interlaced with the letter M between, an early mark of Minton of Stoke. Also on marked Derby porcelain in the Godden Collection.

Mark no. 3 is on a black Egyptian ware tea service, with fables of animals in relief, the Fox and the Grapes, etc., made about 1800; the teapot has on the cover a seated female figure, which forms the handle; in imitation of Wedgwood, the name impressed; formerly in the possession of the author. It also appears on an earthenware plate, blue printed, formerly in the Sheldon Collection. Rogers of Longport (*q.v.*) is believed to have made pottery for Donovan to decorate.

BELFAST. The following account of the Belfast potteries was furnished by the late Mr. W. Pinkerton, F.S.A.:—

" William Sacheverell, that had been Governor of the Isle of Man, made a voyage to Iona at that time. An account of it, entitled ' A Voyage to I-Columb-Kill in the year 1688,' was published at London in 1702. Mr. Sacheverell visited Belfast on his way to I-Columb-Kill, and he tells us that ' The new pottery is a pretty curiosity set up by Mr. Smith, the present sovereign, and his predecessor, Capt. Leather, a man of great ingenuity.'

" This Belfast pottery is also mentioned by Doctor, afterwards Sir Thomas Molyneux, Bart., in a manuscript description of a journey he made from Dublin to the Giant's Causeway in 1708. This manuscript is in Trinity College, Dublin; but, by the kind permission of Dr. Todd, I am now preparing it, with some others of a similar kind, for the press. Speaking of Belfast, Molyneux says : ' Here we saw a very good manufacture of earthenware, which comes nearest to delft of any made in Ireland, and really is not much short of it. It is very clear and pretty, and universally used in the North; and I think not so much owing to any particular happiness in the clay, but rather to the manner of beating and mixing it up.'

" The next pottery that I have any notice of was one set up by the late Victor Coates of Laganville, long before he established the well-known foundry at the same place. I have seen a coarse kind of delf, said to have been made at those works, though I have been traditionally assured that there was only red-pot ware made thereat. Mr. Coates' son is still alive, and may give us some information on that subject, which is not an uninteresting one. On Williamson's map of Belfast, surveyed in 1791, and republished a few years ago by the Messrs. Ward of Donegal Place, we may find ' Coates' Pottery ' marked down on the site of the present foundry, and, next to it, we may see the words ' China Manufactory.' The partners in this Belfast china manufactory were Thomas Gregg, Samuel Stephenson, and John Ashmore. That they carried on the manufacture of china there for some years is certain; for on January 29, 1793, the Earl of Hillsborough presented a petition from them to the Irish House of Commons. The original petition may be seen in the journals of the House. In it the petitioners state that, recognising the great advantages arising from the manufacture of Queen's ware and other fine kinds of ware, such as are made in Staffordshire, they united themselves into a company for producing such wares in Ireland, and by their exertions had carried this manufacture to a greater perfection in the County of Down, near Belfast, than was ever known in this kingdom; that they had been at great expense in erecting buildings, and importing machinery, and in bringing workmen from foreign places; that the difference in the prices of coal between Belfast and Staffordshire had greatly exceeded their expectations; and they now prayed for pecuniary aid. A committee, consisting of the Earl of Hillsborough, Mr. Johnson, and others, was immediately appointed by the House to report on the petition; and on the 2nd of February they reported that the petitioners had fully proved their allegations. The report was then ordered to be laid on the table; but it does not appear that anything was done further in the matter.

" Thus we see that the price of coals in Ireland was the principal obstacle to the success of the Belfast china manufactory, as it has been to our Irish glass manufacturers; and even at Plymouth, Cookworthy, the first maker of hard paste porcelain in England,

was obliged to give up his works there for the very same reason—the price of coals
absorbed the profits of the manufacture.

"A lady in Belfast has several specimens of this manufacture : one, a teapot of
Queen's ware, is decorated with the figure of two armed volunteers, dressed in the
imposing uniform of the First Belfast Company; one volunteer is in the position of
'shoulder arms,' the other at 'charge bayonets'; underneath them are the words
'For my Country.' On another teapot, of similar manufacture, are the words 'Martha
McClelland,' it being formerly a usual mode at the potteries of thus burning in, as it
was technically called, the names of persons to whom articles of ceramic ware were
presented. These two teapots have a history—a regular pedigree it may be termed—
and they are, undoubtedly, of Belfast manufacture. A third teapot, in the possession of
the same lady, is of pure porcelain, painted in blue *en camaieu*."

The following advertisement from a newspaper of the end of the
eighteenth century reveals the existence of a manufactory at Ballymacarret :
"Greg, Stephenson & Ashmore are manufacturing, and have ready for
sale (at their warehouse in Ballymacarret, near Belfast), a great variety
of cream and painted earthenware, which they can assure their friends
and customers is of the best quality, and now equal to any imported. As
their prices are much lower than foreign ware can be laid in for, they
therefore hope for a preference from the dealers therein. Apothecaries
may be supplied with any quantity of gallipots on moderate terms.—
Belfast, November 25, 1793."

In the *Belfast News Letter* of 29th October 1799 the following notice
appears : "The partnership formerly subsisting under the firm of Greg,
Stephenson & Ashmore has been for some time dissolved. Any demands
against the said partnership will be paid by applying to Cunningham
Greg, J. M. Stephenson, and John Ashmore."

BELLEEK (Lough Erne, County Fermanagh). About 1856 some clays
suitable for making both fine pottery or stoneware as well as porcelain
were discovered on the estate of John Caldwell Bloomfield, Esq., of
which Belleek forms a portion. The following announcement appeared
in the *Times* of April 1856 : "Porcelain clay.—To be let, a bed of porcelain
clay and felspar. To be worked on such terms as may be agreed upon.
Water carriage to all parts of the kingdom. Apply to J. Caldwell Bloomfield, Castle Caldwell, Co. Fermanagh, Ireland."

R. W. Armstrong of London, after a series of experiments with these
materials, succeeded in bringing them into working order, and, in conjunction with D. McBirney, a merchant of Dublin, embarked in the year
1857 (or 1863) in the manufacture of ceramic wares, the title of the firm
being D. McBirney & Co., under the immediate superintendence of R. W.
Armstrong. The principal manufactures were at first of a useful character,
such as dinner, breakfast, and toilet services; later the more artistic productions in porcelain and parian were developed. We were first made
acquainted with these at the Dublin Exhibition in 1865, since which time
great advances have been made both in the modelling and finishing of the
decorative pieces. The leading characteristics of design are marine subjects,
such as dolphins, sea-horses, tritons, nereids, aquatic plants, shells, the

sea-urchin, coral, and rockwork; these are produced in parian or biscuit, and a creamy porcelain-like ivory; also covered with a glittering iridescent glaze like mother-of-pearl, similar to that of Brianchon of Paris, who took out a patent in this country in 1857.

Mark no. 4 is printed or stencilled upon the ware in red, brown, or green, and represents one of the Irish round towers, the harp, and the greyhound, as well as the three-leaved shamrock. This china is a real porcelain, the result of the simple vitrification of felspar and china clay, in contradistinction to the phosphate of lime or " bone body " used in England; the abundance of felspar near Belleek, and of pure flint, is a leading element in rendering the manufacture there so cheap. Some of the articles produced at Belleek contain as much as 72 per cent of the local felspar. In addition to the potter's manual art, mechanical means were afterwards introduced, by which an important class of goods is formed in large quantities, such as white and coloured tiles, and porcelain insulators for telegraphic purposes. The Belleek factory is still carried on. Twentieth century examples normally have " Co. FERMANAGH, IRELAND " on a ribbon below the mark. Other self explanatory marks were also used.

YOUGHAL, near Cork. A manufactory of brown ware was established here many years ago.

John Angel, who was secretary to the Dublin Society, in a *General History of Ireland*, published in 1781, says as follows: "The great quantities of pipeclay found in Clonmel and other parts of Ireland have induced many of the manufacturers of Staffordshire to set up in Dublin the manufacture of earthenware, which no doubt will meet with every encouragement from the inhabitants of Ireland." He says again, when speaking of mines and minerals: "Pipeclay has been found in many parts of Ireland, which hath been exported to France and England for the purpose of making that beautiful yellow ware called Paris ware. But in Dublin they make at present this ware, which is much esteemed." "At Carrickfergus," he says, "there used to be considerable quantities of a white bluish clay exported from this town to England for the purpose of making delft ware, which, after being there manufactured, was again imported into Ireland. This business has greatly decreased of late owing to the universal use of Paris yellow ware." "Rostrevor," he says, "is situated on the north side of Carlingford Haven, has a good quay, and ships may with great safety lie here. Here are a salt-house and pottery of the fine potter's clay found near Carrickfergus."

The following paragraph refers to an article called sulphate of barytes, which was largely employed by Josiah Wedgwood in the manufacture of his beautiful jasper ware. Let us hope that this material will be put to a more legitimate use than adulterating the staff of life. It is taken from the *Times* of February 1856:—

" IRISH EXPORTS.—The Cork papers give a timely notice respecting a lucrative but not very creditable trade that has recently sprung up near Bailydehob in that country. It consists in the exportation of large quantities of material called barytes, which is sent to Liverpool for the purpose, it is said, of adulterating flour. This substance—chemically termed sulphate of barytes—is admirably adapted for the adulteration of flour, being an impalpable powder, of perfect whiteness and great density, its weight being nearly equal to that of lead. It is not poisonous, but, being quite indigestible, its effects on the animal economy must be prejudicial if taken in large quantities. Some of it is used for a more laudable purpose—the manufacture of earthenware, for which, in conjunction with other clays of a silicious character, it is well adapted. Manganese is also said to be exported to England to some extent, for the purpose of adulterating black-lead."

LIMERICK. Two rare delft ware plates inscribed "Made by John Stritch, Limerick, 4 June 1761" are illustrated by W. B. Honey in a paper in the *Transactions of the English Ceramic Circle*, vol. 2, no. 8. One of them is illustrated in Godden's *British Pottery and Porcelain, an Illustrated Encyclopædia of Marked Specimens*. In 1762 the Dublin Society awarded a premium of £30 to John Stritch and Christopher Bridson of Limerick " for erecting a manufactory in imitation of delft or white ware."

PORTADOWN (Co. ARMAGH). Since 1953 a new " Irish Porcelain " has been introduced. This ware (a heavy, vitreous porcelain) is produced by Wade (Ulster) Ltd., one of the Wade group, at their Ulster Pottery, Portadown. The designs are simple and attractive. Most pieces are turned on the wheel and have impressed designs which are accentuated by the coloured glazes.

Mark no. 5, impressed, c. 1953+. Mark no. 6, impressed, from October, 1953. " Made in Ireland " added in April, 1954. The " E " is the turner's personal mark. Mark no. 7, printed, from 1954. Die-pressing was introduced about 1956 and such pieces bear an embossed mark no. 8. The " R " is the potter's mark.

ARKLOW POTTERY (ARKLOW, EIRE). The Arklow Pottery Ltd. was established in May, 1935, for the manufacture of domestic earthenware. The various marks include the word ARKLOW or the initials A.P.

SCOTLAND

It would appear that up to 1703 there was not such a thing in Scotland as a pot-work for making earthenware, a want which, of course, occasioned the yearly export of large sums of money out of the kingdom, besides causing all articles of that kind to be sold at double charges to what they cost abroad. William Montgomery of Macbie Hill, and George Linn, merchant in Edinburgh, now made arrangements for setting up a pot-house and all conveniences for making of " laim, purslane," and earthenware, and for bringing in from foreign countries the men required for such a work. As necessary for their encouragement in this undertaking, the Parliament gave them an exclusive right of making laim, purslane, and earthenware for fifteen years.—From Chambers' *Domestic Annals of Scotland;* quoted from *Acts of Scot. Parl.* xi, 3.

In the *London Chronicle* of 1755 we read: " Yesterday four persons well skilled in the making British china were engaged for Scotland, where a new porcelain manufactory is going to be established in the manner of that now carried on at Chelsea, Stratford, and Bow." The date 1755 would seem to be incorrect as the *London Chronicle* did not commence publication until January 1757.

In newspapers of 25th to 27th December, 1764, is a similar intimation: " We hear from Edinburgh that some gentlemen are about to establish a porcelain manufacture in Scotland, and have already wrote up to London to engage proper persons to carry it on."

A further press notice in *St. James's Chronicle*, 10th to 12th September, 1767, reads " Five ingenious mechanics, well skilled in the making of British china, have this week been engaged to Scotland, where a new porcelain manufacture is to be established, in the manner of those at Bow and Chelsea."

It would seem likely that these notices refer to a manufactory (or decorating establishment) set up by William Littler (formerly of the Longton Hall factory) at West Pans, near Musselburgh, in or before 1764. A most interesting receipt, with heading, was discovered by Mr. W. A. Coleridge (of Messrs Knight, Frank & Rutley) at Blair Castle, Perthshire, the seat of the Duke of Atholl and is given here in full:—

Address. " To His Grace The Duke of Atholl at Dunkeld."

Printed   " Bought of Willm. Littler
heading.   CHINA MAKER at West Pans, near Musselburgh
                  in Scotland.
     Where is made all kinds of Usefull and Ornamental China
     Particularly Very Fine Mazareen and Gold Enamel'd China
     Also all kinds of Stone Ware, such as fine Gilded and Japand
     Black and Tortoise Shell Ware etc. . . . ."

Receipt   " His Grace the Duke of Atholl
           1766

		£	s.	d.
To two large Cabbage Leaves fine Mazareen & gold china		2	0	0
Six Pansey Leaves Do....Do....at 9s			2 14	0
a Butter Tub & Stand – – – – – –			1 1	0
2 Doz^n Desart plates at 2.15.0 per D			5 10	0
For the additional work or Expence of ye Crest				
on Each piece of ware – – – – – – – – –			0 18	0
Box containing ye Goods – – – – – –			0 1	6
	Tot. £12	4	6	

Received payment of the Above acct.
by the hand of Mr. Mackenzey—Wm. Littler

My Lord,
    I deliver'd the Same Acct. as Above along with the China to
Mr. MacKenzey in Edenburgh Accordingly as your Grace Left
Directions—and he paid the Acct. I am extreamly happy that the
China has mett with your grace's approbation. I am now at Perth with
a great Assortment of China to Dispose of and my wife sent your Lre
here to me—on which I have immediately Sent your grace the Acct.
and have made bould to Send a Hand Bill—I am—Your Graces
               most Obediently dutifull
                  Servt—Wm Littler
Perth 8th. Oct°—1766 "

    The importance of this document was realised by both Mr. Coleridge
and Mr. E. A. Lane, the Keeper of the Department of Ceramics at the
Victoria and Albert Museum, to whom it was shown. Mr. Lane read a
paper to the English Ceramic Circle based on the discovery of this receipt
and showed various specimens that can now be attributed to Little.'s work
at West Pans. The reader is referred to Mr. Lane's paper printed in
Vol. 5, part 2 of the *Transactions of the English Ceramic Circle*, from which
the following conclusions may be drawn:--
    William Littler was at West Pans in 1764, for on 30th October, 1764

" Mr. Wm. Littler China Manufactorer at West Pans " was made an Honorary Burgess of Musselburgh. His connection with the Longton Hall factory would have ceased in 1760.

Dated examples so far attributed to West Pans include two of 1770 giving a *minimum* period of six years for Littler's Scottish venture. Little is known of his subsequent life, apart from the fact that he died in 1784 at the age of 55, at Burslem, Staffordshire.

Although references are made in the heading here quoted and in the Roll of Honorary Burgesses to " China Maker " and " China Manufactorer " there is no evidence that any wares were *manufactured* by Littler at West Pans. All the examples so far discovered would appear to be salvaged Longton Hall pieces (c. 1750–55), slightly embellished with initials, crests, etc. to special orders. Nevertheless this recent addition to ceramic knowledge is most welcome and may lead to fresh information, or further research on this aspect of Scottish ceramic history.

According to information supplied by Dr. Bernard Watney, a pottery was at West Pans before Littler arrived, because the town council enacted on 10th January, 1754, that Samuel Lambas, potter at West Pans, should pay one pound sterling for clay from Martinmas last to Martinmas next. Littler may well have used the existing pottery in the 1760's.

PORTOBELLO, near Edinburgh. The name SCOTT BROTHERS is found on earthenware dinner and dessert services attributed to the Portobello factory. Examples are usually decorated with yellow designs, leaves, etc., on a chocolate ground, mark no. 9 impressed; also mark no. 10, c. 1786–96. They also made figures, including that of a Scottish fishwife, well modelled of Portobello pottery. N.B.—The name Scott also occurs on pottery made at the Southwick Pottery, Sunderland, and some so-called Scott Bros. chocolate ground Portobello pottery was probably made at Sunderland. The period of many of these pieces is nineteenth not eighteenth century.

BELL. In the International Exhibition of 1851 we find as exhibitors the firm " J. & M. P. Bell & Co., Glasgow, stoneware, porcelain and parian." This firm was established about 1842 and was carried on until about 1928. The standard mark was a bell. Various printed marks also occur with the initials J. & M. P. B. & Co. Porcelain and parian as well as all classes of earthenware were produced in the mid-nineteenth century.

PRESTONPANS. In the early part of the nineteenth century, FOWLER, THOMPSON & Co. had extensive trade with Holland. An earthenware punch-bowl, partly printed in dark blue, with a floral and Greek fret border, and painted with groups of flowers in colours, was painted by Mr. Greig, an employee of the factory, and presented to his sister on her marriage, and marked with her initials, H. T., 22nd June, 1811. Formerly in the possession of Lieut.-Colonel Green, who obtained it from the old lady, living at Stirling. Mark no. 11.

GLASGOW. There were several manufacturers of stoneware here. A butter-boat of white stoneware, good glaze, with three ears of corn in relief has the mark underneath in black " Warranted Stone China,

SCOTT
BROTHERS.

9

SCOTT
PB

10

Fowler Thompson
& Co.

11

R. Cochran & Co.
Glasgow.

12

13

R. Cochran & Co., Glasgow," the royal arms above. Mark no. 12.

Cochran's Verreville Pottery was continued to about 1918. Cochran & Fleming worked the Britannia Pottery, St. Rollox, Glasgow, from about 1857 to 1921. The marks were a representation of the seated Britannia, or the name " Cochran & Fleming." Subsequently this factory was worked by the Britannia Pottery Co. Ltd. until 1935, mark no. 13.

DUNMORE. A manufacture of pottery was established here by Peter Gardner in 1875. Within a few years a great advance was made in the quality of the articles produced. In addition to the brown glazed ware, the proprietor succeeded in obtaining various tints of green and blue, similar to that of Minton, at prices much more reasonable, and flower-baskets, rustic tea-sets, and some elegant forms for vases, furnished by the Countess of Dunmore. It was on the Earl's estate, close to the Airth railway station. From about 1903 the firm was entitled THE DUNMORE POTTERY CO. This firm ceased about 1911. The impressed mark DUNMORE has been recorded.

For full details of the many Scottish potteries, the reader is referred to Fleming's *Scottish Pottery*, 1923.

REGISTRATION MARKS

Many nineteenth century objects are found bearing a diamond shaped stamp. The purpose of this mark was to show that the design (or shape) had been registered with the Patent Office in London and was thereby protected from piracy for an initial period of three years. By using the following chart, the earliest possible date of manufacture can be ascertained.

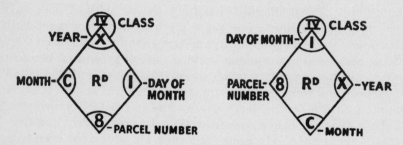

Above are the two patterns of Design Registration Marks that were in current use between the years 1842 and 1883. Keys to "year" and "month" code-letters are given below.

The left-hand diamond was used during the years 1842 to 1867. A change was made in 1868, when the right-hand diamond was adopted.

INDEX TO YEAR AND MONTH LETTERS

1842–67
Year Letter at Top

A = 1845	H = 1843	O = 1862	V = 1850
B = 1858	I = 1846	P = 1851	W = 1865
C = 1844	J = 1854	Q = 1866	X = 1842
D = 1852	K = 1857	R = 1861	Y = 1853
E = 1855	L = 1856	S = 1849	Z = 1860
F = 1847	M = 1859	T = 1867	
G = 1863	N = 1864	U = 1848	

1868–83
Year Letter at Right

MONTHS (BOTH PERIODS)

A	=	1871		A	=	December
C	=	1870		B	=	October
D	=	1878		C or O		January
E	=	1881		D	=	September
F	=	1873		E	=	May
H	=	1869		G	=	February
I	=	1872		H	=	April
J	=	1880		I	=	July
K	=	1883		K	=	November (and
L	=	1882				December 1860)
P	=	1877		M	=	June
S	=	1875		R	=	August (and
U	=	1874				September
V	=	1876				1st–19th 1857)
W	=	(Mar. 1–6)		W	=	March
		1878				
X	=	1868				
Y	=	1879				

From 1884 a simple numerical system was used. The following list gives the registered number for the January of each year from 1884 to 1901 and will show in which year a design was registered.

1884	1	1890	141,273	1896	268,392
1885	19,754	1891	163,767	1897	291,241
1886	40,480	1892	185,713	1898	311,658
1887	64,520	1893	205,240	1899	331,707
1888	90,483	1894	224,720	1900	351,202
1889	116,648	1895	246,975	1901	368,154

The numbers were usually printed under the factory mark and may be prefixed " R^d No."

SELECTED BIBLIOGRAPHY

PRE-NINETEENTH CENTURY WARES

The Ceramic Art of Great Britain. L. Jewitt. 1878. Revised edition 1883.
The Art of the Old English Potter. M. L. Solon. 1883.
A History and Description of English Porcelain. W. Burton. 1902.
English Earthenware and Stoneware. W. Burton. 1904.
Staffordshire Pots and Potters. G. W. & F. A. Rhead. 1906.
The Makers of Black Basaltes. M. H. Grant. 1910.
English Earthenware. A. H. Church. 1911.
The Wood Family of Burslem. F. Falkner. 1912.
Yorkshire Potteries, Pots and Potters. O. Grabham. 1916.
The A.B.C. of English Saltglaze Stoneware. J. F. Blacker. 1922.
Saltglaze with notes of a Collector. C. F. C. Luxmore. 1924.
Guide to Collectors of Pottery and Porcelain. F. Litchfield. 1925.
English Porcelain Figures of the Eighteenth Century. W. King. 1925.
The New Keramic Gallery. W. Chaffers (edited by H. M. Cundall). 1926.
Old English Porcelain. W. B. Honey. 1928. (New edition 1948.)
Catalogue of the Schreiber Collection. Vol. I and II (V. and A.). 1929.
English Pottery and Porcelain. W. B. Honey. 1933, 5th edition 1962.
English Blue and White Porcelain of the Eighteenth Century. S. W. Fisher. 1947.
English Pottery Figures, 1660–1860. R. G. Haggar. 1947.
English Delftware. F. H. Garner. 1948.
English Country Pottery. R. G. Haggar. 1950.
Old English Lustre Pottery. W. D. John. 1951.
Eighteenth Century English Porcelain. G. Savage. 1952.
Staffordshire Chimney Ornaments. R. G. Haggar. 1955.
English Porcelain and Bone China, 1743–1850. G. & T. Hughes. 1955.
The Concise Encyclopædia of English Pottery and Porcelain. R. G. Haggar & W. Mankowitz. 1957.
English Cream-coloured Earthenware. D. Towner. 1957.
British Pottery and Porcelain, an Illustrated Encyclopædia of Marked Specimens. G. A. Godden. In preparation.

NINETEENTH AND TWENTIETH CENTURY WARES

The Ceramic Art of Great Britain. L. Jewitt. 1878. Revised edition 1883.
Staffordshire Pots and Potters. G. W. & F. A. Rhead. 1906.
The A.B.C. of Nineteenth Century Pottery and Porcelain. J. F. Blacker.
    n.d. (c. 1911).
Yorkshire Potteries, Pots and Potters. O. Grabham. 1916.
The A.B.C. of English Saltglaze Stoneware. J. F. Blacker. 1922.
The Cheyne Book of Chelsea Porcelain. Edited by R. Blunt. 1924.
Twentieth Century Ceramics. G. M. Forsyth. 1936.
Catalogue of the Collection of Martinware formed by Mr. Frederick John
    Nettlefold. C. R. Beard. 1936.
The Modern Potter. R. Cooper. 1947.
English Country Pottery. R. G. Haggar. 1950.
The Work of the Modern Potter in England. G. W. Digby. 1952.
Nineteenth Century English Pottery and Porcelain. G. Bemrose. 1952.
Victorian and Edwardian Decorative Arts. Catalogue of V. and A. Ex-
    hibition. 1952.
Artist-Potters in England. M. Rose. 1955.
Staffordshire Chimney Ornaments. R. G. Haggar. 1955.
English Porcelain and Bone China, 1743–1850. G. & T. Hughes. 1955.
British Potters and Pottery Today. C. G. E. Bunt. 1956.
Staffordshire Portrait Figures of the Victorian Age. T. Balston. 1958.
Victorian Pottery and Porcelain. G. B. Hughes. 1959.
Victorian Porcelain. G. A. Godden. 1961.
Victorian Pottery. H. Wakefield. 1962.
British Pottery and Porcelain, 1780–1850. G. A. Godden. 1963.
British Pottery and Porcelain, an Illustrated Encyclopædia of Marked
    Specimens. G. A. Godden. In preparation.

ADAMS

William Adams, an old English Potter. W. Turner. 1904.
The Adams Family. P. W. L. Adams. 1914.
A Pride of Potters. D. Peel. 1959.

BOW

Bow Porcelain. F. Hurlbutt. 1926.
Bow Porcelain, 1744–1776. British Museum Exhibition Catalogue. Com-
    piled by H. Tait. 1959.
See also articles by H. Tait in " Apollo " magazine, Feb., April, June and
    October, 1960.
English Porcelain Figures of the Eighteenth Century. A. Lane. 1961.

BRISTOL

Two Centuries of Ceramic Art in Bristol. H. Owen. 1873.
The Old Bristol Potteries. W. J. Pountney. 1920.
Bristol Porcelain. F. Hurlbutt. 1928.
Champion's Bristol Porcelain. F. S. MacKenna. 1947.
English Porcelain Figures of the Eighteenth Century. A. Lane. 1961.

CHELSEA

Chelsea Porcelain. W. King. 1922.
The Cheyne Book of Chelsea Porcelain. Edited by R. Blunt. 1924.
Chelsea Porcelain Toys. G. F. Bryant. 1925.
Chelsea Porcelain, The Triangle and Raised Anchor Wares. F. S. MacKenna. 1948.
Chelsea Porcelain, The Red Anchor Wares. F. S. MacKenna. 1951.
Chelsea Porcelain, The Gold Anchor Wares. F. S. MacKenna. 1952.
Chelsea and other English Porcelain Pottery and Enamel in the Irwin Untermyer Collection. Y. Hackenbroch. 1957.
English Porcelain Figures of the Eighteenth Century. A Lane. 1961.

COALPORT

A History of the Coalport Porcelain Works. L. Jewitt (reprinted from " Art Journal "). 1862.
Caughley and Coalport Porcelain. F. A. Barrett. 1955.
Victorian Porcelain. G. A. Godden. 1961.

COPELAND

Spode and his Successors. A. Hayden. 1924.
Victorian Porcelain. G. A. Godden. 1961.

DERBY

The Old Derby China Factory. J. Haslem. 1876.
Old Derby Porcelain and its Artist-Workmen. F. Hurlbutt. 1925.
The Derby Pot Manufactory known as Cockpit Hill. F. Williamson. 1931. (See also The Transactions of the English Ceramic Circle. Vol. III, part IV.)
Crown Derby Porcelain. F. B. Gilhespy. 1951.
Derby Porcelain. F. B. Gilhespy. 1961.
Victorian Porcelain. G. A. Godden. 1961.
English Porcelain Figures of the Eighteenth Century. A. Lane. 1961.

LEEDS

Historical Notices of the Leeds Old Pottery. J. R. & F. Kidson. 1892.
A Catalogue of the Boynton Collection of Yorkshire Pottery. A. Hurst. 1922.

Handbook of Leeds Pottery. D. Towner. 1951.
The Leeds Pottery. D. Towner. 1963.

LIVERPOOL

The Liverpool Potteries. C. T. Gatty. 1882.
History of the Art of Pottery in Liverpool. J. Mayer. 1885.
Catalogue of Liverpool Pottery and Porcelain. P. Entwistle. 1907.
Liverpool and her Potters. H. Boswell Lancaster. 1936.

LONGTON HALL

Longton Hall Porcelain. B. Watney. 1957.

LOWESTOFT

Lowestoft China Factory. H. C. Casley. (Proceedings of the Suffolk
    Institute of Archeology and Natural History. Vol. XI, part 3.) 1903.
Lowestoft China. W. W. R. Spelman. 1905.
Lowestoft China Factory. F. A. Crisp. 1907.
Inscribed and Dated Lowestoft Porcelain. A. J. B. Kiddell. (English
    Porcelain Circle Transactions No. III.) 1931.
Early Lowestoft. D. M. Hunting. (Transactions of the English Ceramic
    Circle. Vol. 3, part I.) 1951.
Lowestoft Figures. G. A. Godden. The Connoisseur Year Book. 1957.

MINTON

The Ceramic Art of Great Britain. L. Jewitt. 1878. Revised Edition 1883.
The A.B.C. of Nineteenth Century Pottery and Porcelain. J. F. Blacker.
    n.d. (c. 1911).
Victorian Porcelain. G. A. Godden. 1961.

NANTGARW

The Ceramics of Swansea and Nantgarw. W. Turner. 1897.
The Pottery and Porcelain of Swansea and Nantgarw. E. M. Nance. 1942.
Nantgarw Porcelain. W. D. John. 1948.

NEW HALL

New Hall Porcelain. G. E. Stringer. 1949.

PLYMOUTH

Cookworthy's Plymouth and Bristol Porcelain. F. S. MacKenna. 1946.

SWANSEA

The Ceramics of Swansea and Nantgarw. W. Turner. 1897.
The Pottery and Porcelain of Swansea and Nantgarw. E. M. Nance. 1942.

SPODE

Old Spode. T. G. Cannon. n.d.

Spode and his Successors. A. Hayden. 1924. (See also under Copeland.)

SUNDERLAND

Potteries of Sunderland and District. Edited by J. T. Shaw. Revised edition, 1961.

WEDGWOOD

Life of Josiah Wedgwood. 2 vols. E. Meteyard. 1865–6.
Josiah Wedgwood and his Pottery. W. Burton. 1922.
Wedgwood Ware. W. B. Honey. 1948.
Wedgwood. W. Mankowitz. 1953.
Proceedings of the Wedgwood Society. Edited by G. Wills. 1956—.

WORCESTER

A Century of Potting in the City of Worcester. R. W. Binns. 1865. 2nd edition 1877.
Worcester Pottery and Porcelain, 1751–1851. R. W. Binns. 1877.
Worcester China, 1852–1897. R. W. Binns. 1897.
Worcester Porcelain. R. L. Hobson. 1910.
The Life and Work of Robert Hancock. C. Cook. 1948 (plus supplement 1955).
Worcester Porcelain. F. S. MacKenna. 1950.
Worcester Porcelain. F. A. Barrett. 1953.
Coloured Worcester Porcelain of the First Period. H. Rissik Marshall. 1954.
Victorian Porcelain. G. A. Godden. 1961.

MARK BOOKS

British Pottery Marks. G. W. Rhead. 1920.
Handbook of Pottery and Porcelain Marks. J. P. Cushion & W. B. Honey. 1956.
Encyclopædia of British Pottery and Porcelain Marks. G. A. Godden. 1964.

In addition, the specialised reference books listed above, in the main, contain marks relating to their subject; i.e. Honey's *Wedgwood Ware* contains lists of marks found on Wedgwood objects, Godden's *Victorian Porcelain* contains many nineteenth century marks and information on dating.

TRANSACTIONS OF THE ENGLISH PORCELAIN (LATER CERAMIC) CIRCLE

A large proportion of recent discoveries in the field of English ceramics have been first published in the *Transactions of the English Porcelain* (later *Ceramic*) *Circle*. The main papers are listed below.

TRANSACTIONS OF THE ENGLISH PORCELAIN CIRCLE

No. 1, 1928.

Kaki-emon Designs. W. W. Winkworth.
The Earliest References to Chelsea Porcelain. B. Gardner.
Caughley Porcelain before 1772. A. Hurst.
Sources of Underglaze Blue Decoration. F. C. Dykes.

No. 2, 1929.

Soft-paste Bristol Porcelain—Lowdin's, etc. W. Elliot.
An Early Allusion to English Porcelain, Gouyn's Will, and Some Chelsea
    Models. B. Gardner.
Liverpool Porcelain. B. Rackham & W. B. Honey.
The Early Work of Planché (at Derby) and Duesbury. D. MacAlister.
Life and Work of William Billingsley. W. Tapp.

No. 3, 1931.

Inscribed and Dated Lowestoft Porcelain. A. J. B. Kiddell.
Chelsea Bird Models. B. Gardner.
Caughley Porcelain. R. L. Hobson.
Excavations at Chelsea. A. J. Toppin.
Limehouse China Factory. A. J. Toppin.
A Longton Hall Advertisement. A. J. B. Kiddell.
Inscribed Longton Hall Mugs. D. MacAlister.
Inscribed and Dated " Scratch-Cross " Pieces. H. E. Rhodes.
The Derby Pattern Books and Billingsley's Work. W. H. Tapp.

No. 4, 1932.

Cross-currents in English Porcelain, Glass and Enamels. H. Rhead.
A Chelsea Figure of Aesop. B. Gardner.
Sir Hans Sloane's Plants on Chelsea Porcelain. B. Gardner.
Porcelain as a Sidelight on Battersea Enamels. B. Rackham.
Notes on Janssen and the Artists at the Battersea Factory. A. J. Toppin.
Supplementary Notes on the Battersea Factory. B. Rackham.
John and Robert Brewer, the Derby Painters. W. H. Tapp.
A Bristol Advertisement of Worcester China. J. Calder.

TRANSACTIONS OF THE ENGLISH CERAMIC CIRCLE

Vol. I, no. 1, 1933.

Chelsea Chronology. W. King.
English Saltglazed Stoneware. W. B. Honey.

Bristol Biscuit Plaques. W. Elliot.
The Kentish Town China Factory; James Giles, Enameller; Nicholas
    Crisp, Jeweller and Potter. A. J. Toppin.
Early Staffordshire China. D. MacAlister.
Three Advertisements regarding the Longton Hall Factory. A. J. B.
    Kiddell.

Vol. I, no. 2, 1934.

Elers Ware. W. B. Honey.
Bristol Delftware. G. Mellor.
Worcester Porcelain Figures. W. Elliot.
Robert Hancock and his Sons. A. J. Toppin.

Vol. I, no. 3, 1935.

Lambeth Delft. G. E. Howard.
Chelsea—The Triangle Period. O. Glendenning and D. MacAlister.
The China Trade and some London Chinamen. A. J. Toppin.
Staffordshire Slip Ware. B. Rackham.
Early Polychrome Transfer on Porcelain (Liverpool). N. Neild.
Soaprock Licences. E. M. Nance.
Robert Hancock's Connection with Battersea and Bow. H. W. Hughes.

Vol. I, no. 4, 1937.

Blue Dash Chargers (English delft). R. H. Warren.
English China Collectors of the Past. H. B. Gardner.
Ceramic Construction (Chemical Analysis of Pastes, etc.). A. Hurst.
Lambeth Earthenware (delft type wares). F. H. Garner.
A Bow Porcelain Note-book. L. Ashton.
The Chelsea Fable Painter. W. H. Tapp.

Vol. I, no. 5, 1937.

The Work of James Giles. W. B. Honey.
Some Remarks on Claret Colour. A. H. S. Bunford.
John Dwight (of Fulham), some Contemporary References. F. H. Garner.
Rous & Cullen (of London), Merchants and Potters. A. J. Toppin.
Some Unusual Worcester Pieces. B. Rackham.

Vol. II, no. 6, 1939.

The Trend in English Ceramics. W. W. Winkworth.
Early Tudor Pottery. B. Rackham.
Silvershape in English Porcelain. H. B. Gardner.
Notes on English Salt-Glaze Brown Stoneware. J. Drinkwater.
Further Notes on John Dwight. A. Esdaile.
Thomas Hughes, Enameller, of Clerkenwell. W. H. Tapp.

Vol. II, no. 7, 1939.

Reproductions and Fakes of English Eighteenth Century Ceramics.
  W. Elliot.
The Relations between English and Continental Porcelain. W. B. Honey.
The Virtues of English Pottery. B. Rackham.
Richard Powles, Lowestoft Painter. A. J. B. Kiddell.
Recent Excavations in Bristol. H. W. Maxwell.

Vol. II, no. 8, 1942.

John Wall and the Worcester Porcelain Company. C. W. D. Perrins.
Further History of the Chelsea Porcelain Manufactory. B. Gardner.
A Dated Stoneware Mug. B. Rackham.
Chitqua, The Chinese Modeller, and Wang-y-Tong, The Chinese Boy.
  A. J. Toppin.
Early English (" Girl in the Swing " type) Figures—A Check List. W. A. H.
  King and O. Glendenning.
Limerick Delftware. W. B. Honey.
The Will of Henry Delamain, the Dublin Potter. A. J. Toppin.

Vol. II, no. 9, 1946.

Excavations of 9 Church Street, Chelsea. H. B. Gardner.
Battersea, Ceramic and Kindred Associations. A. J. Toppin.
London Pottery Sites. F. H. Garner.
Armorial Worcester of the First Period. H. R. Marshall.
The Artistic Content of Cookworthy's and Champion's Porcelain. F. S.
  Mackenna.
Notes on Cheam Pottery. G. C. Dunning.

Vol. II, no. 10, 1948.

Fallacies and Mistaken Attributions in English Ceramic Studies. W. B.
  Honey.
Lambeth, Bristol or Liverpool (delftware). F. H. Garner.
Caricature in English Pottery. B. Rackham.
The Origin of some Ceramic Designs. A. J. Toppin.

Vol. III, part 1, 1951.

James Giles, Enameller. H. R. Marshall.
Wedgwood Reconsidered. B. Rackham.
Nineteenth-Century English Ceramics. G. J. V. Bemrose.
The Art of Robert Hancock. C. Cook.
A Ceramic Miscellany—Francis Place, the early Yorkshire Potter; Hold-
  ship's Transfer-Printing at Derby; The Ranelagh Figures. A. J.
  Toppin.
Early Lowestoft. D. M. Hunting.

Notes on the Origins of Worcester Decoration. H. R. Marshall.
Outstanding Pieces in the English Ceramic Collection of the British
  Museum. G. H. Tait.

Vol. IV, part 4, 1959.

David Rhodes, Enameller (of Leeds and London). D. Towner.
William Hopkins Craft, Enamel Painter. A. J. Toppin.
The English Ceramic Collections in the Victoria and Albert Museum.
  A. Lane.

Vol. IV, part 5, 1959.

Some Groups of English Redware (Elers type earthenware). R. Price.
References to John Dwight in a Seventeenth Century Manuscript.
  M. Bimson.
Four Groups of Porcelain, possibly Liverpool, Parts 1 and 2. B. Watney.
The Derby China Factory Sites on Nottingham Road. F. Barrett.
French Influences at Chelsea. T. H. Clarke.
Bernard Palissy and Lambeth Delft. B. Rackham.

Vol. V, part 1, 1960.

English Delftware in the Pharmaceutical Society's Collection. A. Lothian.
Jean Voyez. R. J. Charleston.
Four Groups of Porcelain, possibly Liverpool, Parts 3 and 4. B. Watney.
William Absolon, Junior, of Great Yarmouth. A. J. B. Kiddell.

Vol. V, part 2, 1961.

Liverpool Delftware. F. H. Garner.
William Littler and West Pans, Scotland. A. Lane.
John Dwight. M. Bimson.
Worcester Finds in recent Excavations at Worcester. C. Shingler.
A Historical Survey (Transfer-prints). G. W. Capell.

Vol. V, part 3, 1962.

Girl-in-the-Swing and Chelsea. A. Lane and R. J. Charleston.
The discovery of a new Pottery in Derbyshire—Furnace Farm Pottery,
  Melbourne. F. Barrett and A. L. Thorpe.
Some Groups of English Redware of the mid Eighteenth Century, part 2.
  R. Price.
John Platt of Rotherham, Potter and Mason-Architect. A. J. B. Kiddell.
Some Advertisements of Ceramic Interest. F. E. Burrell.

Vol. V, part 4, 1963.

William Greatbatch and the early Wedgwood Wares. D. Towner.
The Bow Factory under Alderman Arnold and Thomas Frye. H. Tait.

NOTES ON THE AUCTION PRICES
OF CERAMICS

Period 1900–1912
By Frederick Litchfield

As the result of a fairly constant attendance at Messrs. Christie's rooms during a long experience, one may record the comforting reflection for the collector, that there is a gradual and certain appreciation in the value of genuine specimens of the old ceramic factories. Prices vary very considerably according to the *circumstances* of the sale, the name and reputation of the vendor collector, the support by friends and acquaintances who have known and appreciated the particular collection which is to be dispersed, and, above all, the *certainty* that the sale by auction is *bona fide*. When these factors have been taken into account the fact remains that, if we compare the average results with those of ten or even five years ago, there is a steady increase in value. When a dealer's stock of china is sold by auction there is always a suspicion that reserves have been given to the auctioneer, or that some one in the room is present to bid on behalf of the vendor, and the sale will therefore be comparatively a poor one; there will be a lack of spirit in the bidding, and the auctioneer's hammer will be critically and suspiciously watched by the members of the trade. These remarks also apply to the sale of the collection of an owner who is living, and who is likely to take means to protect his sale from the sacrifice incidental to auctions. As an instance of this, it is well known that when the owner is deceased or bankrupt, and the sale takes place on instructions of executors or the official receiver, there is generally a good attendance of the trade, and, although in individual instances there must be bargains for the shrewd and careful buyer, the result may be relied upon for an average of good prices.

Another important influence upon the result of a sale is the fact that the specimens are *fresh*—that is, have not been sold either publicly or privately quite recently. The "trade," who are the real support of the saleroom, prefer to buy specimens which have been in the possession of a private collector for many years previous to their sale by auction, and if there be positive proof of the *bona fides* of such a sale, and the quality of the collection be up to a high standard, then we may be sure that in the hands of a capable auctioneer, the prices realised will rule very high, although the number of buyers is necessarily limited, as must be the case where large sums are given for such *articles de luxe* as specimens of old china. During the year 1907, the sale of the collection of a well-known gentleman took place at Christie's, and an enormous assemblage of works of art, including a great deal of fine Porcelain, were disposed of under the hammer on three separate occasions. The Hon. Mr. Massey-Mainwaring was known to be a good judge, his treasures were sold by order of the trustees, and he died during the progress of the auction. Therefore one would have thought that, the different conditions which I have named being fulfilled, the prices realised should be as high as the quality of the specimens offered would justify. There was, however, one very important reason for the absence of spirited bidding on the part of several of the prominent dealers, in the fact that these specimens were known to have been offered for sale during the owner's lifetime. In some cases they had been placed with one or more dealers for sale on commission, or they had been the subject of more or less recent transactions by way of exchange or barter. They were *not fresh* from the cabinet of a *bona fide* collector, who had bought and kept them for his own pleasure, and the general knowledge by the trade of these circumstances militated against the successful result of the sale, from the vendor's point of view.

It was consequently a great opportunity for the shrewd collector to buy good specimens at moderate prices. In the list of prices quoted from sale catalogues, which follows these pages, the reader will notice, on the list of Worcester specimens, a pair of important hexagonal-shaped vases and covers decorated with exotic birds and flowers on salmon-scale blue ground. These vases cost Mr. Mainwaring, a few years earlier, nearly £700, and at his sale, on April 11, 1907, they realised £535, 10s. They are magnificent specimens of their class and very nearly perfect, and yet, although fine old Worcester of this description has risen in value during the last few years, the price of these vases was influenced by the circumstances to which I have referred. Another reason for poor prices being realised in the Massey-Mainwaring sale was, that, instead of devoting his collecting energies to some particular kind of Pottery or Porcelain, or of Furniture, Bronzes, or Paintings, he was an omnivorous buyer of every sort and kind, good, bad, and indifferent. The result of this promiscuous collecting was that although the catalogue included some fine specimens, such as the Worcester vases noticed above, there was no important quantity of any particular kind of Porcelain to attract a large number of specialists. And this remark brings me to the mention of another point in these notes on sale prices, and that is the advantage of a *special* as opposed to a miscellaneous collection of china. One might naturally think that a great many examples of the same class would cause a glut in the market and therefore a slump in price, but the experience of those who constantly attend sales has proved that this is not the case. "The more the merrier" is a proverbial saying which seems to apply to accumulations of almost any description of valuable old pottery or porcelain. When a few specimens only of any particular kind are included in a general collection of heterogeneous classes, say of Majolica, good, bad, and indifferent; English china, represented by Bow, Chelsea, Derby, and other eighteenth-century factories; Sèvres, and other French porcelains; continental fabrics, such as Dresden, Berlin, Vienna, and so on—such a collection will not realise to so much advantage as a really valuable one of either Majolica, English, Sèvres, or continental porcelain *sui generis*.

One of the reasons for this is, probably, that in the former case there will not be a sufficient number of lots of any particular kind to attract from long distances the best buyers of that description of ware.

There was a notable instance of this when the sale of the celebrated Narford Hall Collection of Majolica took place at Christie's. This important collection of so many of the best productions of the fifteenth century Italian *botegas*, brought over to England the chief continental dealers and many distinguished amateurs, and the result was a list of sensational prices, which, however, would to-day be considerably increased if the collection as such could be resold.

Again, when the Hawkins Collection was sold by Christie's in 1904, including two whole days devoted to the sale of Sèvres porcelain, a precious and costly commodity that one would think only the privileged few could afford to buy, yet there was no falling off in price. The French and German dealers came to compete with their English *confrères*, and one saw no diminution in price of good Sèvres porcelain.

The sale of the Trapnell Collection of Worcester china in 1902, which lasted three days and comprised some five hundred lots and nearly two thousand specimens, gave a similar result, and many other instances could be given.

There are some exceptions to this rule, and the one which occurs to me as noteworthy was the sale of the Cornelius Cox Collection of old Wedgwood ware, a decade and a half ago. This sale occupied four days, and took place on account of the death of the former owner, who had, until shortly before his death, been one of the most keen and liberal purchasers, both by auction on commission, and privately, from the dealers. Some of the prices realised at Christie's were considerably less than those which Mr. Cox had recently given, although since that time the same specimens have been sold for far higher prices.

The reasons for this temporary fall in the price of fine old Wedgwood jasper ware were, firstly, that the trade support was much less spirited than it would have been if a few years had elapsed since the collection had been formed. The dealers did not care to repurchase specimens which they had so recently sold, and in many cases they had given an especially high price, because they knew that in Mr. Cox they had an almost certain customer.

Another reason is that Wedgwood, unlike Majolica, Sèvres, or Dresden, has no continental market, and therefore there was no competition from the French and German collectors, and a four days' sale had to be absorbed by the rather unwilling London dealers, who had by the death of Mr. Cox lost their best client.

The general condition of business, the degrees of prosperity enjoyed by the country, also affect the sale prices, but certainly not to the extent that one would expect. Those who have attended Christie's rooms for the past twenty or thirty years have been surprised at the stability of auction prices, at times when, from the state of politics the conditions of trade and finance, or other passing circumstances, one would naturally have expected a slump, to find, on the contrary, that if the especial conditions of the particular sale were satisfactory, the prices would appear to be but slightly affected by the extraneous causes to which I have alluded.

There is another influence on sale prices which is perhaps of more predominance than any other, and that is the caprice or fashion of the time. It is quite extraordinary how small a number of rich collectors may influence the prices of specimens of old china at auction sales. The trade is so limited that a very little suffices to upset the current price of any particular kind of specimen. I have known instances in which one, two, or three

wealthy French or German amateurs have wanted a certain description of
ceramic specimen, say, the Majolica of Urbino or of Caffaggiolo, and have
purchased such as they could find in the hands of dealers in their own
country. Those foreign dealers would then repair to London and buy all
that they could find from such members of the trade as held specimens of
the kind in demand. Within a month perhaps there would be a sale at
Christie's of a good private collection, and the bidding for such specimens
as would be likely to suit the two or three foreign collectors, would be advanced by twenty or thirty per cent. In some cases the demand even of
one purchaser is sufficient to cause a large advance in price. I well remember, some twenty-five years ago, the instance of a certain nobleman
with a strong penchant for things theatrical, who began the collection of
costumed figures of old china, to gratify the whim of a certain actress whose
good favour he was anxious to enjoy. He called on several of the dealers,
and secured such "Falstaffs," "Garricks," "Othellos," "Kitty Clives," and
other costumed china figures as he could find, and asked to be offered
others which came into the market. There happened to be a sale at
Christie's a short time after this, in which an unusually large and important
figure of Richard Quinn as "Falstaff" was included—and the price which
it realised, instead of being about £15 or £20, which one would have estimated as its normal auction value, suddenly jumped to 60 guineas. Three
or four dealers were all competing on the strength of the noble lord's
request for figures of this kind.

I could give many other similar instances, from which, perhaps, the
observant reader will judge that, if he has some particular requirement, it
is well not to inform more than one dealer of the fact, or he will create a
market against himself.

A little reflection must make it apparent that where the quantity of
any particular kind of china is so restricted, as in the cases I have quoted,
it only requires a very limited amount of influence to raise the price.

The change in the fashion of decorating rooms must also affect the
demand for different kinds of old china, and these changes are reflected in
the saleroom. Within the last fifteen or twenty years collectors have been
more inclined to specialise, and instead of being buyers of all kinds of
specimens of old pottery or porcelain, they have turned more serious attention to some particular description of china. In these cases the collector
generally has more than one dealer who is in constant communication with
him as to desirable specimens, and such are either bought by the dealer on
speculation as an addition to his stock, or on commission for a client. In
such special collections very large sums of money are invested, and, as in
the majority of cases, ample funds are available for the improvement of the
collection, it must necessarily follow that if particularly fine or rare specimens are offered by public sale, there must be active competition and high
prices.

The foregoing remarks by way of explanation may serve to show the
reader that any judgment formed merely upon the perusal of a list of prices
quoted from auction catalogues, requires to be qualified by some knowledge
of the circumstances of the sale. Such extracts will serve to show the
direction of the taste of that section of the public which is interested in the
values of old china. They also serve to some extent to give the standard
prices of some of the many classes into which "Pottery and Porcelain" may

be divided from the collector's point of view, and the notes of reference to previous sales of the same or similar examples may help the amateur to estimate the value of specimens offered to him from time to time.

With regard to the change in values of the different classes of Pottery and Porcelain, I may notice the following as the result of my own observation, confirmed by the marked catalogues of the past five or six years of Christie's sales, which Mr. Albert Amor, my old friend and successor in business, has kindly placed at my disposal.

PERIOD 1921–1931
By T. P. Greig

IN reviewing the prices of old china during the past ten years (1921 to 1931) certain facts stand out very strongly.   At no time in the history of collecting have higher prices been paid in the auction room for the finest productions of the Oriental potter, dispersals such as those of the Benson, Crawford, Johnstone, Alexander and Hirsch Collections indicating that there is apparently no limit to the sums eager collectors are prepared to bid to secure choice early examples.

The long-popular "blue and white" has, it is true, for the time gone **out** of favour, but *famille verte*, *famille rose* and *famille noire* especially have never sold for higher prices, the delightful whole-coloured varieties are increasingly popular, while there is a steadily growing demand for early Chinese pottery of the Sung and other periods.

Continental porcelain, on the other hand, has temporarily called a halt.   Unique and outstanding pieces will still realise high figures, but, on the whole, the excessive sums readily paid for old Sèvres and Dresden porcelain twenty or thirty years ago are now rather the exception than the rule.   When fine Sèvres appears in the London saleroom it is the French dealer who makes the bidding, and often, owing to the lack of opposition from English dealers, he is able to take it back to the country of its origin at much depreciated prices.

Some of the productions of the lesser German factories have shown a considerable increase in value during the past decade, but here again this, too, is due to foreign influence, the German dealers being the principal buyers.

Frankenthal, Fulda, Furstenburg and Hochst are all now greatly in demand, a pair of Frankenthal groups of a lady and gentleman dancing which ten or fifteen years ago might have made £100 to £150, realising over £350 in 1925.

Majolica for the most part has declined in value, and many collectors have suffered a loss when submitting their collections to the ordeal of public sale.   Exceptional pieces, of course, still sell well, such as the Castel Durante bowl in the Newcastle sale, which made 3100 guineas, and the Gubbio dish, for which £2520 was given in the same dispersal.

The recent London exhibition of Persian art was expected to give a fillip to this class of ware, but though a veritable flood of it reached the salerooms, the results on the whole must have been more than disappointing to the sellers.

The English porcelain market, however, has proved the most stable, while the sums given for rare examples of early English pottery have never been equalled.

In 1930, one witnessed the sensational sale of a Chelsea group of a Shepherd and Shepherdess realising the record sum of £3250 at auction, the bidding, however, being mainly confined to two dealers, each of whom apparently had a commission. Such a price as this is not, of course, normal, as is proved by the £580 given for a similar group shortly after this remarkable sale.

Worcester, Bow, Bristol and Plymouth have all well maintained their popularity with collectors, while the productions of less important factories, such as Spode, Davenport and Longton Hall, are in increasing demand.

The value of Swansea and Nantgarw porcelain continues to rise, partly due to the activities of wealthy Welsh collectors, plates which twenty years or so ago were making fifteen to twenty shillings, now making as many pounds.

Great strides have been made by collectors of English pottery, more especially the earlier varieties; and when one witnesses a prosaic if popular Toby Jug realising over £100 at auction, it is only too evident that collectors in this branch of ceramics are becoming more numerous and keener every day.

The early slip-ware, the productions of Whieldon and Astbury, the earlier Staffordshire figures and groups by the Woods and their contemparies, and early salt-glaze, all show a marked *appreciation*, whereas the long-popular Wedgwood shows an undoubted sign of decline in the esteem of the collector.

At the present time, of course, world-wide business depression and financial stringency are having their effect on the china market as a whole, the upheaval of the American financial market in particular affecting every phase of collecting.

There is, in fact, little doubt that the recovery will entail a long period of convalescence.

ENGLISH CERAMICS IN THE NINETEEN-SIXTIES

With the ever increasing demand for perfect specimens of English ceramics of all types, and with the constantly diminishing supply, it is only natural that prices have greatly increased. This trend is particularly noticeable in the earlier wares of each factory: triangle and raised anchor and red anchor period Chelsea is eagerly sought after but the decorative yet academically uninteresting Gold anchor pieces are out of favour today and can usually be purchased for prices less than those ruling thirty or forty years ago.

Longton Hall porcelains of all types have greatly increased in value, no doubt due to the recent research and consequent publicity given to the history and products of this hitherto rather neglected factory. Documentary inscribed and dated specimens of all wares are of the greatest interest and this is reflected in the price such specimens may be expected to realise.

The fine quality of some of our nineteenth century wares is now being appreciated and decorative examples of " Barr, Flight & Barr " and " Flight, Barr & Barr," Worcester command a high price, as do also some of the later Minton, Coalport and " Royal Worcester " wares. The fine Nantgarw and Swansea porcelains remain in favour and have continued to increase in price.

The publicity given in the national press to the high prices paid in the London salerooms should not be allowed to discourage the collector of modest means, for interesting items may still be acquired at reasonable cost. A sale held in November 1960 consisted of 153 lots of English pottery and porcelain, of which number over two-thirds were sold for under thirty pounds, and the majority of these lots contained several items.

Minor damages may be overlooked in the case of very rare, early documentary specimens, but disfiguring blemishes on the more ordinary, or purely decorative specimens, is of importance and affects the price to a great extent. An example of this is cited in the list of sale prices where a Chelsea plate of the red anchor period is listed as realising £160 but two similar plates in a damaged state were sold for £22 the two. The reader is advised to be guarded against skilful modern repairs of damaged specimens, for until the new paint gets discoloured these restorations are extremely difficult to detect.

QUOTATIONS FROM
AUCTIONEERS' CATALOGUES OF SALES
OF REPRESENTATIVE SPECIMENS OF
ENGLISH CERAMICS DURING FIFTY-FIVE YEARS

Prices from 1955 onwards are taken from Sotheby & Co.'s catalogues, and in most cases the examples were illustrated in these catalogues.

BOW

A statuette emblematic of Winter, on green and gold scroll plinth. (Formerly in Dr. Diamond's collection.) Height, 9½ ins. £21.

One figure of an actor wearing a turban. Height 7½ ins. £8 18s. 6d.

Pair of groups, lady and gentleman, playing musical instruments, richly decorated. Height, 9 ins. (From the Wallace Johnstone collection.) Christie, December 9, 1904. £34.

Pair of groups, lady and gentleman, in Eastern costume, standing in flowering bosquets. Height, 9 ins. (From the Wallace Johnstone collection.) Christie, December 9, 1904. £30.

Pair of figures, lady and gentleman, wearing Eastern costume and fur-lined cloak. Height, 7 ins. March 31, 1905. £34 13s.

Pair of figures, lady and gentleman, playing zither and drum. Height, 8 ins. March 31, 1905. £44 2s.

Four figures, "The Continents," with attributes on plinths encrusted with flowers. Height, 13½ ins. June 2, 1905. £120 15s.

Sauce-boat, painted with flower sprays in colours and with branches of fruit in low relief. (From the Walker collection.) Sotheby, June 27, 1905. £2 12s.

Vase and cover, large oviform, painted with flower sprays in colours and richly encrusted with flower branches, surmounted by a bird. (From the Walker collection.) Sotheby, June 27, 1905. £10 10s.

A set of figures emblematic of the Seasons. Height, 6½ inches. Christie, March 20, 1906. £56 14s.

A similar set of figures was sold at Sotheby's rooms, May 4, 1880, for £12.

Pair of figures, of a girl with flowers and a youth with barrel and wine cup, on plinth encrusted with flowers. Height, 7 ins. Christie, June 19, 1906. £46 4s.

Ecuelle cover and stand, painted with fruit in panels with gilt borders on dark blue ground. Christie, June 26, 1906. £152 5s.

Pair of octagonal dishes, painted with flowers and rocks in the Chinese taste. Diameter, 12 ins. Christie, November 15, 1906. £5 5s.

Pair of statuettes, Kitty Clive as "Mrs. Riot," and Woodward as the "Fine Gentleman" in Garrick's "Lethe," white. Height, 10½ ins. Christie, November 15, 1906. £77 14s.

Pair of figures, of a lady and girl, on plinths encrusted with flowers. Height, 7¼ ins. Christie, November 20, 1906. £34 3s.

One figure of a sportsman, standing in a bosquet of flowers. Height, 7 ins. (Formerly in Dr. Diamond's collection.) Christie, April 5, 1907. £8 8s.

A set of three vases and covers, encrusted with flowers and surmounted with birds. Height, 13 ins. and 10 ins. Christie, April 5, 1907. £12 12s.

Vase and two beakers, painted with insects, and encrusted with flowers. Height, 7¼ ins. and 6 ins. (Massey-Mainwaring collection.) Christie, May 9, 1907. £10 10s.

Four figures of birds, on tree stumps encrusted with flowers. Height, 5 ins. Christie, February 7, 1908. £19 19s.

A white figure of a woman, in Eastern costume. Height, 7¾ ins. Christie, February 14, 1908. £3 3s.

A figure of Flora, holding a bouquet of flowers and with a vase at her side, on green, lake, and gold scroll plinth encrusted with flowers. Height, 11¼ ins. Christie, March 19, 1908. £27 6s.

A group of a harlequin and lady, in a bosquet of flowers. Height, 9 ins. Christie, April 30, 1908. £26 5s.

Pair of figures of a lady and gentleman playing the bagpipes, on green, lake, and gold scroll plinths. Height, 9¼ ins. Christie, May 28, 1908. £86 2s.

A group, 15 ins. high, of Venus and Mars standing in front of a bower of trees. London Curio Club, November 15, 1909. £63.

Pair of figures of a girl and youth, with birdcage and nests. Height, 7¼ ins. Christie, February 2, 1911. £17 6s. 6d.

Group of a boy and girl playing musical instruments, with branches of flowers at back. Height, 9 ins. Christie, March 15, 1921. £52 10s.

A pair of figures of sportsman and lady, standing in flowering arbours, on pink, turquoise and gold scroll plinths. Height, 10 ins. Christie, May 9, 1922. £75 12s.

Group of a groom and horse, with branches of flowers at the back, on green and gold scroll plinth. Height, 7¼ ins. Christie, May 7, 1922. £178 10s.

A cream-jug, modelled with the goat and bee and flower sprays in relief, and painted in colour. Height, 4¼ ins. Christie, June 22, 1922. £60 18s.

Another slightly larger made £84.

A figure of General John Manners, in the uniform of a Colonel of the Horse Guards, with military trophies at his feet, on lake plinth. Height, 14 ins. Christie, February 25, 1926. £183 15s.

A figure of General Wolfe, in uniform, on scroll plinth, painted with flowers—impressed mark " To." Height, 13 ins. Christie, February 25, 1926. £210.

A pair of groups of Chinese figures, with monkeys standing in flowering arbours. Height, 9 ins. Christie, February 25, 1926. £99 15s.

A set of four vases and covers, and a pair of beakers, painted with birds on mottled dark blue ground, with lake and gold scroll work round the centres. Height, 13 ins. and 18 ins. Christie, March 13, 1924. £294.

A figure of a cock, in purple, blue, red and yellow. Height, 4 ins. Sotheby, November 11, 1930. £42.

A pair of candlestick bases, formed as a pheasant standing in flowering tree. Height, 9 ins. £26.

A set of The Seasons, Spring and Summer, female figures, with flowers and corn, Autumn a man with a bunch of grapes, Winter an old man before a brazier. Height, 6¾ ins. Sotheby, November 11, 1930. £80.

A pair of deep plates, with knurled borders, painted in Watteau style, in the Chelsea manner, wide dark blue borders, gilt, anchor and dagger marks in gold. 7¾ ins. Sotheby, February 11, 1931. £88.

A tureen in the V. and A. painted by the same hand.

A rare and early pair of white figures of fantastic phoenixes standing against tree stumps, c. 1750. Height, 7 ins. March 26, 1957. £450.

Two early white figures of seated muses—Eraton and Euterpe. Height, 6¼ ins. June 25, 1957. £170.

A rare and primitive standing figure of a peasant girl wearing mob cap and apron. Height, 5¾ ins. July 7, 1959. £110.

A pair of figures of cooks standing on simple early bases, decorated in a soft palette. Height 7½ ins. November 18, 1958. £155.

A pair of circular openwork baskets, the centres painted in the " famille-rose " style with peonies, bamboo and root ornament. Diameter, 7¾ ins. November 24, 1959. £120.

A group of the New Dancers—two children grouped before a floral bocage with candle nozzle over. " To " mark impressed. Height, 10¼ ins. December 22, 1959. £70.

A rare early blue and white bowl with wavy rim, painted with Chinese landscape motifs. Diameter, 3⅛ ins. January 8, 1960. £24.

A bell shaped tankard decorated in underglaze blue with Chinese style landscape pattern. Height, 4¾ ins. January 26, 1960. £22.

An uncoloured white porcelain figure of Henry Woodward in the character of the " Fine Gentleman " in Lethe. Slight damages. Height, 11 ins. February 16, 1960. £150.
A shell sweetmeat dish of three scallop shells on rockwork support, painted in underglaze blue. Height, 8 ins. March 1, 1960. £22.
Figure of Kitty Clive (slightly faulty). February, 1961. (It is interesting to follow the fortune of this figure. In 1874 it sold for £40, in 1875 it fetched £31. In 1880 it sold for £22, and in 1906 with Woodward, the pair realised £77.) £250.

BRISTOL

A group of three boys by a tree. Height, 9 ins. £15 4s. 6d.
Jug, with mask spout, painted with festoons of flowers in green with gold lines across, with pink scale and gold borders, marked with +. Puttick and Simpson, July 6, 1906. £46 4s.
A coffee-pot, decorated in festoons of flowers (marked). Saul, Southport, September 21, 1906. £7 15s.
Oval dish with sprays of flowers in colours on white ground. Diameter, 10 ins. Christie, February 15, 1907. £8 18s. 6d.
A teapot and cover, painted with flowers on white ground, a cup and saucer, with flowers and a laurel wreath. Christie, April 5, 1907. £8 18s. 6d.
A jug, painted with festoons, and sprays of flowers in colours. Height, 9 ins. (Massey-Mainwaring collection.) Christie, April 11, 1907. £14 3s. 6d.
A cabaret, decorated with laurel wreaths and festoons on white ground, comprising tea-pot, milk-pot, saucer, cup and saucer, and oval plateau. (Massey-Mainwaring collection.) Christie, May 8, 1907. £43 1s.

This cabaret was bought in in 1892 by the deceased collector at £63, the sum of £60 having been bid.

Pair of cups and saucers, painted in festoons of green foliage. (Lord Abercromby.) Arber, Rutter, Waghorn and Brown, February 19, 1908. £26 5s.
A teapot and cover, with *famille verte* decoration of flowers in the Oriental taste. Foster, March 19, 1908. £29 8s.
Figure of a river nymph, with fish. Height, 10 ins. (From the Edkins collection.) Christie, December 22, 1908. £23 2s.
A small double sauce-boat, painted with laurel festoons in green, and with foliage in low relief round the lower part. (Merton A. Thoms, Esq.) Christie, February 10, 1910. £50 8s.
Pair of oval dishes, painted with bouquets and sprays of flowers in colours on white ground, and with gilt edges. Width, 10 ins. (Merton A. Thoms, Esq.) Christie, February 10, 1910. £38 17s.
A group of Venus, Adonis, and Cupid, on plinth encrusted with flowers, and with a basket of flowers at the side. Height, 10 ins. (Merton A. Thoms, Esq.) Christie, February 10, 1910. £189
A biscuit portrait of Benjamin Franklin. (Merton A. Thoms, Esq.) Christie, February 10, 1910. £39 18s.
Teacup and saucer, painted with laurel festoons, a coat-of-arms, and initials S.S., with gilt bands round the borders. Part of the Burke Smith Service. Christie, December 16, 1910. £34 13s.

This is part of a different service from that which is known as the " Burke " service.

Tea service, fluted and painted with festoons of flowers in green, 24 pieces. Christie, July 13, 1911. £120 15s.
A teacup and saucer, painted with figures emblematic of Liberty and Plenty, standing beside a pedestal, upon which is painted the arms of Burke impaling Nugent and inscription. (Part of the service presented by R. and J. Champion to Mrs. Burke, and known as the Burke service.) (J. E. Nightingale, Esq., F.S.A.) Christie, December 7, 1911. £178 10s.
Figure of a river goddess by Tebo. Height, 10 ins. Christie, March 15, 1921. £44 2s.
Two plates, painted with flowers and pink and blue ribands round the borders. Christie, June 10, 1925. £13 13s.
Two tea cups and saucers, painted with festoons of flowers in colours. Christie, July 10, 1928. £14 14s.
A bottle, with bulbous neck, painted with a bird and branches in the Hizen taste. Height, 9¼ ins. Christie, December 6, 1928. £19 19s.
Four figures emblematic of the Continents. Height, 13 ins. Christie, July 23, 1929. £99 15s.
Figure of a boy skating. Height, 10 ins. Christie, December 7, 1924. £26 5s.
A cup and saucer from the Smyth service, decorated with classic heads and the mono-gram R. S., with floral festoons and green and gold bands. Sotheby, November 11, 1930. £22.

A figure of Autumn—a woman in white robes with gilt sprigs, coloured base, etc. Goldblatt
Collection. Height, 10¼ ins. May 1, 1956.   £26.
Two figures of milkmaid and goat herd decorated in various colours. Height, 10 and 10½ ins.
May 8, 1956.   £355.
A documentary teapot and cover bearing the initials W I E and date 1777. Painted by
William Stephens with floral festoons. Crossed swords and number " 2 " mark.
Height, 6¼ ins. March 12, 1957.   £250.
A coffee cup and saucer from the celebrated Burke service. March 12, 1957. (A similar cup
and saucer was sold in 1911 for £178 10s.)   £230.
A teapot and cover from the Smith service decorated with Armorial bearings and initials
" S S." Height, 5⅜ ins. March 12, 1957. (A cup and saucer from this service is mentioned
above and was sold in 1910 for £34 13s.)   £135.
Two standing figures, Fire and Water (from the four Elements), variously coloured. Water
has the " To " mark. Height, 11 ins. November 3, 1959.   £215.
A milk jug and cover from the Ludlow of Campden service painted with arms and floral
sprays. Height, 6¼ ins. November 24, 1959.   £90.
A bell shaped mug with ribbed loop handle painted with floral sprays and green and puce
border. Height, 5 ins. January 26, 1960.   £20.
A cylindrical mug painted with floral bouquet, sprays, etc., beneath green ribbon and puce
border. Height, 5¼ ins. May 24, 1960.   £38.

CHELSEA

Pair of candlesticks, the stems encrusted with flowers, and figures of lambs on the
plinths. Height, 9 ins. January 20, 1905.   £4 14s. 6d.
Figure of a dancing girl, in a crinoline. Height, 7 ins. (From the Hardcastle collec-
tion.) January 31, 1905.   £42.
A figure of Diana. Height, 7 ins. Sotheby, February 21, 1905.   £7.
Pair of figures, of girl and youth with baskets of flowers and fruit. Height, 8¾ ins.
February 24, 1905.   £19 19s.
A figure of a lady, holding a bouquet of flowers and carrying a basket of flowers and
fruit, her costume richly decorated, with a figure of a lamb at her feet, and
branches of flowers at the back, on gilt scroll plinth. Height, 11¼ ins. (Dr. W.
O'Neill.) Christie, May 11, 1905.   £105.
Pair of candlesticks, the stems formed as flowering bosquets with birds. Height, 10
ins. June 27, 1905.   £17 17s.
Figure of a youth with a basket of grapes. Height, 6 ins. (From the Walker collection.) June 27, 1905.   £32 11s.
Pair of figures, of a lady and gentleman holding open baskets, on plinths encrusted with
flowers, and with figures of dogs. Height, 7½ ins. (From the Walker collection.)
Sotheby, June 27, 1905.   £65 2s.

The Editor bought at Christie's rooms a precisely similar pair of figures, May 4, 1880, for £13 13s.

Pair of figures, of shepherd and shepherdess, with lamb and dog, on white and gold
plinths encrusted with flowers, modelled by Roubillac; very fine quality. Height,
11½ ins. (From the Walker collection.) Sotheby, June 27, 1905.   £136 10s.
Pair of figures, lady and gentleman with a page, on green and gold scroll plinths en-
crusted with flowers. Height, 10½ ins. (From the Walker collection.) Sotheby,
June 27, 1905.   £75 12s.
Pair of candlesticks, formed as the fables of the " Vain Jackdaw " and the " Cock and
Jewel." in flowering bosquets. July 7, 1905.   £52 10s.
Two figures of Apollo and Urania on turquoise, white and gold scroll pedestals. Part of
the set of ten figures. (Nine Muses and Apollo.) Height, 15 ins. July 7, 1905.
                                                                      £162 15s.

These were somewhat restored. On March 16, 1883, at Christies, there were sold a set of six of these
figures—Apollo, Urania, Thalia, Melpomene, Euterpe, Polymnia—in almost perfect condition for £493 17s.,
But for the condition of those sold in 1905 the price would have been considered to be remarkably low.

Pair of figures, of a lady in draped dress and a man playing a flute, richly decorated
and marked with gold anchor. (From the Broomfield Hall, Sunningdale, collection.)
Chancellor and Sons, March 26, 1906.   £279.

A pair of figures, similar in size, quality, and decoration, but slightly different in subject, sold at Christie's
April 20, 1883, for £171.

A group, the Fortune-tellers. Height, 14 ins. (From the James Cockshut collection.)
Christie, May 4, 1906.   £162 10s.
Service, painted with vegetables, fruit, flowers and large leaves on white ground and
with shaped edges, consisting of fifteen plates, eight large plates and two saucer
dishes. Christie, November 20, 1906.   £32 11s.

Twenty plates, painted with fruit and insects on white ground, and with shaped gilt edges. Diameter, 7½ ins. Christie, November 20, 1906. £20 9s. 6d.

Six plates, similar. Diameter, 9 ins. Christie, November 20, 1906. £26 5s.

A pair of saucer dishes, similar. Diameter, 9½ ins. Christie, November 20, 1906.
£5 15s. 6d.

Four, nearly similar, with birds in centre. Diameter, 9½ ins. Christie, November 20, 1906.
£34 13s.

It should be observed here that the difference in decoration between fruit and insects and good effective " bird " decoration raised the price from about £2 7s. 6d. each to £8 15s. each.

Group of a lady and gentleman seated beneath a tree with Cupid in the branches above. Height, 11 ins. Christie, November 20, 1906. £141 15s.

Two mugs, painted with exotic birds in colours on white ground. Height, 6¼ and 6 ins. Christie, November 30, 1906.
£7 17s.

Pair of important figures, shepherd and shepherdess, richly painted and gilt, with floral background, and on white and gold scroll bases. Marked with the impressed R (for Roubillac, modeller). Height, 13 ins. Knight, Frank and Rutley, March 26, 1907.
£566.

A triple scent-bottle, formed as a group of four hens, on plinth painted with flowers. (In the Von Pannwitz collection; sold at Munich, this scent-bottle realised £21.) (Hermann Zoeppritz.) Christie, May 12, 1908.
£25.

A sweetmeat stand, with seven shell dishes, painted with insects and encrusted with shells and seaweed, on pedestal. Height, 16 ins. Christie, April 23, 1909. £57 15s.

Pair of figures of a girl and youth, with flowers and fruit. Height, 9 ins. (B. Hicklin, Esq.) Christie, June 3, 1909.
£100 16s.

Pair of figures of a lady and gentleman dancing, the latter wearing a mask. Height, 7 ins. (Dr. Dumergue.) Christie, July 9, 1909.
£73 10s.

A figure of Neptune with a dolphin, on plinth encrusted with shells. Height, 10 ins. Christie, February 14, 1910.
£16 5s. 6d.

Pair of vases and covers of square shape, pink ground marbled with gold, each painted with figures of Bacchus, groups of flowers and birds, in panels; the necks pierced with rosettes, and the covers of open trellis design. Height, 13½ ins. (Octavius E. Coope, Esq.) Christie, May 5, 1910.
£1,260.

Pair of groups, each with figures of a lady and gentleman carrying flowers and fruit, emblematic of the Seasons, and standing on white and gold scroll plinths, richly encrusted with coloured flowers, foliage and corn, modelled by Roubillac, and bearing the impressed R. Height, 12¼ ins. Christie, February 17, 1911. £997 10s.

This marks the record of price by auction for a pair of Chelsea groups of this size.

A figure of a lady, wearing a mask, and carrying a hurdy-gurdy, on plinth encrusted with flowers. Height, 7¼ ins. Christie, March 3, 1911. £52 10s.

Large group, of shepherd and shepherdess seated in an arbour of May-blossoms. Height, 15½ ins. Modelled by Roubillac, after Boucher's " Le Mouton Favori." (Sir Alexander Macdonald of the Isles, Bart.) Christie, May 4, 1911. £1,837 10s.

This wonderful group formerly belonged to Louisa, daughter of the Duke of Gloucester, and wife of the eleventh Baronet and third Lord Macdonald.

Pair of groups, emblematic of the Seasons, white and gold plinths encrusted with flowers. Height, 9 ins. Christie, December 13, 1920. £52 10s.

Pair of deep cups, with mottled dark blue ground gilt with birds and trees. Height, 3¾ ins. Christie, December 13, 1920. £99 15s.

Pair of bottles, mottled dark blue ground gilt with birds, the shoulders modelled with satyrs' masks and gilt vine branches. Height, 9½ ins. Christie, December 13, 1920.
£178 10s.

Dessert service, painted with birds, trees and branches of fruit in panels, with gilt scroll borders on mottled dark blue ground, gold anchor mark, 39 pieces. Christie, March 22, 1921.
£609.

A pair of vases and covers, finely painted with Tenier's subjects in mottled dark blue borders, with gilt scroll work. Height, 15½ ins. Christie, July 7, 1921. £1575.

A pair of vases and covers, of oviform shape, painted with Bacchanalian scenes, probably by Donaldson, in panels on pink ground, richly gilt with birds, branches of flowers and scroll work Height, 11¾ ins. Christie, May 9, 1922. £441.

A candlestick with the fable of the Leopard and the Fox, with branches of flowers at the back. Height, 11 ins. Christie, May 30, 1923. £26 5s.

A cream jug, modelled with goats and bee, and painted in colours. Christie, November 24, 1925.
£73 10s.

A pair of bottles, finely gilt with birds and branches on mottled dark blue ground, the shoulders modelled with gilt vine branches in relief, and with satyr's head handles. Height, 9½ ins. Christie, February 2, 1926.
£152 5s.

A figure of Britannia. Height, 12½ ins. Christie, February 25, 1926. £14 14s.

A group of two boys with a fish. Height, 9 ins. Christie, February 25, 1926. £194 5s.

A figure of a nymph seated, holding a falcon, and her foot resting on a tortoise. Height, 11 ins. Christie, February 25, 1926. £199 10s.

A pair of figures, a gardener and girl, seated, holding baskets, encrusted rockwork plinths. Height, 10½ ins. Christie, March 23, 1926. £215 5s.

A watchstand formed as turquoise and gold scrollwork, with figure of Minerva and an owl at base. Height, 13 ins. Christie, March 23, 1926. £63.

La Nourrice : a group of a mother and child. Height, 7¼ ins. Christie, December 13, 1928. £60 18s.

A triple scent bottle, modelled as three hens. Christie, March 5, 1929. £42.

A scent bottle formed as a girl, and Cupid wearing a wig, with tree stump and flowers at back. (Princess Paley.) Christie, July 1, 1929. £136 10s.

There were over fifty scent bottles in this sale realising from £3 to £105.

A group of a shepherd and shepherdess, bearing the gold anchor mark, modelled by Roubillac after Boucher's " Le Mouton Favori." Similar to Macdonald group above. Height, 16 ins. Hurcombs, February 7, 1930. £3250.

A record price for a single piece of English porcelain.

A figure of a pheasant, in red, yellow and brown colourings, on a tree trunk, base encrusted with leaves and flowers, red anchor period. Height, 5½ ins. Sotheby, November 11, 1930. £65.

A sweetmeat stand of six shell dishes on a rocky base, with shells and corals surmounted by a kingfisher. The dishes painted with insects. 6⅜ ins. Sotheby, November 12, 1930. £10 10s.

A rare " red anchor " figure of Barn Owl. Height, 9 ins. June 21, 1955. £900.

A " red anchor " group of two figures dancing, after a Meissen original. June 21, 1955. £250.

A white bust of George II wearing a large wig and loose cloak, c. 1750. Height, 13 ins. May 29, 1956. £1,150.

Four red anchor period standing Seasons, coloured in restrained style. Height, 5¼ ins. March 12, 1957. £530.

An extremely rare pair of " Girl in the swing " class figures of girl and youth with fish, on shaped bases, decorated with floral sprays. Goldblatt Collection. May 1, 1956. £2,500.

A rare early " Girl in the swing " class figure of a standing youth with fish. March 20, 1956. £620.

A triangle marked milk jug of silver pattern decorated with sprigs and insects, band of strawberries and leaves at foot. October 18, 1955. £950.

A Goat and Bee jug picked out in colours. Triangle mark. Height, 4½ ins. June 26, 1956. £320.

A figure of Nourrice seated holding the baby, decorated in restrained style. Raised anchor mark. Height, 7¼ ins. March 12, 1957. £880.

A raised anchor marked teapot and cover painted in a continuous scene with the fable of the " Fox and the Frog." Height, 5⅛ ins. March 12, 1957. £480.

A " Red Anchor " figure of a reclining River God. Length, 7¾ ins. February 18, 1958. £190.

An attractive small figure of a seated Chinese boy holding an oval dish, sparsely decorated. Height, 3½ ins. Raised red anchor mark. November 8, 1960. £700.

A rare pair of raised red anchor mark figures of Little Hawk Owls perched on tree trunks with applied leaves and flowers. Height, 7 ins. July 1, 1958. £1,000.

An important and rare red anchor mark pigeon house perfume pot with cover—a similar piece is recorded in a 1756 Chelsea sale catalogue. Height, 16 ins. May 12, 1959. £580.

A rare and attractive scent bottle in the form of a maiden seated on a green marbled base leaning asleep against a flowered tree. Inscribed " Fidelle me garde." Height, 3 ins. November 3, 1959. £150.

A rare cane handle in the form of a sphinx, the head representing Peg Woffington. Red anchor period. Length, 5 ins. January 26, 1960. £140.

A rare Chelsea scent bottle in the form of a seated monkey wearing tricorn hat and yellow coat, basket on back, variously coloured. Height, 3¼ ins. Blohm Collection. July 14, 1960. (Thirty other fine Chelsea scent bottles from the above Collection were sold for prices ranging from £38 to £580, most examples were in the £100-£300 bracket.) £250.

An attractive small seal of a dancing man wearing tricorn hat, flowered coat, etc. The base inscribed " Toujours Gay." Height, 1¼ ins. Blohm Collection. July 4, 1960. (Seventy-nine other Chelsea seals of various designs were sold for prices ranging from £19 to £155.) £50.

A very important pair of groups of the Seasons, one of Winter and Spring, the other of Summer and Autumn. Richly coloured and gilt on ornate floral encrusted bases. Gold Anchor and " R " mark. Height, both 13¼ ins. November 29, 1960. £980.

A fine botanical plate, the centre painted with large scale blue hollyhock-like flower with leaves and insects. Red anchor mark. Diameter, 8½ ins. November 29, 1960. (Other plates of this type, popularly called " Hans Sloane " decoration, were sold for £140 and

£130, damaged specimens for considerably less—£22 for two. In 1962 six very fine plates of this type were sold for £2,740.) £160.

A fine and rare plate painted in brilliant colours with children playing game of leapfrog type, in landscape, floral spray border. Red anchor mark. Diameter, 9¼ ins. November 29, 1960. (Other examples of these rare plates with similar game subjects were sold for £560, £580, £600 and £650.) £580.

A fine group of the Masked Dancers modelled by Josph Williams, after a Meissen original. The two figures in lively pose, each with one leg kicked back, coloured in attractive subdued palette. Red anchor mark. Height, 7 ins. December 6, 1960. £3,600.

A fine tureen and cover moulded and coloured as a Melon with loop stalk handle. Red anchor mark. Length, 6½ ins. December 20, 1960. £580.

A fine tureen and cover in the form of a bundle of asparagus, c. 1756. Length, 7½ ins. May 22, 1962. £950.

An important early milk jug of silver shape, moulded and coloured floral motifs, etc. Height, 5⅜ ins. Triangle mark incised. This specimen was purchased for £8 in 1866. May 22, 1962. £1,300.

A very good pair of standing figures of shepherd and companion. Richly coloured, on scroll base. Height, 12 ins. Gold anchor mark. May 22, 1962. £750.

A rare head of a baby boy in white, undecorated porcelain. Height, 4¼ ins. July 10, 1962. £1,200.

CHELSEA WITH DARK BLUE AND WITH CRIMSON GROUND COLOURS

Large deep cup or bowl, widening towards the lips, richly gilt with exotic birds and foliage on mottled dark blue ground. Height, 3¾ ins. (From the Hawkins collection.) Christie, May 10, 1904. £80.

A similar cup was sold two years previously for £65.

Pair of plates painted with wreaths of flowers, birds and insects in trefoil shapes, panels and gilt lattice work borders in mottled dark blue ground. (From the Hawkins collection.) Christie, May 10, 1904. £84.

On May 17, 1905, a similar pair of plates in the Louis Huth collection were purchased by Mr. Amor for exactly the same price.

Pair of large cups, crimson ground, richly gilt with birds and festoons of flowers and foliage tied by ribbons and trellis and scrolls round the lip. (From the Hawkins collection.) Christie, June 6, 1905. £263.

These were formerly in the Marjoribanks collection. The form and size of these cups are similar to the single cup described above as sold for £80, but crimson ground instead of blue.

An inkstand, comprising stand, ink and sand vase, pen-case, and taper holder; ground dark blue, pencilled with butterflies and flowers in gold, and with shield-shaped reserved panels painted with exotic birds in polychrome; the handle of the cover of the pen-case is formed as a seated lamb. (From the Massey-Mainwaring collection.) Christie, March 15, 1907. £141 15s.

A similar inkstand to the above, the ground colour being pink. The ink and sand vases missing. (From the Massey-Mainwaring collection.) Christie, March 15, 1907. £204 5s.

It should be observed that although two rather important pieces were missing from this inkstand, the greater rarity of the ground colour caused a much higher price to be given. It is reasonable to suggest that if this specimen had been as complete as the one with blue ground, the price would have exceeded £300.

An ecuelle cover and stand, crimson ground, finely painted with flowers in colours on gold ground, with green, white and gold scroll handles. Christie, March 22, 1907. £336.

Another of similar form, finely painted with sprays of flowers on white ground, and with pink borders of scroll outline. Christie, March 22, 1907. £200 10s.

Pair of vases and covers painted with flowers in colours on gold ground, and with lake borders, enriched with turquoise, white and gold scrolls in relief, the necks and covers of pierced trellis design. Height, 15½ ins. Christie, July 2, 1908. £672.

Pair of cups and saucers, painted with birds and branches in panels, and with alternate mottled blue panels, gilt, with flowers and trellis work. (Lord Amherst.) Christie, December 11, 1908. £120 15s.

Pair of bottles, with mottled dark blue ground, gilt with insects and vine leaves, and modelled with grapes in relief, the handles formed as Satyrs' heads. Height, 10 ins. (J. Cheetham Cockshut, Esq.) Christie, March 23, 1909. £126 5s.

Vase and cover, encrusted with festoons of coloured flowers, and gilt with a bird, etc., with figures of Cupids seated on either side, on boldly modelled scroll-shaped plinth, painted with insects. Height, 13 ins. Christie, July 1, 1909. £399.

Pair of deep bowls or cups, painted with exotic birds, flowers and fruit in colours on gold ground. Height, 3¾ ins. Christie, March 18, 1910. £267 15s.

Pair of deep bowls or cups, with mottled dark blue ground, gilt, with peacock and other birds among branches of foliage. Height, 3½ ins.; diameter, 4⅛ ins. (T. W. Waller, Esq.) Christie, June 8, 1910. £168.

Pair of vases, of pear shape, dark blue mottled ground, gilt, with exotic birds, branches of flowers, the handles modelled as groups of fruit and flowers, painted in natural colours. Height, 16¼ ins. (T. W. Waller, Esq.) Christie, June 8, 1910. £1 890

A superb set of 3 claret ground covered vases, overpainted with flowers. Gold anchor marks. Height, 13¼ ins. by 15½ ins. March 5, 1957. £380.

A mazarin blue cabaret set decorated in gold with Watteau type figures in arbours, etc., and with exotic birds, comprising teapot and cover, sucrier and cover, creamer, two cups and two saucers. Gold anchor marks. July 1, 1958. £270.

A fine pair of covered vases of mottled blue ground with white jasmine in relief. The heart shaped panels painted with Boucher style figures. Gold anchor marks. Height, 9¼ ins. December 2, 1959. £170.

A fine mazarin blue toilet box of heart shape, the cover surmounted by two cupids and lamb, the sides with scattered flowers in gold. Gold anchor period. Length, 5 ins. December 2, 1959. £210.

A pair of plates with wide rose pink borders, the centres painted with single long tailed exotic bird on a gilt leaf spray. Gold anchor marks. Diameter, 8⅝ ins. February 24, 1959. £100.

An attractive vase of quadrangular baluster shape with scroll handles, the bodies painted on either side with a pair of Watteau figures in wooded landscapes on a mazarin blue ground. Gold anchor mark. Height, 7⅜ ins. February 24, 1959. £95.

A pair of mazarin blue ground bottles, the bodies decorated with a frieze of dancing figures in burnished gold. Handle damaged. Gold anchor period. Height, 14½ ins. May 12, 1959. £45.

A beaker of bell shape decorated with birds, etc., in gold on a mazarin blue ground. Gold anchor mark. Height, 3¼ ins. July 5, 1960. £120.

COALBROOKDALE AND COALPORT

Thirteen plates, with green borders richly gilt. Knight, Frank and Rutley, October 26, 1907. £10 10s.

Dessert service, apple green painted in flowers, 18 pieces. Sotheby, December 14, 1905. £8 10s.

Dessert service painted with classical subjects in the centre and panels of flowers on the border on turquoise ground, consisting of two large tazzas, supported by biscuit figures of children. Two etagères, eight tazzas, a pair of sugar tureens and covers, thirty plates. Christie, December 19, 1905. £110 5s.

Pair of plates, the centres painted with views surrounded by turquoise and white borders, on which are designs profusely jewelled. Exhibited at the 1851 Exhibition. Sotheby, February 21, 1906. £9 15s.

Pair of vases and covers, painted with flowers on white ground in dark blue and gold riband borders and with turquoise beading. Height, 12½ ins. Christie, May 4, 1906. £52 10s.

Pair of vases and covers, Sèvres pattern, painted with spiral bands of flowers on pink ground, and with gilt cords in relief. Height, 13 ins. Christie, June 8, 1906. £21.

Pair of boat-shaped vases and covers (vaisseau à mât), painted with panels of flowers in gilt borders on turquoise ground, the shoulders and covers pierced with flowers and foliage, and with white and gold borders. Height, 12½ inches. (Mr. E. J. Stanley.) Christie, January 31, 1908. £47 5s.

Pair of vases, painted with flowers, and encrusted with Cupids, flowers, etc. Height, 13¼ ins. (The Earl of Dunraven.) Christie, January 28, 1910. £15 4s. 6d.

An oblong Coalbrookdale plateau, painted in the Sèvres taste, with children in a landscape, in pink borders gilt with flowers. Width, 16½ ins. Christie, May 9, 1922. £16 16s.

A Coalbrookdale cabaret, painted with dogs on turquoise ground, six pieces. Christie, February 21, 1929. £3 3s.

A pair of Coalport vases, gilt with butterflies and fir cones on a dark blue ground. Height, 17 ins. Christie, May 30, 1923. £10 10s.

A Coalport dessert service, painted with birds and branches in apple green borders, with yellow and gold scrolls, 31 pieces. Christie, July 24, 1924. £8 18s. 6d.

A Coalport tea service, painted with pink roses and other flowers in dark blue borders, richly gilt, 24 pieces. Christie, June 19, 1928. £9 19s. 6d.

Three Coalport Coronation jugs of George IV, painted with flowers, the rose, thistle and shamrock. Christie, March 25, 1930. £19 19s.

A Coalbrookdale floral encrusted inkstand complete with fitting. Stand length, 12½ ins
    October 17, 1959. £50
Two Coalport floral encrusted vases painted with panels of flowers. Height, 14½ ins. and
    14 ins. October 7, 1959. £48
A floral encrusted inkstand, the handle formed as a small wreath of flowers, two flowers in
    the main body form inkwells. Length, 10 ins. July 19, 1960. £30
A fine pair of vases decorated with broad band of roses, hollyhocks and other flowers on a
    dark ground. Large printed circular Society of Arts mark of 1820. Height, 10 ins
    October 25, 1960. £125

COPELAND

Dinner service, gilt and decorated in quaintly coloured oak and other leaves and flowers,
    comprising 162 pieces. Brady and Sons, Perth, September 5, 1906. £20.

        Copeland was the successor of Spode. See the account of this firm.

Dessert centre, with vase supported by four Parian figures and festoons richly gilt.
    Sotheby, November 20, 1906. £7 5s.
A dessert service by Copeland and Garrett, with flowers in colours on buff ground, 19
    pieces. Christie, March 11, 1926. £17 17s.
A Copeland and Garrett dinner service of 106 pieces, each piece bearing a griffin's head crest
    on an apple green ground with gilt edges, etc. Some damages. August 2, 1956. £64.
A Copeland part tea service painted with flowers within panels on a moulded and coloured
    ground comprising 2 plates, 18 cups and 29 saucers. July 23, 1957. £21.
A Copeland and Garrett dessert service decorated with tropical birds within gilt edged
    panels on a turquoise ground comprising centrepiece, sauce tureen and cover, 5 dishes
    and 19 plates. Some staining. January 26, 1960. £32.
A Copeland and Garrett dessert service with apple green borders and bouquets of garden
    flowers comprising centrepiece, 6 dishes and 17 plates. May 29, 1960. £70.

DAVENPORT

Pair of fruit-baskets with stands and side handles, quaintly decorated in English land-
    scape subjects. Brady and Sons, Perth, September 5, 1906. £4 5s.
Set of three vases, with scroll handles, pale green ground, with panels containing birds
    and flowers. Height, 8 ins. (Lord Abercromby.) Arber, Rutter, Waghorn and
    Brown, February 18, 1908. £8 10s.
Dessert service, painted with small panels of landscapes round the border, on pale
    yellow ground, richly gilt, consisting of 17 pieces. Christie, May 10, 1910. £11 11s.
A dinner service, decorated with flower sprays in blue and gold, 76 pieces. Christie,
    May 7, 1925. £18 18s.
A dinner service, decorated with flowers and foliage in red, blue and gold, in narrow
    dark blue and gold borders, 186 pieces. Christie, July 28, 1927. £136 10s.
A dessert service, painted with flowers in colours and gold in the Chinese taste, 35
    pieces. Christie, July 28, 1927. £8 18s. 6d.
A breakfast service, with willow pattern in blue and gilt edges, 98 pieces. Christie,
    June 26, 1928. £16 16s.
A tea service, flower sprays in pink and green, 44 pieces. Christie, June 26, 1928.
    £23 2s.
Dessert service, painted with pink roses and gilt with foliage, 42 pieces; and a tea
    service, *en suite*, 49 pieces. Christie, July 3, 1924. £110 5s.
A decorative porcelain dessert service, each piece painted with different flowers, gilt borders,
    etc., comprising centrepiece, 5 footed dishes and 17 plates. March 22, 1960. £107.
A set of 3 vases of lobed and elongated pear shape, painted with panels of flowers on a claret
    ground. Height, 9 ins. and 8½ ins. May 10, 1960. £13.
A part tea service painted with pink roses and gilt leaves comprising teapot, jug, 12 cups and
    saucers, c. 1850. July 19, 1960. £60.
A yellow ground vase and cover of square section decorated with floral painting, gilt borders,
    etc. Height, 19½ ins. October 25, 1960. £42.
A dessert service of apple green ground, the plates painted with views, comprising 8 footed
    dishes and 16 plates, all richly gilt, c. 1860. June 29, 1962. £105.

DERBY

Plate, painted with a portrait of Charlotte Augusta, Duchess of Leinster, with rosebud
    and laurel border with red, blue and gold edge. (From the Hawkins collection.)
    Christie, June 21, 1904. £24.

Dinner service, painted with flowers and foliage round the borders in red, blue, green and gold, 109 pieces. November 18, 1904. £17 17s.

Dessert service, painted with flowers and ornament in red, blue, green and gold in the oriental taste, 20 pieces. January 20, 1905. £26 5s.

Tea service, with dotted ornament in gold and borders of dark blue, 36 pieces. (From the Huth collection.) Christie, May 23, 1905. £19 19s.

Pair of vases and covers, oviform with striped white and gold ground and dark blue borders, painted with oval panels of nymphs and landscapes in colours. Height, 10½ ins. (From the Huth collection.) Christie, May 23, 1905. £183 15s.

A similar pair of vases in the sale of Mr. Stewart Hodgson's collection some eight or ten years ago realised £150.

Pair of jardinières and covers, painted with turquoise and gold borders and portraits of Louis XVI and M. Antoinette, and flowers in panels on reverse. Sotheby, December 14, 1905. £15.

Coffee-cup and saucer, painted with group of fruit on a pale pink ground, gilt with stars and with small panels of rosebuds, and a coffee-cup and saucer on pink ground with gilt borders. Christie, May 4, 1906. £42.

Set of three jardinières, semicircular shaped, painted with a view of Pembroke town and two landscapes on green ground with gilt borders. Christie, June 19, 1906. £22 1s.

Dessert service, painted with raised views in colours, the borders richly gilt with arabesques; consisting of a pair of sugar tureens, covers and stands, two dessert baskets, twelve shaped dishes and twenty-five plates. Christie, November 15, 1906. £96 12s.

Tea service, nearly similar, consisting of teapot, cover and stand, sugar basin and cover, cream jug, bowl, two dishes, eleven teacups, twelve saucers, three coffee mugs and a large mug. Christie, November 15, 1906. £35 14s.

A set of three jardinières, with pierced covers painted with oblong panels of landscapes on pale green ground. Christie, February 15, 1907. £22 1s.

Pair of figures of "The Mansion House Dwarfs," with inscriptions upon their hats. Height, 7 ins. Christie, July 2, 1908. £28 17s. 6d.

Figure of Garrick as "Richard III." Height, 11 ins. Christie, January 29, 1909. £13 13s.

Pair of figures of boys, with a book and dog 5½ ins. and 6 ins. high. Dresden crossed sword mark. (Dr. Dumergue.) Christie, July 8, 1909. £10 10s.

A biscuit group of a nymph and classical warrior before a statuette of Diana. Height, 14½ ins. Christie, July 22, 1909. £12 12s.

A mug, with initials D.P. in flowers, and royal blue and gold border—marked. London Curio Club, November 15, 1909. £16 5s. 6d.

A miniature teapot and watering-can, encrusted with flowers on a green ground. Christie, December 17, 1909. £28 7s.

Pair of bowls, with scalloped edges, the exteriors painted with exotic birds and trees in colours. Diameter, 8½ ins. Christie, March 18, 1910. £17 17s.

Dessert service, painted with landscapes in colours in the centres, in striped dark blue borders, consisting of 52 pieces. Christie, March 18, 1910. £215 10s.

Pair of vases, encrusted with branches of coloured flowers, and the covers modelled with large bouquets of various flowers in highest relief. Height, 17 ins. (Charles A. O. Baum-Gartner, Esq.) Christie, November 29, 1910. £33 12s.

Figure of a peacock, on plinth encrusted with coloured flowers. Height, 6¾ ins. Christie, November 29, 1910. £12 12s.

A group representing a peep-show, with figures of children. Height, 5¾ ins. Christie, February 24, 1911. £60 18s.

A group of the Tithe Pig. Height, 7¼ ins. Christie, December 1, 1911. £20 9s. 6d.

Dinner service, painted with panels of flowers in dark blue borders, gilt with foliage, 148 pieces. Christie, December 13, 1920. £157 10s.

Some pieces Coalport and Mortlock Copies.

Jug, painted with flower sprays in colours, and the lip modelled with a bust of Admiral Rodney, inscribed "April the 12th, 1782." Height, 7½ ins. Christie, March 15, 1921. £115 10s.

A pair of pastille burners and covers, formed as tripod altars, coloured pink and gold, with rams' heads in relief. Height, 9 ins. Christie, May 30, 1923. £29 8s.

A pair of figures of clowns, with large hats. Height, 6¾ ins. Christie, May 30, 1923. £19 19s.

A figure of a dwarf wearing inscribed hat. Height, 6¾ ins. Christie, February 4, 1926. £13 13s.

Dessert service, painted with coat-of-arms in narrow blue and gold borders, 55 pieces. Christie, March 25, 1926. £84.

Dinner service by Bloor, painted with sprays of cornflowers, 125 pieces. Christie, November 29, 1928. £26 5s.

Dinner service, painted with flowers and foliage in red, blue and gold, 91 pieces. Christie, November 29, 1928. £246 15s.

A pair of plates, with the arms of Pendock-Barry within an oak wreath border of Bill-ingsley roses, black and gold ground, gold mark. Sotheby, November 11, 1930.
£19.

A mug and saucer, cornflower sprig pattern, painted by Banford, with medallion of mother and two children.
£17.

A tankard, painted with a landscape, puce mark. Height, 4¾ ins.
£27.

A pair of cups, covers and saucers, painted with medallions of flowers, puce mark.
£48.

A pair of figures of wild boars. Height, 2¼ ins.
£15.

A pair of goldfinches, standing on a tree trunk encrusted with flowers. Height, 4½ ins.; and another similar, height, 2⅝ ins.
£62.

A " cow " milk-jug, with brown markings on a fluted base, 6¼ ins. long. Sotheby, November 11, 1930.
£13.

A cabaret by Boreman, landscapes, river scenes, cattle and figure subjects within " pearly " beaded borders on canary yellow ground, eight pieces, mark in puce. Sotheby, March 27, 1931.
£64.

A Bloor Derby dessert service, painted with birds, with landscape and river scene back-grounds within dark blue, gilt borders and scallop, gadrooned rims, 42 pieces. Sotheby, November 28, 1930.
£50.

A Duesbury Derby cabaret set comprising tray, teapot and cover, sucrier and cover, milk jug and 2 cups and saucers painted with seascapes within reserves on an apple-green ground. October 18, 1955.
£220.

A pair of figures of Oriental boy and girl as a Sultan and Sultana, after Meissen originals. Height, 7½ ins. and 8 ins. June 2, 1959.
£140.

A rare pair of Blackamoor kneeling figures holding shells, attractively coloured. Height, 7¾ ins. June 2, 1959.
£330.

An early tureen and cover in the form of a melon, naturally moulded and coloured. Length, 10 ins. June 2, 1959.
£480.

An early coffee pot and cover of tapering cylindrical form, painted with Chinaman holding bird. Height, 9 ins. October 17, 1959.
£48.

A pair of standing figures, Gallant and Lady, finely modelled and coloured. Height 9 ins. October 17, 1959.
£195.

A pair of vases of spill vase form, painted with panels of birds (by Dodson) on a blue and gold ground, c. 1820. Height, 7½ ins. March 23, 1960.
£30.

A fine figure of Jupiter riding a two-wheeled chariot with eagle at his side, c. 1770. Height, 10 ins. March 22, 1960.
£150.

A barrel shaped mug with loop handle, painted in underglaze blue with Chinese type river scene. Height, 6¾ ins. March 29, 1960.
£18.

A rare early inkstand, the cover of the pen box surmounted by two children and a goat, the body painted with landscape, butterflies and insects. Length, 9⅞ ins. July 5, 1960.
£180.

A rare early pair of figures of dancers, each standing on one leg with arms raised, variously coloured. Height 6½ ins. November 8, 1960.
£290.

A drinking cup in the form of a fox's head, naturalistically coloured and a ditto in the form of a trout's head. Length, 4⅜ ins. and 5¼ ins. May 10, 1960.
£52.

A fine plate painted with " Marden Blush Rose, Tawny Day Lily and China Aster," by William (Quaker) Pegg. Factory mark. Diameter, 8¾ ins. May 10, 1960.
£45.

A set of three jardinieres with flared lips and mask handles. Painted with continuous freizes of landscapes and panels by George Robertson, c. 1800. Height, 5⅝ ins. and 5¼ ins. May 10, 1960.
£200.

An Admiral Rodney jug of pear-shaped body and mask spout. The body painted with floral sprays and inscribed " April the 12th, 1782." Crowned " D " mark. Height, 7½ ins. May 10, 1960. (A similar example is illustrated in Godden's British Pottery and Porcelain, 1780-1850.)
£48.

A rare oval tray of marbled yellow ground, the centre panel painted with " View in Shen-stone's Walks, Derbyshire." Baton mark. Length 15¼ ins. May 10, 1960.
£145.

A fine cabaret set on shaped tray comprising teapot and cover, covered sugar, creamer and cup and saucer, all of yellow ground painted with panels of views in Derbyshire by Zachariah Boreman. Baton mark, c. 1790. May 10, 1960.
£310.

A very fine pair of Bloor period, c. 1825 vases, the covers naturalistically modelled as bouquet of flowers, the bodies with applied flowers and a rich blue and gold ground. Printed crown and " D " mark. Height, 17 ins. December 20, 1960.
£310

DERBY-CHELSEA

Fine tea service, with crimson ground, gilt with festoons of flowers and turquoise and gold peacock feather decoration round the lower part. Consisting of teapot cover and stand, sugar basin cover and stand, cream jug, bowl, twelve cups and saucers. (Massey-Mainwaring collection.) Christie, April 11, 1907.
£525.

Cabaret of Sèvres pattern painted with Cupids on clouds in pink in panels with gilt borders on turquoise ground, consisting of sucrier cover and stand, cup and saucer, and oval plateau. (Massey-Mainwaring collection.) Christie, April 11, 1907. £71 8s.

It should be noticed that the important pieces of teapot and milk-jug are missing from this little set.

Teapot and cover of Sèvres pattern, painted with panels of cupids on clouds in pink, on white ground, with spiral of turquoise colour. (Lord Melville's collection.) Christie, May 14, 1907. £43 1s.

Pair of cups and saucers, painted with medallion heads and husk festoons in blue and gold borders, and with blue and gold fluted bands. (Lord Melville's collection.) Christie, May 14, 1907. £30 9s.

An oviform vase, painted with the Three Graces in an oval panel, and a spray of flowers on the reverse upon a richly gilt ground, and modelled with winged figured handles. Height, 15 ins. (Lord Abercromby.) Arber, Rutter, Waghorn and Brown, February 18, 1908. £48.

Teapot, cover and stand, painted with flowers and foliage in green, and with ruby coloured stripes, gilt with foliage. (J. Cheetham Cockshut, Esq.) Christie, March 23, 1909. £63.

A group of the Tithe Pig. Height, 6 ins. Christie, February 25, 1910. £11 11s.

The Seasons : a set of four figures of children on pink and gold scroll plinths. Height, 9¼ ins. (Octavius E. Coope, Esq.) Christie, May 4, 1910. £92 8s.

Pair of figures of Shakespeare and Milton. Height, 11½ ins. (Walter Calvert, Esq.) Christie, November 29, 1910. £11 0s. 6d.

A figure of Neptune with a dolphin, on pedestal encrusted with shells. Height, 13 ins. Christie, February 3, 1911. £6 16s. 6d.

Teapot and cover, painted with groups of fruit and wreaths of flowers in panels, on turquoise ground gilt with vines. (John Cockshut, Esq.) Christie, May 4, 1911. £126.

Tea-cup and saucer, and coffee-cup and saucer, painted with green foliage and pink and gold trellis work in turquoise borders. Christie, March 15, 1921. £35 14s.

Group of nymphs festooning bust of a satyr. Height, 12¼ ins. Christie, March 15, 1921. £35 14s.

Group of four cupids round a tree. Height, 9½ ins. Christie, May 9, 1922. £18 18s.

Tea service, painted with classical heads in grisaille on chocolate medallions, and laurel festoons in green, and narrow dark blue and gold borders, 35 pieces. Christie, July 2, 1925. £78 15s.

Four figures of children, emblematic of the Continents. Height, 8¼ ins. Christie, May 7, 1925. £19 19s.

A set emblematic of the Seasons £29 8s.

A garniture of five vases painted with cupids in puce camaieu with white flowers in relief. Height, 7¼ ins. to 9½ ins. June 2, 1959. £58.

A pair of candlestick figures on kneeling blackamoor and companion, candlestick nozzles on the heads. Height, 9¼ ins. June 2, 1960. £150.

A fine ornate pair of candlestick figures of shepherd and shepherdess with bocage background and candle arms at sides. Height, 12 ins. March 22, 1960. £200.

ENGLISH DELFT WARES

Dish, octagonal shaped, decorated in blue and white, and bearing the arms of the Routledge family, whose motto was " Verax atque probis," and crest an oak tree. Dated 1637. Sotheby, February 21, 1906. £7.

Coronation mug, with portrait of Charles II inscribed and dated " C. 2nd, R. 1660." Height, 3½ ins. Bond, Ipswich, April 18, 1906. £38.

Vessel, formed as a cat, painted in blue. Dated 1657. Sotheby, June 25, 1906. £20.

Set of six plates, inscribed. 1. " What is a merry man ?" 2. " Let him do what he cann." 3. " To entertain his guests." 4. " With wine and merry jests." 5. " But if his wife doth frown." 6. " All merriment goes down." All dated 1734. Sotheby, June 25, 1906. £41.

This interesting set of plates are described in Litchfield's *Pottery and Porcelain*, second edition.

A model of a house, decorated in blue and white. Sotheby, November 15, 1906. £3 5s.

A plaque, decorated with the arms of the Apothecaries Company in blue. Christie, November 15, 1906. £9 19s. 6d.

A figure of a lady in embroidered dress, marked with the initials and date in blue, I.S.A. 1619. Sotheby, November 6, 1908. £15 10s.

A bottle, painted with birds and foliage in blue, and dated 1628. Height, 7½ ins. Christie, February 19, 1909. £24 3s.

An octagonal plaque, painted with a coat-of-arms and scroll mantling in blue and yellow. Christie, February 14, 1910. £15 15s.

Small wine bottle, inscribed " Clarit, 1647." Height, 4½ ins. (Sir John Evans.) Christie, February 14, 1911.
£25 4s.

Wine bottle, painted in blue with the crown and cipher of Charles I, and the date, 1648. Height, 6¼ ins. (Sir John Evans.) Christie, February 14, 1911.
£34 13s.

An oval dish, of Palissy design, the centre modelled with Venus and Cupid in relief, painted in blue, yellow and brown, the border modelled with masks and baskets of fruit in relief, and with sunk panels painted with landscapes, the arms of the City of London, the arms of the Embroiderers' Company, initials $\frac{N.}{R.E.}$ and the date, 1661. Width, 19 ins. (Sir John Evans.) Christie, February 14, 1911.
£68 5s.

A jug, oviform, painted with a woman, birds and flowers in colours. Height, 6½ ins. Christie, June 30, 1925.
£44 2s.

A trencher salt of Charles II design, surmounted by three scroll handles, painted with foliage in white on dark blue ground. Christie, July 15, 1929.
£9 9s.

Teapot and cover, painted with landscapes and scrollwork in blue on three shell feet. Christie, February 6, 1923.
£30 9s.

A tankard, decorated in blue with $\frac{B.}{E.\ M.,}$ 1687, and coat of arms. Height, 6¾ ins. £25.

A wine-pot, globular, decorated with a nude child, in blue, yellow and green. Height, 7¼ ins.
£6 10s.

A fuddling cup of three cups joined by twisted handles, decorated in blue. Height, 3 ins. Sotheby, November 11, 1930.
£13 10s.

A Lambeth or Southwark dish, in enamelled earthenware, decorated with seven pomegranates and three bunches of grapes, inscribed under the bottom $\frac{A.}{R.\ M.,}$ 1640. Sotheby, November 11, 1930.
£210.

Four drug jars, inscribed in blue, and dated 1662. Height, 7½ ins. Sotheby, February 11, 1931.
£17.

An armorial wine bottle, painted in blue with the arms of Allen, and inscribed William Allen, and dated 1647. Height, 6⅛ ins.
£43.

Another, painted with the Grocers' arms, initials W. R. and date 1652. Height, 6 ins.
£110.

A set of " Merryman " plates, " 1745."
£45.

A wine bottle, painted in Chinese style, dated 1628. Height, 7¾ ins. Sotheby, February 11, 1931.
£45.

An Adam and Eve charger, dated $\frac{T.}{T.\ M.,}$ 1635, painted in blue, green and yellow, notched blue edge. Height, 19 ins. Sotheby, February 11, 1931.
£82.

An Adam and Eve charger painted in colours, the figures seated. Diameter, 14¾ ins. May 29, 1956.
£95.

A charger painted with view of Charles II's Royal Yacht with initials and date, H W A 1668. May 29, 1956.
£1,550.

A charger with blue dash rim, the centre painted with William III riding on a prancing charger. Diameter, 14 ins. May 29, 1956.
£62.

A wine bottle inscribed " WHIT. 1650. John Tomes," within simple panel, no other decoration. Height, 7⅝ ins. July 24, 1956.
£140.

A Bristol delft bowl decorated in blue with hunting scenes and inscribed " Success to the Miller " and a delft mug also with hunting scene. Diameter of bowl, 10¼ ins. May 3, 1957.
£210.

A very rare Lambeth bleeding bowl inscribed " R.I.E. 1660 " with coloured full-length portrait of Charles I. Diameter, 6⅛ ins. March 24, 1959.
£98.

A rare Lambeth delft mug painted with portraits of King William and Queen Mary and initials W.R. and Q.M. dated 1694. Height, 4 ins. November 3, 1959.
£220.

A Lambeth delft wine bottle inscribed " Sack 1650." Height, 6 ins. October 15, 1959. £60.

A rare dated Lambeth delft armorial goblet of chalice form decorated in blue and inscribed " HE THAT HATH THIS CUP IN HAND DRNKE UP THE BEERE LET IT NOT STAND 1656." " G.E.C." Height, 4¾ ins. May 15, 1959.
£330.

A unique Lambeth delft portrait (three quarter length) wine bottle of Charles II. Height, 6½ ins. December 22, 1959.
£370.

A rare Lambeth delft mug, the body painted in blue with formal Chinese style ducks, weeds and floral motifs. Inscribed on neck " Thomas Balard. 1644." Heights, 6⅜ ins. March 22, 1960.
£300.

A documentary and unique Dublin delft bowl painted with blue panels of landscapes and ruins on a powdered manganese ground. Inscribed on base " Clay got over the Primate's Coals. Dublin 1753." Diameter, 16 ins. May 24, 1960.
£720.

A rare Lambeth delft bottle shaped jug painted in blue with a half-length portrait of Charles II. Inscribed " King Charles the 2/1660/S.B." The side panels with ship and coast scene. Height, 7 ins. October 25, 1960.
£320.

A very rare Lambeth delft octagonal pill slab painted in orange, green and blue with the Arms of the Apothecaries Company with motto. Height, 11 ins. December 20, 1960.
£580.

A rare Lambeth delft oval dish of " Palissy " type moulded with " Le Fecondite " subject. The panels with Arms of the City of London, the Broderer's Company and the initials and date. N.R.E. 1661. Length, 19 ins. December 20, 1960. £480.

A very rare Lambeth delft salt, formed as seated servant with tray, dated 1676. Height, 7½ ins. March 13, 1962. £620.

A fine set of Lambeth delft "Merry Man" plates, each painted with a line of verse, and initials F.M.A. and date 1693. July 10, 1962. £1,200.

LEEDS WARE

Six plates, with coloured transfer birds on cream ware. Sotheby, February 21, 1905. £4 15s.

Teapot and cover, with painted scale decoration, and another, scarlet ground and green leaves. Sotheby, February 21, 1905. £2 2s.

A pottery figure of a horse on oblong coloured plinth. Height, 16 ins. Christie, June 10, 1925. £11 0s. 6d.

Four oval baskets, covers and stands, modelled with rosettes and trellis work, and the covers surmounted by figures of boys. Christie, November 23, 1927. £27 6s.

Puzzle jug, painted with hawk and poultry. Height, 7 ins. Christie, December 15, 1927. £3 13s. 6d.

Teapot and cover, and cream jug, painted with Dutch portraits and flower sprays in colours. Christie, February 6, 1923. £27 6s.

A miniature tea service, 17 pieces. Christie, February 6, 1923. £2 12s. 6d.

A creamware jug with double entwined handle and animal head spout, the body decorated with a sheaf of corn and plough on each side of the inscription "Samuel and Lydia Slaney." Height, 8¾ ins. October 25, 1955. £36.

A creamware coffee service of coffee pot and cover, covered sucrier, 8 cups and 8 saucers. October 22, 1957. £24.

A creamware part tea service, boldly decorated on a brick red ground with vases of flowers and fruit in green and cream comprising teapot and cover, tea caddy and cover, sugar basin and 2 teabowls and saucers. January 20, 1959. £42.

A creamware dessert service of leaf shaped centrepiece, 6 shell shaped dishes and 25 leaf shaped dishes/plates. Impressed mark " Leeds Pottery." July 31, 1962. £140.

LIVERPOOL WARE

Bowl, with a printed ship inside, inscribed " Success to the William and Nancy." Dated 1776. Sotheby, November 13, 1906. £3.

Mug, with printed portrait of William Pitt. Sotheby, November 13, 1906. £2 8s.

Pair of cylindrical mugs, with portraits of George III and Queen Charlotte, supported by scroll work, introducing the Royal Arms, in red. Signed J. Sadler, Liverpool. Height, 6 ins. (Merton A. Thoms, Esq.) Christie, February 11, 1910. £42.

A pair of cylindrical mugs, transfer printed with portrait of George III. and Queen Charlotte, arms and scroll work by I. Sadler. Height, 6 ins. Christie, December 8, 1925. £204 15s.

A jug, moulded with scrolls and painted with exotic birds and flowers in colours. Height, 8½ ins. Sotheby, November 11, 1930. £15 10s.

A set of four octagonal cups and saucers in Chinese style in the Delft manner, in underglaze blue with " lady and jumping boy " pattern, possibly Chaffers' factory, simulated Chinese marks. Sotheby, November 28, 1930. £10 10s.

A pair of bell-shaped mugs attractively painted in the Chinese taste with 2 exotic birds on root ornament with branch, floral sprays, etc. Height, 4¾ ins. April 14, 1959. £90.

A rare small vase and cover with floral motifs in polychrome transfer print. Height, 6¼ ins. October 17, 1959. £24.

A very rare transfer printed teabowl and saucer decorated with gallant and companion walking arm in arm along the banks of a river with maid servant. January 26, 1960. £64.

A fine jug with plain strip loop handle. The body painted with Chinese river scene in underglaze blue with red and gold enrichments. Probably from the Chaffers factory. Height, 9¼ ins. January 26, 1960. £26.

A rare bowl attractively painted with bouquet of flowers and butterflies. Diameter, 6 ins. January 26, 1960. £24.

A rare and attractive moulded pattern cream jug of silver pattern, painted with panels of Chinese figures, etc. Height, 4¾ ins. March 29, 1960. £48.

A very rare blue and white bowl, the interior painted with music and song " Through all the Professions in town," etc. The exterior with Chinese type landscape. Diameter, 9 ins. May 10, 1960. £130.

A rare octagonal squat teapot and cover painted in underglaze blue with Chinese type figures and landscape. Dolphin knob. Height, 4¾ ins. May 10, 1960. £48.

A fluted sauceboat painted in brilliant blue with Chinese figure in landscape. Length 6½ ins. October 25, 1960. £24.

A leaf shaped moulded sauceboat decorated with floral design in underglaze blue. Length, 6¾ ins. October 25, 1960. £22.

A rare saucer dish with fluted sides painted in underglaze blue with " Jumping Boy " pattern. Diameter, 6¼ ins. November 22, 1960. £20.

A very rare dated (1757) bowl. Panels of Chinese styled figures in landscapes, on blue ground. English scene inside bowl. December 12, 1961. £62.

LONGTON HALL

Pair of figures of lady and gentleman with tambourine and lyre, on scroll plinth. Height, 21 ins. (From the Walker collection.) Christie, June 27, 1905. £64.

Vases, set of three, two-handled, bleu du roi ground, gilt floral decorations encrusted with flowers, the panels painted with landscapes, river scenes, and birds. Robinson and Fisher. November 18, 1905. £136 10s.

Pair of vases, painted with panels of exotic birds in gilt borders on dark blue ground. Height, 17 inches. Christie, December 5, 1905. £26 5s.

Pair of figures, boy and girl, on scroll bases. Sotheby, December 14, 1905. £15.

Vase and cover, with dark blue ground painted with exotic birds in colours in emulation of Worcester, in shaped panels with gilt borders. Height, 11¼ ins. (From the Walker collection.) Christie, June 27, 1906. £42.

Pair of figures of leopards. Height, 3¼ ins. (Merton A. Thoms, Esq.) Christie, February 11, 1910. £31 10s.

A figure of a sportsman, with gun, dog, and dead bird. Height, 6¾ ins. Mark, crossed L's. (Merton A. Thoms, Esq.) Christie, February 11, 1910. £53 11s.

Pair of vases and covers, in emulation of Worcester, painted with exotic birds in panels, on mottled dark blue ground, and formal leaves modelled in low relief. Height, 8 ins. Mark A, in blue. (T. W. Waller, Esq.) (Christie, June 8, 1910. £115 10s.

Set of three vases and covers, painted with classical figures, birds, branches in panels, with gilt foliage borders, on mottled blue ground. Height, 11 inches and 10 inches. Christie, April 7, 1911. £225 15s.

Pair of vases, painted with birds and flower sprays, in shaped panels with gilt scroll borders on mottled dark blue ground. Height, 6 ins. Christie, March 15, 1921. £52 10s.

Figure of a shepherd with dog, on red and green square plinth. Height, 9 ins. Christie, March 15, 1921. £23 2s.

Figure of a girl and youth on green square plinth. Height, 10 ins. Christie, March 15, 1921. £42.

Three vases and covers, painted with landscapes and figures in heart-shaped panels, with gilt scroll borders on mottled dark blue ground. Height, 12 ins. and 10½ ins. Christie, June 21, 1922. £215 5s.

A figure of a youth carrying a vase of flowers and leaning against a rock, with a basket of flowers at his side. Christie, February 25, 1926. £63.

A rare seated figure of Britannia, fully coloured. Goldblatt Collection. Height, 11 ins. May 1, 1957. £170.

A pair of plates with leaf borders, the centres painted with castles and towers in landscape. Diameter, 8½ ins. September 16, 1956. £460.

A rare pair of groups of Negro and a Turk leading a horse—after a Meissen original. Height, 8⅝ ins. September 16, 1956. £950.

A rare circular tureen, cover and stand, the body decorated with a deep rich runny blue (Littler's blue), the reserve panels painted with birds and floral sprays. Height, 9 ins. March 25, 1957. £210.

A rare tureen, cover and stand in the form of a cos lettuce, naturally moulded and coloured. Length, 12½ ins. April 15, 1958. £350.

A very rare pair of tureens and covers in the form of bunches of grapes naturalistically modelled and coloured. Length, 4½ ins. June 2, 1959. £320.

A rare tureen and cover in the form of an upright cauliflower, naturalistically modelled and coloured. Height, 6 ins. November 24, 1959. £260.

A fine and rare covered bowl in the form of a basket of flowers, the cover a mound of finely moulded flowers in high relief. Height, 8¾ ins. July 5, 1960. £920.

A very rare pair of candlestick groups—Spring and Autumn. Height, 8½ ins. March 13, 1962. £650.

LOWESTOFT

Bowl, painted with medallion views in brown, and with ribbons and foliage round the border in dark blue and gold. Diameter, 13½ ins. November 18, 1904.   £6 6s.
Child's jar, 1798, shaped, decorated in blue with border inside, at the top and outside with sprigs of flowers, and inscribed, " Onley Harvey, 1798." Bond, Ipswich, April 18, 1906.   £7 10s.
Jug, 1775, decorated with sprays of flowers in blue, marked No. 5 at bottom, inscribed with a cartouche (Ludham in Norfolk) Height, 5 inches. Bond, Ipswich, April 18, 1906.   £20.
Jug, 1778, pear-shaped, decorated in blue with sprays of flowers and insects, inscribed within a " Chippendale " frame (J. Bayfield, 1778). Height, 7 ins. Bond, Ipswich, April 18, 1906.   £17 10s.
Jug, 1786, decorated in blue transfer within a Chippendale design cartouche, a view of a coachman driving a coach with four horses, inscribed and dated below " William Bevine, Lowestoft, coachman, 1786." With this interesting jug is a framed description in the handwriting of the late Mr. W. Mason, of Ipswich. Height, 7½ ins. Bond, Ipswich, April 18, 1906.   £64.
Mug, decorated in rose and pale green colours, inscribed within a 1790 period cartouche. " A trifle from Bungay." Illustrated in Suffolk Arch. XI., Part 3, p. 369. Height, 4¾ ins. Bond, Ipswich, April 18, 1906.   £56.
Plate, 1770, decorated in blue round the edge with sprays of flowers, inscribed within a " Chippendale " frame " William and Mary Ellis." Dated at back, 1770. Diameter, 9 ins. Bond, Ipswich, April 18, 1906.   £23 10s.

  This kind of specimen represents the best work of the factory.

Inkstand, with decoration in blue, and inscribed " A trifle from Lowestoft." Christie, March 11, 1909.   £13 13s.
Coffee jug and cover, painted in blue with panels of Chinese river scenes on powdered-blue ground. Christie, December 3, 1909.   £18 18s.
Large teapot and cover, painted in blue with the royal arms and cipher of George III., and the date 1772; also on the reverse a scroll-shaped panel, enclosing the initials G.B., and the date 1772. (Merton A. Thoms, Esq.) Christie, February 11, 1910.   £26 5s.
A cylindrical mug, painted with a view of a seaport, lighthouse, and shipping, and the arms of Trinity House in colours, on white ground enriched with gilt dots. Height, 5½ ins. (Merton A. Thoms, Esq.) Christie, February 11, 1910. £75 12s.
Teapot and cover, painted with panels of Chinese landscapes in blue, on a ground of raised white flowers, and with initials I.H. and the date 1761 in relief. (Merton A. Thoms, Esq.) Christie, February 11, 1910.   £65 2s.
Mug, inscribed " A Trifle from Lowestoft." Height, 3½ ins. Christie, December 13, 1920.   £29 8s.
Bowl and cover on heater, painted with flower sprays in blue, and the handles modelled with marks. Height, 10 ins. Christie, March 15, 1921.   £32 11s.
A pair of oval dishes, painted with Chinese river scenes in blue, in circular and fan-shaped panels on powder-blue ground. Width, 11 ins. Christie, February 2, 1926.   £25 4s.
Five plates, painted with river scenes in blue in the Chinese taste. Christie, July 21, 1927.   £19 19s.
A pair of bottles, painted with Chinese figures in colours. Height, 4½ ins. Christie, June 31, 1924.   £11 11s.
A teapot decorated with ruins, painted in puce camaieu. Height, 5¾ ins. March, 1, 1955.   £42.
A fine bell shaped mug decorated in underglaze blue with inscription " James Bullard R.A. 1768." Mark " 3." Height, 5¾ ins. December 6, 1955.   £70.
A fine teapot and cover decorated in colours, in the manner of Curtis and inscribed " Willm. and Ann Cobb. Harleston 1790." Height, 5½ ins. December 6, 1955.   £82.
A rare birth tablet decorated in enamel colours, one side inscribed " Ann Redgrave. Born Janry ye 2d 1794." Diameter, 4¼ ins. December 6, 1955.   £70.
A superb set of three cylindrical mugs in graduated sizes, painted in colours with panels of European figures standing on the banks of a river. Height, 5⅞, 5 and 3½ ins. December 6, 1955.   £260.
A jug decorated in underglaze blue, the central cartouche inscribed " John Vince, Great Melton 1791." Height, 7 ins. January 27, 1959.   £100.
A blue and white covered coffee pot and cover inscribed " John Ward. Blofield " with a long verse. Height, 9⅜ ins. January 27, 1959.   £240.
A cylindrical mug the central cartouche inscribed " A Trifle from Lowestoft." Slight floral border in enamel colours. Height, 3½ ins. January 27, 1959.   £58.

A cream ewer decorated in enamel colours inscribed under the base " Mand E. Calder. Norwich 1776." With a matching saucer. January 27, 1959.   £100.
A rare flask painted with scene of two gentlemen seated drinking at a tripod table, the reverse with a sailor and his lass seated on rocks, all in enamel colours. Height, 5⅜ ins. January 27, 1959.   £135.
An oval butter dish and cover decorated with moulded design and panels and other decoration in underglaze blue, c. 1765.   February 10, 1959.   £17.
A rare small figure of a seated cat on oval green base.   Height, 2¼ ins.   July 7, 1959. (Two other examples were sold for £65 and £120 in 1962.)   £65.
A rare figure of a standing putto, scantily draped and coloured. Height, 5½ ins. July 7, 1959.   £66.
A rare coffee cup and saucer from the Ludlow service, painted in black and gold with Lion crest and initials " E.L.," c. 1785.   May 10, 1960.   £20.
A rare circular inkwell inscribed in brown within a puce cartouche " A Trifle from Lowestoft." Height, 2 ins.   May 10, 1960.   (Two mugs bearing this inscription were sold for £52 and £58; similar " trifle " pieces are illustrated in Godden's *British Pottery and Porcelain, an Illustrated Encyclopædia of Marked Specimens.*)   £62.

LUSTRE WARE ·

Two jugs, with resist silver lustre of flowers on canary ground.   Height, 4 ins. and 4½ ins.   £27.
A jug, with band of flowers in resist silver lustre on canary ground.   Height, 5¾ ins.; and a small jug, with floral pattern in silver and red on canary ground.   £33 10s.
A jug, with pattern of birds and foliage in canary on silver lustre.   Height, 6 ins.   £10.
A jug, with pattern of vines in blue on silver lustre.   Height, 5½ ins.   All at Sotheby's, June 4, 1931.   £18.
A fine silver resist pattern jug with vertical sprays of flowers and a cornucopia in blue and silver resist, beneath a wreath in similar technique in blue round the neck.   Height, 5¾ ins.   June 21, 1955.   £80.
A yellow ground silver resist pattern jug, the body decorated with a fine scrolling floral band in lustre.   Height, 6 ins.   June 21, 1955.   £50.
A silver lustre jug with angled handle and lip, the body decorated with pheasant like birds amongst flowers in white resist on a silver ground.   Height, 5¼ ins.   February 18, 1958.   £20.
A silver resist jug with unusual bird's head handle, the body decorated with birds on barred gates, with floral scrolling, in resist on a silver ground.   Height, 5¾ ins.   February 18, 1958.   £34.
A yellow ground earthenware jug decorated with red strawberries with silver lustre leaves and stalks.   Height, 5¼ ins.   June 16, 1959.   £42.

MASON'S IRONSTONE

Pair of large vases, decorated in gold with Kylin tops.   Debenham and Storrs.   January 3, 1906.   £8 5s.
Dinner service, decorated with flowers in colours, consisting of 197 pieces.   Christie, March 2, 1906.   £53 11s.
Two ironstone ewers, painted with landscapes and birds, and gilt with foliage on dark blue ground, with figures of children in high relief.   Height, 27 ins.   Christie, May 30, 1923.   £18 18s.
An ironstone dinner service, painted with flowers in the Oriental taste, 37 pieces. Christie, July 25, 1928.   £8 8s.
An ironstone dessert service, with foliage in red, blue and gold, 31 pieces.   Christie, March 25, 1930.   £15 15s.
An ironstone dinner service, decorated with pagodas and flowers in the Chinese taste, 97 pieces.   Christie, March 25, 1930.   £23 2s.
A large vase, painted with landscapes on a sage green ground, with gilt borders. Height, 28 ins.   Christie, December 9, 1924.   £15 15s.
An Ironstone dinner service decorated in the traditional " Japan " style with red, blue and gilt formal floral pattern comprising 129 pieces—some damaged, c. 1825.   March 6, 1956.   £70.
An Ironstone dinner service decorated in " famille-rose " style within blue borders comprising 103 pieces—some damaged.   Printed marks, c. 1830.   July 10, 1956.   £48.
An Ironstone dessert service decorated with transfer printed and enamelled oriental style formal floral pattern comprising 3 oval dishes, 12 dinner plates and 20 other plates. Printed mark, c. 1830.   February 18, 1958.   £22.

MINTON

Sèvres pattern service, painted with groups of flowers and fruit in centres and panels of birds round the border on *gros bleu* ground, gilt, with flowers, 38 pieces. (From the Duke of Buckingham's collection.) Christie, June 2, 1905. £67 4s.

Pair of vases and covers, Sèvres pattern, painted with Leda and Diana and amatory trophies in panels on turquoise ground, and with white and gold foliage handles and borders. Height, 12 ins. Christie, December 5, 1905. £53 11s.

Harlequin service, variously painted with flowers, figures, etc., consisting of 54 plates. Christie, March 6, 1906. £33 12s.

Pair of Sèvres pattern vases and covers, painted with camp scenes after Morin, and military trophies, in apple green borders on marbled *gros bleu* and gold ground, painted by Boullemin and Leroi. Made for the 1851 Exhibition. Height, 20¼ ins. Christie, March 30, 1906. £136 10s.

Solon ware vases (pair), with chocolate ground and oval panels of nymphs and cupids in white. Height, 16 ins. Christie, May 4, 1906. £22 1s.

Pair of vases and covers, oviform with turquoise ground, painted with panels of children in beaded white and gold borders. Height, 16 ins. Christie, May 4, 1906. £27 6s.

A Solon ware bowl, decorated with nymphs and cupids in white on black ground, and supported by figures of four children. Diameter, 20¼ ins.; height, 24½ ins. (Thomas Wood, Esq.) Christie, April 24, 1908. £38 17s.

Pair of Solon ware vases, with figures of nymphs and cupids before an altar and fountain, in white on black ground, and with decoration in green, blue, chocolate, and gold round the necks and plinths. Height, 20 ins. (Stephen G. Holland, Esq.) Christie, June 30, 1908. £183 15s.

Pair of Sèvres-pattern vases and covers, painted with panels of figures and flowers on pink ground. Height, 15 ins. (Octavius E. Coope, Esq.) Christie, May 4, 1910. £105.

A pair of Minton Sèvres pattern vases and covers, painted with battle scenes and military trophies on marbled pink and blue ground. Height, 20¼ ins. Christie, May 30, 1923. £50 8s.

A Minton Solon ware vase, decorated with a Bacchante and cupids in white on brown ground and richly gilt borders. Christie, July 24, 1924. £35 14s.

A pair of similar vases, decorated in white on a blue ground. Christie, December 15, 1927. £46 4s.

A dessert service, painted with pink rosebuds, pearl ornament and turquoise and red bands in the Sèvres taste, 17 pieces. Christie, July 25, 1928. £18 18s.

A dinner service, decorated with flowers in colours in the Chinese *famille rose* taste, 161 pieces. Christie, April 10, 1924. £36 15s.

A pair of pâte-sur-pâte vases by L. Solon decorated with Cupid and Psyche subjects. February 7, 1956. £98.

A 14 in. pâte-sur-pâte vase and cover by A. Birks decorated with Venus and Cupid subjects. April 10, 1956. £100.

A cabaret set decorated with pâte-sur-pâte panels by Alboine Birks comprising tray and five other pieces. November 13, 1956. £160.

A pair of covered vases 15½ ins. high of mazarin blue ground, the reserve panels painted with birds and trophies in the Sèvres manner, c. 1878. December 16, 1958. £76.

A pair of vases of slender form decorated in the pâte-sur-pâte technique by Alboine Birks, c. 1898. Height, 12 ins. January 12, 1960. £72.

A single large blue ground vase decorated in pâte-sur-pâte technique by L. Solon with Venus and Amor. Gilt mark, c. 1895. Height, 17 ins. November 22, 1960. £160.

A decorative plateau decorated in white and tinted slip by L. Solon. Made for the Paris Exhibition of 1878. Gilt mark, c. 1878. Length, 13 ins. November 22, 1960. £90.

A superb set of three covered vases of Sèvres form. Blue-celeste ground with Watteau type figure subject panels, c. 1875. Height, 13 ins. and 16 ins. June 29, 1962. See Godden's *British Pottery and Porcelain, an Illustrated Encyclopædia of Marked Specimens.* £400.

An important pâte-sur-pâte vase by L. A. Birks. Height, 16 ins. June 29, 1962. £160.

NANTGARW

Four plates, painted with birds in the centre and groups of flowers on the border, and richly gilt with shells and leafage. Impressed mark. (From the Hawkins collection.) Christie, June 2, 1904. £69 10s.

Plates of this same service have been recently sold for £25 each.

Dessert service, in emulation of old Sèvres, painted with bouquets and sprays of flowers and blue lines round the borders, and with raised white flowers. Impressed mark, 11 pieces. (From the Anglesey collection.) Christie, January 12, 1905. £69 6s.

Oval tray, painted with flowers in turquoise and gold borders. Impressed mark. Length, 11 ins. Christie, January 20, 1906. £6 6s.

Plate, painted with doves in the centre and pink rosebuds round the border, on dotted gold ground with raised flower sprays. Impressed mark. Christie, February 27, 1906. £44 2s.

Plate, with hunting scene and flowers, with apple green border. Impressed mark. Christie, February 27, 1906. £21.

Plate, painted with a bird in the centre, raised green branches of flowers and gilt scrolls round the borders. Impressed mark. Christie, April 27, 1906. £30 9s.

Pair of deep plates, painted with rosebuds in the centre and a wreath of roses round the border on dotted gold ground. Impressed mark. Diameter, 10 ins. Christie, May 4, 1906. £29 8s.

Two small cups and saucers, with two handles, painted with rosebuds on white ground and with raised white blossom. Christie, May 18, 1906. £22 1s.

Dessert service, painted with bouquets of flowers in colours and richly gilt with flowers and trellis work. Impressed mark, 21 pieces. Christie, July 7, 1906. £78 15s.

A plate, painted with figures snowballing, in colours in richly gilt border. Impressed mark. (J. E. Wilkinson, Esq.) Christie, April 6, 1909. £26 5s.

Bowl, cover, and stand, painted with rosebuds on dotted gold ground. Impressed mark. Christie, February 1, 1910. £22 1s.

Pair of plates, painted with birds and flowers, and with white scrolls in relief. Impressed mark. Christie, March 4, 1910. £25 4s.

Pair of oval dishes, painted with rosebuds and birds, and richly gilt with foliage, with black medallions round the border. Width, 11½ ins. Impressed mark. Christie, February 3, 1911. £21 10s. 6d.

Pair of plates, painted with bouquets of flowers in colours, the borders modelled with white flowers and scrolls. Impressed mark. Christie, March 7, 1911. £28 7s.

Pair of plates, painted with birds and groups of flowers, and the borders richly gilt with shells and foliage. Diameter, 9¼ ins. Impressed mark. (Montague White, Esq.) Christie, December 15, 1911. £43 1s.

Plate, painted with a view of a park in the centre and small views of country seats round the border, the ground gilt with flowers, and with raised flowers and scrolls. Diameter, 9½ ins. Impressed mark. (Montague White, Esq.) Christie, December 15, 1911. £26 5s.

Dessert service, painted with flower sprays in colours on white ground, and modelled with scrollwork in low relief—impressed mark—37 pieces. Christie, March 15, 1921. £273.

A plate, painted with flowers in centre on a white ground, with groups of fruit round the border on grey ground, with white and gold flower sprays and scrolls in relief. Diameter 9¾ ins.—impressed mark. Christie, June 21, 1922. £21.

A tureen and cover, painted with pink roses on dotted gold ground. Christie, December 15, 1927. £10 10s.

A part service of four dishes, six plates and twenty-four meat plates, painted with bouquets in cobalt, probably by Morris. Sotheby, November 11, 1930. £31.

A plate, with moulded rim, probably by Morris, impressed mark. Diameter, 9½ ins. £8 10s.

A plate, painted with an Elizabethan house, probably by Beddoe. £13.

A pair of plates, painted with birds, by Colclough. Diameter, 9¼ ins. Sotheby, November 11, 1930. £22.

A fine plate, the centre painted with a bullfinch perched on a basket of flowers, probably painted by Thomas Pardoe. Diameter, 10 ins. May 14, 1957. £190.

A typical floral painted plate with raised moulded edges. Impressed mark. Diameter, 8½ ins. May 12, 1959. £65.

An inkstand with cornucopia shaped inkwell and pounce pot and wafer stand. Floral sprays, etc., probably decorated in London, Length of stand, 7¼ ins. October 17, 1959. £80.

A plate with a shaped rim, the centre painted with blue convolvulus and pink roses. Marked. Diameter, 8½ ins. November 24, 1959. £36.

A shaped oval dish with gilt dentil rim, the body painted with sprig pattern and small gilt leaves. Impressed " Nantgarw C.W." mark. Length, 12 ins. March 1, 1960. £48.

A cup and saucer decorated with pink roses connected by gilt scrolls, the cup with swan-neck handle. March 22, 1960. £28.

A rare muffin dish painted with flowers within a dark green border. Impressed " Nantgarw - C.W." mark. Diameter, 8½ ins. November 8, 1960. £65.

A brilliant plate, the centre painted with bouquet of roses, dahlias, honeysuckle, etc., border of roses, etc. Impressed " NANTGARW." mark. Diameter, 10 ins. November 29, 1960. £220.

A good plate with moulded border, the centre painted with country view in the manner of Thomas Pardoe. Impressed Nantgarw C.W. June 26, 1962. £60.

NEW HALL

Tea service, painted with flowers in the Oriental taste, red, blue, green, and gold, consisting of sugar-basin and cover, cream-jug, bowl, dish, ten teacups, twelve coffee-cups, and twelve saucers. Christie, November 20, 1906. £14 3s. 6d.

A tea service, decorated with Chinese figures in landscapes, in red diaper border, 39 pieces. Christie, February 28, 1924. £7 17s. 6d.

A part tea and coffee service painted in colours with vignettes of domestic scenes comprising teapot, cover and stand, sucrier and cover, milk jug, plate, 3 tea cups, 4 coffee cups and 6 saucers, c. 1820. November 28, 1955. £25.

A tea service painted with Chinese figures seated on terraces within ornate border comprising teapot, cover and stand, covered sucrier, milk jug, bowl, 2 plates, 12 tea cups, 8 coffee cups and 12 saucers. July 12, 1955. £32.

A New Hall tea service, transfer printed with views of farms, river scenes, ruins, etc., within oval panels comprising teapot, cover and stand, sucrier and cover, milk jug, bowl, 2 plates, 12 cups and 6 saucers. January 21, 1958. £50.

A New Hall tea set attractively painted with flowers on a grey ground, comprising teapot, (damaged), stand, covered sugar bowl, creamer, 2 saucer plates, 12 coffee cups and saucers and 8 tea cups. February 27, 1962. £130.

PINXTON

A fine yellow ground cream jug. Painted panels of Pinxton Church and Breadsall Church, Derbyshire. June 26, 1962. £260.

A cream jug of similar shape but more ordinary pattern—unnamed views in grey monochrome. June 26, 1962. £40.

An oval teapot and stand and a cup and saucer, painted with border of cabbage roses. Mark P. 131. June 26, 1962. £42.

A plate(?) painted with cottage, etc., in the manner of Cutts. Rare script mark: Pinxton, no. 331. July 31, 1962. £36.

PLYMOUTH

A white shell stand, encrusted with shells. £5 5s.

Half-pint mug, with neatly hand-painted bird and flowers. Saul, Southport, September 21, 1906. £5.

Pair of shell stands of seven dishes, each encrusted with shells, coral, and seaweed. Height, 11¼ ins. And four shell dishes en suite, painted with flowers, the stands encrusted with shells, seaweed, and figures of birds. Christie, March 22, 1907. £100 18s.

A shell, sweetmeat stand, painted with flowers in the Oriental taste, and encrusted with shells. Height, 7½ ins. Christie, April 5, 1907. £25 4s.

Pair of small jugs and covers, painted with panels of Chinese figures in landscapes, on a gilt ground-work of formal flowers. (Percy Arden, Esq.) Christie, December 15, 1909. £27 6s.

Mug, painted with birds and trees in colours. Christie, February 1, 1910. £13 13s.

A large figure, representing Literature and Art, richly decorated. Height, 13¼ ins. Sotheby, November 19, 1910. £23 10s.

Teapot and cover, painted with flowers in colours in the Oriental taste. Christie, November 25, 1910. £21.

A mug, painted with Chinese figures and flowers in colours on white ground. Height, 5½ ins. Christie, March 13, 1924. £52 10s.

Another, similar, £42.

A pair of sauce-boats, painted with Chinese figures, birds and flowers in colours, in raised scroll borders. Christie, March 13, 1924. £18 18s.

A figure of Minerva. Height, 7½ ins. Christie, December 8, 1925. £6 6s.

A group of two children, with a festoon of flowers on lake scroll plinth. Christie, February 25, 1926. £54 12s.

Three white shell stands, encrusted with shells, and with gilt edges. Height, 10 ins. Christie, December 5, 1928. £25 4s.

A shell sweetmeat stand, with ten dishes painted with Chinese figures. Christie, December 5, 1928. £11 11s.

A blue and white teapot and cover decorated in the Chinese taste. Sharp Collection. March 1, 1955.
£26.

A rare coffee pot and cover, the ribbed body decorated with group of Chinese figures in colour. Height, 11½ ins. March 12, 1957.
£140.

A group of 2 putti with goat, bocage background. Height, 7⅝ ins. March 12, 1957. £72.

A set of 4 seasons depicted by standing putti in various poses and dress, coloured. Height, 5½ ins. to 5¾ ins. May 12, 1959.
£200.

A rare bell shaped mug, the central panel finely painted with Chinese figures in a garden, in colours. Height, 6⅛ ins. June 2, 1959.
£145.

Two coloured standing figures of America and Africa from the four continents. Height, 12 ins. October 15, 1959.
£125.

An unusual ribbed and moulded pattern sauce boat, the central panels enamelled with figures in landscape. Length, 7¼ ins. November 24, 1959.
£55.

A pair of hexagonal sauce boats enamelled with floral sprays. Length, 6¾ ins. November 24, 1959.
£65.

A figure of phoenix in white, the bird rising from its ashes, on a square base. Height, 8¼ ins. November 29, 1960.
£75.

A pair of groups of putti, 1 group of 2 putti with goat, coloured and gilt. Height, 6 ins. November 29, 1960.
£90.

ROCKINGHAM

Teapot and cover, large brown, glazed with birds and flowers in colours in relief, and inscribed, " E. Willmott, Christmas, 1800." Sotheby, February 21, 1905. £37 16s.

Twelve plates, octagonal, painted with flowers and birds in colours, in stippled green and red borders, in the Chinese taste. Griffin mark. (From the Huth collection.) Christie, May 23, 1905.
£26 5s.

Tea service, buff, with flower decoration, 44 pieces. Lewendon, Hull, March 9, 1906.
£29 14s.

Pair of figures of a man and woman in Eastern costume. Height, 7¾ ins. Christie, June 22, 1906.
£16 16s.

Dessert service, blue and gold, the centres with landscapes, comprising centre dish, twelve shaped dishes, and twenty-four plates. Puttick and Simpson, July 6, 1906.
£10 10s.

A bowl and stand (2 handles), large, painted with flowers, with deep red and pink borders heightened with gold. Puttick and Simpson, November 5, 1906. £6 16s. 6d.

A dish, encrusted with flowers in colours and centre painted with fruit on a table. Sotheby, November 13, 1906.
£4 12s.

A vase painted with shells and fruit, and richly gilt upon a white ground. Height, 14½ ins. Marked. (Skidmore.) Hepper and Sons, March 4, 1908. £15 4s. 6d.

Pair of plates, painted with the Crown, Lion, Rose, Thistle, and Shamrock, the border gilt, with the Garter motto on dark blue ground. (Said to have belonged to William IV.) Christie, January 29, 1909.
£48 6s.

Vase and cover, painted with a classical river scene and birds, and encrusted with coloured flowers. Height, 12½ ins. Christie, November 25, 1910. £15 4s. 6d.

A plate, painted with the arms of the Earl of Essex, with flower sprays round the border on blue and gold œil-de-perdrix ground—gryphon mark. Christie, July 24, 1924.
£16 16s.

A tea service, painted with flower sprays in colours in buff borders, 43 pieces. Christie, November 24, 1925.
£15 15s.

A dessert service, with apple green borders, gilt with foliage, 74 pieces. Christie, November 24, 1925.
£33 12s.

A pair of beakers, painted with flowers on apple-green ground. Height, 6 ins.; and one with a river scene. Christie, February 4, 1926.
£8 18s. 6d.

A drinking-cup formed as a fox's mask; and one formed as a trout's head. Christie, March 30, 1926.
£11 11s.

A bowl, the interior painted with flowers, in grey borders, richly gilt. Diameter, 10¼ ins. Christie, February 5, 1929.
£5 5s.

A dessert service, painted with landscapes in apple green borders, gilt with foliage and scrollwork, 43 pieces. Christie, November 21, 1929
£120 15s.

A vase, encrusted with flowers. Height, 7½ ins. Christie, November 21, 1929.
£1 11s. 6d.

A pair of porcelain bedposts, now converted into lamp-shades, with griffin mark. Height, of porcelain, 4 ft. 8 ins. Sotheby, November 28, 1930.
£28.

A Rockingham type apple green ground dessert service of 6 various side dishes and 12 plates. All painted with single sprays of botanical flowers, c. 1830. May 8, 1956. £100.

Two Rockingham type vases in the form of an open tulip and a bud with fine green leaves and a mound base. Height, 6¼ ins. and 4 ins. July 10, 1956.
£88.

A large Rockingham dinner service, each piece painted with floral bouquets within sky blue borders and feather moulded rims comprising 2 soup tureens, covers and stands, 2 other tureens, 6 vegetable dishes and 4 covers, 18 dishes, 5 sauce tureens and covers, fruit dish and 119 plates. Some pieces damaged. Some pieces marked with printed " griffin " mark. July 7, 1959. £240.

A Rockingham type dessert service, each piece fine painted with different flowers within a rich blue border comprising centrepiece, 4 dishes and 12 plates, c. 1830. November 3, 1959. £120.

A pair of Rockingham type pot-pourri vases and covers, the bodies painted with landscape and floral and fruit panels on a blue ground. Height, 17½ ins. June 10, 1960. £38.

SALT GLAZE

Tea service, blue, gold, and white, 43 pieces. Lewendon, Hull, March 9, 1906. £20 8s. 6d.

A tea poy, 1770, square-shaped, decorated with scratched flowers in blue, and on one side with a female half-length figure within a " Chippendale " frame holding a cornucopia, inscribed on one side " Marthe Saymore, September ye 25th, 1770." Height, 5¼ ins. Bond, Ipswich, April 18, 1906. £11.

Teapot, crimson ground with white panels, in which are flowers in enamelled colours. Sotheby, June 25, 1906. £26.

Bowl and cover, and a milk-jug decorated in rich blue ground, Sotheby, June 25, 1906. £26.

Teapot and cover, brilliantly enamelled with flowers upon a dark blue ground. Sotheby, June 25, 1906. £25.

Teapot and cover, brilliantly enamelled upon the body with roses, auriculas, and other flowers, with turquoise handle and spout, and painted on the bottom with a sunflower. Sotheby, June 25, 1906. £50.

A figure of a man, wearing Eastern costume, with blue coat and turban. Height, 5½ ins. (J. E. Wilkinson, Esq.) Christie, April 6, 1909. £31 10s.

A figure of Cupid riding a leopard, by Ralph Wood. Height, 8 ins. Christie, December 3, 1909. £36 15s.

A jug, painted in colours, with a lady and gentleman, and buildings in a landscape, and with pink, green, and blue diaper work border. Height, 9½ ins. (Lady Bateman Scott.) Christie, February 22, 1910. £75 12s.

A teapot and cover, painted with flowers in colours on dotted black ground, with branch handle and spout. Christie, February 25, 1910. £16 16s.

A teapot and cover; painted with portrait of the King of Prussia in colours, on a ground of black arrows. (The Rev. A. Willett.) Christie, March 31, 1910. £34 13s.

Teapot and cover, with pink ground and vine branches in low relief, coloured green and purple, branch handle and spout. Christie, April 28, 1911. £48 6s.

A teapot and cover, with portrait of the King of Prussia and the Imperial Eagle in panels, on a ground of black arrow heads. Christie, March 5, 1929. £12 12s.

An equestrian figure. Height, 9 ins. Christie, February 6, 1930. £178 10s.

Two oblong teapots formed as houses. Christie, February 6, 1923. £11 11s.

A figure of a canary, uncoloured, Height, 5¾ ins. £39.

A figure of a hawk, from Chinese original. £38.

A punch kettle, globular, painted with a figure of Bacchus seated on a barrel. Height, 6 ins. £26.

A " pew " group in black and white of a lady seated between two gentlemen on a settee. Partly restored. Height, 6½ ins., width, 6¾ ins. Sotheby, November 11, 1930. £260.

Two others realised £125 and £170.

A teapot decorated with the front panel depicting the King of Prussia, the reverse with black eagle. March 1, 1955. £75.

A teapot painted with floral sprays and green ground panel on which is written " Fine Green Tea." March 1, 1955. £72.

A rare Dog of Fo, after an Oriental original, on rectangular base. Slight brown decoration. Height, 7¾ ins. December 18, 1956. £130.

A fine plate, the border moulded with raised and painted floral sprays, the centre enamelled with standing Chinese lady and kneeling servant with tray of refreshments. Diameter, 9¼ ins. February 10, 1959. £175.

A rare standing white figure of Shou Lao, Taoist God of Longevity (after a Chinese original). Height, 6 ins. October 15, 1959. £140.

A rare and decorative plate with moulded rim, the centre painted in Famille Rose style with Chinese figure in garden. Diameter, 9¼ ins. October 15, 1959. £125.

A very rare large tankard and cover, the moulded body depicting Admiral Vernon, Port o'Bello and H.M.S. Burford. Inscribed " PortoBello taken by Ad. Vernon." Also with Arms, etc., of George II. Height, 9½ ins. October 15, 1959. £780.

A rare and fine period bowl covered with rich blue glaze of Littler type. Diameter, 8¾ ins.
December 11, 1959.
£390.

A well painted and attractive bowl painted with Chinese woman playing a flute, floral
sprays, etc. Diameter, 9¾ ins. February 16, 1960.
£280.

A rare teapot and cover of crimson ground with panels of flowers in red, yellow, blue, pink
and green. Height, 4½ ins. October 25, 1960.
£200.

A fine, rare pair of figures of recumbent horses. Length, 8½ ins. October 24, 1962. £1,450.

A fine jug of silver shape, attractively painted with lovers in a rural landscape. Height,
6¾ ins. November 14, 1961.
£250.

A fine pair of coloured salt glazed wall pockets with moulded motifs, half length figure of
Flora, etc. Height, 11 ins. February 6, 1962.
£350.

A rare and important moulded (uncoloured) saltglaze tankard. Panel portrait of George II
and inscription—God save the King and my Master. Height, 7 ins., mint state.
June 5, 1962.
£250.

SPODE

Pair of vases and covers, hexagonal, painted with panels of flowers in the Oriental
taste, with gilt mask handles. Height, 20 ins. Christie, March 30. £44 2s.

Dessert service, painted with groups of peaches, grapes, and other fruit, in apple green
and gold borders, 113 pieces. (From the Anglesey collection.) Christie, January
12, 1905.
£220 10s.

Tea service, painted with flowers in dark blue, red, and gold, 40 pieces. February 24,
1905.
£11 11s.

Dessert service, painted with panels of flowers and birds on pink ground, and with white
and gold gadrooned edges, comprising centre dish on foot, two square, four shell-
shaped dishes, and eighteen plates. Christie, February 27, 1906. £33 12s.

Dinner service, painted with flowers in the Oriental taste, and with dark blue and gold
panels, 169 pieces. Christie, April 20, 1906.
£38 17s.

Pair of two-handled cups, covers, and saucers, painted with flowers in colours on dark
blue ground, with scale-pattern in gold. Christie, December 10, 1909. £34 13s.

A vase, painted with flowers in colours on gold ground. Height, 6½ ins. Christie,
July 25, 1910.
£8 18s. 6d.

Tea service, decorated with flowers in red, blue, green and gold, 40 pieces. Christie,
December 13, 1920.
£22 1s.

A set of three vases, painted with coast scenes and flowers in colours, with richly gilt
borders and rams' head handles. Height, 11 ins. and 10¼ ins. Christie, May 30,
1931.
£27 6s.

An oblong basket, painted with flowers on dotted gold ground. Christie, November 25,
1925.
£7 17s. 6d.

A dinner service, painted with flowers and vases in red, blue and gold in the Oriental
taste, 214 pieces. Christie, June 10, 1925.
£89 5s.

A pair of plates, painted with flowers in the Worcester taste, in panels, with gilt scroll
borders on dark blue ground. Christie, March 9, 1926.
£18 18s.

A supper set, with Chinese ornament in red and brown on red ground, 12 pieces.
Christie, December 5, 1928.
£25 4s.

A dinner service, decorated with vases of flowers in red, blue and gold in the Chinese
taste, with red, blue and gold panels round the borders, 149 pieces. Christie, May 3,
1928.
£241 10s.

A tripod vase and cover, painted with flowers on dark blue scale pattern ground, with
gilt dolphin supports. Height, 6¼ ins. Christie, March 11, 1926. £28 7s.

A dessert service, painted with flowers in colours on dark blue and gold scale pattern
ground, 25 pieces. Christie, November 27, 1923.
£241 10s.

A small pot-pourri basket and cover of the colourful 1166 pattern, c. 1800. Diameter,
5¼ ins. May 14, 1957.
£30.

A pair of small cups of tulip form. Height, 2¾ ins. May 12, 1959. £65.

A bowl painted in the " Japan " style with formal floral motifs in red, blue, green and gold.
Diameter, 10 ins. November 3, 1959.
£22.

A very rare pottery set of 6 tulip shaped cups on a circular stand of tulip form. Some
slight defects. Impressed " Spode " mark. February 16, 1960.
£360.

A fine pair of porcelain vases of 711 pattern, the bodies painted with flowers on a gold ground.
Height, 6½ ins. April 8, 1960.
£120.

A vase of amphora shape painted with flowers and fruit on an apricot ground. Height,
17¾ ins. November 22, 1960.
£36.

A vase with gilt ground, central panel of scene. Floral sprays over gilt ground. Height,
12¾ ins. Rare mark: Spode & Copeland, in script. July 24, 1962. £50

STAFFORDSHIRE POTTERY

Collection of 59 models of cottages, many coloured and encrusted with flowers. Christie, January 19, 1906. £31 10s.

Group of the Madonna and Child, engraved in Church's *English Earthenware*. Sotheby, February 21, 1906. £8

Barber's jug, 1809, silver lustre, decorated with two medallions, one of a barber and customer in his shop, and another emblematical of Hope, inscribed " William Freeman, 1809." Height, 6¾ ins. Bond, Ipswich, April 18, 1906. £5.

Group of Vicar and Moses, in pulpit translucent colours. Sotheby, November 13, 1906. £8 10s.

Two figures of Falstaff on plinths encrusted with flowers. Height, 9 ins. Christie, November 15, 1906. £5 15s. 6d.

Pair of figures of cupids riding lion and lioness; and inkstand surmounted by an eagle, and a figure of a peasant girl. Christie, November 15, 1906. £20 9s. 6d.

Groups (a pair), the Shoemaker, on pierced blue and white plinths. Height, 12 ins. Christie, November 15, 1906. £27 6s.

Two groups, Hercules and the Bull. Height, 5½ ins. Christie, November 15, 1906. £15 15s.

Large statuette of Cleopatra, height, 22 ins., and a figure of a nymph, height, 17 ins. Christie, November 15, 1906. £19 8s. 6d.

Four Toby fill-pot jugs, formed as gentlemen, and one jug formed as a lady. Christie, November 15, 1906. £30 9s.

Statuette of Sir Walter Raleigh, holding a roll. Height, 21½ ins. (Percy Fitzgerald, Esq., F.S.A.) Christie, January 24, 1908. £21.

Large jug, decorated with a bird and flowers in silver lustre and white, and inscribed, " J. Simpson, Original Staffordshire Warehouse, 1791." (Percy Fitzgerald, Esq., F.S.A.) Christie, January 24, 1908. £14 14s.

A group of lovers, with a lamb, goat, and dog. Height, 10 ins. Christie, December 22, 1908. £18 18s.

A large figure of a nymph, with a dove. Height, 30 ins. (The Rev. A. Willett.) Christie, April 1, 1910. £39 18s.

A voyez jug, modelled with Bacchanalian figures in high relief. Height, 13 ins. Christie, May 26, 1910. £153 5s.

A similar specimen sold at Christie's, July 26, 1910, for £50 8s.

An equestrian figure, by Ralph Wood. Height, 11 ins. Christie, November 25, 1910. £42.

Group of the Madonna and Child. Height, 13½ ins. Christie, February 2, 1911. £12 12s.

Group of a shepherd and shepherdess with lamb, dog, and goat at their feet. Height, 10¾ ins. Christie, March 3, 1911. £9 19s. 6d.

Jug, modelled with Bacchus and an infant satyr in high relief, and with lizard handle, by Ralph Wood. Height, 12 ins. Christie, March 21, 1911. £25 4s.

An equestrian figure, by Ralph Wood. Height, 11½ ins. (Col. Hegan Kennard.) Christie, May 29, 1911. £77 14s.

Figure of a horse. Height, 9 ins. Christie, May 27, 1926. £15 15s.

Astbury figure of a man playing bagpipes. Height, 6 ins. Christie, June 8, 1926. £52 10s.

A jug, formed as a man with a lantern. Christie, June 8, 1926. £5 5s.

A service, painted with classical figures and with vine leaves in green round the borders, eight dishes and seventeen plates. Christie, July 21, 1927. £12 12s.

A collection of forty-nine Toby-Filpot jugs. Christie, July 28, 1927. £252.

An Astbury ewer, formed as the model of a ship with caryatid figure head, the hull incised " Royal George." Christie, July 10, 1928. £44 2s.

Two Toby-Filpot jugs by Ralph Wood. Height, 10 ins. Christie, June 1, 1928. £65 2s.

A punch bowl, painted with flowers. Diameter, 13 ins. Christie, April 4, 1929. £3 3s.

A miniature dinner service, Willow pattern, in brown, 63 pieces. Christie, April 4, 1929. £4 14s. 6d.

Toby-Filpot jug, formed as figure of a woman. Height, 9 ins. Christie, February 6, 1930. £12 12s.

A figure of a soldier. Height, 13 ins. Christie, February 6, 1930. £81 18s.

A supper set by Rogers, painted with landscapes in blue, consisting of a bowl and cover, and four fan-shaped dishes. Christie, February 5, 1924. £10 10s.

A Ralph Wood Toby jug, called " Lord Howe," seated, with dog and pipe. Height, 9½ ins. £30.

A Ralph Wood " Bacchus " jug. Height, 12½ ins. £21.

A " Fair Hebe " jug. Height, 9¼ ins. Sotheby, November 11, 1930. £21.

An important Astbury figure of a cavalryman mounted on a charger, decorated with coloured glazes. Height, 8¼ ins. October 25, 1955. £580.

A rare figure of a cavalryman on a chestnut horse decorated with coloured glazes. Height, 8¼ ins. December 3, 1957. £220.

A fine and rare Astbury-Whieldon type " Fiddler " Toby jug decorated in translucent glazes and inscribed " mak the fidler drink/ for why/ with fidling he is/ dry." Height, 11½ ins. June 21, 1960. £550.

RALPH WOOD FIGURES AND GROUPS. Christie, July 16, 1929.

A pair of a stag and hind, brown, green and drab. Height, 6 ins. £47.
A pair of squirrels, brown and green glazes. Height, 7¼ ins. £100.
Benjamin Franklin, in white. Height, 13 ins. £38.
Bull Baiting, manganese, drab and green. Height, 6⅞ ins. £16.
St. George and the Dragon, green, manganese and orange. Height, 9¾ ins. £50.
The Flute Player, with dog, goat and sheep, green, yellow and manganese. Height, 9½ ins. £22.
The Sweep, after Cyfflé. Height, 6¾ ins. £38.
A Gardener. Height, 7½ ins. £27.
A lady holding handkerchief, drab, yellow and brown. Height, 8 ins. £36.
" The Lost Sheep," green, blue and yellow. Height, 9½ ins. £19.
A Girl Haymaker. Height, 7¾ ins. £20.
A figure of a horse. Height, 6¾ ins. £37 16s.

TOBY JUGS. Sotheby, November 11, 1930.

A small " Hearty Good Fellow " Toby jug, with blue coat, spotted vest and yellow breeches. Height, 6½ ins £9 10s.

A Toby jug, of man with oval face, aquiline nose and short legs, seated, holding jug and wineglass, a dog behind him, vest blue, cuffs, breeches and shoes blue and mottled brown, face and dog spotted with brown, vest plain cream colour. Height, 11¼ ins. £105.

A Ralph Wood Toby jug, man seated on three-cornered chair, holding pipe and jug, coat and vest green. Height, 11 ins. £90.

A Whieldon Toby jug, a man holding jug with both hands, green and pale brown. Height, 9¾ ins. £26.

A Ralph Wood Toby jug, " The Planter," coat olive brown, vest and trousers blue. Height, 12 ins. Sotheby, November 11, 1930 £82.

RALPH WOOD. Sotheby, November 11, 1930.

" The Lost Piece of Money." Height, 8 ins. £19.
" Temperance." Height, 7½ ins. £42.
Apollo, green and blue. Height, 8¾ ins. £40.
Diana, yellow and green. Height, 8½ ins. £46.
Venus, green and blue. Height, 10½ ins. £44.
Shepherd and Shepherdess, a pair, in green, yellow, with dog and lamb. Height, 9 ins. and 8¾ ins. £88.
John Wesley, unglazed bust by Enoch Wood, inscribed. Height, 10¾ ins. £13.

A pair of figures of Fortitude and Patience. Height, 21 ins. Christie, December 9, 1924. £19 19s.

An Astbury teapot, globular raised vine pattern in cream on chocolate ground. Height, 4½ ins. £72.

A figure of a lady seated in high-back chair, raising a cup in right hand and holding saucer in her left, figure cream, chair dark brown. Height, 5¼ ins. Sotheby, November 11, 1930. £56.

A Ralph Wood group of the flute player and shepherdess decorated in translucent glaze. Height, 10 ins. May 10, 1960. £80.

A rare and fine equestrian figure of William III depicted as a Roman Emperor decorated in coloured glazes. Height, 15¼ ins. October 30, 1956. £400.

A Planter Toby jug decorated with translucent coloured glazes. Height, 11¾ ins. October 30, 1956. (A similar example was sold in 1960 for £75.) £47.

A Sailor Toby jug decorated with translucent coloured glazes. Height, 11¼ ins. March 1, 1960. £62.

A figure of haymaker standing with a scythe, his left hand resting on a tree trunk, bright translucent coloured glazes. Height, 7¾ ins. May 24, 1960. £105.

A good Toby jug of normal type attractively decorated with translucent coloured glazes. Height, 9¾ ins. June 26, 1960. £55.

A fine and unusual equestrian group of St. George killing the dragon, with a girl riding pillion behind him. Semi-translucent coloured glazes. Height, 11 ins. July 10, 1962. £360.

STAFFORDSHIRE SLIP WARE

Ralph Toft plate, 17 ins., buff ground, decorated with figure of a soldier in relief, with a sword in each hand and a bust at either side; trellis border. Dated 1677. Warner, Leicester, March 19, 1906. £86.

Brown ware posset pot, two-handled, with lid inscribed in "slip," "William and Mary Goldsmith," date incised on lid "June ye 7th, 1697." Height, 9 ins. Bond, Ipswich, April 18, 1906. £15.

Mug, decorated with a fleur-de-lys, initials "H · I." and date 1668, in yellow on brown ground, with two loop handles. Height, 5½ ins. Christie, March 22, 1921. £52 10s.

A dish, decorated with fleur-de-lys and foliage in brown and yellow. Diameter, 13½ ins. Christie, July 21, 1927. £4 14s. 6d.

A dish of octagonal shape, decorated with pomegranates and fleur-de-lys in relief, in shades of brown on yellow ground, and bearing the initials IS. Diameter, 13½ ins. Christie, March 14, 1929. £21.

A Barnstaple jug, globular, incised patterns of a sunflower, bird and a dog among flowers, and inscriptions, dated 1783. Height, 11¼ ins. Sotheby, November 11, 1930. £15.

A Fremington fuddling cup, with six cups conjoined, with buff, green and brown glaze, and inscribed. Sotheby, November 11, 1930. £5 10s.

A posset-pot in buff earthenware, decorated in yellow and brown slips, with a pattern of tulips and roses, and inscription 1705. Height, 8½ ins. £70.

A baking dish, with toothed edge, with head of Charles II, signed S. M. Diameter, 11¾ ins. Sotheby, November 11, 1930. £36.

A seventeenth century tyg and cover of goblet-shape, with four twisted handles, purplish brown glaze over red buffish ware, with medallions of wyverns in relief. Height, 15 ins. £44.

The "Edward Glover" cup, three loop handles, decorated in white slip on dark brown ground, inscription and date 1730. Height, 9¾ ins. £72.

Charles II. dish by Ralph Simpson, red and brown slip on yellow. Diameter, 17¼ ins. Sotheby, February 11, 1931. £100.

A circular dish by Samuel Malkin depicting "St. George and Dragon." Diameter, 14 ins. May 29, 1956. £90.

A Posset Pot or three handled tyg bearing the name and date "Richard Meir 1687." May 29, 1956. £52.

A fine dish by Ralph Simpson, the centre decorated with a pelican in her piety, the border with the initials "W and R" between the head of William III. Diameter, 18 ins. January 27, 1959. £200.

A fine full length portrait dish by Ralph Simpson, the head flanked by the initials "G.R." inscribed Ralph Simpson. Diameter, 16¾ ins. October 15, 1959. £280.

SWANSEA

Vase and cover, campana-shaped, and pair of oviform vases, painted with wreaths of flowers and with marbled white and gold bands. Height, 6 ins. From Mrs. Hardcastle's collection.) March 31, 1905. £33 12s.

A dessert service, painted with flowered decorations on a richly gilt ground, comprising pair of sucriers, covers, and stands, centre dish, two oval dishes, four square *ditto*, and four circular *ditto*, with nineteen plates. (From Sir R. Wyatt's collection.) April 13, 1905. £472 10s.

Tea service, decorated with flowers in medallions on basket-work ground bordered with blue and gold, and consisting of twelve cups and saucers, sucrier and cover, with jug and slop-basin, 28 pieces. Puttick and Simpson, December 12, 1905. £13 13s.

Plate, painted with roses in white and gold border, and beautifully painted with a seaport scene in the centre. Sotheby, December 14, 1905. £35.

Pair of plates, painted with wreaths of flowers on white ground, and an oblong dessert basket similar. Christie, December 19, 1905. £29 8s.

Dessert service, marked "Dillwyn and Co.," beautifully painted with bouquets of flowers in the centre and richly gilt borders, consisting of eleven plates, four oblong dishes, one oblong centre dish on stand, and two square dishes. Sotheby, June 12, 1906. £33 10s.

Dessert service, marked "Dillwyn and Co.," beautifully painted in bouquets of flowers in centre and richly gilt borders, consisting of eleven plates, four oblong dishes, one oblong centre dish on stand, and two square dishes. Sotheby, November 13, 1906.
£42.

A tea service (part only), painted with sprays of roses and other flowers and insects on white ground, consisting of two sugar-basins and covers, two cream-jugs, a plate, five teacups, one coffee-cup, and two saucers; and three Swansea cups, one saucer, and two dishes nearly similar. Christie, November 15, 1906.
£25.

A biscuit vase and cover, with flowers in relief. Impressed mark. Height, 5¼ ins. Christie, May 26, 1910.
£16 16s.

Jug, painted in colours with the Hanley to Manchester coach, with blue and gold border and initials I.A. (Abel Buckley, Esq.) Christie, May 31, 1910.
£21.

A circular inkstand, painted with flowers in colours. Diameter, 5¼ ins., marked in red. Christie, February 3, 1911.
£8 8s.

A pottery Toby fillpot jug. Height, 9¼ ins. Impressed mark. Christie, February 24, 1911.
£32 11s.

Set of three campana-shaped vases, painted with octagonal panels of flowers, on dark blue ground, gilt with arabesques, and with gilt mask handles. Height, 6¾ ins. and 6 ins. Christie, March 3, 1911.
£47 5s.

A dinner and dessert service, finely painted with baskets of flowers and detached sprays of pink roses, by Billingsley, on white ground with gilt scrollwork round the borders—impressed mark—248 pieces. (Burdett Coutts.) Christie, May 9, 1922.
£1627 10s.

A tea service, painted with flower sprays and richly gilt, 34 pieces. Christie, July 2, 1925.
£43 1s.

A dessert service, painted with flowers in colours, and with gilt vine leaves and grapes in low relief, 35 pieces. Christie, March 25, 1926.
£37 16s.

A two-handled mug, painted with dogs and a bouquet of flowers. Christie, February 5, 1924.
£2 12s. 6d.

A cup and saucer, decorated by Billingsley with fruit and flowers, the former with scroll handles on three feet.
£17.

A pair of plates with moulded rims and scalloped edge, decorated probably by Webster with bouquets. Diameter, 8¼ ins.; and another, with sprays of natural flowers by Pollard. Sotheby, November 11, 1930.
£18.

A dinner service, painted with sprays of flowers in the "Billingsley" manner within moulded borders, 151 pieces. Sotheby, November 28, 1930.
£52.

A fine pair of vases of slender ovoid form with gilt cherub handles, the bodies painted with basket and vase of flowers, floral sprays, etc. Height, 11 ins. December 22, 1959.
£230.

A rectangular dish painted with Mandarin style decoration of figures in a garden, border of vignettes of birds and landscapes. Printed Swansea mark. Length, 12½ ins. May 10, 1960.
£43.

A pair of plates finely painted by William Pollard with a large bouquet of garden flowers. Swansea mark. Diameter, 8¼ ins. November 8, 1960.
£70.

A shell shaped dish with border of formal Japan pattern in red, green, blue and gold. Swansea mark. Diameter, 8½ ins. November 8, 1960.
£30.

A pair of shaped edge plates from the Dynevor service painted by David Evans with wild roses, etc. Impressed Swansea mark. Diameter, 8¼ ins. November 8, 1960. (A plate from the same service was bought for £130.)
£190.

WEDGWOOD

Plaques of Jasper ware

Oval plaque, with nymphs discovering the sleeping Cupid, in white on green ground, with black border 4 ins. wide. (From the Huth collection.) Christie, May 23, 1905.
£5 5s.

Octagonal plaque, with chariot of Cupid in white on buff ground and with black border, and small dark blue plaque, with an equestrian warrior. (From the Huth collection.) Christie, May 23, 1905.
£5 5s.

Oblong plaque, dark blue jasper, with a frieze of dancing "Houris" in relief. Height, 9 ins. by 2½ ins. (From the Huth collection.) Christie, May 23, 1905.
£16 16s.

Oblong plaque of blue jasper, with a classical subject in relief, framed. Height, 14 ins. by 7½ ins. (From the Huth collection.) Christie, May 23, 1905.
£73 10s.

Oblong plaque of blue jasper, with nymphs sacrificing, in relief, framed. Height, 16 ins. by 7 ins. (From the Huth collection.) Christie, May 23, 1905.
£257 5s.

Oblong plaque, with chariot and classical figures in relief, in white on green ground. Height, 15½ ins. by 6 ins. (From the Huth collection.) Christie, May 23, 1905.
£210.

Set of three jardinières, square shape, with festoons in relief. (From the Huth collection.) Christie, May 23, 1906. £27 6s.

Portrait plaque, Edward Bourne, modelled by Hackwood and signed under shoulder of portrait, a fine blue and white portrait in black " basalt " frame. Christie, June 12, 1906. £15 15s.

Oval plaque, Ganymede feeding the Eagle, marked Wedgwood and Bentley. Height, 6½ins. by 5¼ ins. (From the Meyer collection, and later from the Cox collection.) Christie, June 12, 1906. £40 19s.

The most important plaque of this description known to collectors was one measuring 26 inches by 11 inches, with subject, " A Sacrifice to Hymen," which was sold in the Cox collection, May 6, 1880, and realised £415. The finest collection of Jasper ware in existence was that formed by Mr. Marjoribanks, afterwards Lord Tweedmouth, and was recently sold privately by the present Lord Tweedmouth to Mr. Davis, of Bond Street, and is now in the possession of Sir W. H. Lever, M.P. It includes many of the original models in wax by Flaxman, the famous sculptor.

Pair of pillar vases on hexagonal plinths, with reliefs of " blindman's-buff," etc. Christie, June 12, 1906. £42.

Vase, dark blue, with scroll handles, with reliefs of sacrifices, etc., and a round pedestal for the same. Christie, June 12, 1906. £22 1s.

Pair of vases of tripod form, goats' heads and claw supports, lotus leaves on the dome-shaped cover. Christie, June 12, 1906. £32 11s.

Set of three vases, in green ground, modelled by Hackwood, with reliefs of sacrifices, medallions, etc., and three square pedestals for the same. Christie, June 12, 1906. £147.

Pair of vases and covers, black " basalt," with panels of nymphs, rams' heads, and festoons of flowers in relief. Height, 13¾ ins. Christie, December 19, 1906. £12 12s. 10d.

An oblong plaque, modelled with " The Sacrifice of Iphigenia " in white relief on blue ground. Height, 15½ ins. by 6½ ins. Puttick and Simpson, November 4, 1908. £51 9s.

Pair of candlesticks, formed as tree stems, with figures of Cupid in white relief upon a blue ground, emblematic of Summer and Winter, on octagonal plinths. Height, 11 ins. Christie, July 1, 1909. £20 10s.

Pair of black basalt ewers, emblematic of Wine and Water. Height, 15½ ins. Christie, February 24, 1910. £13 13s.

Pair of double seals, formed of blue jasper balusters, with chased gold mounts. Christie, March 18, 1910. £15 15s.

Pair of black basalt figures of Shakespeare and Milton. Height, 16 ins. (The Rev. A. Willett.) Christie, April 1, 1910. £9 9s.

An oval plaque, with figures of nymphs and Cupid in white, on sage-green ground. Height, 6¾ ins. by 8¼ ins. Designed by Lady Templeton. (T. W. Waller, Esq.) Christie, June 7, 1910. £18 18s.

Pair of black basalt busts of Homer and Cicero. Height, 13 ins. Christie, March 7, 1911. £8 18s. 6d.

A copy of the Portland Vase. Height, 9½ ins. Christie, December 8, 1925. £5 5s.

A dessert service, painted with birds and feathers in colours on white ground, 24 pieces. Christie, May 7, 1925. £25 4s.

Black basalt vase and cover, modelled with infant Bacchanals in relief. Height, 12 ins. Christie, March 23, 1926. £2 2s.

Pair of black basalt busts of Scott and Burns. Height, 18 ins.; and a bust of Mercury. Christie, June 9, 1926. £21.

Blue jasper medallions, collection of 86, presented by Wedgwood to Wm. Constable, 1783. Christie, July 19, 1927. £567.

A dinner service, decorated with wreaths round the borders in blue and brown on a cream ground, 146 pieces. Christie, November 22, 1928. £17 17s.

A copy of the Portland Vase, with figures in white on black ground. Height, 10 ins. Christie, July 23, 1929. £17 17s.

A pair of blue jasper jardinières, decorated with star ornament, ribands and ivy leaves. Diameter, 7 ins. Christie, April 25, 1929. £1 11s. 6d.

A tea service, with Egyptian ornament in black on red ground, 9 pieces; a black basalt tripod vase; and a small copy of Portland Vase. Christie, May 26, 1929. £4 4s.

A dinner service, decorated with flowers and foliage in red, blue and gold in the Chinese taste, 190 pieces. Christie, February 5, 1924. £36 15s.

A set of chessmen. Christie, May 8, 1923. £15 15s.

A cream ware dinner service, painted with oak-leaf and acorn intertwined borders, 234 pieces (12 faulty). Sotheby, November 28, 1930. £40.

A fine pair of portrait plaques of George III and Queen Charlotte, modelled by William Hackwood and signed with the initials " W.H." in white on a light blue jasper ground. November 7, 1955. £145.

An original copy of the Portland vase in black basalt body with white figure reliefs. Height, 9½ ins. October 30, 1956. £480.

A Wedgwood & Bentley black basalt oval bust portrait plaque of Catherine the Great. Height, 3¼ ins. March 24, 1959.
£42.

A nineteenth century copy of the famous Portland vase, blue jasper ground with white reliefs. Height, 10½ ins. June 16, 1959. (A similar example sold in 1960 fetched £36. Many copies in various sizes and colours have been made by Wedgwoods and other firms.)
£24.

Two Wedgwood creamware framed plaques painted by Emile Lessore with typical figure subjects. Size, 19¼ ins. by 15¼ ins. (and another plaque by J. Eyre). May 15, 1959.
£44.

A rare Wedgwood & Bentley portrait medallion of Captain Cook in white on a blue jasper ground. In carved wood frame. May 15, 1959.
£78.

A Wedgwood & Bentley oval plaque of Victory on a blue ground. Height, 3¾ ins. May 15, 1959.
£26.

An oval shaped edge creamware tray attractively painted with pastoral scene by Emile Lessore, c. 1875. Length, 16¾ ins. January 12, 1960.
£50.

A pair of Wedgwood & Bentley agate ware vases on square black bases. Impressed mark. Height, 7¾ ins. January 12, 1960.
£70.

A pair of Wedgwood & Bentley marbled vases and covers with mask handles on black basalt bases. Impressed mark. Height, 9½ ins. November 22, 1960.
£145.

A pair of Wedgwood & Bentley basalt busts of Horace and Virgil. Height, 19 ins. April 18, 1961.
£290.

WEDGWOOD'S PRINTED WARE

Dinner service, with pale pink borders, decorated with wreaths of foliage and berries in green and red, 158 pieces. (From the Huth collection.) Christie, May 23, 1905.
£15 15s.

Service, with flowers in blue in the style of old Nankin, 90 pieces. (From the Huth collection.) Christie, May 23, 1905.
£16 16s.

Dinner service, with birds and flowers in colours in the Oriental taste, consisting of 140 pieces. Christie, December 1, 1905.
£26 5s.

WHIELDON WARE

Tea poy, square shaped, dated " 1799," cream coloured, very slightly tinted in places with green, on three sides a female embossed figure with cornucopia, and the fourth side inscribed " Abraham Randell," " Alice Randell." Bond, Ipswich, April 18, 1906.
£7 10s.

An agate ware teapot, modelled with shells. Christie, June 19, 1906. £12 1s. 6d.

Figure of a lady. Height, 7 ins. Puttick and Simpson, November 5, 1906. £4 10s.

A plaque, with portrait of Sarah Malcolm Saunders, executed in 1733, very rare, taken from the picture by Hogarth. Sotheby, November 13, 1906. £2 10s.

Three figures of musicians. Christie, November 15, 1906. £13 2s. 6d.

An agate ware teapot and cover, modelled with shells, and surmounted by a figure of a lion, the handle and spout formed as dolphins. (J. E. Wilkinson, Esq.) Christie, April 6, 1909.
£13 13s.

An agate ware figure of a cat; and a figure of a dog. Height, 4 ins. (J. E. Wilkinson, Esq.) Christie, April 6, 1909.
£22 1s.

Pair of equestrian figures, mottled with tortoiseshell and green. Height, 10½ ins. Christie, May 25, 1909.
£37 16s.

A jug, formed as a figure of a sailor seated on a chest. Height, 11½ ins. Christie, May 9, 1922.
£105.

A Toby-Filpot jug. Height, 9½ ins. Christie, March 25, 1926. £19 19s.

A pair of figures of birds. Height, 7½ ins. Christie, March 30, 1926. £10 10s.

A pair of hanging flower vases, splashed with green and brown. Height, 7½ ins. Christie, July 14, 1927.
£13 13s.

A group of Vicar and Moses. Height, 9½ ins. Christie, December 5, 1928. £28 7s.

A pair of figures of cats. Height, 7 ins. Christie, April 16, 1927. £8 8s.

A figure of a shepherd on green scroll plinth. Height, 9 ins. Christie, February 6, 1930.
£50 9s.

A figure of shepherd carrying a lamb. Height, 8½ ins. Christie, February 6, 1930.
£32 11s.

A figure of a boy with pack at his foot. Height, 7½ ins. Christie, February 6, 1930.
£58 16s.

A group of lady and gentleman, seated, with lamb and dog at feet. Height, 11¼ ins. Christie, February 6, 1930.
£42.

A Toby-Filpot jug, with seated figure of a man holding jug and cup. Height, 12 ins. Christie, February 6, 1930.
£44 2s.

An agate ware tea service, decorated with marbling in blue, brown and grey, 10 pieces. Christie, February 6, 1923. £84.

In the same sale two agate ware cream jugs £28 7s. ; two teapots £38 17s. ; and a sauce boat £21.

A figure of a thrush on tree trunk, in brown, yellow and green glaze. Height, 8¾ ins. £72.

A figure of an owl perched on a rock, bird cream, rock tortoiseshell. Height, 8½ ins. Sotheby, November 11, 1930. £130.

A teapot and cover, globular, rustic handle and spout, applied mouldings in white clay touched with purple and bluish grey on a deep buff ground. Height, 4½ ins. Sotheby, November 11, 1930. £51.

A figure of a cavalryman, manganese coat, white breeches and yellow-lined casque with initials " G.R. " in front, saddle cloth green, horse grey and white splashed glazes. Height, 9 ins. Sotheby, June 4, 1931. £88.

A Whieldon-Wedgwood rustic teapot with a medallion with a bust portrait of the King of Prussia coloured in manganese, green, blue, yellow and grey. Height, 4½ ins. March 1, 1955. £72.

A Whieldon-Wedgwood teapot and cover moulded in low relief with overlapping leaves in green, cream, yellow and pale manganese. Rabbit knob. Height, 4⅜ ins. March 1, 1955. £52.

A fine Whieldon figure of an owl in perching attitude on a hollow rockwork base, cream glaze with traces of aubergne and grey, the base mottled manganese. Height, 9 ins. October 25, 1955. £260.

A rare Whieldon wall vase of moulded rococo form, the central panel bearing Robert Hancock's Milkmaid print, the main body coloured with mottled green, grey, yellow and manganese glazes. Height, 9½ ins. October 25, 1955. £70.

A Whieldon cow creamer, the cow suckling a calf, decorated with typical manganese, brown and green splashed markings. Length, 6¼ ins. December 17, 1957. £65.

A rare Whieldon cow creamer standing on a low rough rectangular base, the whole with a pale green lead glaze. Length, 5¼ ins. April 15, 1958. £160.

A rare tray of rectangular shape with double twig handles, the upper surface decorated with manganese, brown, green and yellow splashes. Length, 11 ins. October 15, 1959. £50.

A group of milkmaid and cow in cream glaze except on skirt and hat, mounted on square hollow base. Height, 4¼ ins. October 15, 1959. £43.

WORCESTER

Transfer Decoration

Jug painted with portrait of the King of Prussia and military trophies. Height, 7½ ins. Sotheby, November 11, 1904. £7 7s.

Bowl, transfer decoration hunting scene. Saul, Southport, September 21, 1906. £4 15s.

A shaped mug, printed with a portrait of the King of Prussia and military trophies. Christie, April 30, 1908. £12 12s.

A cylindrical mug, printed with a portrait of the Marquis of Granby, Britannia, Fame, and Cupid. Height, 5½ ins. Christie, May 12, 1909. £28 7s.

An oviform vase, transfer printed in colours and grisaille, with an equestrian figure, a ship, small landscapes, a military trophy and harlequin figures on white ground, by R. Hancock. Height, 10 ins. Christie, May 26, 1909. £115 10s.

A cylindrical mug, with portrait of George II., a ship, a military trophy, etc., by R. Hancock, signed with monogram. Height, 6¼ ins. (Merton A. Thoms, Esq.) Christie, February 10, 1910. £32 11s.

Pair of oviform vases, with portrait of the King of Prussia, with a battle scene in the background, and a military trophy on the reverse, by R. Hancock, 1757, signed with monogram. Height, 7 ins. (Merton A. Thoms, Esq.) Christie, February 10, 1910. £86 2s.

A cylindrical mug, with a parrot and branch of currants. Height, 3¼ ins., signed R. Hancock, fecit, in one of the branches. The subject taken from plate 74 in " The Ladies' Amusements." (Merton A. Thoms, Esq.) Christie, February 10, 1910. £23 2s.

A shaped mug, transfer printed with portrait of the King of Prussia, by R. Hancock. Height, 4¾ ins.; and a sugar basin. Christie, December 13, 1920. £18 18s.

A transfer printed mug, with straight sides, transfer printed in chocolate with bust portrait of George III., signed J. Sadler; Liverpool. Height, 5¾ ins. Sotheby, November 11, 1930. £24.

A jug transfer printed with the King of Prussia subject by Hancock. Height, 7¼ ins. May 14, 1957. £37.

A small bell shaped mug transfer printed in black with Hancock's famous King of Prussia subject. Dated 1757. Height, 3⅜ ins. June 23, 1959. £26

A rare vase painted with the same King of Prussia subject. Height, 7 ins.   June 23, 1959.
£52.
A rare cylindrical mug bearing sepia transfer print of children playing marbles. Height,
4½ ins.   June 23, 1959.   £210.
A bowl printed in sepia with naval views and inscribed " Cape Breton," " Guadaloupe " and
" Senegal."   Diameter, 7⅜ ins.   May 10, 1960.
£46.

BLUE SALMON SCALE DECORATIONS

Three large coffee cups and saucers, exotic birds and insects in panels enclosed by gilt
borders on dark blue scale pattern ground. Christie, March 29, 1904.   £73 10s.
Bowl, blue salmon scale ground, gilt decorations, the panels painted in flowers (square
mark).   Robinson and Fisher, November 18, 1904.   £33 1s. 6d.
Jug, moulded with leaves and painted with exotic birds and insects in panels, with gilt
borders on a dark blue scale pattern ground and with mask modelled beneath the
spout (square mark). Height 11½ ins. (From the Menzies collection.) Christie,
February 24, 1905.   £199 10s.
Canisters and covers (pair), oviform, blue salmon scale ground, birds in panels, with
gilt scroll borders. Height, 6¼ ins. (From the Huth collection.) Christie, May 23,
1905.   £165 18s.
Pair of hexagonal vases and covers, with dark blue scale pattern ground panels of exotic
birds and insects (square mark). Height, 13¾ ins. (From the Sir Everard Cayley
collection.) Christie, December 8, 1905.   £798.
Pair of vases and covers of hexagonal shape, finely painted with exotic birds, flowers,
fruit and insects in panels, with gilt scroll borders on dark blue scale pattern
ground. Height, 12 ins. (From the Keele Hall collection.) Christie, May 22,
1906.   £493 10s.
Set of three vases and covers, hexagonal, finely painted with exotic birds in landscapes,
flights of birds, buterflies, and other insects in variously shaped panels with gilt
borders on dark blue salmon scale pattern ground. Height, 13¾ ins. and 11½ ins.
(From the Walker collection.) Christie, June 27, 1906.   £504.
Mugs, pair of, cylindrical, with dark blue salmon scale ground, painted with exotic
birds and insects in panels with gilt scroll borders. Height, 5 ins. (From the
Walker collection.) Christie, June 27, 1906.   £115 10s.

A single mug, precisely similar, was sold at Christie's from Mr. Leyburn Popham's collection, in
March 1882, for £42.

Teapot and stand, with dark blue salmon scale ground, painted with exotic birds and
insects in scroll panels with gilt borders. (From the Walker collection.) Christie,
June 27, 1906.   £19 19s.
Teapot and cover, painted with exotic birds and insects in panels of gold. Christie,
November 20, 1906.   £33 12s.
Sugar-basin and cover, similar. Christie, November 20, 1906.   £32 11s.
Coffee-pot and cover, similar. Christie, November 20, 1906.   £63.
Cylindrical mug, similar decoration. Height, 5¾ ins. Christie, November 30, 1906.
£57 15s.
Pair of hexagonal vases and covers, with dark blue scale pattern ground, painted with
exotic birds, branches, and insects in scroll panels with gilt borders. Height, 13 ins.
(Massey-Mainwaring collection.) Christie, April 11, 1907.   £535 10s.
An oval dish, painted with birds and insects in gilt scroll borders. Width, 10¼ ins.
Christie, April 3, 1908.   £44 2s.
A vase and cover of hexagonal shape, painted with exotic birds and branches, in scroll
panels, with gilt borders. Height, 12 ins. (Mrs. Arthur Bristowe.) Christie,
February 19, 1909.   £262 10s.
Large jug, painted with exotic birds and insects in scroll panels, with gilt borders, the
spout modelled with a mask. Height, 11½ ins. (J. Cheetham Cockshut, Esq.)
Christie, March 23, 1909.   £215 5s.
Pair of large hexagonal vases and covers, painted with exotic birds in landscapes, insects,
and sprays of flowers, in scroll panels, with gilt borders. Height, 16½ ins. (J.
Cheetham Cockshut, Esq.) Christie, March 23, 1909.   £945.
A two-handled cup and saucer, painted with birds and flowers in scroll panels, richly
gilt with flowers and foliage. Christie, April 23, 1909.   £60 18s.
Hexagonal vase and cover, finely painted with a Chinese lady and gentleman, seated in
arbours of foliage, in scroll panels, with gilt borders, and with smaller panels round
the neck, enclosing flying birds, buterflies, and other insects. Height, 13½ ins.
Christie, July 1, 1909.   £640 10s.
A mug, painted with exotic birds and insects in scroll panels with gilt borders. (Mrs.
R. S. Fairbank.) Christie, March 11, 1910.   £117 12s.
Pair of baskets, with pierced trellis sides painted in the centre with exotic birds. Width,
7¼ ins. Christie, May 10, 1910.   £69 6s.
Teacup and saucer, painted with birds in scroll panels with gilt borders. Christie,
March 3, 1911.   £16 5s. 6d.

Pair of plates, painted with flowers in scroll borders. Diameter, 7½ ins. Christie, March 3, 1911. **£23 2s.**

A coffee-cup and saucer, painted with a camel and bison, by O'Neale, in gilt borders on dark blue ground. (J. E. Nightingale, Esq., F.S.A.) Christie, December 7, 1911. **£33 12s.**

A two-handled cup and saucer, painted with Watteau figures, birds and flowers, in scroll-shaped panels, with gilt borders, on dark blue scale pattern ground. (J. E. Nightingale, Esq., F.S.A.) Christie, December 7, 1911. **£222 12s.**

Pair of mugs, painted with medallion views and festoons of fruit, in turquoise, dark blue and gold borders. Height, 5 ins. Christie, July 13, 1911. **£131 5s.**

A sugar-basin and cover, painted with flowers in circular and fan-shaped panels on powdered-blue ground, gilt with sprays of flowers and foliage. (Montague White, Esq.) Christie, December 15, 1911. **£39 18s.**

A tea service, painted with groups of flowers, and with dark blue bands gilt with flowers, 10 pieces. (Montague White, Esq.) Christie, December 15, 1911. **£178 10s.**

A large jug, painted with exotic birds and landscapes in scroll panels with gilt borders, the spout modelled as a mask. Height, 11½ ins. Christie, June 21, 1922. **£141 5s.**

A smaller jug, similar, £89 5s.

A pair of two-handled cups, covers and saucers, painted with Watteau subjects. Christie, June 21, 1921. **£157 10s.**

A large hexagonal vase and cover, painted with garden scenes and figures in colours by Donaldson. Height, 17 ins. Christie, June 21, 1922. **£2730.**

From the Trapnell Collection,

A bowl and cover, painted with birds and insects in scroll panels with gilt borders. Christie, April 29, 1926. **£32 11s.**

A pair of hexagonal vases and covers, painted with exotic birds and trees in red, blue and green in the Oriental taste, blue scale pattern ground. Height, 16½ ins. Christie, February 2, 1926. **£451 10s.**

A pair of hexagonal vases and covers, painted with exotic birds and insects in shaped panels with gilt scroll borders and dark blue scale pattern ground. Height, 16½ ins. Christie, July 3, 1924. **£1575.**

A pair of smaller ditto, 11½ ins., £557 10s.

A teapot and cover, with panels of exotic birds and insects on scale blue, square mark. Height, 6¾ ins. **£28.**

A jug, with mask spout, decorated with two large panels of exotic birds, also with butterflies, on scale blue, square mark. Height, 11¾ ins. Sotheby, November 11, 1930. **£85.**

A tea service, painted with flowers in the Oriental taste, blue scale pattern ground, 33 pieces. Christie, December 13, 1920. **£141 15s.**

A service, finely painted with birds and insects in scroll panels with gilt borders, on dark blue scale pattern ground. Christie, December 9, 1920. **£2318.**

Sold in forty lots, ninety-eight pieces.

A tea service, painted with exotic birds and insects in scroll panels with gilt borders, on dark blue scale pattern ground, 18 pieces. Christie, March 5, 1929. **£210.**

A pair of bough pots of rococo form with pierced tops decorated with scale blue ground with panels of exotic birds, etc. Square marks. Height, 6¾ ins., length, 8⅜ ins. May 10, 1960. **£400.**

A fine pear shaped teapot and cover and stand of richly gilt scale blue ground and panels of exotic birds and flowers. Blue crescent and "W" marks. Height, 6½ ins. May 10, 1960. **£310.**

A fine basket, cover and stand of lobed oval shape, the interior with scale blue ground and floral panels, the exterior moulded with basket work and painted yellow. Square marks. Length, 11 ins. November 8, 1960. **£430.**

A cream jug with pear shaped body and pinched lip, the reserve panels painted with dishevelled birds, of a well known type. Height, 4½ ins. November 29, 1960. **£28.**

A fine blue scale ground chocolate cup and saucer, the reserve panels painted with musicians in the manner of Pillemont (very rare). Smaller panels of birds and insects. Seal marks. November 29, 1960. **£400.**

A pair of plates with scalloped rims, the reserve panels painted with brightly coloured swags of garden flowers. Seal marks. Diameter, 7½ ins. November 29, 1960. **£56.**

A kidney shaped dish of similar and typical pattern. Crescent mark. Length, 10½ ins. November 29, 1960. **£34.**

MOTTLED BLUE AND OTHER COLOURED GROUNDS

Jug, with canary yellow ground, painted with bouquets of flowers in colours, the spout modelled with a mask. Height, 7¾ ins. Christie, June 26, 1905. **£131**

Vase and cover, oviform, painted with festoons of flowers in heart-shaped panels, richly
　　gilt foliage and scroll borders on mottled dark blue ground. Height, 9½ ins.
　　February 24, 1905. £252

Three vases, comprising a pair of hexagonal vases and covers, and an oviform vase with
　　pierced cover, painted with flowers in red, green, and gold in the Oriental taste, in
　　scroll panels, with gilt borders on mottled blue ground marbled with gold. Height,
　　11½ ins. and 10¾ ins. (From the Walker collection.) Christie, June 27, 1905. £462.

Tea service, part of, with alternate crimson and turquoise stripes gilt with festoons of
　　flowers, consisting of sugar basin and cover, canister, nine cups and eight saucers.
　　Christie, November 20, 1906. £126.

Vase, painted with exotic birds in gilt borders on mottled blue ground, with white and
　　gold scroll handles. Height, 8½ ins. Christie, November 23, 1906. £105.

A cylindrical mug, painted with exotic birds and trees in scroll panels, with gilt borders
　　upon apple-green ground. Height, 6 ins. Christie, February 7, 1908. £115 10s.

Pair of plates, painted with fan ornament in the Japanese taste. Christie, April 30, 1908.
　　£21.

Tea poy and cover, apple-green ground, with panels of exotic birds in gilt scrolls.
　　Sotheby, March 9, 1909. £56.

Coffee-pot and cover, painted with peasant figures in landscapes, in colours on white
　　ground. (The teapot and cover and the milk-jug and cover of this service realised
　　£36 15s. and £22 respectively.) (J. Cheetham Cockshut, Esq.) Christie, March 23,
　　1909. £94 10s.

Teapot and cover, in emulation of the old Chinese *famille verte,* painted with flowers
　　and rocks in panels, on stippled-green ground. (J. Cheetham Cockshut, Esq.)
　　Christie, March 23, 1909. £50 8s.

Sugar-basin and cover, painted with the arms, coronet, and crest of Lord Nelson, and
　　green and gold oak-leaves, by Baxter. (The bowl and a large cup and saucer of
　　this service realised £22 and £30 respectively.) Christie, May 12, 1909. £32 11s.

Milk-jug and cover, painted with exotic birds and branches in colours on white ground,
　　and with pink festoons and green trellis panels round the borders. Christie, July 22,
　　1909. £50 8s.

Teapot and cover, painted with flowers in colours, in shaped apple-green borders. (Mrs.
　　R. S. Fairbank.) Christie, March 11, 1910. £60 18s.

Sugar-basin and cover, painted with flowers in circular and fan-shaped panels, on
　　powdered blue ground, gilt with foliage. (Charles Procter, Esq.) Christie,
　　November 29, 1910. £25 4s.

Jug, painted with a portrait of George III., Britannia, and Fame, in blue. Height,
　　4¾ ins. Christie, March 3, 1911. £26 5s.

A teapot, painted with figure of Iachimo and on the reverse Imogen. Height, 5¾ ins.
　　£36.

A claret ground plate, bouquet in centre, and at sides in four panels exotic birds on
　　crimson ground with heavy gold sprays. Diameter, 9¾ ins. £98.

A yellow ground plate, decorated with flower sprays in colours on yellow ground.
　　Diameter, 8 ins. £35.

A chocolate cup, cover and saucer, with apple green borders painted with fruit and
　　insects, marks crossed swords and 9. £68.

A pair of tea poys, oviform, painted with exotic birds and insects on plain royal blue
　　ground, 5½ ins., one with square mark. All at Sotheby's, November 11, 1930. £25.

A bottle and basin, painted with exotic birds and insects on mottled dark blue ground
　　gilt with sprays of foliage. Bottle, 10 ins. high, basin, 11 ins. diam. Christie,
　　July 25, 1927. £126.

A teapot and cover, painted with flower sprays in colours on a yellow ground, and with
　　a fox and " Tally Ho " in two panels. Christie, June 21, 1922. £231.

Oviform vase and cover, painted with birds and insects in scroll panels on apple green
　　ground. Height, 10 ins. Christie, March 5, 1929. £346 10s.

　　　　A pair of canisters and covers, similar, £110 5s.

A pair of plates, painted with birds and flowers in shaped panels on a crimson ground,
　　richly gilt with flowers and foliage. Diameter, 7¾ ins. Christie, March 5, 1929.
　　£136 10s.

　　　　A ten inch dish, similar, £120 15s.

A pair of campana-shaped vases by the same, painted with panels of shells and richly
　　gilt with arabesques. Height, 10 ins. Christie, March 5, 1929. £25 4s.

A pair of plates by Flight, painted with Lady Hamilton as " Hope " in grisaille in
　　dark blue and gold borders. Diameter, 9¾ ins. (Part of the Nelson Service.)
　　Christie, March 5, 1929. £31 10s.

A coffee cup and saucer, painted with flowers in colours on striped gold ground, Dresden
　　mark. Christie, March 5, 1929. £34 13s.

A pair of oviform vases, painted with exotic birds and landscapes. Height, 8 ins.
　　Christie, June 21, 1922. £262 10s.

　　　　A set of three beakers, similar, £441.

Three oviform vases and one cover, painted with flowers and fruit in colours, in scroll panels with gilt borders on apple green ground. Height, 10 ins. and 7 ins. Christie, December 13, 1920. £157 10s.

A jug, similar, made £168 and a mug £152 5s.

A dessert service, painted with groups of flowers in panels, with gilt scroll borders on mottled dark blue ground, 51 pieces. Christie, May 9, 1922. £556 10s.

A jug, with yellow ground, transfer printed with pastoral scenes in colours in panels with lake scroll borders, the neck painted with flowers and insects in colours, and the spout modelled with a mask. Height, 8¼ ins. Christie, May 9, 1922. £152 5s.

A tea service, painted with fruit and flowers, mark, the Dresden crossed swords in blue, 47 pieces. Christie, June 21, 1922. £378.

A circular dish nearly similar £57 15s.

A yellow scale ground teapot and cover with reserve panels of exotic birds, butterflies and insects. May 8, 1956. (Two cups and saucers from the same service fetched £440.) £1,000.

A yellow ground circular junket dish with reserve panels painted with flowers. Diameter, 9 ins. December 18, 1956. £280.

A jug with mask spout decorated with apple green ground, the reserve panels decorated with exotic birds in landscape. Height, 7¼ ins. April 9, 1957. £110.

A covered vase of gros bleu ground, the panels painted with putti, probably painted by John Donaldson. Height, 9 ins. April 9, 1957. £90.

A fine and rare blue bordered plate, the centre painted with the Fable subject—The Monkey and the Owl by O'Neale. Diameter, 9⅛ ins. March 4, 1958. £440.

A fine yellow ground cabbage-leaf mask head jug with panels of Chinese lake scenes and figures in puce monochrome. Height, 1½ ins. December 2, 1958. £420.

A fine yellow ground bell shaped mug, the panels painted with Chinese figures in landscape, in puce. Floral sprays over the yellow body. Height, 3⅜ ins. January 26, 1960. £210.

A fine apple green ground bowl, painted with exotic birds in landscape. Diameter, 9 ins. March 28, 1961. £360.

OTHER WORCESTER PORCELAIN OF THE FIRST PERIOD

A rare standing figure of a female Turk, dressed in coloured costume, the base with applied floral sprays of " hot cross bun " type. Height, 5⅛ ins. June 26, 1956. £420.

A fine coffee pot and cover painted with figure subjects in the style of James Giles. Height, 8⅝ ins. April 9, 1957. £770.

A similar coffee pot and cover painted with exotic birds in landscape. Height, 8¼ ins. April 9, 1957. £400.

A pair of small tureens and covers in the form of cauliflowers, naturalistically moulded and coloured. Height 4¾ ins. May 12, 1959. £160.

A pair of leaf shaped dishes transfer printed in underglaze blue with floral sprays. Length, 9¾ ins. June 23, 1959. £32.

A documentary bell shaped mug, superbly painted in soft enamels with birds, landscape, etc. Signed on base " I. Rogers' Pinxit 1757." Height, 3¼ ins. June 23, 1959. £600.

An early double handled sauceboat of silver shape painted in underglaze blue within moulded panels, etc. Length, 7½ ins. October 20, 1959. £19.

A rare small tureen and cover in the form of a partridge, slightly gilt. Length, 6¼ ins. October 20, 1959. £380.

A rare, inscribed and dated " Frances James 1770 " mug decorated in underglaze blue. Height, 2½ ins. October 17, 1959. £58.

A fine soup plate from the Duke of Gloucester service boldy painted with various fruits. the border with panels of insects, etc. Gold crescent mark. Diameter, 8⅞ ins. May 10, 1960. £310.

" GRAINGER " WORCESTER

Set of three vases, lavender blue ground, painted with flowers in panel, richly gilt, marked " Grainger, Lee and Co.". Height, 15½ ins. and 12¼ ins. Saul, Southport, September 21, 1906. £20.

A set of three vases and covers, painted with views on dark blue ground, richly gilt. Height, 12 ins. and 14 ins. Christie, April 24, 1908. £21.

A pair of pink ground vases of pilgrim flask shape, panels of views of Worcester and Malvern, gilt feet and handles, c. 1860. Height, 8½ ins. November 8, 1960. £16.

CHAMBERLAIN'S WORCESTER

Tea service, painted with flowers in the Oriental taste, and with dark blue and gold bands, consisting of sugar-basin and cover, cream-jug, bowl, two dishes, twelve teacups and saucers, and ten coffee-cups. Christie, November 20, 1906.　£30 9s.

A dessert service, painted with flowers in colours on dark blue ground, and with grapes in yellow and gold, consisting of an oblong centre dish, twelve shaped dishes, a pair of vase-shaped sugar tureens and covers, and twenty-four plates. Christie, December 18, 1908.　£48 6s.

A jug, painted with a coursing scene, on grey ground, the border gilt with foliage. Height, 6 ins. Christie, July 19, 1910.　£5 15s. 6d.

Pair of vases, painted with panels of exotic birds and insects, on dark blue ground, with gilt lions' mask handles. Height, 6 ins.　Christie, November 25, 1910. £18 18s.

Chamberlain Worcester dinner service, painted with flowers in a scroll panel on richly gilt ground of royal blue, 132 pieces. Sotheby, December 3, 1926.　£370.

Another, one hundred and thirty-seven pieces, £480.

A pair of urns and covers with gilt handles, supported on three gilt dolphins, decorated with floral sprays on a blue ground, the covers with parkland scenes. Damages. Height, 14 ins. May 10, 1960.　£34.

A fine lilac ground jug, the panels painted by Humphrey Chamberlain with a huntsmen's carousing scene and small panels of trophies, dead game, etc. Red script mark. " Regent " china body. Height, 9¾ ins. November 8, 1960.　£360.

A decorative basket, the centre painted with views of Osterley Park, the sides encrusted with shells. Length, 10½ ins. November 22, 1960.　£78.

BARR, FLIGHT & BARR AND FLIGHT, BARR & BARR, WORCESTER

Pair of vases and covers, green and gold ground, painted with hunting subjects. Sotheby, November 13, 1906.　£26 10s.

A beaker, painted with a nymph before an altar, by Humphrey Chamberlain, on marbled salmon pink and gold ground. Height, 5 ins. Christie, March 19, 1908.　£17 6s. 6d.

Pair of oval dishes, painted with Lady Hamilton as Hope, in grisaille, and with dark blue and gold borders. Width, 19½ ins. Christie, May 12, 1909.　£42.

Vase and cover, painted with a portrait of Shakespeare, and Mrs. Siddons as The Tragic Muse, in two panels, on dark blue ground, richly gilt. Height, 20½ ins. Christie, February 1, 1910.　£68 5s.

Cup and saucer, painted with panels of birds and insects in gilt borders, on dark blue scale pattern ground. (W. L. Chew, Esq.) Christie, June 15, 1910.　£15 4s. 6d.

Vase, painted with shells, and gilt with bands of arabesque foliage, on pale blue and white ground. Christie, January 27, 1911.　£17 17s.

Vase and cover, by Flight, Barr and Barr, painted with flower sprays on pale yellow ground, with gilt serpent handles. Height, 9½ ins. Christie, March 5, 1929. £21.

Vase, by Flight, Barr and Barr, painted with subjects from Milton's " Comus " in panels, with gilt borders on apple green ground, and with gilt horses' head handles. Height, 20 ins. Christie, May 7, 1929.　£18 18s.

Dessert service, Flight, Barr and Barr, painted with Chinese figures and pagodas in colours and gold, 28 pieces. Christie, July 28, 1927.　£105.

A fine Flight, Barr & Barr period porcelain plaque painted with vase of flowers, possibly by Thomas Baxter. Height, 7½ ins. April 14, 1959.　£240.

A fine pair of Flight, Barr & Barr vases of apple green ground, the central panels painted with landscapes. Height, 11¾ ins. December 22, 1959.　£220.

A pair of campana shape Flight, Barr & Barr vases with gilt handles, the bodies painted with landscape and floral panels on a puce ground. Height, 13¼ ins. May 10, 1960.　£75.

A fine set of three campana shaped open Flight, Barr & Barr vases with gilt handles, painted with panels of shells on a claret ground. Script marks. Height 6½ ins. and 4¼ ins. May 10, 1960.　£200.

A pair of campana shaped Flight, Barr and Barr vases and covers, with gilt handles, painted with landscape panels on a claret ground. Impressed and script marks. Height, 8½ ins. May 10, 1960.　£195.

A pair of crater shaped Flight, Barr & Barr vases, the panels painted with Shakespearian figure subjects, possibly by Thomas Baxter. Slight faults. Script marks. Height, 10 ins. December 20, 1960.　£125.

A Barr, Flight & Barr coffee can and saucer, the panels painted with feathers (by Thomas Baxter), grey marbled ground.　£90.

A similar coffee can and saucer, the panels painted with sea shells. Both items sold November 28, 1961.　£70.

WROTHAM WARE

A four-handled loving cup, an unusually fine specimen, decorated with dots, bosses, initials $_{L.\ R.}^{W.}$ and H. I., and dated 1656. Sotheby, January 25, 1906. £56.

A wine jug, brown body with yellow slip, inscribed "Samuel Hugheson." Dated 1618. Height, 8 ins. Sotheby, June 12, 1906. £10.

A slip-ware posset-pot, inscribed, "Richard Mier, His Cup, 1708." Diameter, 9½ ins. (The Rev. A. Willett.) Christie, April 1, 1910. £56 14s.

A slip-ware flower-pot, decorated with a stag-hunt, and dated 1714. Height, 11 ins. Christie, March 3, 1911. £5 15s. 6d.

Three slip-ware dishes, decorated with trellis and other ornament in brown and yellow. Christie, November 23, 1927. £8 18s. 6d.

A tyg and cover, with brown glaze incised with an inscription and date 1701. Height, 12½ ins. Christie, March 14, 1929. £10 10s.

A rare slipware tyg of beaker shape covered with a yellowish-brown glaze and with four double loop handles. Inscribed in relief T.I. and dated 1643. (Other examples by Thomas Ifield are recorded.) Height, 5⅝ ins. June 25, 1957. £260.

A rare globular tyg decorated with cream coloured slip on a brown ground and inscribed " 1709. Wrotham. I.E." Height, 6¼ ins. March 18, 1958. £330.

A rare slipware tyg by John Livermore, with four double loop handles, dated 1631, initials I.L. and N.H. Height, 7⅛ ins. February 6, 1962. £460.

YARMOUTH

Six plates, inscribed in the centre, "Thomas and Mary Bingham in Yarmouth, 1742," with zigzag ornament in blue round the borders. Christie, November 15, 1906. £25 4s.

Dish and two plates with fruit and foliage in blue, and inscribed "John Elesbeth Andis, 1759," with a plate inscribed "God Save King George, 1737." Christie, November 15, 1906. £13 13s.

Although described in Christie's catalogue as Yarmouth, it is probable that these pieces were of Lowestoft manufacture.

A creamware coffee pot and cover painted by Absolon (signed Absolon, Yarmo) with farm-yard scene. Inscribed "Success to Farming" and " For my dear Father." Height, 8¼ ins. November 3, 1959. £42.

A creamware vase, painted by Absolon with a view of Yarmouth church. Height, 8½ ins. Marked: Absolon. Yarm. January 23, 1962. £36.

ADVICE TO COLLECTORS

By FREDERICK LITCHFIELD

THE following suggestions are offered with some diffidence, because the writer recognises the fact that a book like Chaffers' is not generally bought by the young and inexperienced collector, but is rather the standard library work which the possessor of a valuable collection keeps for reference. Such advice, or rather hints and suggestions, are given for what they may be worth, and will occupy but a small space, and need only be read by those who feel that they are likely to benefit from their consideration.

MAKING A COLLECTION

The mere acquisition of a great number of specimens, even if genuine and valuable, does not constitute a "collection." It is quite possible to spend a very large sum of money and yet not to have a collection, and a comparatively small sum of money, *but an infinite amount of care and attention*, and to acquire a collection of either pottery or porcelain of the greatest interest. To attain this object it is necessary to acquire a knowledge of the history and vicissitudes of the factories, the specimens of which are to be collected, and to steadily build up and gradually obtain and render complete, a chronological sequence of the different efforts and products of the factory or factories. There are sidelights also on the history of many ceramic factories which can be obtained by the acquisition of specimens of other factories, which show the inspiration from which sometimes a later and sometimes a contemporary undertaking, drew its *motifs* of form and decoration.

In another work on this subject I have termed such pieces "link" specimens, and I will give an illustration of my meaning. The earlier efforts of the Dresden, Bow, Chelsea, Worcester, and some other factories all derived their first ideas of decoration from Oriental porcelain, then, during the Dr. Wall period of the Worcester factory, there was a time when the imitation of old Venetian porcelain was affected, at others Dresden china was imitated, and similar instances may be noticed with regard to all the old ceramic industries. If, therefore, an original Oriental, Venetian, or Dresden specimen be acquired and compared with the example of which it is the prototype, one may term such a piece a "link." These specimens add materially to the interest of a collection, and they increase the amateur's knowledge of different pastes and glazes by careful comparison, and are material aids to gaining experience.

DESCRIPTIVE INVOICES

I have always advised collectors when making purchases to insist upon having a properly descriptive invoice of the specimen bought. Mistakes must sometimes happen and fraud must also be guarded against. In case of either the one or the other, where an exchange of the article or a return of the purchase money is sought to be obtained, the written invoice will be found a most material piece of evidence.

Frequently I am consulted about an unsatisfactory purchase, and ask to see the invoice, when I find that the so-called Chelsea or old Dresden specimen is described as a "china" figure or a "richly decorated" cup and saucer; whereas if the proper description had been in writing I could have helped my client to much readier redress. The collector should remember the Latin maxim, *Litera scripta manet*.

PURCHASES AT AUCTION

For several reasons the purchase of specimens at sales by auction is not recommended for amateurs of limited experience. Of course, there is always the fascination and excitement of bidding, and the expectation of saving the dealers' profit. As a set off against these inducements there are many disadvantages. To begin with, one generally misses the purchase of the particular lots which were selected on view day, and at the end of the sale finds oneself the owner of some lots which were not examined, but which appeared to be going so much below their value, that the temptation to make a bid was irresistible. In the result specimens are acquired which could have been done without, and their cost much more satisfactorily expended in examples which were really requisite to render more complete the *methodical* collection of specimens of any particular factory.

Those of us who are conversant with some of the secrets of the sale-room know how many are the pitfalls prepared for the unwary bargain-hunter. Sales are "rigged"—that is, composed of lots put in by dealers anxious to realise the cost of some of their old "shop-keepers"—and there is generally some one in the room on the vendor's behalf on the look-out for an inexperienced bidder who is opposed, as far as discretion or daring permits. Not infrequently, when the protecting bidder goes just too far and the lot is knocked down to him, he will deny that he made the bid, and the amateur will then be expected to take the lot if he was the previous bidder.

If the collector prefers to purchase at auctions rather than to make his selections quietly and deliberately from the stock of a reliable dealer, my advice is to view the sale carefully, and then to seek the assistance of a dealer of repute whose judgment can be relied upon. Such a man will advise as to the price which ought to be given for any of the specimens selected, and he may also prevent a foolish purchase by pointing out some good reason for its rejection. The commission usually charged is five per cent. on the amount given, or a shilling in the pound, and as this charge is inclusive of personal attendance and advice on the view day, and of collection and delivery, it seems well worth the comparatively small addition to the cost of really desirable specimens.

Where very large amounts are given for lots some more favourable arrangement than five per cent. may be made, if it is considered desirable to do so, but we must always remember that in order to be well served we must pay generously.

It is much better and more satisfactory in every way to make one's purchases through the same dealer, and not vary one's patronage by employing sometimes one, and sometimes another agent, or, still more unwisely, to give the commissions to the casual "touter" one is addressed by in the saleroom. There are some good reasons for this caution. In the first place a respectable dealer will appreciate the confidence of a regular client and will do his best for his interest, while if he has a suspicion that a rival is being employed, he may show some resentment of what he considers unfair treatment by increasing the cost by bidding or perhaps by buying the lot. The casual commission agent may have the advantage of being on the spot, and thus save a little extra trouble, but there is a good deal of risk in employing him, and the amateur collector cannot be too strongly urged to first make a careful choice of the member of the trade who can be thoroughly trusted to act for him, and then, even at the cost of some extra personal trouble in making an appointment or in writing instructions, to make it worth his while by giving him all his commissions. If the prices or values suggested are, as they should be, in the collector's interest, moderate and well judged, it must necessarily follow that only a portion of the selected lots will be purchased, and therefore there must be many disappointments where the commission earned is only trifling in amount or the result of the sale may be a blank. If the agent knows that he has his client's full confidence, he will put up with this in the hope that he will be more fortunate upon the next occasion. It is sometimes desirable in one's own interest to see matters from another man's point of view, and this is one of many instances in which a due consideration for the agent employed will be for the ultimate benefit of the collector.

RESTORATIONS

It is almost impossible to expect that fragile china groups and figures can escape the penalty exacted by time and careless handling, but if we buy restored specimens we like to know that we do so, and the extent of the repair. I have found two means of detection—one by smell; a recently repaired piece can be detected by holding the specimen close to one's nasal organ, when the odour of paint will be apparent. The other remedy is to tap the suspected part with a coin or the blunt edge of a knife. China will give out a ring and composition will not.

IMITATIONS

The law of supply and demand must inevitably bring about imitations of anything that is valuable or desirable. Apart from the pecuniary loss, the annoyance at being the victim of fraud or deception is irritating. The best suggestion I can offer is only to deal with firms of established honesty and reputation. There are many dealers who are entirely reliable, and although I cannot give here names or recommendations, such may always be obtained from connoisseur friends, or from myself by consultation.

Imitations are of various kinds. There are the obvious German and

French spurious manufactures, purporting to be old Chelsea, Worcester, and Oriental porcelain, and there are others much more subtle and difficult to detect.

Of the former, many really ought not to deceive any one of ordinary powers of observation, for their inferiority to the work of which they purport to be imitations, is so palpable. There is a garish meretricious appearance which should act as a danger-signal to the eye of a cultivated man or woman, and if the details of painting and gilding be examined they will be found to be quite different from the decorative treatment of genuine old pieces. These remarks apply to the more ambitious imitations, that is, the imitations of fine scale Worcester, richly coloured Chelsea or fine old Sèvres, but the imitations of the humble kinds of old china are not so easily detected.

Collectors should be careful to avoid the imitation of the old Carl Theodor and Ludwigsburg groups and figures which have been lately produced in Germany, and which bear a mark which very closely resembles that which is found on the original productions of these fine old fabrics.

Oriental china is counterfeited to an enormous extent. The imitations of the more valuable kinds, such as *famille verte, famille rose*, and the ruby-backed eggshell, are made by M. Samson of Paris, and there is also some clever work of the modern Chinese factories in vases and services in the style of the seventeenth century. These sometimes bear marks which would appear to be those of the earlier time.

Nothing but experience can enable the amateur to detect the more carefully prepared imitations, but one may offer a suggestion that will be found of practical use, and that is to buy from well-known dealers pieces of high quality and about which there can be no doubt. If such pieces are placed in the cabinet and constantly seen, they will be the best witnesses in themselves against fraud, and when "a jackdaw in peacock's feathers" is placed near the real peacock the difference will become apparent to a collector of very moderate experience. There is no severer test for a sham than to be placed in the company of the real, and, for the rest, intelligence and experience must be trusted to protect the young collector from growing tares with wheat.

Speaking generally of the various imitations of old china which occasionally come before the expert for examination and report, there is a class of production which is sometimes of a puzzling character. The specimen submitted is obviously not the ordinary sham, made for purposes of fraud or deception, and yet as obviously it is not a product of the factory which it represents.

I have seen well made and carefully finished vases and portions of services, purporting to be Sèvres, Dresden, Chelsea, or Worcester, sometimes bearing a misleading mark and frequently having no mark whatever. In numerous cases the explanation of the mystery is that at some time, perhaps as long as fifty or sixty years ago, the owner has required to make up his service, which has suffered from breakage, and a pattern has been sent to the Coalport, Minton, or perhaps the Spode or Derby works, and portions made to match in every respect the pattern as regards decoration and general appearance. There is a difference in the paste or body, a slight variation in the treatment of the details of decoration, which require very close inspection under a magnifying-glass before one can give an opinion as to the place of origin. I remember very well that when Lord Lonsdale's china was sold at Christie's, some ten or fifteen years ago, some dozens of old Sèvres plates of the decoration known as "horse shoe" pattern were followed in the catalogue by some other dozens of plates similar as to decoration, but unmistakably of Coalport make instead of Sèvres. They had been made to render the table service of sufficient quantity for the use of a larger dinner-party. The trade, knowing the difference, gave some £30 to £40 a dozen for the first on the list, which were genuine old Sèvres, and about £2 10s. a dozen for the ones which followed, and a collecting friend, who happened to be standing near me, was astonished at the great difference in price until the reason was explained to him.

This kind of imitative work, though honest in its purpose, has led to many difficulties, as the different kinds of china get sometimes mixed, owing to want of care or knowledge, therefore services which are offered for sale should be carefully examined piece by piece before a purchase is decided upon.

Chelsea and Worcester vases which have lost their covers, and in some cases even, when one of a set of three has been missing, have been completed in this way; and, unless the buyer has had some experience of "make ups" of this kind, he may be deceived to a serious extent, since the value of vases and covers is considerably lessened if they have covers made at a later time or are the product of a different factory.

The above notes for collectors were written by Frederick Litchfield in 1912 and are reprinted again, as the advice given is just as appropriate now as it was then.

SOME OF THE IMITATIONS AND MISLEADING MARKS ON CHINA

WITH reference to the marks upon some of the imitations of favourite descriptions of old china, it should be obvious that in the majority of cases, a more or less exact copy of the genuine mark is added to render the imposition more attractive. There are, however, several marks of a misleading character which are apt to puzzle the collector, since they are not to be found amongst those which appear in the body of this volume as representative of the various fabriques of which notices are given.

It may be useful, therefore, to add a list of such marks as have come under the Editor's observation, together with some notes which, taken together with the caution given above, may place the amateur upon his guard, and inform him as to their origin.

IMITATIONS OF OLD LOWESTOFT

The Editor has already given his views on the vexed question of Lowestoft, and the more recent experience and writings of expert authorities confirm what has been said with regard to the greater quantity of "Armorial" china.

The popularity of Armorial china has led to the production of a vast quantity of reproductions. The best of these, both as regards the quality of the china itself, and also the painting of the coats of arms, which form the principal ornament, are the work of Samson of Paris, already mentioned, but there are other makers, both in France and Germany, whose work one sees frequently exposed for sale. Only careful examination, made with some knowledge of pastes and glazes, can enable the amateur to discriminate between the better and older imitations, and those of Oriental china decorated with the coats of arms and crests of the families of the eighteenth century, who ordered these services through the officers of the old East India Company.

Then again, to mark the distinction between that which is Oriental and that which is genuine old Lowestoft, is a still more difficult task, and must be generally left to an experienced collecting friend or to a trade expert. The Lowestoft paste was soft, and the Oriental, without exception, very hard.

The Lowestoft factory, with a few exceptions, did not achieve the greatest measure of success, and there are certain signs of crudeness which will never be found in good Oriental porcelain; one of these is the clumsiness in the under-rim of cups and saucers and plates and dishes of Lowestoft as contrasted with the "clean," thinner, and better potted work from an old Chinese porcelain kiln.

Neither real or imitation Lowestoft bears any fabric mark.

WORCESTER, CHELSEA, BOW IMITATIONS

The imitations of the products of the most sought after of the English china factories are also of various kinds and degrees. The commoner and cheaper descriptions of "old Worcester," with the salmon scale ground and panels of exotic birds, which are made in France and Germany, are of such an ambitious character that they should at once arouse suspicion. The paste is coarse, the painting bad, the glaze entirely different from that of real Worcester, and the same may be said of the sham figures and vases bearing the gold anchor and purporting to be Chelsea, or with the Bow mark to imitate the latter factory.

These shams are not difficult to detect, but there are other more carefully-made imitations of the less important kinds of specimens which require a more careful examination, and the best advice which it occurs to me to offer is that which I mentioned in the earlier portions of these remarks. It is to procure from a dealer of good repute certain test pieces of undoubted merit and to use such for comparison with doubtful pieces.

The mark shown, which has appeared on the market since about 1907, requires some explanation to prevent mistakes. The ware is fine earthenware decorated with the blue flowers and insects on a white ground in the manner of the early productions of the Dr. Wall period of old Worcester china. The models of oval and round basket dishes, and also of leaf-shaped trinket-stands, are also similar to those of the old Worcester factory. The mark is said to be the monogram of Charles Bowers, manager of Booths Ltd. of Tunstall but, looked at carelessly and without some explanation, it might easily be mistaken for the Crescent and the W., which the reader will find amongst the early Worcester marks.

There was also placed on the market another imitation of old Worcester china, the patterns with the famous apple-green ground and paintings of exotic birds being the most successful. This ware is also made by Booths Limited, of Church and Swan Works, Tunstall. When critically examined this will be found to be only a superior earthenware with a glaze which resembles that of Worcester. The collector must also be on his guard against redecorated and refired Worcester. This can generally be detected by carefully examining the details of the decoration, which will show a certain amount of clumsiness in application, the new colours being more opaque in appearance, and the paste or body will show splutterings, that is, tiny black spots, as the result of refiring. Good genuine old Worcester china is invariably well potted, carefully painted and finished.

THE VALUE OF A MARK

Perhaps it may not be out of place to conclude these remarks by saying that, inasmuch as the easiest part of an imitation to produce is a fraudulent copy of a mark, we should for that reason not place, too much reliance on the mark itself. Let us consider a mark *not the evidence* of genuineness but the *confirmation* of other evidence. Thus if a specimen possess all the characteristics of a certain factory—paste, glaze, form, colour, quality—then if marked so much the better; it confirms all the evidence of its being the specimen we think it is, but the mark should come last, and not first, as a factor in forming a decision upon a doubtful specimen.

To the collector the marks and monograms on the different examples of the various factories in his cabinets have a special value. The many points of specific interest, the helps and indications which they afford in deciding the particular period of the factory's history, or the individual potter, modeller, artist, or gilder who formed or decorated the specimen— in all these matters of detail, which add so infinitely to the personal fascination of collecting china, the mark, the monogram, even a scratched or incised number or initial, has " points." The object of these cautionary observations is not to belittle the importance of the mark, but to warn the inexperienced collector that he should first of all be satisfied that the specimen is a genuine one *by its having the merits* of its kind. Then when this main issue is decided, the added interest of the mark, whether of fabrique, artist, or workman, gives an extra charm and value to the possession.

FREDERICK LITCHFIELD.

The above remarks regarding fakes and the value of marks were written by Frederick Litchfield in 1912 and apply mainly to the eighteenth century wares. The marks of the nineteenth century are rarely forged (Rockingham, Swansea and Nantgarw are exceptions) and afford a convenient means of identification and dating.   G.G.

BRITISH POTTERY MANUFACTURERS IN 1900

(Compiled from *The Pottery Gazette Diary Directory* and reproduced by permission of the proprietors—Messrs. Scott, Greenwood & Son Ltd.)

William Adams & Co., Greenfield and Greengates Potteries, Tunstall, Stoke-on-Trent.
Wm. A. Adderley & Co., Daisy Bank Works, Longton, Stoke-on-Trent.
Ainsworth Brothers, Stockton Pottery, Stockton-on-Tees.
Albert Pottery Co., Victoria Terrace, St. Philip's Marsh, Bristol.
H. Alcock & Co., Waterloo Road, Cobridge, Stoke-on-Trent.
Aller Vale Art Potteries, Newton Abbott.
Charles Allerton & Sons, Park Works, High Street, Longton, Stoke-on-Trent.
Charles Amison, Stanley Pottery, Anchor Road, Longton, Stoke-on-Trent.
W. J. Arlidge, The Old Pottery, Donyatt, Ilminster.
Arrowsmith & Co., Central Works, Longton, Stoke-on-Trent.
Art Pottery Co., Anchor Works, Hanley, Stoke-on-Trent.
Edward Asbury & Co., Prince of Wales' Works, Longton, Stoke-on-Trent.
G. L. Ashworth & Bros., Broad Street, Hanley, Stoke-on-Trent.
William Ault, Swadlincote, Burton-on-Trent.
Aylesford Pottery Co., Aylesford, Kent.
H. Aynsley & Co., Commerce Works, Longton, Stoke-on-Trent.
John Aynsley & Sons, Portland Works, Longton, Stoke-on-Trent.

C. F. Bailey, Burslem Pottery Co., Scotia Works, Burslem, Stoke-on-Trent.
W. & J. A. Bailey, Alloa Pottery, Alloa, Scotland.
Baker & Co. Ltd., Fenton Potteries, Fenton, Stoke-on-Trent.
J. Baker, Kingsfield Pottery, Newcastle, Staffs.
J. Baker, Hoo Pottery, Werburgh, Rochester.
J. H. Bale, 174 Westbourne Grove, London.
A. Balfour & Co., North British Pottery, Glasgow.
Ball Bros., Deptford Pottery, Sunderland.
J. Barber, Gladstone Works, Burslem, Stoke-on-Trent.
Barker Bros., Meir Works, Longton, Stoke-on-Trent.

H. K. Barker, Rubian Art Pottery, Fenton, Stoke-on-Trent.
Barker Pottery Co., New Brampton, Chesterfield.
Barkers & Kent Ltd., Foley Pottery, Fenton, Stoke-on-Trent.
T. W. Barlow & Son, Coronation Works, Longton, Stoke-on-Trent.
W. L. Baron, Rolle's Quay, Barnstaple.
Bates, Dewsberry & Co. (Tiles), Mayer Street, Hanley, Stoke-on-Trent.
R. Bateson, Stoneware, Burton-in-Lonsdale, Yorks.
Beehive Pottery Co., Chatsworth Road, Chesterfield.
Belfield & Co., Prestonpans Pottery, Prestonpans, Scotland.
J. & M. P. Bell & Co. Ltd., Glasgow Pottery, Glasgow.
Belleek Pottery Co., Belleek, Co. Fermanagh, Ireland.
Bennett & Shenton, Pelham Street Works, Hanley, Stoke-on-Trent.
W. Bennett, Cleveland Works, Victoria Road, Hanley, Stoke-on-Trent.
Benthall Pottery Co., Benthall, Broseley.
G. L. Bentley & Co., Cyples Old Pottery, Longton, Stoke-on-Trent.
Beresford Bros., Victoria Works, Longton, Stoke-on-Trent.
J. W. Beswick, Gold Street Works, Longton, Stoke-on-Trent.
W. Bettaney, 41 Hope Street, Hanley, Stoke-on-Trent.
T. Betteridge, Woodville Pottery, Burton-on-Trent.
H. & W. Billington (Decorators), Waterloo Road, Burslem, Stoke-on-Trent.
Bilston Pottery Co., Mount Pleasant, Bilston.
Biltons Ltd., London Road Works, Stoke-on-Trent.
E. Bingham (The Hedingham Ware Art Pottery), Castle Hedingham, Essex.
Birch Tile Co. Ltd., 22 Clarence Street, Hanley, Stoke-on-Trent.
L. A. Birks & Co., The Vine Pottery, Stoke-on-Trent.
Bishop & Stonier, High Street, Hanley, Stoke-on-Trent.
Blackhurst & Hulme, Belgrave Works, Longton, Stoke-on-Trent.
Blair & Co., Beaconsfield Pottery, Longton, Stoke-on-Trent.
T. &. R. Boote Ltd., Waterloo Potteries, Burslem, Stoke-on-Trent.
Booths Ltd., High Street, Tunstall, Stoke-on-Trent.
G. Borgfeldt & Co., 36 Glebe Street, Stoke-on-Trent.
Boulton & Co., Edensor Road, Longton, Stoke-on-Trent.
Boulton & Floyd, Lovatt & Hall Street Works, Stoke-on-Trent.
E. J. E. Leigh Bourne, Albion Pottery, Burslem, Stoke-on-Trent.
J. Bourne & Son, Denby Pottery, Near Derby.
J. Bourne & Son, New St. Pancras Station, London.
Bovey Pottery Co. Ltd., Bovey Tracy.
Bradshaw & Co., Lount Pottery, Osbaston, Nuneaton.
C. H. Brannam, The Pottery, Barnstaple.
Brayne & Mansfield, Victoria Pottery, Leigh, Essex.
F. Brayne & Co., Bow Pottery, Bromley-by-Bow, London.
T. Brian, Church Street, Longton, Stoke-on-Trent.
B. W. H. Bridges, Boship Pottery Works, Hellingly, Sussex.
Bridgett & Bates, King Street, Longton, Stoke-on-Trent.
S. Bridgwood & Son, Anchor Pottery, Longton, Stoke-on-Trent.
R. Bridgwood, Granville Works, Longton, Stoke-on-Trent.

Britannia China Co., Edensor Road, Longton, Stoke-on-Trent.
British Anchor Pottery Co. Ltd., Anchor Road, Longton, Stoke-on-Trent.
James Broadhurst & Sons, Victoria Road, Fenton, Stoke-on-Trent.
J. Bromley, Barker Street, Longton, Stoke-on-Trent.
Brooks & Co., Normacott Road, Longton, Stoke-on-Trent.
J. W. Brough, Wharf Street Pottery, Stoke-on-Trent.
J. Brown, Mount Blue Pottery, Camlachie, Glasgow.
Brown-Westhead, Moore & Co., Cauldon Place, Stoke-on-Trent.
A. W. Buchan & Co., Waverley Potteries, Portobello, Scotland.
L. Buist & Sons, Sinclairtown Pottery, Kirkcaldy.
Bullers Ltd., Joiners Square Works, Hanley, Stoke-on-Trent.
A. Bullock & Co., Waterloo Works, Hanley, Stoke-on-Trent.
Burgess & Leigh, Middleport and Hill Potteries, Burslem, Stoke-on-Trent.
Burnside Bros., Lime Street Pottery, Ouseburn, Newcastle-on-Tyne.
G. & T. Burton, Registry Street Works, Stoke-on-Trent.

Caledonian Pottery Co. Ltd., Caledonian Pottery, Rutherglen, Near
　　Glasgow.
Campbell Tile Co., London Road, Stoke-on-Trent.
Campbellfield Pottery Co. Ltd., Springburn, Near Glasgow.
Capper & Wood, Bradwell Works, Longport, Stoke-on-Trent.
Carder & Sons, Lays Pottery, Brierley Hill.
Carder & Sons, Mount Pleasant, Bilston.
J. Carr & Sons, Low Lights, North Shields.
Carter & Co., Poole and Hamworthy Potteries, Poole, Dorset.
Cartlidge & Matthias, Chelsea Works, Hanley, Stoke-on-Trent.
F. Cartlidge & Co., Normacott Road, Longton, Stoke-on-Trent.
Carlton Pottery Co., 20 Glebe Buildings, Stoke-on-Trent.
Cartwright & Edwards, Borough Pottery, Longton, Stoke-on-Trent.
Ceramic Art Company Ltd. (Decorators), Stoke Road, Hanley, Stoke-on-
　　Trent.
D. Chapman & Sons, Atlas China Works, Longton, Stoke-on-Trent.
Clarence Potteries Co. Ltd., Norton, Stockton-on-Tees.
Clark & Mottishaw, Newbold Pottery, Chesterfield.
H. Clark, Dicker Pottery Works, Hellingly, Sussex.
Clementson Bros., Phoenix and Bell Works, Hanley, Stoke-on-Trent.
Clokie & Sons, Castleford Potteries, Castleford.
Clyde Pottery Co., Pottery Street, Greenock.
Coalport China Co. (John Rose & Co.) Ltd., Ironbridge, Shropshire.
T. Coates, Burton-in-Lonsdale, Yorks.
Cochran & Fleming, Britannia Pottery, Glasgow.
R. Cochrane & Co., Verreville Pottery, Glasgow.
Codling & Bainbridge, Wolviston, Near Stockton-on-Tees.
Colclough & Co., Goddard Works, Longton, Stoke-on-Trent.
Collier, Grovelands Potteries, Reading.
Collingwood Bros., Stafford Street, Longton, Stoke-on-Trent.
T. Cone, Alma Works, Longton, Stoke-on-Trent.

J. H. Cope & Co., Wellington Works, Longport, Stoke-on-Trent.
W. T. Copeland & Sons, High Street, Stoke-on-Trent.
W. & E. Corn, Top Bridge Works, Longport, Stoke-on-Trent.
Corr & McNally, Coalisland, Ireland.
E. Cotton, Nelson Road and Commercial Road, Hanley, Stoke-on-Trent.
Craven, Dunnill & Co. Ltd. (Tiles), Jackfield Works, Jackfield, Shropshire.
G. M. Creyke (Decorator), Newhall Street Works, Hanley, Stoke-on-Trent.
Cross Bros., Jubilee Works, Church Gresley, Burton-on-Trent.
Crowther & Wangler, The Alexandra Pottery Co., Maindee, Newport, Mon.
Cumnock Pottery Co., Old Cumnock, Cumnock, Scotland.
D. Davies, Gas Works Road, Neath, South Wales.
R. Davies, Sutton Heath Pottery, Sutton Heath, St. Helens.
Davison & Sons, Bleak Hill Works, Burslem, Stoke-on-Trent.
M. Dean, Ranelagh Street, Hanley, Stoke-on-Trent.
T. Dean, Black Works, Stoke-on-Trent.
Decorative Art Tile Co. Ltd., Bryan Street, Hanley, Stoke-on-Trent.
Della Robbia Pottery Ltd., Paice Street, Birkenhead.
H. Dennis (Tiles), Ruabon, North Wales.
Dewes & Copestake, Viaduct Works, Longton, Stoke-on-Trent.
J. Dimmock & Co., Albion Works, Hanley, Stoke-on-Trent.
T. J. Doe. Wattisfield, Diss, Norfolk.
Doulton & Co. Ltd., Nile Street Works, Burslem, Stoke-on-Trent.
Doulton & Co. Ltd., Lambeth Pottery, London.
Down & Pennington, The Pottery, Cheam Common, Worcester Park, Surrey.
Dresden Porcelain Co., Blythe Works, Longton, Stoke-on-Trent.
T. & R. Duckworth, Broughton Barn Pottery, Oswaldtwistle, Lancs.
Dudson Bros., Hope Street, Hanley, Stoke-on-Trent.
J. Dunbar, Clay Flats, Workington, Cumberland.
Dunn, Bennett & Co., Royal Victoria Pottery, Burslem, Stoke-on-Trent.

Edge, Malkin & Co. Ltd., Newport Pottery, Burslem, Stoke-on-Trent.
Edwards Bros., Albion Works, Burslem, Stoke-on-Trent.
G. Edwards, Sheridan Works, Longton, Stoke-on-Trent.
J. C. Edwards (Tiles and Terra Cotta), Ruabon, North Wales.
W. Edwards & Sons, Hadderidge Pottery, Burslem, Stoke-on-Trent.
W. J. Edwards, Warren Place, Longton, Stoke-on-Trent.
Edwards & Brown, High Street, Longton, Stoke-on-Trent.
E. H. Elton, Sunflower Pottery, Clevedon, Somerset.
J. F. Elton & Co., Archer Works, Stoke-on-Trent.
Empire Porcelain Co., Empire Works, Stoke-on-Trent.
Exeter Art Pottery, Okehampton Street, Exeter.

D. Farrance. High Halden, Ashford.
S. Fielding & Co., Railway Pottery, Stoke-on-Trent.
W. Fielding, Cannon Street Works, Hanley, Stoke-on-Trent.
G. Finch, Gestingthorpe, Halstead, Essex.

E. B. Fishley, Fremington, Devonshire.
Ford & Sons, Newcastle Street, Burslem, Stoke-on-Trent.
C. Ford, Cannon Street, Hanley, Stoke-on-Trent.
D. Ford & Co. (Decorators), Empress Pottery, Hanley, Stoke-on-Trent.
S. Ford & Co., Lincoln Pottery, Burslem, Stoke-on-Trent.
T. Forester & Sons Ltd., Phoenix Works, Longton, Stoke-on-Trent.
H. Foster, East Grinstead Pottery, East Grinstead, Surrey.
J. Foxton, Littlethorpe, Ripon, Yorkshire.
Furnivals Ltd., Cobridge, Stoke-on-Trent.

P. Gardner, Dunmore Pottery, Near Stirling, Scotland.
Gaskell & Grocott, Whitehall Works, Longport, Stoke-on-Trent.
Gater, Hall & Co., New Gordon Pottery, Tunstall, Stoke-on-Trent.
Gibson & Sons, Moorland Road, Burslem, Stoke-on-Trent.
W. Gill & Sons, Providence Potteries, Castleford.
Gilmore Bros., Fountain Place Works, Fenton, Stoke-on-Trent.
Glastonbury Pottery Co. Ltd., Wells Road, Glastonbury, Somerset.
J. Godwin, Stoddard & Co., China Works, Foley, Longton, Stoke-on-Trent.
A. E. Goodwin, The Potteries, Cheltenham, Gloucestershire.
W. H. Goss, London Road, Stoke-on-Trent.
G. Grainger & Co., Royal China Works, Worcester.
H. Gravett, St. John's Pottery, Burgess Hill, Sussex.
Gray & Co., Britannia Pottery, Hanley, Stoke-on-Trent.
W. A. Gray & Sons, Midlothian Potteries, Portobello, Scotland.
T. A. & S. Green, Minerva Works, Fenton, Stoke-on-Trent.
T. G. Green & Co. Ltd., Church Gresley Potteries, Burton-on-Trent.
T. W. Green, Albion Potteries, New Whittington, Chesterfield.
J. T. Greenrod & Son, Pottery Lane, Brentford.
Grimwades Ltd., Winton, Stoke and Elgin Potteries, Stoke-on-Trent.
W. H. Grindley & Co., Woodland Pottery, Tunstall, Stoke-on-Trent.
Grinhaff & Co., Coleorton Pottery, Ashby-de-la-Zouch, Leicester.
Grosvenor & Son, Eagle Pottery, Bridgeton, Glasgow.
Grove & Co., Palissy Works, Longton, Stoke-on-Trent.
Guest & Dewsberry, South Wales Pottery, Llanelly, Wales.

A. G. Hackney, Slippery Lane, Hanley, Stoke-on-Trent.
J. Hadley & Son, High Street and Lower Bath Road, Worcester.
S. S. Hall, Plaskynaston Potteries, Wrexham, Denbighshire.
J. & R. Hammersley, New Street, Hanley, Stoke-on-Trent.
R. Hammersley & Son, Wedgwood Place, Burslem, Stoke-on-Trent.
Hammond & Munday, Poling, Sussex.
S. Hancock, Old Crown Derby China Works, King Street, Derby.
S. Hancock & Sons, Wolfe Street, Stoke-on-Trent.
Hanley China Company, Burton Place, Hanley, Stoke-on-Trent.
Harling & Son, Whitwood Mere, Castleford.

A. Harris, Pottery Works, Wrecclesham, Farnham.

Harrop & Burgess, Mount Pleasant Works, Tinkersclough, Hanley, Stoke-on-Trent.

Hawley Bros., Northfield Pottery, Rotherham and Low Pottery, Near Rotherham.

Hawley & Co., Temple Backs, Bristol.

Hawley, Webberley & Co., Garfield Works, Longton, Stoke-on-Trent.

H. Hayes, Old Ewloe Pottery, Chester.

F. Heath, Woodville, Burton-on-Trent.

T. Heath, Albion Works, Longton, Stoke-on-Trent.

Hepworth & Heald, Kilnhurst Pottery, Kilnhurst, Near Rotherham.

R. Heron & Son, Fife Pottery, Sinclairtown, Kirkcaldy, Scotland.

Hexter, Humpherson & Co., The Potteries, Newton Abbot.

Hill & Co., St. James's Place, Longton, Stoke-on-Trent.

Hines Bros., Heron Cross Pottery, Fenton, Stoke-on-Trent.

G. & J. Hobson, Albert Street Pottery, Burslem, Stoke-on-Trent.

J. Hodgett & Co., Lea Brook, Wednesbury.

Holdcroft & Co., George Street Pottery, Tunstall, Stoke-on-Trent.

J. Holdcroft, Sutherland Pottery, Longton, Stoke-on-Trent.

J. Holding & Sons, Broadfield Pottery, Oswaldtwistle, Lancs.

Hollinshead & Griffiths, Chelsea Works, Burslem, Stoke-on-Trent.

Hollinshead & Kirkham, Unicorn Pottery, Tunstall, Stoke-on-Trent.

J. Hollinson, High Street, Longton, Stoke-on-Trent.

Holmes & Son, Clayton Street, Longton, Stoke-on-Trent.

J. W. Holt, Victoria Works, Longton, Stoke-on-Trent.

Horn Bros., Australian Pottery, Ferrybridge, Yorkshire.

J. Howlett & Co., Northwood Pottery, Hanley, Stoke-on-Trent.

Howsons & Sons Ltd., Hallfield Pottery, Hanley, Stoke-on-Trent.

W. Hudson, Normacott Road, Longton, Stoke-on-Trent.

E. Hughes & Co., Opal China Works, Fenton, Stoke-on-Trent.

T. Hughes & Son, Longport, Stoke-on-Trent.

A. J. Hull, King Street Pottery, Longton, Stoke-on-Trent.

Hulme & Christie, Sutherland Pottery, Fenton, Stoke-on-Trent.

W. Hulme, Wedgwood Works, Burslem, Stoke-on-Trent.

W. Hutchings & Co., Pipe Lane, Bristol.

Jackson & Gosling, Grosvenor Works, Foley, Fenton, Stoke-on-Trent.

J. Jeavons & Sons, Brettell Lane, Brierley Hill, Staffordshire.

G. Jennings, South Western Pottery, Parkstone, Dorset.

Johnson Bros. Ltd., Alexandra Pottery, Tunstall, Stoke-on-Trent.

Johnson Bros. Hanley Ltd., Hanley Pottery, Hanley, Stoke-on-Trent.

Johnson, McAlister Tile Co., Adelaide Street, Burslem, Stoke-on-Trent.

S. Johnson, Hill Pottery, Burslem, Stoke-on-Trent.

Johnson & Riley, Bradley Fold Pottery, Little Lever, Bolton, Lancs.

A. Jones, Church Gresley, Burton-on-Trent.

A. B. Jones & Sons, Grafton Works, Longton, Stoke-on-Trent.

G. Jones & Sons Ltd., Trent Potteries, Stoke-on-Trent.

W. Jones, Ebenezer Works, Longton, Stoke-on-Trent.
Jones & Gerrard, Ewloe Green Potteries, Buckley, Chester.

T. Kay & Son, Holbeck Moor Pottery, Holbeck, Leeds.
Kay & Grieves, Canny Hill Pottery, Bishop Auckland, Durham.
Keeling & Co., Dale Hall Works, Burslem, Stoke-on-Trent.
H. T. K. Kelly Pottery Ltd., Parkstone, Dorset.
J. Kelly, Ginns, Whitehaven, Cumberland.
H. Kennedy & Sons, Barrowfield Potteries, Glasgow.
J. Kent, The Old Foley Pottery, Longton, Stoke-on-Trent.
W. Kent, Novelty Works, Burslem, Stoke-on-Trent.
King & Barrett, Bournes Bank Pottery, Burslem, Stoke-on-Trent.
W. Kirkham, London Road, Stoke-on-Trent.
Kirkland & Co., Albion Pottery, Etruria, Hanley, Stoke-on-Trent.
Kitsons & Whitworth, Woodman House Pottery Works, Elland, Yorks.
Knight & Sproston, Keele Street, Stoke-on-Trent.
M. Knowles & Son, Welshpool and Payne Potteries, Brampton Moor, Chesterfield.

Lancaster & Sons, Dresden Works, Tinkersclough, Hanley, Stoke-on-Trent.
S. M. Lancaster, Wheeldon Mill, Chesterfield, Derbyshire.
T. Lawrence, Falcon Works, Longton, Stoke-on-Trent.
R. Lax, Evenword, Bishop Auckland, Durham.
Lea & Bolton, The Art Tileries, Tunstall, Stoke-on-Trent.
T. Ledgar, Heathcote Pottery, Longton, Stoke-on-Trent.
Leeds Art Pottery & Tile Co. Ltd., Hunslet, Leeds.
Leeds Fireclay Co. Ltd., Burmantofts Works, Burmantofts, Leeds.
C. H. Lewis, Kew Road, Clevedon, Somerset.
Lingard & Webster, Swan Bank Pottery, Tunstall, Stoke-on-Trent.
J. Lockett & Co., Chancery Lane, Longton, Stoke-on-Trent.
Long Park Fine Art Terra Cotta Co., St. Marychurch, Torquay.
S. Longbottom, The Potteries, Nafferton, Hull.
Longton Porcelain Co., Victoria Works, Longton, Stoke-on-Trent.
Lovatt & Lovatt, The Pottery, Langley Mill, Near Nottingham.
S. Lowe & Sons, Alma and Brunswick Potteries, Brampton, Chesterfield, Derbyshire.
W. Lowe, Sydney Works, Longton, Stoke-on-Trent.

A. Machin & Co., Chancery Lane, Longton, Stoke-on-Trent.
W. Machin, George Street Works, Hanley, Stoke-on-Trent.
J. Macintyre & Co. Ltd., Washington Works, Burslem, Stoke-on-Trent.
A. Mackee, Foley Works, Longton, Stoke-on-Trent.
J. Maddock & Sons Ltd., Newcastle Street, Burslem, Stoke-on-Trent.
C. T. Maling & Sons, A. and B. Ford Potteries, Newcastle-on-Tyne.
F. Malkin (Decorator), Belle Works, Burslem, Stoke-on-Trent.
Malkin Tile Works Co., Newport Lane, Burslem, Stoke-on-Trent.

Marsden Tile Co. Ltd., Fairfield and Ducal Works, Burslem, Stoke-on-Trent.

R. W. Martin & Bros., Southall Pottery, Southall, London.

W. Mason & Co., Pool Pottery, Church Gresley, Burton-on-Trent.

J. F. Matthews, Milton, Stoke-on-Trent.

Maw & Co. Ltd. (Tiles), Benthall Works, Jackfield, Near Ironbridge, Shropshire.

McDougall & Sons (Nautilus Porcelain Co.), Buchanan Street, Glasgow.

C. W. McNay, Bridgeness Pottery, Boness, Scotland.

McNeal & Co., Stanley Pottery, Longton, Stoke-on-Trent.

A. Meakin Ltd., Royal Albert, Victoria and Highgate Pottery, Tunstall, Stoke-on-Trent.

J. & G. Meakin Ltd., Eastwood Works and Eagle Pottery, Hanley, Stoke-on-Trent.

Meller, Taylor & Co., Waterloo Road, Burslem, Stoke-on-Trent.

J. Mercer & Son, Kingston Pottery, Norbiton, Surrey.

D. Methven & Sons, Kirkcaldy Pottery, Kirkcaldy, Scotland.

J. H. Middleton, Bagnall Street China Works, Longton, Stoke-on-Trent.

Midland Pottery Co., Old Hall Street, Liverpool.

Minton, Hollins & Co., Patent Tile Works, Stoke-on-Trent.

Mintons Ltd., London Road, Stoke-on-Trent.

F. Mitchell, Belle Vue Pottery, Rye, Sussex.

H. Moorcraft, Wood Green Potteries, Waltham Abbey, Essex.

Moore Bros., St. Mary's Works, Longton, Stoke-on-Trent.

M. Moore & Co., Victoria Works, Hanley, Stoke-on-Trent.

W. Morley, Salopian Works, Fenton, Stoke-on-Trent.

Morris & Co., Earthen Joiners Square, Hanley, Stoke-on-Trent.

T. Morris, Anchor Road Works, Longton, Stoke-on-Trent.

T. Morris, Regent Works, Longton, Stoke-on-Trent.

Morris & Davies, High Street, Longton, Stoke-on-Trent.

Morrison & Crawford, Rosslyn Pottery, Gallatown, Kirkcaldy, Scotland.

E. Morton & Sons, Salendinenook, Lindley, Huddersfield.

J. Morton & Sons, Lindley Moor Pottery, Lindley, Huddersfield.

A. J. Mountford, Salisbury Works, Burslem, Stoke-on-Trent.

Myott, Son & Co., Alexander Pottery, Stoke-on-Trent.

T. Nadin, Hartshorn Pottery, Woodville, Stoke-on-Trent.

New Hall Porcelain Co., New Hall Works, Hanley, Stoke-on-Trent.

Newport Pottery Co., Albany Street, Newport, Monmouth.

E. & R. Norman, Chailey Potteries, Chailey, Sussex.

R. & N. Norman, St. John's Works, Burgess Hill, Sussex.

Old Hall Porcelain Works Ltd., Hill Street, Hanley, Stoke-on-Trent.

C. W. Outram & Co., Woodville, Near Burton-on-Trent.

Pardoe Bros., Nantgarw, South Wales.

J. Parker, Burton-in-Lonsdale, Yorkshire.

Patman & Co., Ginns Pottery, Whitehaven, Cumberland.
Patterson & Gray, Sodhouse Bank, Sheriff's Hill, Gateshead-on-Tyne.
G. Patterson, Sheriff's Hill Pottery, Gateshead-on-Tyne.
T. Patterson & Co., Pottery Bank, St. Anthony's, Newcastle-on-Tyne.
J. Peake, New Park Works, Hanley, Stoke-on-Trent.
S. Peake, Gillow Heath Pottery, Near Congleton, Cheshire.
S. A. Peake, Rectory Road, Shelton, Hanley, Stoke-on-Trent.
Pearl Pottery Co., Brook Street, Hanley, Stoke-on-Trent.
Pearson & Co., Whittington Moor Potteries, Chesterfield, Derbyshire.
J. Pearson, Oldfield and London Potteries, Chesterfield, Derbyshire.
C. Phillips & Son, Whitwood Mere, Castleford.
Pidduck, Rushton & Co., Prospect Pottery, Cobridge, Stoke-on-Trent.
Pilkington's Tile & Pottery Co. Ltd., Clifton Junction, Near Manchester.
Pitcairns Ltd., Pinnox Pottery, Tunstall, Stoke-on-Trent.
Plant Bros., Stanley Works, Longton, Stoke-on-Trent.
E. Plant, Crown Pottery, Burslem, Stoke-on-Trent.
R. Plant & Sons, Warwick Works, Longton, Stoke-on-Trent.
R. H. & S. L. Plant, Tuscan Works, Longton, Stoke-on-Trent.
Plowright Bros., New Brampton, Chesterfield, Derbyshire.
J. Plummer, Fareham Potteries, Fareham.
Pointon & Co. Ltd., Norfolk Works, Hanley, Stoke-on-Trent.
T. Poole, Cobden Works, Longton, Stoke-on-Trent.
Porcelain Tile Co., Crystal Porcelain Tile Works, Cobridge, Stoke-on-Trent.
Port Dundas Pottery Co., Bishop Street, Port Dundas, Glasgow.
Possil Pottery Co., Denmark Street, Possil Park, Glasgow.
Poulson Bros., West Riding Pottery, Ferrybridge, Yorkshire.
Pountney & Co. Ltd., Bristol Victoria Pottery, Bristol.
I. & W. Powell, Ewloe Pottery, Alltammy, Near Mold, Flintshire.
W. Powell & Sons, Templegate Potteries, Bristol.
F. & R. Pratt & Co., High Street East, Fenton, Stoke-on-Trent.
Price Bros., Crown Works, Burslem, Stoke-on-Trent.
Price, Sons & Co., The Old Stoneware Potteries, Bristol.
Priest's (George) Pottery & Stone Ware Manufacturing Co. (Cardiff) Ltd.,
    Cardiff, Wales.
G. Proctor & Co., Gladstone Pottery, Longton, Stoke-on-Trent.

S. Radford, High Street, Fenton, Stoke-on-Trent.
Ratcliffe & Co., Clarence Works, Longton, Stoke-on-Trent.
T. Rathbone & Co., Newfield Pottery, Tunstall, Stoke-on-Trent.
Redfern & Drakeford, Chatfield Works, Longton, Stoke-on-Trent.
J. Reeves, Victoria Works, Fenton, Stoke-on-Trent.
J. J. Rickaby & Co., Monkwearmouth Pottery, Monkwearmouth, Sunder-
    land.
Ridgways, Bedford Works, Shelton, Hanley, Stoke-on-Trent.
Rigby & Stevenson, Boston Works, Hanley, Stoke-on-Trent.
D. Roberts, Bath Street, Hanley, Stoke-on-Trent.
Robinson Bros., Castleford and Allerton Potteries, Castleford.

B. Robinson, Church Gresley, Burton-on-Trent.
Robinson & Leadbetter, Wolfe Street, Stoke-on-Trent.
Robinson & Son, Foley China Works, Longton, Stoke-on-Trent.
T. Robinson, Coxhoe, Durham.
W. Robinson & Sons, Jack Lane Pottery, Hunslet, Leeds.
Rowley & Newton Ltd., Park Place Works, Longton, Stoke-on-Trent.
Royal Art Pottery Co., Waterloo Works, Longton, Stoke-on-Trent.
Royal Crown Derby Porcelain Co. Ltd., Osmaston Road, Derby.

Sadler & Son, Well Street Pottery, Tunstall, Stoke-on-Trent.
J. Sadler & Sons, Newport Street, Burslem, Stoke-on-Trent.
Salopian Art Pottery Co., Broseley, Shropshire.
Salt Bros., Brownhills Pottery, Tunstall, Stoke-on-Trent.
W. Sandland, Litchfield Pottery and Broad Street Works, Hanley, Stoke-on-Trent.
W. Sants, Milk Street, Bath.
Mrs. M. Saunders & Son, Chalfont St. Peter, Gerrards Cross, Buckinghamshire.
Sefton & Brown, Ferrybridge Pottery, Ferrybridge, Yorkshire.
Sharp, Jones & Co., Bourne Valley Pottery, Parkstone, Dorset.
W. H. Sharp, Canning Street Pottery, Fenton, Stoke-on-Trent.
F. Sharpe, Bourne Valley Works, Near Poole, Dorset.
Shaw & Sons, Sandyfield Pottery, Tunstall, Stoke-on-Trent.
G. Shaw & Sons, The Holmes Pottery, Rotherham, Yorkshire.
Sheaf Pottery Co., Commerce Street, Longton, Stoke-on-Trent.
Sherwin & Cotton, Tile Works, Hanley, Stoke-on-Trent.
J. Shore & Co., Edensor Works, Longton, Stoke-on-Trent.
Shorter & Boulton, Copeland Street, Stoke-on-Trent.
T. A. Simpson & Co. Ltd. (Tiles), Cliff Bank Works, Stoke-on-Trent.
G. Skey & Co. Ltd., Wilnecote Works, Near Tamworth, Staffordshire.
Smith Bros., Littlethorn Pottery, Woodville, Burton-on-Trent.
Smith & Co., Victoria Road, Hanley, Stoke-on-Trent.
J. Smith, Glebe Street Pottery, Stoke-on-Trent.
S. Smith, Sutherland Works, Longton, Stoke-on-Trent.
W. T. H. Smith & Co., The Cable Pottery, Longton, Stoke-on-Trent.
J. & J. Snow, Cauldron Place, Hanley, Stoke-on-Trent.
C. E. Snowdon & Co., Bridge Pottery, Sheepfolds, Near Sunderland.
Soho Pottery Co., Soho Pottery, Tunstall, Stoke-on-Trent.
T. B. Spencer, Kingswood Green Pottery, Wrenbury, Nantwich, Cheshire.
Star China Co., St. Gregory's Works, Longton, Stoke-on-Trent.
J. Stiff & Sons, London Pottery, Lambeth, London.
W. H. Stockwell, St. Sampson, Guernsey, Channel Islands.
Stone & Co. Ltd., Tile Works and Potteries, Epsom, Surrey.
Street Bros., Cruicks Terra Cotta Works, Inverkeithing, Fifeshire.
R. Sudlow & Sons, Adelaide Street, Burslem, Stoke-on-Trent.
Sykes & Dickinson, Lane End Pottery, Holbeck, Leeds.

J. Tams, Crown Pottery, Longton, Stoke-on-Trent.
Taylor Bros., Alltammy, Mold, Flintshire.
Taylor & Kent, Florence Works, Longton, Stoke-on-Trent.
Taylor, Tunnicliff & Co., Eastwood, Hanley, Stoke-on-Trent.
N. Taylor, Denholme Pottery, Cullingworth, Bradford, Yorkshire.
Thomas U. & Co., Marlborough Works, Hanley, Stoke-on-Trent.
Thompson & Co., Wethericks Pottery, Clifton, Penrith, Cumberland.
Thornaby Pottery Co. Ltd., The Pottery, Thornaby-on-Tees.
R. Till & Bates, Commerce Street, Longton, Stoke-on-Trent.
T. Till & Sons, Sytch Pottery, Burslem, Stoke-on-Trent.
Tilstone Bros., Bournes Bank, Burslem, Stoke-on-Trent.
Timmis & Co., Stour Fire Clay Works, Lye, Stourbridge.
J. Timmis & Sons, Bradwell Wood Tileries, Tunstall, Stoke-on-Trent.
Tooth & Co., Bretby Art Pottery, Woodville, Near Burton-on-Trent.
Torquay Terra Cotta Co. Ltd., Hele Cross, Torquay, Devon.
E. R. Tunnicliffe, Victoria Pottery, Woodville, Near Burton-on-Trent.
A. Turner & Sons, Bradley Pottery, Bilston, Staffordshire.
R. H. Twist, Sutton Heath Potteries, Sutton Heath, St. Helens, Lancs.

J. Unwin & Co., Cornhill Works, Longton, Stoke-on-Trent.
Upper Hanley Pottery Co., High Street, Hanley, Stoke-on-Trent.

E. D. Venn, St. Austell Street, Truro, Cornwall.
Victoria Pottery Co., High Street, Hanley, Stoke-on-Trent.
Vivian & Sons, Morriston Potteries, Morriston, Glamorgan.

Wade & Co., High Street Works, Burslem, Stoke-on-Trent.
J. & W. Wade & Co., Flaxman Art Tile Works, Burslem, Stoke-on-Trent.
Wagstaff & Brunt, Richmond Pottery, Longton, Stoke-on-Trent.
C. Waine, Sutherland Road, Longton, Stoke-on-Trent.
C. Wakefield, South Street, Stoke, Coventry.
J. Walder & Sons, Crowhurst Pottery, Near Battle, Sussex.
Wallace & Co., Foundry Lane, Ouseburn, Newcastle-on-Tyne.
T. Walters, St. Martins Lane, Longton, Stoke-on-Trent.
Walton Pottery Co., New Brampton, Longton, Stoke-on-Trent.
Wardlaw, Johnston, Star Pottery, Glasgow.
Wardle & Co., Washington Works, Hanley, Stoke-on-Trent.
G. Warrilow & Sons, Queen's Pottery, Longton, Stoke-on-Trent.
Watcombe Pottery Co., Watcombe, Near Torquay, Devon.
H. & J. Watson, Wattisfield Pottery, Diss, Norfolk.
J. H. Weatherby & Sons, Falcon Pottery, Hanley, Stoke-on-Trent.
Webbs Worcester Tileries Co. Ltd., Tunnel Hill, Worcester.
Josiah Wedgwood & Sons Ltd., Etruria, Hanley, Stoke-on-Trent.
Wellington Pottery Co., Commercial Road, Hanley, Stoke-on-Trent.
West Lothian Pottery Co. Ltd., Hamilton Street, Boness, Scotland.
Wheeler & Co., Kew Kiln, Tilehurst, Reading, Berkshire.

T. Wild & Co., Albert Works, Longton, Stoke-on-Trent.

Wildblood, Heath & Sons, Peel and Clifton Works, Longton, Stoke-on-Trent.

Wileman & Co., The Foley China Works, Longton, Stoke-on-Trent.

A. J. Wilkinson Ltd., Royal Staffordshire Pottery, Burslem, Stoke-on-Trent.

H. M. Williamson & Sons, Bridge Pottery, Longton, Stoke-on-Trent.

J. Wilson & Sons, Park Works, Fenton, Stoke-on-Trent.

Wiltshaw & Robinson, Copeland Street Works, Stoke-on-Trent.

F. Winkle & Co., Colonial Pottery, Stoke-on-Trent.

Wood & Barker Ltd., Queen Street Pottery, Burslem, Stoke-on-Trent.

H. J. Wood, Alexandra Pottery, Burslem, Stoke-on-Trent.

Wood & Hulme, Garfield Pottery, Burslem, Stoke-on-Trent.

J. Wood & Son, Friarton, Perth, Scotland.

J. Wood & Co. Ltd., Stepney Pottery, Newcastle-on-Tyne.

J. B. Wood & Co., Edensor Road, Longton, Stoke-on-Trent.

Wood & Son, Trent and New Wharf Potteries, Burslem, Stoke-on-Trent.

W. Wood & Co., Albert Street Works, Burslem, Stoke-on-Trent.

H. Woodfield, Thurmaston Pottery, Thurmaston, Leicester.

J. Woodward, Swadlincote, Burton-on-Trent.

Wooldridge & Walley, Knowle Works, Burslem, Stoke-on-Trent.

G. Woolliscraft & Son, Patent Tile Works, Hanley, Stoke-on-Trent.

Worcester Royal Porcelain Co. Ltd., Royal Porcelain Works, Worcester.

E. Wright & Co. Ltd., Wheat Bridge Potteries, New Brampton, Derbyshire.

G. M. Yates & Co., Moor Lane, Brierley Hill, Staffordshire.

C. Yeomans, Cove Green Pottery, Farnborough, Hants.

BRITISH POTTERY MANUFACTURERS IN 1964

(Compiled from the *Pottery Gazette Reference Book and Directory* by permission of the proprietors, Messrs. Scott Greenwood & Son Ltd.)

Abbeydale New Bone China Co. Ltd., Duffield, Derbyshire.

Adams, Wm., & Sons (Potters) Ltd., Tunstall, Stoke-on-Trent.

Adderley Floral China Works (Ridgway Potteries, Ltd.), Sutherland Road, Longton, Stoke-on-Trent.

Alcock, Lindley & Bloore Ltd., Clough Street, Hanley, Stoke-on-Trent.

Aldridge Pottery Co. (Longton) Ltd., Normacot Road, Longton, Stoke-on-Trent.

Alton Towers Handcraft Pottery (Staffs.) Ltd., Alton Towers, Stoke-on-Trent.

Aristocrat Florals & Fancies, Heathcote Works, Heathcote Road, Longton, Stoke-on-Trent.

Ashworth, Geo. L. & Bros. Ltd., Broad Street Works, Hanley, Stoke-on-Trent.

Ault Potteries Ltd., Swadlincote, Near Burton-on-Trent.

Avon Art Pottery Ltd., Jubilee Works, off Uttoxeter Road, Longton, Stoke-on-Trent.

Aynsley, H. & Co. Ltd., Commerce Works, Commerce Street, Longton, Stoke-on-Trent.

Aynsley, John & Sons Ltd., Portland Works, Sutherland Road, Longton, Stoke-on-Trent.

Babbacombe Pottery Ltd., Babbacombe Road, Torquay.

Baggaley, E., Ltd., Branksome China Works, Westbourne, Hants.

Bairstow, P. E. & Co., Mount Pleasant, Shelton, Stoke-on-Trent.

Barker Bros. Ltd., Meir Works, Barker Street, Longton, Stoke-on-Trent.

Barratt's of Staffordshire Ltd., Royal Overhouse Pottery, Burslem, Stoke-on-Trent.

Belleek Pottery, The, Ltd., Belleek, Co. Fermanagh, N. Ireland.

Beswick, John, Ltd., Gold Street, Longton, Stoke-on-Trent.

Biltons (1912) Ltd., London Road, Stoke-on-Trent.

Blue John Pottery Ltd., Union Street, Hanley, Stoke-on-Trent.
Blyth Pottery (Longton) Ltd., Blyth Works, Uttoxeter Road, Longton, Stoke-on-Trent.
Bossons, W. H. (Sales) Ltd., Brook Mills, Congleton, Cheshire.
Bourne, Joseph, & Son, Ltd., Denby Pottery, Near Derby.
Brannam, C. H., Ltd., Litchdon Pottery, Barnstaple, Devon.
Braunton Pottery Co. Ltd., Station Road, Braunton, N. Devon.
Bretby Brick & Stoneware Co. Ltd., Newhall, near Burton-on-Trent.
Bridge Pottery, Lamberhurst, Kent.
Bridgwood, Sampson & Son Ltd., Anchor Pottery, Longton, Stoke-on-Trent.
Briglin Pottery Ltd., 22 Crawford Street, London, W.1.
Britannia Designs Ltd., Townstal, Dartmouth, Devon.
British Anchor Pottery Co. Ltd., Anchor Road, Longton, Stoke-on-Trent.
Broadhurst, James, & Sons Ltd., Portland Pottery, Frederick Street, Fenton, Stoke-on-Trent.
Bron Border Pottery (Peebles) Ltd., Eastgate, Peebles, Scotland.
Brown, T., & Sons Ltd., Ferrybridge Pottery, Ferrybridge, Knottingley, Yorks.
Buchan, A. W., & Co. Ltd., Thistle Potteries, Portobello, Edinburgh, 9, Scotland.
Bullers Ltd., Tipton, Staffs.
Burgess & Leigh Ltd., Middleport Pottery, Burslem, Stoke-on-Trent.

Cambrian Pottery Co. Ltd., Llandudno, N. Wales.
Cara China Co., Uttoxeter Road, Longton, Stoke-on-Trent.
Cardew, Michael, Wenford Bridge Pottery, St. Tudy, Bodmin, Cornwall.
Carlton Ware Ltd., Carlton Works, Stoke-on-Trent.
Cartwright & Edwards Ltd., Newborough and Sutherland Potteries, Longton, Stoke-on-Trent.
Castle Wynd Potteries Co., Gifford, East Lothian, Scotland.
Cauldon Potteries Ltd., Fishponds, Bristol.
Chapmans, Longton Ltd., Albert Works, Uttoxeter Road, Longton, Stoke-on-Trent.
Chelsea Pottery (Rawnsley Academy Ltd.), Radnor Walk, Chelsea, London, S.W.3.
Chinaware Ltd., Meir Airport, Stoke-on-Trent.
Cinque Ports Pottery, The Mint, Rye, Sussex.
Clough's Royal Art Pottery Ltd., Longton, Stoke-on-Trent.
Coalbrook Potteries, Cleveland Works, College Road, Shelton, Hanley, Stoke-on-Trent.
Coalport China Ltd., Stoke-on-Trent.
Cone, Thomas, Ltd., Alma Works, Uttoxeter Road, Longton, Stoke-on-Trent.
Conway Pottery Co. Ltd., Park Lane, Fenton, Stoke-on-Trent.
Co-operative Wholesale Society Ltd., Crown Clarence Pottery, 493 King Street, Longton, Stoke-on-Trent.

Co-operative Wholesale Society Ltd., Windsor Pottery, Clayton Street, Longton, Stoke-on-Trent.

Cooper Ltd., Susie, Crown Works, Burslem, Stoke-on-Trent.

Copeland, W. T., & Sons Ltd., Spode Works, Stoke-on-Trent.

Cotton, Elijah, Ltd., Nelson Pottery, Hanley, Stoke-on-Trent.

Crown Staffordshire China Co. Ltd., Minerva Works, Fenton, Stoke-on-Trent.

Dartmouth Pottery Ltd., Dartmouth, Devon.

Dennis (Fenton) Ltd., Alexandra Works, King Street, Fenton, Stoke-on-Trent.

Denton China (Longton) Ltd., Upper Normacot Road, Longton, Stoke-on-Trent.

Devonmoor Art Pottery Ltd., Liverton, Newton Abbott, Devon.

Devonshire Potteries Ltd., Bovey Tracey, Near Newton Abbot, Devon.

Doulton Fine China Ltd., Royal Doulton Potteries, Nile Street, Burslem, Stoke-on-Trent.

Dudson Bros. Ltd., Hanley, Stoke-on-Trent.

Dunn, Bennett & Co. Ltd., Dalehall Works, Burslem, Stoke-on-Trent.

Eastgate Potteries, Withernsea, Yorks.

Elektra Porcelain Co. Ltd., Edensor Road, Longton, Stoke-on-Trent.

Ellgreave Pottery Co. Ltd., Aitken Street, Burslem, Stoke-on-Trent.

Empire Porcelain Co., Empire Works, Stoke-on-Trent.

Everett Raymond Pottery, Rye, Sussex.

Everson, Ronald, 64 Vicarage Road, Leyton, London, E.10.

Fieldhouse, Murray, Pendley Pottery, Pendley Manor, Tring, Herts.

Fielding, S., & Co. Ltd., Devon Pottery, Stoke-on-Trent.

Finney, A. T., & Sons Ltd., Duchess China Works, Longton, Stoke-on-Trent.

Five Towns China Co. Ltd., Milvale Street, Middleport, Stoke-on-Trent.

Ford & Sons (Crownford) Ltd., Newcastle Street, Burslem, Stoke-on-Trent.

Foy, Peggy E., Ltd., Harvest Bank Road, West Wickham, Kent.

Fryer, J., Ltd., Roundwell Street, Tunstall, Stoke-on-Trent.

Fulham Pottery & Cheavin Filter Co. Ltd., 210 New King's Road, Fulham, London, S.W.6.

Furnivals (1913) Ltd., Cobridge, Stoke-on-Trent.

Gibson & Sons Ltd., Albany Pottery, Burslem, Stoke-on-Trent.

Gladstone China, Uttoxeter Road, Longton, Stoke-on-Trent.

Goddard, Elaine, Ltd., Discove, Bruton, Somerset.

Govancroft Potteries Ltd., 1855 London Road, Tollcross, Glasgow, E.2.

Green, T. G., & Co. Ltd., Church Gresley Potteries, Near Burton-on-Trent.

Grimwades Ltd., Royal Winton Potteries, Stoke-on-Trent.

Grindley Hotel Ware Co. Ltd., Globe Pottery, Scotia Road, P.O. Box
    No. 7, Tunstall, Stoke-on-Trent.
Grindley, W. H., & Co. Ltd., Woodland Pottery, Tunstall, Stoke-on-Trent.
Grosvenor China Ltd., Chelson Street, Longton, Stoke-on-Trent.

Hall Bros. (Longton) Ltd., Radnor Works, Ayshford Street, Longton,
    Stoke-on-Trent.
Hammersley & Co. (Longton) Ltd., Alsager Pottery, Sutherland Road,
    Longton, Stoke-on-Trent.
Harris, A., & Sons, Farnham Potteries, Wrecclesham, Farnham, Surrey.
Hastings Pottery, Hastings, Sussex.
Heath, J. E., Ltd., Albert Potteries, Burslem, Stoke-on-Trent.
Heatherley Fine China Ltd., Hook Road, Chessington, Surrey.
Holding Bros., The Potteries, Oswaldtwistle, Near Accrington, Lancs.
Holdsworth, Peter, Holdsworth Potteries, Ramsbury, Near Marlborough,
    Wilts.
Holkham Pottery Ltd., Holkham, Wells, Norfolk.
Holland, Fishley, The Pottery, Clevedon, Somerset.
Honiton Potteries Ltd., Honiton, Devon.
Hornsea Pottery Co. Ltd., Edenfield Works, Marlborough Avenue, Hornsea,
    E. Yorks.
Howard Pottery Co. Ltd., Norfolk Street, Shelton, Stoke-on-Trent.
Hudson & Middleton Ltd., Sutherland Pottery, Longton, Stoke-on-Trent.

Iden Pottery, Rye, Sussex.

Jackson & Gosling Ltd., Chelson Street, Longton, Stoke-onTrent.
Jenkins, David J., & Sons, Ewenny Pottery, Near Bridgend, Glamorgan,
    S. Wales.
Jersey Potteries (Home Decorations Ltd.), Gorey Village, Jersey, Channel
    Islands.
Johnson Bros. (Hanley) Ltd., Hanley Pottery, Stoke-on-Trent.
Jones, A. B., & Sons Ltd., Grafton Works, Longton, Stoke-on-Trent.
Kaposvary, John A., 16 Inglewood Grove, Porthill, Newcastle, Staffs.
Keele Street Pottery Co. Ltd., Meir Airport, Longton, Stoke-on-Trent.
Kent, James, Ltd., The Old Foley Pottery, Longton, Stoke-on-Trent.
Kirklands (Staffordshire) Ltd., Albion Pottery, Brick Kiln Lane, Etruria,
    Stoke-on-Trent.

Lake, W. H., & Son Ltd., Chapel Hill Pottery, Truro, Cornwall.
Lamorna Pottery, Lamorna, Penzance, Cornwall.
Lancaster & Sandland Ltd., Dresden Works, Tinkersclough, Hanley,
    Stoke-on-Trent.
Lawrence, Thomas (Longton), Ltd., Sylvan Works, Longton, Stoke-on-
    Trent.
Leach Pottery, Higher Stennack, St. Ives, Cornwall.

Leaper Pottery, Fore Street, Newlyn, Cornwall.

Lewis, Reginald A., Glympton Studio, Water Orton, Near Birmingham.

Lingard, Webster & Co. Ltd., Swan Pottery, Hunt Street, Tunstall, Stoke-on-Trent.

Lockett, John, & Co., Middleport Pottery, Burslem, Stoke-on-Trent.

Longton New Art Pottery Co. Ltd., Gordon Pottery, Forrister Street, Longton, Stoke-on-Trent.

Lovatt's Potteries Ltd., The Pottery, Langley Mill, Near Nottingham.

Maddock, John, & Sons Ltd., Newcastle Street Pottery, Burslem, Stoke-on-Trent.

Mason, Cash & Co. Ltd., Pool Potteries, Church Gresley, Near Burton-on-Trent.

Matthews, Basil, F.R.S.A., M.S.I.A., The Studio, Langley Road, Merryhill, Wolverhampton, Staffs.

Maund, Geoffrey, Pottery Ltd., 138 Upper Shirley Road, Shirley Hills, Croydon, Surrey.

Mayer, Thomas (Elton Pottery) Ltd., Vinebank Street, off London Road, Stoke-on-Trent.

Meakin, Alfred (Tunstall) Ltd., Royal Albert and Newfield Potteries, Tunstall, Stoke-on-Trent.

Meakin, J. & G., Ltd., Eagle Pottery, Hanley, Stoke-on-Trent.

Midwinter, W. R., Ltd., Albion & Hadderidge Potteries, Burslem, Stoke-on-Trent.

Milland Pottery, Milland, Liphook, Hants.

Mintons Ltd., China Works, Stoke-on-Trent.

Moira Pottery Co. Ltd., Moira, Near Burton-on-Trent.

Moorcroft, W., Ltd., Burslem, Stoke-on-Trent.

Morton, Enos, & Son, Lindley Moor Pottery, Laund Road, Salendine Nook, Near Huddersfield, Yorks.

Myott, Son & Co. Ltd., Alexander Potteries, Hanley, Stoke-on-Trent.

New Devon Pottery Ltd., Forde Road, Newton Abbot, Devon.

Newbridge Pottery, Fenton, Stoke-on-Trent.

Newport Pottery Co. Ltd., Newport Pottery, Burslem, Stoke-on-Trent.

Norfolk Pottery Co. Ltd., Norfolk Street, Shelton, Stoke-on-Trent.

Northwood Pottery, Festing Street, Hanley, Stoke-on-Trent.

Palissy Pottery, Ltd., Chancery Lane, Longton, Stoke-on-Trent.

Paragon China Ltd., " Atlas Works," Beech Street, Longton, Stoke-on-Trent.

Paramount Pottery Co. Ltd., Meir Airport, Longton, Stoke-on-Trent.

Pearson & Co. (Chesterfield) Ltd., The Potteries, Whittington Moor, Chesterfield, Derbyshire.

Pearson, James, Ltd., Oldfield Pottery, Chesterfield, Derbyshire.

Plant, R. H. & S. L., Ltd., Tuscan Works, Forrister Street, Longton, Stoke-on-Trent.

Poole Pottery Ltd., Poole, Dorset.
Portmeirion Potteries Ltd., Kirkham Street, Stoke-on-Trent.
Pountney & Co. Ltd., The Bristol Pottery, Fishponds, Bristol.
Price & Kensington Potteries Ltd., Trubshaw Cross, Longport, Stoke-on-Trent.
Price, Powell & Co., 1 Upton Road, Bristol, 3.
Prince William Pottery Co., Liverpool 5.
Prinknash Benedictines, Prinknash Abbey, Gloucester.

Quinnell, Richard, Ltd., Rowhurst Works, Oxshott Road, Leatherhead, Surrey.

Rainham Pottery Ltd., 327 High Street, Rainham, Kent.
Regency China Ltd., Sutherland Road, Longton, Stoke-on-Trent.
Richardson, A. G., & Co. Ltd., Britannia Pottery, Cobridge, Stoke-on-Trent.
Ridgway Potteries Ltd., Ash Hall, Stoke-on-Trent.
Rosemary Art Ware Co., 307 and 78 King Street, Fenton, Stoke-on-Trent.
Rosina China Co. Ltd., Queen's Pottery, Sutherland Road, Longton, Stoke-on-Trent.
Roslyn China, Park Place Works, Uttoxeter Road, Longton, Stoke-on-Trent.
Royal Crown Derby Porcelain Co. Ltd., Osmaston Road, Derby.
Royal Stafford China, Cooke Street, Longton, Stoke-on-Trent.
Rustington Pottery, Brookside Avenue, Worthing Road, Rustington, Sussex.
Rye Pottery, Ferry Road, Rye, Sussex.

Sadler, James, & Sons Ltd., Wellington and Central Potteries, Market Place, Burslem, Stoke-on-Trent.
Salisbury China Co. Ltd., Edensor Road, Longton, Stoke-on-Trent.
Sandygate Pottery Ltd., St. Michael's Works, Kingsteignton, Near Newton Abbot, Devon.
Schofield, A., Wetheriggs Pottery, Near Penrith, Cumberland.
Shaw & Copestake Ltd., Sylvan Works, Longton, Stoke-on-Trent.
Shelley Potteries Ltd., Longton, Stoke-on-Trent.
Shore & Coggins Ltd., Greendock Street, Longton, Stoke-on-Trent.
Shorter & Son Ltd., Copeland Street, Stoke-on-Trent.
Simmill, Donald, 53 Summerville Road, Trent Vale, Stoke-on-Trent.
Simpsons (Potters) Ltd., Elder Works, Cobridge, Stoke-on-Trent.
Solly, John, 36 London Road, Maidstone.
Southcliffe, R. G., & Co. Ltd., Creigiau, Near Cardiff, S. Wales.
Staffordshire Potteries (Export) Ltd., Meir, Stoke-on-Trent.
Staffordshire Potteries Ltd., Meir Airport, Longton, Stoke-on-Trent.
Staffordshire Tea Set Co. Ltd., Plex Street, Tunstall, Stoke-on-Trent.
Studio Szeiler Ltd., Moorland Road, Burslem, Stoke-on-Trent.

Sudlow, R., & Sons Ltd., Adelaide Pottery, Moorland Road, Burslem, Stoke-on-Trent.

Summerbank Pottery Ltd., Butterfield Place, Tunstall, Stoke-on-Trent.

Sunfield Pottery, Clent Grove, Clent, Near Stourbridge, Worcester.

Swincraft Productions, 80 Hagley Road, Oldswinford, Stourbridge, Worcestershire.

Swinnertons Ltd., Clough Street, Hanley, Stoke-on-Trent.

Sylvan Pottery Ltd., Ratton Street, off Huntbach Street, Hanley, Stoke-on-Trent.

Tams, John, Ltd., Crown Pottery, Longton, Stoke-on-Trent.

Taylor & Kent Ltd., Florence Works, 209 Uttoxeter Road, Longton, Stoke-on-Trent.

Thorley China Ltd., Wellington Works, The Strand, Longton, Stoke-on-Trent.

Tintagel Pottery, Tintagel, Cornwall.

Toni Raymond Pottery, Torquay.

Tooth & Co. Ltd., Bretby Art Pottery, Woodville, Near Burton-on-Trent.

Wade, George, & Son Ltd., Manchester Pottery, Greenhead Street, Burslem, Stoke-on-Trent.

Wade, Heath & Co. Ltd., Royal Victoria Pottery, Burslem, Stoke-on-Trent.

Wade (Ulster) Ltd., Ulster Pottery, Portadown, Co. Armagh, N. Ireland.

Wain, H. A., & Sons Ltd., Melba Works, Hurst Street, Longton, Stoke-on-Trent.

Watson's, Henry, Potteries Ltd., Wattisfield, Suffolk.

Weatherby, J. H., & Sons Ltd., Falcon Pottery, Hanley, Stoke-on-Trent.

Wedgwood & Co. Ltd., Tunstall, Stoke-on-Trent.

Wedgwood, Josiah, & Sons Ltd., Barlaston, Stoke-on-Trent.

Weetman Figures, High Street, Sandyford, Tunstall, Stoke-on-Trent.

West Surrey Ceramic Co. Ltd., Wormley, Near Godalming, Surrey.

Wild, Thos. C., & Sons Ltd., St. Mary's China Works, Longton, Stoke-on-Trent.

Wilkinson, A. J., Ltd., Royal Staffordshire Pottery, Burslem, Stoke-on-Trent.

Wood, Arthur, & Son (Longport) Ltd., Bradwell Works, Longport, Stoke-on-Trent.

Wood, H. J., Ltd., Alexandra Pottery, Furlong Lane, Burslem, Stoke-on-Trent.

Washington Pottery (Staffordshire) Ltd., College Road, Shelton, Stoke-on-Trent.

Wood & Sons Ltd., Burslem, Stoke-on-Trent.

Worcester Royal Porcelain Co., Ltd., Royal Porcelain Works, Worcester.

JACKFIELD WARES

A very large class of earthenware useful wares—jugs, coffee pots, tea-wares etc.,—are covered by the general term " Jackfield " when they are decorated with an all-over rich shiny black glaze. For many years these objects have been attributed to Jackfield in Shropshire although many specimens would seem to have been produced in the Staffordshire Potteries. Broken fragments of this type of ware have been excavated in the Stafford-shire Potteries (at or near Whieldon's Works at Fenton Low).

It is not generally known that the name Jackfield is also that of an estate at Burslem in the Staffordshire Potteries, so that the oft quoted reference to potters " from Jackfield " may never have been intended to mean the Shropshire town of this name. A potter, Thomas Malkin, of the Staffordshire Jackfield is recorded as making black pottery early in the 18th century. The full story of the decorative black glazed so-called " Jackfield " wares would bear fuller study, although it will probably be found that these wares represent a standard form of decoration made at several different potteries in the middle of the 18th century.

INDEX

Note.—*Manufacturers are denoted by large capitals: potters' marks by italics. References to volume one are preceded by figure i, and references to volume two are preceded by figure ii.*

Collector's Handbook of Marks and
Monograms on Pottery and Porcelain of
the Renaissance and Modern Periods

By Wm. Chaffers

Revised by F. Litchfield

7½ × 5 ins. Fourth Edition. Pp. viii, 367, 1968

The authoritative, world-famous handbook containing over 5,000
marks and monograms, plus a ready reference index. The marks,
signatures and monograms of factories of Fayence, Delft, Majolica,
Pottery and Porcelain, with a large section on Chinese and Japanese
are given, in many cases with the dates of time of existence, from
thirteenth to twentieth century. It is a book for every collector,
student, hobbyist and dealer.

Handbook to Hall Marks on Gold and
Silver Plate of Great Britain and Ireland

By Wm. Chaffers

WILLIAM REEVES
LONDON